# Higher Education
# Service-Learning Sourcebook

Robin J. Crews

**Oryx Press**
Westport, Connecticut · London

*The rare Arabian Oryx is believed to have inspired the myth of the unicorn. This desert antelope became virtually extinct in the early 1960s. At that time, several groups of international conservationists arranged to have 9 animals sent to the Phoenix Zoo to be the nucleus of a captive-breeding herd. Today the Oryx population is over 1,000, and 500 have been returned to reserves in the Middle East.*

**Library of Congress Cataloging-in-Publication Data**

Crews, Robin Jeffrey
  Higher education service-learning sourcebook / Robin J. Crews.
    p. cm.
  Includes bibliographical references and index.
  ISBN 1-57356-253-X (alk. paper)
  1. Student service—United States—Directories. 2. Student volunteers in social service—United States—Directories. 3. Community and college—United States—Directories. 4. Experiential learning—United States—Directories. I. Title.

LC220.5.C73 2002
378.1'03—dc21                                                                 00-011692


British Library Cataloguing in Publication Data is available.

Library of Congress Catalog Card Number: 00-011692
ISBN: 1-57356-253-X

First published in 2002

Oryx Press, 88 Post Road West, Westport, CT 06881
An imprint of Greenwood Publishing Group, Inc.
www.oryxpress.com

Printed in the United States of America

♾™

The paper used in this book complies with the Permanent Paper Standard issued by the National Information Standards Organization (Z39.48-1984).

10  9  8  7  6  5  4  3  2  1

# Table of Contents

**Preface**       v

**Introduction**       vii

**1. Definitions of Terms and Concepts**       1

**2. Literature and Online Resources**       45

Monographs: An Annotated Selection of "Essential Texts"       45

Journals       49

Bibliographies       52

Online Resources: Internet Discussion Groups and World Wide
Web Sites       55

**3. Colleges and Universities with Service-Learning Programs
or Courses**       63

Overview: The Status of Service-Learning in Higher Education       63

Summary of Findings       64

Directory of Colleges and Universities with Service-Learning
Programs or Courses       66

**4. Service-Learning and Service Organizations, Associations,
and Networks**       245

Service-Learning Organizations, Associations, and Networks       245

Service Organizations, Associations, and Networks       251

**5. Conferences, Colloquia, Institutes, and Academies**       265

Conferences and Colloquia       265

Institutes and Academies       271

**6. Awards, Scholarships, Fellowships, Internships,
and Grants**       275

Awards: Service-Learning       275

Awards: Service       276

Scholarships       278

Fellowships        278

Internships        279

Grants        280

**Appendix: E-mail Questionnaire Used for Directory Entries        283**

**Bibliography        285**

**Index        295**

# Preface

Service-learning in higher education involves teaching and learning that blends personal experience and wisdom gained from community-based service with knowledge arising out of more traditional coursework within academe. As service-learning in higher education has grown dramatically as a pedagogy in the past decade, so have its practitioners, its proponents, and its literatures. In fact, so many service-learning groups and programs have come into being and so much has been written about this relatively young pedagogy in the past few years that newcomers to service-learning may find the task of becoming acquainted with the field and its constituencies a somewhat daunting enterprise.

This is complicated by the fact that service-learning, by definition, exists not only on college and university campuses and in relevant professional academic associations, but also within thousands of governmental and non-governmental agencies, organizations, associations and networks in communities across North America and around the world.

The primary purpose of this sourcebook is twofold: (1) for newcomers, to serve as a navigable introduction to service-learning in higher education; and (2) to organize the wealth of information about service-learning concepts and components, theories, courses and programs in colleges and universities, publications, research, organizations and networks, conferences, training opportunities, funding, and awards. At the dawning of the third millennium, one can find as much (if not more) of this information online, i.e., on the Internet and World Wide Web, as in non-virtual publica-

tions. Accordingly, this source book is a comprehensive guide to print and online information and resources, and research for it was conducted both online and in print.

The Introduction provides a brief, descriptive introduction to service-learning: a non-theoretical, conceptual sketch, consisting primarily of a few definitions of the construct and phenomenon. This is followed by a list of common terms, concepts, and issues (Chapter 1). Chapter 2 describes primary information resources found in monographs, journals, bibliographies, and online resources (i.e., Internet discussion groups and World Wide Web sites). Chapter 3 includes an overview of the status of service-learning in higher education (i.e., a summary of individual entries that comprise the rest of the chapter), and a comprehensive directory of college and universities where service-learning can be found in lesser or greater degrees. Chapter 4 moves the reader off campus by introducing: (a) organizations, associations, and networks that promote and support service-learning in higher education; and (b) selected service organizations that are relevant to service learning, including some which facilitate or oversee placement of students. Chapter 5 provides an overview of conferences, institutes, and training opportunities for those interested in service-learning in higher education. Finally, Chapter 6 summarizes awards, scholarships, fellowships, internships, and grants in the field.

It is important to note at the outset that factual information in this book is taken directly from brochures, Web sites, e-mail messages (both personal correspondence and messages sent to the author's Service-Learning

Discussion Group by subscribers), conversations with the author's colleagues, other authors, representatives of organizations, and others, and is supplemented by the author's personal knowledge when appropriate. The information on college and university service-learning programs in Chapter 3 comes entirely from responses to questionnaires sent out in an extensive, 18-month long survey conducted by e-mail and is supplemented by researching program Web sites. This book would not exist without the participation of hundreds of individuals who supplied information about their work, and the author wishes to acknowledge and thank everyone who participated in the survey or in other aspects of the research and ultimately made this book possible.

# Introduction

Service-learning is called by many names and is defined in many different ways. The debate about what to call service-learning is decades old. At present, there are those who favor "community service learning" (e.g., as in *Michigan Journal of Community Service Learning*). Others, who see "service" and "community service" as problematic, but want to retain "community," prefer "community-based learning." According to Giles and Eyler, the name "service-learning" "grew out of the work of Robert Sigmon and William Ramsey at the Southern Regional Education Board" in 1967. Among those who have settled upon "service-learning," some want it hyphenated while others do not.

Once past the name debate, the term still has many meanings: it may refer to learning, pedagogy, or to both. In addition, its meaning may shift depending on whether the context is educational philosophy, philosophy, politics, discussions of social justice and social change (including educational reform and the realignment of higher education to confront societal problems and contribute directly to their resolution), or the means by which universities traditionally contribute to their local communities and/or engage in institutional outreach as a part of their mission statements. Definitions also vary depending upon who is employing the term (teachers, students, program staff, community partners, university administrators, politicians, government agencies, etc.), for what purpose, and the nature of expectations about intended outcomes of its use as pedagogy or engine of social change.

Within the context of learning, some interpret the construct quite broadly to include any learning, however personal, unstructured or unmeasurable, accomplished by anyone engaged in any kind of volunteer work or service to one's community. A second school of thought holds that service-learning is essentially curricular in nature, i.e., integrated into, and structured within, courses. In this view, service and volunteering—and any learning that accrues during these processes—are highly valued, but are not synonymous with service-learning. In order for service-learning to occur, a number of criteria must be met. A third view allows for both curricular and co-curricular manifestations of service-learning, including semester break and immersion programs and even one-time service events. (Sometimes, semester break and immersion programs are integrated into courses and offer academic credit, e.g., at the University of Notre Dame, in which case they fall within the curricular view of service-learning.) The author favors curricular definitions of service-learning but also believes that the quality of service-learning experiences (for all of the parties involved) is of much greater concern than the boundaries of the curricular vs. co-curricular debates. It is possible to have disastrous curriculum-based service-learning and excellent co-curricular service-learning. Descriptions of immersion and semester break programs are included in this sourcebook because a number of them exist in higher education programs and some of the colleges and universities in the directory (see Chapter 3) include them in their entries.

As described in the Preface, service-learning involves learning that blends personal experience and wisdom gained from community-based service with knowledge arising out of more traditional course work within academe. It is a subset of experiential learning, in which service complements and enhances other modes of traditional learning. Service is necessary, but not sufficient, for the learning in a service-learning course to take place. However, service-learning is more than learning. It is also pedagogy; some would say there are a variety of service-learning pedagogies. Given its flexibility and the many different ways in which it is being experimented with in vastly different contexts and communities, service-learning certainly can be seen as a set of pedagogies. These various pedagogies have several characteristics in common: they integrate out-of-classroom service and learning with traditional teaching and learning; they allow students the freedom to connect the constructs and methods of more formal academic worldviews with the experiences and perspectives students have outside of college and within the many communities they inhabit as students; they offer students the opportunity to more fully participate in their own learning (see "collaborative and cooperative learning"); and they invite more open-ended learning agendas (thus working against a teacher's control of what is learned and how it is learned).

As pedagogy, service-learning is used by instructors as a powerful means of teaching: teaching that has the potential to breathe life into any subject matter for students. It also has other uses beyond the particular discipline or subject matter in question: it can introduce students to worlds beyond the campus that students may migrate through but not necessarily belong to or contribute to as members. In so doing, it can raise awareness, inculcate values, and invite critical thinking about issues of social justice, citizenship, civic and social responsibility, and ethical and moral choices in increasingly complex local and global communities. Or it can be used to teach leadership and social skills, train students for subsequent employment, or open the door to various career paths. Some teachers employ service-learning purely as a pedagogical means of enhancing students' learning about a specific subject matter and not for any of the other purposes mentioned above. Other teachers embrace service-learning not as a means of teaching course content, but for the more indirect purposes related to consciousness-raising, ethical development, skills-building, etc. A third community of teachers uses service-learning for all the reasons above. In conclusion, it is fair to say that, among faculty and academics who have more than a casual familiarity with service-learning theory, method and history, a significant number appear to view the goals of service and learning as equally important. The following definitions and descriptions of service-learning are relatively recent and come from leaders in the field; accordingly, they may prove useful as examples of how others see service-learning today. Stanton, Giles, and Cruz see "service" as inclusive of "community action": "Service-learning joins two complex concepts: community action, the 'service,' and efforts to learn from that action and connect what is learned to existing knowledge, the 'learning.'" Jacoby and Associates stress the importance of learning and service and also emphasize structure, reflection, and reciprocity:

> Service-learning is a form of experiential education in which students engage in activities that address human and community needs together with structured opportunities intentionally designed to promote student learning and development. Reflection and reciprocity are key concepts of service-learning.

Similarly, Thomas Ehrlich identifies service-learning as

> the various pedagogies that link community service and academic study so that each strengthens the other. The basic theory of service-learning is Dewey's: the interaction of knowledge and skills with experience is key to learning. Students learn best not by reading the Great Books in a closed room but by opening the doors and windows of experience. Learning starts with a problem and

continues with the application of increasingly complex ideas and increasingly sophisticated skills to increasingly complicated problems.

Finally, in its *Series on Service-Learning in the Disciplines*, The American Association for Higher Education (AAHE) defines service-learning as

> a method under which students learn and develop through thoughtfully-organized service that: is conducted in and meets the needs of a community and is coordinated with an institution of higher education, and with the community; helps foster civic responsibility; is integrated into and enhances the academic curriculum of the students enrolled; and includes structured time for students to reflect on the service experience.

## References

American Association for Higher Education (AAHE). *Service-Learning in the Disciplines*. Monograph Series. Washington, DC: AAHE, 1997–2000.

Ehrlich, Thomas. "Foreword." In *Service-Learning in Higher Education: Concepts and Practices*, ed. Barbara Jacoby and Associates. San Francisco: Jossey-Bass, 1996.

Giles, Jr., Dwight E., and Janet Eyler. "The Theoretical Roots of Service-Learning in John Dewey: Toward a Theory of Service-Learning." *Michigan Journal of Community Service Learning* 1, no. 1 (1994): 77–85.

Jacoby, Barbara, and Associates, eds. *Service-Learning in Higher Education: Concepts and Practices*. San Francisco: Jossey-Bass, 1996.

Stanton, Timothy K., Dwight E. Giles, Jr., and Nadinne I. Cruz. *Service-Learning: A Movement's Pioneers Reflect on Its Origins, Practice, and Future*. San Francisco: Jossey-Bass, 1999.

# 1
# Definitions of Terms and Concepts

This section of the book is a primer on key terms, concepts, issues, programs, research, types of service, and references for further information. Taken together these comprise the basis of a conceptual infrastructure of service-learning. Entries are organized alphabetically; some entries (key subjects which are themselves the focus of other chapters, e.g., awards and honors) refer the reader to other chapters in the book.

## Academic Credit

Should academic credit be awarded for the service portion of work completed for a service-learning course? This question is central to a larger debate over service-learning's comparative validity as a pedagogy and its acceptance within academia. Critics argue that work performed outside the classroom or outside the purview of the instructor either cannot, or should not, be considered as part of a student's total grade for a given course. The argument here is that instructors can not reasonably evaluate student performance they do not witness. Others argue that the problem goes beyond the issue of an instructor's inability to evaluate performance they do not witness: the issue is more fundamental and involves the claim that service itself is not academic and therefore is not learning and therefore does not merit an academic grade.

The debate is further complicated by the fact that some may want to pay students for part or all of their service (or subsidize some of the costs incurred by some students) through wages,

stipends, honoraria, grants, scholarships, or reimbursement for operational expenses (e.g., travel to the service site, etc.). Thus, questions over academic credit vs. pay and concerns about the legality and ethics of receiving both academic credit and pay have exacerbated the larger debate over academic credit in service-learning.

In the first instance, proponents of service-learning have pointed out that other pedagogies involving coursework performed outside the classroom (internships, fieldwork, action research and many other forms of experiential education and learning) are generally accepted by academia and that service-learning should not be singled out or judged by different standards. Moreover, many in service-learning have developed assessment and evaluation methods and forms for evaluating the service and performance of students at their service sites.

In response to the second argument (i.e., that service is not academic and therefore does not merit a grade), proponents of service-learning have embraced one of three approaches. First, some have criticized the claim as invalid, biased, or based on faulty assumptions (e.g., that those who see one pedagogy as non-academic are not explaining their terms or are favoring their own pedagogical preferences over others). A second response involves research on learning and cognition: some rely on the work of Kolb and others to argue that learning processes and styles vary greatly among students, that more traditional modes of academic teaching do not meet the learning needs of a significant percentage of students, and that other

**Complete List of
Terms and Concepts:**
Academic Credit
Academic Legitimacy
Alternative Break Programs
America Reads and America Counts
    Programs
AmeriCorps
Assessment and Evaluation
Awards
Benefits and Outcomes of Service-
    Learning
Bibliographies
Books and Journals
Citizenship, Civic and Social
    Responsibility, and Civil Education
Co-curricular Service, Community
    Service, and Volunteering
Colleges and Universities with Service-
    Learning Programs or Courses
Conferences, Colloquia, Institutes, and
    Academies
Contemporary Issues and Topics in
    Service-Learning
Corporation For National Service (CNS)
Course Criteria and Designations
Course Development
Degrees in Service-Learning
Documenting Service
Faculty Development
Faculty Fellows
Faculty Incentives
Fellowships
Foundations
Fourth Credit Options

Funding
Grants
Immersion Programs
Institutionalizing Service-Learning on
    Campus
Integrating Service-Learning into the
    Curriculum
International Service-Learning
Internships
Leadership
Learn and Serve America—Higher
    Education
Learning Agreements and Service
    Contracts
Learning Circles
Liability
Mandatory vs. Voluntary Service-
    Learning
The Martin Luther King Day of Service
Mentoring and Tutoring
National Senior Service Corps
Online Resources: Internet Discussion
    Groups and World Wide Web Sites
Organizations, Associations, and Networks
    (Service-Learning and Service-Related)
Partnerships
Peace Studies and Service-Learning
Placement Issues
Principles of Good Practice
Problem-Based Learning (PBL)
Reflection
Residence Halls and Theme Housing
Scholarships
Service-Learning: Definitions
Types of Service

pedagogies, including service-learning, do). A third type of response involves citing guidelines and "principles of good practice" that have been developed over the years by professional educational organizations, faculty, and practitioners. The first of Howard's ten "Principles of Good Practice in Community Service Learning Pedagogy" specifically addresses this concern: "Academic Credit is for Learning, Not for Service." Many in service-learning appear to be satisfied that the research and literature on learning styles and the principles of good practice respond adequately to the argument that service should not be graded because it is not academic.

Finally, the question of academic credit vs. pay or credit plus pay may appear on the horizon from time to time, but generally it is accepted that students may receive pay or academic credit, but not both. Given that the service in service-learning takes place in the context of coursework, it is most likely that the reward will be academic credit and not financial remuneration. *See also* Academic Legitimacy; Principles of Good Practice.

**References**

Howard, Jeffrey. "Community Service Learning in the Curriculum." In *Praxis I: A Faculty Casebook on Community Service Learning,* edited by Jeffrey Howard, 3–12. Ann Arbor: University of Michigan, OCSL Press, 1993.

Kolb, David A. *Experiential Learning: Experience as the Source of Learning and Development.* Englewood Cliffs: Prentice-Hall, 1984.

## Academic Legitimacy

Service-learning has been saddled with the unpleasant burden of proving its own legitimacy to others in academia simultaneous with its own nascency, i.e., at the same time it is being introduced, explored, and tested by early adopters. In addition to those reasons cited above (*see* Academic Credit), service-learning struggles with its own legitimacy for at least five reasons.

First, it suffers from the fact that it is relatively new (even unknown) to the majority of teachers in higher education, despite the view some have of it as a broad movement with a healthy history of some decades (e.g., Stanton, Giles, and Cruz). The new and the unknown in academia may be embraced by early adopters but are often threatening to the majority.

Second, service-learning is currently in its adolescent stages of growth, and it is adapting and developing quite quickly. Something new and fluid is even harder to grasp, appreciate, and apply than something new and static.

Third, it is a pedagogy or set of pedagogies, rather than a discipline, subject, content area, or theory. While pedagogy is an essential part of academia and often fascinates those who love teaching, it may not captivate the minds of many in academia the same way that non-pedagogical theories, ideas, and models seem to do.

Fourth, service-learning is applicable to all disciplines and is developing across the disciplines, rather than being specific to only one discipline. Thus, like other interdisciplinary or transdisciplinary fields or areas of interest, service-learning is devalued and disadvantaged by the rigid status quo of an academia structured predominantly by disciplines.

Fifth, the service components of service-learning are rarely value-neutral and most often assume a compassionate, progressive, radical, or religious social, economic, or political agenda on the part of the teacher, the course, the departmen, or the institution.

For the traditional professoriate who are more comfortable with what Boyer calls the "German university tradition" and see the university as a venue for knowledge and the pursuit of "truth," social change, action, activism, volunteering, and community benefit are anathema.

Consequently, the speed and extent to which colleges and universities embrace service-learning is not dependent entirely upon service-learning itself.

**References**

Boyer, Ernest L. "Creating the New American College." *Chronicle of Higher Education* (Mar 9, 1994): 48.

Boyer, Ernest L. *Scholarship Reconsidered: Priorities of the Professoriate.* Princeton: Carnegie Foundation for the Advancement of Teaching, 1990.

Stanton, Timothy K., Dwight E. Giles, Jr., and Nadinne I. Cruz. *Service-Learning: A Movement's Pioneers Reflect on Its Origins, Practice, and Future.* San Francisco: Jossey-Bass, 1999.

## Alternative Break Programs

During summers and academic semester breaks, many students participate in alternative break programs that involve service-learning. According to Break Away, an organization that promotes alternative break programs, such programs offer students the chance to "perform short term projects for community agencies and learn about issues such as literacy, poverty, racism, hunger, homelessness and the environment." Whether alternative break programs offer service or service-learning depends upon the service-learning definitions and criteria employed. Break Away has developed eight criteria for good alternative break programs:

1. Strong Direct Service: Programs provide an opportunity for participants to engage in direct or "hands-on" service that addresses critical but unmet social needs.

2. Orientation: Participants are oriented to the mission and objectives of both the break program and the host agency or organization with which they will be working.

3. Education: Programs establish and achieve educational objectives to give participants a sense of context and understanding of both the region in which they will be working and of the problems they will be addressing during the break.

4. Training: Participants are provided with adequate training in skills necessary to carry out tasks and projects during the trip. Ideally this training should take place prior to departure, although in some instances it may occur once participants have reached their site.

5. Reflection: During the trip, participants reflect upon the experiences they are having. Applying classroom learning and integrating many academic disciplines should also occur. The site leaders should set aside time for reflection to take place, both individually and in a group setting.

6. Reorientation: Upon return to campus, there should be a reorientation session for all participants where they can share their break experiences with one another and with the greater campus community and are actively encouraged to translate this experience into a lifelong commitment to service.

7. Diversity: Strong alternative break programs include participants representing the range of students present in the campus community. Coordinators should recruit, design, implement and evaluate their program with this end in mind.

8. Alcohol and Other Drug-Free: Programs must be aware that issues of legality, liability, and personal safety and group cohesion are of concern when alcohol and other drugs are consumed on an alternative break. Programs should provide education and training on alcohol and other drug-related issues as well as develop a policy on how these issues will be dealt with on an alternative break.

**Reference**

*Break Away*, http://www.alternativebreaks.com, January 2000.

## America Reads and America Counts Programs

The America Reads and America Counts Programs are designed to improve children's interest and skills in reading and students' interest and skills in mathematics, respectively. President Clinton announced the America Reads Program in August of 1996. Its overall objective is to foster in children a love of reading and help every child in the U.S. read by the end of the third grade. The program has many facets, and helping children read happens in many ways: parents can read with their children; teachers, principals, and librarians can offer "after-school, summer and weekend literacy programs," etc. But the primary strategies involve tutoring and mentoring, which are performed by "AmeriCorps members. . . , Foster Grandparents, RSVP volunteers and Learn and Serve College students," and many others. The U.S. Department of Education and the Corporation for National Service (CNS) are partners in the initiative, and the program makes use of the diverse service programs and networks of volunteers and partner organizations funded by CNS.

The America Counts Program, a more recent effort, is similar in some ways to the America Reads Program, but also quite different. A joint program of the Department of Education and the National Science Foundation, it seeks to improve mathematics learning and teaching in the U.S. by pursuing six "strategic goals": train better teachers, "[p]rovide personal attention and additional learning time for students," support better research, "build public understanding of the mathematics today's students must master," improve curricula and standards, and ensure the best use of resources. Service and service-learning come in to play in the second goal. Tutoring and mentoring (by college students and others) are activities that enhance personal attention and assist younger students in learning mathematics.

### References

*Corporation for National Service*, http://www. nationalservice.org, April 2000.

*America Reads*, http://www.nationalservice.org/ areads/index.html; http://www.ed.gov/inits/ americareads/, April 2000.

*America Counts*, http://www.ed.gov/americacounts/, April 2000.

## AmeriCorps

AmeriCorps is an umbrella program within the Corporation for National Service (CNS), under which hundreds of different service programs are supported. AmeriCorps was created along with CNS in 1993 and is one of the Corporation's three primary programs. AmeriCorps programs are essentially service programs, not service-learning programs, although some argue that it is hard to delineate between the two in some AmeriCorps programs.

Two of the programs, AmeriCorps*VISTA (Volunteers in Service to America) and AmeriCorps*NCCC (the National Civilian Community Corps) are administered nationally. In AmeriCorps*VISTA, volunteers assist low-income communities in a variety of ways, e.g., by developing community-service programs. This is a one-year, full-time commitment for those who choose to serve. In AmeriCorps*NCCC, volunteers (aged 18 to 24) join a 10-month residential national service program and engage in full-time work projects away from home, doing everything from trail-building to tutoring. A third program,

AmeriCorps National Direct (or just AmeriCorps), is a network of hundreds of local to national service programs supported in part by AmeriCorps funding.

Recently, CNS added a new member to the AmeriCorps family: the AmeriCorps Promise Fellows Program, which is intended for "fellows" who wish to work for a year with human service agencies on projects that specifically improve the lives of children and youth. All AmeriCorps members receive health insurance and, at the completion of their service, earn an education award. Full-time AmeriCorps members earn a "modest living allowance." Other benefits vary depending on the program, time served, student status, etc.

### Reference

*Corporation for National Service*, http://www. nationalservice.org, January, 2000.

## Assessment and Evaluation

Assessment and evaluation play a prominent role in service-learning courses, programs, and literatures. Often, these terms are used synonymously. They refer to the measurement of many different phenomena: the effect of service on student learning; the effectiveness of the service-learning component of a particular course vis-a-vis the course content and goals; prior learning; learning outcomes and other benefits of service-learning courses; students' performance of service at a service site; faculty performance; courses (e.g., students' end-of-term evaluations of courses); program effectiveness; community and agency needs and perceptions; and the quality and quantity of service provided in a community by service-learning courses or programs.

Assessment is the focus of at least three conferences a year, i.e., the AAHE Assessment Conference, the Assessment Institute, and the Race Conference (Relevance of Assessment and Culture in Evaluation). In addition, most service-learning conferences, institutes, and workshops have at least one session on assessment or evaluation. Assessment also shows up as a topic of many conversations in the Service-Learning Discussion Group.

Two early sets of standards for assessing learning in general have been widely adopted in service-learning:

**Standards for Quality Assurance in Assessing Learning for Credit**

1. Credit should be awarded only for learning, and not for experience.
2. College credit should be awarded only for college-level learning.
3. Credit should be awarded only for learning that has a balance, appropriate to the subject, between theory and practical application.
4. The determination of competence levels and of credit awards must be made by appropriate subject matter and academic experts.
5. Credit should be appropriate to the academic context in which it is accepted.

(Whitaker, 1989)

**Principles of Good Practice for Assessing Student Learning**

1. The assessment of student learning begins with educational values.
2. Assessment is most effective when it reflects an understanding of learning as multidimensional, integrated, and revealed in performance over time.
3. Assessment works best when the programs it seeks to improve have clear, explicitly stated purposes.
4. Assessment requires attention to outcomes but also and equally to the experiences that lead to those outcomes.
5. Assessment works best when it is ongoing, not episodic.
6. Assessment fosters wider improvement when representatives from across the educational community are involved.
7. Assessment makes a difference when it begins with issues of use and illuminates questions that people really care about.
8. Assessment is most likely to lead to improvement when it is part of larger set of conditions that promote change.
9. Through assessment, educators meet responsibilities to students and to the public.

(AAHE, 1992)

In addition, today there is an array of studies, models, articles, and guides in the literature and online to assist those with an interest in assessment itself or in the results of assessment studies. Kraft and Krug (1994) provide a comprehensive review of the research on and evaluation of service-learning through 1993. Their review includes "General Surveys," "Social Growth Investigations," "Psychological Development Investigations," "Moral Judgement Studies," "Intellectual Learning Investigations," "Community Impact and Effects on Those Served," and "Evaluation of Colorado Service Learning Programs."

In *Connecting Cognition and Action: Evaluation of Student Performance in Service Learning Courses* (1995), Troppe explores a "Philosophy of Evaluation in Service Learning Courses" and Bradley proposes "A Model for Evaluating Student Learning in Academically Based Service." Hesser (1995) investigates "Faculty Assessment of Student Learning. . ." and discovers that faculty are beginning to embrace experiential education and service-learning. He identifies ten factors that "explain the current widespread practice of experiential education/service-learning." Driscoll et al. (1996) propose a "comprehensive case study model of assessment. . . [that] responds to the need to measure the impact of service-learning on four constituencies (student, faculty, community, and institution)."

Assessment studies often provide practitioners with two kinds of much-needed information: results about outcomes, and details about assessment research designs and strategies. For example, the learning and development assessment studies by Astin et al., Eyler and Giles, Eyler et al., and Gray et al. produce substantive findings from longitudinal assessment research on service-learning, and, at the same time, inform the reader about the assessment process in general and about assessing service-learning in particular.

Recent publications in service-learning assessment include a book by McElhaney and Kezar on "community service learning focusing on outcomes assessment. . . [in which] one of the findings is that service-learning develops some unique outcomes that are not necessarily measured through traditional outcomes assessment or methods of evaluation. . . [The authors] explain the need to utilize alternative forms of assessment in service learning that captures these outcomes."

Cumbo and Vadeboncouer (1999) argue in a similar vein, and develop a model for integrating service-learning, "standards based educational reform, and authentic assessment." The authors claim that it "is now widely accepted that multiple-choice, norm-reference "traditional" tests fail to measure many important dimensions of learning and do not adequately promote effective teaching." Accordingly, they embrace "alternative" or "authentic assessments"—"'authentic' in that they engage students in real-world tasks that occur in real-life contexts."

Vernon and Ward (1999) point out that much assessment research on service-learning "tends to emphasize student learning outcomes and pedagogical issues and de-emphasize the community voice. To be true to the dual responsibility of service-learning to both campus and community constituencies, research must include both campus and community viewpoints."

Assessment workbooks also exist: the Center for Academic Excellence at Portland State University publishes *Assessing the Impact of Service Learning: A Workbook of Strategies and Methods*. The workbook is intended as a "guide to assist faculty, students, institutional leaders and community partners in understanding and assessing the impact of community-based service learning. It includes an overview of assessment measures, guides for the administration of each measure, and suggestions for how to use assessment data to further improve teaching and learning."

Finally, there are online resources available as well. For information on assessment in general, the Educational Resources Information Center (ERIC) Clearinghouse on Assessment and Evaluation (http://ericae.net/ftlib.htm) has "links to some of the best full-text books, reports, journal articles, newsletter articles and papers on the Internet that address educational measurement, evaluation and learning theory." It includes publications on educational quality, learning theory, evaluation, student evaluation, tests and testing, research, and statistical analysis. In addition, the Greater Kalamazoo Evaluation Project publishes a newsletter, *Evaluation for Learning*, to "foster evaluation throughout the Kalamazoo area. . . , enabling all organizations to continually improve their effectiveness and to communicate their outcomes to the rest of the community." The newsletters, beginning with the Winter 1998 issue, are available online at http://www.wmich.edu/evalctr/eval_nsltr/evalnsltr.htm.

There are also online resources specific to service-learning assessment and evaluation.

The Service-Learning Research and Development Center at the University of California—Berkeley (http://www-gse.berkeley.edu/research/slc/servicelearning.html) conducts research and evaluations of various service-learning programs (in K-12 and higher education) in California. The center has developed its own "Evaluation System for Experiential Education (ESEE), a comprehensive system to assess the impact of Service-Learning on students, faculty, educational institutions, and communities." A number of the ESEE evaluation instruments (surveys, etc.) are available online at: http://www-gse.berkeley.edu/research/slc/eval.htm. *See also* Benefits and Outcomes; "Conferences, Colloquia, Institutes, and Academies" in Chapter 5.

### References

American Association for Higher Education Assessment Forum, "Principles of Good Practice for Assessing Student Learning." Washington, DC: AAHE, 1992.

Astin, Alexander W., Lori J. Vogelgesang, Elaine K. Ikeda, and Jennifer A. Yee. *How Service Learning Affects Students: Executive Summary*. Los Angeles: Service Learning Clearinghouse Project, Higher Education Research Institute, University of California. January 2000. http://www.gseis. ucla.edu/slc/rhowas.html, April 2000.

*Corporation for National Service: Learn & Serve America!*, http://www.nationalservice. org/learn/index.html, April 2000.

*Corporation for National Service, Learn & Serve:Research,*http://www.nationalservice. org/learn/research/index.html, April 2000.

Cumbo, Kathryn Blash, and Jennifer A. Vadeboncouer. "What are Students Learning? Assessing Cognitive Outcomes in K-12 Service-Learning." *Michigan Journal of Community Service Learning* 6 (1999): 84–96.

Driscoll, Amy, Barbara Holland, Sherril Gelmon, and Seanna Kerrigan. "An Assessment Model for Service-Learning: Comprehensive Case Studies of Impact on Faculty, Students, Community, and Institution." *Michigan Journal of Community Service Learning* 3 (1996): 66–71.

Eyler, Janet, and Dwight E. Giles, Jr. *Where's the Learning in Service-Learning?* San Francisco: Jossey-Bass, 1999.

Eyler, Janet, Dwight E. Giles, Jr., and John Braxton. "The Impact of Service-Learning on College Students." *Michigan Journal of Community Service Learning* 4 (1997): 5–15.

Gray, Maryann J., Elizabeth H. Ondaatje, and Laura Zakaras. *Combining Service and Learning in Higher Education: Summary Report*. Santa Monica: Rand, 1999.

Hesser, Garry. "Faculty Assessment of Student Learning: Outcomes Attributed to Service-Learning and Evidence of Changes in Faculty Attitudes About Experiential Education." *Michigan Journal of Community Service Learning* 2 (1995): 33–42.

Ikeda, Elaine. E-mail message to the Service-Learning Discussion Group ("Evaluation

& Assessment Resources"). 13 February 2000.

Kezar, Adrianna. E-mail message to the Service-Learning Discussion Group ("Outcomes Assessment"). 20 July 1999.

McElhaney, Kellie, and Adrianna Kezar, A. *Community Service Learning in Higher Education: Outcomes Reassessed and Assessment Realigned.* ASHE-ERIC Higher Education Report Series. San Francisco: Jossey-Bass, 2001.

Kraft, Richard J., and James Krug. "Review of Research and Evaluation on Service Learning in Public and Higher Education." In *Building Community: Service Learning in the Academic Disciplines*, ed. Richard J. Kraft and Marc Swadener. Denver: Colorado Campus Compact,1994.

Miller, Jerry. "The Impact of Service-Learning Experiences on Students' Sense of Power." *Michigan Journal of Community Service Learning* 4 (1997): 16–21.

Miller, Jerry. "Linking Traditional and Service-Learning Courses: Outcome Evaluations Utilizing Two Pedagogically Distinct Models." *Michigan Journal of Community Service Learning* 1 (1994): 29–36.

*Portland State University, Center for Academic Excellence*, http://www.oaa.pdx.edu/cae/, May 2000.

Portland State University, Center for Academic Excellence. *Assessing the Impact of Service Learning: A Workbook of Strategies and Methods*. Portland. OR: Portland State University, Center for Academic Excellence, 1998.

Renner, Tanya, and Michele Bush. *Evaluation and Assessment in Service-Learning.* Mesa: Campus Compact National Center for Community Colleges, 1997.

Seifer, Sarena. E-mail message to the Service-Learning Discussion Group ("National Learn and Serve Evaluation"). 21 June 1996.

Troppe, Marie, ed. *Connecting Cognition and Action: Evaluation of Student Performance in Service Learning Courses*. Providence: Campus Compact, 1995.

Vernon, Andrea, and Kelly Ward. "Campus and Community Partnerships: Assessing Impacts and Strengthening Connections." *Michigan Journal of Community Service Learning* 6 (1999): 30–37.

Whitaker, Urban. *Assessing Learning: Standards, Principles, and Procedures*. Chicago: Council for Adult and Experiential Learning (CAEL), 1989.

Willingham, Warren W. *Principles of Good Practice in Assessing Experiential Learning*. Chicago: Council for Adult and Experiential Learning (CAEL), 1977.

**Awards.** *See* **Chapter 6.**

## Benefits and Outcomes of Service-Learning

From a pedagogical perspective, the primary reason to integrate service-learning into one's teaching is that it benefits students and their learning in ways that other pedagogies do not (or not as well as service-learning). In addition, its proponents argue that service-learning also contributes to non-academic dimensions of students' personal development. Over the years, many claims have been made about the benefits and outcomes of service-learning, some of them more reliable than others. How much—and in what ways—does service-learning actually benefit students?

A number of studies have been conducted to assess various outcomes of service and service-learning. In a recent study, "How Service Learning Affects Students," Astin, Vogelgesang, Ikeda, and Yee explored the effects of service and service-learning on the "cognitive and affective development" of a large sample (22,236) of college undergraduates. The study's authors conclude that participation in service "shows significant positive effects on all [of the] outcome measures [in the study]: academic performance (GPA, writing skills, critical thinking skills), values (commitment to activism and to promoting racial understanding), self-efficacy, leadership (leadership activities, self-rated leadership ability, interpersonal skills), choice of a service career, and plans to participate in service after college."

Moreover, they find that "[p]erforming service as part of a course (service learning) adds significantly to the benefits associated with community service for all outcomes except interpersonal skills, self-efficacy and leadership. . . .Benefits associated with course-based service were strongest for the academic outcomes, especially writing skills."

Several factors affect the extent to which service enhances learning and service-learning benefits the students: the "degree of [their] interest in the subject matter," how much "the professor encourages class discussion," how much the students "process the service experience with each other," and "the frequency with which professors connect the service experience to the course subject matter."

According to the study's authors, the "qualitative findings suggest that service learning is effective in part because it facilitates four types of outcomes: an increased sense of personal efficacy, an increased awareness of the world, an increased awareness of one's personal values, and increased engagement in the classroom experience . . . [and] that both faculty and students develop a heightened sense of civic responsibility and personal effectiveness through participation in service-learning courses."

A 1997 study of 286 community college students by Berson found that service-learning students "achieved higher final course grades and reported greater satisfaction with the course, the instructor, the reading assignments, and the grading system, and. . . had fewer absences. . . .In addition, the faculty members reported that. . . class discussions were more stimulating, the sections seemed more vital in terms of student involvement, the students seemed more challenged academically, more motivated to learn, and seemed to exert more effort in the course."

In 1996, after the first year of Learn and Serve America, Higher Education (LSAHE) programs, a national evaluation of the programs by Rand and UCLA concluded that "participation in service was associated with gains in student learning and development. Students participating in service showed greater increases in civic responsibility, academic achievement, and life skills than did non-participating students." In addition, "community organizations strongly valued the contributions of student volunteers and perceived the students as highly effective in meeting both organizational and client needs" (Seifer).

In 1999, Gray, Ondaatje, and Zakaras authored a *Summary Report* of Rand's evaluation of LSAHE's first three years (fiscal years 1995–97), and discovered "a strong correlation between student participation in a service-learning course and increased civic responsibility." However, while "[s]tudents were highly satisfied with their service-learning courses[,] . . . evidence of only modest gains in student development [was found]." The authors state that there was "no association between participation in a service-learning course and improvement in a student's academic abilities or career preparation. Correlation did emerge, however, when certain 'good practices' were employed—such as establishing strong links between the service experience and the course content, having student volunteers serve for more than 20 hours per semester, and discussing service in class."

In "The Impact of Service-Learning Experiences on Students' Sense of Power," Miller (1997) discovers that, contrary to his expectations, "students perceived people to have less power than before the [service-learning] experience." While these findings appear to be disappointing on their surface, Miller sees them in a positive light: "service-learning experiences may contribute to undergraduate education. . . [by] helping students to develop a more realistic sense of their own place and power in the world."

In "The Impact of Service-Learning on College Students," Eyler, Giles, and Braxton found that students "who chose to participate in serv-ice-learning experiences and those who did not differ significantly on virtually every outcome measure at the beginning of the service semester. Students who chose these activities were already higher on each of these measures with the exception of valuing attaining great wealth; in many cases these differences prior to choosing service-learning are greater than any changes that subsequently take place during a relatively brief exposure to service-learning."

As Schultz notes in his review of *Where's the Learning in Service-Learning?*, Eyler and Giles discuss learning outcomes in the following: personal and interpersonal development; understanding and applying knowledge; engagement, curiosity, and reflective practice; critical thinking; perspective transformation; and citizenship. Among other findings, the authors observe that service-learning "leads to the values, knowledge, skills, efficacy, and commitment that underlie effective citizenship," and that service-learning "make[s] a difference in student learning." Not unlike the authors of the second Rand study, Eyler and Giles point out that learning outcomes improve with improved service-learning courses and programs. This means "good community placements, applications of service to course work, extensive reflection, [and] diversity and community voice".

In summary, studies agree and disagree about the effect of service-learning on students' learning outcomes. Their results vary with different samples, study designs, etc. The main area of agreements are: (1) the extent to which service-learning is complex and therefore learning and development connected with it are difficult to measure; and (2) improved learning outcomes occur when there is better integration of service-learning into courses and programs. Of course, learning outcomes are just one of the benefits of—and students are just one group of beneficiaries in—service-learning. Most of the studies mentioned above also explore the many positive impacts of student service on their communities and their universities, including the thousands of hours of service performed, and strengthened community relations. *See also* Assessment and Evaluation.

## References

Astin, Alexander W., Lori J. Vogelgesang, Elaine K. Ikeda, and Jennifer A. Yee. *How Service Learning Affects Students: Executive Summary*. Los Angeles: Service Learning Clearinghouse Project, Higher Education Research Institute, University of California. January 2000. http://www.gseis.ucla.edu/slc/rhowas.html, April 2000.

Berson, Judith S. E-mail message to the Service-Learning Discussion Group ("Study Results Announced"). 25 August 1997.

*Corporation for National Service: Learn & Serve America!*, http://www.nationalservice.org/learn/index.html, April 2000.

*Corporation for National Service, Learn & Serve: Research*, http://www.nationalservice.org/learn/research/index.html, April 2000.

Eyler, Janet, and Dwight E. Giles, Jr. *Where's the Learning in Service-Learning?* San Francisco: Jossey-Bass, 1999.

Eyler, Janet, Dwight E. Giles, Jr., and John Braxton. "The Impact of Service-Learning on College Students." *Michigan Journal of Community Service Learning* 4 (1997): 5–15.

Gray, Maryann J., Elizabeth H. Ondaatje, and Laura Zakaras. *Combining Service and Learning in Higher Education: Summary Report*. Santa Monica: Rand, 1999.

Miller, Jerry. "The Impact of Service-Learning Experiences on Students' Sense of Power." *Michigan Journal of Community Service Learning* 4 (1997): 16–21.

Schultz, Steven. "Book Review: Where's the Learning in Service-Learning?" *Michigan Journal of Community Service Learning* 6 (1999): 142–143.

Seifer, Sarena. E-mail message to the Service-Learning Discussion Group ("National Learn and Serve Evaluation"). 21 June 1996.

*Service-Learning: The Home of Service-Learning on the World Wide Web: Benefits of Service-Learning*, http://csf.colorado.edu/sl/benefits.html, April 2000.

## Bibliographies. *See* Chapter 2.

## Books and Journals. *See* Chapter 2.

## Citizenship, Civic and Social Responsibility, and Civil Education

One of the main claims of service-learning is that it contributes (or seeks to contribute) to the enhancement of students' concepts of citizenship, civic and social responsibility, and civil education. Some proponents of service-learning also wish to achieve these goals by transforming education itself into something more civil than it appears to its critics to be at times.

Evidence of these themes in service-learning can be found in numerous places: the names of academic programs and courses, topics within courses, literatures embraced by service-learning, assessment and evaluation studies, and declarations. For example, there is the "Citizenship and Service Learning" program at Southwest Missouri State University, the "University College of Citizenship and Public Service" at Tufts University, the "Honors Civic Engagement Project" at Florida International University, the "Center for Civic Education and Service" at Florida State University, and "Civic House" at the University of Pennsylvania.

Boyer's work on "Scholarship Reconsidered" and "Creating the New American College" focuses on the larger intellectual effort necessary for reviving, re-discovering, and in some cases, reinventing the academy in ways that make it a viable venue for civic—and civil—education.

Two recent "declarations" also attest to the "civic mission" of our colleges and universities, and call on leadership and laypersons alike to commit or re-commit to this vision and mission of the academy. The first is the "Wingspread Declaration on Renewing the Civic Mission of the American Research University"

(Boyte and Hollander), which calls on research universities to "make democracy come alive" by "renewing the civic mission of American higher education". The second is the "Presidents' Fourth of July Declaration on the Civic Responsibility of Higher Education Declaration" (Ehrlich and Hollander), which seeks to "articulate the commitment of all sectors of higher education, public and private, two- and four-year, to their civic purposes and to identify the behaviors that will make that commitment manifest."

## References

Boyer, Ernest L. "Creating the New American College." *Chronicle of Higher Education* (Mar. 9, 1994): 48.

Boyer, Ernest L. *Scholarship Reconsidered: Priorities of the Professoriate.* Princeton: Carnegie Foundation for the Advancement of Teaching, 1990.

Boyte, Harry, and Elizabeth Hollander. "Wingspread Declaration on Renewing the Civic Mission of the American Research University." 1998–99. *Campus Compact*, http://www.compact.org, January 2000.

Ehrlich, Thomas, and Elizabeth Hollander. "Presidents' Fourth of July Declaration on the Civic Responsibility of Higher Education Declaration." 1999. *Campus Compact*, http://www.compact.org, January, 2000.

## Co-curricular Service, Community Service, and Volunteering

Are co-curricular service, community service, and volunteering service-learning? This question is at the heart of one of the fundamental debates in service-learning. Co-curricular service is (community) service or volunteering performed by students outside the curriculum. As Scheuermann notes, "From the YMCA to fraternity and sorority philanthropic activities, from Circle K to organizations affiliated with campus ministries, community service has long been an integral part of student life outside the classroom."

More recent attempts to add structure and reflection components to certain kinds of co-curricular service (e.g., semester break and immersion programs, and one-time service events) may begin to approach service-learning and deserve our attention. Some even use the term "co-curricular service-learning" now.

Nonetheless, the various "Principles of Good Practice" at the core of the field and specific sets of service-learning criteria designed and employed by numerous colleges and universities are all testimony to the fact that service-learning is something unique and that there are boundaries beyond which it is not useful to claim that service (simply because it takes place at school or on a college campus and is conducted by students) is service-learning. In general, co-curricular service, community service, and volunteering are essential to service-learning, but are not synonymous with it. Similar debates involve internships and service-learning. Campus Outreach Opportunity League (COOL) developed five "critical elements of thoughtful community service"(sometimes called "meaningful" or "quality" community service) to guide and improve the quality of service:

### Community Voice

Community voice is essential if we are to build bridges, make change, and solve problems. Any community service organization should make sure that the voice and needs of the community are included in the development of the community service program.

### Orientation and Training

Orientation and training are important first steps for any community service experience. Information should be provided for student volunteers about the community, the issue, and the agency or community group.

### Meaningful Action

Meaningful action means that the service being done is necessary and valuable to the community itself. Meaningful action makes people feel like what they did made a difference in a measurable way and that their time was utilized well. Without this, people will not want to continue their service no matter how well we do with the other four elements.

### Reflection

Reflection is a crucial component of the community service learning experience. Reflection should happen immediately after the experience to discuss it—reactions, stories, feelings, and facts about the issues which may dispel any stereotypes or an individual's alienation from service—and reflection should place the experience into a broader context.

### Evaluation

Evaluation measures the impact of the student's learning experience and the effectiveness of the service in the community. Students should evaluate their learning experience and agencies should evaluate the effectiveness of the student's service. Evaluation gives direction for improvement, growth, and change.

(Campus Outreach Opportunity League, 1993)

*See also* Internships.

### References

Campus Outreach Opportunity League. *Into the Streets: Organizing Manual.* St. Paul: COOL Press, 1993.

Scheuermann, Cesie Delve. "Ongoing Cocurricular Service-Learning." In *Service-Learning in Higher Education: Concepts and Practices*, edited by Barbara Jacoby and Associates. San Francisco: Jossey-Bass, 1996.

## Colleges and Universities with Service-Learning Programs or Courses. *See* Chapter 3.

## Conferences, Colloquia, Institutes, and Academies. *See* Chapter 5.

## Contemporary Issues and Topics in Service-Learning

In addition to the diverse array of service-learning topics and issues involving pedagogy, program development, institutionalization, and partnering with community agencies, a wide variety of substantive, contemporary issues come into play in service-learning courses, campus service-learning center projects, community agencies, and service-learning conferences. They also are the subjects of many conversations among subscribers to the author's Service-Learning Discussion Group (the "SL List") and other Internet listservs related to service or service-learning.

Some examples of these topics and issues include action, activism, and apathy; anti-nuclear legislation; the arts; the Balkan war and war in general; battering and domestic violence; child/youth development; citizenship, civic values and civil society; consumption and materialism; conflict resolution; democracy; diversity and multiculturalism; disability issues; disaster relief; drugs and substance abuse; economic development; education; environment and ecology; fundraising for nonprofits; HIV/AIDS prevention; housing and homelessness; human rights; hunger and food recycling; leadership; native American issues; Nike and Third World Exploitation; philanthropy; poverty; power, disempowerment, and empowerment; prejudice, racism, and discrimination; prison reform; school-to-work programs; sexism, women's rights and issues of gender; social justice; social responsibility; urbanism and urban issues; youth violence and violence in general.

Given that courses across the curriculum engage students in the problems of communities and cultures, and human service agencies pursue their mandates to assist those in need, these issues and topics are not surprising. This immense sweep of contemporary challenges and crises facing the world which one encounters in the field of service-learning reflects, as well, service-learning's relevance and integrative value in higher education today. *See also* Peace Studies and Service-Learning.

### Reference

*Service-Learning: The Home of Service-Learning on the World Wide Web: Service-Learning Discussion Group,* http://csf.colorado. edu/mail/sl, April 2000.

**Corporation For National Service (CNS).** *See* **"Corporation For National Service" in Chapter 4.**

## Course Criteria and Designations

Course criteria and designations can help distinguish, identify, and denote service-learning courses in the curriculum. What makes a course a service-learning course? What distinguishes it from other courses? What is unique to a service-learning course? What are the necessary components or pedagogical strategies required? These questions are among those central to all aspects of service-learning's success in higher education.

This quest for identity in service-learning is ubiquitous: throughout the literature; in conferences, workshops, and institutes; in the years of ongoing conversations taking place on Internet discussion groups; and in the plethora of constantly revised strategic plans for institutionalizing service-learning on college and university campuses across the U.S. While definitions and boundaries of service-learning will continue to be discussed and re-framed for a long time to come, in the present, some guidelines may help students, faculty and institutions identify service-learning courses in their curricula.

A logical response to this problem has been the development of criteria to be met in order for a course to be considered a service-learning course. Beyond the various "principles of good practice," the first university to develop such criteria for its own courses was the University of Utah in 1990 to 1991. When a course meets the criteria, it is designated as a "service-learning" course in the course schedule. Thus, in addition to helping with the issue of identity, criteria contribute to course designation, which in turn, contributes to the integration of service-learning courses into the curriculum. At the University of Utah, faculty interested in having a course designated as a service-learning course: "(1) submit a current syllabus with an indication of how service would be incorporated; (2)

include a one-paragraph description of the class; [and] (3) describe, in one page, how the class will meet the. . . nine criteria." A faculty committee is charged with reviewing proposals and approving "service-learning" designations.

As colleges and universities continue to institutionalize service-learning on their campuses and integrate it into the curriculum, the need to identify service-learning courses through the use of criteria, "SL" designations, and other means will increase. On the one hand, faculty and administrators will want to know what constitutes a service-learning course, and also which ones are service-learning courses. On the other hand, for purposes of enrollment, students will want to know which courses in the curriculum (or in their major) are service-learning courses.

A related issue involves the fact that instructors teach their courses differently: one professor may teach a course as a service-learning course one semester or year, and another professor may not do so the following semester or year. Course criteria and designations (and the decision to make a course a service-learning course in a given curriculum) may work in the direction of requiring all faculty who teach such a course to learn how to teach it as a service-learning course. Or they may be designed so that faculty continue to teach these courses the way they prefer (i.e., differently from one another).

In the past, the traditions and restrictions of print versions of college catalogs and semester course schedules (e.g., publication lead times of up to one year, and the limitations on space for new codes and text) have mitigated against the addition of "SL" course designations. The rapid growth of departmental and campus service-learning center Web sites has begun to make the task of identifying and advertising service-learning courses easier. The flexibility and potential for constant revision of Web sites allow for these courses to be taught in different ways by different instructors, and also for information about service-learning courses to be included in schedules and disseminated widely on campuses.

**Criteria for Designation of Service-Learning Classes (Lowell Bennion Community Service Center, University of Utah)**

1. Students in the class provide a needed service to individuals, organizations, schools, or other entities in the community.

2. The service experience relates to the subject matter of the course.

3. Activities in the class provide a method or methods for students to think about what they learned through the service experience and how these learnings related to the subject of the class.

4. The course offers a method to assess the learning derived from the service. Credit is given for the learning and its relation to the course, not for the service alone.

5. Service interactions in the community recognize the needs of service recipients, and offer an opportunity for recipients to be involved in the evaluation of the service.

6. The service opportunities are aimed at the development of the civic education of students even though they may also be focused on career preparation.

7. Knowledge from the discipline informs the service experiences with which the students are involved.

8. The class offers a way to learn from other class members as well as from the instructor.

9. Course options ensure that no student is required to participate in a service placement that creates a religious, political, and/or moral conflict for the student.

**Reference**

*Bennion Center, University of Utah,* http://www.bennioncenter.org, February 2000.

## Course Development

Course development involves producing an academic course which includes service-learning: it is a fundamental step in integrating service-learning into one's teaching and into the curriculum. As is the case with faculty development, course development can happen in a variety of ways and is enhanced through contact with service-learning staff or faculty, attending conferences, institutes, and workshops, and making use of Web sites and discussion groups. A significant percentage of service-learning literature is devoted to course development, implementation, and assessment. In addition, reviewing syllabi of existing service-learning courses (which can be found in the literature and online) can be of assistance to newcomers.

There are essentially two ways to develop a service-learning course: (1) create an entirely new course from the bottom up, and (2) transform an existing course into a service-learning course by integrating service-learning into it. Sometimes it is not possible to do the latter, but when it is, this approach has many advantages: the resulting service-learning course is already familiar to the teacher, it is much less work than developing a new course, and it avoids the procedural, political, and budgetary difficulties of getting a new course approved within a given curriculum.

Whatever the approach, faculty developing service-learning courses generally ask themselves a number of questions. For example, what are the learning goals of the course and in what way is the service component relevant to these goals? What kinds of service and which community agencies best fit the subject matter and learning goals of the course? Will service-learning be an option or will all students be required to engage in it? In courses where service-learning is optional, what will the course requirements be for each group of students in the class? How much time each week will students be expected to engage in service? How will service site supervisors evaluate student service? Which assessment techniques will be used to evaluate the service-learning aspects of the course? How much class time will be needed for reflection?

Identifying and contacting community agencies and potential service sites can be accomplished by faculty on their own, or in cooperation with service-learning staff and offices on campus, depending on the campus. There are a number of issues and concerns involved in this aspect of the process (e.g., Does an agency have a demonstrated need for volunteers? Is it interested in having students as service-learners? Are agency staff willing to become service-learning partners and supervisors of students engaged in service-learning?), and many guidelines have been developed to assist faculty in this part of the process. *See also* Faculty Development; Principles of Good Practice.

**References**

Bonar, Linda, Renee Buchanan, Irene Fisher, and Ann Wechsler, *Service-Learning in the Curriculum: A Faculty Guide to Course Development*. The Lowell Bennion Community Service Center, University of Utah, 1996.

Kraft, Richard J., and Marc Swadener, eds. *Building Community: Service Learning in the Academic Disciplines*. Denver: Colorado Campus Compact, 1994.

Jackson, Katherine, ed. *Redesigning Curricula: Models of Service Learning Syllabi*. Providence: Campus Compact, 1994.

Kupiec, Tamar Y., ed. *Rethinking Tradition: Integrating Service and Academic Study on College Campuses*. Providence: Campus Compact, 1993.

Student Employment and Service-Learning Center. *The University of Colorado at Boulder Service-Learning Handbook*. Boulder: University of Colorado—Boulder, 1995, 1996.

## Degrees in Service-Learning

Are there degrees in service-learning? Should there be? In the introduction to this book, service-learning is described as either learning, or pedagogy, or both. To many, this covers all aspects of service-learning. However, some people also see service-learning as an academic subject (even a discipline) unto itself. Certainly, there are related intellectual concerns, e.g., leadership, public service, and philanthropy, that have become subjects within higher education. Whether they are disciplines (like English, math, art, and biology) is for others to argue elsewhere. And, even though the academic status of service-learning is not synony-

mous with that of public service or leadership or biology, it involves public service, sometimes includes leadership and philanthropy, and can be used to teach biology. To date, there is no census on the status of service-learning as an academic subject.

Given that traditional academia (i.e., organized primarily by disciplines) has a habit of offering majors, minors, and degrees only in academic subjects (and sometimes only in disciplines), it is not surprising to learn that (as of June 2000) there are no graduate degrees or undergraduate majors in service-learning (that the author is aware of), only two undergraduate minors, and there are as few as seven colleges and universities that offer certificates in service-learning, designate service-learning on students' academic records, or honor students at graduation. Perhaps this will change; perhaps it will not. In order for change to occur, however, at least one of three changes will need to happen: those in favor of casting service-learning as an academic subject will have to convince enough of their colleagues that it is one; academic institutions will need to shed even more of their dependence on disciplines as their organizing principle and cornerstone of awarding degrees; or service-learning will have to become overwhelmingly popular among students as an area of study (not just a means of learning), and then enrollment numbers will subsequently shape academic budgets.

Education, as a subject and a field, warrants its own degrees, departments, and even schools and colleges. Over the years, advancements and innovations in educational theory, method and research have manifested themselves in various specializations within the larger field of education (e.g., special education, experiential education, etc.). If service-learning were to have its own "home" within academe, education seems a likely fit. *See also* Faculty Development; Principles of Good Practice; Chapter 3.

## Documenting Service

Documenting service conducted by students in service-learning courses is necessary for many reasons. First, faculty and service-learning centers must ensure that students show up at the service site and perform their service hours on a regular basis, as agreed. Second, service-learning centers and their respective colleges or universities must document and report out the number of total hours of service accomplished by their students each semester or year. This need is often prompted by grant requirements, institutional public relations, state and federal agency mandates, or the desire of service-learning faculty and centers to inform colleagues and administrators about the quantitative results of service-learning. Third, all partners in a service-learning relationship have an interest in monitoring and evaluating the quality of the service performed by students. Fourth, some colleges and universities want to include this kind of information in permanent student records or dossiers. This is especially relevant to those institutions that require service or service-learning to graduate. Finally, some institutions have record-keeping needs related to their practice of awarding certificates of service of one kind or another to graduating students.

California State University, Chico has a 4th-credit option. For credit to be awarded, student timesheets "have to be signed by a site supervisor of some sort (parent, teacher, etc.) Without proof of hours, no credit is given." At SUNY College at Oneonta, there is a "Record of Service which contains dates of service, position(s) held, and hours."

Gainesville College uses a "co-curricular transcript. . . an official document that records verifiable student activities which occur outside the classroom." Similarly, Gonzaga University developed a "co-curricular transcript that would include appropriate volunteer and service-learning experiences." Pace University has developed its own "Student Development Transcript." Brevard Community College has "implemented academic notation of service-learning on. . . [students'] academic transcript[s]."

The Service-Learning Center at Virginia Polytechnic Institute and State University gathers information in three ways: student timesheets, service-learning site supervisor evaluation forms, and end-of-semester faculty activity reports.

The timesheets are for logging hours and are completed by students. The supervisor evaluation forms, which also have a question about hours worked, are completed by supervisors for each student supervised. In the faculty activity reports, instructors include "the number of students who served in. . . class and the number of required hours." This provides "a good estimate of the total number of hours completed. . . [and t]he student timesheets and supervisor forms are good back ups."

At the College of St. Benedict/St. John's University, students "report through email and public folders on [their] computer network system." Responses are highest, however, "in classes where the students will be docked a few points if they do not respond on a weekly basis."

Many service-learning faculty and center staff have struggled with the issues of documenting service hours. The examples above illustrate some of the different types of forms that have been developed to address varying needs. Ultimately, however, each campus has to devise or adopt methods that suit its own needs best. *See also* Learning Agreements and Service Contracts.

## References

Berg, Deanna. E-mail message to the Service-Learning Discussion Group ("Collecting Service Hours"). 24 February 1999.

*Gainesville College Co-Curricular Transcript*, http://troy.gc.peachnet.edu/www/ssmith/cct/what.html, April 2000.

James-Deramo, Michele. E-mail message to Deanna Berg; included in Deanna Berg's message to the Service-Learning Discussion Group ("Collecting Service Hours"). 24 February 1999.

Masters, Ellen L. E-mail message to the Service-Learning Discussion Group ("Co-curricular Transcripts"). 15 November 1999.

Thorpe, Sima. E-mail message to the Service-Learning Discussion Group ("Co-curricular transcript development"). 27 July 1999.

## Faculty Development

Faculty development is an essential aspect of institutionalizing service-learning on college and university campuses. It involves introducing faculty to its benefits, concepts, theories, and methods; training them in course development, implementation, and assessment; and connecting them to existing service-learning and service infrastructures on campus, in the community, and across the country. Faculty development occurs through contact with service-learning staff or faculty, at conferences, institutes, and workshops, and via Web sites online and discussion groups.

The Center for Public Service and Leadership at Indiana University–Purdue University Indianapolis (IUPUI) pursues faculty development by "offering course development stipends, offering faculty development workshops, assisting in the design of service learning courses, identifying community service opportunities, and linking faculty to regional and national organizations."

One aspect of faculty development involves seeing how service-learning might be effective in one's own discipline, and, more specifically, one's own courses. Providing faculty with service-learning syllabi in their respective disciplines is one means of accomplishing this task. Syllabi are included in much of the literature. In addition, online course lists and syllabi have been available or the author's Internet/Web site since 1993. Today, a growing number of college and university service-learning program Web sites are including their own course lists and syllabi online. Sharing syllabi is not the only way to help faculty visualize service-learning in their disciplines: the American Association for Higher Education (AAHE) is engaged in the production of an 18-volume monograph series on *Service-Learning in the Disciplines*. Each monograph focuses on service-learning in one discipline or field.

After initial explorations in service-learning, staff and faculty at many colleges and universities develop their own publications (e.g., handbooks, manuals, and guides) to facilitate faculty development on their campus. Some of the publications remain in-house; others are shared in print format and via the Web. One such publication is *The University of Colorado at Boulder Service-Learning Handbook*. Another is the *Service-Learning Faculty Manual*, developed by the Office for Service-Learning and Volunteer Programs' Service Integration Project at Colorado State University. IUPUI's Center for Public Service and Leadership has developed a number of publications, including "A Service-Learning Curriculum for Faculty," "Engaging and Supporting Faculty in Service Learning," *Service Learning Curriculum Guide for Campus-Based Workshops*, and *Service Learning Tips Sheets: A Faculty Resource Guide*.

Kendall's three-volume anthology, *Combining Service and Learning*, continues to be an essential resource on all aspects of service-learning, and every essay contributes in one way or another to faculty development. Finally, Campus Compact has published an *Introductory Service-Learning Toolkit*, which includes "readings and bibliographies on: Definitions and principles, Theory, Pedagogy, Community Partnerships, Reflection, Academic Culture, Student Development, Assessment, Tenure and Promotion, Model Programs, [and] Redesigning Curriculum." *See also* American Association for Higher Education, *Service-Learning in the Disciplines* in the "Monographs" section of Chapter 2; Course Development in this chapter.

### References

Bonar, Linda, Renee Buchanan, Irene Fisher, and Ann Wechsler, *Service-Learning in the Curriculum: A Faculty Guide to Course Development*. The Lowell Bennion Community Service Center, University of Utah, 1996.

Bringle, R.G., and J.A. Hatcher. "A Service-Learning Curriculum for Faculty." *Michigan Journal of Community Service Learning* 2 (1995): 112–122.

Bringle, R.G., J.A. Hatcher, and R. Games. "Engaging and Supporting Faculty in Service Learning." *Journal of Public Service and Outreach* 2 (1997): 43–51.

Campus Compact, *Introductory Service-Learning Toolkit*. Providence: Campus Compact, 1999. *Campus Compact*, http://www. compact.org/toolkit_new.html, May 2000.

Colorado State University, Office for Service-Learning and Volunteer Programs, Service Integration Project. *SIP Manual*. http://www.colostate.edu/Depts/SLVP/sipman.htm.

Foos, C., and J.A. Hatcher. *Service Learning Curriculum Guide for Campus-Based Workshops*. Indianapolis: Indiana Campus Compact, 1999.

Galiardi, Shari. E-mail message to the Service-Learning Discussion Group ("Here's what they said. . . ''). 13 March 2000.

Giles, Jr., Dwight E., and Janet Eyler. "The Theoretical Roots of Service-Learning in John Dewey: Toward a Theory of Service-Learning." *Michigan Journal of Community Service Learning* 1, no.1 (1994): 77–85.

Hatcher, J.A., ed. *Service Learning Tips Sheets: A Faculty Resource Guide*. Indianapolis: Indiana Campus Compact, 1998.

Ikeda, Elaine. E-mail message to the Service-Learning Discussion Group ("Evaluation & Assessment Resources"). 13 February 2000.

Jackson, Katherine, ed. *Redesigning Curricula: Models of Service Learning Syllabi*. Providence: Campus Compact, 1994.

Kendall, Jane C., and Associates, eds. *Combining Service and Learning: A Resource Book for Community and Public Service*. Volumes I-III. Raleigh: National Society for Internships and Experiential Education, 1990.

Kraft, Richard J., and Marc Swadener, eds. *Building Community: Service Learning in the Academic Disciplines*. Denver: Colorado Campus Compact, 1994.

Kupiec, Tamar Y., ed. *Rethinking Tradition: Integrating Service and Academic Study on College Campuses*. Providence: Campus Compact, 1993.

Office for Service-Learning and Volunteer Programs, Service Integration Project. *Service-Learning Faculty Manual*. Fort Collins: Colorado State University, 1996.

*Service-Learning: The Home of Service-Learning on the World Wide Web: Service-Learning Handbooks and Manuals*, http://csf.colorado.edu/sl/handbooks.html,April 2000.

Student Employment and Service-Learning Center. *The University of Colorado at Boulder Service-Learning Handbook*. Boulder: University of Colorado–Boulder, 1995, 1996.

*UCLA Service-Learning Clearinghouse Project*, http://www.gseis.ucla.edu/slc/, April 2000.

## Faculty Fellows

In general, faculty fellows are faculty members of a college or university who are awarded, or selected for, some kind of special status for a period of time (e.g., a semester or academic year). The purpose is usually faculty development or enhancing opportunities to engage in course development, research, or writing. Faculty fellows often receive some reduction in teaching load, additional research funding, or some other means of extra support.

In service-learning, this approach has become a useful faculty development tool as well as an innovative means of introducing service-learning to faculty, making service-learning more visible on campuses, and uniting faculty already engaged in it. Faculty familiar with service-learning are often alone in their interest or are members of extremely small minorities: their interests in service-learning are often invisible or barely visible to their colleagues, departmental leadership, and administrations. This phenomenon is magnified on larger campuses, where knowing all faculty members and their interests is not possible anyway. In such situations, faculty engaged in service-learning in their own classes and disciplines may often be unaware that others with similar interests or experiences exist at their institutions. Faculty fellows programs identify and bring together sometimes isolated individuals, thereby creating a community of scholars. Thus, service-learning faculty fellows programs serve many functions.

The Center for Public Service and Leadership at Indiana University-Purdue University Indianapolis (IUPUI) has one of the first and most extensive faculty fellows programs in service-learning: it supports "faculty in integrating professional service and outreach with research and teaching, and in documenting service in such a way that it can be evaluated and rewarded in the promotion, tenure, and review process."

There are four different kinds of faculty fellows programs at IUPUI: (1) HUD COPC, which works with the HUD Community Outreach Partnership Center and partners five faculty members and three neighborhoods over a three-year period; (2) the IU Strategic Direction Initiative, the focus of which is the "documentation of service and using and developing criteria to evaluate professional service"; (3) Indiana Campus Compact's Faculty Fellows Project, "a statewide program which gives faculty the opportunity to create stronger ties to their communities by integrating community service into teaching, research and service"; and (4) the Kellogg Peer Review of Professional Service, "a national program which identifies faculty who have engaged in significant community outreach and works with them to develop documentation that will allow effective peer review and evaluation." These programs are described more fully in, R.G. Bringle, et al., "Faculty Fellows Program: Enhancing Integrated Professional Development through Community Service."

Another excellent example of service-learning faculty fellows programs can be found at the University of Utah. The Bennion Center has a "Public Service Professorship" with funding designed to "cover release time to one or more faculty members annually who are selected by the Bennion Center's Faculty Advisory Board to carry out a community project or develop a service-learning course." The Bennion Center also offers an annual "Borchard Service-Learning Faculty Fellow Award" "to an experienced service-learning faculty member so that s/he can mentor other faculty members new to service-learning. Responsibilities of the fellow vary annually, based on the interests and skills of the fellow and the needs of the Center and include organizing sessions around service-learning topics, facilitating a service-learning discussion group on a campus network, and meeting one-on-one with faculty as needed."

Faculty Fellows programs can be found at a number of colleges and universities, including Cornell University, Eastern Michigan University, Mount St. Mary's College, and Wake Forest University. At Wheaton College, a "Faculty Fellow for Service Learning" is a member of the faculty who works with the Filene Center for Work & Learning and helps his or her colleagues in "course design and ongoing course/project evaluation."

Virginia Campus Outreach Opportunity League (VA COOL) has a statewide Faculty Fellows Program, in which "up to seven faculty [each year] from diverse disciplines and colleges across Virginia are selected through a competitive process to design a service-learning course and mentor other Virginia faculty interested in service-learning. Fellows join one another three times annually to develop and refine their service-learning efforts and to evolve as mentors to their peers." The program is funded by a grant from the Corporation for National Service Learn and Serve America: Higher Education.

## References

Bringle, R.G., R. Games, C. Ludlum, R. Osgood, and R. Osborne. "Faculty Fellows Program: Enhancing Integrated Professional Development through Community Service." *American Behavioral Scientist* 43, no. 5 (2000): 882–894.

*The Center for Public Service and Leadership*, http://cpsl.iupui.edu, April 2000.

Lowell Bennion Community Service Center. *Building An Engaged Campus: A Four-Year Plan to Strengthen Community Partnerships and Service-Learning and Encourage Community-Based Scholarship at the University of Utah*. Salt Lake City: University of Utah. December 1998.

*VA COOL*, http://www.student.richmond.edu/ ~jmarsh/, April 2000.

## Faculty Incentives

What incentives are there for faculty to learn about service-learning and integrate it into their teaching and courses? Proponents and critics alike have observed that there is ample work involved in the faculty development, course development, and teaching aspects of service-learning. When the common complaints among faculty are that they are overworked, underpaid, and short on time, why would any college teacher consider learning new ways of teaching, taking on more work, and not receiving additional compensation for any of it?

The issue of incentives is compounded by the fact that review, promotion, and tenure concerns put considerable pressure on faculty to publish and do research in their own disciplines and areas of specialty, not in a pedagogy that appears to be substantively unrelated to their fields or, at best, applicable across the disciplines.

There are at least four different categories of incentives for faculty to explore service-learning, all of which can be viewed as benefits of service-learning: those that accrue to the teacher, the student, the community, and the college or university.

The first category of faculty incentives can be divided into four subsets. The first relates to a teacher's interest in learning and teaching, e.g., a teacher's interest in making the course and learning experience better for students; enjoyment of the increased participation and excitement of students; desire to be a better teacher and to enjoy teaching more; and delight in continuing to learn, oneself. The second subset involves the benefits of better teaching that accrue to a teacher: improved course evaluations, increased recognition and visibility on campus, and perhaps even awards. The third subset includes possible faculty development grants and course reductions that might be available as a result of efforts on campus to institutionalize service-learning. The fourth subset has to do with review, promotion and tenure. Although much progress remains to be

made in this area, sometimes service-learning can be integrated into the curriculum and institution in such a way as to contribute to promotion, and tenure. In particular, some institutions with general-education curricula require faculty to participate in them in order to receive promotions and tenure. At Saint Francis College, for example, including a service-learning component in a course is one of the ways faculty can meet their general-education participation requirements.

The remaining three categories are benefits to students, community, and institution, yet all are ultimately incentives to faculty as well. These benefits include everything from student empowerment and personalized education to improved community health and education to enhanced campus-community relationships and collaboration. *See also* Benefits and Outcomes of Service-Learning.

### References

*Benefits of Service-Learning, Service-Learning Home Web site*, http://csf.colorado. edu/sl/benefits.html, April 2000.

Mitzel, Meg. E-mail message to the Service-Learning Discussion Group (''Faculty Incentives''). 12 May 1999.

## Fellowships. *See* Chapter 6.

## Foundations. *See* Chapter 6.

## Fourth Credit Options

One way to increase the number of service-learning courses on campus and integrate service-learning across the curriculum is the Fourth Credit Option (sometimes called a ''One Credit Option''), whereby instructors offer an extra hour of academic credit (i.e., a fourth credit, when added to a traditional three-credit course) to students interested in additional service-learning work connected to the course. This approach circumvents many of the problems often associated with getting new courses developed and approved by numerous committees and offices.

A number of colleges and universities employ this approach. Examples include California State University, Chico, Goucher College, Kean University, Mount St. Mary's College, and Northern State University. A creative variation of this theme can be found in the at Ethics Program at Villanova University (http://www.villanova.edu/servlet/Web2000): a fourth hour of class and credit for service-learning have been added to a regular course to transform it into a four-credit service-learning course. But here, the entire class is involved. The professor meets with the students three hours per week for "the more formal classroom discussion and one hour a week, in smaller groups, for reflection on their experience."

Even though the development of new courses can be avoided by adding a fourth-credit option to existing courses, teachers still must learn about service-learning and how to incorporate it into their courses. A simple add-on without course integration would most likely prove disastrous for all involved. In particular, when offering service-learning as extra credit in a class where the majority of students are not involved in the service or the service-learning, special care is needed to successfully integrate the service and the learning into the course. *See also* "Directory of Colleges and Universities with Service-Learning Programs or Courses" in Chapter 3.

**References**

Berg, Deanna. E-mail message to the Service-Learning Discussion Group ("Collecting Service Hours"). 24 February 1999.

Doorley, Mark. E-mail message to the Service-Learning Discussion Group ("A Request"). 15 September 1999.

*Villanova University*, http://www.villanova.edu/servlet/Web2000, February 2000.

**Funding.** *See* **Chapter 6.**

**Grants.** *See* **Chapter 6.**

**Immersion Programs**

Immersion Programs take students out of familiar surroundings and routines and "immerse" them in new ones. They are not unique to service-learning, of course, but appear to be one of the many forms service-learning takes. Immersion programs are often found in foreign-language instruction. In service-learning, they vary in form and duration, lasting anywhere from one or two days to a semester or summer. Alternative break programs represent one kind of immersion program. An excellent example can be found at the University of Notre Dame. Their Center for Social Concerns has a one-credit seminar called the "Urban Plunge," "a 48-hour immersion in inner-city life during winter vacation, preceded by readings and a workshop on justice issues, followed by discussion with faculty. . . .Alumni provide opportunities for discussion during the immersion experience, and faculty host follow-up sessions in their homes to facilitate further reflection. The Plunge experience often prompts further academic investigation into the root causes of poverty and urban concerns as well as exploration of potential solutions."

A number of service-learning institutions have immersion programs, including Augsburg College, Baldwin-Wallace College, Creighton University, Gettysburg College, Goshen College, Loyola College in Maryland, Rice University, Saint Francis Xavier University, Saint Mary's University, and Tusculum College. Baldwin-Wallace College offers a "semester-long urban immersion program. . . [in which] students live and study in an urban neighborhood while working in an internship with a nonprofit organization." The Center for Public Service at Gettysburg College has a service-learning immersion program "which functions somewhat like an Alternative Break program with trips to domestic and international sites during winter and spring break." At Loyola College in Maryland, the Service Leadership program "requires one course be an immersion program."

Rice University's Community Involvement Center offers an International Summer Service Project, an Alternative Spring Break Program, and a summer Urban Immersion Program ("a week-long service intensive orientation to Houston's cultural and social issues"). At Saint Francis Xavier University, "Immersion SL. . .

[involves] intense service experiences in communities which include inner city settings and international locations. . . Students may also choose to integrate an immersion experience with their chosen field of study through research for course credit, or specifically through [a] course. . . : Immersion Service Learning.'' Saint Mary's University provides "regional and international service immersion trips.'' And Tusculum College offers a two-to-three week "Service-Learning Immersion,'' in which students "immerse themselves in service projects and reflection.''

The power of such programs emanates from the ability to immerse students in another (often quite foreign) social, economic, or cultural context. As one might infer from the name chosen by the Center For Social Concerns for its seminar, the students' experience is not unlike diving into a body of cold (or hot) water: the immersion is a jolt that awakens the senses and raises awareness.

The potential problems in such approaches arise when they are administered without sufficient orientation and preparation prior to the immersion or the essential reflection and integration of the learning after the immersion. In addition, there are the prior curricular challenges of integrating co-curricular immersion experiences into the academic curriculum in general and the pedagogical challenges of integrating the specific immersion experience and learning into a specific course. Immersion programs also run other risks: precluding real service opportunities and learning due to abbreviated time frames; turning service and learning into field trips that transform those in need into "things" to see rather than people to serve; and leaving communities feeling invaded by armies of observers instead of feeling more integrated as the result of substantive relationship- and community-building. *See also* Alternative Break Programs.

### References

*Center For Social Concerns*, http://www.nd.edu/~ndcntrsc, April 2000.

Buckley, Honora. E-mail message to the Service-Learning Discussion Group ("Curriculum-Based Immersion Programs''). 29 April 1999.

Grusky, Sara. E-mail message to the Service-Learning Discussion Group ("international sl''). 15 May, 1998.

Syrett, Heather C. E-mail message to the Service-Learning Discussion Group ("Position Announcement''). 1 April 1998.

## Institutionalizing Service-Learning on Campus

An essential task of campus administrations and service-learning faculty and staff is to institutionalize service-learning, i.e., create and nurture programs and courses that become part of the fabric of their institutions. One approach to introducing and institutionalizing service-learning on college and university campuses involves reminding and reawakening the leadership of these institutions of the historic purpose and mission of higher education in the United States. Boyer's work on "Scholarship Reconsidered'' and "Creating the New American College'' contributes significantly to this larger intellectual effort.

In addition, Campus Compact has been successful in this arena: as a membership organization at the level of college and university presidents and chancellors, it recruits presidents (and thus institutions) into the fold. The Campus Compact "President's Statement of Principles,'' endorsed by member presidents in 1996, commits them and their institutions to value and work toward a commendable array of individual and public goals and goods, including: "personal and social responsibility''; "public and community service''; "the social and economic well-being of America's communities''; "the common good of American and global society''; "the quality of civic discourse''; "productive collaborations between colleges and communities''; "democratic participation by citizens''; "the application of the intellectual and material resources of higher education to help address the challenges that confront communities''; "student, faculty, staff and alumni involvement in citizenship-building service activities''; and "support [for] service learning because it enables students and faculty to integrate academic study with service through responsible and reflective involvement in the life of the community.''

The strategy is not foolproof, of course. One disadvantage is that institutional commitment on many campuses, as a result of scarce resources, often takes the form of presidential testimonies and revised mission statements proclaiming the importance of citizenship education, civic responsibility, service to community, and service-learning as a means of achieving these nebulous goals. Implementation of the commitment in the form of programs, staffing, budgets, and courses may or may not follow.

A second structural problem for some is that Campus Compact's access to, and communication with, presidents and chancellors, while advantageous in many ways, may not be advantages shared by lower-level staff in educational bureaucracies who are charged with the task of implementing service-learning on their campuses. This has the potential to create diffused and confused loci of responsibility and leadership, and parallel tracks of communication and implementation, with one track led by parties external to the campus community.

A third issue for some is limited resources: monies allocated to healthy membership dues in organizations like Campus Compact diminish or eliminate potential service-learning-program operating budgets. The benefits of this top-down/bottom-up approach, however, have been considerable, and presidential commitments alone, even if purely symbolic, are a significant accomplishment in that they raise awareness, educate, and make the leadership of educational institutions accountable for agendas that often compete with those arising out of the business of education.

Other significant issues which dominate the process of institutionalization are academic credit and legitimacy, perceived and actual benefits of service-learning, course development and curricular concerns connected with integration, faculty development, resource availability, and the structural and physical location of responsibility for service-learning within an institution and on campus. All of these issues, except for the last two are addressed in their own entries in this section of the book.

With regard to resource availability, everything and nothing can be said about this. Without the necessary resources, interdisciplinary initiatives perceived as "new" by many stand no chance of competing for the hearts and minds of faculty, staff, administrators, and alumnae. As a result, subsequent commitments to courses, classrooms, programs, and reasonable budgets remain elusive, if not unattainable. Resource availability depends primarily on campus commitment. The latter can be enhanced and assuaged by outside funding, often in the form of one-to-three-year seed grants for the purpose of institutionalization, but service-learning cannot ultimately survive on its own with external funding. Like all academic pursuits, it requires internal institutional commitments and resources to thrive and hold its own in the highly competitive marketplace of disciplines and departments that characterize the modern-day university. Moreover, however much external funding helps in the short term, it also has a tendency to undercut the legitimacy of service-learning on campus: the lack of institutional commitment is usually a visible sign to all that service-learning is valued less than are other curricular endeavors.

Finally, the importance of institutional location of service-learning varies greatly on campuses. Judging by the number of times this issue has been raised and thoroughly discussed by contributors to the Service-Learning Discussion Group over the years, it certainly is quite important to many. Conversely, plenty of campuses have not had to worry about it at all, perhaps because sufficient support and momentum have come from their mission statements, administrations, faculty, or existing centers or programs on campus, and the salience of location as an issue has been minimized.

For those who have found location to be a significant issue, however, it has often taken the form of a dilemma. Because it bridges the divide between academics and action, thinking and doing, campus and community, service-learning needs to be housed in such a way that both "sides" of the divide are honored and represented. However, on many campuses, there is a pre-existing structural separation between academics and student life or student services. This separation is personified, for example, in "divisions" and deans (academic deans and deans of students) and manifested in respective budgets and political turf, all of which, when joined by similar "divisions" of departments and professors competing for scarce academic resources, account for the lion's share of the enmity and intransigence of university politics. In other words, without wanting or meaning to do so, service-learning unfortunately falls directly into a pre-existing ideological, political, and bureaucratic quagmire and, in doing so, falls victim to powerful forces that keep it from reaching its full potential for campus and community alike.

To be perceived as academically legitimate, service-learning needs to be located on the academic "side" of an institution. Yet, to be able to work well with campus volunteer centers and staff, community agencies and partners, and the community at large, service-learning is better off on the student services "side" of a college or university. In practice, some service-learning offices have found it best to locate on one 'side' or the other. In some cases, these offices start in student services and over time decide to move to the academic "side"—or vice versa. Other campuses attempt to have service-learning straddle the divide from the outset.

In the author's view, one of service-learning's potential contributions to higher education is its inherent ability to help campuses move beyond the segregation, discrimination, and competition inherent in discipline-based, departmental, and divisional hierarchies to truly collaborative, interdisciplinary education. This, of course, is an immense agenda, embraced by a relatively small minority in academia, that goes far beyond the domain of service-learning. Nonetheless, if campuses can appreciate service-learning as a shared, collaborative educational endeavor that has ramifications for the curriculum as well as the soul of its stu-

dent body, then this is a first step toward that larger agenda. Thus, a collaborative approach to locating service-learning within an institution seems to offer the greatest long-term rewards. However, a shared location will have its conflicts and does not guarantee success. *See also* Campus Compact in "Service-Learning Organizations, Associations, and Networks" in Chapter 4.

## References

Boyer, Ernest L. "Creating the New American College." *Chronicle of Higher Education* (Mar 9, 1994): 48.

Boyer, Ernest L. *Scholarship Reconsidered: Priorities of the Professoriate.* Princeton: Carnegie Foundation for the Advancement of Teaching, 1990.

*Campus Compact*, http://www.compact.org, January 2000.

## Integrating Service-Learning into the Curriculum

Integrating service-learning into the curriculum is an essential part of intsitutionalizing service-learning on college and university campuses. Curricular integration requires initial institutional and faculty awareness of, and commitment to, service-learning (including the commitment of additional resources), acceptance of the idea of adopting new pedagogies, faculty development, and course development. Usually, service-learning courses are developed in one of three ways: through the addition of fourth-credit options to existing courses, by redesigning existing courses to include service-learning in a comprehensive fashion, and by developing new courses that are service-learning courses from the outset. Internships, practica, immersion programs, and alternative break programs are additional mechanisms for integrating service-learning into the curriculum. All of the strategies and processes mentioned above are discussed in detail in other entries. *See also* Faculty Development; Fourth Credit Options; Institutionalizing Service-Learning on Campus.

## International Service-Learning

While most service-learning occurs in communities throughout the United States, international service-learning has been around for a long time and is a gaining in visibility and popularity today. Given service-learning's reciprocal relationship between institutions of higher learning and their communities and community partners, most of the time service-learning is assumed to be a local, rather than international, enterprise. In addition to reciprocity, the coordination and integration of service and classes limits, to some extent, the geographic possibilities of traditional campus-based courses. For some, these limitations are invitations to creativity, not obstacles. For others, a wider view of service-learning eliminates the problem altogether. Moreover, adding global literacy and citizenship, multicultural education and experience, and international community-building to the mix of benefits in service-learning's already impressive portfolio is hard to resist.

International internships, study-abroad programs, and semester and summer break programs comprise the majority of international service-learning opportunities for U.S. students. Instead of struggling with the difficulties posed by linking international service with courses on campus, one approach simply involves sending students off to do study abroad or international internships—with service-learning or service components as part of the package. If the programs are already part of one's university (or external to it but already approved), transferring credit is not an issue. If this is not the case, then the only significant institutional challenge is approving the transferral of academic credit. The same is true for semester and summer break programs if academic credit is expected or desired by student participants. Bentley College, for example, is integrating service-learning into all of its study-abroad and international programs. Its pilot program is an international service-learning program in Budapest. Rice University, on the other hand, has its own Summer International Service Learning Trip.

Whether any program or experience is international service-learning or international service will depend on one's definition of service-learning. There is a large and growing number of organizations and venues that offer international service opportunities for students and non-students alike. In contrast, there are few organizations that offer international service-learning opportunities. The oldest and best-known among these is the International Partnership for Service-Learning, which offers service with academic study programs in the Czech Republic, Ecuador, England, France, India, Israel, Jamaica, Mexico, the Philippines, Scotland, and South Dakota in the United States. It also administers a one-year (British) master's degree program in International Service, in cooperation with affiliated universities in Great Britain, Mexico, and Jamaica.

A second organization is UK Centres for Experiential Learning, which offers a service-learning program through Westminster College, Oxford University, in addition to international community service and internships. In a slightly different vein, the School for International Training in Brattleboro, Vermont, offers a maste's degree in "International and Intercultural Service" and also arranges study-abroad and international-exchange programs. Finally, the Office of Community Outreach and Service Learning at University of Natal (Durban, KwaZulu-Natal, South Africa) administers its service-learning program for its own students and also engages in partnerships with tertiary institutions around the world to offer six-week service-learning courses to international students during the northern-hemisphere summer. *See also* "Service Organizations, Associations, and Networks" in Chapter 4; "Service-Learning Organizations, Associations, and Networks" in Chapter 4.

### References

*International Partnership for Service-Learning*, http://www.ipsl.org, April 2000.

*Office of Community Outreach and Service Learning, University of Natal*, http://www.und.ac.za/und/cadds/cosl.htm, February 2000.

*School for International Training in Brattleboro*, http://www.sit.edu, February 2000.

*UK Centres for Experiential Learning,* http://www.btinternet.com/~ukcentres, February 2000.

## Internships

Internships are one kind of experiential learning opportunity. They take many forms: some involve courses that students take for academic credit and/or financial remuneration; others are not connected with a curriculum, or at times, even with an educational institution. The kinds of internships relevant, here, are those that occur as academic courses.

Is an internship a service-learning course? The debate surrounding this question is close to the one surrounding co-curricular service, community service, and volunteering service-learning, i.e., are they service-learning? There are arguments on all sides of the debate, many reminiscent of those involving co-curricular service, community service, and volunteering. In the case of internships, it would appear that some internships clearly are service-learning, and some clearly are not. Those that fall in the latter category may simply be job training, or pre-employment opportunities for students about to pursue careers, i.e., there is no academic course content, about which students are learning through service. Or, there may be no service in the internship, e.g., when a student is simply being paid a wage to work temporarily for a company or a nonprofit organization like any other employee. Or, as is noted in the entry on co-curricular service, community service, and volunteering, internships may not include structured reflection or meet all of the criteria inherent in the various "Principles of Good Practice" in service-learning.

On the other hand, if they do meet these criteria, if there is service (not just employment), and if the internship is a means of learning outside the classroom about subject matter covered in the course, then an internship may be service-learning. Enos and Troppe suggest at least two differences between service-learning internships and traditional internships: "The opportunity for structured reflection with an emphasis on ties to the academic curriculum, so that students see connections between

their actions on the job and their work in the classroom, is one important distinction. Another. . . relates to some of the purposes that many argue are the ultimate goals of service-learning: the development of civic responsibility and moral character." Albert notes that service-learning internships offer "intensive" service-learning experiences, and discusses appropriate reflection strategies for them. *See also* Co-curricular Service, Community Service, and Volunteering.

### References

Albert, Gail. "Intensive Service-Learning Experiences." In *Service-Learning in Higher Education: Concepts and Practices*, edited by Barbara Jacoby and Associates. San Francisco: Jossey-Bass, 1996.

Enos, Sandra L., and Marie L. Troppe. "Service-Learning in the Curriculum." In *Service-Learning in Higher Education: Concepts and Practices*, edited by Barbara Jacoby and Associates. San Francisco: Jossey-Bass, 1996.

## Leadership

Leadership is often seen as one manifestation of service, and, it is argued, the best leaders are servants. The study of leadership has its own place in academia and its own literature. As service-learning has grown in higher education in recent years, however, many proponents have coupled it with leadership and leadership studies: conceptually as well as programmatically. Leadership development is not uncommon as a component of service-learning courses and programs, and leadership skills are frequently cited as benefits and outcomes of service-learning activities.

Althaus suggests that service-learning is a pedagogy for leadership development. In particular, she sees service-learning as part of a "curriculum for introducing students to nontraditional leadership styles, including those that are not based on power, authority, and hierarchy. Billingsley agrees: in the Presidents Leadership Class, at the University of Colorado at Boulder, "service is a basic objective and experientially based service learning is a fundamental part of the pedagogy.''

About ten percent of the service-learning programs in this book's directory of colleges and universities have ''leadership'' in their names, have leadership programs within them, or collaborate with other leadership programs or schools on their campuses. Examples of such programs are Ball State University (Office of Leadership and Service Programs); George Mason University (Center for Service and Leadership); Indiana University of Pennsylvania (Office for Service Leadership); Indiana University–Purdue University Indianapolis (Office of Service Learning, Center for Public Service and Leadership); James Madison University (Community Service-Learning, Center for Leadership, Service and Transitions); LaGrange College (Servant Leadership Initiative); Seattle University (Leadership and Service Office); University of Colorado at Boulder (the Service Learning Program, the Student Leadership Institute, and the Presidents Leadership Class); University of Detroit Mercy (Leadership Development Institute); University of Washington (Edward E. Carlson Leadership and Public Service Center); and Waynesburg College (Center for Service Leadership). Another ten percent or so mention leadership as part of the mission or work of their service-learning programs.

A few colleges and universities with service-learning programs also offer degrees or certificates in leadership. At Loyola College in Maryland, the Center for Values and Service has a new Service Leadership Program, through which students can earn the Service Leadership Program Certificate. Humboldt State University has a Service Learning/Experiential Education program and also offers a Leadership Studies minor, which involves service-learning courses and opportunities. Royal Roads University (British Columbia) offers a master of arts in Leadership and Training. In a related vein, the Jepson School of Leadership Studies at the University of Richmond requires service learning of all majors (the university also has a Service-Learning Program on its campus). *See also* ''Directory of Colleges and Universities with Service-Learning Programs or Courses'' in Chapter 3.

**References**

Althaus, Jennifer. ''Service-Learning and Leadership Development: Posing Questions Not Answers.'' *Michigan Journal of Community Service Learning* 4 (1997): 122–129.

Althaus, Jennifer. ''Service-Learning and Leadership Development: Posing Questions Not Answers Billingsley, Ronald G. ''Leadership Training and Service Learning.'' In *Building Community: Service Learning in the Academic Disciplines*, ed. Richard J. Kraft and Marc Swadener. Denver: Colorado Campus Compact, 1994.

Althaus, Jennifer. ''Service-Learning and Leadership Development: Posing Questions Not Answers Thorne, Wesley E. E-mail message to the Service-Learning Discussion Group (''Leadership & Service Resources''). 10 January 2000.

## Learn and Serve America—Higher Education

Learn and Serve America–Higher Education is one of three major programs of the Corporation for National Service. It is a grant program that helps support service-learning programs and training in schools and communities throughout the United States. As its name implies, Learn and Serve America–Higher Education, supports service-learning programs in higher education. Grants fund new programs, the replication of some existing programs that are highly successful, training, faculty development, etc. Grants are given both directly (colleges and universities) and indirectly (to some agencies, organizations, and Indian tribes) to support service-learning programs. In the last few years, Learn and Serve America has also started funding a National Service Learning Clearinghouse.

**References:**
*Corporation for National Service*, http://www. nationalservice.org, January 2000.

## Learning Agreements and Service Contracts

Learning agreements and service contracts (or student-supervisor contracts) are agreements between service-learning students and their teachers, educational institutions, and/or service agencies. They articulate and formalize understandings about learning objectives and outcomes, the nature and responsibilities of student service, and the expectations by all parties involved in service-learning relationships. Learning agreements or contracts are also techniques used by teachers of traditional (i.e., non-service-learning) courses to negotiate agreements with students about course performance, expectations, and grades. They can be used in this fashion in service-learning courses as well, but they also have the added function of serving to identify and concretize the expected learning outcomes related to service. In addition, service and learning contracts (along with waivers of various kinds) can become components of the liability procedures of service-learning programs. Finally, learning agreements and service contracts are often a necessary part of, or contribute to, assessment and evaluation procedures in service sites and service-learning courses.

Examples of learning agreements and service contracts are located throughout the literature and course syllabi (in print and on-line). Discussions and samples of service-learning agreements and contracts can be found in print in *Combining Service and Learning: A Resource Book for Community and Public Service, Volume II* (Kendall), and "Hunger for Justice: Service-Learning in Feminist/Liberation Theology" (James-Deramo). A number of college and university service-learning program Web sites have service-learning agreements and contracts online—either in the general program Web site or as part of their online service-learning course syllabi. See Gonzaga University's Office of Service-Learning Web site. (http://www.gonzaga.edu/service/gvs/service_learning/courses/index.html) and *Service-Learning: The Home of Service-Learning on the World Wide Web: Service-Learning Syllabi By Discipline* (http://csf.colorado.edu/sl/syllabi/index.html) for examples. *See also* Documenting Service.

### References

*Gonzaga University Office of Service-Learning*, http://www.gonzaga.edu/service/gvs/service_learning/courses/index.html, May 2000.

James-Deramo, Michele. "Hunger for Justice: Service-Learning in Feminist/Liberation Theology." In *Teaching for Justice: Concepts and Models for Service-Learning in Peace Studies*, edited by Kathleen Maas Weigert and Robin J. Crews. Washington, DC: American Association for Higher Education, 1999.

Kendall, Jane C., and Associates, eds. *Combining Service and Learning: A Resource Book for Community and Public Service*. Volume II. Raleigh: National Society for Internships and Experiential Education, 1990.

*Service-Learning: The Home of Service-Learning on the World Wide Web: Service-Learning Syllabi By Discipline*, http://csf.colorado.edu/sl/syllabi/index.html, May 2000.

## Learning Circles

According to Cynthia Scheinberg and the Bylaws of the Invisible College, learning circles are an "innovation" of their organization. They are "'small, on-going gatherings of people who come together to share their ideals, goals, practices and honest experiences in service learning. In all cases, learning circles seek to be free spaces where open discussion of hard questions can take place in a collaborative and enriching environment that brings together people from different constituencies.'" All Invisible College members join a learning circle, "'each of which shall maintain its own listserv for electronic discussion and collaboration. Each learning circle shall have a coordinator, responsible for facilitating discussion and collaboration. Learning circles can be organized around different themes, regions and interests. . . ' (Article IV, Section 2)." Thus learning circles serve a unique role among members of the Invisible College, yet may also be seen as a generic phenomenon, in which people attempt to maintain small-group communications via electronic mail. *See also* Invisible College in "Service-Learning Organizations, Associations, and Networks" in Chapter 4.

### Reference

Scheinberg, Cynthia. "Learning Circles." *Invisible College*, http://www.selu.edu/orgs/ic/learning.htm.

## Liability

Liability issues attract significant attention in service-learning. For example, are service-learning students employees of the university? Of the service agency? Are they entitled to health insurance or worker's compensation? Students can be injured while engaging in service, or while traveling to and from service sites. Similarly, students can unintentionally injure others while performing service. Programs involving international travel and service have additional liability concerns.

On one hand, service-learning faculty, staff, and their host institutions are encouraged to do all they can to anticipate and prevent potential liability problems in advance. They must also understand the basic legal issues surrounding liability and protect themselves against possible legal actions resulting from accidents, negligence, or insufficient risk management.

On the other hand, some colleges and universities treat service-learning courses and programs as they would any other academic course or program. As a result, injuries to others by students during the course of service-learning are covered by normal university insurance policies in the same way that internships, field experience and practica are covered. Student injuries are covered by student or parental health insurance.

Faculty and educational institutions interested in service-learning are fortunate to have a wealth of information available to them in this area. Liability and risk management continue to be constant session themes at most service-

learning conferences, institutes, and workshops. The various sets of "Principles of Good Practice" serve as useful guides to maximizing benefits and minimizing risks and liability. Volume II of Kendall's *Combining Service and Learning*, includes two helpful essays on the subject: "Legal Issues in Combining Service and Learning" (Goldstein et al.) and "Practical Issues for Youth Programs: Recruitment, Liability, Transportation" (Hedin and Conrad).

The Nonprofit Risk Management Center (Washington, DC; http://www.nonprofitrisk.org; e-mail: info@nonprofitrisk.org) has a *Community Service Briefs* series on liability and risk management that was written for grantees of the Corporation for National Service. The entire series is available online (Each publication can be downloaded free.). Titles include: *Avoiding a Crash Course: Auto Liability, Insurance and Safety for Nonprofits*; *Crisis Prevention: Effective AmeriCorps Program Management*; *Grievance Procedures for AmeriCorps\*USA*; *Insurance Basics for Community-Serving Programs*; *Legal Barriers to Volunteer Service*; *Legal Issues for Service-Learning Programs*; *Managing Volunteers Within the Law*; *Negotiating the Legal Maze to Volunteer Service*; and *State Liability Laws for Charitable Organizations and Volunteers*.

Programs with international service-learning can benefit from organizations like the Association of International Educators (NAFSA). NAFSA (Washington, DC; http://www.nafsa.org) "promotes the exchange of students and scholars to and from the United States. . . [and] sets and upholds standards of good practice. . . that strengthen[s] institutional programs and services related to international educational exchange." NAFSA's Standards and Policies include: statements on "International Educational Exchange," "Professional Competencies," "Health Insurance for Foreign Students," "AIDS and International Education Issues," principles for the "Administration of Sponsored Student Programs," and "International Educational Exchange," and a "Code of Ethics and Procedures for Filing and Investigating an Ethics Related Complaint."

## References

Cooper, Mark. *The Big Dummy's Guide to Service-Learning: 27 Simple Answers to Good Questions on: Faculty, Programmatic, Student, Administrative, & Non-Profit Issues*. Miami: Volunteer Action Center, Florida International University, http://www.fiu.edu/~time4chg/Library/bigdummy.html, May 2000.

Flueckiger, Anne. E-mail message to the Service-Learning Discussion Group ("Waivers, etc. for Overseas Travel"). 4 April 2000.

Nonprofit Risk Management Center, *State Liability Laws for Charitable Organizations and Volunteers*. Washington, DC: Nonprofit Risk Management Center, 1996.

Roufs, Andrea. E-mail message to the Service-Learning Discussion Group ("FAQ: Risk Management, Liability, Insurance and Service"). 13 December 1999.

Rypkema, Pam. *Avoiding a Crash Course: Auto Liability, Insurance and Safety for Nonprofits*. Washington, DC: Nonprofit Risk Management Center, 1995.

Rypkema, Pamela J., Herschel Dungey, and Eileen Cronin. *Grievance Procedures for AmeriCorps\*USA*. Washington, DC: Nonprofit Risk Management Center, 1997.

Rypkema, Pamela J., and Melanie L. Herman. *Crisis Prevention: Effective AmeriCorps Program Management*. Washington, DC: Nonprofit Risk Management Center, 1997.

Seidman, Anna. *Negotiating the Legal Maze to Volunteer Service*. Washington, DC: Nonprofit Risk Management Center, 1998.

Seidman, Anna, and Charles Tremper. *Legal Issues for Service-Learning Programs*. Washington, DC: Nonprofit Risk Management Center, 1994.

Tremper, Charles, and Anna Seidman. *Special Legal Issues for AmeriCorps\*USA*. Washington, DC: Nonprofit Risk Management Center, 1994.

Tremper, Charles, Anna Seidman, and Suzanne Tufts. *Managing Volunteers Within the Law*. Washington, DC: Nonprofit Risk Management Center, 1994.

Tremper, Charles, and Pamela Rypkema. *Insurance Basics for Community-Serving Programs*. Washington, DC: Nonprofit Risk Management Center, 1994.

Tufts, Suzanne, and Charles Tremper. *Legal Barriers to Volunteer Service*. Washington, DC: Nonprofit Risk Management Center, 1994.

## Mandatory vs. Voluntary Service-Learning

What happens when service (i.e., volunteering) is required in a service-learning course? Is it no longer volunteering? Is a special quality of service lost if it is mandatory? Should service-learning be optional in a course, or should it be required? These questions have challenged service-learning practitioners for years. Arguments both for and against mandating service and service-learning are compelling. Some arguments focus on the legitimacy of requiring service-learning in a course, others focus on the issue of requiring service and/or service-learning for graduation, and others involve the rights of school systems and states to mandate service and/or service-learning.

In the first instance, those who believe it is legitimate to require service-learning in a course argue that requiring service as a means of learning is essentially no different than requiring lab work, field work, or library research in order to complete a course. Moreover, it is not the service that is awarded a grade, but the overall learning and performance of a student in the course. In short, faculty mandate all kinds of things in a course (e.g., what to read, what kinds of papers to write, what kinds of exams students must take, what kinds of films to watch, what lab work to do, etc.) and the same standards should apply to service-learning.

Those opposed to requiring service-learning in a course have numerous concerns. First, volunteering is no longer volunteering once it is required. Second, some of the benefits of service-learning involve a student choosing to serve, and turning service into yet another course requirement reduces the possibility that a student will be excited about the experience. Third, service-learning puts additional demands on students outside of normal class hours and requiring it places an unequal burden on those students who have families or work to put themselves through school. Fourth, there are finite limits to the number of hours students can engage in service per week or semester; therefore students would be limited in the number of service-learning courses they could enroll in at one time, and thus their ability to select courses and graduate on time would be curtailed. Finally, service requirements may have a negative impact on some students' interest in future service: e.g., for those students "who are not willing or ready to volunteer," mandating service may diminish their willingness to volunteer in the future.

Fewer than ten percent of the colleges and universities included in this book's directory require service and/or service-learning to graduate. In addition, a few other institutions require service or service-learning in an honors program or in a specific program, college, or school within their university. Finally, a small number are considering proposals to mandate service or service-learning in the future. In religious institutions, serving others is often a central element of the mission of the school, and this is translated into graduation requirements for all students. In secular institutions, service and/or service-learning requirements exist for various reasons: some having do to with the service or outreach components of institutional missions and some arising out of pedagogical or programmatic developments within an institution. Requirements of this kind are easier to create in private colleges and universities, but they are found in public institutions as well.

All of the arguments for and against requiring service-learning in a course are also found in debates about institution-wide requirements. In addition, some proponents of service-learning fear the loss of some of its transformative power as pedagogy and social change agent if it moves from the margins of academia to the center, i.e, if it becomes institutionalized. For this group, there are inherent dangers in succeeding too much. Accordingly, there is a tension between seeking further legitimation, visibility, and resources, on the one hand, and achieving institutional acceptance and stability on the other hand.

Debates over the rights of school systems and states to mandate service and/or service-learning involve K-12 education. The author knows of no states that have passed laws requiring service or service-learning in public higher education. States "that have opted to adopt policies that involve fully integrated [K-12] service-learning"include California, Kentucky, Ohio, South Carolina, and Vermont. *See also* "Overview" and "Directory of Colleges and Universities with Service-Learning Programs or Courses" in Chapter 3.

### References

Ikeda, Elaine K. E-mail message to the Service-Learning Discussion Group ("Mandatory Community Service"). 20 February 2000.

*Mandatory Community Service: Citizenship Education or Involuntary Servitude?* Issue Paper. Denver: Education Commission of the States 1999.

Stukas, A. A., M. Snyder, and E. G. Clary. "The Effects of 'Mandatory Volunteerism' on Intentions to Volunteer." *Psychological Science* 10, no.1 (1999): 59–64.

Stukas, Art. E-mail message to the Service-Learning Discussion Group ("Mandatory Community Service"). 20 February 2000.

## The Martin Luther King Day of Service

The Martin Luther King Day of Service is a way to honor the memory of Dr. Martin Luther King, Jr. by engaging in service (and service-learning) on the national holiday in January that is named after the African American who championed nonviolence as the only means to justice and peace. Each year, thousands of people engage in service that benefits their local communities as part of this celebration of Dr. King, nonviolence, and service. According to Dr. King, "Everybody can be great, because everybody can serve."

Sponsors include the Corporation for National Service; the Martin Luther King, Jr. Center for Nonviolent Social Change, Inc.; Best Buy Co. Inc.; Do Something Kindness & Justice Challenge (an educational and interactive introduction to character education. In the two weeks following the federal holiday, students will perform millions of Acts of Kindness (helping others) and Acts of Justice (standing up for what is right); First Book (a national nonprofit organization. . . give[s] disadvantaged children the opportunity to read and own their first new books); Habitat for Humanity International; the Points of Light Foundation; United Way of America; and Youth Service America. CNS has an e-mail address for questions specific to MLK Day of Service: mlkday@cns.gov.

**References:**

*Corporation for National Service, Martin Luther King Day*, http://www.mlkday.org, April 2000.

## Mentoring and Tutoring

Often the service that college students do as part of their service-learning courses takes the form of mentoring and tutoring K-12 students. Mentoring (serving as a more experienced helper, guide, or role model) and tutoring (providing individual or specialized instruction) are a logical fit for students in search of service. Why? In the case of tutoring, a student majoring in Spanish can tutor younger students who are also learning the language (or help Spanish-speaking students learn English). A math student can help others who are struggling with their arithmetic or mathematics classes. And so on. There really is no subject matter or discipline that cannot be taught using service-learning: tutoring is always an option as a possible form of service.

Mentoring takes many forms in service-learning, and college students can serve as mentors in numerous ways: as Big Sisters or Big Brothers, teaching assistants, house builders in Habitat For Humanity, and so on. Students can even be mentors while serving as tutors. In some service-learning programs, roles are reversed and college students are mentored by others: "Through the Visiting Mentor Program, the Haas Center for Public Service at Stanford University invites individuals from the community to help students consider career and lifestyle issues. The purpose of the program is to enable experienced persons from various careers in the community and public service to interact with students informally" (Fisher). In addition, faculty often serve as mentors for students. In another variation, some colleges and universities have service-learning faculty mentors who serve as advisors for faculty new to service-learning.

University faculty and staff can also have "theoretical" service-learning mentors: in their study of the "pioneers" of the service-learning "movement," Stanton, Giles, and Cruz observe that most service-learning pioneers "felt a need both to theorize about their work and connect it to larger theories related to human, organization, and community development. They identified numerous public leaders and theoretical mentors as helping to show them the way in service-learning."

The service-learning literature on mentoring is ample. For example, Campus Compact alone has three publications on specifically on mentoring: *Best Practices in Campus-Based Mentoring: Linking College Students and At-Risk Youth, Resource Manual for Campus-Based Youth Mentoring Programs*, and *Knowing You've Made a Difference: Strengthening Campus-Based Mentoring Programs through Evaluation and Research*. The Learn and Serve America National Service-Learning Clearinghouse (University of Minnesota) has over 90 listings with the keyword, "mentoring," and 135 listings for the keyword, "mentor." Nearly nine percent of the colleges and universities in this book's directory mention mentoring as a part of their service-learning programs. Finally, many faculty handbooks and manuals in service-learning have sections on mentoring. See also "Directory of Colleges and Universities with Service-Learning Programs or Courses" in Chapter 3.

**References**

Campus Compact, *Best Practices in Campus-Based Mentoring: Linking College Students and At-Risk Youth*. Providence: Campus Compact, 1993.

Campus Compact, *Knowing You've Made a Difference: Strengthening Campus-Based Mentoring Programs through Evaluation and Research*. Providence: Campus Compact, 1990.

Campus Compact, *Resource Manual for Campus-Based Youth Mentoring Programs*. Providence: Campus Compact, 1993.

Fisher, Irene S. "Integrating Service-Learning Experiences into Postcollege Choices." In *Service-Learning in Higher Education: Concepts and Practices*, edited by Barbara Jacoby and Associates. San Francisco: Jossey-Bass, 1996.

Stanton, Timothy K., Dwight E. Giles, Jr., and Nadinne I. Cruz. "Helps, Hindrances, and Accomplishments." In *Service-Learning: A Movement's Pioneers Reflect on Its Origins, Practice, and Future*, ed. Timothy K. Stanton, Dwight E. Giles, Jr., and Nadinne I. Cruz. San Francisco: Jossey-Bass, 1999.

Vue-Benson, Robin, and Robert Shumer. *Topic Bibliography on Sources Related to Mentoring and Service*. National Service-Learning Cooperative Clearinghouse (NSLC), 1994. (Online: NSLC, http://www.nicsl.coled.umn.edu/res/bibs/bibs.htm).

## National Senior Service Corps

The National Senior Service Corps is the third main area of programs funded and overseen by the Corporation for National Service. In existence for more than thirty years, the Senior Corps includes the Foster Grandparent Program, the Senior Companion Program, and the Retired and Senior Volunteer Program (RSVP). Foster Grandparents volunteer to help children "with special or exceptional needs." They "offer. . . emotional support to child victims of abuse and neglect, tutor. . . children who lag behind in reading, mentor. . . troubled teenagers and young mothers, and car[e]. . . for premature infants and children with physical disabilities and severe illnesses."

In the Senior Companion Program, Senior Companions "reach out to adults, who need extra assistance to live independently in their own homes or communities." They "provide companionship and friendship to isolated frail seniors, assist with simple chores, provide transportation, and add richness to their clients' lives. Senior Companions serve frail older adults and their caregivers, adults with disabilities, and those with terminal illnesses."

In the Retired and Senior Volunteer Program (RSVP), Senior Volunteers perform many kinds of service in their communities: they "tutor children in reading and math, help to build houses, help get children immunized, model parenting skills to teen parents, participate in neighborhood watch programs, plan community gardens, deliver meals, offer disaster relief to victims of natural disasters, and help community organizations operate more efficiently."

**References**

*Corporation for National Service*, http://www.nationalservice.org, January 2000.

*Senior Service Corps*, http://www.nationalservice.org/senior/index.html, April 2000.

## Online Resources: Internet Discussion Groups and World Wide Web Sites. *See* Chapter 2.

## Organizations, Associations, and Networks (Service-Learning and Service-Related). *See* Chapter 4.

## Partnerships

Partnerships are the collaborative relationships (between faculty, students, service-learning staff, a college or university, community-service agencies, their constituencies, the larger community, and funding agencies or institutions) that are necessary for service-learning to work. "Partner" and "partnerships" appear to have joined the service-learning lexicon in the 1990s. The term partner even metamorphosed into a verb (''to partner'') and a gerund (''partnering'') along with ''mentoring'' and ''tutoring.'' In part, this might have come about as a result of the recognition by some campus-based service-learning initiatives that they were developing without actually knowing the needs of, or collaborating with, those community-based agencies and constituencies in their communities, upon which they depended for their service placements. Nonetheless, awareness and appreciation of partners was a logical step in the evolution of service-learning.

Community-Campus Partnerships for Health not only includes the word in its organizational name, it developed a working definition of partnership: ''a close mutual cooperation between parties having common interests, responsibilities, privileges and power.'' In addition, CCPH developed the following ''Principles of Good Community-Campus Partnerships,'' intended to guide the relationships and service shared by campus and community:

**Principles of Good Community-Campus Partnerships:**

- Partners have agreed upon mission, values, goals, and measurable outcomes for the partnership.
- The relationship between partners is characterized by mutual trust, respect, genuineness, and commitment.
- The partnership builds upon identified strengths and assets, but also addresses areas that need improvement.
- The partnership balances power among partners and enables resources among partners to be shared.
- There is clear, open and accessible communication between partners, making it an ongoing priority to listen to each need, develop a common language, and validate/clarify the meaning of terms.
- Roles, norms, and processes for the partnership are established with the input and agreement of all partners.
- There is feedback to, among, and from all

stakeholders in the partnership, with the goal of continuously improving the partnership and its outcomes.

- Partners share the credit for the partnership's accomplishments.
- Partnerships take time to develop and evolve over time.

(Community-Campus Partnerships for Health, 1998)

While service-learning has strengthened campus-community relationships, and actual partnerships between campuses and communities have improved significantly over the years, the assessment literature suggests that there is room for further refinement. In ''Campus and Community Partnerships: Assessing Impacts and Strengthening Connections,'' Vernon and Ward make four recommendations for improving service-learning partnerships: (1) ''[c]ommunication lines need to be opened between different parties involved in identifying service opportunities for students''; (2) ''[c]ampuses need to open their doors to community partners''; (3) [c]ampuses and communities need to jointly approach issues associated with recruitment, training, and retention of service providers''; and (4) [c]ampuses need to develop guidelines that clearly outline the purpose and expectations of different campus-based service initiatives.''

### References

Community-Campus Partnerships for Health, ''Principles of Good Community-Campus Partnerships,'' *Community-Campus Partnerships for Health*, http://futurehealth. ucsf.edu/ccph.html, January 2000.

Vernon, Andrea, and Kelly Ward. ''Campus and Community Partnerships: Assessing Impacts and Strengthening Connections.'' *Michigan Journal of Community Service Learning* 6, (1999): 30–37.

### Peace Studies and Service-Learning

Peace Studies is a broad interdisciplinary field that covers the pursuit of justice, the development of peace, and conflict analysis and resolution at all levels (intrapersonal to global). Thus, it includes many foci: social movements and social change; theories and methods of nonviolence; human rights; hunger, poverty, and economic justice; the analysis of power; security (environmental, economic, and more traditional strategic concerns); and the study of violence.

While interest in peace and justice is not a prerequisite for faculty who employ service-learning purely as a means of teaching their courses, there is a large overlap between the academic and intellectual objectives of peace studies and the pedagogical goals of service-learning. Even today, awareness of, and familiarity with, the academic field of peace studies by practitioners of service-learning is limited at best. The same can be said of academics in peace studies about service-learning. However, in the mid-1990s, interest in social justice on the part of some in service-learning led to initial explorations of peace studies. At NSEE's 1995 National Conference in New Orleans, not only was there increased interest in, and conversation about, service-learning among those in experiential education, there were discussions of peace studies and social justice and a roundtable presentation on "Service-Learning and Peace Studies Connections Between Academic Neighbors." One year later, at the NSEE's National Conference in Snowbird, Utah, there was a roundtable presentation on "Reflections on the Causes of Injustice and Their Relationship to Service-Learning Programs," and ad hoc discussions on the need for a separate listserv and a separate NSEE Special Interest Group (SIG) for those interested in social justice. Similarly, at the Peace Studies Association's Eighth Annual Meeting in April 1996, one of the roundtable choices was "Peace Studies and Service-Learning: Pedagogy and Possibilities." No doubt additional examples of shared interest and convergence can be found in the proceedings of other conferences and gatherings.

Today, this convergence is becoming increasingly institutionalized organizationally and in the literature. "Social Justice" is one of NSEE's 11 Social Interest Groups (SIGs); "Service-Learning" is another. The Social Justice SIG "[a]ddresses questions relating to social justice issues and their relationship to experiential education." In the literature, for example, peace studies joins accounting, biology, communication studies, composition, engineering, environmental studies, history, management, medical education, nursing, philosophy, political science, psychology, sociology, Spanish, teacher education, and women's studies in the American Association for Higher Education's 18-volume series on *Service-Learning in the Disciplines*. As more and more faculty in peace studies are introduced to service-learning and explore its applications as an ideal set of pedagogies for peace studies—and as more practitioners of service-learning discover the theoretical and real-world contributions of peace studies, the potential for "education for justice" to be part of constructive, nonviolent social change will grow considerably.

## References

Crews, Robin J. "Peace Studies, Pedagogy, and Social Change." In *Teaching for Justice: Concepts and Models for Service-Learning in Peace Studies*, edited by Kathleen Maas Weigert and Robin J. Crews, 23–32. Washington, DC: American Association for Higher Education, 1999.

Crews, Robin J., and Kathleen Maas Weigert. "Peace Studies and Service-Learning: Pedagogy and Possibilities." Roundtable, Eighth Annual Meeting of the Peace Studies Association. Richmond, IN: Earlham College, April 1996.

Crews, Robin J., Kathleen Maas Weigert, Nadinne Cruz, Dale Bryan, and Robert Seidel. "Service-Learning and Peace Studies: Connections Between Academic Neighbors." Roundtable, NSEE National Conference. New Orleans: November 1995.

*National Society for Experiential Education*, http://www.nsee.org/sigs.htm, January 2000.

O'Meara, KerryAnn, Robin J. Crews, and Carol Maybach. "Reflections on the Causes of Injustice and Their Relationship to Service-Learning Programs." Roundtable,

NSEE National Conference. Snowbird, UT: October 1996.

Weigert, Kathleen Maas, and Crews, Robin J., eds. *Teaching for Justice: Concepts and Models for Service-Learning in Peace Studies.* Washington, DC: American Association for Higher Education, 1999.

## Placement Issues

Faculty, administrators, and campus service-learning centers new to service-learning have questions and concerns about placing their students in service settings and are interested in developing guidelines about placements. As service-learning has matured, campuses have become more sensitive to their community partners' reciprocal concerns about college students being placed in their organizations. Accordingly, campuses have embraced more collaborative approaches to the development of placement guidelines. Most issues, of course, can be resolved quite successfully through good communication and collaborative skills, and through learning and service contracts.

Faculty and students need to understand the needs and expectations of community-service agencies and the constituencies they serve. They also need to prepare students for their service experience prior to showing up at a service site. Because courses and instructors vary significantly from one another, it is also important for community partners to understand the needs and expectations of instructors and students.

In addition to the needs and expectations of all parties, from the perspective of the university, there is the question of how much service is necessary per academic credit. Larger placement concerns within the university involve economic and logistical issues (e.g., related to transportation), the nature and purpose of organizations for which students might serve, university endorsement of student service that might appear to some as political acts, the liability of the university for student behavior during service, and so on.

When the author served as director of service-learning at the University of Colorado–

Boulder, the university's Service-Learning Faculty Council struggled with various placement issues, and in 1995 designed and approved a "Policy on Service-Learning Placements." The policy, which was "intended to assist faculty as they placed students in service-learning settings," benefitted from established regulations at the state level (i.e., from the Colorado Commission on Higher Education) governing university internships. For example, because internships required "three hours of work per week for each hour of credit," any "service-learning placements that take the form of internships" would need to do likewise. The internship regulations and service-learning policy, along with other factors and service-learning norms nationwide, contributed to an informal understanding that students in service-learning courses at the university would usually engage in three hours of service per week as part of their coursework. The policy also advised faculty that "[s]ervice placements should have a range that is circumscribed by the content of the course, be of a duration sufficient to enable the fulfillment of learning goals, and have the potential to stimulate course-relevant learning."

The larger issues related to university endorsement and liability were addressed by acknowledging that the "placement of students in a given organization is primarily for academic purposes, and therefore does not constitute an endorsement of that organization's principles by the University''; that the actions of students or agencies were their own and not the university's, and that "placement should terminate if these actions seriously jeopardize the academic purposes of the placement." Each college and university must address placement issues in its own way. Quite a few have done so by incorporating placement-related guidelines in their own service-learning handbooks and Web sites. *See also* Learning and Service Contracts.

**Reference**

Service-Learning Faculty Council. "Policy on Service-Learning Placements." In *The University of Colorado at Boulder Service-Learning Handbook.* Boulder: Student

Employment & Service-Learning Center, University of Colorado–Boulder, 1995.

## Principles of Good Practice

Principles of Good Practice are guidelines for understanding and designing good service-learning activities, courses, and programs. As service-learning has grown, its practitioners have reflected on their own experiences, hoping to learn from them and improve all aspects of service and learning. In doing so, they have established guidelines and principles along the way that both help to define service-learning and assist others in engaging in it as constructively as possible.

Some principles focus on those served, while others focus on the service itself. There are also principles that seek to define service-learning and delineate effective service-learning or service-learning programs. Other types of principles are devoted to service-learning pedagogies and/or ways to integrate service-learning into a course. The following six sets of principles, most of them quite well-known in service-learning circles, are salient examples of such guidelines.

### Service-Learning: Three Principles

1. Those being served control the service(s) provided;

2. Those being served become better able to serve and be served by their own actions; and

3. Those who serve also are learners and have significant control over what is expected to be learned.

(Sigmon, 1979)

### The Wingspread Principles of Good Practice for Combining Service and Learning an Effective Program:

1. engages people in responsible and challenging actions for the common good.

2. provides structured opportunities for people to reflect critically on their service experience.

3. articulates clear service and learning goals for everyone involved.

4. allows for those with needs to define those needs.

5. clarifies the responsibilities of each person and organization involved.

6. matches service providers and service needs through a process that recognizes changing circumstances.

7. expects genuine, active, and sustained organizational commitment.

8. includes training, supervision, monitoring, support, recognition, and evaluation to meet service and learning goals.

9. insures that the time commitment for service and learning is flexible, appropriate, and in the best interests of all involved.

10. is committed to program participation by and with diverse populations

(Porter Honnet and Poulsen, 1989)

### Principles of Good Practice in Community Service Learning Pedagogy

1. Academic Credit is for Learning, not for Service.

2. Do Not Compromise Academic Rigor.

3. Set Learning Goals for Students.

4. Establish Criteria for the Selection of Community Service Placements.

5. Provide Educationally-Sound Mechanisms to Harvest the Community Learning.

6. Provide Supports for Students to Learn how to Harvest the Community Learning.

7. Minimize the Distinction between the Student's Community Learning Role and the Classroom Learning Role.

8. Re-Think the Faculty Instructional Role.

9. Be Prepared for Uncertainty and Variation in Student Learning Outcomes.

10. Maximize the Community Responsibility Orientation of the Course.

(Howard, 1993).

**Essential Characteristics for Course Inclusion
in the Service Integration Project**

1. The syllabus is developed or revised to incorporate the service experience into the teaching and learning objectives of the course.

2. Involve students in at least 5 hours of service in the community for each hour of credit they are receiving for the course.

3. Students do not receive credit for the time spent performing service, but for their knowledge in connecting their service experience with the course content.

4. The service experience must be connected to the course through readings and presentation in class.

5. Reflection on the service experience includes dialogue about social, psychological, political and ethical considerations involved in the service and the need for the service.

6. The faculty member is willing to become acquainted with each community agency (understands the agency mission, clientele, location and student role) that students are placed with. This knowledge could be obtained through the Service Integration Project or through direct contact with the agency.

7. The course will provide students with information about the agency and the clients and/or issue area that it serves before the service begins.

8. Students, faculty and community agencies participate in an evaluation process provided by the Service Integration Project.

(*Essential Characteristics. . .* , 1994)

**Diversity Principles of Good Practice in
Combining Service and Learning**

A program committed to diversity:

1. Engages people to notice, reflect on, and participate in dialogues about dialogues about differences in defining, interpreting and expressing concepts of "responsibility," "action," and "common good."

2. Encourages a variety of ways to "do" and express "reflection," including nondirective discussion, story-telling, varieties of artistic expression in various media. . . in addition to analytic modes more commonly regarded as "legitimate" especially in the academy.

3. Respects and acknowledges different cultural practices that shape how people define "goals," develop them, and feel a comfort level with precise definitions or lack thereof. In addition, a program committed to diversity provides time and structure for participants to experience together a process of struggling across differences in coming to consensus and/or principled disagreement in defining what is to be accomplished and what is to be learned.

4. Recognizes that some people may not view themselves primarily in terms of "need," and that the concept of "need" may be contested by those who view themselves as having borne the costs of historical legacies of colonialism, slavery, patriarchy, and other forms of subjugation or oppression.

5. Honors varying organizational cultures, some of which may define responsibilities more formally and explicitly according to a more rational-legal model, while others may be organized in more fluid, informal ways.

6. Respects the different cultural approaches that inform different participants about who is to be "matched," by whom, with whom, and how.

7. Respects varying ways by which "commitment" is culturally defined and expressed, and accounts for the possibility that failure to honor commitments may unequally and negatively affect different people involved in the program.

8. Respects culturally different ways by which training, supervision, monitor-

ing, support, recognition, and evaluation are defined and expressed.

9. Makes possible the effective participation of low-income working people, single parents, and others who experience
constraints defined by different economic and cultural realities.

10. Commits the necessary resources to encourage expression of voices of diverse
participants who hold to competing in-
terpretations of the "Principles of Good
Practice in Service-Learning" and to
competing assumptions that underlie
them.

(Cruz, 1996; intended to accompany the Wingspread "Principles of Good Practice" as
"Alternative Diversity Principles")

### References

Cruz, Nadinne. "Proposed Diversity Principles of Good Practice in Combining Service and Learning." In *Service-Learning in
Higher Education: Concepts and Practices*, edited by Barbara Jacoby and Associates. San Francisco: Jossey-Bass, 1996.

*Essential Characteristics for Course Inclusion
in the Service Integration Project*. Fort
Collins: Colorado State University, 1994.

Howard, Jeffrey. "Community Service Learn-
ing in the Curriculum." In *Praxis I: A
Faculty Casebook on Community Service
Learning,* edited by Jeffrey Howard. Ann
Arbor: University of Michigan, OCSL
Press, 1993.

Porter Honnet, Ellen, and Susan J. Poulsen.
*Principles of Good Practice for Combin-
ing Service and Learning. Wingspread
Special Report*. Racine: Johnson Foundation, 1989.

Sigmon, Robert. "Service-Learning: Three Principles." *Synergist* 8, no.1 (1979): 10.

## Problem-Based Learning (PBL)

According to the Center for Problem-Based
Learning Research and Communications at
Samford University and Howard S. Barrows,
problem-based learning is "an instructional
strategy that promotes active learning." In PBL,
learning is student centered and occurs in small
groups. "Teachers are facilitators or guides.
Problems form the organizing focus and stimulus for learning. . . [and] are a vehicle for the
development of clinical problem-solving skills.
New information is acquired through self-directed learning."

Citing Barrows, the center lists a number of
PBL objectives and outcomes (which appear to
be shared, at least collectively, by other progressive pedagogies, e.g., active learning, service-learning, cooperative and collaborative learning, and experiential education):

- Problem-solving skills
- Self-directed learning skills
- Ability to find and use appropriate resources
- Critical thinking
- Measurable knowledge base
- Performance ability
- Social and ethical skills
- Self-sufficient and self-motivated
- Facility with computer
- Leadership skills
- Ability to work on a team
- Communication skills
- Proactive thinking
- Congruence with workplace skills

In "Connecting Service- and Classroom-
Based Learning: The Use of Problem-Based
Learning," Whitfield argues that problem-based
learning can "strengthen service-learning curricula" and help students "connect academic
and community-based learning." PBL has existed since the 1950s, primarily in university
health-science programs.

### References

*Center for Problem-Based Learning Research
and Communications*, http://www.samford.
edu/pbl, February 2000.

Barrows, Howard S. "Problem-Based Learn-
ing in Medicine and Beyond: A Brief
Overview." In *Bringing Problem-Based
Higher Education: Theory and Practice:
New Directions for Teaching and Learn-*

*ing*, edited by L. Wilkerson and W. H. Gijselaers. San Francisco: Jossey-Bass, 1996.

Whitfield, Toni S. "Connecting Service- and Classroom-Based Learning: The Use of Problem-Based Learning." *Michigan Journal of Community Service Learning* 6 (1999): 106–111.

## Reflection

Reflection is a fundamental component of all service-learning courses and programs. Eyler, Giles, and Schmiede describe it as "a process specifically structured to help examine the frameworks that we use to interpret experience; critical reflection pushes us to step outside of the old and familiar and to reframe our questions and our conclusions in innovative and more effective terms." Stanton, Giles, and Cruz echo this view in their description of reflection: it is "stepping back from intense social engagement to learn from it in order to be more effective the next time, and the connecting of these reflections with existing theoretical knowledge."

Eyler, Giles, and Schmiede note that Dewey argued that "reflective thinking" was part of "reflective activity," and that the latter consists of five phases: "suggestion," "intellectualization," "the hypothesis," "reasoning," and "testing the hypothesis in action." From their research involving in-depth interviews of students, the authors discover that "effective critical reflection is continuous, connected, challenging, [and] contextualized." That is to say, it is "[c]ontinuous in time frame, [c]onnected to the 'big picture' information provided by academic pursuits, [c]hallenging to assumptions and complacency, and [c]ontextualized in terms of design and setting."

Everyone benefits from normal, everyday, unstructured reflection; it occurs as part of students' service experiences, too. However, the various forms of reflection so often discussed and employed in service-learning are of a different kind: they are intentional, structured, and formal. While reflection can be employed in traditional and service-learning pedagogies in many aspects of students' learning and development processes, its primary use in service-learning is as a means of learning from the (service) experience and integrating it with students' course-based learning. As Jacoby notes, "Reflection can take many forms: individual and group, oral and written, directly related to discipline-based course material or not." Written reflection can occur through journals, daily or weekly written assignments, short essays, integrative papers, and even e-mail discussions (Crews). At the University of Utah, a "theoretically based template for implementing written reflection. . . [leads students] to reflect on the following aspects of the service-learning program: the [a]ffect (which involves exploration of feelings and emotions), [b]ehavior (meaning the actions taken before, during, and after the service-learning project), and [c]ognition or [c]ontent (information, concepts, or skills examined)."

While they were writing *A Practitioner's Guide to Reflection in Service-Learning: Student Voices & Reflections*, Eyler, Giles, and Schmiede observed that, "with the exception of Harry Silcox's book, (1993) very little literature on reflection in service-learning existed." However, the literature on reflection has grown considerably in recent years: those interested in learning about reflection today have many resources available to them. Most service-learning faculty guides and manuals include a section on reflection. The Learn and Serve America National Service-Learning Clearinghouse literature database includes over 40 listings for monographs, book chapters, or serial articles with "reflection" in the title; over 240 have "reflection" as a keyword in the citation. Reflection is also an important topic in discussions on the Service-Learning Discussion Group: keyword searches of the SL List's archives produce many hundreds of messages which include "reflection" in their discussions. Finally, information about reflection appears in a large majority of all college and university service-learning Web sites. *See also* "Directory of Colleges and Universities with Service-Learning Programs or Courses" in Chapter 3.

**References**

Crews, Robin J. "Learning About Peace Through Service: Introduction to Peace and Conflict Studies at the University of Colorado at Boulder." In *Teaching for Justice: Concepts and Models for Service-Learning in Peace Studies*, edited by Kathleen Maas Weigert and Robin J. Crews. Washington, DC: American Association for Higher Education, 1999.

Dewey, John. *How We Think*. Boston: Heath, 1933.

Dewey, John. *Experience and Education*. New York: Collier Books, 1938.

Eyler, Janet, Dwight E. Giles, Jr., and Angela Schmiede. *A Practitioner's Guide to Reflection in Service-Learning: Student Voices & Reflections*. Nashville: Vanderbilt University, 1996.

Jacoby, Barbara. "Service-Learning in Today's Higher Education." In *Service-Learning in Higher Education: Concepts and Practices*, edited by Barbara Jacoby and Associates. San Francisco: Jossey-Bass, 1996.

Kolb, David A. *Experiential Learning: Experience as the Source of Learning and Development*. Englewood Cliffs: Prentice-Hall, 1984.

Scheuermann, Cesie Delve. "Ongoing Cocurricular Service-Learning." In *Service-Learning in Higher Education: Concepts and Practices*, edited by Barbara Jacoby and Associates. San Francisco: Jossey-Bass, 1996.

Silcox, H. C. *A How-To Guide to Reflection: Adding Cognitive Learning to Community Service Programs*. Philadelphia: Brighton Press, 1993.

Stanton, Timothy K., Dwight E. Giles, Jr., and Nadinne I. Cruz. "Helps, Hindrances, and Accomplishments." In *Service-Learning: A Movement's Pioneers Reflect on Its Origins, Practice, and Future*, ed. Stanton, Timothy K., Dwight E. Giles, Jr., and Nadinne I. Cruz. San Francisco: Jossey-Bass, 1999.

Treacy, Ann. E-mail message to the Service-Learning Discussion Group ("Articles on Service-Learning [NSEE Quarterly]"). 24 January 2000.

Welch, M. "The ABCs of Reflection: A Template for Students and Instructors to Implement Written Reflection in Service-Learning." *NSEE Quarterly*, 25, no. 2 (1999): 23–25.

## Residence Halls and Theme Housing

An innovative approach to institutionalizing service-learning on campus involves dedicating a residence hall or other student housing to service-learning. Theme housing in general is commonplace on college campuses, and adding service-learning to the mix of themes is a useful way to educate students about service-learning. Students in service-learning halls then become informal service-learning ambassadors on campus: they communicate their interest to other students and to their instructors.

It is not difficult to imagine how students in a house dedicated to community service would manifest their commitment. Most likely, they would engage in various service projects in the community and on campus. The service might be conducted in collaboration with other service-related groups on campus, e.g., Alpha Phi Omega or the campus volunteer center. What do service-learning halls or houses do? Just as honors dorms may have honors seminars taught on site (with enrollment restricted to residents), service-learning courses are taught to students in some service-learning halls. Service projects required in such courses may be conducted as hall service projects. In other cases, service-learning is a joint theme (e.g., with leadership). Courses taught in these halls may focus primarily on another theme and incorporate service-learning as a means of teaching the courses.

Roughly 25 percent of the colleges and universities included in this book's directory indicate that they have service-learning residence halls or theme houses. The actual amount may be significantly smaller, as many of the responses may be referring to housing with community service—rather than service-learning—

themes (or service-learning may be connected indirectly to the main theme of a house, e.g., the "Peace and Social Justice floor" of a residence hall at the University of Detroit Mercy. *See also* "Directory of Colleges and Universities with Service-Learning Programs or Courses" in Chapter 3.

**Scholarships.** *See* **Chapter 6.**

**Service-Learning: Definitions.** *See* **Introduction.**

## Types of Service

One way to measure the applicability of service-learning across the curriculum is to explore the many types of service possible. The following categories or "areas of focus" come from the Idealist Web site, which lists volunteer opportunities at some 20,000 organizations in 140 countries: arts; children and youth; community building and renewal; community (Internet) networks; community service and volunteering; computers and technology; consumer protection; crime and safety; disability issues; disaster relief; economic development; education; energy conservation; environment; family and parenting; farming and agriculture; foundations and fundraising; coalitions; gay, lesbian, and bisexual issues; government oversight and reform; health; housing and homelessness; human rights and civil liberties; immigration; job training and workplace issues; legal assistance; library or resource centers; media; men's issues; mental health; multiservice community agencies; networks of nonprofit organizations; peace and conflict resolution; personal finance; poverty and hunger; prison reform; race and ethnicity; recovery, addiction, and abuse; recreation and leisure;

religion; rural issues; seniors and retirement issues; spiritual and metaphysical issues; veterans of wars; voting and democracy; wildlife and animal welfare; and women's issues.

Types of service can be categorized in many different ways: these areas of focus represent just one way to do so. For example, the area of "education," above, is huge, and might be further divided into: (1) primary, secondary, and higher education, or (2) subject areas, e.g., English, foreign-language instruction, tutoring in reading, writing, or mathematics, etc. Similarly, the category of "health" appears to include the entire spectrum of medicine, hospitals, physical therapy, fitness, sports, etc. "Peace and conflict resolution" encompasses everything from justice, nonviolence, and social change to international security and arms control; from interpersonal conflict resolution, mediation, and dispute resolution (in the legal system) to ethnic, civil, and international conflict resolution. Moreover, if one were to add categories like "international" or "multicultural," the range of possible service venues would grow even more.

No community is likely to have a full complement of service opportunities, but every community is likely to have some. Most often, every community has more needs than it can meet and human-service agencies devoted to helping meet those needs. In other words, usually significant need exists in every community to satisfy the demands of service-learning courses in local colleges and universities. And, as is evident from the diverse categories above, there are plenty of types of service to meets the service-learning needs of all disciplines in academia.

### Reference
*Idealist*, http://www.idealist.org, April 2000.

# 2
# Literature and Online Resources

## Monographs: An Annotated Selection of "Essential Texts"

Despite the fact that it is a relatively new discipline, service-learning has a large and growing literature. Much of this literature is identified repeatedly in bibliographies in nearly every new service-learning article, book, or publication. This section does not attempt to survey or reproduce such bibliographies (although the third section, below, is a compilation of individually published bibliographies of service-learning). Instead, the following 11 annotated entries offer a selection of 32 volumes considered by the author to be essential for any service-learning library or scholar. While only monographs are annotated here, the *Michigan Journal of Community Service Learning* is also essential reading (see the Journals section, below, for a complete entry). It should be noted that "The Theoretical Roots of Service-Learning in John Dewey: Toward a Theory of Service-Learning" (Giles and Eyler), in the journal's inaugural issue, deserves particular attention.

**American Association for Higher Education (AAHE).** *Service-Learning in the Disciplines.* **Monograph Series. Washington, DC: AAHE, 1997–2000.**
This is an ambitious 18-volume series that illustrates the universality of service-learning across disciplines and interdisciplinary fields, with each volume serving as a guide to instructors within a discipline or field. The monographs greatly assist those interested in integrating service-learning into a particular discipline, who otherwise would have to search

journal articles, papers, and conversations on the Net for relevant (often anecdotal) information. The subtitle for each volume is *Concepts and Models for Service-Learning in [discipline]*. For example, the full title of the peace studies volume is *Teaching for Justice: Concepts and Models for Service-Learning in Peace Studies*. Discipline/field, volume editor(s), title (when known) and (expected) date of each publication are as follows:

Accounting: D.V. Rama, ed. 1998. *Learning by Doing.*

Biology: Brubaker, Dave, and Joel Ostroff, eds. Expected 2002. *Life, Learning & the Community.*

Communication Studies: Droge, David, and Bren Ortega Murphy, eds. 1999. *Voices of Strong Democracy.*

Composition: Adler-Kassner, Linda, Robert Crooks, and Ann Watters, eds. 1997. *Writing the Community.*

Engineering: Tsang, Edmund, ed. 2000. *Projects That Matter.*

Environmental Studies: Harold Ward, ed. 1999. *Acting Locally.*

History: Donovan, Bill, and Ira Harkavy, eds. 2000. *Connecting Past and Present.*

Management: Godfrey., Paul C., and Edward T. Grasso, eds. 2000. *Learning by Serving.*

Medical Education: Seifer, Sarena D., Kris Hermanns, and Judy Lewis, eds. 1999. *Creating Community-Responsive Physicians.*

Nursing: Norbeck, Jane S., Charlene Connolly, and JoEllen Koerner, eds. 1998. *Caring and Community*.

Peace Studies: Weigert, Kathleen Maas, and Robin J. Crews, eds. 1999. *Teaching for Justice*.

Philosophy: Lisman, C. David, and Irene E. Harvey, eds. 2000. *Beyond the Tower*.

Political Science: Battistoni, Richard M., and William E. Hudson, eds. 1997. *Experiencing Citizenship*.

Psychology: Bringle, Robert G., and Donna K. Duffy, eds. 1998. *With Service in Mind*.

Sociology: Ostrow, James, Gerry Hesser, and Sandra Enos, eds. 1999. *Cultivating the Sociological Imagination*.

Spanish: Hellebrandt, Josef, and Lucia T. Varona, eds. 1999. *Construyendo Puentes (Building Bridges)*.

Teacher Education: Erickson, Joseph A., and Jeffrey B. Anderson, eds. 1997. *Learning With the Community*.

Women's Studies: Balliet, Barbara, and Kerry Heffernan, eds. Expected 2002.

Edward Zlotkowski, series editor. $28.50 per volume ($24.50 for AAHE members); $405 for the entire series (prices include cost of shipping to U.S. destinations). Additional online information about the series: http://www. aahe.org/service/series.htm. Questions and order information: AAHE Publications Orders Desk, (202) 293–6440 x11, or by e-mail: rstarks@aahe.org.

**Bonar, Linda, Renee Buchanan, Irene Fisher, and Ann Wechsler,** *Service-Learning in the Curriculum: A Faculty Guide to Course Development*. **The Lowell Bennion Community Service Center, University of Utah, 1996.**

The authors wrote this guide "for faculty of the University of Utah as an aid to discover, explore, and develop service-learning in the curriculum." The guide's intended audience and objectives may be local, but its usefulness

is universal and faculty from all colleges and universities will find it extraordinarily helpful. Its three sections ("Service-Learning Defined and Described," "A Rationale for Institutionalizing Service-Learning," and "Service-Learning for Practitioners") provide information on every aspect of service-learning necessary for newcomers and experienced practitioners, including background and histories, benefits, a conceptual model, course development, definitions, evaluation, key elements, reflection, risk management, and issues surrounding working with one's community. Among its nine appendices are "Criteria for Designation of Service-Learning Classes," "Officially Designated Service-Learning Classes," "Surveys of Student Attitudes Toward Service-Learning," "Journal Examples," and "Sample Student Performance Evaluation." The publication also contains an annotated bibliography.

***Community Service in Higher Education: A Decade of Development.* Providence: Providence College, 1996.**

This small publication and the narrative documentary on service-learning's "pioneers" by Stanton et al (see entry below) are two important, and quite different, contributions towards a larger, collective history of service-learning. This text is a review of the preceding decade, of the "community service movement" beginning in 1985. It takes the shape of an initial, reflective essay by Goodwin Liu, which is followed up by a nine responses from 11 of the 17 participants who came together in July 1995 to discuss and respond to Liu's essay as a group. The publication closes with an afterword by Liu, which takes into account the critiques and concerns of the responses to his initial essay. The result is a personal yet analytical account that is highly informative.

**Eyler, Janet, Dwight E. Giles, Jr., and Angela Schmiede.** *A Practitioner's Guide to Reflection in Service-Learning: Student Voices & Reflections*. **Nashville: Vanderbilt University, 1996.**

After its publication, this book quickly became the essential text on reflection. The authors, who are known for their many contributions to the service-learning literature on assessment and evaluation, have transformed their expertise in interviews, surveys, and data collection into a highly readable and useful guide to reflection. Much of the book recounts students' stories of "successful reflection and. . . translate[s] their stories into practice." The authors collected these stories via interviews of 67 students at eight different colleges and universities. The guide is, in fact, highly practical, as the title of the last chapter ("Putting Reflection Into Action") attests. It includes reflection activities which employ "reading, writing, doing, [and] telling." Earlier chapters ("Reflection and Service-Learning," "Student Voices on the Value of Reflection," and "Different Ways to Reflect and Learn") explore how we learn from experience, different learning styles, the principles of reflection, how reflection links service to learning, and "putting theory to use." In addition, they give voice to student perceptions of how service-learning: "motivates students to learn," "aids personal development," "helps students connect to others," "helps students develop commitment to active citizenship," "enhances understanding of issues and subject matter," "helps students apply knowledge and skills they learn in one setting to other settings," and "helps students reframe the way they think about complex social issues." The guide's appendices include a bibliography on reflection, and separate lists of reflection guides and handbooks, and other "helpful readings for reflection."

**Jackson, Katherine, ed.** *Redesigning Curricula: Models of Service Learning Syllabi.* **Providence: Campus Compact, 1994.**

Although one can find plenty of newer service-learning syllabi on the Web today, the 24 syllabi and five commentaries in this collection are as useful to faculty today as they were at the time of publication. The syllabi represent courses in business and economics, education and social theory, writing and the humanities, sociology, and health and sciences. This volume is seen as a "companion" to *Rethinking Tradition: Integrating Service and Academic Study on College Campuses* (Kupiec), which Campus Compact published one year earlier. *Rethinking Tradition* includes essays on various aspects of service-learning as well as 13 course syllabi (see separate entry, below).

**Jacoby, Barbara, and Associates, eds.** *Service-Learning in Higher Education: Concepts and Practices.* **San Francisco: Jossey-Bass, 1996.**

This comprehensive reader is a major contribution to the field. It serves as both a monograph and a guide, and it covers literally every aspect of service-learning in higher education, from "Principles of Good Practice" to issues and methods of integrating service-learning into the curriculum and institutionalizing it on campus. It is comprised of 14 chapters by 17 contributors, most of whom are well known in the service-learning community. The text is divided into three main parts: "Foundations and Principles of Service-Learning," "Designing a Spectrum of Service-Learning Experiences," and "Organizational, Administrative, and Policy Issues." It has two appendices: "National Organizations that Support Service-Learning," and "Programs and Resources Useful in Helping Students Make Postcollege Service and Career Choices." The Foreword is by Thomas Ehrlich.

**Kendall, Jane C., and Associates, eds.** *Combining Service and Learning: A Resource Book for Community and Public Service.* **Volumes I-II. Raleigh: National Society for Internships and Experiential Education, 1990.**

**Luce, Janet, ed.** *Service-Learning: An Annotated Bibliography. Linking Public Service with the Curriculum.* **Volume III of** *Combining Service and Learning: A Resource Book for Community and Public Service.* **Raleigh: National Society for Internships and Experiential Education, 1988.**

As Frances Moore Lappe writes in the Preface of *Volume I, Combining Service and Learning* is "a treasure trove" of information about aspects of the phenomena and pedagogies that have come to be called service-learning. Volumes I and II total more than 1,200 pages of essential principles, rationales and theories, public and institutional policy issues and guides, a "history and future of the service-learning movement," "practical issues and ideas for programs and courses that combine service and learning," "profiles of programs and courses that combine service and learning," and "profiles of programs that combine service and learning in community-based organizations, government, and youth-serving agencies." Volume III is an annotated bibliography of service-learning literatures. This three-volume set comprises a comprehensive reference collection all by itself.

**Kraft, Richard J., and Marc Swadener, eds.** *Building Community: Service Learning in the Academic Disciplines*. **Denver: Colorado Campus Compact, 1994.**

This is a valuable anthology of essays on service-learning in the early 1990s. It differs from the Jacoby text (above) in that, rather than examining every aspect of service-learning, it explores service-learning in four diverse areas: (1) programs; (2) service-learning in the liberal arts; (3) service-learning in professional schools; and (4) research, evaluation, program activities, and bibliography. With one exception, all of the chapters are written by service-learning faculty and staff at colleges and universities in Colorado (or at Colorado Campus Compact).

**Kupiec, Tamar Y., ed.** *Rethinking Tradition: Integrating Service and Academic Study on College Campuses*. **Providence: Campus Compact, 1993.**

*Rethinking Tradition* is a successful hybrid that combines essays on strategies, pedagogies and institutional development of service-learning with 13 syllabi for courses ranging from "Homelessness and Public Policy" to "The Artist in Society." As noted above, Campus Compact followed this a year later with its "companion volume," *Redesigning Curricula: Models of Service Learning Syllabi* (Jackson). The book includes essays by Parker Palmer, Keith Morton, Irene Fisher, Ira Harkavy, and many others.

**Stanton, Timothy K., Dwight E. Giles, Jr., and Nadinne I. Cruz.** *Service-Learning: A Movement's Pioneers Reflect on Its Origins, Practice, and Future.* **San Francisco: Jossey-Bass, 1999.**

The authors' purpose in writing this book was twofold: to discover, publicize, and celebrate the stories and work of the "pioneers" of service-learning; and, by locating contemporary efforts in this larger history, enhance the perspective, meaning, and value of the work of those in the service-learning "movement" today. The pioneers are "thirty-three advocates, scholars, and practitioners of service-learning throughout the 1960s and beyond." The text is a mix of the pioneers' stories and the authors' narratives and analysis. One of the appendices, "An Organizational Journey to Service-Learning," is actually an innovative, graphed timeline by Robert L. Sigmon that includes events and developments in the following categories: governmental initiatives, higher education and secondary education, business and philanthropy, education associations and religious groups, and "intellectual markers." The "journey" begins in the nineteenth and early twentieth centuries with and progresses to 1995. The book is more than a look back in time: as its subtitle suggest, it also "reflect[s] on its. . . practice, and future."

**The Praxis Series:**

**Howard, Jeffrey, ed.** *Praxis I: A Faculty Casebook on Community Service Learning.* **Ann Arbor: University of Michigan, OCSL Press, 1993.**

**Galura, Joseph, Rachel Meiland, Randy Ross, Mary Jo Callan, and Rick Smith, eds.** *Praxis II: Service-Learning Resources for University Students, Staff and Faculty.* **Ann Arbor: University of Michigan, OCSL Press, 1993.**

**Galura, Joseph, Jeffrey Howard, Dave Waterhouse, and Randy Ross.** *Praxis III: Voices in Dialogue.* **Ann Arbor: University of Michigan, OCSL Press, 1995.**

These three monographs are treated together here, as they comprise the *Praxis* series, a trilogy published by the Office of Community Service Learning at the University of Michigan in Ann Arbor from 1993 to 1995. The editors of *Praxis III* state that the first two volumes were intended to "develop and publish service-learning curriculum and co-curricular models which had been 'road tested' by University of Michigan faculty, staff and students. . . ." Accordingly, the first volume, *Praxis I*, discusses so-called "generic" issues (e.g., service-learning in the curriculum and "preparing students to learn from the experience of community service"), and then focuses on undergraduate and graduate course models. *Praxis II* and *III* cover a wide, diverse terrain that is challenging to summarize briefly. *Praxis II*'s sections are entitled "The Meaning of Praxis," "Service-Learning at the University Level: Some Guiding Principles," "Off to See the Wizard," "Service-Learning Projects Affiliated with Sociology 389," "Service-Learning Projects Not Affiliated with Sociology 389," and "Reflections." *Praxis III* is designed to "broaden. . . and deepen. . . the dialogue initiated in the first two books." It contains the transcripts of conference speeches, descriptions of service-learning courses, and brown-bag lunch presentations. The last section of the book occupies more than half the volume, and is about the university's service-learning courses (Sociology 389 and Education 317). This section includes "overviews of the course," "replication manuals," "technological applications," and "longitudinal reflections."

Individually or together, these three volumes are considered to be classics in the service-learning literature.

## Journals

Given its relative youth as a visible academic field, service-learning has just two peer-reviewed academic journals devoted entirely to service-learning in higher education. The *Michigan Journal of Community Service Learning* addresses all disciplines in, and dimensions of, service-learning. A recent addition, *Reflections on Community-Based Writing Instruction*, specializes in service-learning in one specific academic area (composition). Some periodicals, like the *NSEE Quarterly*, cover service-learning as part of their focus on experiential education or related fields. Other journals in higher education touch upon service-learning to a lesser degree; it is not their primary focus. For example, *Academic Exchange Quarterly (AEQ)* and *Journal on Excellence in College Teaching* focus on pedagogy and important issues in teaching and higher education. *Education and Urban Society* is concerned with social research and its relevance to public policy. *The Journal of Public Service & Outreach* covers institutional service and outreach in academe (not to be confused with teaching courses using service-learning pedagogies). *Community College Journal* covers community college issues and trends. One of its recent issues is devoted to the theme of service-learning. Finally, journals like *The Generator: Journal of Service-Learning and Service Leadership* include service-learning as a focus, but are not limited to higher education and are not academic journals. These nine journals are described more fully below.

In addition to those above, a large number of academic journals in education or other disciplines are relevant to service-learning in that they include at least one article on service-learning. In a message to the Service-Learning Discussion Group, Vincent Peters (1999) shared his compilation of these journals with articles on service-learning. Journals in education (with dates indicating the year articles in service-learning appeared) include the following: *Action in Teacher Education* (1988), *Alternative Higher Education* (1978), *American Educator* (1992), *American Journal of Education* (1980), *American Journal Research Journal* (1994), *College Teaching* (1987), *Curriculum Inquiry* (1987), *Democracy and Education* (1994), *Education* (1994), *Education Digest* (1990), *Education Week on the Web*, *Educational Evaluation and Policy Analysis* (1993), *Educational Leadership* (1993), *Educational Record* (1987), *Experiential Education* (1998), *Generator* (1993), *Harvard Educational Review* (1981), *Innovative Higher Education* (1985), *Instructor* (1991), *Journal of College Student Development* (1991, 1995), *Journal of Cooperative Education* (1990, 1991), *Journal of Higher Education* (1979), *Journal of Moral Education* (1994), *Journal of Research and Development in Education* (1990), *Metropolitan Universities* (1996), *Phi Delta Kappan* (1991, 1996, 2000), *Theory and Research in Social Education* (1981). Two additional journals in this category, which can be found in the records of the National Service-Learning Clearinghouse (http://www.nicsl.coled.umn.edu/), are: *Community Education Journal. Perfect Match: Community Education and Service Learning* (1997) and *Service: a Journal for Academically Based Public Service* (1995).

Peters' (1999) found the following discipline-specific journals that have included service-learning articles: *Adolescence* (1990), *American Psychologist* (1991), *Business Communication Quarterly* (1997), *College Composition and Communication* (1994), *Journal of Adolescence* (1990), *Journal of Adolescent Research* (1988), *Journal of Business Education* (1985), *Journal of Business Ethics* (1996), *Journal of Health Education* (1995, 1997), *Journal of Nursing Education* (1995), *Journalism Educator* (1994), *Liberal Education* (1988, 1990, 1994), *PS: Political Science and Politics* (1993), *Teaching Sociology* (1994). Finally, miscellaneous journals with service-learning articles include *American Behavioral Scientist* (1998), *Change* (1987), *Journal of Career Development* (1994), *Social Policy* (1987), *Synergist* (1981), and *Thrust* (1986).

### Academic Exchange Quarterly (AEQ)
Chattanooga State, 4501 Amnicola Highway
Chattanooga, TN 37406–1097

First published in 1997, *Academic Exchange Quarterly* "is dedicated to the presentation of ideas, research, and methods leading to effective instruction and learning regardless of level or subject." *AEQ* is a blind-refereed academic journal. While not specifically about service-learning, *AEQ* devotes its Winter 1999 issue to a "Review of Service Learning," and its Winter 2000 issue to "Guide to Service-Learning" (http://ww.higher-ed.org/AEQ/redak3. htm). Three prior issues (Spring 1998, 2:1; Spring 1999, 3:1; and Summer 1999, 3:2) include one article each on service-learning.

### Community College Journal
American Association of Community Colleges (AACC)
One Dupont Circle, NW, Suite 410
Washington, DC 20036–1176
(202) 728–0200, ext 215
fax: (202) 223–9390
e-mail: cgamble@aacc.nche.edu
http://www.aacc.nche.edu/books/journal/ journalindex.htm

Begun in 1930, the *Community College Journal* is "devoted exclusively to community college issues." Objective essays on the "problems and solutions of contemporary community colleges" are preferred over empirical research. All articles are reviewed by an editorial board. The *Journal* is published six times a year; each issue has a specific theme. The focus of the December 1999/January 2000 issue (vol. 70, no. 3 ) is service-learning.

### Education and Urban Society
Education and Urban Society
Corwin Press, Inc., A Sage Publications Company
2455 Teller Road
Thousand Oaks, CA 91320

*Education and Urban Society* is "an independent quarterly journal of social research with implications for public policy." Each issue is devoted to a special topic. The February 1996 (vol. 28, no. 2) issue's special topic is "Learning by Service and Doing." The guest editor is Richard J. Kraft (School of Education, University of Colorado at Boulder), an early pioneer in the field and a recipient of the Thomas Ehrlich Faculty Award for Service Learning.

### The Generator: Journal of Service-Learning and Service Leadership
National Youth Leadership Council (NYLC)
1910 West County Road B
Saint Paul, MN 55113
(651) 631–3672
fax: (651) 631–2955
e-mail: nylcinfo@nylc.org
http://www.nylc.org/sec.pubs.Generator.html

NYLC (the National Youth Leadership Council) publishes a variety of monographs, handbooks, and resource guides. *The Generator: Journal of Service-Learning and Service Leadership* was their biannual service-learning and service journal (free to NYLC's membership). The theme of the Fall 1998 issue, for example, is "Service-Learning and Social Justice." The latest (and final) issue was published in 2000.

### The Journal of Public Service & Outreach

Office of the Vice President for Public
  Service & Outreach
The University of Georgia
Athens, GA 30602–1692
http://www.uga.edu/~jpso/
E-mail: JPSO@uga.cc.uga.edu

*The Journal of Public Service & Outreach*, another peer-reviewed journal, is "the first interdisciplinary journal dedicated to the third mission of the academy," i.e., service. Academe's traditional use of the term "service" usually implies "public service" in the form of: (a) faculty service to the university (often in the form of committee work), or (b) university outreach to community and society. As such, "service" to date has rarely included or implied service-learning, i.e., service integrated into curriculum as pedagogy and learning opportunity. This perception is changing somewhat, as service-learning becomes more visible and more valuable within academe. *JPSO* is about the larger, traditional concern with service and outreach. Nonetheless, service-learning is not excluded from its purview. For example, the inaugural issue includes an essay on "The Scholarship of Engagement" (1966: 11–20) by the late Ernest L. Boyer, who is seen as a founding father of the service-learning movement. *JPSO* is published by the University of Georgia, Athens.

### Journal on Excellence in College Teaching

Journal on Excellence in College Teaching
6953 Highway. 144
Owensboro, KY 42303
http://ject.lib.muohio.edu/
E-mail: ject@compuserve.com

The *Journal on Excellence in College Teaching*, published at Miami University, is a peer-reviewed journal about pedagogy in higher education. Readers looking for articles specifically on service-learning may be disappointed, but the journal is relevant to service-learning to the extent that many articles focus on cooperative and collaborative teaching and learning, reflection, journals, portfolios, and other pedagogical philosophies and techniques shared by service-learning.

### Michigan Journal of Community Service Learning

OCSL Press
University of Michigan
1024 Hill Street
Ann Arbor, MI 48109–3310
http://www.umich.edu/~ocsl/MJCSL/
E-mail: mjcsl@umich.edu

The *Michigan Journal of Community Service Learning (MJCSL)* is the first and only peer-reviewed academic journal for the entire field of service-learning in higher education. Published once a year in the fall, there are six volumes to date, beginning in 1994. The goals of the *MJCSL* are to "provide a venue to intellectually stimulate educators around the issues pertinent to academic service-learning, and. . . provide a venue to publish scholarly articles specifically for a service-learning audience" (http://www.umich.edu/~ocsl/MJCSL/about.htm). To accomplish these goals, the MJCSL seeks to "widen the community of service-learning educators, . . . sustain the intellectual vigor of those in this community, . . . encourage research and pedagogical scholarship around service-learning, and ultimately, . . . increase the number of students who have a chance to experience the rich learning benefits that accrue to service-learning participants" (http://www.umich.edu/~ocsl/MJCSL/about.htm). Each issue usually contains three sections: "Research and Theory," "Pedagogy," and "Forum." Articles in these sections are academic in content, style, and format.

### NSEE Quarterly

National Society for Experiential Education (NSEE)
1703 North Beauregard Street
Alexandria, VA 22311–1714

(703) 933–0017
fax: (603) 250–5852
e-mail: info@nsee.org
http://www.nsee.org

Members of the National Society for Experiential Education receive the *NSEE Quarterly* as a benefit of membership. As an organizational publication, the *NSEE Quarterly* serves various purposes. It communicates organizational news, publicizes calendar-related information, and prints excerpts of keynote speeches from past annual conferences and other organizational gatherings. In addition, each issue includes a number of brief articles on "issues in experiential education, program models, publications, research, and professional development opportunities." A healthy number of the articles are on service-learning. All articles are authored by NSEE members and "potential members."

### *Reflections on Community-Based Writing Instruction*

Conference on College Composition and
  Communication
c/o Nora Bacon
English Department
University of Nebraska at Omaha
6001 Dodge Street
Omaha, NE 68182
e-mail: Nora_Bacon@unomaha.edu

*Reflections on Community-Based Writing Instruction* is the newest journal in service-learning: the first issue was published in April 2000. It is "intended to disseminate current news about service-learning in composition, to showcase innovative programs and best practices, to discuss learning assessment and program evaluation, and to open a forum for sharing service-learning scholarship." Articles "describ[e] service-learning courses or assignments or explor[e] the practical, theoretical, political, and ethical implications of community-based writing instruction." *Reflections* is published three times a year and is peer-reviewed. [Reference: Roswell, Barbara. E-mail message to the Service-Learning Discussion Group ("Reflections—Call for Papers"). 14 February 2000.]

## Bibliographies

A number of useful bibliographies of service-learning can found in the literature. Bibliographies accompany most published articles, essays, and monographs, of course. With few exceptions, however, the bibliographies below are published as bibliographies, i.e., they are individual publications. References to many bibliographies can be found online, and some full-text bibliographies are also online. Online references and full-texts are identified as such, below. The remainder can be found in print. A number of the bibliographies cover service-learning in general; others are topical. Some bibliographies are annotated; others are not.

### General Bibliographies—Annotated

*American Association of Community Colleges Service Learning Clearinghouse: Resources/Publications*, http://199.75.76.16/initiatives/SERVICE/b_resour.htm, May 2000. (Online).

*An Annotated Bibliography of Service-Learning: A Partial List of Resources Held by the Center for Teaching Library*, (Center for Teaching Library, Vanderbilt University, October 1998), http://www.vanderbilt.edu/cft/sl/bibliography.pdf, May, 2000. (Online. This is a "pdf" file: Adobe Acrobat software is needed to read this file).

Bonar, Linda, Renee Buchanan, Irene Fisher, and Ann Wechsler, "Annotated Bibliography." In *Service-Learning in the Curriculum: A Faculty Guide to Course Development,* Linda Bonar, Renee Buchanan, Irene Fisher, and Ann Wechsler. The Lowell Bennion Community Service Center, University of Utah, 1996.

Council of Chief State School Officers. *Service Learning Annotated Bibliography*. Washington DC: Council of Chief State School Officers, 1993.

Luce, Janet, ed. *Service-Learning: An Annotated Bibliography. Linking Public Service with the Curriculum.* Volume III of *Combining Service and Learning: A Resource Book for Community and Public Service.* Raleigh: National Society for

Internships and Experiential Education, 1988.

Moore, Amanda. *Annotated Bibliography: Service Learning and Related Issues.* Columbia, SC: University of South Carolina, 1996.

**General Bibliographies—Not Annotated**

Belbas, Brad, and Robert D. Shumer. *Frequently Cited Sources in Service Learning.* St. Paul: National Service-Learning Cooperative Clearinghouse (NSLC), 1993. (Online: NSLC, http://www.nicsl.coled.umn.edu/res/bibs/bibs.htm).

Campus Compact, *Community Service Learning: Essential Reading Bibliography.* Caron, Barbara. E-mail message to the Service-Learning Discussion Group ("'Best of' resources for Service Learning/Heidi Bitter's request"). 21 December 1999. (Online: *Service-Learning: The Home of Service-Learning on the World Wide Web: The Service-Learning Discussion Group*, http://csf.colorado.edu/mail/service-learning/, December 1999.)

Galura, Joseph, Rachel Meiland, Randy Ross, Mary Jo Callan, and Rick Smith, eds. "Bibliography" in *Praxis II: Service-Learning Resources for University Students, Staff and Faculty.* Ann Arbor: University of Michigan, OCSL Press, 1993.

Hockenbrought, Charles D. *Service-Learning Bibliography.* E-mail message to Robin Crews ("Bibliography"). 14 April 1995. (Online: *Service-Learning: The Home of Service-Learning on the World Wide Web: Service-Learning Bibliographies*, http://csf.colorado.edu/sl/biblios.html, February 1999.)

Howard, Jeffrey. "Bibliography." In *Praxis I: A Faculty Casebook on Community Service Learning,* edited by Jeffrey Howard. Ann Arbor: University of Michigan, OCSL Press, 1993.

Kraft, Richard J. "A Comprehensive Resource List/Bibliography." In *Building Community: Service Learning in the Academic Disciplines,* ed. Richard J. Kraft and Marc Swadener. Denver: Colorado Campus Compact, 1994.

*University of Wisconsin-Green Bay Service Learning Site Bibliography*, http://gbms01.uwgb.edu/~service/biblio.htm, May, 2000. (Online).

**Topical Bibliographies—Annotated**

Some of the 18 monographs in the recent American Association for Higher Education (AAHE) series, *Service-Learning in the Disciplines*, have annotated bibliographies at the end of the volume. The monograph by Battistoni and Hudson, immediately below, is one of those that has an annotated bibliography.

Battistoni, Richard M., and William E. Hudson, eds. *Experiencing Citizenship: Concepts and Models for Service-Learning in Political Science.* Washington, DC: American Association for Higher Education, 1997.

Cook, Charles C. *African-American, Hispanic, and Latino Youth in Service Topic Bibliography.* National Service-Learning Cooperative Clearinghouse (NSLC), 1999. (Online: NSLC, http://www.nicsl.coled.umn.edu/res/bibs/bibs.htm).

Cook, Charles C., and Robert Shumer. *Literacy and Service-Learning: A "Links" Piece, Connecting Theory and Practice.* National Service-Learning Cooperative Clearinghouse (NSLC), 1998. (Online: NSLC, http://www.nicsl.coled.umn.edu/res/bibs/bibs.htm).

Eyler, Janet, Dwight E. Giles, Jr, and Charlene J. Gray. *At A Glance: What We Know about The Effects of Service-Learning on Students, Faculty, Institutions and Communities, 1993–1999.* National Service-Learning Cooperative Clearinghouse (NSLC), 1999. (Online: NSLC, http://www.nicsl.coled.umn.edu/res/bibs/bibs.htm).

Hengel, Madeleine S., and Robert Shumer. *School-To-Work and Service-Learning: A "Links" Piece, Connecting Theory and Practice.* National Service-Learning Cooperative Clearinghouse (NSLC), 1997. (Online: NSLC, http://www.nicsl.coled.umn. edu/res/bibs/bibs.htm).

Hengel, Madeleine S., and Robert Shumer. *A Summit Summary: An Annotated Bibliography on Civic Service-Learning, National Service, Education, and Character Education*. National Service-Learning Cooperative Clearinghouse (NSLC), 1997. (Online: NSLC, http://www.nicsl.coled.umn. edu/res/bibs/bibs.htm).

*Impacts and Effects of Service-Learning*. National Service-Learning Cooperative Clearinghouse (NSLC), No date. (Online: NSLC, http://www.nicsl.coled.umn.edu/ res/bibs/bibs.htm).

Kendall, Jane C., and Associates, eds. *Combining Service and Learning: A Resource Book for Community and Public Service*. Volumes III. Raleigh: National Society for Internships and Experiential Education, 1990.

Klosterman, Gail. *Guides to Developing Service-Learning Programs*. National Service-Learning Cooperative Clearinghouse (NSLC), 1996. (Online: NSLC, http:// www.nicsl.coled.umn.edu/res/bibs/bibs. htm). (This is a ''pdf'' file: Adobe Acrobat software is needed to read this file).

*Service-Learning and Evaluation: A Brief Review of Issues and the Literature. A ''Link'' Piece: Connecting Theory With Practice*. National Service-Learning Cooperative Clearinghouse (NSLC), No date. (Online: NSLC, http://www.nicsl.coled. umn.edu/res/bibs/bibs.htm).

Smith, Marilyn W. *Bibliography and Annotated Bibliography of Research: The Effects of Service Learning Participation on Students Who Serve*. St Paul: Minnesota Commission on National and Community Service, 1992.

Treacy, Ann. *Service Learning as a Tool for Violence Prevention: An Annotated Topic Bibliography*. National Service-Learning Cooperative Clearinghouse (NSLC), 1999. (Online: NSLC, http://www.nicsl.coled. umn.edu/res/bibs/bibs.htm).

Vue-Benson, Robin, and Robert Shumer. *Individuals with Disabilities Performing Service Topic Bibliography*. 1994. Updated by Madeleine S. Hengel and Craig Hollander in 1997. National Service-Learning Cooperative Clearinghouse (NSLC), 1994, 1997. (Online: NSLC, http://www.nicsl.coled. umn.edu/res/bibs/bibs.htm).

———. *Intergenerational Service Topic Bibliography*. 1995. Revised by Madeleine S. Hengel and Craig Hollander in 1997. National Service-Learning Cooperative Clearinghouse (NSLC), 1995, 1997. (Online: NSLC, http://www.nicsl.coled.umn. edu/res/bibs/bibs.htm).

———. *Topic Bibliography of Sources Related to Service-Learning by ESL/Bilingual Students*. National Service-Learning Cooperative Clearinghouse (NSLC), 1994. (Online: NSLC, http://www.nicsl.coled. umn.edu/res/bibs/bibs.htm).

———. *Topic Bibliography on English Language Arts and Service*. National Service-Learning Cooperative Clearinghouse (NSLC), 1995. (Online: NSLC, http:// www.nicsl.coled.umn.edu/res/bibs/bibs. htm).

———. *Topic Bibliography on Resiliency and ''At Risk'' Youth*. National Service-Learning Cooperative Clearinghouse (NSLC), 1994. (Online: NSLC, http://www.nicsl. coled.umn.edu/res/bibs/bibs.htm).

———. *Topic Bibliography on Service with Math and Science Education*. National Service-Learning Cooperative Clearinghouse (NSLC), 1994. (Online: NSLC, http:// www.nicsl.coled.umn.edu/res/bibs/bibs. htm).

———. *Topic Bibliography on Sources Related to Mentoring and Service*. National Service-Learning Cooperative Clearinghouse (NSLC), 1994. (Online: NSLC, http:// www.nicsl.coled.umn.edu/res/bibs/bibs. htm).

———. *Topic Bibliography on Sources Related to Service and the Environment*. National Service-Learning Cooperative Clearinghouse (NSLC), 1994. (Online:

NSLC,http://www.nicsl.coled.umn.edu/res/bibs/bibs.htm).

## Topical Bibliographies—Not Annotated

Constitutional Rights Foundation. *Civic Participation Service Learning: a Brief Bibliography*. Los Angeles: Constitutional Rights Foundation, 1994.

ERIC Clearinghouse on Higher Education. *Community Service Learning. ERIC Critical Issues Bibliography*. 1997. (Online: ERIC Clearinghouse on Higher Education, http://www.gwu.edu/~eriche/Library/CRIB59a2.html).

Eyler, Janet, Dwight E. Giles, Jr., and Angela Schmiede. "Reflection Bibliography." In *A Practitioner's Guide to Reflection in Service-Learning: Student Voices & Reflections*, Janet Eyler, Dwight E. Giles, Jr., and Angela Schmiede. Nashville: Vanderbilt University, 1996.

Bonar, Linda, Renee Buchanan, Irene Fisher, and Ann Wechsler. "Annotated Bibliography." In *Service-Learning in the Curriculum: A Faculty Guide to Course Development*, Linda Bonar, Renee Buchanan, Irene Fisher, and Ann Wechsler. The Lowell Bennion Community Service Center, University of Utah, 1996.

*Shelf List of Research Resources*. National Service-Learning Cooperative Clearinghouse (NSLC), 1996. (Online: NSLC, http://www.nicsl.coled.umn.edu/res/bibs/bibs.htm).

Smith, Marilyn W. *Bibliography and Annotated Bibliography of Research: the Effects of Service Learning Participation on Students Who Serve*. St Paul: Minnesota Commission on National and Community Service, 1992.

## Online Resources: Internet Discussion Groups and World Wide Web Sites

This section includes listings for discussion groups on the Internet and Web sites devoted to service-learning in higher education. Global information networks like the Internet and World Wide Web have immense potential for service-learning and some of its goals (e.g., educating socially responsible global citizens). This potential is only beginning to be explored. Beyond the use of discussion groups and Web sites, of course, there is the immense, uncharted terrain of using information technologies in ways that benefit service-learning teaching and learning experiences. In recognition of these two categories of applications (i.e., using the web and Internet to disseminate information about service-learning, and integrating them into the actual teaching of service-learning courses), it is perhaps worth noting here that Corporation for National Service published *The Internet Guide To National Service Networking* in 1996, and the Virginia Tech Service-Learning Center at Virginia Polytechnic Institute and State University published *Best Practices in Cyber-Serve: Integrating Technology With Service-Learning Instruction* in 1999.

## Service-Learning Discussion Groups or "Listservs"

Today many service-learning organizations and campus-based service-learning programs have their own listservs to facilitate organizational business and communications among staff and members, or staff, faculty, students, and community partners. For information on a specific organization's listserv, visit the organization's Web site (see Chapter 4 for Web site addresses of service-learning and service organizations). To learn more about the listserv of a service-learning program at a particular college or university, see the program's Web site (visit the author's online "Guide To: College and University Service-Learning Programs Including Links to Online Course Lists and Syllabi" (http://csf.colorado.edu/sl/academic.html) for direct links to all college and university service-learning program Web sites). This section focuses solely on discussion groups on service-learning in higher education.

### California State University Service Learning Internet Community (SLIC)

Host: California State University
Homepage: http://www.slic.calstate.edu
Comments and Feedback:
  efreihage@calstate.edu

Help: jkg7001@humboldt.edu

SLIC is a new statewide Web site for service-learning programs on campuses throughout the California State University system. It describes itself as an "Online Community for CSU Service-Learning Programs." The Web site, "developed in collaboration with the CSU Center for Distributed Learning and the EOE Foundation," includes the following kinds of information specific to the CSU system: courses and projects, member profiles, news and events, partnerships, funding and awards, and resources and materials. Its "Courses and Projects Library" is slated to include CSU syllabi, projects, lessons, and reflection activities. In June 2000, there were 19 course syllabi in ten disciplines/fields: Communications, Computer Science, Earth Sciences, Economics & Business, Education, General Science, Generalities, Political Science, Social Sciences, and Sports & Games. The "Resources Library" is intended to include articles, bibliographies, books, book reviews, campus service-learning Web sites, evaluation forms, institutional policies, newsletters, professional papers, reports, research studies, responsibility agreements, training manuals, and other Web sites.

### The JSL List (*Journal of Service-Learning*)

List Owner and Founder: Robin J. Crews (crews@csf.colorado.edu)

Host: Communications For A Sustainable Future (CSF)

Listserv Archives: http://csf.colorado.edu/mail/jsl/

The JSL List was intended to serve as a co-moderated version of the Service-Learning Discussion Group. It existed from January 1996 to January 1998. The JSL List's purpose was to serve as a venue for substantive contributions to service-learning (whereas the Service-Learning List was a mix of serious discussion, lighter conversation, and announcements), and to be an interim step between the Service-Learning List's discussions and, ultimately, the *Journal of Service-Learning*: the first online, refereed service-learning journal. The latter still remains a possible project for the future. The JSL List's archives are searchable.

### The Learn & Serve America National Service-Learning Clearinghouse

Host: University of Minnesota, Dept. of Work, Community & Family Education

Homepage: http://www.nicsl.coled.umn.edu

E-mail: serve@tc.umn.edu

Based at the University of Minnesota, the Learn & Serve America National Service-Learning Clearinghouse was originally the National Service-Learning Cooperative/Clearinghouse. It provided K-12 service and service-learning information via a 1–800 phone number. In the mid-1990s, funded by a grant from the Corporation for National Service, it created a K-12 Web site and K-12 listserv (the listserv is discussed in an earlier entry). In 1998, with funding from another large CNS grant, it took on the responsibilities of being the clearinghouse for the corporation's Learn & Serve program. It is now called the Learn & Serve America National Service-Learning Clearinghouse, and is part of a "consortium of thirteen other institutions and organizations." At this time, it expanded its mission to include K-16 service-learning partnerships. The Web site contains a number of searchable databases (on current events, past events, literature, and programs); a resources section (which includes "FAQs," a listserv, bibliographies, monographs, newsletters, state reports, videos, and a publications list); and links section. The service-learning-related literature database is quite extensive, and is searchable by title, keyword, author, or subject.

### The NSLCK-12 Listserv

Host: Learn & Serve America National Service-Learning Clearinghouse (serve@tc.umn.edu)

Listserv Homepage: http://www.nicsl.coled.umn.edu/

Listserv Archives: http://mail.tc.umn.edu/archives/nslck-12.html

Listserv e-mail address: nslck-12@vm1.spcs.umn.edu

Subscription address: listserv@tc.umn.edu

To subscribe, send the message: sub nslck-12 YourFirstName YourLastName Organization to: listserv@tc.umn.edu

While this chapter is devoted to literature and online resources for service-learning in higher education, contact and subscription information for the NSLCK-12 Listserv is worth including here, as it is the primary discussion group for the K-12 service-learning community. Message digests are available. Listserv messages are archived in a searchable database.

### Service-Learning and Writing

Host: National Council of Teachers of English (NCTE)

Listserv Homepage: http://www.ncte.org/ lists/service-learning/

Listserv Archives: http://www.ncte.org/ lists/service-learning/archives.shtml

List Manager: listmgr@lists.ncte.org

This listserv is described as ''an open list for discussing service learning projects and approaches.'' It appears to be a ''quiet'' listserv, with an average of less than one message per day. Message digests do not appear to be available.

### The Service-Learning Discussion Group (or ''Service-Learning List'')

List Owner and Founder: Robin J. Crews (crews@csf.colorado.edu)

Host: Communications For A Sustainable Future (CSF)

Listserv Homepage (URL): http://csf. colorado.edu/sl/

Listserv Archives: http://csf.colorado.edu/ mail/service?learning/

Listserv e-mail address: service-learning@csf.colorado.edu

Subscription address: majordomo@csf.colorado.edu

To subscribe, send the message: subscribe service-learning to: majordomo@csf.colorado.edu

In the Spring of 1993, the author created this Internet-wide discussion group and companion Internet/Web site as a service to those interested in service-learning, with a primary emphasis on higher education. The idea came from having done the same for the field of peace studies a year-and-a-half earlier. It was the author's hope that the discussion group and Web site would enhance communication, information-sharing and learning across large distances, and help to nurture a rapidly growing national service-learning community.

The goal was to develop a seamless, online resource, with conversations on the discussion group for debates on, and analysis of, service-learning pedagogies and issues (e.g., in theory, philosophy, curriculum, practice, politics, research, institutionalization, current work, etc.) and an online service-learning library on the Internet site. With the advent of the World Wide Web, the Internet site became a Web site and onsite document files gave way to ''links'' to service-learning document files and Web sites on the Web.

The Service-Learning Discussion Group was the first listserv about service-learning on the Internet. In subsequent years, a K-12 listserv (now called the ''NSLCK-12 ListServ'') was created by the (K-12) National Service-Learning Cooperative/Clearinghouse (now called the Learn & Serve America National Service-Learning Clearinghouse), and the Service-Learning Discussion Group's primary emphasis on service-learning in higher education became even more pronounced as subscribers in K-12 education moved to that discussion group. Other listservs on service-learning and specific educational areas (e.g., writing) or for specific geographic regions also have been created in recent years, but the Service-Learning Discussion Group remains the only comprehensive Internet-wide listserv for service-learning in higher education.

The Service-Learning List maintains a subscriber base of about 1,200 faculty, students, staff, community partners, representatives of national service-learning (and service) organizations, and friends of service-learning across the country. Conversations touch upon every aspect of service-learning found in this book, from analysis, research, debates, and syllabi sharing to announcements about new programs, conferences, employment, sources of funding, and legislation. The discussion group's archives (http://csf.colorado.edu/mail/service-learning) include all years, are keyword searchable, and can be immediately indexed by author, date, and thread (the latter allows viewers to follow conversations on specific subjects chronologically). As such, the archives represent an essential teaching and research service-learning database for subscribers and non-subscribers alike. Message digests (aggregations of individual messages) are available.

The Service-Learning Discussion Group is one of about 35 progressive listservs hosted by Communications for a Sustainable Future (CSF), which in turn is hosted at the University of Colorado at Boulder. The author created and continues to own and manage his peace studies and service-learning discussion groups on a volunteer basis in his capacity as a founding editor, list owner, and Web site developer of Communications for a Sustainable Future. Don Roper (Professor of Economics, University of Colorado at Boulder), a colleague and close friend of the author's, created and heads Communications for a Sustainable Future. The Service-Learning Discussion Group and Web site would not exist without Professor Roper's dedication, assistance, support, and guidance during the past ten years of collaboration.

Over the years, the author created—and often managed—numerous other service-learning related discussion groups (which CSF has also hosted). Most are private listservs for national organizations (e.g., the American Association of Community Colleges, Campus Compact, COOL, the Invisible College, CNS's Learn and Serve America Higher Education (LSAHE) List, etc.), all of which are now managed by representatives of these organizations—even though some of these listservs are still hosted by CSF today.

## Service-Learning Web Sites

The early years of the World Wide Web saw few service-learning Web sites. However, the number of service-learning sites has skyrocketed in recent years. Once colleges and universities developed their own Web sites, it eventually became possible for their academic departments and service-learning programs to do likewise. About 77 percent of the 325 college and university service-learning programs listed in the Directory in Chapter 3 now have their own Web sites. Web site addresses (''URLs'') are included in directory entries (although addresses are known to change from time to time). Direct links to all college and university service-learning program Web sites can be found at the author's online ''Guide To: College and University Service-Learning Programs Including Links to Online Course Lists and Syllabi'' (http://csf.colorado.edu/sl/academic.html).

Service-learning organizations also have a strong presence on the web today. Each Web site includes information and resources specific to the mission and membership (if any) of a service-learning organization. The best way to explore these resources is to visit organizational Web sites (see Chapter 4 for Web site addresses). With a few exceptions, this section does not duplicate organizations or Web sites mentioned in Chapter 4. Instead, it focuses only on Web sites that serve as primary resources and guides for everyone involved service-learning in higher education.

## Service-Learning: The Home of Service-Learning on the World Wide Web

Web site Owner and Founder: Robin J.
 Crews (crews@csf.colorado.edu)
Host: Communications For A Sustainable
 Future (CSF)
Homepage: http://csf.colorado.edu/sl/

As described above, in ''The Service-Learning Discussion Group,'' this Internet/Web site and the discussion group were created by the author in the Spring of 1993. At the time, it was an ftp and gopher site on the Internet. The purpose of the site was to serve as a free online guide to, and library of, service-learning. The goal was a virtual library containing archives of all conversations on the discussion group; articles; bibliographies; a comprehensive calendar of conferences and events; definitions of service-learning; descriptions and directories of college and university service-learning programs; directories of organizations, networks, and resources; dissertations; essays; funding sources; handbooks and manuals; job announcements; journals; papers; publications and publishers; syllabi for service-learning courses; topical sections on assessment, benefits, reflection, research, etc.; useful bookmarks; and so on. With the advent of the World Wide Web, the Internet site was transformed quickly into a Web site and the collection and cataloging of many onsite document files gave way to "links" to service-learning document files and sites elsewhere on the Web. As was the case with the Service-Learning Discussion Group, the idea for the Internet/Web site came from having done the same for the field of peace studies a year-and-a-half earlier.

"Service-Learning: The Home of Service-Learning on the World Wide Web" was the first (and for quite some time, the only) service-learning site on the Internet/Web. Like the Service-Learning Discussion Group, it was intended to serve everyone interested in service-learning, with its primary emphasis on higher education. When the National Service-Learning Cooperative/Clearinghouse in Minnesota developed a K-12 Web site, the "Service-Learning" Web site became exclusively devoted to service-learning in higher education. Further expansions of the clearinghouse and its mission occurred in 1998 (see entry below). As noted above, there are now hundreds of Web sites related to service-learning in higher education (belonging to campus-based service-learning programs and organizations). Nonetheless, "Service-Learning: The Home of Service-Learning on the World Wide Web" continues to be the only comprehensive Web site solely for service-learning in higher education.

Today, the primary components of the site are the "Guide To College and University Service-Learning Programs, Including Links to Online Course Lists and Syllabi"; the Service-Learning Discussion Group's Archives; the "Guide to Service-Learning Organizations, Networks, Venues, and Resources"; the online library of "Service-Learning Syllabi" organized by discipline (with some 168 syllabi in 36–40 disciplines); bibliographies; journals; handbooks and manuals; international service-learning; definitions and benefits of service-learning; and useful bookmarks to help navigate the web. The calendar and employment sections have languished in recent years, therefore the best way to find out about service-learning conferences, events, and employment opportunities is to subscribe to the Service-Learning Discussion Group, or search its archives for these announcements.

"Service-Learning: The Home of Service-Learning on the World Wide Web" is one of the major Web sites hosted by Communications for a Sustainable Future (CSF), which in turn is hosted at the University of Colorado at Boulder. CSF also hosts the International Studies Association's (ISA) Web site. As noted above, the author created, and continues to own and manage, his peace studies and service-learning Web sites on a volunteer basis in his capacity as a founding editor, list owner, and Web site developer of Communications for a Sustainable Future.

The Web site would not exist without Don Roper's many years of mentoring and support.

## UCLA Service-Learning Clearinghouse Project

Webmaster: Kejian Jin (kjin@ucla.edu)

Project Director: Elaine Ikeda (esaito@ucla.edu)

E-mail: Emailheslcp@gseis.ucla.edu

Host: UCLA Graduate School of Education and Information Studies Department, Higher Education Research Institute

Homepage: http://www.gseis.ucla.edu/slc/

The Service-Learning Clearinghouse Project is a partner of the Learn and Serve America National Service-Learning Clearinghouse, and is funded by it and the Corporation for National Service. Its mission is to "provide resources and support to Learn and Serve America Higher Education grantees and subgrantees, as well as the higher education service-learning field at large." The project is located at UCLA in the Graduate School of Education and Information Studies Department, within the Higher Education Research Institute. The Web site includes information on assessment and evaluation, faculty issues, K-H partnerships, service-learning research, and training and technical assistance. In addition, it has its own online newsletters (beginning Summer 1999), listserv subscription information, and links to other service-learning Web sites.

## Service Web Sites

### Idealist

Sponsor: Action Without Borders

Homepage: http://www.idealist.org

E-mail: info@idealist.org

Idealist is a project of Action Without Borders. As noted in the organizational description of Action Without Borders in Chapter 4, Idealist is the most comprehensive service site on the Web, with listings of 20,000 community and nonprofit organizations in 140 countries. It is a virtual "community of nonprofit and volunteering resources," which also provides a Web presence to those without Web sites. The organizations can be searched or browsed by name, location, or mission. The site also includes a significant list of organizations that promote global volunteering (i.e., beyond the huge list of organizations where volunteers are placed); job and internship listings in its Nonprofit Career Center; "a directory of companies and consultants that provide products and services to nonprofit organizations; links to the most useful resources. . . on the Web for managing and funding a nonprofit organization; a collection of the most informative and frequently updated Nonprofit News Sites on the Web; and a global directory of Public Internet Access Points in hundreds of schools, libraries, community centers and Internet cafes."

### Impact Online, Inc.

Homepage: http://www.impactonline.org

E-mail: respond@impactonline.org

Impact Online, founded in 1994, is a nonprofit organization that assists volunteerism through the Internet. Visitors to this Web site will find "VolunteerMatch," a matching service for volunteers and nonprofits, "Virtual Volunteering," a research project on volunteer activities which can be completed over the Internet, and information and resources on volunteerism. (See Chapter 2: "Online Resources.")

### The Odyssey: World Trek for Service and Education

Homepage: http://www.worldtrek.org

E-mail: worldtrek@hotmail.com

The Odyssey Web site is listed here as a unique—an innovative—example of the potential of the World Wide Web in education in general and in service-learning in particular. Indeed, it is a wholly different approach to service-learning altogether: it is learning at a distance (i.e., distance learning) from the service of others around the world, and then combining and integrating this with local service-learning experiences. The Odyssey is an Internet-based nonprofit whose mission is "to promote global awareness among youth and involve them in activities to create positive change in the world." Their current major project is the "World Trek," which started in January 1999. The World Trek "takes students on. . . a two-year Trek around the world. . . via the Odyssey Web site, their connection to a Team of five educators doing a real two-year World Trek. The Team is visiting ten major non-western countries to document their histories and cultures: Guatemala, Peru, Zimbabwe, Mali, Egypt, Israel, Turkey, Iran, India, and China." Odyssey team members engage in six weeks of service in partnership with "grassroots organizations in or near each of the ten destination cities. . . .The work of the organizations and the volunteers [is] captured on video, audio and text and shared with the students via the Student Site on the World Wide Web."

The World Trek is designed to "bring critical global issues into the classroom." The educational themes of these issues include the Internet and society; community; indigenous people; wealth and poverty; the environment and development; the global community; the nature of conflict; gender roles and representations; youth and society; social change in theory and practice. "The skills and knowledge that students gain will be put into practice through service learning activities. This will sometimes mean joining a letter-writing campaign regarding a current Odyssey topic. It will sometimes mean working with local organizations partnered with The Odyssey. It will at other times mean working on projects that come from the students themselves in response to their own immediate concerns.''

## SERVEnet

Sponsor: Youth Service America (YSA)

Homepage: http://www.servenet.org

E-mail: feedback@ysa.org

SERVEnet is a Web site that brings ''volunteers and community organizations together online.'' It is a program of Youth Service America, a resource center and alliance of over 200 organizations working to increase ''the quantity and quality of opportunities for young Americans to serve locally, nationally, or globally.'' The Web site functions to ''encourage more citizens to become actively engaged in their communities by volunteering; . . . provide volunteer-based nonprofit organizations the best resources available to them in a quick and easy manner; and, . . . match the skills, experience, and enthusiasm of dedicated volunteers with nonprofit organizations who need their participation.''

## Studyabroad.com

Sponsor: Educational Directories Unlimited, Inc.

Homepage: http://www.studyabroad.com

E-mail: webmaster@studyabroad.com

Studyabroad.com is a comprehensive ''online study abroad information resource.'' It is a service of Educational Directories Unlimited, Inc. (a campus marketing firm). The Web site includes listings for a very large number of study-abroad programs in over 100 countries. Visitors to the site can search for programs by academic year and semester programs by country; summer programs by country; winter/spring intersession programs; academic programs by subject; intensive language programs by language; English as a second language programs; TEFL certificate programs; experiential/internship programs; programs for high school students; summer law programs; and summer graduate business programs. In addition, the site includes an online Handbook (travel guide), a ''Marketplace'' (with information on financial aid, health insurance, student ID cards, merchandise, long-distance service, and travel services), a Book Store, and the Study Abroad Forum. Studyabroad.com is included here and in Chapter 4 under ''Organizations with International Service Opportunities'' primarily because of its ''experiential/internship programs'' listings, which are useful to students interested in designing overseas service-learning experiences. In addition, the site's information about traveling abroad (including country-specific concerns) is helpful to any student anticipating an overseas service-learning opportunity.

## References

Corporation for National Service. *The Internet Guide To National Service Networking.* Washington, DC: Corporation for National Service, 1996.

*Best Practices in Cyber-Serve: Integrating Technology With Service-Learning Instruction.* Blacksburg, VA: Virginia Tech Service-Learning Center, Virginia Polytechnic Institute and State University, 1999.

# 3

# Colleges and Universities with Service-Learning Programs or Courses

## Overview: The Status of Service-Learning in Higher Education

The Directory of Colleges and Universities with Service-Learning Programs or Courses in this chapter includes 324 entries. They represent a significant amount of all service-learning in higher education, and offer up a fascinating, in-depth, and comprehensive look at service-learning in higher education at the beginning of the third millennium.

### Interpreting the Findings:

For several reasons, the entries should be seen as illustrative and descriptive, not definitive. First, the one constant dimension of service-learning on college and university campuses is the amazing amount of change and fluidity in programs, initiatives, courses, budgets, and Web sites, e-mail addresses, and contact information. While most well-known programs appear to evolve and grow steadily, many others experience an extraordinary amount of constant transformation (purpose, institutional location, and/or name) and turnover in staffing. Finding, corresponding with, and collecting information from individuals and programs under such conditions is a labyrinthian undertaking. The quantity and quality of constant change suggests that no entry is current for very long.

Second, as mentioned in the Preface, the information in these entries comes from responses to questionnaires that were part of an extensive, 18-month-long survey conducted by e-mail between late January 1999 and June 2000; it is supplemented by follow-up e-mail correspondence and further research involving program Web sites. Given the time necessary for editorial review and publication, it is wise to assume that no published directory is ever completely current.

Third, while this directory is a comprehensive listing of service-learning programs in higher education, there are a healthy number of colleges and universities known or rumored to have service-learning that did not respond to the surveys and repeated requests for information. This is quite understandable, given how busy campus service-learning programs are and the frequency with which they are asked to collect and disseminate data about their own campuses. It is also worth noting that service-learning does not exist at many colleges and universities rumored to have it in one form or another (this conclusion is based directly on responses received from many of these institutions). Others, in the early stages of contemplating or planning service-learning programs, chose not to be included in the directory at this time because they felt they had nothing yet to include in an entry.

Finally, it is important to note that all numerical answers (e.g., the number of service-learning courses, instructors, and staff) should be seen as approximate. Often respondents indicated that these kinds of answers were approximate at best. And, as noted above, they are quite likely to change from one semester to the next, and from one year to the next. For all of these reasons, it is useful to interpret the descriptive and quantitative information in this directory as realistic and concrete, yet, at the same time, illustrative and fluid. The initial questionnaire may be found in the Appendix.

In nearly every instance, a college or university is represented by one entry. In a few cases, where two or more different programs or areas of a university have service-learning and provided sufficient information on each program, there are two entries for the university.

## Summary of Findings

All but six of the institutions are in the United States. Of these six, three are in Canada: Lethbridge Community College (Lethbridge, Alberta), Royal Roads University (Victoria, British Columbia), and Saint Francis Xavier University (Antigonish, Nova Scotia). The remaining three are the University of Balamand (Tripoli, Lebanon), the University of Natal (Durban, KwaZulu-Natal, South Africa), and the University of Surrey Roehampton (London, UK).

The majority of the programs are at public institutions of higher education (55 percent public vs. 45 percent private), and on university campuses (61 percent universities vs. 25 percent colleges vs. 14 percent community colleges). In addition, a majority of the institutions are secular (63 percent secular vs. 37 percent religious).

Two hundred and sixty-seven (or 82 percent) of the 325 entries represent colleges and universities which collectively offer between 7,380 and 7,741 service-learning courses at the undergraduate level; 94 entries (29 percent) offer 764 to 799 graduate level service-learning courses. Most of these are courses taught using service-learning pedagogies; only a few are courses solely about service-learning. Between 6,665 and 6,843 faculty members teach these courses, i.e., an average of 20.5 to 21 instructors per entry.

Just under 10 percent of the institutions in this directory require all students to take service-learning courses in order to graduate (in a few entries this requirement is just for students in a graduate program or professional school program listed); fewer than two percent require service-learning now for certain majors or honors programs; and fewer than one percent indicated that service-learning requirements for graduation were under consideration for the future.

Service is required of all students for graduation at fewer than nine percent of the entries; another 1.5 percent require service in specific majors or honors programs; and one university is considering requiring service of all students in the future. Three-quarters (76 percent) of the programs in the directory are at institutions that also offer co-curricular service opportunities. Twenty-five percent have service-learning residence halls or theme houses (although this figure may be high, as respondents may have included service as well as service-learning theme residences in their answers to this question), and just over one percent have plans for them in the near future.

In discussions of service-learning programs and degrees, it may be helpful to distinguish among the following: (1) academic programs (including degree programs—master's, majors, minors, concentrations, or certificates) that include service-learning courses vs programs that require such courses for successful completion; and (2) master's, majors, minors, concentrations, or certificates in service-learning.

At the undergraduate level, there are no major degree programs in service-learning at responding institutions (and none are planned for the future). However, as noted below, graduate students in the field of education can do a self-designed major in service-learning at the University of Pittsburgh. At three universities, service-learning courses are part of other majors: in Human Services at George Washington University; in health education, nursing, social work, education, and psychology at North Carolina Central University; and in elementary education at Slippery Rock University. At one college (Providence College and its Feinstein Institute for Public Service), a Bachelor of Arts degree is offered in "Public and Community Service Studies" (not in service-learning, per se). Students can also minor in it.

There are two academic minors in service-learning: "Community Service and Service-Learning" at Slippery Rock University and a minor through the "American Humanics" major at the University of Texas-San Antonio.

Minors in service-learning are planned or being considered at two other institutions: Bentley College and the University of Minnesota-Twin Cities. Service-learning currently appears to be required in other minors at four institutions: the Leadership Studies minor at Humboldt State University; the Peace and Conflict Studies minor and the Feminist Studies minor at Pacific University; the "Public and Community Service Studies" minor at Providence College (mentioned above); and in a number of minors at the University of Denver.

Seven colleges and universities either: (1) offer certificates in service-learning, (2) designate service-learning on students' academic records, or (3) honor students at graduation: Chattanooga State Technical Community College, MiraCosta College, Mount Wachusett Community College, Salt Lake Community College, State University of New York/College at Oneonta, the University of Texas-San Antonio, and the University of Utah. Five institutions require service-learning as part of certificates in community service or other disciplines.

At the graduate school level, the author knows of no Ph.D. or M.A. programs in service-learning (as of June 2000). There are, however, a handful of M.A. programs that include or require service-learning courses, and offer degrees in related fields: International Service, International and Intercultural Service, and Leadership and Training. Specifically, the University of Surrey Roehampton (London,UK) has an M.A. and a Graduate Diploma in International Service (and serves as the degree-granting institution for the M.A. in International Service offered by the International Partnership for Service-Learning (New York); the School For International Training (Brattleboro, VT) has an M.A. Program in International and Intercultural Service; and Royal Roads University (Victoria, British Columbia) has an M.A. Program in Leadership and Training.

Chatham College has a number of graduate programs in the health sciences that all have large service-learning components. Ohio State University's Higher Education and Student Affairs graduate program offers a service-learn-ing track in the curriculum which provides students with an opportunity for coursework in service-learning (and graduate assistantship opportunities in service-learning are available). At the University of Louisville, most graduate programs (particularly programs through the Kent School of Social Work, the School of Education, Allied Health, Urban Studies and the Medical, Dental, and Nursing Schools) have an internship or practicum requirement in which students apply what they are learning in a community setting. At the University of Pittsburgh, graduate students in the field of education can do a self-designed major in service-learning.

In terms of program access and visibility on the World Wide Web, 77 percent of the service-learning programs now have their own Web sites. When they exist, Web site addresses ("URLs") are included in directory entries (although addresses are known to change from time to time). Direct links to all college and university service-learning program Web sites can be found at the author's online "Guide To: College and University Service-Learning Programs Including Links to Online Course Lists and Syllabi" (http://csf.colorado.edu/sl/academic.html). About 30 percent of the programs have lists of service-learning courses online, and nearly 8 percent have service-learning course syllabi online.

The directory below is a photo album—not a snapshot—of service-learning in higher education. It paints a mural made up of diverse and often contrasting, individual paintings, rather than a unified family portrait. There is nothing monolithic about service-learning in higher education today: some of the best colleges and universities in the country have had strong service-learning programs for many years, while others may never develop service-learning programs on their campuses. Some campuses have programs with no staff or funding, and yet others have healthy funding and staffing levels. Some "service-learning" centers appear to devote all their energies to co-curricular service programs and could not identify any service-learning courses on campus, while others distinguish clearly between service-learning (as academic and integrated into courses and curricula) and other service and volunteer initiatives. Even within the genre of (academic) service-learning, service-learning takes many different forms.

There are 324 different faces of service-learning identified in the entries below. And, almost as if it were a harbinger of good tidings for service-learning at the beginning of this new century and millennium, one of them received news in June 2000 of a $1 million grant for the first endowed professorship in service-learning in the country (at least to the author's knowledge): Goucher College (Baltimore, MD) received a grant from the France-Merrick Foundation of Baltimore, and Carol Weinberg, faculty member and coordinator of community service, will be the first chair holder.

## Directory of Colleges and Universities with Service-Learning Programs or Courses

### Adrian College
110 S Madison, Rush Union, Adrian, MI 49221–2575
*University/College URL:* http://www.adrian.edu
*Type of Institution:* private, college, teaching, religious
*SL Program/Center Name:* Office of Student Activities & Volunteerism
*Contact Person Name and Title:* Merritt Olsen, Dir, Student Activities
*Contact Phone Number:* (517) 264–3811
*Contact Fax Number:* (517) 264–3331
*Contact Email Address:* molsen@adrian.edu
*SL Program/Center URL:* http://www.adrian.edu/studentaffairs/stdtact.htm
*Description:* The Office of Student Activities and Volunteerism is the liaison between faculty and community agencies. The director of Student Activities consults with faculty about potential agency opportunities for service-learning projects and conducts related consultations with agencies. Some recent activities have been funded through Michigan Campus Compact Venture Grant funds; otherwise there is no specified budget within Student Affairs.

*SL Required for Graduation (all students)?* No
*Service Required for Graduation (all students)?* No
*Any Co-curricular Service?* Yes
*Any SL Residence Halls or Theme Houses?* No
*Number of Undergraduate SL Courses Offered Per Year:* 4–5
*Number of Graduate SL Courses Offered Per Year:* 0
*Total Number of SL Courses Offered Per Year:* 4–5
*Number of Instructors Teaching SL Courses Per Year:* 4–5
*Number of Full-time SL Staff on Campus (not counting instructors):* 1 (Service/Service-Learning is about 1/3 of the director's job responsibilities)
*Number of Part-time SL Staff on Campus (not counting instructors):* 0

### Albuquerque TVI Community College
525 Buena Vista, SE, Albuquerque, NM 87106
*University/College URL:* http://www.tvi.cc.nm.us
*Type of Institution:* public, community college, teaching
*SL Program/Center Name:* Service Learning Program
*Contact Person Name and Title:* Rudy M. Garcia, Dir, Experiential Education
*Contact Phone Number:* (505) 224–3068
*Contact Fax Number:* (505) 224–3073
*Contact Email Address:* rudyg@tvi.cc.nm.us
*Description:* The TVI Service Learning Program provides students with opportunities to learn their coursework while serving the community. Students learn that they can make a difference in the community and that learning goes beyond the boundaries of the classroom. The program provides students with experiences that allow them to build upon critical thinking, analytical problem solving, team building, and leadership skills. Through reflection exercises students realize how their academic coursework, when applied through service, can relate to their degrees and chosen career fields.

*SL Required for Graduation (all
students)?* No
*Service Required for Graduation (all stu-
dents)?* No
*Any Co-curricular Service?* No
*Any SL Residence Halls or Theme
Houses?* No
*Number of Undergraduate SL Courses
Offered Per Year:* 30
*Total Number of SL Courses Offered Per
Year:* 30
*Number of Instructors Teaching SL Courses
Per Year:* 30
*Number of Full-time SL Staff on Campus
(not counting instructors):* 2
*Number of Part-time SL Staff on Campus
(not counting instructors):* 0

## Allan Hancock College

800 South College Dr, Santa Maria, CA
93454–6399
*University/College URL:* http://www.
hancock.cc.ca.us
*Type of Institution:* public, community col-
lege, teaching
*Contact Person Name and Title:* Deborah
Brasket, Service Learning Grant Coord
*Contact Phone Number:* (805) 922–6966,
ext 2102
*Contact Fax Number:* (805)347–8715
*Contact Email Address:* dbrasket@sbceo.org
*Description:* Allan Hancock College received
grant funding in July 1999 from the State
Chancellor's office to develop a service-learning program. Since then, a Service Learning
Advisory Board has been established, service-
learning has been integrated into the nursing
program, and a survey and brochure have been
developed and will be sent to service agencies
in the area to introduce the concept of service-
learning and assess volunteer needs in the community. A service learning database, Web site,
and introductory video are being developed.
Near-term objectives include a service-learning center and coordinator to help interested
faculty develop service-learning courses and
find appropriate placement sites in the community. Service-learning courses are currently offered in the nursing program and in composition (two courses). In Fall 2000, the college
anticipates offering service-learning in two ad-
ditional composition courses, as well as in art,
math, business, and social science courses.
*SL Required for Graduation (all
students)?* No
*Service Required for Graduation (all stu-
dents)?* No
*Any Co-curricular Service?* No
*Any SL Residence Halls or Theme
Houses?* No
*Number of Undergraduate SL Courses
Offered Per Year:* 14
*Number of Graduate SL Courses Offered
Per Year:* 0
*Total Number of SL Courses Offered Per
Year:* 14
*Number of Instructors Teaching SL Courses
Per Year:* 5
*Number of Full-time SL Staff on Campus
(not counting instructors):* 0
*Number of Part-time SL Staff on Campus
(not counting instructors):* 1

## Alma College

614 W Superior, Alma, MI 48801
*University/College URL:* http://www.
alma.edu
*Type of Institution:* private, college, teach-
ing, research
*SL Program/Center Name:* Service Learning
Program
*Contact Person Name and Title:* Anne Ritz,
Service Learning Coord
*Contact Phone Number:* (517) 463–7366
*Contact Fax Number:* (517) 463–7073
*Contact Email Address:* ritz@alma.edu
*SL Program/Center URL:* http://www.alma.
edu/academics/servicelearning/
*SL Online Course Description URL:* http://
www.alma.edu/academics/
servicelearning/courses.htm
*SL Online Syllabi URL:* http://www.alma.
edu/academics/servicelearning/oldcourses.
htm
*Description:* The Alma College Service Learning Program introduces students to the value of
service as a way of gaining focus and meaning
in studies. The program provides service-learning opportunities for students through curricular and co-curricular offerings, practical expe-

rience, global service options, and work-study experiences.

*SL Required for Graduation (all students)?* No

*Service Required for Graduation (all students)?* No

*Any Co-curricular Service?* Yes

*Any SL Residence Halls or Theme Houses?* No

*Number of Undergraduate SL Courses Offered Per Year:* 30

*Number of Graduate SL Courses Offered Per Year:* 0

*Total Number of SL Courses Offered Per Year:* 30

*Number of Instructors Teaching SL Courses Per Year:* 20

*Number of Full-time SL Staff on Campus (not counting instructors):* 0

*Number of Part-time SL Staff on Campus (not counting instructors):* 2

### Alvernia College
400 Saint Bernardine St, Reading, PA 19607

*University/College URL:* http://www.alvernia.edu

*Type of Institution:* private, college, religious

*SL Program/Center Name:* Community Service Program

*Contact Person Name and Title:* Ellen Engler, Dir, Community Service

*Contact Phone Number:* (610) 796–8285

*Contact Fax Number:* (610) 796–8381

*Contact Email Address:* engleel@alvernia.edu

*SL Program/Center URL:* http://www.alvernia.edu/campu5.htm

*Description:* Alvernia College requires all baccalaureate students to complete 40 hours of approved service to others. Students in the associate degree program must complete 20 hours of service. All service must be approved by the director of Community Service. The service requirement upholds the college's Franciscan tradition of service to others. The Community Service Program is funded by the college.

*SL Required for Graduation (all students)?* No

*Service Required for Graduation (all students)?* Yes

*Any Co-curricular Service?* Yes

*Any SL Residence Halls or Theme Houses?* No

*Number of Undergraduate SL Courses Offered Per Year:* 10

*Number of Graduate SL Courses Offered Per Year:* 0

*Total Number of SL Courses Offered Per Year:* 10

*Number of Instructors Teaching SL Courses Per Year:* 10

*Number of Full-time SL Staff on Campus (not counting instructors):* 1

*Number of Part-time SL Staff on Campus (not counting instructors):* 0

### American University
4400 Massachusetts Ave, NW, Washington, DC 20009

*University/College URL:* http://www.american.edu

*Type of Institution:* private, university, teaching

*SL Program/Center Name:* Community Service Learning Program

*Contact Person Name and Title:* Karyn A. Cassella, Coord for Community Service

*Contact Phone Number:* (202) 885–3395

*Contact Fax Number:* (202) 885–1560

*Contact Email Address:* kcassel@american.edu

*SL Program/Center URL:* http://www.american.edu/volunteer/cslphome.html

*Description:* The Community Service Learning Program is one of several programs in the Office of Community Service. The program is a one-credit pass/fail opportunity for students who complete 40 hours of approved community work that complements a three-credit course. The grade is assigned based on the quality of an academic project designed by the student and advising faculty on a case-by-case basis.

*SL Required for Graduation (all students)?* No (However, service-learning will soon be required of undergraduate students in School of Education)

*Service Required for Graduation (all students)?* No

*Any Co-curricular Service?* Yes

*Any SL Residence Halls or Theme Houses?* Yes

*Number of Undergraduate SL Courses Offered Per Year:* 4–10

*Total Number of SL Courses Offered Per Year:* 4–10

*Number of Instructors Teaching SL Courses Per Year:* 4–8

*Number of Full-time SL Staff on Campus (not counting instructors):* 1

*Number of Part-time SL Staff on Campus (not counting instructors):* 0.5

## American University

4400 Massachusetts Ave, NW, School of International Service, Washington, DC 20016–8071

*University/College URL:* http://www. american.edu

*Type of Institution:* private, university, teaching, research, religious

*SL Program/Center Name:* Project PEN (Providing for Educational Needs)

*Contact Person Name and Title:* Heather E. Prichard, Dir

*Contact Phone Number:* (202) 885–2014

*Contact Fax Number:* (202) 885–1661/2494

*Contact Email Address:* pen@american.edu

*SL Program/Center URL:* http://www. american.edu/academic.depts/sis/level3/ PAGE1.HTM

*Description:* Project PEN is a conflict-resolution education internship and professional-development experience for American University students studying peace and conflict resolution, education, psychology, justice, and related fields. PEN interns work alongside Washington, D.C. public school teachers to infuse conflict resolution and peace education concepts, skills and lessons into traditional classes such as social studies, history, psychology, ESL, and literature. During class time, interns and teachers help high school students think about conflict from a variety of perspectives, while gaining experience with active listening, perspective taking, and effective problem solving. It is believed that students who refine their conflict-resolution competencies while learning more about the world in which they live, are better positioned to fully participate as active, engaged citizens in their local and global communities. Beyond in-class work, PEN encourages all members of the school community to use and practice conflict-resolution skills in their everyday lives in order to build a caring climate in and around the school.

*SL Required for Graduation (all students)?* Yes

*Any SL Residence Halls or Theme Houses?* Yes

## Appalachian State University

231 Plemmons Student Union, ACT Community Outreach Center, Boone, NC 28608

*University/College URL:* http://www. appstate.edu

*Type of Institution:* public, university, teaching, research, secular

*SL Program/Center Name:* ACT Community Outreach Center, Service-Learning Program

*Contact Person Name and Title:* Shari Galiardi, ACT Service-Learning Coord

*Contact Phone Number:* (828) 262–2193

*Contact Fax Number:* (828) 262–2937

*Contact Email Address:* galiardisl@appstate.edu

*SL Program/Center URL:* http://www. appstate.edu/www_docs/student/act/SL/ index.html

*SL Online Course Description URL:* http:// www.appstate.edu/www_docs/student/act/ courses.html

*Description:* The ACT (Appalachian and the Community Together) Community Outreach Center is ASU's clearinghouse for community service and service-learning opportunities in Watauga County. The center offers diverse opportunities for individual and student groups involvement in human services and environmental advocacy. It also assists faculty members with integrating community-service projects into their academic courses. ACT's Peer Counselors and professional staff members help students locate local, national, and international service opportunities. The center provides students with information and educational resources about social issues and answers questions about community service and service-learning.

*SL Required for Graduation (all students)?* No

*Service Required for Graduation (all students)?* No (But, a service requirement is under consideration right now.)

*Any Co-curricular Service?* Yes

*Any SL Residence Halls or Theme Houses?* No

*Number of Full-time SL Staff on Campus (not counting instructors):* 2 (1 for service-learning, 1 for community service)

*Number of Part-time SL Staff on Campus (not counting instructors):* 5 + 12 (1 graduate assistant and 4 undergraduates); also 12 volunteers who do campus outreach for the center

**Arizona State University**

Division of Undergraduate Academic Services, PO Box 873801, Tempe, AZ 85282–3801

*University/College URL:* http://www.asu.edu

*Type of Institution:* public, university, research, secular

*SL Program/Center Name:* The Service Learning Program

*Contact Person Name and Title:* Dr. Gay W. Brack, Dir

*Contact Phone Number:* (602) 965–8238

*Contact Fax Number:* (602) 965–1091

*Contact Email Address:* gay.brack@asu.edu

*SL Program/Center URL:* http://www.asu.edu/duas/servlearn

*SL Online Course Description URL:* http://www.asu.edu/duas/servlearn

*SL Online Syllabi URL:* http://www.asu.edu/duas/servlearn

*Description:* The Service Learning Project involves course-linked internships and provides one-on-one and classroom tutoring in math, physical geography, geology, plant biology, multicultural education, nursing, and English. In addition, pilot projects include medieval and renaissance studies and microbiology. The project is located at 11 school and agency sites. Approximately 2,000 Arizona State University students, participating in course-linked intern-

ships, have contributed more than 200,00 hours of tutoring and mentoring children and youth whose environments put them at risk of academic failure. Primary funding is provided by community funding partners.

*SL Required for Graduation (all students)?* No

*Service Required for Graduation (all students)?* No

*Any Co-curricular Service?* Yes

*Any SL Residence Halls or Theme Houses?* No

*Number of Undergraduate SL Courses Offered Per Year:* 15–20 course-linked internships

*Number of Graduate SL Courses Offered Per Year:* 0

*Total Number of SL Courses Offered Per Year:* 12–15

*Number of Instructors Teaching SL Courses Per Year:* 12–15

*Number of Full-time SL Staff on Campus (not counting instructors):* 3

*Number of Part-time SL Staff on Campus (not counting instructors):* 4

**Ashland University**

401 College Ave, Ashland, OH 44805

*University/College URL:* http://www.ashland.edu

*Type of Institution:* private, university, teaching, religious

*SL Program/Center Name:* Office of Community Service

*Contact Person Name and Title:* Rebecca Rio, Dir, Study Abroad & Community Service

*Contact Phone Number:* (419) 289–5064

*Contact Fax Number:* (419) 289–5071

*Contact Email Address:* rrio@ashland.edu

*SL Program/Center URL:* http://www.ashland.edu/cardev

*Description:* Ashland University's Service Learning Advisory Council is made up of faculty members and is coordinated by the Director of Community Service. The council promotes service-learning on campus, coordinates training sessions, writes articles, has created $500 planning grants, and recently developed a Service Learning Elective Credit (plus one credit) program. The Elective Credit currently is being promoted among faculty and students. The council's budget (administrative costs) is covered by the Community Service Office.

*SL Required for Graduation (all students)?* No

*Service Required for Graduation (all students)?* No

*Any Co-curricular Service?* Yes

*Any SL Residence Halls or Theme Houses?* No

*Number of Undergraduate SL Courses Offered Per Year:* 8–12 (4–6 a semester)

*Total Number of SL Courses Offered Per Year:* 8–12

*Number of Instructors Teaching SL Courses Per Year:* 4–6

*Number of Full-time SL Staff on Campus (not counting instructors):* 0

*Number of Part-time SL Staff on Campus (not counting instructors):* 1

## Auburn University, School of Pharmacy, Auburn University, AL 36849

*University/College URL:* http://www. pharmacy.auburn.edu

*Type of Institution:* public, university, teaching, research

*SL Program/Center Name:* Pharmacy Practice Experience Program, School of Pharmacy

*Contact Person Name and Title:* Janelle Krueger, Coord, Early Experiential Education

*Contact Phone Number:* (334) 844–2988

*Contact Fax Number:* (334) 844–8353

*Contact Email Address:* kruegjl@auburn.edu

*Description:* The Pharmacy Practice Experience Program is a continuous experiential course (involving nine quarters—or three school years), and is a requirement of all pharmacy students at Auburn University. The service-learning experience is a component of the curriculum (as opposed to being part of an individual course). Students spend time each week communicating, establishing relationships, and providing pharmaceutical care to individuals within the community. They assist individuals identified through community-service agencies or those who have asked/agreed to be a part of the

program. The emphasis is on care provision within the community setting. Therefore, students are exposed to the idea that pharmaceutical care practice does not always have to occur within the four walls of a pharmacy. The level of care provided expands with the knowledge base of the student. Students are required to submit written documentation and reflection following each visit. In addition, each student is placed on a team comprised of first-, second-, and third-year pharmacy students that is guided by two faculty mentors. Teams meet weekly to review patient cases, reflect upon experiences, discuss issues related to professionalism and ethics, and link classroom learning with community experiences. This longitudinal service-learning experience is taken along with a full didactic load.

*SL Required for Graduation (all students)?* Yes

*Service Required for Graduation (all students)?* Yes

*Any Co-curricular Service?* No

*Any SL Residence Halls or Theme Houses?* No

*Number of Undergraduate SL Courses Offered Per Year:* 0

*Number of Graduate SL Courses Offered Per Year:* 9 (Professional School)

*Total Number of SL Courses Offered Per Year:* 9

*Number of Instructors Teaching SL Courses Per Year:* 40 (1 primary faculty member, 39 other faculty participants)

*Number of Full-time SL Staff on Campus (not counting instructors):* 1

*Number of Part-time SL Staff on Campus (not counting instructors):* 0

## Augsburg College

2211 Riverside Ave, PO Box 108, Minneapolis, MN 55454

*University/College URL:* http://www. augsburg.edu

*Type of Institution:* private, college, religious

*SL Program/Center Name:* Center for Service, Work and Learning

*Contact Person Name and Title:* Mary Laurel True, Assoc Dir; Merrie Benasutti, Program Coord

*Contact Phone Number:* (612)330–1775
*Contact Fax Number:* (612)330–1649
*Contact Email Address:*
 Truem@augsburg.edu;
 Benasutt@augsburg.edu
*SL Program/Center URL:* http://www.
 augsburg.edu/cswl/srvlrn.html
*Description:* Service-Learning at Augsburg is
an educational approach where students learn
from and about the community and society in
which they live by participating in service
experiences that are integrated into Augsburg
courses or done as part of campus life and
activities. The program's goals include build-
ing personal commitment to life-long service
and citizenship.
*SL Required for Graduation (all*
 *students)?* No
*Service Required for Graduation (all stu-*
 *dents)?* No
*Any Co-curricular Service?* Yes
*Any SL Residence Halls or Theme*
 *Houses?* Yes
*Number of Undergraduate SL Courses*
 *Offered Per Year:* 15
*Number of Graduate SL Courses Offered*
 *Per Year:* 1 (in Education)
*Total Number of SL Courses Offered Per*
 *Year:* 30
*Number of Instructors Teaching SL Courses*
 *Per Year:* 20
*Number of Full-time SL Staff on Campus*
 *(not counting instructors):* 1 VISTA
 volunteer
*Number of Part-time SL Staff on Campus*
 *(not counting instructors):* 2

**Augustana College**
2001 S Summit Ave, Sioux Falls, SD 57197
*University/College URL:* http://www.
 augie.edu
*Type of Institution:* private, college, teach-
 ing, religious
*SL Program/Center Name:* Teagle Service-
 Learning Grant
*Contact Person Name and Title:* Dr. Richard
 A. Hanson, VP for Academic Affairs,
 Dean of the College
*Contact Phone Number:* (605) 336–5417
*Contact Fax Number:* (605) 336–4450

*Contact Email Address:*
 rhanson@inst.augie.edu
*Description:* Augustana College has a faculty-
development program in service-learning. It
features all-day faculty workshops led by experts in service-learning, mini-grants to support summer work by faculty developing service-learning components for specific courses,
and newsletters and e-mail announcements to
keep faculty informed and to share experiences
and ideas. The three-year program is intended
to help make service to the community an
integral part of the college's liberal arts curriculum. The new program is supported by a
$41,000 grant from the Teagle Foundation.
*SL Required for Graduation (all*
 *students)?* No
*Service Required for Graduation (all stu-*
 *dents)?* No
*Any Co-curricular Service?* Yes
*Any SL Residence Halls or Theme*
 *Houses?* No
*Number of Full-time SL Staff on Campus*
 *(not counting instructors):* 1

**Azusa Pacific University**
901 East Alosta Ave, PO Box 7000, Azusa,
 CA 91702
*University/College URL:* http://www.apu.edu
*Type of Institution:* private, university, teach-
 ing, religious
*SL Program/Center Name:* Office of Com-
 munity Service Learning
*Contact Person Name and Title:* Joy Bianchi
 Brown, Dir
*Contact Phone Number:* (626) 815–6000,
 ext 3780
*Contact Fax Number:* (626) 815–3801
*Contact Email Address:* jmbbrown@apu.edu
*SL Program/Center URL:* http://www.apu.
 edu/ocsl/
*SL Online Course Description URL:* http://
 home.apu.edu/~jmbbrown/newpages/sf.
 htm
*Description:* The Office of Community Service Learning exists to provide quality service
opportunities for students that will inspire and
motivate them to become lifelong learners and
to have a life of continual awareness and involvement in the community. Goals include

serving faculty, empowering students, and building community. The office is run primarily by students who take an interest in learning through serving. They work directly with faculty to promote this pedagogy and act as advocates to assist them with any logistical details for their service-learning projects.

*SL Required for Graduation (all students)?* No

*Service Required for Graduation (all students)?* Yes (30 hours per year)

*Any Co-curricular Service?* Yes

*Any SL Residence Halls or Theme Houses?* No

*Number of Undergraduate SL Courses Offered Per Year:* 45–50

*Number of Graduate SL Courses Offered Per Year:* 3–5

*Total Number of SL Courses Offered Per Year:* 45–50

*Number of Instructors Teaching SL Courses Per Year:* 40–45

*Number of Full-time SL Staff on Campus (not counting instructors):* 1

*Number of Part-time SL Staff on Campus (not counting instructors):* 10

## Baldwin-Wallace College

275 Eastland Dr, Berea, OH 44017–2088

*University/College URL:* http://www.bw.edu

*Type of Institution:* private, college, teaching, religious

*SL Program/Center Name:* Office of Community Outreach

*Contact Person Name and Title:* Margaret O'Gorman, Dir

*Contact Phone Number:* (440) 826–2301

*Contact Fax Number:* (440) 826–2075

*Contact Email Address:* mogorman@bw.edu

*SL Program/Center URL:* http://www.bw.edu/~outreach/

*Description:* The Office of Community Outreach is primarily a center for co-curricular service opportunities, including weekly volunteer opportunities at more than 12 different agencies in the Cleveland area. The office is run primarily by students. Student staff serve as links between the college and community. The office is expanding its opportunities for service through some service-learning courses (prima-

rily in education and social sciences) and has created a semester-long urban-immersion program. In this program, students live and study in an urban neighborhood while working in an internship with a nonprofit organization. This program will be modeled after a six-week summer immersion program that has been operating successfully for the past five years. The Office of Community Outreach also serves as the home for the college's America Reads program.

*SL Required for Graduation (all students)?* No

*Service Required for Graduation (all students)?* No

*Any Co-curricular Service?* Yes

*Any SL Residence Halls or Theme Houses?* Yes

*Number of Undergraduate SL Courses Offered Per Year:* 5–7

*Total Number of SL Courses Offered Per Year:* 5–7

*Number of Instructors Teaching SL Courses Per Year:* 5

*Number of Full-time SL Staff on Campus (not counting instructors):* 1

*Number of Part-time SL Staff on Campus (not counting instructors):* 2 (graduate student assistants)

## Ball State University

2000 W University Ave, Muncie, IN 47306

*University/College URL:* http://www.bsu.edu

*Type of Institution:* public, university, teaching

*SL Program/Center Name:* Office of Leadership and Service Programs

*Contact Person Name and Title:* Peter Young, Assoc Dir

*Contact Phone Number:* (765) 285–2621

*Contact Fax Number:* (765) 285–2855

*Contact Email Address:* pyoung@bsu.edu

*SL Program/Center URL:* http://www.bsu.edu/students/slsp

*Description:* Student Voluntary Services, a unit of the Office of Leadership and Service Programs, provides students with educationally valuable experiences through community service and service-learning. Student Voluntary Services collaborates with more than 120 local service agencies, student organizations, and academic departments to offer students opportunities to engage in meaningful service.

*SL Required for Graduation (all students)?* No

*Service Required for Graduation (all students)?* No

*Any Co-curricular Service?* Yes

*Any SL Residence Halls or Theme Houses?* No

*Number of Undergraduate SL Courses Offered Per Year:* 45

*Number of Graduate SL Courses Offered Per Year:* 5

*Total Number of SL Courses Offered Per Year:* 50

*Number of Instructors Teaching SL Courses Per Year:* 35

*Number of Full-time SL Staff on Campus (not counting instructors):* 4 (1 professional staff, 1 support staff, 2 AmeriCorps members)

*Number of Part-time SL Staff on Campus (not counting instructors):* 11 (10 part-time AmeriCorps members (students); 1 graduate assistant)

### Barry University

547 NE 58th St, Miami, FL 33161

*University/College URL:* http://www.barry.edu

*Type of Institution:* private, university, teaching, religious

*SL Program/Center Name:* Academy for Better Communities

*Contact Person Name and Title:* Jacqueline B. Mondros, DSW, Prof and Dir

*Contact Phone Number:* (305) 899–3909

*Contact Fax Number:* (305) 899–4783

*Contact Email Address:* jmondros@mail.barry.edu

*Description:* The Academy for Better Communities is the university's outreach arm to low-income communities of South Florida and the organizations and agencies that serve them. It facilitates partnerships between university faculty and students and local communities, in order to solve pressing urban problems the communities face. Service-learning is included as part of field experience credits, which are

linked to other courses in which students discuss their experiences and learn how to improve their own skills and the environments in which they work.

*SL Required for Graduation (all students)?* No

*Service Required for Graduation (all students)?* No

*Any Co-curricular Service?* No

*Any SL Residence Halls or Theme Houses?* No

*Number of Undergraduate SL Courses Offered Per Year:* 0

*Number of Graduate SL Courses Offered Per Year:* 5

*Total Number of SL Courses Offered Per Year:* 5

*Number of Instructors Teaching SL Courses Per Year:* 5

*Number of Full-time SL Staff on Campus (not counting instructors):* 26

*Number of Part-time SL Staff on Campus (not counting instructors):* 0

### Barstow College

2700 Barstow Rd, Barstow, CA 92311

*University/College URL:* http://www.barstow.cc.ca.us

*Type of Institution:* public, community college, teaching

*Contact Person Name and Title:* Joann Jelly, EdD, Psychology

*Contact Phone Number:* (760) 252–2411

*Contact Email Address:* jjelly@barstow.cc.ca.us

*Description:* The Service Learning program is delivered through one three-unit course and through "bonus activities" in most psychology classes. Students perform internships at various agencies in the city based on their interests and majors. The course and related activities are intended for students who need electives and for agencies which have indicated an interest to work with the program. Eventually the course may be required for graduation. Funding for meetings, conferences, publications, etc. comes from the general budget.

*SL Required for Graduation (all students)?* No

*Service Required for Graduation (all students)?* No
*Any Co-curricular Service?* No
*Any SL Residence Halls or Theme Houses?* No
*Number of Undergraduate SL Courses Offered Per Year:* 3
*Total Number of SL Courses Offered Per Year:* 3
*Number of Instructors Teaching SL Courses Per Year:* 2
*Number of Full-time SL Staff on Campus (not counting instructors):* 0
*Number of Part-time SL Staff on Campus (not counting instructors):* 0

## Bates College

Center for Service-Learning, 163 Wood St, Lewiston, ME 04240
*University/College URL:* http://www.bates.edu
*Type of Institution:* private, college, secular
*SL Program/Center Name:* Center for Service-Learning
*Contact Person Name and Title:* Peggy Rotundo, Assoc Dir
*Contact Phone Number:* (207) 786–8273
*Contact Fax Number:* (207) 786–8282
*Contact Email Address:* mrotundo@bates.edu
*SL Program/Center URL:* http://abacus.bates.edu/pubs/NS.brochures/Service-Learning.html/
*Description:* The Center for Service-Learning provides opportunities for students and faculty to incorporate community-service projects into their learning and teaching. The center helps students set up independent studies, summer opportunities, and internships which incorporate service-learning. It also helps students set up reflective opportunities on the nature and purpose of community involvement.
*SL Required for Graduation (all students)?* No
*Service Required for Graduation (all students)?* No
*Any Co-curricular Service?* Yes
*Any SL Residence Halls or Theme Houses?* Yes

*Number of Undergraduate SL Courses Offered Per Year:* 31
*Total Number of SL Courses Offered Per Year:* 31
*Number of Instructors Teaching SL Courses Per Year:* 31
*Number of Full-time SL Staff on Campus (not counting instructors):* 2
*Number of Part-time SL Staff on Campus (not counting instructors):* 3

## Belmont University

1900 Belmont Blvd, Nashville, TN 37212–3757
*University/College URL:* http://www.belmont.edu
*Type of Institution:* private, university, teaching, religious
*SL Program/Center Name:* Service Learning Task Force
*Contact Person Name and Title:* Tim Stewart, Coord for Service Learning
*Contact Phone Number:* (615) 460–5431/5423
*Contact Fax Number:* (615) 460–6446
*Contact Email Address:* stewartt@mail.belmont.edu; mcdonaldm@mail.belmont.edu
*Description:* Service-learning courses at Belmont are offered in the following areas: accounting, English, journalism, sociology, occupational therapy, nursing, religion, and Spanish. Faculty who teach these courses have formed the Service Learning Task Force to foster service-learning on campus, to exchange ideas and resources, and to assess the effectiveness of service-learning courses. Individual courses are innovative, and faculty in journalism, nursing, and English have made contributions to the national discussion on service-learning. Sites for service-learning classes include the neighborhood adjacent to campus (where several collaborative programs have been developed), a retirement center near campus, local service agencies, and study-abroad sites in Central America. Links continue to be developed between service programs that form part of students' graduation requirements and service-learning academic courses. In 1999–2000, staffing includes a part-time posi-

tion for Coordinator of Service Learning, a position within the Teaching Center.

*SL Required for Graduation (all students)?* No

*Service Required for Graduation (all students)?* Yes

*Any Co-curricular Service?* Yes

*Any SL Residence Halls or Theme Houses?* No

*Number of Undergraduate SL Courses Offered Per Year:* 10

*Number of Graduate SL Courses Offered Per Year:* 1

*Total Number of SL Courses Offered Per Year:* 11

*Number of Instructors Teaching SL Courses Per Year:* 9

*Number of Full-time SL Staff on Campus (not counting instructors):* 0

*Number of Part-time SL Staff on Campus (not counting instructors):* 1

**Bentley College**

175 Forest St, Waltham, MA 02452

*University/College URL:* http://www. bentley.edu

*Type of Institution:* private, college, teaching, secular

*SL Program/Center Name:* Bentley Service-Learning Center

*Contact Person Name and Title:* Robert E. Koulish Dir

*Contact Phone Number:* (781) 891–2652

*Contact Fax Number:* (781) 891–3410

*Contact Email Address:* rkoulish@bentley.edu

*SL Program/Center URL:* http://ecampus. bentley.edu/dept/bslc/index.html

*Description:* The primary goal of the Bentley Service-Learning Center is educational: through service-learning, students discover that community involvement outside the classroom contributes significantly to what they have learned within it. The center seeks to enhance students' abilities and dispositions to become socially responsible working professionals. At the same time, the center pursues the social goal of developing projects that serve the human needs and interests of the Greater Boston community. In this way, the center endeavors to balance

service and learning. It helps partner organizations in Waltham and the Boston area to serve their constituencies as effectively as possible, while also helping faculty to integrate these projects into their course objectives. Under the center's banner, every first-year student has a service-learning requirement, and hundreds of undergraduates annually take advantage of the fourth-credit option to deepen their involvement as part of class-specific service projects. The BSLC receives internal funding and external grants.

*SL Required for Graduation (all students)?* Noo, but now included as required part of First Year Initiative

*Service Required for Graduation (all students)?* No

*Any Co-curricular Service?* Yes

*Any SL Residence Halls or Theme Houses?* No

*SL Degrees Offered:* Minor in development

*Number of Undergraduate SL Courses Offered Per Year:* 30

*Total Number of SL Courses Offered Per Year:* 30

*Number of Instructors Teaching SL Courses Per Year:* 30

*Number of Full-time SL Staff on Campus (not counting instructors):* 3

*Number of Part-time SL Staff on Campus (not counting instructors):* 2

**Bethel College**

3900 Bethel Dr, Saint Paul, MN 55112

*University/College URL:* http://www. bethel.edu

*Type of Institution:* private, college, teaching, religious

*SL Program/Center Name:* Service-Learning at Bethel

*Contact Person Name and Title:* Vincent Peters, Prof, Social Work, Dir, Service-Learning

*Contact Phone Number:* (651) 638–6124

*Contact Fax Number:* (651) 638–6001

*Contact Email Address:* v-peters@bethel.edu

*SL Program/Center URL:* http://www.bethel. edu/Academics/Service_Learning/sl. mainpage.html

*Description:* Bethel College provides learning

opportunities through the service-learning program that motivate students in exploring solutions to problems and in understanding their distinctive roles and responsibilities in enacting social transformation, spiritual growth, and community well-being as future leaders. Commitment to service-learning among students, faculty, and administrators is part of the college's Christian commitment to service.

*SL Required for Graduation (all students)?* No

*Service Required for Graduation (all students)?* No

*Any Co-curricular Service?* Yes

*Any SL Residence Halls or Theme Houses?* Yes

*Number of Undergraduate SL Courses Offered Per Year:* 35–40

*Number of Instructors Teaching SL Courses Per Year:* 20–25

*Number of Full-time SL Staff on Campus (not counting instructors):* 3

*Number of Part-time SL Staff on Campus (not counting instructors):* 2.5

## Binghamton University

PO Box 6000, Binghamton, NY 13902
*University/College URL:* http://www.binghamton.edu
*Type of Institution:* public, university, research, secular
*SL Program/Center Name:* Experiential Education Advisory Committee
*Contact Person Name and Title:* Meg Mitzel, Experiential Education Coord
*Contact Phone Number:* (607) 777–2400
*Contact Fax Number:* (607) 777–4499
*Contact Email Address:* mmitzel@binghamton.edu
*Description:* The Experiential Education Advisory Committee promotes the development and coordination of experiential education activities in both credit and non-credit bearing settings, including internships, community service, service-learning, co-ops, projects, and similar activities at Binghamton University.
*SL Required for Graduation (all students)?* No

*Service Required for Graduation (all students)?* No

## Birmingham-Southern College

900 Arkadelphia, Box 549065, Birmingham, AL 35254
*University/College URL:* http://www.bsc.edu
*Type of Institution:* private, college, teaching, religious
*SL Program/Center Name:* Hess Center for Leadership and Service
*Contact Person Name and Title:* Rachel Estes, Dir of Service-Learning
*Contact Phone Number:* (205) 226–4720
*Contact Fax Number:* (205) 226–3073
*Contact Email Address:* restes@bsc.edi
*SL Program/Center URL:* http://www.bsc.edu/specialprogram/hessctrservice/default.htm
*Description:* The Office of Service Learning, housed in the Hess Center for Leadership and Service, facilitates 12 ongoing local service programs. These programs are student-initiated, student-run and student-maintained. The goal of the office is to provide students with the opportunity to develop a sense of commitment and relationship through these service programs. Alternative Spring Breaks and International Service-Learning trips are an integral part of the office's programming. Trips to Calcutta, Africa, Latin America, as well as national trips, have encouraged students to experience other cultures through service.
*SL Required for Graduation (all students)?* No

*Service Required for Graduation (all students)?* No

*Any Co-curricular Service?* Yes

*Any SL Residence Halls or Theme Houses?* No

*Number of Undergraduate SL Courses Offered Per Year:* 3–5

*Total Number of SL Courses Offered Per Year:* 3–5

*Number of Instructors Teaching SL Courses Per Year:* 2

*Number of Full-time SL Staff on Campus (not counting instructors):* 2

*Number of Part-time SL Staff on Campus (not counting instructors):* 1

**Bloomsburg University of Pennsylvania**
400 East Second St, Bloomsburg, PA 17815
*University/College URL:* http://www.
  bloomu.edu
*Type of Institution:* public, university,
  teaching
*SL Program/Center Name:* Students Organ-
  ized to Learn through Volunteerism and
  Employment (SOLVE) Office
*Contact Person Name and Title:* Jean
  Downing, Dir
*Contact Phone Number:* (570) 389 4788
*Contact Fax Number:* (570) 387 4278
*Contact Email Address:*
  jdowning@bloomu.edu
*SL Program/Center URL:* http://www.
  bloomu.edu/departments/solve/pages/
  index.htm
*SL Online Course Description URL:* http://
  www.bloomu.edu/departments/solve/
  pages/serv.htm
*SL Online Syllabi URL:* http://www.bloomu.
  edu/departments/solve/pages/serv.htm
*Description:* Students Organized to Learn
through Volunteerism and Employment
(SOLVE) is the university's office of community service, student employment, and student
volunteerism. Begun in 1992, SOLVE is a
campus-wide service-learning resource center
which endeavors to develop service as an integral part of the education process. Service-
learning is a teaching strategy used by some
faculty individually and encouraged by some
departments (e.g., nursing, education, and special education). In such courses, students are
generally required to spend 10–20 hours in a
community-service project. They engage in
reflection through journals, class discussion
and reaction papers. In 1998–1999, more than
2,500 students volunteered at more than 50
community organizations in programs ranging
from tutoring elementary children to therapeu-
tic horseback riding for physically challenged
individuals. Over 100 students earn their federal college work-study award at schools and
nonprofit agencies through the PHEAA Off-
Campus Community Service program.
*SL Required for Graduation (all
  students)?* No

*Service Required for Graduation (all stu-
  dents)?* No
*Any Co-curricular Service?* Yes
*Any SL Residence Halls or Theme
  Houses?* No

**Boston College**
140 Commonwealth Ave, McElroy 117,
  Chestnut Hill, MA 02467–3805
*University/College URL:* http://www.bc.edu
*Type of Institution:* private, university, teach-
  ing, research, religious
*SL Program/Center Name:* PULSE Program
*Contact Person Name and Title:* David J.
  McMenamin, PhD, Dir
*Contact Phone Number:* (617) 552–3495
*Contact Fax Number:* (617) 552–2885
*Contact Email Address:* pulse@bc.edu
*SL Program/Center URL:* http://www.bc.
  edu/pulse
*SL Online Course Description URL:* http://
  www.bc.edu/pulse/courseofferings.html
*Description:* The PULSE program provides
students with the opportunity to combine supervised social service or social advocacy field
work with the study of philosophy, theology,
and other disciplines. In light of classical philosophical and theological texts, PULSE students
address the relationship of self and society, the
nature of community, the mystery of suffering,
and the practical difficulties of developing a
just society. The majority of the students enrolled in the program take a 12-credit, year-
long core-level course in philosophy and theology entitled "Person and Social Responsibility." A limited number of PULSE elective
courses are also offered each year. Begun in the
Spring of 1970 as a result of the initiative of the
Undergraduate Government of Boston College, the program is currently celebrating its
30th anniversary.
*SL Required for Graduation (all
  students)?* No
*Service Required for Graduation (all stu-
  dents)?* No
*Any Co-curricular Service?* Yes
*Any SL Residence Halls or Theme
  Houses?* Yes
*Number of Undergraduate SL Courses
  Offered Per Year:* 12

*Number of Graduate SL Courses Offered Per Year:* 0

*Total Number of SL Courses Offered Per Year:* 12

*Number of Instructors Teaching SL Courses Per Year:* 11

*Number of Full-time SL Staff on Campus (not counting instructors):* 2

*Number of Part-time SL Staff on Campus (not counting instructors):* 0

## Brevard Community College

1519 Clearlake Rd, Student Center Room 214, Cocoa, FL 32922

*University/College URL:* http://www.brevard.cc.fl.us

*Type of Institution:* public, community college primary emphasis:, teaching, secular

*SL Program/Center Name:* Center for Service-Learning

*Contact Person Name and Title:* Roger Henry, Dir

*Contact Phone Number:* (407) 632–1111, ext 33150

*Contact Fax Number:* (407) 632–1111, ext 32112

*Contact Email Address:* henryr@brevard.cc.fl.us

*SL Program/Center URL:* http://www.brevard.cc.fl.us/CSL/

*SL Online Syllabi URL:* http://www.brevard.cc.fl.us/CSL/07Syllabi/

*Description:* The Center for Service-Learning creates and enhances public-service opportunities for students and develops an expectation of service as an integral part of the college experience. The center recruits, places, and supports students in meaningful and reciprocal service-learning projects and experiences. It works in partnership with hundreds of community projects and organizations and sets as a priority the integration of service and academic study.

*SL Required for Graduation (all students)?* No (But a proposal to require service-learning is being considered for implementation in Fall 2000.)

*Service Required for Graduation (all students)?* No

*Any Co-curricular Service?* Yes

*Any SL Residence Halls or Theme Houses?* No

*Number of Undergraduate SL Courses Offered Per Year:* 125

*Total Number of SL Courses Offered Per Year:* 125

*Number of Instructors Teaching SL Courses Per Year:* 115

*Number of Full-time SL Staff on Campus (not counting instructors):* 4

*Number of Part-time SL Staff on Campus (not counting instructors):* 2

## Bridgewater College

402 East College St, Box 133, Bridgewater, VA 22812

*University/College URL:* http://www.bridgewater.edu

*Type of Institution:* private, college, teaching, religious

*SL Program/Center Name:* Service-Learning Center

*Contact Person Name and Title:* Robbie Miller, Dir of Service-Learning

*Contact Phone Number:* (540) 828–5674

*Contact Fax Number:* (540) 828–5479

*Contact Email Address:* service.learning@bridgewater.edu

*SL Program/Center URL:* http://www.bridgewater.edu/departments/servlearn/index.html

*Description:* The Service-Learning Center links students, faculty, and staff with community needs and promotes opportunities for learning through service. Every student at Bridgewater is required to complete a minimum of 10 service-learning hours each academic year.

*SL Required for Graduation (all students)?* Yes

*Service Required for Graduation (all students)?* No

*Any Co-curricular Service?* No

*Any SL Residence Halls or Theme Houses?* No

*Number of Undergraduate SL Courses Offered Per Year:* 0

*Total Number of SL Courses Offered Per Year:* 0

*Number of Instructors Teaching SL Courses Per Year:* 0

*Number of Full-time SL Staff on Campus
(not counting instructors):* 0
*Number of Part-time SL Staff on Campus
(not counting instructors):* 2

**Brigham Young University**
PO Box 27908, Provo, UT 84602
*University/College URL:* http://www.byu.edu
*Type of Institution:* private, university, teaching, religious
*SL Program/Center Name:* The Jacobsen
Center for Service and Learning
*Contact Person Name and Title:* Jim
Backman, Dir
*Contact Phone Number:* (801) 378–8686
*Contact Fax Number:* (801) 378–1291
*Contact Email Address:*
jim_backman@byu.edu
*SL Program/Center URL:* http://www.byu.
edu/stlife/campuslife/slc/index.htm
*Description:* The Jacobsen Center for Service
and Learning helps students see service as a
valuable part of their own learning experience,
better understand their responsibility to extend
the benefits of their learning to members of the
LDS Church in all parts of the world, and create
friends for the university and the LDS Church.
The center also facilitates joint efforts between
Student Life and the academic arm of the
University; helps faculty develop valuable service-learning components in their courses; and
assists in organizing, coordinating, and supporting the existing service efforts of the University. The Jacobsen Center is involved with
the full spectrum of student involvement in
service and learning. In the non-academic area
of service, it provides office space and support
to the Student Association's 28 Community
Service programs and assumes functions of the
Campus Involvement Center (5000 students).
The center contributes support to programs for
academic credit, such as Academic Internships
in more than 60 departments (5000 students)
and international programs (2000 students) managed through the Kennedy Center International
Study Programs office. In addition, service-learning courses are developed by faculty with
help from the Jacobsen Center and Faculty
Center. The center has a director, assistant
director, staff, an executive committee, a faculty committee, and coordinating council and
community committee. Funding comes from a
private endowment and donor contributions
through the university's Development Office.
*SL Required for Graduation (all
students)?* No
*Service Required for Graduation (all students)?* No
*Any Co-curricular Service?* Yes
*Any SL Residence Halls or Theme
Houses?* No
*Number of Undergraduate SL Courses
Offered Per Year:* 40
*Number of Graduate SL Courses Offered
Per Year:* 13
*Total Number of SL Courses Offered Per
Year:* 53
*Number of Instructors Teaching SL Courses
Per Year:* 37
*Number of Full-time SL Staff on Campus
(not counting instructors):* 2
*Number of Part-time SL Staff on Campus
(not counting instructors):* 6

**Brooklyn College of the City University of
New York**
2900 Bedford Ave, Brooklyn, NY
11210–2889
*University/College URL:* http://www.brooklyn.cuny.edu
*Type of Institution:* public, university, teaching, research, secular
*SL Program/Center Name:* Brooklyn College
Community Partnership for Research and
Learning
*Contact Person Name and Title:* Nancy
Romer, Dir, and Prof, Psychology
*Contact Phone Number:* (718) 951–5015
*Contact Fax Number:* (718) 951–5927
*Contact Email Address:*
nromer@brooklyn.cuny.edu
*Description:* Community Partnership for
Research and Learning sponsors service-learning courses, faculty-development seminars, and
action research. At present, it offers three service-learning courses a semester (on average)
and plans significant expansion with increased
college support and grants. CPRL has organized a CUNY-wide conference (and an organization that grew out of the conference) on

community outreach with service-learning as a primary mode. The program is aimed primarily at undergraduate liberal arts majors. The work is directed by a Community Advisory Board of local school administrators, CBO staff, parents, and teachers. It is funded through college tax-levied funds and has also conducted work under a CNS Learn and Serve America–Higher Education grant and a HUD Community Outreach Partnership grant.

*SL Required for Graduation (all students)?* No
*Service Required for Graduation (all students)?* No
*Any Co-curricular Service?* No
*Any SL Residence Halls or Theme Houses?* No
*Number of Undergraduate SL Courses Offered Per Year:* 6
*Number of Graduate SL Courses Offered Per Year:* 0
*Total Number of SL Courses Offered Per Year:* 6
*Number of Instructors Teaching SL Courses Per Year:* 4
*Number of Full-time SL Staff on Campus (not counting instructors):* 2 (one admin & one admin assist: service learning is only part of their duties)
*Number of Part-time SL Staff on Campus (not counting instructors):* 0

**Brown University**
25 George St, Box 1974, Providence, RI 02912
*University/College URL:* http://www.brown.edu
*Type of Institution:* private, university, teaching, research
*SL Program/Center Name:* Howard R. Swearer Center for Public Service
*Contact Person Name and Title:* Peter Hocking, Dir
*Contact Phone Number:* (401) 863–2338
*Contact Fax Number:* (401) 863–3094
*Contact Email Address:* Peter_Hocking@Brown.edu
*SL Program/Center URL:* http://www.brown.edu/Departments/Swearer_Center
*SL Online Course Description URL:* http://

www.brown.edu/Departments/Swearer_Center/academics/course-search.shtml
*Description:* The Swearer Center considers active community participation and social responsibility to be central concerns of a liberal education. Students are seen as being capable of making valuable social contributions while learning. This approach reflects the university's public trust to both prepare its students for meaningful engagement in the American democracy and to be of service to the world at large. Over the past decade these beliefs have been informed by experience, and the center has become an intersection between service, vital community, and social change. This intersection is seen as forming a crossroads where the theory of the classroom meets the practice of living in the world.
*SL Required for Graduation (all students)?* No
*Service Required for Graduation (all students)?* No
*Any SL Residence Halls or Theme Houses?* No
*Number of Undergraduate SL Courses Offered Per Year:* 10–15
*Total Number of SL Courses Offered Per Year:* 10–15
*Number of Instructors Teaching SL Courses Per Year:* 10–15

**Brown University**
Curriculum Affairs Office, School of Medicine, Box G-B232, Providence, RI 02912
*University/College URL:* http://biomed.brown.edu/Medicine.html
*Type of Institution:* private, university, teaching, research, secular
*SL Program/Center Name:* Curriculum Affairs Office, School of Medicine
*Contact Person Name and Title:* Judith Boss, Assist Dir of Curriculum Affairs; Bettye Williams, Service Learning Admin
*Contact Phone Number:* (401) 863–3992
*Contact Fax Number:* (401) 863–3562
*Contact Email Address:* Judith_Boss@Brown.EDU
*Description:* The Service Learning Program in the Medical School's Curriculum Affairs Office assists premedical and medical students in find-

ing community service-learning opportunities through courses or at community sites in the greater Providence area that fulfill Ability VII credit ("Social and Community Contexts of Health Care"). The center also assists students who have done community service on their own to obtain credit for their service-learning. All medical students are required to demonstrate competence in the "Social and Community Contexts of Health Care." They can complete the beginning levels of this competency as undergraduate pre-med students or during their first two years of medical school. One beginning level of this competency is usually, though not always, satisfied through participation in community service-learning programs such as the student-run Community Health Advocacy Program (CHAP), the Student National Medical Association (SNMA), Swearer Center Community Partnerships, or AMA Community Context programs.

*SL Required for Graduation (all students)?* Yes

*Service Required for Graduation (all students)?* Yes

*Any Co-curricular Service?* No

*Any SL Residence Halls or Theme Houses?* No

*Number of Undergraduate SL Courses Offered Per Year:* 0

*Total Number of SL Courses Offered Per Year:* 0

*Number of Full-time SL Staff on Campus (not counting instructors):* 2

*Number of Part-time SL Staff on Campus (not counting instructors):* 0

## Bucknell University

Lewisburg, PA 17837

*University/College URL:* http://www.bucknell.edu

*Type of Institution:* private, college, teaching, secular

*SL Program/Center Name:* Concentration in Human Services, Dept of Sociology and Anthropology

*Contact Person Name and Title:* Carl Milofsky, Prof

*Contact Phone Number:* (570) 577–3468

*Contact Fax Number:* (570) 577–3543

*Contact Email Address:* milofsky@bucknell.edu

*SL Program/Center URL:* http://www.facstaff.bucknell.edu/milofsky/

*SL Online Course Description URL:* http://www.facstaff.bucknell.edu/milofsky/Community/

*SL Online Syllabi URL:* http://www.facstaff.bucknell.edu/milofsky/HumServSys/, http://www.facstaff.bucknell.edu/milofsky/Nonprofits/

*Description:* Service Learning at Bucknell College grows out of departmental activities in both the academic and student services areas. There is no formal program and funding comes out of regular budget lines. However, the college has many diverse courses and many co-curricular activities. Teaching and volunteer service are emphasized. Active action-research projects are operational with a wide variety of community agencies that provide opportunities for internships, student consulting, and publishing in which students co-author papers with faculty or make their own presentations at professional conferences.

*SL Required for Graduation (all students)?* No

*Service Required for Graduation (all students)?* No

*Any Co-curricular Service?* Yes

*Any SL Residence Halls or Theme Houses?* Yes (although generally service-learning is one of several aspects)

*SL Degrees Offered:* Concentration in Human Services (as part of the Sociology major)

*Number of Undergraduate SL Courses Offered Per Year:* 10–15

*Number of Graduate SL Courses Offered Per Year:* 3

*Total Number of SL Courses Offered Per Year:* 10–15

*Number of Instructors Teaching SL Courses Per Year:* 10–15

*Number of Full-time SL Staff on Campus (not counting instructors):* 2 (There is no

formal program or staff; the Associate Dean of Students and an Internship coordinator in Career Development do substantial work on service-learning.)
*Number of Part-time SL Staff on Campus (not counting instructors):* 0

**California Polytechnic State University**
c/o Student Life, San Luis Obispo, CA 93407
*University/College URL:* http://www.calpoly.edu
*Type of Institution:* public, university, teaching, secular
*SL Program/Center Name:* Community Service & Learning Center
*Contact Person Name and Title:* Sam Lutrin, Coord, Community Service Programs
*Contact Phone Number:* (805) 756–5839
*Contact Fax Number:* (805) 756–5836
*Contact Email Address:* plutrin@calpoly.edu
*SL Program/Center URL:* http://www.calpoly.edu/~slad/csl
*SL Online Course Description URL:* http://www.calpoly.edu/~slad/csl/syllabi.html
*SL Online Syllabi URL:* http://www.calpoly.edu/~slad/csl/syllabi.html
*Description:* Class & Community Connections is the service-learning program in the Community Service and Learning Center. Begun in 1996–97, the program is looking at adding service components to general-education courses. Nearly 600 students enroll in one of these courses each year. Program staffing includes faculty, trained and paid Student Mentors, and the Coordinator of Community Service Programs. Funding is provided by student fees, an internal grant, a small external grant, the Instructionally-Related Activities Committee and the Office of Student Life.
*SL Required for Graduation (all students)?* No
*Service Required for Graduation (all students)?* No
*Any Co-curricular Service?* Yes
*Any SL Residence Halls or Theme Houses?* No
*Number of Undergraduate SL Courses Offered Per Year:* 20

*Number of Graduate SL Courses Offered Per Year:* 0
*Total Number of SL Courses Offered Per Year:* 20
*Number of Instructors Teaching SL Courses Per Year:* 20
*Number of Full-time SL Staff on Campus (not counting instructors):* 0.5
*Number of Part-time SL Staff on Campus (not counting instructors):* 4 (10 hours per week each)

**California State Polytechnic University, Pomona (Cal Poly Pomona)**
3801 W Temple Ave, Pomona, CA 91768
*University/College URL:* http://www.csupomona.edu
*Type of Institution:* public, university, teaching
*SL Program/Center Name:* Human Corps Volunteer Center
*Contact Person Name and Title:* David E. Johnson, Interim Dir, Judicial Affairs
*Contact Phone Number:* (909) 869–3257
*Contact Fax Number:* (909) 869–4390
*Contact Email Address:* dejohnson@csupomona.edu
*Description:* Human Corps Volunteer Center works to match volunteers with agencies for both community service and service-learning opportunities.
*SL Required for Graduation (all students)?* No
*Service Required for Graduation (all students)?* No
*Any Co-curricular Service?* Yes
*Any SL Residence Halls or Theme Houses?* No
*Number of Undergraduate SL Courses Offered Per Year:* 6–8
*Number of Graduate SL Courses Offered Per Year:* 1–3
*Total Number of SL Courses Offered Per Year:* 7–11
*Number of Instructors Teaching SL Courses Per Year:* 3–4
*Number of Full-time SL Staff on Campus (not counting instructors):* 1

**California State University**

400 Golden Shore, Suite 317, Office of Community Service Learning, Long Beach, CA 90802

*University/College URL:* http://www. co. calstate.edu

*Type of Institution:* public, university, teaching, secular

*SL Program/Center Name:* Office of Community Service Learning

*Contact Person Name and Title:* Erika Freihage, Coord, Community Service Learning

*Contact Phone Number:* (562) 985–2713

*Contact Fax Number:* (562) 985–2120

*Contact Email Address:* efreihage@calstate.edu

*SL Program/Center URL:* http://www. calstate.edu/tier3/csl/

*Description:* The Office of Community Service Learning in the CSU Chancellor's Office provides support and assistance to service-learning and community-service programs at the 22 campuses of the CSU system. The office works to develop institutional support for service-learning pedagogy so that each CSU student can have the opportunity to participate in a service-learning course before he or she graduates.

*SL Required for Graduation (all students)?* No

*Service Required for Graduation (all students)?* No

*Any Co-curricular Service?* Yes

*Any SL Residence Halls or Theme Houses?* Yes

**California State University, Chico**

W 2nd & Cherry St, Chico, CA 95929–0750

*University/College URL:* http://www. csuchico.edu

*Type of Institution:* public, university, teaching, secular

*SL Program/Center Name:* Community Action Volunteers in Education (CAVE)

*Contact Person Name and Title:* Nan Timmons, Exec Dir

*Contact Phone Number:* (530) 898–5817

*Contact Fax Number:* (530) 898–6431

*Contact Email Address:* Ntimmons@csuchico.edu

*SL Program/Center URL:* GOTOBUTTON BM_- http://www.csuchico.edu/cave

*Description:* Community Action Volunteers in Education (CAVE) is the largest student-run organization on campus funded primarily by the Associated Students. CAVE is a community-service organization with 23 different programs and a student staff of over 75. In recent years, CAVE has been converting many of its strictly community-service programs into service-learning opportunities with the help of key faculty who use service-learning as a teaching pedagogy. None of the courses are officially designated as service-learning classes. Faculty members choose individually to use service-learning as a teaching pedagogy. Service-learning is a part of the university's strategic plan, but no formal structure is in place to recognize it.

*SL Required for Graduation (all students)?* No

*Service Required for Graduation (all students)?* No

*Any Co-curricular Service?* Yes

*Any SL Residence Halls or Theme Houses?* No

*Number of Instructors Teaching SL Courses Per Year:* 12–15

**California State University, Fresno**

5150 N Maple Ave, M/S JA 120, Fresno, CA 93740–8026

*University/College URL:* http://www. csufresno.edu

*Type of Institution:* public, university, teaching, secular

*SL Program/Center Name:* Students for Community Service

*Contact Person Name and Title:* Chris Fiorentino, Instruct/Coord

*Contact Phone Number:* (559) 278–7079

*Contact Fax Number:* (559) 278–6483

*Contact Email Address:* chrisf@csufresno.edu

*SL Program/Center URL:* http://www. csufresno.edu/scs

*SL Online Course Description URL:* http:// www.csufresno.edu/scs

*SL Online Syllabi URL:* http://www. csufresno.edu/scs

*Description:* Students for Community Service is dedicated to promoting the value and importance of community service and service-learning to students, faculty, and staff. SCS is responsible for all activities related to the university's role in establishing service-oriented partnerships between the university, other educational institutions, and the served community. SCS seeks to provide students with quality volunteer experiences that cultivate a lifelong service-ethic which will stimulate and enhance the educational experience at all levels.

*SL Required for Graduation (all students)?* No

*Service Required for Graduation (all students)?* No

*Any Co-curricular Service?* Yes

*Any SL Residence Halls or Theme Houses?* No

*Number of Undergraduate SL Courses Offered Per Year:* 50

*Total Number of SL Courses Offered Per Year:* 50+

*Number of Instructors Teaching SL Courses Per Year:* 48

*Number of Full-time SL Staff on Campus (not counting instructors):* 1

*Number of Part-time SL Staff on Campus (not counting instructors):* 1

## California State University, Fullerton

800 N State College Blvd, TSU 245, PO Box 6830, Fullerton, CA 92887–6830

*University/College URL:* http://www. fullerton.edu

*Type of Institution:* public, university, teaching, secular

*SL Program/Center Name:* Community-based Learning and Service Center

*Contact Person Name and Title:* Jeannie Kim-Han, Coord, Community-based Learning Programs

*Contact Phone Number:* (714) 278–3211

*Contact Fax Number:* (714) 278–5109

*Contact Email Address:* jkim-han@fullerton.edu

*Description:* The Community-based Learning And Service Center assists faculty in developing service-learning courses, identifies appropriate site placements for students to complete service-learning requirements, houses 10 student-run service projects and is responsible for special service events for all campus members to participate in. The center is currently working on an undergraduate certificate program in nonprofit management in concert with American Humanics.

*SL Required for Graduation (all students)?* No

*Service Required for Graduation (all students)?* No

*Any Co-curricular Service?* Yes

*Any SL Residence Halls or Theme Houses?* No

*Number of Undergraduate SL Courses Offered Per Year:* 10–15

*Number of Graduate SL Courses Offered Per Year:* 3–5

*Total Number of SL Courses Offered Per Year:* 13–20

*Number of Instructors Teaching SL Courses Per Year:* 10–15

*Number of Full-time SL Staff on Campus (not counting instructors):* 1

*Number of Part-time SL Staff on Campus (not counting instructors):* 0

## California State University, Long Beach

Community Service Learning Center, 5th Floor Library, 1250 Bellflower Blvd, Long Beach, CA 90840

*University/College URL:* http://www. csulb.edu

*Type of Institution:* public, university, teaching, research, secular

*SL Program/Center Name:* Community Service Learning Center

*Contact Person Name and Title:* Patricia D. Rozee, Dir

*Contact Phone Number:* (562) 985–7131

*Contact Fax Number:* (562) 985–5721

*Contact Email Address:* prozee@csulb.edu

*SL Program/Center URL:* http://www.csulb. edu/centers/cslc

*SL Online Course Description URL:* http:// www.csulb.edu/centers/cslc

*Description:* The Community Service Learning Center serves a student body of 28,000.

There are currently 106 service-learning courses in more than 15 disciplines. As part of this effort, students are placed in nonprofit community-based or governmental agencies.

*SL Required for Graduation (all students)?* No

*Service Required for Graduation (all students)?* No

*Any Co-curricular Service?* Yes

*Any SL Residence Halls or Theme Houses?* No

*Total Number of SL Courses Offered Per Year:* 106

*Number of Full-time SL Staff on Campus (not counting instructors):* 0

*Number of Part-time SL Staff on Campus (not counting instructors):* 4

### California State University, Los Angeles

5151 State University Dr, Los Angeles, CA 90032

*University/College URL:* _ http://www.calstatela.edu

*Type of Institution:* public, university, teaching, research

*SL Program/Center Name:* University Service Learning

*Contact Person Name and Title:* Ed Forde, Prof, Coord, Service Learning

*Contact Phone Number:* (323) 343 4036

*Contact Fax Number:* (323) 343 4045

*Contact Email Address:* eforde@calstatela.edu

*SL Program/Center URL:* http://www.calstatela.edu/centers/cetl/service_learning.html

*Description:* Building on a 30-year history of student community service, the university currently offers service-learning courses in several departments and academic majors. These include psychology, history, political science, art, business, and education. The campus has specified the increased development of service-learning as one of its Strategic Plan Initiatives and priorities. Community service-learning is being integrated into the curriculum at many levels, to achieve the goal of offering every student the opportunity to enroll in a least one service-learning course during his or her undergraduate education.

*SL Required for Graduation (all students)?* No

*Service Required for Graduation (all students)?* No

*Any Co-curricular Service?* No

*Any SL Residence Halls or Theme Houses?* No

*Number of Undergraduate SL Courses Offered Per Year:* 12

*Number of Graduate SL Courses Offered Per Year:* 0

*Total Number of SL Courses Offered Per Year:* 12

*Number of Instructors Teaching SL Courses Per Year:* 12

*Number of Full-time SL Staff on Campus (not counting instructors):* 0

*Number of Part-time SL Staff on Campus (not counting instructors):* 0

### California State University at Monterey Bay

Service Learning Institute, 100 Campus Center, Bldg 8, Seaside, CA 93955

*University/College URL:* http://www.monterey.edu

*Type of Institution:* public, university, teaching, secular

*SL Program/Center Name:* The Service Learning Institute

*Contact Person Name and Title:* Stewart Jenkins, Information Specialist

*Contact Phone Number:* (831) 582–3644

*Contact Fax Number:* (831) 582–3568

*Contact Email Address:* service_learning_institute@monterey.edu

*SL Program/Center URL:* http://service.monterey.edu

*SL Online Course Description URL:* http://service.monterey.edu

*SL Online Syllabi URL:* http://service.monterey.edu

*Description:* The Service Learning Institute serves as an instructional unit and a resource center for faculty members, students, and community representatives interested in service-learning. One may research organizations on the institute's database, participate in student leadership activities, or gain training in teaching a course with a service-learning component. The institute teaches one course, "Introduction to Service in Multicultural Communities," which all undergraduates are required to take if they transfer in with less than 56 units of credit. All undergraduates, regardless of how many units they have earned when they transfer, are required to take a course within their major that has a service-learning component. The Service Learning Institute supports faculty and departments develop new courses that meet institute criteria for a service-learning course.

University Service Advocates (USAs): Students who participate in the Summer of Service Leadership Academy (SOSLA) learn how to be advocates for community partners and offer assistance to professors who would like to deepen the service-learning component of their courses. After participating in SOSLA students apply to become a University Service Advocate.

*Number of Undergraduate SL Courses Offered Per Year:* 79

*SL Required for Graduation (all students)?* Yes

*Service Required for Graduation (all students)?* Yes

*Any SL Residence Halls or Theme Houses?* No

*Number of Graduate SL Courses Offered Per Year:* 0

*Total Number of SL Courses Offered Per Year:* 79

*Number of Instructors Teaching SL Courses Per Year:* 70

*Number of Full-time SL Staff on Campus (not counting instructors):* 6

*Number of Part-time SL Staff on Campus (not counting instructors):* 12

## California State University, Northridge
8111 Nordhoff St, Northridge, CA 91330–8370

*University/College URL:* http://www.csun.edu

*Type of Institution:* public, university, teaching, secular

*SL Program/Center Name:* Center for Community Service-Learning

*Contact Person Name and Title:* Maureen Rubin, Dir, Prof, Journalism

*Contact Phone Number:* (818) 677–7395

*Contact Fax Number:* (818) 677–5935

*Contact Email Address:* maureen.rubin@csun.edu

*SL Program/Center URL:* http://www.csun.edu/~ocls99

*SL Online Course Description URL:* http://www.csun.edu/~ocls99/depts.html

*Description:* Established in 1998, the Center for Community Service-Learning at California State University, Northridge was created to inspire, encourage, and support students and faculty in their pursuit of academic excellence though involvement in community service. Through the identification of, and partnership with, educational institutions and both public and private nonprofit organizations, the center serves as the liaison for the revitalization of citizenship by improving students' sense of commitment, connection, and responsibility to community needs. The center works to facilitate cooperation between faculty and community partners, focused on improving student learning while addressing Los Angeles County needs. It helps to coordinate service-learning courses on campus, provide outreach services for community partners, and design curricula to better facilitate community collaboration with the university. The center is funded through a combination of the Undergraduate Studies budget and public/private grants.

*SL Required for Graduation (all students)?* No

*Service Required for Graduation (all students)?* No

*Any Co-curricular Service?* Yes

*Any SL Residence Halls or Theme Houses?* No

*Number of Undergraduate SL Courses Offered Per Year:* 80+ (During any given semester, there are over 60 service-learning classes in 28 departments; approximately 30% are at the graduate level.)

*Number of Graduate SL Courses Offered Per Year:* 40+

*Total Number of SL Courses Offered Per Year:* 120+

*Number of Instructors Teaching SL Courses
   Per Year:* 200
*Number of Full-time SL Staff on Campus
   (not counting instructors):* 2+ (The direc-
   tor has 8/10 release time from the
   Journalism Department; plus a full-time
   Admin Analyst/Assist Dir; and for Spring
   2000, one tenured faculty member was
   given 3 units of release time to act as
   Assistant Director.)
*Number of Part-time SL Staff on Campus
   (not counting instructors):* 2

**California State University, Sacramento**
6000 J St, Office of Community Collabora-
   tion, Sacramento, CA 95819
*University/College URL:* http://www.csus.
   edu
*Type of Institution:* public, university, teach-
   ing, secular
*SL Program/Center Name:* Office of Community Collaboration
*Contact Person Name and Title:* Charlotte
   Cook, Coord
*Contact Phone Number:* (916) 278–4610
*Contact Fax Number:* (916) 278–4836
*Contact Email Address:* occ@csus.edu
*SL Program/Center URL:* http://www.occ.
   csus.edu
*SL Online Course Description URL:* http://
   www.occ.csus.edu
*Description:* The Office of Community Collaboration (OCC) serves as a community-university contact point, and is charged with pro-
moting community-based learning of all types
as well as faculty scholarship with a regional
focus. Activities include linkage, workshops
on service-learning, assistance with community placements and integration of community-
based learning with academic learning.
*SL Required for Graduation (all
   students)?* No
*Service Required for Graduation (all stu-
   dents)?* No
*Any Co-curricular Service?* Yes
*Any SL Residence Halls or Theme
   Houses?* No
*Number of Undergraduate SL Courses
   Offered Per Year:* 24

*Number of Graduate SL Courses Offered
   Per Year:* 5
*Total Number of SL Courses Offered Per
   Year:* 29
*Number of Instructors Teaching SL Courses
   Per Year:* 25
*Number of Full-time SL Staff on Campus
   (not counting instructors):* 1 (The coordi-
   nator is a faculty member assigned to
   OCC 3/4-time.)
*Number of Part-time SL Staff on Campus
   (not counting instructors):* 6 (A half-time
   community liaison, a half-time secretary,
   and 4 student assistants)

**California State University, San Marcos**
333 Twin Oaks Rd, San Marcos, CA 92082
*University/College URL:* http://www.
   csusm.edu
*Type of Institution:* public, university, teach-
   ing, secular
*SL Program/Center Name:* Office of Com-
   munity Service-Learning
*Contact Person Name and Title:* Dr. Lynda
   Gaynor, Dir
*Contact Phone Number:* (760) 750–4055
*Contact Fax Number:* (760) 750–3550
*Contact Email Address:*
   lgaynor@mailhost1.csusm.edu
*SL Program/Center URL:* http://ww2.csusm.
   edu/ocsl/
*Description:* The Office of Community Service-Learning (OCSL) is part of the Division of
Academic Affairs. It facilitates the development of academic courses that include service
in the meeting of course learning objectives.
Currently there are 70 courses, involving 1000
students, that include some service-learning.
The OCSL maintains a database of over 250
community opportunities for these courses and
maintains relationships with Community Partners who are represented by a regularly meeting Community Partners Advisory Board. The
OCSL also receives advice and assistance from
a Service Learning Committee with representa-
tion of faculty from all colleges, Student Affairs,
and students. Each year the OCSL creates various events to further service-learning and community service in general, for example: workshops for faculty development, an on campus

fair for Community Partners to showcase the projects they have available for volunteers, and a "Celebration of Service" event for awarding recognition for outstanding community service to not only university students but to students of all ages, within the local community.

*SL Required for Graduation (all students)?* No

*Service Required for Graduation (all students)?* No

*Any Co-curricular Service?* Yes

*Any SL Residence Halls or Theme Houses?* No

*Number of Undergraduate SL Courses Offered Per Year:* 49

*Number of Graduate SL Courses Offered Per Year:* 21

*Total Number of SL Courses Offered Per Year:* 70

*Number of Full-time SL Staff on Campus (not counting instructors):* 1

*Number of Part-time SL Staff on Campus (not counting instructors):* 1

## Calvin College

3201 Burton SE, Grand Rapids, MI 49503

*University/College URL:* _ http://www.calvin.edu

*Type of Institution:* private, college, teaching, religious

*SL Program/Center Name:* Service-Learning Center

*Contact Person Name and Title:* Rhonda Berg, Dir

*Contact Phone Number:* (616) 957–6455

*Contact Fax Number:* (616) 957–6644

*Contact Email Address:* Berg@Calvin.edu

*SL Program/Center URL:* _ http://www.calvin.edu/admin/slc/

*SL Online Course Description URL:* http://www.calvin.edu/admin/slc/99acad.htm

*Description:* The Service-Learning Center is the locus for Calvin College's involvement in the community. Approximately 1200–1500 students are involved in "Academically-Based Service-Learning" (through their courses) and about 300 are engaged in various kinds of co-curricular service. In addition, all first-year students (approximately 1000) participate in "StreetFest," an orientation to the service mission of the college which involves doing service projects at 60 community sites within a two-day period during the Fall semester. The center has a director, a 5/7-time associate director, a 2/3-time office coordinator and twelve 1/4-time student coordinators. Within the Service-Learning Center a team of six students works with the director on co-curricular service. Much of their emphasis is on coordinating the efforts of student leaders for a variety of partnerships and projects, including involvement in the Federal Service-Learning Work-Study program and America Reads. The associate director heads a team of six students to coordinate the Academically-Based Service-Learning efforts. The Service-Learning Center directors work in close partnership with the Academic Division through the Dean for Instruction. Four faculty members receive a modest stipend to promote and support the development of Academically-Based Service-Learning. The center is primarily funded through the general operating budget of the college.

*SL Required for Graduation (all students)?* No

*Service Required for Graduation (all students)?* No

*Any Co-curricular Service?* Yes

*Any SL Residence Halls or Theme Houses?* Yes

*Number of Undergraduate SL Courses Offered Per Year:* 80

*Total Number of SL Courses Offered Per Year:* 80

*Number of Instructors Teaching SL Courses Per Year:* 40

*Number of Full-time SL Staff on Campus (not counting instructors):* 1

*Number of Part-time SL Staff on Campus (not counting instructors):* 14 (one 5/7-time assoc dir, one 2/3-time office coord; twelve 1/4-time student coords)

## Case Western Reserve University

10900 Euclid Ave, Cleveland, OH 44106

*University/College URL:* http://www.cwru.edu

*Type of Institution:* private, university, research

*SL Program/Center Name:* Office of Student Community Service
*Contact Person Name and Title:* Glenn Odenbrett, Dir
*Contact Phone Number:* (216) 368–6960
*Contact Fax Number:* (216) 368–0839
*Contact Email Address:* gxo2@po.cwru.edu
*SL Program/Center URL:* http://ess.cwru.edu/oscs
*SL Online Course Description URL:* http://ess.cwru.edu/oscs/sl
*Description:* The Office of Student Community Service (OSCS) provides both curricular and co-curricular service-learning opportunities to students in the areas of literacy, the environment, public health, and bridging the digital divide. For example, through OSCS-sponsored literacy and mentoring programs, students in psychology and sociology classes can complete a practicum in adolescent development, and students majoring in English can complete a practicum in the teaching of developmental reading and writing. The office also serves as the manager of long-term community partnerships from which service-learning projects in other disciplines are generated. For example, the office solicits engineering design problems from the community which are then evaluated and referred to the School of Engineering for ''adoption'' either at the freshman (in the context of a newly-introduced community-service-based freshman design course) or senior level (as a senior design project). Projects have included a custom-designed indoor greenhouse for an inner-city recreation center, puppets for children with severe physical handicaps, a ventilator platform for a juvenile wheelchair, interactive Web sites for local nonprofit organizations, and a flood gauge for a watershed stewardship project at a local nature center.
*SL Required for Graduation (all students)?* No
*Service Required for Graduation (all students)?* No
*Any Co-curricular Service?* Yes
*Any SL Residence Halls or Theme Houses?* No
*Number of Undergraduate SL Courses Offered Per Year:* 7

*Number of Graduate SL Courses Offered Per Year:* 0 (However, a service-learning-based graduate curriculum in nursing is being developed.)
*Total Number of SL Courses Offered Per Year:* 7
*Number of Instructors Teaching SL Courses Per Year:* 7
*Number of Full-time SL Staff on Campus (not counting instructors):* 4
*Number of Part-time SL Staff on Campus (not counting instructors):* 0

## Centenary College of Louisiana
2911 Centenary Blvd, PO Box 41188, Shreveport, LA 71134–1188
*University/College URL:* http://www.centenary.edu
*Type of Institution:* private, college, teaching
*SL Program/Center Name:* Service-Learning Program
*Contact Person Name and Title:* Dian Tooke, Dir
*Contact Phone Number:* (318) 869–5542
*Contact Fax Number:* (318) 859–5199
*Contact Email Address:* dtooke@centenary.edu
*SL Program/Center URL:* http://personal.centenary.edu/~dtooke/plan.html
*SL Online Course Description URL:* http://personal.centenary.edu/~dtooke/agencylist.html
*Description:* All students must successfully complete a 30-hour minimum service-learning project in an approved agency, which should be completed the semester before the student intends to graduate. The college's Service-Learning Program, Church Careers, and academic departments with service-learning projects, courses and/or modules offer opportunities to fill this graduation requirement. There is a list of projects approved for service-learning credit available through the Service-Learning Office. Independent projects are considered on a pre-approved basis.
*SL Required for Graduation (all students)?* Yes
*Service Required for Graduation (all students)?* No
*Any Co-curricular Service?* Yes

*Any SL Residence Halls or Theme Houses?*
No (However, one of the female residence halls is oriented toward community service.)

*Number of Undergraduate SL Courses Offered Per Year:* 1–2 (usually 3-week modules)

*Number of Graduate SL Courses Offered Per Year:* 0

*Total Number of SL Courses Offered Per Year:* 1–2

*Number of Instructors Teaching SL Courses Per Year:* 1–2

*Number of Full-time SL Staff on Campus (not counting instructors):* 1

*Number of Part-time SL Staff on Campus (not counting instructors):* 1–2 work study students

**Chaminade University of Honolulu**
3140 Waialae Ave, Honolulu, HI 96816–1578

*University/College URL:* http://www.chaminade.edu

*Type of Institution:* private, university, teaching, religious

*SL Program/Center Name:* Community Service Program

*Contact Person Name and Title:* Thomas Spring, SM, Coord

*Contact Phone Number:* (808) 735–4895

*Contact Fax Number:* (808) 735–7748

*Contact Email Address:* tspring@chaminade.edu

*SL Program/Center URL:* http://www.chaminade.edu/academic.php3?articleno=211

*SL Online Course Description URL:* http://www.chaminade.edu/academic.php3?articleno=211

*Description:* Currently, Chaminade's service-learning program is part of the Community Service Program, which operates out of Campus Ministry. About 10 professors offer service-learning courses in a wide variety of disciplines. All of these are coordinated by the Coordinator of the Community Service Program, which is a half-time position.

*SL Required for Graduation (all students)?* No

*Service Required for Graduation (all students)?* No

*Any Co-curricular Service?* Yes

*Any SL Residence Halls or Theme Houses?* No

*Number of Undergraduate SL Courses Offered Per Year:* 20

*Number of Graduate SL Courses Offered Per Year:* 0

*Total Number of SL Courses Offered Per Year:* 20

*Number of Instructors Teaching SL Courses Per Year:* 11

*Number of Full-time SL Staff on Campus (not counting instructors):* 0

*Number of Part-time SL Staff on Campus (not counting instructors):* 1

**Chandler-Gilbert Community College**
2626 E Pecos Rd, Chandler, AZ 85225

*University/College URL:* http://www.cgc.maricopa.edu

*Type of Institution:* public, community college, teaching

*SL Program/Center Name:* Service Learning Program

*Contact Person Name and Title:* Duane Oakes, Dir, Office of Student Life

*Contact Phone Number:* (480) 732–7146

*Contact Fax Number:* (408) 732–7090

*Contact Email Address:* oakes@cgc.maricopa.edu

*SL Program/Center URL:* http://www.cgc.maricopa.edu/pecos/community/service_learning/

*SL Online Course Description URL:* http://www.cgc.maricopa.edu/pecos/community/service_learning/

*Description:* At Chandler-Gilbert Community College, service-learning combines community service with academic instruction, focusing on critical thinking and problem solving, values clarification, social and personal development, and civic and community responsibility.

*SL Required for Graduation (all students)?* No

*Service Required for Graduation (all students)?* No

*Any Co-curricular Service?* Yes

*Any SL Residence Halls or Theme
    Houses?* No
*Number of Undergraduate SL Courses
    Offered Per Year:* 50+ course sections
*Total Number of SL Courses Offered Per
    Year:* 50+ course sections
*Number of Instructors Teaching SL Courses
    Per Year:* 25
*Number of Full-time SL Staff on Campus
    (not counting instructors):* 1
*Number of Part-time SL Staff on Campus
    (not counting instructors):* 0

## Chapman University

One University Dr, Orange, CA 92866
*University/College URL:* http://www.
    chapman.edu
*Type of Institution:* private, university,
    teaching
*SL Program/Center Name:* GIVE (Getting
    Involved in Volunteer Efforts)
*Contact Person Name and Title:* Chris
    Hutchison, Assist Dir, Student Activities
    and Organizations
*Contact Phone Number:* (714) 628–7227
*Contact Fax Number:* (714) 997–6852
*Contact Email Address:*
    hutchiso@chapman.edu
*SL Program/Center URL:* http://www.
    chapman.edu/studlife/sao/saogive.html
*Description:* GIVE is Chapman University's
volunteer program. It is a part of the Office of
Student Activities and Organizations. It sponsors a variety of volunteer events that are open
to students, faculty, and staff. The mission of
GIVE is to promote and raise awareness of
community service and volunteerism by planning and implementing campus-wide community-service programs and events; building connections with the local community; serving as a
liaison and referral source between volunteer
agencies and the Chapman community; and
creating an environment which supports service-learning.

Freshman Seminar Program: The Freshman
Seminar is a required course for all incoming
freshman students. Its title is "The Global
Citizen" and is designed to educate students on
global issues and to uphold Chapman's mission
statement which includes developing global

citizens. It is a single-syllabus course taught by
27 faculty. All sections do a service activity
that lasts a half-day to a full day. Examples of
the service activities include helping with construction work on an orphanage in Tijuana,
Mexico, tutoring at a community center, feed-
ing the homeless, and participating in beach
clean-ups. Faculty integrate the service activity
into the course so that it is not merely a stand-
alone service activity.
*SL Required for Graduation (all
    students)?* No
*Service Required for Graduation (all stu-
    dents)?* No
*Any Co-curricular Service?* Yes
*Any SL Residence Halls or Theme
    Houses?* No
*Number of Undergraduate SL Courses
    Offered Per Year:* 1 (Freshman Seminar)
*Total Number of SL Courses Offered
    Per Year:* 1

## Chatham College

Woodland Rd, Pittsburgh, PA 15232
*University/College URL:* http://www.
    chatham.edu
*Type of Institution:* private, college, teach-
    ing, secular
*SL Program/Center Name:* Office of Serv-
    ice-Learning
*Contact Person Name and Title:* Gretchen
    Fairley, Coord, Service-Learning
*Contact Phone Number:* (412) 365–1280
*Contact Fax Number:* (412) 365–1142
*Contact Email Address:*
    fairley@chatham.edu
*Description:* The Office of Service-Learning
coordinates most of the service programs on
campus including "A Day of Service" during
new-student orientation, a two-week service-
learning program for the First Year Writing
Seminar, off-campus community service work-
study positions, community partnerships, and
co-curricular service projects.

First Year Writing Seminar: All first-year
students are required to take the First Year
Writing Seminar which includes an 8–10 hour
service-learning component during the month
of October. The project focus is on women's
health and the environment in conjunction with

the text, Refuge, by Terry Tempest Williams. In 1999, 145 students participated in 81 service-learning events around the city of Pittsburgh.

Graduate Health Sciences programs: Chatham College has a number of new co-ed graduate programs in the health sciences that all have large service-learning components. The Physical Therapy program has a one-credit, 2–1/2 week service-learning project during the last clinical experience. In 1998, physical therapy students contributed over 4,000 hours of service. The Physician's Assistants program takes a problem-based learning approach to service, where students work in small groups to address community health needs. Students in the Occupational Therapy program spend a semester working in community-service agencies while gaining professional experience.

*SL Required for Graduation (all students)?* Yes
*Service Required for Graduation (all students)?* No
*Any Co-curricular Service?* Yes
*Any SL Residence Halls or Theme Houses?* No
*Number of Undergraduate SL Courses Offered Per Year:* 18
*Number of Graduate SL Courses Offered Per Year:* 4
*Total Number of SL Courses Offered Per Year:* 22
*Number of Instructors Teaching SL Courses Per Year:* 22
*Number of Full-time SL Staff on Campus (not counting instructors):* 0
*Number of Part-time SL Staff on Campus (not counting instructors):* 1

## Chattanooga State Technical Community College

4501 Amnicola Hwy, Chattanooga, TN 37343
*University/College URL:* http://www.cstcc.cc.tn.us
*Type of Institution:* public, community college, teaching, secular
*SL Program/Center Name:* Chattanooga State Learn and Serve
*Contact Person Name and Title:* Kathy Williamson, Learn and Serve Coord
*Contact Phone Number:* (423) 697–2507
*Contact Email Address:* kwilliamson@cstcc.cc.tn.us
*Description:* The Learn and Serve office recruits faculty members to become involved in service-learning initiatives, acts as a liaison between students and potential placement sites, and coordinates one-time service activities for students campus-wide. The office is run by a part-time coordinator, a position funded by a grant from the East Tennessee Consortium on Service-Learning.
*SL Required for Graduation (all students)?* No
*Service Required for Graduation (all students)?* No
*Any Co-curricular Service?* No
*Any SL Residence Halls or Theme Houses?* No
*SL Degrees Offered:* Institutional Certificate of Advancement in Service-Learning: 18-hour program of study which includes 12 hours of core humanities classes with service-learning emphasis and two 3-hour pure service-learning courses.
*Number of Undergraduate SL Courses Offered Per Year:* 10
*Total Number of SL Courses Offered Per Year:* 10
*Number of Instructors Teaching SL Courses Per Year:* 10
*Number of Full-time SL Staff on Campus (not counting instructors):* 0
*Number of Part-time SL Staff on Campus (not counting instructors):* 1

## City College of San Francisco

50 Phelan Ave, B403, San Francisco, CA 94112
*University/College URL:* http://www.ccsf.cc.ca.us
*Type of Institution:* community college, teaching
*SL Program/Center Name:* Service Learning in the OMI Community
*Contact Person Name and Title:* Service Learning Coordinator
*Contact Phone Number:* (415) 239–3281
*Contact Fax Number:* (415) 239–3514
*Contact Email Address:* lleung@ccsf.cc.ca.us

*Description:* As part of its strategy to develop service-learning at City College of San Francisco, the Service Learning in the Oceanview-Merced Heights-Ingleside community program makes efforts to expand the number of instructors who modify their curricula to meet needs in the neighboring community. Under this project, students enrolled in psychology and sociology are placed in organizations serving senior citizens and youth in after-school activities; students enrolled in architecture provide design options to improve public access and usage of public land. It is funded through the Western Region California Campus Office.

*SL Required for Graduation (all students)?* No

*Service Required for Graduation (all students)?* No

*Any Co-curricular Service?* No

*Any SL Residence Halls or Theme Houses?* No

*Number of Undergraduate SL Courses Offered Per Year:* 32 (16 per semester)

*Total Number of SL Courses Offered Per Year:* 32 (16 per semester)

*Number of Instructors Teaching SL Courses Per Year:* 10

*Number of Full-time SL Staff on Campus (not counting instructors):* 1 (1/3-time to service-learning)

*Number of Part-time SL Staff on Campus (not counting instructors):* 0

## Clarion University

840 Wood St, 247 Gemmell Student Center, Clarion, PA 16214–1232

*University/College URL:* http://www.clarion.edu

*Type of Institution:* public, university, teaching

*SL Program/Center Name:* Community Service-Learning Office

*Contact Person Name and Title:* Diana Lynn Anderson, Dir

*Contact Phone Number:* 814) 393–1865

*Contact Fax Number:* (814) 393–2707

*Contact Email Address:* Anderson@clarion.edu

*SL Program/Center URL:* http://www.clarion.edu/student/studentaffairs/cslhome.htm

*Description:* The Community Service-Learning (CSL) Office serves as a clearinghouse to provide students, faculty, and staff with "one-stop shopping" for information regarding community service, service-learning, and volunteerism. It is responsible for the coordination of volunteer and service-learning programs and activities within the Student Affairs Division; promotion of service-related opportunities to the university community; and coordination of the off-campus service-learning federal work-study program. The goals of the office are: (1) to clarify service-learning and volunteer interests; (2) to identify community and human-service-agency needs; and (3) to facilitate the placement of university volunteers in appropriate community-service settings with respect to their personal interests, course requirements, or career-exploration needs.

Services include service counselors (staff and volunteers), who assist with the registration and placement of university volunteers and the promotion of CSL events and activities; the Service Opportunities Directory, a detailed listing of the programs and projects of agencies, civic groups, service organizations, businesses, and special programs that seek university volunteers; the Service Opportunities Newsletter (published monthly), which lists "short term" or "one time" volunteer opportunities; the Community Service-Learning Federal Work-Study Program, with on- and off-campus federal work-study positions which provide students with work-learning opportunities related to their educational or career goals; Outreach and Workshops (staff are available to speak to organizations and provide presentations ranging from five minutes to an extensive workshop on Leadership and Volunteerism); Volunteer Transcripts (records of student service activities to meet personal goals or to complement resumes); Volunteer Recognition Reception (students, university employees, and agencies are recognized for service at the end of each academic year; "Excellence in Service" awards are presented for "Outstanding Student Volunteer," "Outstanding Employee Volunteer," "Outstanding Service Project"); and the Resource Library, which includes an extensive collection of reference books, articles, and journals on service-learning, community service, and volunteerism. Additionally, staff compile notebooks of courses, internships, and field experiences which include service as a component. These materials are available to the university community for projects, classroom-related research or personal enrichment.

Special projects include the Adopt-A-School Partnership, which provides tutoring and mentoring opportunities with children at the Immaculate Conception Elementary School and the Clarion Area Jr/Sr High School; Alternative Service Breaks, e.g. the "Service in the City" spring-break trip provides an opportunity for students to experience a week of service in New York City, work in a soup kitchen, tutor elementary school students, observe an AIDS support group, and assist with an adult literacy program; and "The Plunge," held each semester, in which students and university employees commit to a day of service with local community groups or human-service agencies.

A Service Advisory Board serves in an advisory capacity to the CSL office. It promotes service-learning on campus among students, faculty, and staff. It also provides a forum for cooperation and collaboration among the various programs, departments, and individuals involved in service-learning and volunteerism.

*SL Required for Graduation (all students)?* No

*Service Required for Graduation (all students)?* No

*Any Co-curricular Service?* No

*Any SL Residence Halls or Theme Houses?* No

*Number of Undergraduate SL Courses Offered Per Year:* 33

*Number of Graduate SL Courses Offered Per Year:* 2

*Total Number of SL Courses Offered Per Year:* 35

*Number of Instructors Teaching SL Courses Per Year:* 33

*Number of Full-time SL Staff on Campus (not counting instructors):* 2

*Number of Part-time SL Staff on Campus (not counting instructors):* 7

**Clark College**

1800 McLoughlin Blvd, Student Program Office, Gaiser Hall, Room 153F, MS 37, Vancouver, WA 98663–3598

*University/College URL:* http://www.clark.edu

*Type of Institution:* public, college, community college, teaching

*SL Program/Center Name:* Student Programs–Service Learning Project

*Contact Person Name and Title:* Pete Anderson, Service Learning Project Coord

*Contact Fax Number:* (360) 992–2859

*Contact Email Address:* panderson@clark.edu

*SL Program/Center URL:* http://www.pacifier.com/~petea

*Description:* Placing students as volunteers with community-based not-for-profit organizations. Some students are entitled to an education award for a required amount of volunteer hours.

*SL Required for Graduation (all students)?* No

*Service Required for Graduation (all students)?* No

*Any Co-curricular Service?* No

*Any SL Residence Halls or Theme Houses?* No

**Clemson University**

Service Learning Collaborative, c/o National Dropout Prevention Center, 209 Martin St, Clemson, SC 29631–1555

*University/College URL:* _ http://www.clemson.edu

*Type of Institution:* public, university, teaching, research, secular

*SL Program/Center Name:* Service Learning Collaborative

*Contact Person Name and Title:* Marty Duckenfield, Coord

*Contact Phone Number:* (864) 656–2599

*Contact Fax Number:* (864) 656–0136

*Contact Email Address:* mbdck@clemson.edu

*SL Program/Center URL:* http://www.clemson.edu/learning

*SL Online Course Description URL:* http://www.clemson.edu/learning/syllabi.htm

*SL Online Syllabi URL:* http://www.clemson.
edu/learning/syllabi.htm

*Description:* The Service Learning Collaborative is an initiative originally funded through the Provost's office by an Innovation Fund grant to encourage Clemson University faculty to adopt service-learning as a teaching methodology; to facilitate training opportunities for these faculty; and to act as a catalyst for seeking service-learning funding for Clemson University. Members include faculty and student representatives from each of the five colleges.

*SL Required for Graduation (all
    students)?* No

*Service Required for Graduation (all students)?* No

*Any Co-curricular Service?* Yes

*Any SL Residence Halls or Theme
    Houses?* No

*Number of Undergraduate SL Courses
    Offered Per Year:* 65

*Number of Graduate SL Courses Offered
    Per Year:* 5

*Total Number of SL Courses Offered Per
    Year:* 70

*Number of Instructors Teaching SL Courses
    Per Year:* 50

*Number of Full-time SL Staff on Campus
    (not counting instructors):* 0

*Number of Part-time SL Staff on Campus
    (not counting instructors):* 0

## Colby College

4140 Mayflower Hill Dr, Waterville, ME
    04901–8841

*University/College URL:* http://www.
    colby.edu

*Type of Institution:* private, college, secular

*Contact Person Name and Title:*
    AmeriCorps VISTA Member

*Contact Phone Number:* (207) 872–3098

*Contact Fax Number:* (207) 872–3524

*Description:* While there is no institutionalized service-learning program or center at Colby, there is a small but growing number of faculty in various disciplines who are practicing a service-learning pedagogy on their own prerogative at multiple course levels. Service-learning courses, while not always recognized or publicized as such, are currently offered within the English, sociology, economics, psychology, education, and environmental science departments.

*SL Required for Graduation (all
    students)?* No

*Service Required for Graduation (all students)?* No

*Any Co-curricular Service?* No

*Any SL Residence Halls or Theme
    Houses?* No

*Number of Undergraduate SL Courses
    Offered Per Year:* 6–12

*Total Number of SL Courses Offered Per
    Year:* 6–12

*Number of Instructors Teaching SL Courses
    Per Year:* 6–12

*Number of Full-time SL Staff on Campus
    (not counting instructors):* 1
    (AmeriCorps VISTA)

*Number of Part-time SL Staff on Campus
    (not counting instructors):* 0

## College of Eastern Utah

451 East 400 North, Price, UT 84501

*University/College URL:* http://www.ceu.edu

*Type of Institution:* public, community college, teaching

*SL Program/Center Name:* SUN Center

*Contact Person Name and Title:* Kathy
    Murray, Dir, Career and Volunteer
    Services

*Contact Phone Number:* (435) 613–5284

*Contact Fax Number:* (435) 613–5814

*Contact Email Address:* kmurray@ceu.edu

*SL Program/Center URL:* http://www.ceu.
    edu/suncenter/volunteer/default.htm

*Description:* The SUN Center's mission is to enhance, promote, support, and teach the value of effective volunteerism. The center develops partnerships with existing community agencies and leaders to identify the needs of the community and create solutions to meet those needs. It serves as a catalyst to inspire volunteerism in the community. It advocates and facilitates the inclusion of service-learning programs within the college curriculum. It empowers the students, faculty, and staff to become a part of the solution to community problems.

*SL Required for Graduation (all
    students)?* No

*Service Required for Graduation (all students)?* No

*Any Co-curricular Service?* No

*Any SL Residence Halls or Theme Houses?* No

*Number of Undergraduate SL Courses Offered Per Year:* 3

*Number of Graduate SL Courses Offered Per Year:* 0

*Total Number of SL Courses Offered Per Year:* 3

*Number of Instructors Teaching SL Courses Per Year:* 2

*Number of Full-time SL Staff on Campus (not counting instructors):* 0

*Number of Part-time SL Staff on Campus (not counting instructors):* 1

## College of Saint Benedict/Saint Johns University

37 S College Ave/none, Saint Joseph/ Collegeville, MN 56374/56321

*University/College URL:* http://www. csbsju.edu

*Type of Institution:* private, university, college, religious

*SL Program/Center Name:* The Liemandt Family Service Learning Program

*Contact Person Name and Title:* Cindy Pederson, Service Learning Coord

*Contact Phone Number:* (320) 363–5117

*Contact Fax Number:* (320) 363–6096

*Contact Email Address:* cpederson@csbsju.edu

*SL Program/Center URL:* http://www.csbsju. edu/servicelearning

*Description:* The Liemandt Family Service Learning Program fosters the integration of learning through service by assisting in the development of curricular and co-curricular programs that explicitly integrate the Benedictine character of service to others with the institutional commitment to a liberal arts education that fosters students' life-long respect for learning and for socially responsible leadership in the broader community. The program resulted from two years of research (conducted by a committee created by the president of Saint Johns University). A three-year start-up grant from a university regent covered the full-time SL Coordinator's salary. The program now has a part-time secretary (covered through an additional grant by the same regent), a full-time VISTA, and eight work-study students. In 1999–2000, there were approximately 30 courses (there were eight in 1997–1998) with a service-learning component. In addition, staff administer an America Reads program and a Community Service Work Study Program that follows a service learning model. In 1999–2000, the Liemandt Family Service Learning Program will impact between 750 and 1000 students. Program staff report to the Provost for Academic Affairs. Program funding and the SL Coordinator's salary are now institutionalized.

*SL Required for Graduation (all students)?* No

*Service Required for Graduation (all students)?* No

*Any Co-curricular Service?* Yes

*Any SL Residence Halls or Theme Houses?* Yes (The Global Initiative Group)

*SL Undergraduate Program Name:* The Liemandt Family Service Learning Program

*Number of Undergraduate SL Courses Offered Per Year:* 30

*Number of Graduate SL Courses Offered Per Year:* 0

*Total Number of SL Courses Offered Per Year:* 30

*Number of Instructors Teaching SL Courses Per Year:* 10

*Number of Full-time SL Staff on Campus (not counting instructors):* 1

*Number of Part-time SL Staff on Campus (not counting instructors):* 10 (a part-time secretary—covered through an additional grant by the same regent, a full-time VISTA, and eight work-study students)

## College of the Atlantic

105 Eden St, Bar Harbor, ME 04609

*University/College URL:* http://www.coa.edu

*Type of Institution:* private, college, teaching, research, secular

*SL Program/Center Name:* Internship Program Office

*Contact Person Name and Title:* Jill Barlow-

Kelley, Dir, Internships, Career and
Alumni Services
*Contact Phone Number:* (207) 288–
5015, ext 236
*Contact Fax Number:* (207) 288–4126
*Contact Email Address:*
JBK@ecology.coa.edu
*SL Program/Center URL:* http://www.coa.
edu/INTERNSHIPS/
*Description:* The Internship Program Office
assists all students in completing a required,
10-week, 40-hour internship prior to graduation. The internship is a component of a student's academic program and allows for skills
and knowledge gained through coursework to
be applied to the work world. Students are
responsible for designing their own internship
experience with support and information from
the Internship Director. There is no curriculum
or formalized coursework for either the internship or community-service component. The
Internship Program Office houses numerous
publications, Web sites, and contacts including
an extensive alumni pool available to help with
connections and networking. Students choose
whether to do a non-credit or credit internship.
Credit-bearing internships require full tuition
plus fees. Internships may be completed during
any of the three academic terms or summers.
*SL Required for Graduation (all students)?*
Yes (Internships)
*Service Required for Graduation (all stu-
dents)?* Yes
*Any Co-curricular Service?* Yes (may be
linked with community-service
requirement)
*Any SL Residence Halls or Theme
Houses?* No
*Number of Full-time SL Staff on Campus
(not counting instructors):* 1
*Number of Part-time SL Staff on Campus
(not counting instructors):* 0

## College of William and Mary
Campus Center Room 207, PO Box 8795,
Williamsburg, VA 23187
*University/College URL:* http://www.wm.edu
*Type of Institution:* public, university,
teaching

*SL Program/Center Name:* Office of Student
Volunteer Services
*Contact Person Name and Title:* Drew
Stelljes, Coord
*Contact Phone Number:* (757) 221–3263
*Contact Fax Number:* (757) 221–3451
*Contact Email Address:* adstel@wm.edu;
volsvs@wm.edu
*SL Program/Center URL:* http://www.wm.
edu/OSA/activ/service
*Description:* The mission of the Office of Student Volunteer Services (OSVS) is to promote
a culture of service at the college, increase
participation in public and community service,
and develop service involvement as an educational experience. This builds upon the college's tradition of public and community service. Students, faculty, and administrators see
the value of finding ways to integrate academic
pursuits with the social issues that impact society. A report from the president's task force on
service states, ''The College considers public
service to be a vehicle for accomplishing its
educational aims and for improving its overall
effectiveness as well as a means through which
individuals may develop personally and professionally.'' The goal of the college and OSVS
is to ensure that students are provided with
opportunities to make a difference in the lives
of others while learning, growing, and developing a greater sense of responsibility to their
community.
*SL Required for Graduation (all
students)?* No
*Service Required for Graduation (all stu-
dents)?* No
*Any Co-curricular Service?* Yes
*Any SL Residence Halls or Theme
Houses?* No
*Number of Undergraduate SL Courses
Offered Per Year:* 11
*Total Number of SL Courses Offered Per
Year:* 11
*Number of Instructors Teaching SL Courses
Per Year:* 11
*Number of Full-time SL Staff on Campus
(not counting instructors):* 1
*Number of Part-time SL Staff on Campus
(not counting instructors):* 41 (3 graduate

assistants, 1 graduate intern, 2 student employees, 35 student volunteers)

**Collin County Community College**
2200 W University, McKinney, TX 75070
*University/College URL:* http://www. ccccd.edu
*Type of Institution:* public, community college, teaching, secular
*SL Program/Center Name:* Service Learning Program
*Contact Person Name and Title:* Regina M. Hughes, Coord, Service Learning
*Contact Phone Number:* (972) 548–6739
*Contact Fax Number:* (972) 548–6801
*Contact Email Address:* rhughes@ccccd.edu
*SL Program/Center URL:* http://www.ccccd. edu/divisions/ssps/service/servlrn.htm
*Description:* The Service Learning Program began in1995. As of September 1999, it is operating with a full-time coordinator of Service Learning and three faculty liaisons. Collin County Community College is a multi-campus institution serving approximately 31,000 credit and non-credit students. The primary goal of the Service Learning Program is to offer all students the best learning opportunities available while providing needed services to the community. Currently, the program works with approximately 200 agencies in Collin County. It is beginning to explore international service-learning, alternative spring breaks, and ways to incorporate service-learning in learning-community courses. As a result of commitment on the part of faculty and the administration, participation rates of students and faculty continue to increase each semester.
*Any Co-curricular Service?* No
*Any SL Residence Halls or Theme Houses?* No
*Number of Undergraduate SL Courses Offered Per Year:* 110 (55 per semester); 280 sections (140 per semester)
*Total Number of SL Courses Offered Per Year:* 110; 280 sections
*Number of Instructors Teaching SL Courses Per Year:* 70 (35 per semester)
*Number of Full-time SL Staff on Campus (not counting instructors):* 1 (Coord of Service Learning)

*Number of Part-time SL Staff on Campus (not counting instructors):* 3 (Faculty Coords/Liaisons)

**Colorado College**
24 E Cache La Poudre, Colorado Springs, CO 80903
*University/College URL:* http://www. coloradocollege.edu
*Type of Institution:* private, college, teaching, secular
*SL Program/Center Name:* The Center for Community Service
*Contact Person Name and Title:* Gay Victoria, Dir
*Contact Phone Number:* (719) 389–6846
*Contact Fax Number:* (719) 389–6137
*Contact Email Address:* gvictoria@coloradocollege.edu
*SL Program/Center URL:* _ http://www. coloradocollege.edu/students/ communityservice/
*Description:* The Center for Community Service at Colorado College was created to promote an ethic of service and to develop civic-minded leadership among all members of the college community. Its purpose is to recognize and understand the civic and social challenges of the world and to act with others in the pursuit of a just society.
*SL Required for Graduation (all students)?* No
*Service Required for Graduation (all students)?* No
*Any Co-curricular Service?* No
*Any SL Residence Halls or Theme Houses?* No
*Number of Full-time SL Staff on Campus (not counting instructors):* 1
*Number of Part-time SL Staff on Campus (not counting instructors):* 0

**Colorado Mountain College**
3000 County Rd 114, Glenwood Springs, CO 81601
*University/College URL:* http://www. coloradomtn.edu
*Type of Institution:* community college

*SL Program/Center Name:* Service Learning Abroad
*Contact Person Name and Title:* Dave Harmon
*Contact Phone Number:* (970) 947–8262
*Contact Fax Number:* (970) 945–1227
*Contact Email Address:* dharmon@coloradomtn.edu
*Description:* Nicaragua and El Salvador service-learning courses include study tours of select communities. Students are exposed to major aspects of social, political, economic, and cultural life which contribute to the shape of the social institutions that define the life experiences of people in these countries.
*SL Required for Graduation (all students)?* No
*Service Required for Graduation (all students)?* No
*Any Co-curricular Service?* No
*Any SL Residence Halls or Theme Houses?* No
*Number of Undergraduate SL Courses Offered Per Year:* 2
*Number of Graduate SL Courses Offered Per Year:* 0
*Total Number of SL Courses Offered Per Year:* 2
*Number of Instructors Teaching SL Courses Per Year:* 2
*Number of Full-time SL Staff on Campus (not counting instructors):* 0
*Number of Part-time SL Staff on Campus (not counting instructors):* 0

**Colorado State University**
Lower Level, Lory Student Center, Fort Collins, CO 80523–8033
*University/College URL:* http://www.colostate.edu
*Type of Institution:* public, university, research
*SL Program/Center Name:* Office for Service-Learning and Volunteer Programs
*Contact Person Name and Title:* Victoria Keller, Dir
*Contact Phone Number:* (970) 491–1682
*Contact Fax Number:* (970) 491–2826
*Contact Email Address:* vkeller@lamar.colostate.edu

*SL Program/Center URL:* http://www.colostate.edu/depts/SLVP/
*SL Online Course Description URL:* http://www.colostate.edu/Depts/SLVP/courses.htm
*Description:* The Office for Service-Learning and Volunteer Programs builds and maintains partnerships between the campus community and broader communities. Towards this end, staff design and implement meaningful service projects that address community-defined needs, contribute to student learning, and encourage student leadership.
*SL Required for Graduation (all students)?* No
*Service Required for Graduation (all students)?* No
*Any Co-curricular Service?* Yes
*Any SL Residence Halls or Theme Houses?* Yes
*Number of Undergraduate SL Courses Offered Per Year:* 60
*Number of Graduate SL Courses Offered Per Year:* 10
*Total Number of SL Courses Offered Per Year:* 70
*Number of Instructors Teaching SL Courses Per Year:* 62
*Number of Full-time SL Staff on Campus (not counting instructors):* 4
*Number of Part-time SL Staff on Campus (not counting instructors):* 6

**Community College of Aurora**
9125 E 10th Dr, Bldg 859, Aurora, CO 80010
*University/College URL:* http://www.cca.cccoes.edu
*Type of Institution:* public, community college, secular
*SL Program/Center Name:* Service-Learning Center
*Contact Person Name and Title:* Paula J. Bonell, Service Learning Coord
*Contact Phone Number:* (303) 340–7051
*Contact Fax Number:* (303) 340–7080
*Contact Email Address:* Paula.Bonell@cca.cccoes.edu
*Description:* The Service Learning Center supports approximately 30 faculty, offering courses

that integrate service-learning in support of academic achievement. Each year, over 300 students work on community-defined needs which relate directly to course material. The center provides placement sites for service-learning and helps design special service projects to meet instructors' needs. For example, biology students identify and classify fossils at the Denver Natural History Museum; advanced art students design a mural for a local elementary school, and ethics students tutor children at an apartment complex. Outreach efforts to the community have increased through AmeriCorps. Three CCA AmeriCorps members tutor children during literacy blocks at a local elementary school located in a diverse, low-income area. Faculty, students, and community are the cornerstone of all partnerships. Faculty work with community partners to help them reinforce course outcomes and students work with both faculty and partners in a mentorship learning environment. CCA has evolved considerably as it continues to define service and community, gather institutional support, establish partnerships, and implement effective programming.

*SL Required for Graduation (all students)?* No

*Service Required for Graduation (all students)?* No

*Any Co-curricular Service?* No

*Any SL Residence Halls or Theme Houses?* No

*Number of Undergraduate SL Courses Offered Per Year:* 30

*Number of Graduate SL Courses Offered Per Year:* 0

*Total Number of SL Courses Offered Per Year:* 30

*Number of Instructors Teaching SL Courses Per Year:* 30

*Number of Full-time SL Staff on Campus (not counting instructors):* 0

*Number of Part-time SL Staff on Campus (not counting instructors):* 2

## Community College of Denver

Campus Box 650, PO Box 173363, Denver, CO 80217–3363

*University/College URL:* http://ccd. rightchoice.org

*Type of Institution:* public, community college, teaching

*SL Program/Center Name:* CCD Office for Service Learning

*Contact Person Name and Title:* Darilyn Carroll, Coord

*Contact Phone Number:* (303) 556–3848

*Contact Fax Number:* (303) 556–4583

*Contact Email Address:* dlc30@hotmail.com

*SL Program/Center URL:* http://ccd. rightchoice.org/serv_lrn

*Description:* The Office for Service Learning contributes to the Community College of Denver's overall mission as a learning-centered college. Service-learning is used as a teaching tool but also as a means to increase student retention, particularly for first-generation or other high-risk students. Service-learning collaborations exist with both community partners and with other college programs. The Office for Service Learning is a self-funded program.

*SL Required for Graduation (all students)?* No

*Service Required for Graduation (all students)?* No

*Any Co-curricular Service?* Yes

*Number of Undergraduate SL Courses Offered Per Year:* 10

*Total Number of SL Courses Offered Per Year:* 10

*Number of Instructors Teaching SL Courses Per Year:* 10

*Number of Full-time SL Staff on Campus (not counting instructors):* 0

*Number of Part-time SL Staff on Campus (not counting instructors):* 1

## Community College of Rhode Island

Lincoln Campus, 1762 Louiscuisett Pike, Lincoln, RI 02865

*University/College URL:* http://www.ccri. cc.ri.us

*Type of Institution:* public, community college

*Contact Person Name and Title:* Thomas Morrissey

*Contact Phone Number:* (401) 333–7270

*Contact Fax Number:* (401) 333–7111

*Contact Email Address:*
    tmorrissey@ccri.cc.ri.us
*Description:* Service-learning is optional for
faculty who are interested. Related programs
include AmeriCorps, Vista, America Reads,
and AACC Horizons Mentors.
*SL Required for Graduation (all*
    *students)?* No
*Service Required for Graduation (all stu-*
    *dents)?* No
*Any Co-curricular Service?* No
*Any SL Residence Halls or Theme*
    *Houses?* No
*Number of Undergraduate SL Courses*
    *Offered Per Year:* 60+
*Number of Instructors Teaching SL Courses*
    *Per Year:* 60+
*Number of Full-time SL Staff on Campus*
    *(not counting instructors):* 0
*Number of Part-time SL Staff on Campus*
    *(not counting instructors):* 2

### Connecticut College

270 Mohegan Ave, Box 5277, New London,
    CT 06320
*University/College URL:* http://www.
    conncoll.edu
*Type of Institution:* private, college, teach-
    ing, secular
*SL Program/Center Name:* Holleran Center
    for Community Challenges
*Contact Person Name and Title:* Tracee
    Reiser, Assoc Dir
*Contact Phone Number:* (860) 439–2456
*Contact Fax Number:* (860) 439–5408
*Contact Email Address:* tlrei@conncoll.edu
*SL Program/Center URL:* http://camel2.
    conncoll.edu/academics/centers/
    hollerancenter/INDEX.HTM
*SL Online Syllabi URL:* http://camel2.
    conncoll.edu/academics/centers/
    hollerancenter/service-learning/syllabi.
    html
*Description:* The Holleran Center for Commu-
nity Challenges is a multidisciplinary, aca-
demic center that is dedicated to teaching,
research, and community collaborations that
foster active citizenship and community leadership in a multicultural, democratic society.
Directed by an advisory board composed of

college and community representatives, the Center oversees three major areas: the Program in
Community Action; Service Learning Course
Development; and College-Community Partnerships. With the center's guidance, students,
faculty, staff, community members, and alumni
work togther in a spirit of reciprocal learning
and community enhancement.
    Program in Community Action: The center's
certificate for the Program in Community Action (PICA) is awarded at graduation to students who successfully supplement a major
with a set of requirements organized around a
senior integrative project that addresses a specific community challenge. These requirements
include four courses outside the major (service-
learning courses where appropriate), a summer
internship, and the senior project, which is an
independent study or honors thesis in the student's major field. PICA scholars also participate in a series of workshops (the Leadership
Cluster) that develop their skills in negotiation,
mediation, public speaking, interviewing, nonprofit management, and electronic networking.
*SL Required for Graduation (all*
    *students)?* No
*Service Required for Graduation (all stu-*
    *dents)?* No
*Any Co-curricular Service?* Yes (The Office
    of Volunteers for Community Service
    places over 500 students per year in
    volunteer positions; approximately half
    participate through service-learning
    courses.)
*Any SL Residence Halls or Theme Houses?*
    No (But there is a community-service
    representative in each residence hall.)
*SL Degrees Offered:* Certificate in Commu-
    nity Action
*Number of Undergraduate SL Courses*
    *Offered Per Year:* 23
*Number of Graduate SL Courses Offered*
    *Per Year:* 1
*Total Number of SL Courses Offered Per*
    *Year:* 24
*Number of Instructors Teaching SL Courses*
    *Per Year:* 14
*Number of Full-time SL Staff on Campus*
    *(not counting instructors):* 1

*Number of Part-time SL Staff on Campus
(not counting instructors):* 1

## Cornell University

Ithaca, NY 14853
*University/College URL:* http://www.
cornell.edu
*Type of Institution:* private, university, teach-
ing, research, secular
*SL Program/Center Name:* Public Serv-
ice Center
*Contact Person Name and Title:* Leonardo
Vargas-Mendez, Interim Dir
*Contact Phone Number:* (607) 255–1148
*Contact Fax Number:* (607) 255–9550
*Contact Email Address:* LJV1@cornell.edu;
cupsc@cornell.edu
*SL Program/Center URL:* http://www.psc.
cornell.edu
*Description:* Founded in 1991, the mission of
the Public Service Center is to promote the
university's commitment to service as essential
to active citizenship. To fulfill this mission,
the Public Service Center selected service-
learning as the educational philosophy that
guides its programs. Service-learning fosters
service to others, community development and
empowerment, and reciprocal learning through
participants' social and educational interactions. The center, an academic initiative of
Cornell University's division of Student and
Academic Services, strives to provide a complete and diverse experience for students through
service that both complements and is an integral part of the academic experience. All of
these efforts aim to provide service in partnership with the larger community. The center
offers curricular and co-curricular service-learning initiatives that involve more than 3,700
Cornell students each year (over one-third of
the university undergraduate population). Curricular efforts have been developed by the
Faculty Fellows in Service program and involve over 32 service-learning courses in all
seven colleges.
*SL Required for Graduation (all
students)?* No
*Service Required for Graduation (all stu-
dents)?* No
*Any Co-curricular Service?* Yes

*Any SL Residence Halls or Theme
Houses?* No
*Number of Undergraduate SL Courses
Offered Per Year:* 35
*Number of Graduate SL Courses Offered
Per Year:* 3
*Total Number of SL Courses Offered Per
Year:* 38
*Number of Instructors Teaching SL Courses
Per Year:* 30
*Number of Full-time SL Staff on Campus
(not counting instructors):* 1 (Note: This
answer reflects only the staff person who
works directly with faculty in developing
course and other curricular service-learning initiatives (credit-based independent
projects). The Center co-curricular service-learning initiatives are supported by 5
other professionals: 3 full-time and 2
part-time.)
*Number of Part-time SL Staff on Campus
(not counting instructors):* 1 (administrative staff)

## Cowley College

125 S 2nd St, PO Box 1147, Arkansas City,
KS 67005
*University/College URL:* http://cowley.cc.
ks.us
*Type of Institution:* public, community col-
lege, teaching, secular
*SL Program/Center Name:* Service Learning
Central
*Contact Person Name and Title:* Mark
L. Jarvis
*Contact Phone Number:* (800) 593–2222,
ext 5202
*Contact Fax Number:* (316)441–5350
*Contact Email Address:*
jarvis@cowley.cc.ks.us
*SL Program/Center URL:* http://www.
slcserves.com
*Description:* Begun in 1991, Service Learning
Central provides resources, organization, and
the stimulus for citizen volunteerism and experiential learning, positively impacting area communities. A nine-member Board of Directors,
composed equally of students and community
members, establishes policy, solicits support,
fields ideas, and guides all programming. This

programming encompasses the Corporation for National Service's "streams of service," and has initiated a local volunteer service club. The heart of programming is mentoring a number of students on volunteer service scholarships (at present, 56 are on this roster). These students enroll in service-learning courses every semester and are required to serve in a service site on a weekly basis for 50–100 hours per semester. The center also introduces students to meaningful service through a volunteer fair, classroom visits, and campaigning and tabling. The clearinghouse places approximately half of the main campus student body in 100 sites in a five-county area. On a monthly basis, the office engages students in field experiences called "Do Good Days," which are often coupled with national days of service. Significant support is provided by the college, including scholarships, office space, salary, and a conservative operating budget.

*SL Required for Graduation (all students)?* No

*Service Required for Graduation (all students)?* No

*Any Co-curricular Service?* Yes

*Any SL Residence Halls or Theme Houses?* Yes

*Number of Undergraduate SL Courses Offered Per Year:* 14–18 (8 "stand-alone" service learning courses; 6–10 courses integrating service components)

*Total Number of SL Courses Offered Per Year:* 8

*Number of Instructors Teaching SL Courses Per Year:* 4–6

*Number of Full-time SL Staff on Campus (not counting instructors):* 0

*Number of Part-time SL Staff on Campus (not counting instructors):* 3

**Creighton University**
Creighton Center for Service and Justice, 2500 California Plaza, Omaha, NE 68178
*University/College URL:* http://www.creighton.edu
*Type of Institution:* private, university, teaching, research, religious
*SL Program/Center Name:* Creighton Center for Service and Justice

*Contact Person Name and Title:* Maria Teresa Gaston, Dir
*Contact Phone Number:* (402) 280–1290
*Contact Fax Number:* (402) 280–4732
*Contact Email Address:* mtgaston@creighton.edu
*SL Program/Center URL:* http://www.creighton.edu/ccsj
*Description:* At this time Creighton University does not have an academic service-learning center. The Creighton Center for Service and Justice (CCSJ) is the temporary home for connecting Creighton professors with community organizations for the purpose of integrating service-learning into their courses. In addition, the CCSJ facilitates many co-curricular opportunities for service, reflection, and social analysis such as Spring Break Service Trips and local Omaha Immersions.

*SL Required for Graduation (all students)?* No

*Service Required for Graduation (all students)?* No

*Any Co-curricular Service?* Yes

*Any SL Residence Halls or Theme Houses?* Yes

*Number of Undergraduate SL Courses Offered Per Year:* 5

*Number of Instructors Teaching SL Courses Per Year:* 5

**Del Mar College**
101 Baldwin Blvd, Corpus Christi, TX 78404
*University/College URL:* http://www.delmar.edu
*Type of Institution:* public, community college
*SL Program/Center Name:* Service Learning Program
*Contact Person Name and Title:* Anne Stewart, Coord of SL
*Contact Phone Number:* (361) 698–1336
*Contact Fax Number:* (361) 698–1936
*Contact Email Address:* astewart@delmar.edu
*Description:* The Service Learning Program provides information to students, faculty, staff, and the community regarding the college's commitment to the development of civic re-

sponsibility through instructional and other student development activities. The SL Coordinator convenes an advisory committee for program review and recommendations, presents training sessions for faculty and students, collects syllabi from participating faculty members to share with others, and shares information pertaining to SL from conferences and professional publications. Funding is provided through the Teaching and Learning Center, the Dean of Student Development, and the Dean of Arts and Sciences.

*SL Required for Graduation (all students)?* No

*Service Required for Graduation (all students)?* No

*Any Co-curricular Service?* No

*Any SL Residence Halls or Theme Houses?* No

*Number of Undergraduate SL Courses Offered Per Year:* 2

*Number of Graduate SL Courses Offered Per Year:* 0

*Total Number of SL Courses Offered Per Year:* 2

*Number of Instructors Teaching SL Courses Per Year:* 6

*Number of Full-time SL Staff on Campus (not counting instructors):* 0

*Number of Part-time SL Staff on Campus (not counting instructors):* 1

**Denison University**

1 Main St, PO Box M, Granville, OH 43023

*University/College URL:* http://www.denison.edu

*Type of Institution:* private, college, teaching, secular

*SL Program/Center Name:* Alford Center for Service-Learning

*Contact Person Name and Title:* Dr. David T. Ball, Dir

*Contact Phone Number:* (740) 587–6474

*Contact Fax Number:* (740) 587–6386

*Contact Email Address:* ball@denison.edu

*SL Program/Center URL:* http://www.denison.edu/service-learning/

*SL Online Course Description URL:* http://www.denison.edu/service-learning/courses.html

*Description:* The Alford Center for Service-Learning is a place where students, faculty, and administrators can access resources for a wide variety of community-service projects. Center staff plan and implement campus-wide, co-curricular service-learning programs; support a 500-plus member student-run community-service organization; coordinate with faculty in designing service-learning components for academic courses; and administer the America Reads tutoring program. Ongoing contact with groups and agencies is maintained in order to be responsive to genuine community needs. The Center is primarily funded by the endowment of the late John W. Alford, supplemented for certain programs by student government and general budget allocations.

*SL Required for Graduation (all students)?* No

*Service Required for Graduation (all students)?* No

*Any Co-curricular Service?* Yes

*Any SL Residence Halls or Theme Houses?* Yes

*Number of Undergraduate SL Courses Offered Per Year:* 25

*Total Number of SL Courses Offered Per Year:* 25

*Number of Instructors Teaching SL Courses Per Year:* 22

*Number of Full-time SL Staff on Campus (not counting instructors):* 1

*Number of Part-time SL Staff on Campus (not counting instructors):* 3

**DePaul University**

2233 N Kenmore Ave, Chicago, IL 60614

*University/College URL:* http://www.depaul.edu

*Type of Institution:* private, university, teaching, religious

*SL Program/Center Name:* Office of Community-based Service Learning

*Contact Person Name and Title:* Laurie Worrall, Dir

*Contact Phone Number:* (773) 325–7457

*Contact Fax Number:* (773) 325–7459

*Contact Email Address:* cbsl@wppost.depaul.edu

*SL Program/Center URL:* http://www.depaul.edu/~cbsl

*SL Online Course Description URL:* http://
www.depaul.edu/~cbsl
*Description:* Individual DePaul faculty have
been teaching service-learning courses for five
years or more. In October 1998, DePaul made
an institutional commitment to encourage the
development of service-learning courses as a
way of developing and strengthening university-community partnerships by establishing the
Office of Community-based Service Learning.
CbSL facilitates the development of partnerships between DePaul and community-based
organizations by encouraging the teaching of
service-learning courses and the consistent place-
ment of students at partner organizations.
*SL Required for Graduation (all
  students)?* No
*Service Required for Graduation (all stu-
  dents)?* No
*Any Co-curricular Service?* Yes
*Any SL Residence Halls or Theme
  Houses?* Yes
*SL Degrees Offered:* DePaul is currently
  developing an undergraduate Community
  Service Minor.
*Number of Undergraduate SL Courses
  Offered Per Year:* 25–35
*Number of Graduate SL Courses Offered
  Per Year:* 2–4
*Total Number of SL Courses Offered Per
  Year:* 25–35
*Number of Instructors Teaching SL Courses
  Per Year:* 20–25
*Number of Full-time SL Staff on Campus
  (not counting instructors):* 3
*Number of Part-time SL Staff on Campus
  (not counting instructors):* 7

**Duke University**
102 West Duke, PO Box 90431, Durham,
  NC 27708
*University/College URL:* http://www.
  duke.edu
*Type of Institution:* private, university, teach-
  ing, research
*SL Program/Center Name:* Kenan Ethics
  Program
*Contact Person Name and Title:* Betsy
  Alden, Coord for Service-Learning
*Contact Phone Number:* (919) 660–3199

*Contact Fax Number:* (919) 660–3049
*Contact Email Address:* alden@duke.edu
*SL Program/Center URL:* http://kenan.ethics.
  duke.edu
*Description:* Service-Learning at Duke is a
collaborative effort between the Kenan Ethics
Program, the Community Service Center, the
Hart Leadership Program, and the Center for
Documentary Studies. This collaborative effort
offers rigorous integration of community-service experiences with students' academic work
in a particular undergraduate course. Initiated
in 1997, the Kenan Ethics Program now has
over 500 students per year (from a student body
of 6000) participating in service-learning. A
student organization, LEAPS (Learning Through
Experience, Action, Partnership, and Service),
supports the program by recruiting, training,
and overseeing 25 student facilitators, who
work closely with assigned faculty in a specific
course to offer peer-led reflection sessions
throughout the semester. The Coordinator for
Service-Learning works with faculty and community partners to determine and provide appropriate placement sites and to develop and
maintain these relationships, as well as with
LEAPS to maintain databases and develop student leadership. The Kenan Ethics Program
offers a multi-tiered approach to service-learning: opportunities for students to be introduced
to during their first two years, then enrollment
in a year-long course which includes an intensive summer service experience, followed by
reflection and research in the fall semester
(Service Opportunities in Leadership). Several new approaches are underway in first-
year FOCUS programs and Research Service-
Learning.
*SL Required for Graduation (all
  students)?* No
*Service Required for Graduation (all stu-
  dents)?* No
*Any Co-curricular Service?* Yes
*Any SL Residence Halls or Theme
  Houses?* No
*Number of Undergraduate SL Courses
  Offered Per Year:* 20
*Total Number of SL Courses Offered Per
  Year:* 20

*Number of Instructors Teaching SL Courses
Per Year:* 15
*Number of Full-time SL Staff on Campus
(not counting instructors):* 1
*Number of Part-time SL Staff on Campus
(not counting instructors):* 1

## Earlham College
801 National Rd West, Drawer 195, Rich-
mond, IN 47374
*University/College URL:* http://www.
earlham.edu
*Type of Institution:* private, college, teaching
*SL Program/Center Name:* Service Learning
Program
*Contact Person Name and Title:* Theresa
Ludwig, Dir
*Contact Phone Number:* (765) 983–1317
*Contact Fax Number:* (765) 983–1234
*Contact Email Address:*
ludwite@earlham.edu
*SL Program/Center URL:* http://www.
earlham.edu/%7Eesl/
*Description:* Earlham's Service Learning Program (SLP) serves as a resource and advising
unit to student-initiated service efforts, and it
assists with matching students and their skills
and interests to the needs of the community.
SLP provides orientation, leadership training,
specialized workshops, and opportunities for
reflection for students to ensure that quality
learning occurs with their community-service
experiences. An annual Service Celebration
pulls together campus and community to hail
the efforts of all volunteers.
*SL Required for Graduation (all
students)?* No
*Service Required for Graduation (all stu-
dents)?* No
*Any Co-curricular Service?* Yes
*Any SL Residence Halls or Theme Houses?*
Yes (Woodman House)
*Number of Undergraduate SL Courses
Offered Per Year:* 10–15
*Number of Graduate SL Courses Offered
Per Year:* 0
*Total Number of SL Courses Offered Per
Year:* 10–15
*Number of Instructors Teaching SL Courses
Per Year:* 10

*Number of Full-time SL Staff on Campus
(not counting instructors):* 1
*Number of Part-time SL Staff on Campus
(not counting instructors):* 3

## Eastern College
1300 Eagle Rd, Saint Davids, PA
19087–3696
*University/College URL:* http://www.
eastern.edu
*Type of Institution:* private, college, teaching, religious
*SL Program/Center Name:* Service Learning
and Campus Ministries
*Contact Person Name and Title:* Kimberlee
Johnson, Coord
*Contact Phone Number:* (610) 341–1830
*Contact Fax Number:* (610) 341–1705
*Contact Email Address:*
kjohnso2@eastern.edu
*Description:* The philosophy of service-learning at Eastern College flows from its mission to
be a Christian college dedicated to the preparation of students for thoughtful and productive
lives of Christian faith and service. Because the
college is committed to developing students
who follow Christ and become increasingly
transformed into His image, it initially provides
means by which students can integrate faith,
learning, and praxis.

First Year Student Seminar: Service Learning is an integral part of the first-year student
seminar ("Living and Learning in Community:
The Transforming Vision"), and comprises 30
percent of the grade for the course. Twenty
hours must be spent at one community location
throughout the semester. These hours are veri-
fied by the site supervisor. A paper must be
submitted requiring critical reflection of the
service as it relates to the objectives of the
course. Opportunities for reflection and proc-
essing of the community experience are provided during class as well.
*SL Required for Graduation (all
students)?* Yes
*Service Required for Graduation (all stu-
dents)?* Yes
*Any Co-curricular Service?* Yes
*Any SL Residence Halls or Theme
Houses?* No

*Number of Undergraduate SL Courses
   Offered Per Year:* 1+
*Number of Graduate SL Courses Offered
   Per Year:* 0
*Total Number of SL Courses Offered Per
   Year:* 1+ (In addition to the first-year
   student seminar, some other courses exist
   with a service learning component)
*Number of Instructors Teaching SL Courses
   Per Year:* 16
*Number of Full-time SL Staff on Campus
   (not counting instructors):* 1
*Number of Part-time SL Staff on Campus
   (not counting instructors):* 0

**Eastern Michigan University**
233 Rackham, Office of Academic Service-
   Learning, Ypsilanti, MI 48197
*University/College URL:* http://www.
   emich.edu
*Type of Institution:* public, university, teach-
   ing, secular
*SL Program/Center Name:* Office of Aca-
   demic Service-Learning
*Contact Person Name and Title:* Dale L.
   Rice, PhD, Dir
*Contact Phone Number:* (734) 487–3300
*Contact Fax Number:* (734) 480–1319
*Contact Email Address:* dale.rice@emich.edu
*SL Program/Center URL:* http://www.emich.
   edu/public/office_asl/home.html
*Description:* The Office of Academic Service-
Learning was created to support the growth of
academic service-learning at Eastern Michigan
University. The mission of the office is to build
an infrastructure that will support students,
faculty, administrators, and community members in their efforts to implement academic
service-learning. The office provides several
services to its constituents. These include Faculty Fellow Development Seminars, a Resource
Center, Workshops for K-12 teachers, community links, and research opportunities. The office supports several research efforts including
America Reads and an Eisenhower project.
*SL Required for Graduation (all
   students)?* No
*Service Required for Graduation (all stu-
   dents)?* No (Honors students must com-

plete 30 hours of service to graduate with
honors.)
*Any Co-curricular Service?* Yes
*Any SL Residence Halls or Theme
   Houses?* No
*Number of Undergraduate SL Courses
   Offered Per Year:* 83
*Number of Graduate SL Courses Offered
   Per Year:* 24
*Total Number of SL Courses Offered Per
   Year:* 107
*Number of Instructors Teaching SL Courses
   Per Year:* 0
*Number of Full-time SL Staff on Campus
   (not counting instructors):* 45
*Number of Part-time SL Staff on Campus
   (not counting instructors):* 8

**Eckerd College**
4200 54th Ave South, Saint Petersburg,
   FL 33711
*University/College URL:* http://www.
   eckerd.edu
*Type of Institution:* private, college, teach-
   ing, religious
*SL Program/Center Name:* Center for the
   Applied Liberal Arts
*Contact Person Name and Title:* James J.
   Annarelli, PhD, Assoc Dean & Dir
*Contact Phone Number:* (727) 864–7676
*Contact Fax Number:* (727) 864–7995
*Contact Email Address:*
   calamail@eckerd.edu
*Description:* Through its Center for the Applied
Liberal Arts (CALA), Eckerd College provides
off-campus and experiential-learning opportunities aimed at enhancing students' academic
and personal development, and bridging their
transition from college to graduate study or
employment. The programs of the center include study-abroad experiences, domestic and
international internships, service-learning opportunities, career-planning assistance, and
graduate and professional school admissions
resources. Students may pursue community
service as a co-curricular volunteer activity or
as a part of a class that has been designed by the
professor with a service option or requirement.
Such a class integrates a relevant service experience into the work of the course in ways that

address specific community needs while furthering the learning objectives of the course. Courses that have a service-learning option or requirement have been offered both on campus and in conjunction with travel experiences to other regions of the country or the world.

*SL Required for Graduation (all students)?* Yes (All seniors must complete a course entitled "Quest for Meaning," which includes a 40-hour service-learning component)

*Service Required for Graduation (all students)?* No

*Any Co-curricular Service?* Yes

*Any SL Residence Halls or Theme Houses?* No

*Number of Undergraduate SL Courses Offered Per Year:* 5 [About 18 sections of one of these courses (QFM) are offered each Fall]

*Number of Graduate SL Courses Offered Per Year:* 0

*Total Number of SL Courses Offered Per Year:* 5

*Number of Instructors Teaching SL Courses Per Year:* 22

*Number of Full-time SL Staff on Campus (not counting instructors):* 2 (split duties)

*Number of Part-time SL Staff on Campus (not counting instructors):* 0

## Elizabethtown College

One Alpha Dr, Elizabethtown, PA 17022

*University/College URL:* http://www.etown.edu

*Type of Institution:* private, college, teaching

*SL Program/Center Name:* Elizabethtown College Learning Center

*Contact Person Name and Title:* Shirley Deichert, Dir, Learning Center

*Contact Phone Number:* (717) 361–1227

*Contact Fax Number:* (717) 361–1390

*Contact Email Address:* deichesa@etown.edu

*SL Program/Center URL:* http://www.etown.edu/learningcenter

*Description:* Elizabethtown College Learning Center offers a network for service-learning opportunities, as well as academic support services. As a service-learning network, the center

links the needs of the community with the service needs of the students/staff. The center provides service-learning opportunities for volunteers, work-study students, and service-learning courses. The Learning Center is funded through the College Life division.

*SL Required for Graduation (all students)?* No

*Service Required for Graduation (all students)?* No

*Any Co-curricular Service?* Yes

*Any SL Residence Halls or Theme Houses?* Yes

*Number of Undergraduate SL Courses Offered Per Year:* 13

*Total Number of SL Courses Offered Per Year:* 13

*Number of Instructors Teaching SL Courses Per Year:* 10

*Number of Full-time SL Staff on Campus (not counting instructors):* 2 (each with half-time responsibilities to service-learning)

*Number of Part-time SL Staff on Campus (not counting instructors):* 0

## Elon College

101 Haggard Ave, 2700 Campus Box, Elon, NC 27244

*University/College URL:* http://www.elon.edu

*Type of Institution:* private, college, teaching, religious

*SL Program/Center Name:* Kernodle Center for Service Learning

*Contact Person Name and Title:* Kathy Manning, Dir

*Contact Phone Number:* (336) 584–2102

*Contact Fax Number:* (336) 538–2673

*Contact Email Address:* Kathy.Manning@elon.edu

*SL Program/Center URL:* http://www.elon.edu/service/

*Description:* The Kernodle Center for Service Learning seeks to provide all members of the Elon College campus the opportunity to develop an ethic of service by connecting campus and community through service experiences. The center's Course-Linked Service Learning Program helps professors link service with their curricula and provides an experiential-learning opportunity for students. Students perform a certain number of hours with a service agency in the community and reflect on the service in the classroom. The Kernodle Center for Service Learning provides administrative support for the placements. Through course-linked service learning, students learn about their community, themselves, and others.

*SL Required for Graduation (all students)?* No

*Service Required for Graduation (all students)?* No

*Any Co-curricular Service?* Yes

*Any SL Residence Halls or Theme Houses?* Yes

*Number of Undergraduate SL Courses Offered Per Year:* 22

*Total Number of SL Courses Offered Per Year:* 22

*Number of Instructors Teaching SL Courses Per Year:* 13

*Number of Full-time SL Staff on Campus (not counting instructors):* 1

*Number of Part-time SL Staff on Campus (not counting instructors):* 0

## Emory University

Theory Practice Learning Program, Center for Teaching and Curriculum—Candler Library, Atlanta, GA 30322

*University/College URL:* http://www. emory.edu

*Type of Institution:* private, university, teaching, research, secular

*SL Program/Center Name:* Theory Practice Learning Program

*Contact Person Name and Title:* Dr. Bobbi Patterson, Dir, Lecturer, Religion Dept

*Contact Phone Number:* (404) 727–6730/2541

*Contact Fax Number:* (404) 727–7597

*Contact Email Address:* bpatter@emory.edu

*Description:* The TPL program provides faculty and students with resources for understanding the theories and methods of experience-based and community-based teaching and learning. TPL provides workshops, colleague groups, and consultation on class development, design, implementation, and evaluation. It also

develops and sustains a relationship for theory and practice with community partners who help teach and/or work with TPL classes. Finally, it maintains a library of resources available to faculty and students interested in this pedagogy. Funding is all Emory based.

*SL Required for Graduation (all students)?* No

*Service Required for Graduation (all students)?* No

*Any Co-curricular Service?* Yes

*Any SL Residence Halls or Theme Houses?* Yes

*Total Number of SL Courses Offered Per Year:* (Unknown; however, every department in the college has at least one, usually several, TPL courses; 1–1/2 years ago, the estimate was 48 courses in the college.)

*Number of Full-time SL Staff on Campus (not counting instructors):* 1

*Number of Part-time SL Staff on Campus (not counting instructors):* 0

## Florida Atlantic University

777 Glades Rd, Boca Raton, FL 33431

*University/College URL:* http://www.fau.edu

*Type of Institution:* public, university, teaching, secular

*SL Program/Center Name:* Campus Volunteer Center

*Contact Person Name and Title:* Carol Clyde, Senior Coord

*Contact Phone Number:* (561) 297–3607

*Contact Fax Number:* (561) 297–1004

*Contact Email Address:* cclyde@fau.edu

*SL Program/Center URL:* http://www.fau. edu/volunteer

*Description:* The Campus Volunteer Center works to promote an ethic of volunteerism among the campus community. The center acts as a clearinghouse to more than 2,000 local agencies, and hosts a number of specialized programs including: Service Owls (a transcript program), Project HOPE (community mentoring), Alternative Break, and other activities.

*SL Required for Graduation (all students)?* No

*Service Required for Graduation (all students)?* No

*Any Co-curricular Service?* Yes

*Any SL Residence Halls or Theme Houses?* No

*Number of Undergraduate SL Courses Offered Per Year:* 17

*Number of Graduate SL Courses Offered Per Year:* 0

*Total Number of SL Courses Offered Per Year:* 17

*Number of Instructors Teaching SL Courses Per Year:* 87

*Number of Full-time SL Staff on Campus (not counting instructors):* 1

*Number of Part-time SL Staff on Campus (not counting instructors):* 2

## Florida Gulf Coast University

10501 Ben Hill Griffin Prkwy, Fort Myers, FL 33904

*University/College URL:* http://www.fgcu.edu

*Type of Institution:* public, university, teaching, secular

*SL Program/Center Name:* EaglesConnect/ Office of Community Learning and Special Programs

*Contact Person Name and Title:* Linda Summers, Coord

*Contact Phone Number:* (941) 590–7016

*Contact Fax Number:* (941) 590–7024

*Contact Email Address:* lsummers@fgcu.edu

*SL Program/Center URL:* http://www.fgcu.edu/connect/

*Description:* Florida Gulf Coast University has an undergraduate service-learning graduation requirement (for students graduating after May 1999). Students may fulfill this requirement through service-learning courses or through stand-alone service-learning activities. The Office of Community Learning and Special Programs is designed to offer the infrastructure necessary to support this requirement. The coordinator works with a campus advisory board to develop policies and procedures and offer a review process for student appeals, and is also responsible for developing service opportunities and approving service-learning experiences that students develop on their own. The Office

of Community Learning and Special Programs includes the coordinator, a program assistant who provides initial contact with students and handles clerical tasks, and a part-time student assistant who acts as a liaison for America Reads, for student organizations and for the Student Government Association. University funding pays salaries of both full-time staff members, matching monies for work-study funds and for operational expenses.

*SL Required for Graduation (all students)?* Yes (for undergraduate students)

*Service Required for Graduation (all students)?* Yes

*Any Co-curricular Service?* Yes

*Any SL Residence Halls or Theme Houses?* No

*Number of Undergraduate SL Courses Offered Per Year:* 12

*Number of Graduate SL Courses Offered Per Year:* 0

*Total Number of SL Courses Offered Per Year:* 12

*Number of Instructors Teaching SL Courses Per Year:* 8

*Number of Full-time SL Staff on Campus (not counting instructors):* 2

*Number of Part-time SL Staff on Campus (not counting instructors):* 1 (Student Assistant)

## Florida International University

10700 SW 8 St, (Honors College), Miami, FL 33199

*University/College URL:* http://www.fiu.edu/~Honors

*Type of Institution:* public, university, teaching, research, secular

*SL Program/Center Name:* Honors Civic Engagement Project, Honors College

*Contact Person Name and Title:* Robert Hogner

*Contact Phone Number:* (305) 348–2571

*Contact Fax Number:* (305) 348 3792

*Contact Email Address:* rhogner@fiu.edu

*SL Program/Center URL:* http://cba.fiu.edu/mktg/service

*Description:* The Honors College operates Foodrunners (a community service-learning project serving Miami's homeless communities;

http://www.fiu.edu/~foodrun), the Health & Social Justice Project (a community service-learning program for pre-med Honors College students developing in collaboration with the UM Medical School); the Art Reaching Children Project (which links Honors College education, social science, art, and music students with children at Miami's homeless families centers); and the Step Up/Step-Out Project, in which students serve as mentors of lower-income-family high school students. All projects except for Foodrunners operate in conjunction with a fourth-year Honors College course, "Lives, Livelihood and Community." Foodrunners is a collaborative effort of the Honors College and the College of Business Administration.

*SL Required for Graduation (all students)?* No
*Service Required for Graduation (all students)?* No
*Any SL Residence Halls or Theme Houses?* No

**Florida International University**
University Park, Graham Center 340, Miami $5FL 33199
*University/College URL:* http://www.fiu.edu
*Type of Institution:* public, university, teaching, research
*SL Program/Center Name:* Volunteer Action Center
*Contact Person Name and Title:* Anna Tang, Coord
*Contact Phone Number:* (305) 348–2149
*Contact Fax Number:* (305) 348–3823
*Contact Email Address:* time4chg@fiu.edu
*SL Program/Center URL:* http://www.fiu. edu/~time4chg
*Description:* The Volunteer Action Center is the central office for volunteerism on campus. It works closely with service-learning professors, as well as with multiple community agencies throughout Miami and the nation.
*SL Required for Graduation (all students)?* No
*Service Required for Graduation (all students)?* No
*Any Co-curricular Service?* No

*Any SL Residence Halls or Theme Houses?* No
*Number of Undergraduate SL Courses Offered Per Year:* 40
*Number of Graduate SL Courses Offered Per Year:* 4
*Total Number of SL Courses Offered Per Year:* 40–50
*Number of Instructors Teaching SL Courses Per Year:* 17

**Florida State University**
Center for Civic Education and Service, 930 West Park Ave, MC 4180, Tallahassee, FL 32306–4180
*University/College URL:* http://www.fsu.edu
*Type of Institution:* public, university, research, secular
*SL Program/Center Name:* Center for Civic Education and Service
*Contact Person Name and Title:* Bill Moeller, Dir
*Contact Phone Number:* (850) 644–3342
*Contact Fax Number:* (850) 644–3362
*Contact Email Address:* bmoeller@admin.fsu.edu
*SL Program/Center URL:* http://www.fsu. edu/~service
*Description:* The Center for Civic Education and Service aims to promote community involvement and civic responsibility as integral elements of a liberal arts education at Florida State University. By providing service opportunities for students and faculty, promoting the linking of service to classroom learning through service-learning options, and arranging and participating in collaborative community-improvement projects, the center expects to make a significant contribution to the education outcomes of students and to the well-being of the communities the university reaches.
*SL Required for Graduation (all students)?* No
*Service Required for Graduation (all students)?* No
*Any Co-curricular Service?* Yes
*Any SL Residence Halls or Theme Houses?* No
*Number of Undergraduate SL Courses Offered Per Year:* 83

*Number of Graduate SL Courses Offered Per Year:* 14

*Total Number of SL Courses Offered Per Year:* 97

*Number of Instructors Teaching SL Courses Per Year:* 48

*Number of Full-time SL Staff on Campus (not counting instructors):* 3

*Number of Part-time SL Staff on Campus (not counting instructors):* 6

**Fort Lewis College**

71 Reed Lib, 1000 Rim Dr, Durango, CO 81301

*University/College URL:* http://www. fortlewis.edu

*Type of Institution:* public, college, teaching

*SL Program/Center Name:* Center for Service Learning

*Contact Person Name and Title:* Kalin Grigg

*Contact Phone Number:* (970) 247–7641

*Contact Fax Number:* (970) 247–7198

*Contact Email Address:* grigg_k@fortlewis.edu

*SL Program/Center URL:* http://www. fortlewis.edu/acad-aff/geninfo/acadsupp. html#service

*Description:* The Center for Service Learning supports faculty and students in their efforts to integrate academic study with responsible service and activism in local and regional communities. Focusing academic resources on pressing social, environmental, economic, and civic issues links campuses to communities in a dynamic partnership that both enhances students' educational experience and assists community-based groups in their vital work.

*SL Required for Graduation (all students)?* No

*Service Required for Graduation (all students)?* No

*Any Co-curricular Service?* Yes

*Any SL Residence Halls or Theme Houses?* No

*Number of Undergraduate SL Courses Offered Per Year:* 20–25

*Number of Graduate SL Courses Offered Per Year:* 0

*Total Number of SL Courses Offered Per Year:* 20–25

*Number of Instructors Teaching SL Courses Per Year:* 12–15

*Number of Full-time SL Staff on Campus (not counting instructors):* 0

*Number of Part-time SL Staff on Campus (not counting instructors):* 2

**Gadsden State Community College**

1001 Wallace Dr, PO Box 227, Gadsden, AL 35902

*University/College URL:* http://www. gadsdenst.cc.al.us

*Type of Institution:* public, community college, teaching

*SL Program/Center Name:* Learning And Serving Education & Reflection

*Contact Person Name and Title:* Laura Salmon, Public Relations Dir

*Contact Phone Number:* (256) 549–8224

*Contact Fax Number:* (256) 549–8444

*Contact Email Address:* lsalmon@gadsdenst.cc.al.us

*SL Program/Center URL:* http://www. gadsdenst.cc.al.us/pr/lrnsrv.htm

*SL Online Course Description URL:* http:// www.gadsdenst.cc.al.us/pr/classes.htm

*Description:* The college offers a service-learning course entitled "Community Awareness Through Service Learning" (ORI 101). Classes began Spring 1998. The focus is on teaching students about critical thinking, values clarification, social development, and civic responsibility in the context of developing an awareness of social needs and service opportunities available in their community. The course includes information about agencies' opportunities for students to acquire field experiences and particular requirements of the various agencies for service volunteers. Students who volunteer through the college's student service corps are required to take ORI 101. In addition to ORI 101, service-learning courses are offered in electrical engineering technology, nursing, mechanical engineering technology, and environmental science.

One way for the agencies to communicate their service needs and opportunities is through Web Pages for Community Agencies, which instructs agencies in Web-page development. These Web pages are added to the college's

Web site in a directory of community agencies which provide service-learning opportunities in the community. Students are then able to scan agency listings in search of service-learning placements that best suit their individual academic goals. Co-curricular service opportunities include the "Mock Wreck" alcohol/drug abuse prevention activity, "Make A Difference Day," "World AIDS Day" and the "Martin Luther King Birthday Initiative" observed in three separate events: Community Health Fair, Volunteer Agencies Festival in the Mall, and Youth Service Day.

*SL Required for Graduation (all students)?* No

*Service Required for Graduation (all students)?* No

*Any Co-curricular Service?* Yes

*Any SL Residence Halls or Theme Houses?* No

*Number of Undergraduate SL Courses Offered Per Year:* 8

*Number of Graduate SL Courses Offered Per Year:* 0

*Total Number of SL Courses Offered Per Year:* 8

*Number of Instructors Teaching SL Courses Per Year:* 6

*Number of Full-time SL Staff on Campus (not counting instructors):* 0

*Number of Part-time SL Staff on Campus (not counting instructors):* 4

**Gainesville College**

3820 Mundy Mill Rd, PO Box 1358, Gainesville, GA 30503

*University/College URL:* http://www.gc. peachnet.edu

*Type of Institution:* public, community college, teaching

*Contact Person Name and Title:* Dr. Janie Wolf-Smith, Prof, Sociology and Social Work

*Contact Phone Number:* (770) 718–3670

*Contact Fax Number:* (770) 718–3832

*Contact Email Address:* jwsmith@hermes.gc.peachnet.edu

*Description:* At Gainesville College, a faculty member has been designated as the service-learning coordinator on campus. The coordina-

tor assists faculty who are interested in service-learning and compiles statistics on the number of faculty using it, the number of students participating, and the number of hours served. Faculty members who chose to do so can incorporate it as a part of their courses. It may be a required component or optional or used as extra credit. Gainesville College also uses co-curricular transcripts and lists service-learning on transcripts. A "stand alone" service-learning course for credit is planned for the 2000–2001 academic year.

*SL Required for Graduation (all students)?* No

*Service Required for Graduation (all students)?* No

*Any Co-curricular Service?* Yes

*Any SL Residence Halls or Theme Houses?* No

*Total Number of SL Courses Offered Per Year:* 0

*Number of Instructors Teaching SL Courses Per Year:* 0

*Number of Full-time SL Staff on Campus (not counting instructors):* 0

*Number of Part-time SL Staff on Campus (not counting instructors):* 0

**Gannon University**

109 University Square, Erie, PA 16541

*University/College URL:* http://www. gannon.edu

*Type of Institution:* private, university, teaching, religious

*SL Program/Center Name:* Center for Social Concerns

*Contact Person Name and Title:* Anne McCarthy, OSB, Dir

*Contact Phone Number:* (814) 871–7433

*Contact Fax Number:* (814) 871–7344

*Contact Email Address:* mccarthy002@gannon.edu

*SL Program/Center URL:* http://www. gannon.edu/resource/student/socconcerns

*Description:* Gannon's Center for Social Concerns, part of the Chaplain's Department, fosters service and learning by Gannon students in the Erie community and furthers Gannon's mission by working for social justice locally and globally. As an urban campus anchored in the inner city, Gannon's Center for Social Concerns facilitates a wide variety of community-service projects, most within walking distance of the campus. The center serves as a resource for faculty in developing service-learning course components and advises five student organizations including SOUL, a service-learning community. Alternative break service trips are organized by the Center during winter, spring, and summer breaks. The Center participates in advocacy coalitions and organizations in the local community, the neighborhood, nationally, and internationally.

Staff include one full-time director and two graduate assistants.

*SL Required for Graduation (all students)?* No

*Service Required for Graduation (all students)?* No

*Any Co-curricular Service?* No

*Any SL Residence Halls or Theme Houses?* Yes

*Total Number of SL Courses Offered Per Year:* 35

*Number of Instructors Teaching SL Courses Per Year:* 27

*Number of Full-time SL Staff on Campus (not counting instructors):* 1

*Number of Part-time SL Staff on Campus (not counting instructors):* 2

**GateWay Community College**
108 North 40th St, Phoenix, AZ 85034
*University/College URL:* http://www.gwc.maricopa.edu
*Type of Institution:* public, community college
*SL Program/Center Name:* Community Partnership Programs
*Contact Person Name and Title:* Michele Bush, Dir
*Contact Phone Number:* (602) 392–5185
*Contact Fax Number:* (602) 392–5329
*Contact Email Address:* bush_m@gwc.maricopa.edu
*SL Program/Center URL:* http://www.gwc.maricopa.edu/partnerships/community.html
*Description:* The coordination of Service-Learning activities at GWCC is the responsibility of

the director of Community Partnership Programs, who reports directly to the Dean of School and Community Relations. Documentation and tracking of SL activities is the responsibility of the Office of Student Activities. A Service-Learning standing committee made up of faculty, related staff, and students meets monthly to oversee activities and make recommendations to the administration. Faculty, staff, and community partners collaborate to integrate academic instruction with community service to address unmet community needs while fostering civic and challenging students to think critically about social issues, their career choices, and their options.

*SL Required for Graduation (all students)?* No

*Service Required for Graduation (all students)?* No

*Any Co-curricular Service?* Yes

*Any SL Residence Halls or Theme Houses?* No

*Number of Undergraduate SL Courses Offered Per Year:* 21

*Total Number of SL Courses Offered Per Year:* 21

*Number of Instructors Teaching SL Courses Per Year:* 24

*Number of Full-time SL Staff on Campus (not counting instructors):* 1 (Service-learning is only part of duties.)

*Number of Part-time SL Staff on Campus (not counting instructors):* 0

**George Fox University**
8660 W Emerald St, Suite 112, Boise, ID 83704–8201
*University/College URL:* http://www.georgefox.edu/academics/graduate.shtml
*Type of Institution:* private, university, teaching, religious
*SL Program/Center Name:* Master of Arts in Organizational Leadership (MAOL) degree program at the George Fox University Boise Center, Idaho
*Contact Person Name and Title:* John S. DeJoy, PhD, Dir, Graduate Studies, Assist Prof, Management
*Contact Phone Number:* (208) 375–3900
*Contact Fax Number:* (208) 375–3564

*Contact Email Address:*
jdejoy@georgefox.edu
*SL Program/Center URL:* http://www.
georgefox.edu/academics/graduate.shtml
*Description:* The George Fox University Boise
(Idaho) Center offers an M.A. in Organizational Leadership. All students are required to
complete a course entitled "Service Learning
Project" for which they receive two graduate
semester credits. This requirement is a year-
long, team service project where students work
with a public-benefit organization to apply
skills, theory, course concepts, and research-
based decision-making skills. The faculty mentor structures the learning, coordinates with the
cooperating organizations, assesses the level
and the significance of learning, and monitors
the overall experience.
*SL Required for Graduation (all students)?*
Yes (for all MAOL students)
*Service Required for Graduation (all stu-
dents)?* Yes (for all MAOL students)
*Any Co-curricular Service?* No
*Any SL Residence Halls or Theme
Houses?* No
*Number of Graduate SL Courses Offered
Per Year:* 1 (a 2-semester course which is
conducted over a 12-month period)
*Total Number of SL Courses Offered
Per Year:* 1
*Number of Instructors Teaching SL Courses
Per Year:* 1
*Number of Full-time SL Staff on Campus
(not counting instructors):* 0
*Number of Part-time SL Staff on Campus
(not counting instructors):* 0

**George Mason University**
MSN 2F3, Fairfax, VA 22030
*University/College URL:* http://www.
gmu.edu
*Type of Institution:* public, university, re-
search, secular
*SL Program/Center Name:* Center for Serv-
ice and Leadership
*Contact Person Name and Title:* Laura
Gaither, Dir
*Contact Phone Number:* (703) 993–2900
*Contact Fax Number:* (703) 993–2117
*Contact Email Address:* lgaither@gmu.edu

*SL Program/Center URL:* http://www.gmu.
edu/student/csl
*SL Online Course Description URL:* http://
www.gmu.edu/student/csl/courses.html
*Description:* The Center for Service and Leadership promotes positive change and civic responsibility by combining academic study, leadership development, and direct community
service. The center provides leadership development and service-learning opportunities in a
variety of formats including courses, conferences, workshops, retreats, and one-on-one consultations. The center assists students in understanding social issues that may impact upon
different areas of community service. It provides information on service-learning placements and volunteer opportunities for students,
faculty, and staff and serves as the central point
of contact for the university on leadership development and service-learning initiatives. The
center houses a 500-plus volume library for
students, faculty and staff.
    Service-Learning Partners Program: Aca-
demic credit is offered to students in classes
where faculty add a service-learning component to their students' educational experience.
Reflection sessions, writing, and 45 service
hours per academic credit are available. The
university offers independent study, fourth-
credit add-on and service-learning community
options.
*SL Required for Graduation (all
students)?* No
*Service Required for Graduation (all stu-
dents)?* No
*Any Co-curricular Service?* Yes
*Any SL Residence Halls or Theme Houses?*
No (But one is planned for a freshman
learning community next year.)
*SL Degrees Offered:* Service-learning is a
component of the Leadership Studies
Certificate.
*Number of Undergraduate SL Courses
Offered Per Year:* 20
*Number of Graduate SL Courses Offered
Per Year:* 1–2 (depending on cross-
listings)
*Total Number of SL Courses Offered Per
Year:* 22

*Number of Instructors Teaching SL Courses
Per Year:* 20
*Number of Full-time SL Staff on Campus
(not counting instructors):* 1
*Number of Part-time SL Staff on Campus
(not counting instructors):* 2 (student
workers)

**George Washington University**
Human Services Program
801 22nd St NW, Rome Hall 456, Washington, DC 20052
*University/College URL:* http://www.gwu.edu
*Type of Institution:* public, university, teaching, research
*SL Program/Center Name:* Human Services Program
*Contact Person Name and Title:* Honey W. Nashman, Dir, Prof, Sociology Dept
*Contact Phone Number:* (202) 994–6167
*Contact Fax Number:* (202) 994–1512
*Contact Email Address:* hnashman@gwu.edu
*SL Program/Center URL:* http://gwis2.circ.gwu.edu/~hmsr
*SL Online Course Description URL:* http://gwis2.circ.gwu.edu/~hmsr/courses.html
*Description:* The George Washington University Human Services Program prepares undergraduate students to assume effective leadership roles in not-for profit agencies supporting or serving people and communities who are experiencing need. It is an academic, service-learning program applying concepts learned in the classroom to contemporary societal problems.
*SL Required for Graduation (all
students)?* No
*Service Required for Graduation (all students)?* No
*Any Co-curricular Service?* Yes
*Any SL Residence Halls or Theme
Houses?* Yes
*SL Degrees Offered:* Human Services Program is a Degree Program (B.A.)
*Number of Undergraduate SL Courses
Offered Per Year:* 8
*Number of Graduate SL Courses Offered
Per Year:* 0

*Total Number of SL Courses Offered
Per Year:* 8
*Number of Instructors Teaching SL Courses
Per Year:* 8
*Number of Full-time SL Staff on Campus
(not counting instructors):* 1
*Number of Part-time SL Staff on Campus
(not counting instructors):* 0

**George Washington University**
800 21st St NW, Suite 427, Washington, DC 20052
*University/College URL:* http://www.gwu.edu
*Type of Institution:* public, university, teaching, research, secular
*SL Program/Center Name:* Office of Community Service
*Contact Person Name and Title:* Amiko Matsumoto, Dir
*Contact Phone Number:* (202) 994–5492
*Contact Fax Number:* (202) 994–6102
*Contact Email Address:* amatsumo@gwu.edu
*SL Program/Center URL:* http://gwired.gwu.edu/sac/service.html
*Description:* The Office of Community Service exists to facilitate, coordinate, enhance, and recognize the service efforts of students, staff, faculty, and alumni with community agencies and organizations in the DC Metropolitan area. The OCS provides the GW community with a clearinghouse where individuals and groups in search of service opportunities can seek out a broad range of initiatives. Both long-term and short-term placements are listed. OCS staff coordinate an assortment of larger service projects which bring participants together to serve with the community. In addition, OCS works with academic schools, departments, and individual faculty to identify the type of service-learning programs and projects which best assist students to meet their course requirements.
*SL Required for Graduation (all
students)?* No
*Service Required for Graduation (all students)?* No
*Any Co-curricular Service?* Yes
*Any SL Residence Halls or Theme Houses?*
Yes (One floor in a residence hall)
*SL Undergraduate Program Name:* Human

Services Program (see separate
entry, above)
*Number of Instructors Teaching SL Courses
Per Year:* 5
*Number of Full-time SL Staff on Campus
(not counting instructors):* 3
*Number of Part-time SL Staff on Campus
(not counting instructors):* 0

**Georgetown University**
37th and O St, NW, Washington, DC 20057
*University/College URL:* http://www.
georgetown.edu
*Type of Institution:* private, university, re-
search, religious
*SL Program/Center Name:* The Volunteer
and Public Service Center
*Contact Person Name and Title:* Service
Learning Coord
*Contact Phone Number:* (202) 687–3703
*Contact Fax Number:* (202) 687–8980
*Contact Email Address:*
vps@gunet.georgetown.edu
*SL Program/Center URL:* http://www.
georgetown.edu/outreach/vps
*SL Online Course Description URL:* http://
www.georgetown.edu/outreach/vps/
service-learn/s-l_classes.html
*SL Online Syllabi URL:* http://www.george-
town.edu/outreach/vps/service-learn/s-l_
classes.html
*Description:* Founded in 1978, the Volunteer
and Public Service Center, a division of the
Georgetown University Office of Student
Affairs, has sought to engage members of the
Georgetown University community in service
opportunities that address issues of social justice on the local, national, and international
levels. Respectful of diversity of faith, philosophy, and culture, the center upholds the
distinctiveness of the Georgetown Jesuit mission to educate men and women for others.
Community involvement is integral to the University's educational mission, and the center
contributes to this mission by linking academic
theory with practical experience and encouraging students to use their education to respond to
human needs. The center also offers the Service-Learning Credit, an established and popular
program for service learning at Georgetown.

Students arrange to link 40 hours of community
service to any Main Campus course offering.
With the consent of the professor, the student's
home college, and the center, a service-learning
grade is awarded for demonstrated learning
(not for the service itself). The center coordi-
nates guided reflection sessions and e-mail
discussion groups for all Service Learning Credit
participants.
*SL Required for Graduation (all
students)?* No
*Service Required for Graduation (all stu-
dents)?* No
*Any Co-curricular Service?* Yes
*Any SL Residence Halls or Theme
Houses?* Yes
*Number of Undergraduate SL Courses
Offered Per Year:* 8
*Number of Graduate SL Courses Offered
Per Year:* 1
*Total Number of SL Courses Offered
Per Year:* 9
*Number of Instructors Teaching SL Courses
Per Year:* 7
*Number of Full-time SL Staff on Campus
(not counting instructors):* 1
*Number of Part-time SL Staff on Campus
(not counting instructors):* 4

**Georgia State University**
Department of English, University Plaza,
Atlanta, GA 30303–3083
*University/College URL:* http://www.gsu.edu
*Type of Institution:* public, university, re-
search, secular
*SL Program/Center Name:* Service Learning
in Technical and Professional Writing
*Contact Person Name and Title:* Jeff Grabill,
Assist Prof of English
*Contact Phone Number:* (404) 651–2900
*Contact Fax Number:* (404) 651–1710
*Contact Email Address:* jgrabill@gsu.edu
*SL Program/Center URL:* http://www.gsu.
edu/~engjtg
*Description:* Service Learning in Technical
and Professional writing is part of the larger
writing program. Students are provided opportunities to work with community-based organizations to help them solve writing-related prob-
lems. These opportunities are typically situ-

ated in business-writing and technical-writing classes, courses which serve junior and senior level majors and non-majors. The initiative is unfunded.

*SL Required for Graduation (all students)?* No

*Service Required for Graduation (all students)?* No

*Any Co-curricular Service?* No

**Gettysburg College**
300 N Washington St, Gettysburg, PA 17325
*University/College URL:* http://www.gettysburg.edu
*Type of Institution:* private, college, teaching
*SL Program/Center Name:* Center for Public Service
*Contact Person Name and Title:* Karl Mattson, Dir; Gretchen Carlson Natter, Assoc Dir; David Crowner, Faculty Coord for Service-Learning
*Contact Phone Number:* (717) 337–6490
*Contact Fax Number:* (717) 337–6496
*Contact Email Address:* kmattson@gettysburg.edu; gnatter@gettysburg.edu; crowner@gettysburg.edu
*SL Program/Center URL:* http://www.gettysburg.edu/college_life/cps
*SL Online Course Description URL:* http://www.gettysburg.edu/college_life/cps/courses.html
*Description:* In keeping with the college's mission to educate young people to think critically and to act compassionately, the Center for Public Service promotes, organizes, and supports public and community service by members of the Gettysburg College community. In this context, the center tries to accomplish three goals that help students become responsible citizens: to respond strategically to community needs as identified by community members (community action); to develop in students the requisite knowledge, skills, and commitment for a lifetime of effective engagement with social issues (service learning); and to connect community needs with academic scholarship in a way that expands students' intellectual development and provides effective assist-

ance to off-campus communities (curriculum development).

*SL Required for Graduation (all students)?* No

*Service Required for Graduation (all students)?* No

*Any Co-curricular Service?* Yes

*Any SL Residence Halls or Theme Houses?* Yes

*Number of Undergraduate SL Courses Offered Per Year:* 5–8

*Total Number of SL Courses Offered Per Year:* 5–8

*Number of Instructors Teaching SL Courses Per Year:* 5

*Number of Full-time SL Staff on Campus (not counting instructors):* 2

**Gonzaga University**
E 502 Boone, MSC 2472, Spokane, WA 99258
*University/College URL:* http://www.gonzaga.edu
*Type of Institution:* private, university, religious
*SL Program/Center Name:* Office of Service-Learning
*Contact Person Name and Title:* Mari Morando, Service-Learning Coord
*Contact Phone Number:* (509) 323–6396
*Contact Fax Number:* (509) 323–5872
*Contact Email Address:* morando@gu.gonzaga.edu
*SL Program/Center URL:* http://www.gonzaga.edu/service/gvs/service_learning/
*SL Online Course Description URL:* http://www.gonzaga.edu/service/gas/Service_Learning/courses/index.html
*SL Online Syllabi URL:* http://www.gonzaga.edu/service/gas/Service_Learning/courses/index.html
*Description:* The Service-Learning program, guided by the Service-Learning Committee and the Office of Service-Learning, has been developed in 11 academic departments and the Law School. The Office of Service-Learning, housed in the Center for Community Action & Service-Learning (CASSEL), acts as a resource for

students, faculty, and staff involved in service-learning. CASSEL sponsors events including the Community Service Fair, a semi-annual event occurring at the beginning of each semester offering students the opportunity to interact with local community nonprofit agencies. Students also participate in the Volunteer Voices Forums to informally reflect on and share their stories of service with one another.

*SL Required for Graduation (all*
   *students)?* No
*Service Required for Graduation (all stu-*
   *dents)?* No
*Any Co-curricular Service?* Yes
*Any SL Residence Halls or Theme*
   *Houses?* Yes
*Number of Undergraduate SL Courses*
   *Offered Per Year:* 14
*Number of Graduate SL Courses Offered*
   *Per Year:* 2
*Total Number of SL Courses Offered Per*
   *Year:* 16
*Number of Instructors Teaching SL Courses*
   *Per Year:* 12
*Number of Full-time SL Staff on Campus*
   *(not counting instructors):* 1
*Number of Part-time SL Staff on Campus*
   *(not counting instructors):* 2

**Goucher College**
1021 Dulaney Valley Rd, Towson,
   MD 21204
*University/College URL:* http://www.
   goucher.edu
*Type of Institution:* private, college, teaching
*SL Program/Center Name:* Community
   Service Program
*Contact Person Name and Title:* Carol
   Weinberg, Coord, Community Service
*Contact Phone Number:* (410) 337–6483
*Contact Fax Number:* (410) 337–6405
*Contact Email Address:*
   cweinber@goucher.edu
*Description:* Service is integrated into approximately 30 courses each year. This is done in several ways. Some classes each semester offer a service-credit option where students can elect to take an additional credit and do 30 hours of service at a site that relates to the course content. The service is integrated into the course through written assignments given by the professor. To date, this approach has been used in sociology, Spanish, education, English, theater, history, politics, and public policy. Some courses (including anthropology, chemistry, psychology) include a service component in which all class members do some work in the community and incorporate that service into the classroom discussion. Still other courses have been designed around a shared group service project which meets a need in the community and puts to use the skills that the students have developed. Included are courses in urban policy, survey research, and a unique interdisciplinary senior capstone course entitled ''Making Connections: A Service-Learning Liberal Arts Capstone.''

In June 2000, Goucher College received a $1 million grant from the France-Merrick Foundation of Baltimore for an endowed professorship in service-learning. The France-Merrick grant will be used to ensure the academic quality of Goucher's service-learning efforts by creating an endowed professorship that will give the program continuity and leadership. Goucher faculty member Carol Weinberg, coordinator of community service, will be the first chair holder.

*SL Required for Graduation (all*
   *students)?* No
*Service Required for Graduation (all stu-*
   *dents)?* No
*Any Co-curricular Service?* Yes
*Any SL Residence Halls or Theme*
   *Houses?* No
*Number of Undergraduate SL Courses*
   *Offered Per Year:* 30
*Number of Graduate SL Courses Offered*
   *Per Year:* 0
*Total Number of SL Courses Offered Per*
   *Year:* 30
*Number of Instructors Teaching SL Courses*
   *Per Year:* 25
*Number of Full-time SL Staff on Campus*
   *(not counting instructors):* 0
*Number of Part-time SL Staff on Campus*
   *(not counting instructors):* 1

## Grand Rapids Community College

143 Bostwick NE, Service Learning Center, Grand Rapids, MI 49503

*University/College URL:* http://www.grcc. cc.mi.us

*Type of Institution:* public, community college, teaching

*SL Program/Center Name:* Service Learning Center

*Contact Person Name and Title:* Martha Cox, Coord of Service Learning

*Contact Phone Number:* (616) 234–4162

*Contact Fax Number:* (616) 234–4019

*Contact Email Address:* mcox@grcc.cc.mi.us

*SL Program/Center URL:* http://www.grcc. cc.mi.us/studentservices/index. html#Student

*Description:* The Service Learning Center provides opportunities for students to develop their sense of social responsibility through active participation in organized volunteer experiences at community-based organizations. It assists faculty who offer service-learning options in their courses by placing the students at agencies, organizations, or schools in the community. The center also offers a Community Plunge during the Fall semester for incoming freshmen and other students, four Alternative Spring Break trips and one weekend trip each year. It participates in the America Reads, America Counts nationwide tutoring program. The center partners with an elementary school in the community in supporting children as they increase reading and math scores and with the school's student council with special projects such as beautification projects and fundraisers. The center is six years old and is operated out of the Student Activities Office. Initially started with a Venture Grant from Michigan Campus Compact, it is now funded by the college. It assists approximately 500 students per semester.

*SL Required for Graduation (all students)?* No

*Service Required for Graduation (all students)?* Yes

*Any Co-curricular Service?* Yes

*Any SL Residence Halls or Theme Houses?* No

*Number of Undergraduate SL Courses Offered Per Year:* 11

*Total Number of SL Courses Offered Per Year:* 11

*Number of Instructors Teaching SL Courses Per Year:* 11

## Grand Valley State University

One College Landing, Student Life Office, Kirkhof Center, Allendale, MI 49401

*University/College URL:* http://www. gvsu.edu

*Type of Institution:* public, university, teaching, secular

*SL Program/Center Name:* Volunteer GVSU, a service learning project

*Contact Person Name and Title:* Jay Cooper, Assoc Dir, Student Life

*Contact Phone Number:* (616) 895–2345

*Contact Fax Number:* (616) 895–2355

*Contact Email Address:* Cooperj@gvsu.edu

*SL Program/Center URL:* http://www4.gvsu. edu/alumni/volunteer/index.htm

*Description:* Volunteer GVSU, a student-run service-learning project, is made up of 13 issue-based organizations: Alternative Spring Break, Best Buddies, Disabilities, Environment, Health and AIDS, Hunger and Homeless, Habitat for Humanity, Literacy, Seniors, Substance Abuse, Volunteer Corps, and Youth. Students involved in the issues gain valuable leadership skills, coordinate direct service projects in the community, and coordinate many on-campus educational programs. In addition to Volunteer GVSU, the Leadership and Volunteer Center (LAVC) houses the GVSU Leadership Program, a variety of non-credit leadership experiences for students. LAVC also serves as a resource to faculty and staff interested in developing academic-based service-learning through disseminating grant information, international service-learning opportunities, and housing an extensive service-learning library and bibliography.

*SL Required for Graduation (all students)?* No

*Service Required for Graduation (all students)?* No

*Any Co-curricular Service?* Yes

*Any SL Residence Halls or Theme Houses?* No

*Number of Undergraduate SL Courses Offered Per Year:* 35

*Number of Graduate SL Courses Offered Per Year:* 5

*Total Number of SL Courses Offered Per Year:* 40

*Number of Instructors Teaching SL Courses Per Year:* 25

*Number of Full-time SL Staff on Campus (not counting instructors):* 0

*Number of Part-time SL Staff on Campus (not counting instructors):* 3 (2 part-time staff and 1 graduate assistant)

## Grossmont College

8800 Grossmont College Dr, El Cajon, CA 92020–1799

*University/College URL:* http://grossmont. gcccd.cc.ca.us

*Type of Institution:* public, college, community college, teaching, secular

*SL Program/Center Name:* Community Service Learning Center

*Contact Person Name and Title:* Cassandra Evans, Prog Specialist

*Contact Phone Number:* (619) 644–7821

*Contact Fax Number:* (619) 644–7934

*Contact Email Address:* cassandra.evans@gcccd.net

*SL Program/Center URL:* http://www. grossmont.net/csl

*Description:* The Community Service Learning Center serves faculty, students, and community-based organizations by assisting with the development of meaningful service-learning activities that meet the needs of the community and enhance the students' learning process. The college has a strong cross-cultural studies program, which utilizes two Native American Indian reservations in the district as significant placement sites. The center also has an AmeriCorps/America Reads program. Grossmont faculty have been interested in or involved in service-learning for about five years, and understanding and support of service-learning on campus is strong. The center is housed under the Dean of Humanities, Social and Behav-

ioral Sciences, and International Programs. It is funded through a California State Chancellor's Office Fund for Student Success grant in 1999. This grant supports a three-year institutionalization project.

*SL Required for Graduation (all students)?* No

*Service Required for Graduation (all students)?* No

*Any Co-curricular Service?* No

*Any SL Residence Halls or Theme Houses?* No

*Number of Undergraduate SL Courses Offered Per Year:* 30

*Total Number of SL Courses Offered Per Year:* 30

*Number of Instructors Teaching SL Courses Per Year:* 15

*Number of Full-time SL Staff on Campus (not counting instructors):* 2

*Number of Part-time SL Staff on Campus (not counting instructors):* 0

## Hamline University

536 Hewitt Ave, Saint Paul, MN 55104

*University/College URL:* http://www. hamline.edu

*Type of Institution:* private, university, teaching, secular

*SL Program/Center Name:* Office of Service-Learning and Volunteerism

*Contact Person Name and Title:* Sharon Jaffe, Coord

*Contact Phone Number:* (651) 523–2483

*Contact Fax Number:* (651) 523- 2956

*Contact Email Address:* service-learning@gw.hamline.edu

*SL Program/Center URL:* http://web. hamline.edu/~jdart/volunteer.html

*Description:* In Fall 2000, the Office of Service-Learning and Volunteerism (OSLV) became the Wesley Center For Community Involvement. The mission of the Wesley Center is to connect campus and community through learning and action in order to promote a just and sustainable society. Each activity of the OSLV/Wesley Center is coordinated and advised by a group of students, faculty/staff, and community members. The Wesley Center continues the work of the OSLV in three areas:

community-service, academic service-learning, and applied research. Community service includes assisting people who participate in community service, producing a monthly newsletter, and supporting student activities such as an annual volunteer fair, community-service day, Second Saturday service days, and alternative spring breaks. Academic service-learning includes providing resources for faculty to use service-learning in first-year seminars and LEAD (leadership, education and development) classes, which are required for graduation. In the area of applied research, the center promotes research that mutually benefits students, faculty, and communities.

*SL Required for Graduation (all students)?* No
*Service Required for Graduation (all students)?* No
*Any Co-curricular Service?* Yes
*Any SL Residence Halls or Theme Houses?* No
*Number of Undergraduate SL Courses Offered Per Year:* 5 (The First Year Seminars have service-learning.)
*Number of Graduate SL Courses Offered Per Year:* 0
*Total Number of SL Courses Offered Per Year:* 5
*Number of Instructors Teaching SL Courses Per Year:* 5
*Number of Full-time SL Staff on Campus (not counting instructors):* 1
*Number of Part-time SL Staff on Campus (not counting instructors):* 1

**Hocking College**
3301 Hocking Prkwy, Nelsonville, OH 45764
*University/College URL:* http://www.hocking.edu
*Type of Institution:* public, community college, teaching, secular
*SL Program/Center Name:* HOPE (Hocking Outreach Program Experience) Center
*Contact Person Name and Title:* Elaine Dabelko, Dir, Service-Learning; Suzanne Brooks, Center Coord
*Contact Phone Number:* (740) 753–3591, ext 2272; ext 2334

*Contact Fax Number:* (740) 753–4852
*Contact Email Address:* dabelko_e@hocking.edu; brooks_s@hocking.edu
*Description:* The HOPE Center plans and implements service-learning activities and assists faculty in incorporating service-learning into the curriculum. The HOPE Center works with area agencies, schools, churches, and organizations to develop appropriate service-learning sites; coordinates the America Reads program and Kids on Campus; and promotes service-learning to the campus and general public.
*SL Required for Graduation (all students)?* No
*Service Required for Graduation (all students)?* No
*Any Co-curricular Service?* Yes
*Any SL Residence Halls or Theme Houses?* No
*Number of Undergraduate SL Courses Offered Per Year:* 12
*Number of Graduate SL Courses Offered Per Year:* 0
*Total Number of SL Courses Offered Per Year:* 12
*Number of Instructors Teaching SL Courses Per Year:* 15–20
*Number of Full-time SL Staff on Campus (not counting instructors):* 0
*Number of Part-time SL Staff on Campus (not counting instructors):* 2

**Holyoke Community College**
303 Homestead Ave, Holyoke, MA 01040–1099
*University/College URL:* http://www.hcc.mass.edu
*Type of Institution:* public, community college, teaching, secular
*SL Program/Center Name:* Community Service-Learning Center
*Contact Person Name and Title:* Joan Mikalson, Dir
*Contact Phone Number:* (413) 552–2714
*Contact Fax Number:* (413) 534–8975
*Contact Email Address:* jmikalson@hcc.mass.edu
*SL Program/Center URL:* http://www.hcc.mass.edu/g_k/html/service_learning.html
*Description:* Community Service Learning at

Holyoke Community College is in its third year of development. The program is faculty-driven and course-based across disciplines. Students elect to participate in community-service projects, events or activities in the community—off campus or on campus. Federal work-study eligible students are placed in the community as tutors or mentors. Although service is not required for graduation, in order to receive funding, half of the membership of student clubs must participate in one community-service project per year. Community Service Learning is funded by a Massachusetts Campus Compact (Learn and Serve) grant and a Perkins grant. Half of the director's position is institutionalized, with plans for full institutional funding in the upcoming financial year.

*SL Required for Graduation (all students)?* No
*Service Required for Graduation (all students)?* No
*Any Co-curricular Service?* Yes
*Any SL Residence Halls or Theme Houses?* No
*Number of Undergraduate SL Courses Offered Per Year:* 60
*Number of Graduate SL Courses Offered Per Year:* 0
*Total Number of SL Courses Offered Per Year:* 60
*Number of Instructors Teaching SL Courses Per Year:* 30
*Number of Full-time SL Staff on Campus (not counting instructors):* 1
*Number of Part-time SL Staff on Campus (not counting instructors):* 1

### Honolulu Community College
874 Dillingham Blvd, Honolulu, HI 96817
*University/College URL:* http://www.hcc.hawaii.edu
*Type of Institution:* public, community college, teaching, secular
*SL Program/Center Name:* HCC Service Learning
*Contact Person Name and Title:* Grace R. Ihara
*Contact Phone Number:* (808) 845–9262
*Contact Email Address:* grace@hcc.hawaii.edu

*SL Program/Center URL:* http://www.hcc.hawaii.edu/servicelearning/index.html
*SL Online Course Description URL:* http://www.hcc.hawaii.edu/servicelearning/index.html
*Description:* HCC is in the process of integrating service-learning projects into several classes in various areas. This includes mentoring, tutorials, community issues, environmental issues, and leadership development for all participants. Classes with service-learning are in the areas of early childhood, human services, associate of justice, history, sociology, speech, and political science.

*SL Required for Graduation (all students)?* No
*Service Required for Graduation (all students)?* No
*Any Co-curricular Service?* Yes
*Any SL Residence Halls or Theme Houses?* No
*Number of Undergraduate SL Courses Offered Per Year:* 10
*Number of Graduate SL Courses Offered Per Year:* 0
*Total Number of SL Courses Offered Per Year:* 10
*Number of Full-time SL Staff on Campus (not counting instructors):* 4

### Humboldt State University
House 91, 1 Harpst St, Arcata, CA 95521–8299
*University/College URL:* http://www.humboldt.edu
*Type of Institution:* public, university, teaching
*SL Program/Center Name:* Service Learning/Experiential Education
*Contact Person Name and Title:* Annie Bolick, Coord
*Contact Phone Number:* 707) 826–4965
*Contact Fax Number:* (707) 826–5558
*Contact Email Address:* amb2@axe.humboldt.edu
*SL Program/Center URL:* http://www.humboldt.edu/~slee; http://www.humboldt.edu/~yes
*SL Online Course Description URL:* http://

www.humboldt.edu/~slee/html/courses.
shtml

*Description:* Service Learning/Experiential Education is a campus-wide initiative that promotes and supports a continuum of volunteer, community service, and service-learning programs across campus. Youth Educational Services (YES) is a co-curricular student-run community-service learning organization currently offering fifteen different community-service programs.

*SL Required for Graduation (all
    students)?* No

*Service Required for Graduation (all students)?* No

*Any Co-curricular Service?* Yes

*Any SL Residence Halls or Theme
    Houses?* Yes

*SL Degrees Offered:* Leadership Studies Minor (an interdisciplinary minor with an emphasis phase featuring service-learning courses and opportunities)

*Number of Full-time SL Staff on Campus
    (not counting instructors):* 1

*Number of Part-time SL Staff on Campus
    (not counting instructors):* 8

## Indiana University, Bloomington

618 E Third St, Bloomington, IN 47429

*University/College URL:* http://www.
    indiana.edu/iub

*Type of Institution:* public, university, research, secular

*SL Program/Center Name:* Office of Community Partnerships in Service-Learning

*Contact Person Name and Title:* JoAnn
    Campbell, Dir

*Contact Phone Number:* (812) 856–6011

*Contact Fax Number:* (812) 855–3315

*Contact Email Address:*
    jocampbe@indiana.edu

*SL Program/Center URL:* http://www.
    indiana.edu/~ocpsl/

*SL Online Course Description URL:* http://
    www.indiana.edu/~ocpsl/courses.html

*Description:* The Office for Community Partnerships in Service-Learning was established to develop community partnerships in support of course-based service-learning and to serve as a clearinghouse of related information. As a part of both the IU Center on Philanthropy and the Dean of Faculties Office, it aims to strengthen its partners, enrich academic experiences, and expand the amount of time, energy, and skill devoted to building a healthy community.

*SL Required for Graduation (all
    students)?* No

*Service Required for Graduation (all students)?* No

*Any Co-curricular Service?* Yes

*Any SL Residence Halls or Theme
    Houses?* Yes

*Number of Undergraduate SL Courses
    Offered Per Year:* 38

*Number of Graduate SL Courses Offered
    Per Year:* 11

*Total Number of SL Courses Offered Per
    Year:* 49

*Number of Instructors Teaching SL Courses
    Per Year:* 50

*Number of Full-time SL Staff on Campus
    (not counting instructors):* 4

*Number of Part-time SL Staff on Campus
    (not counting instructors):* 2

## Indiana University of Pennsylvania

104 Pratt Hall, 201 Pratt Dr, Indiana,
    PA 15701

*University/College URL:* http://www.iup.edu

*Type of Institution:* public, university, teaching

*SL Program/Center Name:* Student Community Services

*Contact Person Name and Title:* Tammy
    Patterson Manko, Dir, Office for Service Leadership

*Contact Phone Number:* (724) 357–2598

*Contact Fax Number:* (724) 357–2593

*Contact Email Address:*
    Tammym@grove.iup.edu

*SL Program/Center URL:* http://www.iup.
    edu/sao/stucomm.htmlx

*Description:* The Office for Service Leadership at IUP works with a variety of projects and programs. Staff assist faculty with incorporating service into their classes, help students with community service, and organize campus community-service events. The office is a component of the Department of Student Activities and Organizations, which provides operational funding.

*SL Required for Graduation (all students)?* No

*Service Required for Graduation (all students)?* No

*Any SL Residence Halls or Theme Houses?* Yes

*Total Number of SL Courses Offered Per Year:* 60+

*Number of Instructors Teaching SL Courses Per Year:* 44

*Number of Full-time SL Staff on Campus (not counting instructors):* 3 (1 professional with shared responsibilities; 1 clerk with shared responsibilities; 1 AmeriCorps member)

*Number of Part-time SL Staff on Campus (not counting instructors):* 8 (1 half-time graduate assistant; 7 undergraduate work-study students)

## Indiana University-Purdue University Indianapolis

Center for Public Service and Leadership, 815 West Michigan St, LY 3116, Indianapolis, IN 46202–5146

*University/College URL:* http://www.iupui.edu

*Type of Institution:* public, university, teaching, research, secular

*SL Program/Center Name:* Center for Public Service and Leadership, Office of Service Learning

*Contact Person Name and Title:* Robert G. Bringle, Dir; Julie Hatcher, Assoc Dir

*Contact Phone Number:* (317) 278–2370

*Contact Fax Number:* (317) 278–7683

*Contact Email Address:* rbringle@iupui.edu

*SL Program/Center URL:* http://cpsl.iupui.edu

*SL Online Course Description URL:* http://cpsl.iupui.edu/servcla.htm

*Description:* The mission of the Center for Public Service and Leadership is to make service an integral and distinct aspect of the educational culture of IUPUI. The Office of Service Learning supports the development of service-learning classes and scholarship associated with service-learning.

*SL Required for Graduation (all students)?* No

*Service Required for Graduation (all students)?* No

*Any Co-curricular Service?* No

*Any SL Residence Halls or Theme Houses?* No

*Number of Undergraduate SL Courses Offered Per Year:* 35

*Number of Graduate SL Courses Offered Per Year:* 5

*Total Number of SL Courses Offered Per Year:* 40

*Number of Instructors Teaching SL Courses Per Year:* 30

*Number of Full-time SL Staff on Campus (not counting instructors):* 1

*Number of Part-time SL Staff on Campus (not counting instructors):* 6

## International Partnership for Service-Learning

815 Second Ave, Suite 315, New York, NY 10017

*University/College URL:* http://www.ipsl.org $8 (Nonprofit educational organization)

*SL Program/Center Name:* International Partnership for Service-Learning

*Contact Person Name and Title:* Howard A. Berry, Pres

*Contact Phone Number:* (212) 986–0989

*Contact Fax Number:* (212) 986–5039

*Contact Email Address:* pslny@aol.com

*SL Program/Center URL:* http://www.ipsl.org

*SL Online Course Description URL:* http://www.ipsl.org

*SL Online Syllabi URL:* http://www.ipsl.org

*Description:* The International Partnership for Service-Learning is a nonprofit educational organization that conducts undergraduate and graduate programs (for a semester, year, or summer) which join academic studies and substantive community service in 11 countries: the Czech Republic, Ecuador, England, France, India, Israel, Jamaica, Mexico, the Philippines, Scotland, and South Dakota, USA (with Native Americans). Students come from over 400 U.S. and other colleges and universities. Most are undergraduates, but an increasing number are graduate students. The IPSL is basically funded by student fees, but some support from foundations allows development activities. There is a minority participation of 22 percent.

*SL Undergraduate Program Name:* International Service-Learning

*SL Undergraduate Program Description:* 12–15 credits a semester. 6–9 credits for summer. All programs are based at an in-country university. Financial aid applies.

*SL Graduate Program Name:* M.A. Degree in International Service

*SL Graduate Program Description:* The M.A. program is designed to prepare students for careers in the field of international nonprofit organizations. Students spend a semester in either Mexico or Jamaica doing graduate studies and research on nonprofit service organizations combined with actual community-service experience. All students join in the second semester in England at the degree-granting institution, University of Surrey Roehampton. They continue graduate studies about management and organization of nonprofits, and continue their service agency experience. A thesis topic is developed with thesis tutors during both semesters. The thesis incorporates aspects from both semesters, and it is written in the form of policy and/or funding recommendations showing understanding of the issues, needs, and management of nonprofit organizations.

*SL Degrees Offered:* M.A. Degree in International Service

*Number of Undergraduate SL Courses Offered Per Year:* 50

*Number of Graduate SL Courses Offered Per Year:* 10

*Total Number of SL Courses Offered Per Year:* 60

*Number of Instructors Teaching SL Courses Per Year:* 50

## Iowa Wesleyan College

601 North Main St, Mount Pleasant, IA 52641

*University/College URL:* http://www.iwc.edu

*Type of Institution:* private, college, teaching

*SL Program/Center Name:* Responsible Social Involvement Program

*Contact Person Name and Title:* Jerry Naylor, Dir

*Contact Phone Number:* (319) 385–6362

*Contact Fax Number:* (319) 385–6363

*Contact Email Address:* iwcrsi@iwc.edu

*SL Program/Center URL:* http://www.iwc.edu/Common%20Pages/Site%20Map/index.htm

*Description:* Responsible Social Involvement (RSI) is a special form of experiential learning. It requires a community-service project, a major academic paper, and a presentation to a faculty committee, based on the learning and discoveries made by the student during the project. RSI has been requirement for all college graduates for over 30 years. RSI is housed directly under the Academic Dean.

*SL Required for Graduation (all students)?* Yes

*Service Required for Graduation (all students)?* No

*Any Co-curricular Service?* No

*Any SL Residence Halls or Theme Houses?* No

*Total Number of SL Courses Offered Per Year:* 0

*Number of Instructors Teaching SL Courses Per Year:* 0

*Number of Full-time SL Staff on Campus (not counting instructors):* 2 (Dir and Admin Assist)

*Number of Part-time SL Staff on Campus (not counting instructors):* 0

## Jacksonville University

2800 University Blvd North, Jacksonville, FL 32211–3394

*University/College URL:* http://www.ju.edu

*Type of Institution:* private, university

*SL Program/Center Name:* Community Service Center

*Contact Person Name and Title:* Christine Tyler, Dir, Community Service

*Contact Phone Number:* (904) 745–7234

*Contact Fax Number:* (904) 745–7154

*Contact Email Address:* ctyler@ju.edu

*SL Program/Center URL:* http://lake.ju.edu/communitysvc

*Description:* The Community Service Center is committed to enhancing student learning and development and social action through community service that allow students to acquire leadership skills, grow in social responsibility, assess personal values, and develop critical-thinking skills. The center employs a director who advises and guides undergraduate students about fulfilling their 50-hour community-service requirement. A Community Service Student Leadership Team assists with specific projects, recruits students, and provides other support to the director. The center publishes an annual guide to more than 100 service opportunities in the greater metropolitan area as well as develops monthly group projects. In addition, the center created and leads annual projects such as "Days of Thanks & Giving," a week of activities that address hunger and homelessness each November; an Alternative Spring Break program; and the Summer Service Corps, which places work-study students as a team in a nonprofit agency each summer. The center promotes leadership, cultural diversity, and citizenship through service projects, reflection sessions, and other community-building activities.

*SL Required for Graduation (all students)?* No

*Service Required for Graduation (all students)?* Yes (50 hours of community service is required of all undergraduates before graduation)

*Any Co-curricular Service?* No

*Any SL Residence Halls or Theme Houses?* No

## James Madison University

South Main Street, Harrisonburg, VA 22807

*University/College URL:* http://www.jmu.edu

*Type of Institution:* public, university, teaching, secular

*SL Program/Center Name:* Community Service-Learning

*Contact Person Name and Title:* Rich Harris, Assoc Dir, Center for Leadership, Service and Transitions

*Contact Phone Number:* (540) 568–3463

*Contact Fax Number:* (540) 568–6719

*Contact Email Address:* harrisra@jmu.edu

*SL Program/Center URL:* http://www.jmu. edu/clst/CS-L/

*Description:* Community Service-Learning (CS-L) is located in the Center for Leadership, Service and Transitions. CS-L is a partnership between Student and Academic Affairs. Its learning goals include linking the service experience to the academic curriculum, personal development, and developing lifelong service involvement. CS-L accomplishes these learning goals through the following kinds of partnerships and programs: faculty development through grants and training; student leadership through paid service staff positions; leadership training; service-learning courses; alternative spring break; action research and community development through grants; and partnerships with over 100 community partners.

*SL Required for Graduation (all students)?* No

*Service Required for Graduation (all students)?* No

*Any Co-curricular Service?* Yes

*Any SL Residence Halls or Theme Houses?* No

*Number of Undergraduate SL Courses Offered Per Year:* 30

*Number of Graduate SL Courses Offered Per Year:* 0

*Total Number of SL Courses Offered Per Year:* 30

*Number of Instructors Teaching SL Courses Per Year:* 30

*Number of Full-time SL Staff on Campus (not counting instructors):* 1

*Number of Part-time SL Staff on Campus (not counting instructors):* 13 (12 undergraduate students and 1 graduate student staff the center)

## John Carroll University

20700 North Park Blvd, University Heights, OH 44118

*University/College URL:* http://www.jcu.edu

*Type of Institution:* private, university, teaching, research, religious

*SL Program/Center Name:* Center for Community Service

*Contact Person Name and Title:* Dr. Mark C. Falbo

*Contact Phone Number:* (216) 397–4698
*Contact Fax Number:* (216) 397–1661
*Contact Email Address:* mfalbo@jcu.edu
*SL Program/Center URL:* http://www.jcu.edu/COMSERV/index.htm
*SL Online Course Description URL:* http://www.jcu.edu/COMSERV/sl01.htm
*Description:* The Center for Community Service was founded in 1992 to promote the integration of service and learning at John Carroll University. The center supports faculty by developing service activities and opportunities related to course goals and objectives, by scheduling transportation and creating service-learning partnerships with community-based organizations and agencies. The center is committed to providing high-quality community-service opportunities for students, faculty, and staff, especially in support of faculty service-learning that meets real community needs, in particular the needs of the most vulnerable members of local communities.
*SL Required for Graduation (all students)?* No
*Service Required for Graduation (all students)?* No
*Any Co-curricular Service?* Yes
*Any SL Residence Halls or Theme Houses?* No
*Number of Undergraduate SL Courses Offered Per Year:* 20–25
*Number of Graduate SL Courses Offered Per Year:* 5
*Total Number of SL Courses Offered Per Year:* 25–30
*Number of Instructors Teaching SL Courses Per Year:* 40
*Number of Full-time SL Staff on Campus (not counting instructors):* 2
*Number of Part-time SL Staff on Campus (not counting instructors):* 2

**Johnson & Wales University**
8 Abbott Park Pl, Providence, RI 02903–3703
*University/College URL:* http://www.jwu.edu
*Type of Institution:* private, university, teaching
*SL Program/Center Name:* Alan Shawn Feinstein Community Service Center

*Contact Person Name and Title:* Judith Turchetta, Dir, The Alan Shawn Feinstein Enriching America Program, Community Service Learning, and Assoc Prof, Social Sciences
*Contact Phone Number:* (401) 598–1266
*Contact Fax Number:* (401) 598–1277
*Description:* Johnson & Wales University made a commitment to the Feinstein Community Service Learning Center in September 1996, with the inclusion of Community Service Learning (CSL) options in all university programs, the creation of a 10-hour CSL theoretical course, and the adoption of a policy requirement that students complete a CSL experiential component, in conjunction with a course or practicum experience. Students begin the academic program by taking a 10-hour course in their freshman year that introduces them to the underlying philosophies associated with community service-learning. They are then required to complete an experiential component in conjunction with one of their academic classes or "practicum" programs. Through the experiential component, students agree to volunteer approximately 10 to 20 hours of service to a not-for-profit agency, over the course of one academic term. Students choose their own site placements from a predesignated list of offerings that have been matched to specific courses, through which the volunteer options are offered. Students earn minimal credit for their volunteer work. Instead, they are more heavily evaluated on the academic project that is assigned to them in class that links their service to the content taught in the respective course. Students reflect upon their volunteer experience in a weekly-reflection log-in booklet. Through their participation in CSL, students strengthen their understanding of civic responsibility through hands-on experience with complicated social issues that might otherwise remain intangible to them. Fulfillment of the graduation requirement is fully contingent upon successful completion of all of the above-stated components.
*SL Required for Graduation (all students)?* Yes

*Service Required for Graduation (all students)?* No

*Any Co-curricular Service?* No

*Any SL Residence Halls or Theme Houses?* No

*Number of Undergraduate SL Courses Offered Per Year:* 79

*Number of Graduate SL Courses Offered Per Year:* 0 (But CSL will be offered in graduate courses in the future.)

*Total Number of SL Courses Offered Per Year:* 79

*Number of Instructors Teaching SL Courses Per Year:* 85

*Number of Full-time SL Staff on Campus (not counting instructors):* 6

*Number of Part-time SL Staff on Campus (not counting instructors):* 1

**Johnson County Community College**
12345 College Blvd, Overland Park, KS 66210

*University/College URL:* http://www. johnco.cc.ks.us

*Type of Institution:* public, community college, teaching

*SL Program/Center Name:* Service-Learning Program

*Contact Person Name and Title:* Marcia Shideler, Service-Learning Coord

*Contact Phone Number:* (913) 469–8500, ext 3570

*Contact Fax Number:* (913) 469–3825

*Contact Email Address:* shideler@jccc.net

*SL Program/Center URL:* http://www.jccc. net/careers/serv_learn

*Description:* Since 1993, service-learning opportunities have been offered at Johnson County Community College. Through a variety of courses and programs, students have combined academic instruction with service at over 100 community sites in the Kansas City area, thus increasing participant understanding, skills, and involvement in and addressing of community needs. A co-curricular, international service-learning project sends a team of students, faculty, and staff each year to the developing community of Las Pintas, Mexico.

*SL Required for Graduation (all students)?* No

*Service Required for Graduation (all students)?* No

*Any Co-curricular Service?* Yes

*Any SL Residence Halls or Theme Houses?* No

*Number of Undergraduate SL Courses Offered Per Year:* 25–30

*Number of Graduate SL Courses Offered Per Year:* 0

*Total Number of SL Courses Offered Per Year:* 25–30

*Number of Instructors Teaching SL Courses Per Year:* 30–35

*Number of Full-time SL Staff on Campus (not counting instructors):* 0

*Number of Part-time SL Staff on Campus (not counting instructors):* 1

**Juniata College**
1700 Moore St, Huntingdon, PA 16652

*University/College URL:* http://www. juniata.edu

*Type of Institution:* private, college

*Contact Person Name and Title:* Jenell J. Patton, Community Service Coord

*Contact Phone Number:* (814) 641–3365

*Contact Fax Number:* (814) 641–3317

*Contact Email Address:* pattonj@juniata.edu

*Description:* Juniata College is currently in the process of developing its service-learning program. At present, it operates out of the Campus Ministry Office and budget. Juniata offers a one-credit service-learning course open to second-semester freshmen, juniors, and seniors. Students can take this course four times throughout their college career. They volunteer 27 hours of service and have three hours of class time (pre, during, and post reflective exercises). The college is in the process of determining which courses already offer service-learning components and which courses are likely candidates for service-learning. The college also sponsors a service-learning trip during Spring Break. The trip alternates between domestic to international destinations every other year.

*SL Required for Graduation (all students)?* No

*Service Required for Graduation (all students)?* No

*Any Co-curricular Service?* Yes
*Any SL Residence Halls or Theme Houses?* No
*Number of Undergraduate SL Courses Offered Per Year:* 2
*Number of Graduate SL Courses Offered Per Year:* 0
*Total Number of SL Courses Offered Per Year:* 2
*Number of Instructors Teaching SL Courses Per Year:* 1
*Number of Full-time SL Staff on Campus (not counting instructors):* 0
*Number of Part-time SL Staff on Campus (not counting instructors):* 1

**Kansas State University**
119 Anderson Hall, (Office of Admissions), Manhattan, KS 66506
*University/College URL:* http://www.ksu.edu
*Type of Institution:* public, university, research
*SL Program/Center Name:* Community Service Program
*Contact Person Name and Title:* Carol Peak, Dir
*Contact Phone Number:* (785) 532–5701
*Contact Fax Number:* (785) 532–0671
*Contact Email Address:* ksuserve@ksu.edu
*SL Program/Center URL:* http://www. ksu.edu/csp
*SL Online Course Description URL:* http:// www.ksu.edu/csp/lands/courses.html
*Description:* The Community Service Program allows students with various majors and backgrounds to participate in meaningful and challenging service-learning projects in the community, the state of Kansas, and international sites. The CSP houses six student-run programs, including International Summer Teams, Kansas Summer Teams, CSP Tutoring, America Reads/America Counts, Learn and Serve, and CALL (Community Action for Leadership and Learning). All programs use the service-learning model of preparation, service participation, and meaningful reflection to enhance students' participation in programs that address local and international needs.
*SL Required for Graduation (all students)?* No

*Service Required for Graduation (all students)?* No
*Any Co-curricular Service?* Yes
*Any SL Residence Halls or Theme Houses?* No
*Number of Undergraduate SL Courses Offered Per Year:* 11
*Number of Graduate SL Courses Offered Per Year:* 0
*Total Number of SL Courses Offered Per Year:* 11
*Number of Instructors Teaching SL Courses Per Year:* 12
*Number of Full-time SL Staff on Campus (not counting instructors):* 2
*Number of Part-time SL Staff on Campus (not counting instructors):* 7

**Kean University**
1000 Morris Ave, Union, NJ 07083
*University/College URL:* http://www. kean.edu
*Type of Institution:* public, university, teaching
*SL Program/Center Name:* Kean in Community—Service-Learning Program
*Contact Person Name and Title:* Heather Sullivan-Catlin, Dir, Asst Prof, Sociology
*Contact Phone Number:* (908) 527–2090
*Contact Fax Number:* (908) 527–9014
*Contact Email Address:* sullcat@worldnet.att.net
*Description:* The current service-learning program at Kean is very new and is still in its pilot stage. Its goal is to create service-learning courses across the curriculum. The program employs a fourth-credit model. Service-learning sections of undergraduate and graduate courses have a co-requisite one-credit module in recognition of the additional work required. Faculty wishing to incorporate service-learning into an existing course do so by developing a service-learning project and working with the director of Cooperative Education to establish community partners. The program has two part-time staff members. The faculty director works with faculty to develop new courses and is compensated by a one-course reduction in teaching load. The director of the cooperative-education program also works on service-learn-

ing by developing relationships with community partners and matching students with them. A service-learning advisory board (made up primarily of faculty involved with service-learning) has also been established to help develop policies for the program. It is funded through the university president's strategic-initiatives program.

*SL Required for Graduation (all students)?* No

*Service Required for Graduation (all students)?* No

*Any Co-curricular Service?* Yes

*Any SL Residence Halls or Theme Houses?* No

*Number of Undergraduate SL Courses Offered Per Year:* 10

*Number of Graduate SL Courses Offered Per Year:* 4

*Total Number of SL Courses Offered Per Year:* 14

*Number of Instructors Teaching SL Courses Per Year:* 14

*Number of Full-time SL Staff on Campus (not counting instructors):* 0

*Number of Part-time SL Staff on Campus (not counting instructors):* 2

**Kennebec Valley Technical College**
92 Western Ave, Fairfield, ME 04937
*University/College URL:* http://www.kvtc.net
*Type of Institution:* public, college, teaching
*Contact Person Name and Title:* Ann M. Davis, RN, MSN, Service Learning Supervisor
*Contact Phone Number:* (207) 459–5193
*Contact Fax Number:* (207) 453–5194
*Contact Email Address:* kadavis@kvtc.net
*Description:* Norridgewock Central Grade School Afterschool Program is a primary locus of service-learning at Kennebec Valley Technical College. It was designed to benefit children, communities, and KVTC students. A steering committee determined the focus of the program, which began in Fall 1999. The program was funded by the Corporation for National and Community Service. In addition to Norridgewock Central Grade School Afterschool Program, service-learning occurs through America Reads and America Counts

programs, as well as through other service-learning opportunities.

*SL Required for Graduation (all students)?* No

*Service Required for Graduation (all students)?* No

*Any Co-curricular Service?* Yes

*Any SL Residence Halls or Theme Houses?* No

*Number of Undergraduate SL Courses Offered Per Year:* 8

*Number of Graduate SL Courses Offered Per Year:* 0

*Total Number of SL Courses Offered Per Year:* 8

*Number of Instructors Teaching SL Courses Per Year:* 5

*Number of Full-time SL Staff on Campus (not counting instructors):* 1

*Number of Part-time SL Staff on Campus (not counting instructors):* 0

**La Salle University**
1900 W Olney Ave, PO Box 829, Philadelphia, PA 19141
*University/College URL:* http://www.lasalle.edu
*Type of Institution:* private, university, teaching, religious
*SL Program/Center Name:* Center for Community Service and Learning
*Contact Person Name and Title:* Louise Giugliano, Dir
*Contact Phone Number:* (215) 951–1804
*Contact Fax Number:* 215) 951–1411
*Contact Email Address:* Giugliano@lasalle.edu
*SL Program/Center URL:* http://www.lasalle.edu/services/comlearn/comlearn.htm
*Description:* The Center for Community Service and Learning's mission is to prepare La Salle students for service and progressive leadership in their communities and to assist community members to reach their own personal goals of academic achievement. The ultimate outcome sought is to join the forces of personal and collective engagement to achieve a better life for the community and beyond. The center's community-service-learning approach is one based on the values of equality, justice, and

civic responsibility. Community-service-learning puts theory into practice. Participants meet community needs while developing their ability to think critically, solve problems collectively, and deepen their commitment to improving life for all.

*SL Required for Graduation (all students)?* No

*Service Required for Graduation (all students)?* No

*Any Co-curricular Service?* Yes

*Any SL Residence Halls or Theme Houses?* No

*Number of Full-time SL Staff on Campus (not counting instructors):* 2

*Number of Part-time SL Staff on Campus (not counting instructors):* 1

## Lafayette College
Easton, PA 18042

*University/College URL:* http://www.lafayette.edu

*Type of Institution:* private, college, teaching

*SL Program/Center Name:* Community Outreach Center

*Contact Person Name and Title:* Gary R. Miller, Chaplain

*Contact Phone Number:* (610) 330–5320

*Contact Fax Number:* (610) 330–5509

*Contact Email Address:* millerg@lafayette.edu

*SL Program/Center URL:* http://www.lafayette.edu/outreach/home.html

*SL Online Course Description URL:* http://www.lafayette.edu/outreach/courses.html

*SL Online Syllabi URL:* http://www.lafayette.edu/millerg/fys/fyshome.html

*Description:* The Community Outreach Center provides opportunities for student volunteer work in the local community. The center offers over twenty volunteer programs for working with children of all ages, prison inmates, nursing home residents, shelter residents and environmental concerns. The center is staffed with a community outreach coordinator and a student intern staff of 20.

*SL Required for Graduation (all students)?* No

*Service Required for Graduation (all students)?* No

*Any Co-curricular Service?* Yes

*Any SL Residence Halls or Theme Houses?* Yes

*Number of Undergraduate SL Courses Offered Per Year:* 6

*Number of Graduate SL Courses Offered Per Year:* 0

*Total Number of SL Courses Offered Per Year:* 6

*Number of Instructors Teaching SL Courses Per Year:* 5

*Number of Full-time SL Staff on Campus (not counting instructors):* 0

*Number of Part-time SL Staff on Campus (not counting instructors):* 21 (one coordinator and twenty student interns)

## LaGrange College
601 Broad St, LaGrange, GA 30240

*University/College URL:* http://www.lgc.edu

*Type of Institution:* private, college, teaching, religious

*SL Program/Center Name:* Servant Leadership Initiative

*Contact Person Name and Title:* Bob Thomas, Dir

*Contact Phone Number:* (706) 812–7248

*Contact Email Address:* rthomas@lgc.edu

*Description:* The Servant Leadership Initiative, funded by a grant from the Bradley-Turner Foundation, aims to integrate the principles of servant leadership throughout the college community through outreach and education of faculty, students, staff, and community leaders in the city of LaGrange. Servant leadership, service learning, and community service are intertwined throughout the curriculum and student life offerings of the college.

*SL Required for Graduation (all students)?* Yes

*Service Required for Graduation (all students)?* Yes

*Any Co-curricular Service?* Yes

*Any SL Residence Halls or Theme Houses?* No

*Number of Undergraduate SL Courses Offered Per Year:* 2

*Total Number of SL Courses Offered Per Year:* 2

*Number of Instructors Teaching SL Courses Per Year:* 15

*Number of Full-time SL Staff on Campus (not counting instructors):* 1

*Number of Part-time SL Staff on Campus (not counting instructors):* 0

## Lehigh University

27 Memorial Dr West, Bethlehem, PA 18015–3000

*University/College URL:* http://www.lehigh.edu

*Type of Institution:* private, university, teaching, secular

*SL Program/Center Name:* Community Service Program; Provost's Ventures Program

*Contact Person Name and Title:* Julie De Motte, Community Service Program Coord; Dr. Todd Watkins, Assoc Prof of Economics, Faculty Fellow, The Ventures Program; Dr. Henry Odi, Dir, Adj Prof, Office of Academic Outreach

*Contact Phone Number:* (610) 758–5445

*Contact Fax Number:* (610) 758–6692

*Contact Email Address:* service@lehigh.edu; jud2@lehigh.edu; taw4@lehigh.edu; huo0@lehigh.edu

*SL Program/Center URL:* http://www.lehigh.edu/~service/center.html; http://www2.lehigh.edu/page.asp?page=ventures; http://www2.lehigh.edu/page.asp?page=academicoutreach

*SL Online Course Description URL:* http://www.lehigh.edu/~service/csfaculty2.htm

*Description:* Service learning is supported primarily by three different areas of the university. The Office of Academic Outreach sponsors campus-based service projects. The Provost's Ventures Program funds experiential and service-learning faculty initiatives. Finally, the Community Service Center supports faculty with the implementation of their courses. The Provost's Venture Program is run by faculty and has recently produced some creative service-learning initiatives including ''Chempals'' (an interdisciplinary effort to mentor children using e-mail) and a Prejudice Reduction Theatre Troupe that works with neighborhood children.

*SL Required for Graduation (all students)?* No

*Service Required for Graduation (all students)?* No

*Any Co-curricular Service?* Yes

*Any SL Residence Halls or Theme Houses?* No

*Number of Undergraduate SL Courses Offered Per Year:* 20

*Number of Graduate SL Courses Offered Per Year:* 10

*Total Number of SL Courses Offered Per Year:* 30

*Number of Instructors Teaching SL Courses Per Year:* 25

*Number of Full-time SL Staff on Campus (not counting instructors):* 1

*Number of Part-time SL Staff on Campus (not counting instructors):* 4

## Lethbridge Community College

3000 College Drive South, Lethbridge, Alberta, Canada T1K 1L6

*University/College URL:* http://www.lethbridgecollege.ab.ca

*Type of Institution:* community college, teaching, research

*SL Program/Center Name:* Community Service Learning

*Contact Person Name and Title:* Vicki-Lynn Hegedus, Placement Specialist

*Contact Phone Number:* (403) 320–3283

*Contact Fax Number:* (403) 317–3503

*Contact Email Address:* vlhegedu@raptor.lethbridgec.ab.ca

*SL Program/Center URL:* http://www.lethbridgecollege.ab.ca/serc/cso.html

*Description:* Community Service Learning is a program which connects the curriculum to volunteerism within the community. This program operates in the context of the general-education curriculum, and, unlike traditional work experience or practicum models of industry placements, Community Service Learning connects learners with not-for-profit organizations or public-service agencies. Community Service Learning offers learners academically based experiences of volunteerism which focus on such values as understanding, human diversity, social justice, human solidarity, and engaged citizenship. Community Service Learning is funded by the Wild Rose Foundation of Alberta, and a grant from the G.L. Talbot Educational Endowment.

*SL Required for Graduation (all students)?* No

*Service Required for Graduation (all students)?* No

*Any Co-curricular Service?* Yes

*Any SL Residence Halls or Theme Houses?* No

*Number of Undergraduate SL Courses Offered Per Year:* 3–5

*Total Number of SL Courses Offered Per Year:* 3–5

*Number of Instructors Teaching SL Courses Per Year:* 7

*Number of Full-time SL Staff on Campus (not counting instructors):* 0

*Number of Part-time SL Staff on Campus (not counting instructors):* 1

**Longwood College**

201 High St, Lancaster 158, Farmville, VA 23909

*University/College URL:* http://www.lwc.edu

*Type of Institution:* public, college, teaching

*SL Program/Center Name:* GIVE Office (Groups & Individuals Volunteering Efforts)

*Contact Person Name and Title:* Ellen L. Masters, Coord of Volunteer, Service-Learning

*Contact Phone Number:* (804) 395–2397

*Contact Fax Number:* (804) 395–2347

*Contact Email Address:* emasters@longwood.lwc.edu; givelwc@longwood.lwc.edu

*Description:* The GIVE Office is a branch of Student Affairs which provides the Longwood Community (consisting of faculty, staff, administrators, alumni, and ultimately students) with volunteer and service-learning placements in Farmville and surrounding communities. The purpose of GIVE is to positively affect the Longwood community by promoting and enhancing campus-based community service and service-learning. Volunteers give of their time and abilities, independently or with student groups, to help local service agencies that have

requested assistance. The goal of the GIVE Program is to enable students to help others while incorporating service into the learning component of their classroom experiences. GIVE is committed to the concept, vision, and process of learning through the practice of career development, experiential learning, and related disciplines.

*SL Required for Graduation (all students)?* No (However, it is required for some majors.)

*Service Required for Graduation (all students)?* No

*Any Co-curricular Service?* Yes

*Any SL Residence Halls or Theme Houses?* No

*Number of Undergraduate SL Courses Offered Per Year:* 1

*Number of Graduate SL Courses Offered Per Year:* 0

*Total Number of SL Courses Offered Per Year:* 1

*Number of Instructors Teaching SL Courses Per Year:* 3

*Number of Full-time SL Staff on Campus (not counting instructors):* 1

*Number of Part-time SL Staff on Campus (not counting instructors):* 1 (an AmeriCorps VCCC member)

**Louisiana State University**

Learning Assistance Center, B-31 Coates Hall, Baton Rouge, LA 70803

*University/College URL:* http://www.lsu.edu

*Type of Institution:* public, university, research

*SL Program/Center Name:* LSU PLUS (Program of Learning ThrU Service)

*Contact Person Name and Title:* Bobbie Shaffett, Service Learning Coord

*Contact Phone Number:* (225)388–2872

*Contact Fax Number:* (225)388–5762

*Contact Email Address:* bshaffe@lsu.edu

*SL Program/Center URL:* http://www.lac.lsu.edu/lsuplus/lsuplus.htm

*SL Online Course Description URL:* http://www.lac.lsu.edu/lsuplus/courses.html

*Description:* Learning ThrU Service (LSU PLUS) helps students apply complex course concepts to real-life situations in the Baton

Rouge community. Instructors in selected courses in English, philosophy, speech, and sociology integrate optional or required service-learning projects into academic assignments. LSU PLUS office staff assist students, faculty, and community agencies by matching needs, facilitating partnerships, tracking service hours or projects, and training new faculty or agency partners.

*SL Required for Graduation (all students)?* No

*Service Required for Graduation (all students)?* No

*Any Co-curricular Service?* Yes

*Any SL Residence Halls or Theme Houses?* No

*Number of Undergraduate SL Courses Offered Per Year:* 25

*Number of Graduate SL Courses Offered Per Year:* 0

*Total Number of SL Courses Offered Per Year:* 25

*Number of Instructors Teaching SL Courses Per Year:* 13

*Number of Full-time SL Staff on Campus (not counting instructors):* 1

*Number of Part-time SL Staff on Campus (not counting instructors):* 0

**Loyola College in Maryland**
4501 N Charles St, Cohn 3, Baltimore, MD 21201

*University/College URL:* http://www. loyola.edu

*Type of Institution:* private, university, religious

*SL Program/Center Name:* Center for Values and Service

*Contact Person Name and Title:* Susan Burton, Assoc Dir of Service-learning

*Contact Phone Number:* (410) 617–2092

*Contact Fax Number:* (410) 617–2052

*Contact Email Address:* sburton@loyola.edu

*SL Program/Center URL:* http://nmc. loyola.edu/cvs/

*Description:* The Center for Values and Service provides opportunities for Loyola students, faculty, and staff to incorporate service into

their education through work with over 70 community-based organizations and programs in and around Baltimore. It also organizes service-immersion programs and promotes social-justice education through reflection discussions, lecture series, and the integration of service into the academic curriculum (service-learning).

Service Leadership Program: This is a new (1998) program designed to provide rigorous academic experience for students who are drawn to community service and issues of social justice. Built on Loyola's tradition in service-learning, the program combines a series of required and elective components that creates an integrated experience in service and leadership. Over four years, participating students pursue their own separate disciplinary interests while coming together in a series of one-credit practica (e.g. Immersion Experience) and, finally, a capstone seminar. The core issues addressed throughout the program are social justice; the relationship between individual and community as it is has been variously understood; the notion of "good community"; civic literacy; the application of leadership theories to the challenges of service; and, service itself— exploring its roots, its methods and its hazards.

*SL Required for Graduation (all students)?* No

*Service Required for Graduation (all students)?* No

*Any Co-curricular Service?* Yes

*Any SL Residence Halls or Theme Houses?* No

*SL Degrees Offered:* Service Leadership Program Certificate

*Number of Undergraduate SL Courses Offered Per Year:* 55–60

*Number of Graduate SL Courses Offered Per Year:* 0–1

*Total Number of SL Courses Offered Per Year:* 55–60

*Number of Instructors Teaching SL Courses Per Year:* 30–35

*Number of Full-time SL Staff on Campus (not counting instructors):* 1

*Number of Part-time SL Staff on Campus (not counting instructors):* 4

**Loyola University Chicago**

Center for Urban Research and Learning, 820 N Michigan Ave, 10th floor, Chicago, IL 60611

*University/College URL:* http://www.luc.edu

*Type of Institution:* private, university, research, religious

*SL Program/Center Name:* Service Learning Program

*Contact Person Name and Title:* Kimberly Fox, Service Learning Coord

*Contact Phone Number:* (312) 915–7765

*Contact Fax Number:* (312) 915–7770

*Contact Email Address:* kfox1@luc.edu

*SL Program/Center URL:* http://www.luc.edu/depts/servicelearning

*Description:* Service-learning at Loyola University Chicago offers students the opportunity to engage in course-relevant, community-focused service that connects academic pursuits and community action. The Chicago location provides a wide variety of activities and a vibrant urban environment for students to meet community needs and advance their education. Service-learning is available in a variety of fields as either an option or course requirement. While completion of service-learning courses is not a requirement for graduation, it offers students the opportunity to fulfill the mission of Loyola University Chicago's Jesuit heritage and obtain knowledge in the service of humanity.

*SL Required for Graduation (all students)?* No

*Service Required for Graduation (all students)?* No

*Any Co-curricular Service?* Yes

*Any SL Residence Halls or Theme Houses?* Yes

*Number of Undergraduate SL Courses Offered Per Year:* 25–30

*Number of Graduate SL Courses Offered Per Year:* 0

*Total Number of SL Courses Offered Per Year:* 25–30

*Number of Instructors Teaching SL Courses Per Year:* 15–20

*Number of Full-time SL Staff on Campus (not counting instructors):* 1

*Number of Part-time SL Staff on Campus (not counting instructors):* 0

**Lycoming College**

700 College Pl, Campus Box 149, Williamsport, PA 17701

*University/College URL:* http://www.lycoming.edu

*Type of Institution:* private, college, teaching

*SL Program/Center Name:* Community Service Center

*Contact Person Name and Title:* Marco Hunsberger, Dir

*Contact Phone Number:* (570) 321–4165

*Contact Fax Number:* (570) 321–4337

*Contact Email Address:* hunsberg@lycoming.edu

*SL Program/Center URL:* http://www.lycoming.edu/dept/cscenter

*Description:* The Community Service Center of Lycoming College acts as a liaison between students, faculty, and staff and community organizations in the greater Williamsport area. The center provides an environment for student learning through service and reflection. It helps students looking for volunteer opportunities to find local agencies best suited for them. The center maintains contact with local agencies in order to keep informed of their work and to be aware of the types of student who best fit their needs.

*SL Required for Graduation (all students)?* No

*Service Required for Graduation (all students)?* No

*Any Co-curricular Service?* Yes

*Any SL Residence Halls or Theme Houses?* No

*Number of Undergraduate SL Courses Offered Per Year:* 4

*Total Number of SL Courses Offered Per Year:* 4

*Number of Instructors Teaching SL Courses Per Year:* 5

**Macalester College**

1600 Grand Ave, St. Paul, MN 55105

*University/College URL:* http://www.macalester.edu

*Type of Institution:* private, college, teaching, secular(historically Presbyterian but nonsectarian)

*SL Program/Center Name:* Community Service Office

*Contact Person Name and Title:* Karin Trail-Johnson, Dir

*Contact Phone Number:* (651) 696–6040

*Contact Fax Number:* (651) 696–6030

*Contact Email Address:* trailjohnson@macalester.edu

*SL Program/Center URL:* http://www.macalester.edu/~cso

*Description:* The Community Service Office encourages members of the Macalester community to engage in community work by sponsoring weekly volunteer opportunities as well as several one-time events. The office also coordinates the Off-Campus Student Employment Program (work study), works with faculty who include a service-learning or action-research component in their courses, and provides guidance to student and alumni groups and campus offices interested in service activities.

*SL Required for Graduation (all students)?* No

*Service Required for Graduation (all students)?* No

*Any Co-curricular Service?* Yes

*Any SL Residence Halls or Theme Houses?* No

*Number of Undergraduate SL Courses Offered Per Year:* 10

*Total Number of SL Courses Offered Per Year:* 10

*Number of Instructors Teaching SL Courses Per Year:* 15

*Number of Full-time SL Staff on Campus (not counting instructors):* 3 (2 + 1 VISTA)

*Number of Part-time SL Staff on Campus (not counting instructors):* 1 (support staff)

**Marian College**

3200 Cold Spring Rd, Indianapolis, IN 46222–1997

*University/College URL:* http://www.marian.edu

*Type of Institution:* private, college, teaching, religious

*Contact Person Name and Title:* Sr. Norma Rocklage, VP for Mission Effectiveness

*Contact Phone Number:* (317) 955–6378

*Contact Fax Number:* (317) 955–6448

*Description:* Marian College has several mentoring programs which work with adolescents and children in the Indianapolis area. Many professors embed service-learning into their courses. The Education Department has been working for three years to embed service-learning into its coursework for beginning teachers.

*SL Required for Graduation (all students)?* No

*Service Required for Graduation (all students)?* No

*Any Co-curricular Service?* No

*Any SL Residence Halls or Theme Houses?* No

*Number of Undergraduate SL Courses Offered Per Year:* 6+

*Total Number of SL Courses Offered Per Year:* 6+

*Number of Instructors Teaching SL Courses Per Year:* 5–7

*Number of Full-time SL Staff on Campus (not counting instructors):* 1

*Number of Part-time SL Staff on Campus (not counting instructors):* 2

**Marquette University**

Brooks Hall 100, PO Box 1881, Milwaukee, WI 53201–1881

*University/College URL:* http://www.mu.edu

*Type of Institution:* private, university, teaching, religious

*SL Program/Center Name:* Service Learning Program

*Contact Person Name and Title:* Bobbi Timberlake, SLP Admin

*Contact Phone Number:* (414) 288–3261

*Contact Fax Number:* (414) 288–3259

*Contact Email Address:* Barbara.Timberlake@marquette.edu

*SL Program/Center URL:* http://www.marquette.edu/servicelearning/

*Description:* Service Learning at Marquette is housed within the Institute for Urban Life, under the Division of Academic Affairs. Each semester, about 700 students from 40–50 courses perform service at 75–90 community agencies. Students choosing the service-learning option are required to produce some evidence for their professors that they learned something about the course by working in the community. They are graded on this demonstration of knowledge, not on the service provided. The Service Learning Program has a staff of 2 professionals and 14 students. Program operations include recruitment and training of faculty, setting up placements and maintaining relationships with community partners, registering service learners and assisting them as they begin their service work, addressing problems, collecting feedback from service learners, faculty, and community agency representatives. The program is fully institutionalized within the university budget.

*SL Required for Graduation (all students)?* No

*Service Required for Graduation (all students)?* No

*Any Co-curricular Service?* Yes

*Any SL Residence Halls or Theme Houses?* No

*Number of Undergraduate SL Courses Offered Per Year:* 70–85

*Number of Graduate SL Courses Offered Per Year:* 0

*Total Number of SL Courses Offered Per Year:* 70–85

*Number of Instructors Teaching SL Courses Per Year:* 57

*Number of Full-time SL Staff on Campus (not counting instructors):* 2

*Number of Part-time SL Staff on Campus (not counting instructors):* 14

## Marywood University (and the University of Scranton)

Scranton, PA 18510

*University/College URL:* http://www.uofs. edu

*Type of Institution:* private, university

*SL Program/Center Name:* Collegiate Volunteers of Marywood University and the University of Scranton

*Contact Person Name and Title:* Catherine Mascelli, Service Learning Coord

*Contact Phone Number:* (570) 941–7429

*Contact Fax Number:* (570) 941–7963

*Contact Email Address:* Collegiate-Vols@uofs.edu

*SL Program/Center URL:* http://academic. scranton.edu/department/ministry/volunt. html

*Description:* Collegiate Volunteers is a collaborative program between the University of Scranton and Marywood University. It maintains information on over 125 community organizations and agencies where students can choose to do their service-learning. In addition to assisting students in the selection of a service site, Collegiate Volunteers assists faculty in designing service-learning components for their courses. Collegiate Volunteers helps with reflection activities and training events. The program is partially funded through a private endowment.

*SL Required for Graduation (all students)?* No

*Service Required for Graduation (all students)?* No

*Any Co-curricular Service?* Yes

*Any SL Residence Halls or Theme Houses?* Yes

*Number of Undergraduate SL Courses Offered Per Year:* 30

*Total Number of SL Courses Offered Per Year:* 30

*Number of Instructors Teaching SL Courses Per Year:* 15

*Number of Full-time SL Staff on Campus (not counting instructors):* 1

*Number of Part-time SL Staff on Campus (not counting instructors):* 3

## Massachusetts College of Liberal Arts

375 Church St, North Adams, MA 01247

*University/College URL:* http://www.mcla. mass.edu

*Type of Institution:* public, college, teaching, research

*SL Program/Center Name:* Learn and Serve and the Center for Service and Citizenship

*Contact Person Name and Title:* Dr. Myles Whitney

*Contact Phone Number:* (314) 662–5473

*Contact Email Address:* mwhitney@mcla.mass.edu

*Description:* Service-learning experiences are interwoven in many courses as well as out-of-class experiences at Massachusetts College of Liberal Arts. It is, therefore, a reasonably well-integrated campus life experience with staff, faculty, and students working with community-based agencies to select, implement, and assess learning and service work. While the college is the primary funding agent, grants from the Massachusetts Campus Compact and Service Alliance support the work as well.

*SL Required for Graduation (all students)?* No

*Service Required for Graduation (all students)?* No

*Any Co-curricular Service?* Yes

*Any SL Residence Halls or Theme Houses?* Yes

*Number of Undergraduate SL Courses Offered Per Year:* 12

*Total Number of SL Courses Offered Per Year:* 12

*Number of Instructors Teaching SL Courses Per Year:* 10

*Number of Full-time SL Staff on Campus (not counting instructors):* 1

*Number of Part-time SL Staff on Campus (not counting instructors):* 0

## Massachusetts College of Pharmacy and Health Sciences, School of Pharmacy-Worcester

66 Vernon St, Worcester, MA 01610

*University/College URL:* http://www.mcp.edu

*Type of Institution:* private, college, teaching, secular

*SL Program/Center Name:* Service Learning Program

*Contact Person Name and Title:* Kevin R. Kearney, Ph.D., Dir of Service Learning, Assoc Prof of Biochemistry

*Contact Phone Number:* (508) 363–2302

*Contact Fax Number:* (508) 755–6215

*Contact Email Address:* kkearney@mcp.edu

*SL Program/Center URL:* http://www.mcp.edu

*Description:* All students in the first year of the three-year Pharm.D. degree program (beginning September 2000) are required to enroll in a one-quarter (out of a four-quarter academic year) service-learning course. Students undertake service work in the local community and reflect on that work in the classroom part of the course.

*SL Required for Graduation (all students)?* Yes

*Service Required for Graduation (all students)?* Yes

*Any Co-curricular Service?* Yes

*Any SL Residence Halls or Theme Houses?* No

*Number of Undergraduate SL Courses Offered Per Year:* 0

*Number of Graduate SL Courses Offered Per Year:* 1

*Total Number of SL Courses Offered Per Year:* 1

*Number of Instructors Teaching SL Courses Per Year:* 1

*Number of Full-time SL Staff on Campus (not counting instructors):* 0

*Number of Part-time SL Staff on Campus (not counting instructors):* 1

## McHenry County College

8900 US Hwy 14, Crystal Lake, IL 60012–2761

*University/College URL:* http://www.mchenry.cc.il.us

*Type of Institution:* public, community college, teaching, secular

*SL Program/Center Name:* Service-Learning

*Contact Person Name and Title:* Dr. Jeanne McDonald, English Instructor

*Contact Phone Number:* (815) 455–8946

*Contact Fax Number:* (815) 455–3762

*Contact Email Address:* jmcdonal@pobox.mchenry.cc.il.us

*Description:* Service-learning is at the core of the college's Composition II course, and service-learning components are included in psychology, speech, Composition I, sociology, health and fitness, and early-childhood-development classes. The college also has a Phi

Theta Kappa chapter, and a Staff Development Day in October, which is given over to community-service projects. All full-time faculty, staff, administrators, and many students participate. In October 1999, over 500 participants worked at 70 project sites throughout McHenry County.
*SL Required for Graduation (all students)?* No
*Service Required for Graduation (all students)?* No
*Any Co-curricular Service?* Yes (Phi Theta Kappa; Staff Development Day)
*Any SL Residence Halls or Theme Houses?* No
*Number of Undergraduate SL Courses Offered Per Year:* 20
*Number of Graduate SL Courses Offered Per Year:* 0
*Total Number of SL Courses Offered Per Year:* 20
*Number of Instructors Teaching SL Courses Per Year:* 9
*Number of Full-time SL Staff on Campus (not counting instructors):* 0
*Number of Part-time SL Staff on Campus (not counting instructors):* 1

**Mesa Community College**
1833 W Southern Ave, Mesa, AZ 85202
*University/College URL:* http://www.mc.maricopa.edu
*Type of Institution:* public, community college
*SL Program/Center Name:* Center for Public Policy and Service
*Contact Person Name and Title:* Susan McGill
*Contact Phone Number:* (480) 461–7393
*Contact Fax Number:* (480) 461–7816
*Contact Email Address:* mcgill@mc.maricopa.edu
*SL Program/Center URL:* http://www.mc.maricopa.edu/stuserv/cppolicy
*Description:* The mission of the Center for Public Policy and Service is to promote service-learning and active participation in the social and political process as an integral part of a community college education in a democracy. The service-learning program provides students with educational opportunities in community

service by placement in government agencies, educational entities, civic organizations, or citizen advocacy groups. Students get involved in service-learning through independent modules offered in 25 disciplines and through courses that integrate service-learning. Students in the Honors Program are required to complete one service-learning credit. The service-learning program provides opportunities in America Reads, the CONNECTOR program, and the 2+4 Grant focusing on welfare reform.
*SL Required for Graduation (all students)?* No (But any student in the honors program must complete one credit of service-learning.)
*Service Required for Graduation (all students)?* No
*Any Co-curricular Service?* No
*Any SL Residence Halls or Theme Houses?* No
*Number of Undergraduate SL Courses Offered Per Year:* 50 (25 courses each semester)
*Number of Graduate SL Courses Offered Per Year:* 0
*Total Number of SL Courses Offered Per Year:* 50 (25 courses each semester)
*Number of Instructors Teaching SL Courses Per Year:* 20

**Messiah College**
1 College Ave, Grantham, PA 17027
*University/College URL:* http://www.messiah.edu
*Type of Institution:* private, college, teaching, religious
*SL Program/Center Name:* Agape Center for Service and Learning
*Contact Person Name and Title:* John W. Eby, Prof, Sociology, Dir, Service-Learning
*Contact Phone Number:* (717) 766–2511
*Contact Fax Number:* (717) 691–6040
*Contact Email Address:* JEby@Messiah.edu
*SL Program/Center URL:* http://www.messiah.edu/ministry/mission-service-home.htm
*SL Online Course Description URL:* http://www.messiah.edu/acdept/epicntr/programs/servlea.htm

*SL Online Syllabi URL:* http://www.messiah.
  edu/hpages/facstaff/jeby/ServlrnI.htm
*Description:* The Agape Center for Service and
Learning coordinates curricular and co-curricular service programs in the local community and around the world: Academic Service-
Learning, Summer Service/Mission Teams,
Community Volunteer Service, Service Teams
during breaks, World Christian Fellowship,
and the West Africa Project sponsored by the
Engineering Department. The Agape Center is
a "one stop" resource for faculty incorporating
service into classes and for students doing
volunteer service.
*SL Required for Graduation (all*
  *students)?* No
*Service Required for Graduation (all stu-*
  *dents)?* No
*Any Co-curricular Service?* Yes (Both "fac-
  ulty"- and student-run)
*Any SL Residence Halls or Theme Houses?*
  Yes [Serving and Living Together
  (SALT) House]
*Number of Undergraduate SL Courses*
  *Offered Per Year:* 20
*Number of Graduate SL Courses Offered*
  *Per Year:* 0
*Total Number of SL Courses Offered Per*
  *Year:* 20
*Number of Instructors Teaching SL Courses*
  *Per Year:* 14
*Number of Full-time SL Staff on Campus*
  *(not counting instructors):* 2
*Number of Part-time SL Staff on Campus*
  *(not counting instructors):* 0.5

**Metropolitan State College of Denver**
Campus Box 7—PO Box 173362, Denver,
  CO 80217–3362
*University/College URL:* http://www.
  mscd.edu
*Type of Institution:* public, college, teaching
*SL Program/Center Name:* Cooperative Edu-
  cation Internship Center
*Contact Person Name and Title:* Dr. Susan
  Warren Lanman, Dir; Ms. Jayne James,
  Assoc Dir
*Contact Phone Number:* (303) 556–3290
*Contact Fax Number:* (303) 556–2091

*Contact Email Address:* lanmans@mscd.edu;
  jamesj@mscd.edu
*Description:* The Service Learning program is
one of three programs in the Cooperative Education Internship Center. It positively integrates
the college with the surrounding community
and fosters an ethic of social responsibility
among students. Students earn credit in their
major or minor field of study while working in
volunteer public and community service related to their academic training. The Service
Learning Program is housed under Academic
Affairs and is funded by the institution.
*SL Required for Graduation (all*
  *students)?* No
*Service Required for Graduation (all stu-*
  *dents)?* No
*Any Co-curricular Service?* No
*Any SL Residence Halls or Theme*
  *Houses?* No
*Number of Instructors Teaching SL Courses*
  *Per Year:* 78
*Number of Full-time SL Staff on Campus*
  *(not counting instructors):* 8.6 (6.6 pro-
  fessional staff, for whom Service-Learn-
  ing is only one-third of their responsibili-
  ties; 2 clerical staff)
*Number of Part-time SL Staff on Campus*
  *(not counting instructors):* 0

**Miami University**
Oxford, OH 45056
*University/College URL:* http://www.
  muohio.edu
*Type of Institution:* public, university, teach-
  ing, secular
*SL Program/Center Name:* Office of Student
  Leadership and Service Learning
*Contact Person Name and Title:* Elizabeth
  O'Reggio-Wilson, Dir
*Contact Phone Number:* (513) 529–2961
*Contact Fax Number:* (513) 529–3445
*Contact Email Address:*
  oreggie@muohio.edu
*SL Program/Center URL:* http://www.
  muohio.edu/mlc/
*Description:* The mission of the Office of Stu-
dent Leadership and Service Learning is to: (a)
engage and support students in classroom and
out-of-classroom opportunities which encour-

age critical self- reflection on and practical application of their exercise of leadership and service on campus and in the surrounding community; (b) prepare students for thoughtful and effective leadership and service to the communities to which they will graduate; and (c) encourage and advance the development of innovative educational opportunities through financial support to and collaboration with faculty, staff, students, alumni, and community members. The office seeks to fulfill this mission in the broadest sense through courses taught; programs designed, implemented, and directed; student staff recruited, trained, and supervised; publications designed and disseminated; grants awarded; and collaboration with campus and community colleagues.

*SL Required for Graduation (all students)?* No

*Service Required for Graduation (all students)?* No

*Any Co-curricular Service?* No

*Any SL Residence Halls or Theme Houses?* Yes (the Residential Service-Learning Program)

*Number of Undergraduate SL Courses Offered Per Year:* 1+ (at least; other discipline-based courses include service-learning as a component)

*Number of Graduate SL Courses Offered Per Year:* 0

*Total Number of SL Courses Offered Per Year:* 1+

*Number of Full-time SL Staff on Campus (not counting instructors):* 2

*Number of Part-time SL Staff on Campus (not counting instructors):* 2 (graduate assistants)

## Miami-Dade Community College

300 NE 2nd Ave, Miami, FL 33132

*University/College URL:* http://www.mdcc.edu

*Type of Institution:* public, community college, teaching

*SL Program/Center Name:* Center for Community Involvement

*Contact Person Name and Title:* Josh Young, Prog Dir

*Contact Phone Number:* (305) 237–3848/ 0859/1820

*Contact Fax Number:* (305) 237–7580

*Contact Email Address:* jyoung@mdcc.edu

*SL Program/Center URL:* http://www.mdcc.edu/servicelearning/

*Description:* The Center for Community Involvement is housed within the Academic Division of the college. The center is responsible for all service-learning, the America Reads program, and experiential-education activities at the college. In addition, it functions as a volunteer clearinghouse for students, staff, and faculty who wish to get involved in community service. There are full-service centers at three of the college's campuses and outreach programs at all campuses.

*SL Required for Graduation (all students)?* No

*Service Required for Graduation (all students)?* No

*Any Co-curricular Service?* Yes

*Any SL Residence Halls or Theme Houses?* No

*Number of Undergraduate SL Courses Offered Per Year:* 250

*Number of Graduate SL Courses Offered Per Year:* 0

*Total Number of SL Courses Offered Per Year:* 250

*Number of Instructors Teaching SL Courses Per Year:* 125

*Number of Full-time SL Staff on Campus (not counting instructors):* 4

*Number of Part-time SL Staff on Campus (not counting instructors):* 18

## Michigan State University

Service-Learning Center, Rm 27 Student Services, East Lansing, MI 48824–1113

*University/College URL:* http://www.msu.edu

*Type of Institution:* public, university, teaching, research

*SL Program/Center Name:* Service-Learning Center

*Contact Person Name and Title:* Georgia Davidson, Acting Dir

*Contact Phone Number:* (517) 353–4400

*Contact Fax Number:* ( 517) 353–3336

*Contact Email Address:* servlrn@msu.edu or davids16@msu.edu

*SL Program/Center URL:* http://www.csp. msu.edu/slc

*Description:* Established by the MSU Board of Trustees in 1967 as the Office of Volunteer Programs, the office was renamed the Service-Learning Center in 1987 to reflect the integration of active learning through career and civic development. The mission of the Service-Learning Center is to inform and prepare students for career and civic involvement through community service. The center has three categories of placements: service-learning which is integrated with MSU classes, or academic programs through independent study (internship) options; civic and career development for pre-professional students in medicine, pre-vet medicine, human-or public service-careers; and co-curricular community service through student leadership with community organizations. Over 5,000 students applied for 1,000 local area opportunities to serve during the 1999–2000 year.

The Liberty Hyde Bailey Scholars Program: This program is for students in MSU's College of Agriculture and Natural Resources. See http://www.bsp.msu.edu/bailey/background/overview. htm for a full description of the program.

The American Thought and Language Writing Project is part of the Service-Learning Writing Project (SLWP), which is a joint endeavor of Michigan State University's College of Arts and Letters, the Department of American Thought and Language, the Service-Learning Center (a division of Student Services), and the Writing Center. See http://www.msu.edu/~atl/community.html for information about the project.

*SL Required for Graduation (all students)?* No

*Service Required for Graduation (all students)?* No

*Any Co-curricular Service?* Yes

*Any SL Residence Halls or Theme Houses?* Yes

*Number of Undergraduate SL Courses Offered Per Year:* 62

*Number of Graduate SL Courses Offered Per Year:* 1

*Total Number of SL Courses Offered Per Year:* 63

*Number of Instructors Teaching SL Courses Per Year:* 20

*Number of Full-time SL Staff on Campus (not counting instructors):* 3

*Number of Part-time SL Staff on Campus (not counting instructors):* 3

**Millikin University**

1184 W Main, Decatur, IL 62522

*University/College URL:* http://www. millikin.edu

*Type of Institution:* private, university

*SL Program/Center Name:* Center for Service Learning

*Contact Person Name and Title:* Michel Wakeland, Dir

*Contact Phone Number:* (217) 362 6463

*Contact Fax Number:* (217) 424 3544

*Contact Email Address:* mwakeland@mail.millikin.edu

*SL Program/Center URL:* http://www. millikin.edu/academics/ UniversityWidePrograms/slmain.html

*SL Online Course Description URL:* http:// www.millikin.edu/academics/ UniversityWidePrograms/slcourses.html

*Description:* The Center for Service Learning exists to help students incorporate community-service experiences into their education, assist faculty in adopting creative, experiential community-based teaching methods, carry out the civic-education portion of the university's mission, and make a positive impact upon Decatur and the other communities in which students serve. There is one full-time program staffer and one full-time support staff person. Other staff include eight Service Learning Scholars and students employed in the Community Work Study program.

*SL Required for Graduation (all students)?* Yes

*Service Required for Graduation (all students)?* No

*Any Co-curricular Service?* Yes

*Any SL Residence Halls or Theme Houses?* No

*SL Undergraduate Program Description:*
Students encounter service-learning in a
required first-year experience class, may
encounter it in upper-division majors, and
will choose service either on or off
campus as part of a senior interdisciplinary capstone. Often students undertake
service-learning as part of a three-credit
off-campus learning requirement.

*Number of Undergraduate SL Courses
Offered Per Year:* 48

*Number of Graduate SL Courses Offered
Per Year:* 0

*Total Number of SL Courses Offered Per
Year:* 48

*Number of Instructors Teaching SL Courses
Per Year:* 23

*Number of Full-time SL Staff on Campus
(not counting instructors):* 2

*Number of Part-time SL Staff on Campus
(not counting instructors):* 8

## Mills College

5000 MacArthur Blvd, Oakland, CA 94613

*University/College URL:* http://www.
mills.edu

*Type of Institution:* private, college, teaching, secular

*SL Program/Center Name:* Mills C.A.R.E.S.
(Community Action Reciprocal Education
and Service)

*Contact Person Name and Title:* Dave
Donahue, Dir

*Contact Phone Number:* (510) 430–3154

*Contact Fax Number:* (510) 430–3119

*Contact Email Address:*
millscares@mills.edu

*SL Program/Center URL:* http://www.mills.
edu/PROV/MCAR/mcar.homepage.html

*Description:* The Mills CARES (Community
Action, Reciprocal Education and Service) Center serves as the hub of community service and
service-learning for the College. This student-coordinated center is administered by faculty
directors appointed by the Office of the Provost. It provides three functions: linking students, faculty, and staff to community-service
opportunities; supporting faculty engaged in
service-learning; and serving as a clearinghouse for agencies seeking volunteers.

Service in Culturally Diverse Communities:
Mills College does not have a course devoted
entirely to service-learning; instead, service-learning is incorporated into courses in the
college's academic departments. To support
students in such courses, the college offers a
series of eight workshops entitled "Service in
Culturally Diverse Communities" each semester. Through journal writing, activities, readings, and discussions in the workshops, students learn to enter, participate, and leave a
community-service placement responsibly and
sensitively; develop a personal philosophy of
and commitment to service; understand and
value the perspective of people in the community on issues connected to their service; and
integrate their service experience with the academic content of their college courses.

*SL Required for Graduation (all
students)?* No

*Service Required for Graduation (all students)?* No

*Any Co-curricular Service?* Yes

*Any SL Residence Halls or Theme
Houses?* No

*Number of Undergraduate SL Courses
Offered Per Year:* 12–15

*Number of Graduate SL Courses Offered
Per Year:* 1

*Total Number of SL Courses Offered Per
Year:* 13–16

*Number of Instructors Teaching SL Courses
Per Year:* 12

*Number of Full-time SL Staff on Campus
(not counting instructors):* 0

*Number of Part-time SL Staff on Campus
(not counting instructors):* 5

## MiraCosta College

One Barnard Dr, Mail Station 13, Oceanside,
CA 92056–3899

*University/College URL:* http://www.
miracosta.cc.ca.us

*Type of Institution:* public, community college, teaching, secular

*SL Program/Center Name:* Service Learning
and Volunteer Center (SLVC)

*Contact Person Name and Title:* Cassandra
Evans, Coord

*Contact Phone Number:* (760) 757–2121,
   ext 6355
*Contact Fax Number:* (760) 757–6773
*Contact Email Address:*
   cevans@yar.miracosta.cc.ca.us
*SL Program/Center URL:* http://www.
   miracosta.cc.ca.us/info/admin/studserv/
   ServLrn/
*SL Online Course Description URL:* http://
   www.miracosta.cc.ca.us/info/admin/
   studserv/ServLrn/courses.htm
*Description:* The Service Learning and Volunteer Center helps students integrate volunteerism
and community service with academic instruction. Students work with their instructors and
the Service Learning coordinator to find meaningful placements in the community related to
what they are learning in class, at the same time
fine-tuning their critical-thinking skills. Currently, 35 faculty members offer the service-
learning component in more than 45 class
sections.
*SL Required for Graduation (all*
   *students)?* No
*Service Required for Graduation (all stu-*
   *dents)?* No
*Any Co-curricular Service?* Yes
*Any SL Residence Halls or Theme*
   *Houses?* No
*SL Degrees Offered:* All students who
   complete a Service Learning project
   receive a certificate, which is signed by
   the president of the college.
*Number of Undergraduate SL Courses*
   *Offered Per Year:* 80–100 (45 each
   semester; 5–10 in the summer)
*Number of Graduate SL Courses Offered*
   *Per Year:* 0
*Total Number of SL Courses Offered Per*
   *Year:* 80–100
*Number of Instructors Teaching SL Courses*
   *Per Year:* 70 (30 to 35 each semester;
   5–10 in the summer)
*Number of Full-time SL Staff on Campus*
   *(not counting instructors):* 1
*Number of Part-time SL Staff on Campus*
   *(not counting instructors):* 3 (2 adminis-
   trators and 1 student worker)

**Moravian College**
1200 Main St, Bethlehem, PA 18018
*University/College URL:* http://www.
   moravian.edu
*Type of Institution:* private, college, teach-
   ing, religious
*SL Program/Center Name:* Moravian College Community Service Center
*Contact Person Name and Title:* Chris
   Giesler, Chaplain
*Contact Phone Number:* (610) 861–1411
*Contact Fax Number:* (610) 807–3830
*Contact Email Address:*
   chrisg@moravian.edu
*SL Program/Center URL:* http://www.
   moravian.edu/arc/student/community.htm
*Description:* The Community Service Center
serves the campus by providing a variety of
community-service options for students, faculty, and staff. It is funded through the college's
general budget; however, two programs are
funded by outside sources. The aim of the
center is to provide students with opportunities
for doing community service and aiding faculty
in making service-learning a part of their
curriculum.
*SL Required for Graduation (all*
   *students)?* No
*Service Required for Graduation (all stu-*
   *dents)?* No
*Any Co-curricular Service?* No
*Any SL Residence Halls or Theme*
   *Houses?* Yes
*Number of Undergraduate SL Courses*
   *Offered Per Year:* 2
*Total Number of SL Courses Offered*
   *Per Year:* 2
*Number of Instructors Teaching SL Courses*
   *Per Year:* 2
*Number of Full-time SL Staff on Campus*
   *(not counting instructors):* 0
*Number of Part-time SL Staff on Campus*
   *(not counting instructors):* 1

**Mount St. Mary's College**
12001 Chalon Rd, Los Angeles, CA 90049
*University/College URL:* http://www.
   msmc.la.edu
*Type of Institution:* private, university,
   teaching

*SL Program/Center Name:* Service-Learning
Program

*Contact Person Name and Title:* Dr. Pam
Haldeman, Dir

*Contact Phone Number:* (310) 954–4366

*Contact Fax Number:* (310) 954–4019

*Contact Email Address:*
phaldeman@msmc.la.edu

*SL Program/Center URL:* http://www.msmc.
la.edu/Academics/Service_Learning/
service_learning.htm

*Description:* In 1998, Mount St. Mary's College was awarded a generous grant from the
William and Flora Hewlett Foundation for the
purpose of significantly enhancing the institution's long tradition of community service
through the development of a curriculum-based
program of service-learning. Through the Center for Urban Partnerships, service-learning activities associated with courses are coordinated.
In May 1999, 10 Service-Learning Faculty
Fellowships were awarded to teachers who
have become innovators and leaders in the
service-learning arena on the college's campuses. They come from a range of disciplines,
including art, math, sociology, psychology, education, nursing, business, and history. Each has
redesigned a course they regularly teach to
include a service-learning component in them.
The center's goal is to infuse service-learning
throughout the curriculum so that each student
upon graduation will have experienced service-
learning in their academic career.

*SL Required for Graduation (all
students)?* No

*Service Required for Graduation (all stu-
dents)?* No

*Any Co-curricular Service?* Yes

*Any SL Residence Halls or Theme
Houses?* Yes

*Number of Undergraduate SL Courses
Offered Per Year:* 18

*Number of Graduate SL Courses Offered
Per Year:* 0

*Total Number of SL Courses Offered Per
Year:* 18

*Number of Instructors Teaching SL Courses
Per Year:* 15

*Number of Full-time SL Staff on Campus
(not counting instructors):* 4

*Number of Part-time SL Staff on Campus
(not counting instructors):* 10

**Mount St. Mary's College**

16300 Old Emmitsburg Rd, Emmitsburg,
MD 21727

*University/College URL:* http://www.
msmary.edu

*Type of Institution:* private, college, teaching, religious

*SL Program/Center Name:* Office of Community Service

*Contact Person Name and Title:* Joseph
T. Purello, Dir, Community Service
Learning

*Contact Phone Number:* (301) 447–5223

*Contact Fax Number:* (301) 447–5818

*Contact Email Address:*
purello@msmary.edu

*Description:* The Office of Community Service provides students with a wide variety of
service-outreach activities. Students can volunteer in the local community or may choose to
participate in service trips offered during academic break periods. The director of Community Service and Service Learning (CSSL) serves
as a resource for students seeking volunteer
placements during the school year, summer,
and after graduation. The director assists faculty in developing and administering the service component of service-learning coursework
and advises students on service-learning opportunities and procedures. The Office of Community Service works with the Office of Student Development in offering community-
service theme housing, organizing service events
for student clubs, and inculcating an early appreciation of service among students by sponsoring team service projects during freshman
orientation.

Upon consultation and agreement with the
professor of a particular course, students have
the opportunity to integrate meaningful community service within their academic studies
through the "One Credit Option in Service
Learning" program. The additional academic
effort associated with fulfilling the service-
learning requirements of the course is recog-

nized by the awarding of one credit in service-learning in addition to the disciplinary credits earned. In addition to the One Credit Option in Service Learning, three-credit service-learning courses are periodically offered.

*SL Required for Graduation (all students)?* No

*Service Required for Graduation (all students)?* No

*Any Co-curricular Service?* Yes

*Any SL Residence Halls or Theme Houses?* Yes

*Number of Undergraduate SL Courses Offered Per Year:* 12

*Number of Graduate SL Courses Offered Per Year:* 0

*Total Number of SL Courses Offered Per Year:* 12

*Number of Instructors Teaching SL Courses Per Year:* 9

*Number of Full-time SL Staff on Campus (not counting instructors):* 1

*Number of Part-time SL Staff on Campus (not counting instructors):* 0

## Mount Wachusett Community College

444 Green St, Gardner, MA 01440

*University/College URL:* http://www.mwcc.mass.edu

*Type of Institution:* public, community college, teaching

*SL Program/Center Name:* MWCC Service-Learning Office

*Contact Person Name and Title:* Susan Staniewicz McAlpine, Dir, Cooperative Education & Service Learning

*Contact Phone Number:* (978) 632–6600, ext 219

*Contact Fax Number:* (978) 632–6155

*Contact Email Address:* s_mcalpine@mwcc.mass.edu

*SL Program/Center URL:* http://www.mwcc.mass.edu/HTML/ServLearning.html

*Description:* Service Learning at Mount Wachusett Community College officially began three years ago, and it has developed into a strong, exciting program that includes interdepartmental collaborations. Faculty offer students an opportunity to participate in service-learning experiences for a total of 20 hours of service each semester. Service-learning is funded through a Massachusetts Campus Compact/Learn & Serve grant and college funds.

*SL Required for Graduation (all students)?* No

*Service Required for Graduation (all students)?* No

*Any Co-curricular Service?* Yes

*Any SL Residence Halls or Theme Houses?* No

*SL Degrees Offered:* Certificates are offered to students who complete service-learning and are indicated on student transcripts.

*Number of Undergraduate SL Courses Offered Per Year:* 20+

*Total Number of SL Courses Offered Per Year:* 20–30

*Number of Instructors Teaching SL Courses Per Year:* 15–20

## Nebraska Methodist College of Nursing and Allied Health

8501 W Dodge Rd, Omaha, NE 68114

*University/College URL:* http://www.nmhs.org

*Type of Institution:* private, college, teaching

*SL Program/Center Name:* Service Learning

*Contact Person Name and Title:* Jennifer Reed-Bouley, PhD, Coord, Service Learning

*Contact Phone Number:* (402) 354–4919

*Contact Fax Number:* (402) 354–8875

*Contact Email Address:* jreed@nmhs.org

*Description:* The coordinator of Service Learning consults with faculty who are developing service-learning courses and offers ongoing faculty development to those who are already employing service-learning as a pedagogy in their courses. Faculty invite the coordinator to their classes to assist with student orientation to service-learning and ongoing reflection on community experiences. The coordinator co-directs a student leadership-development group and sponsors co-curricular community-service opportunities for faculty, staff, and students.

*SL Required for Graduation (all students)?* No (However, a proposal is currently being considered for including service-learning in a required general education course.)

*Service Required for Graduation (all students)?* No

*Any Co-curricular Service?* Yes

*Any SL Residence Halls or Theme Houses?* No

*Number of Undergraduate SL Courses Offered Per Year:* 8

*Number of Graduate SL Courses Offered Per Year:* 0

*Total Number of SL Courses Offered Per Year:* 8

*Number of Instructors Teaching SL Courses Per Year:* 8

*Number of Full-time SL Staff on Campus (not counting instructors):* 0

*Number of Part-time SL Staff on Campus (not counting instructors):* 1

## Neumann College

One Neumann Dr, Aston, PA 19012–1298

*University/College URL:* http://www.neumann.edu

*Type of Institution:* private, college, religious

*SL Program/Center Name:* Career Development

*Contact Person Name and Title:* Charlotte Ryan, Experiential Education Coord

*Contact Phone Number:* (610) 558–5527

*Contact Fax Number:* (610) 361–5475

*Contact Email Address:* ryanc@neumann.edu

*SL Program/Center URL:* http://www.neumann.edu/Services/CareerDv/carexper.htm

*SL Online Course Description URL:* http://www.neumann.edu/Services/CareerDv/carexper.htm

*Description:* The Service Learning Experience at Neumann College combines theoretical classroom learning with service-based learning in the community. A Service-Learning Experience serves as a valuable and integral part of the student's total learning experience for a specific course or can be pursued as an independent study. This type of experience supports the student's intellectual, ethical, career, civic, and personal development as well as enhances a sense of social responsibility. Service placements are established to address unmet needs in the community. Examples of service-learning experiences include the college's out-

reach to Native American children who live at the Acoma and Laguna Pueblos in New Mexico; School Yard Lab, which involves teaching local elementary students environmental values; a Servant Leadership course; and VITA, a volunteer income tax assistance program. Service-learning opportunities are available to the student under the guidance of the coordinator of Experiential Education Programs. The program is funded by the institution.

*SL Required for Graduation (all students)?* No

*Service Required for Graduation (all students)?* No

*Any Co-curricular Service?* Yes

*Any SL Residence Halls or Theme Houses?* No

*Number of Undergraduate SL Courses Offered Per Year:* 16–20

*Total Number of SL Courses Offered Per Year:* 16–20

*Number of Instructors Teaching SL Courses Per Year:* 9

*Number of Full-time SL Staff on Campus (not counting instructors):* 1 (The Experiential Education coordinator services the co-op, internship, and service learning programs.)

*Number of Part-time SL Staff on Campus (not counting instructors):* 0

## New College of USF (University of South Florida)

5700 N Tamiami Trail, Sarasota, FL 34243

*University/College URL:* http://www.newcollege.usf.edu

*Type of Institution:* public, college

*SL Program/Center Name:* Center for Service Learning

*Contact Person Name and Title:* Alena Scandura, Coord, Student Activities

*Contact Phone Number:* (941) 359–4266

*Contact Fax Number:* (941) 359–4308

*Contact Email Address:* ascandur@virtu.sar.usf.edu; csl@virtu.sar.usf.edu

*SL Program/Center URL:* http://www.sar.usf.edu/~csl/

*Description:* The center assists students in developing service-learning projects by conducting biannual fairs, maintaining a resource file, publicizing projects and sites, assisting faculty, and coordinating service and alternate break projects. New College is a liberal arts undergraduate program. There is no core curriculum, and there are no grades or credit hours. Students are free to design a program of study that meets with their academic goals/objectives. Students may or may not include a service-learning project as a means to achieving their goals. The goals/objectives are written as a contract which is evaluated by the faculty advisor. Students may take classes, conduct independent reading/study projects, and organize a tutorial. Therefore, it is never known from year to year what service-learning ''classes'' will take place.

*SL Required for Graduation (all students)?* No

*Service Required for Graduation (all students)?* No

*Any Co-curricular Service?* Yes

*Any SL Residence Halls or Theme Houses?* No

*Number of Instructors Teaching SL Courses Per Year:* 4–6 (out of 45 full-time faculty on campus)

*Number of Full-time SL Staff on Campus (not counting instructors):* 1 (Service-learning is only part of this person's duties.)

*Number of Part-time SL Staff on Campus (not counting instructors):* 0

**Niagara University**
PO Box 1906, Niagara University, NY 14109–1906

*University/College URL:* http://www.niagara.edu

*Type of Institution:* private, university, teaching, religious

*SL Program/Center Name:* Learn and Serve Niagara

*Contact Person Name and Title:* Marilynn P. Fleckenstein, PhD, Dir

*Contact Phone Number:* (716) 286–8573

*Contact Fax Number:* (716) 286–8753

*Contact Email Address:* mpf@niagara.edu

*SL Program/Center URL:* http://www.niagara.edu/learnserve/

*Description:* Learn and Serve Niagara students are involved in a variety of community-service projects, including mentoring at-risk elementary and high school students, providing health assessment, and working in community-service agencies that address needs such as domestic violence, homelessness, and other child and family services.

*SL Required for Graduation (all students)?* No

*Service Required for Graduation (all students)?* No

*Any Co-curricular Service?* Yes

*Any SL Residence Halls or Theme Houses?* No

*Number of Undergraduate SL Courses Offered Per Year:* 20–25

*Number of Graduate SL Courses Offered Per Year:* 5–6

*Total Number of SL Courses Offered Per Year:* 25–31

*Number of Instructors Teaching SL Courses Per Year:* 15–20

*Number of Full-time SL Staff on Campus (not counting instructors):* 3

*Number of Part-time SL Staff on Campus (not counting instructors):* 2

**North Carolina Central University**
1801 Fayetteville St, PO Box 19738, Durham, NC 27707

*University/College URL:* GOTOBUTTON BM_- http://www.nccu.edu

*Type of Institution:* public, university, teaching, research, secular

*SL Program/Center Name:* Academic Community Service Learning Program

*Contact Person Name and Title:* Dr. Theodore Parrish, Dir; Mrs. Rosa S. Anderson, Assoc Dir

*Contact Phone Number:* (919) 560–6404; (919) 530–7078

*Contact Fax Number:* (919) 560–5385

*Contact Email Address:* tparrish@wpo.nccu.edu; rand@wpo.nccu.edu

*SL Program/Center URL:* http://www.nccu.edu/commserv/serve.htm

*SL Online Course Description URL:* http://

www.nccu.edu/commserv/SerLea/
slreport.htm

*Description:* The Academic Community Service Learning Program (ACSLP) was mandated by Chancellor Julius Chambers in 1995. Undergraduate students learn and develop through active participation in service-learning activities conducted in the community. Students are enabled to develop skills that foster service to their campus as well as the greater community. Community Service Learning Scholarships are available. Since the fall semester of 1995, all new full-time and transfer students are required to complete 15 clock hours of community service per semester, unless otherwise stipulated by a scholarship. Every student is expected to provide community-service hours until a total of 120 clock hours are fulfilled. Students must register with ACSLP for each service experience. Students may complete a minimum of 15 clock hours of service per semester by working with community/campus agencies; enrolling in courses with actual service-learning components; conducting community-based research; and participating in university-community initiatives that promote service-learning as approved by the director of the ACSLP. The program is funded by the university and through grants from foundations and other charitable organizations.

Service Learning Ambassadors is an ACSLP project which recruits highly motivated students to help market service-learning and participate in the design and implementation of projects and further promote the Academic Community Service Learning Program both on campus and off. This initiative operates under "GRASP" (Generating Resources To Address Social Problems), the university's blanket service-learning project, from which other service-learning projects emanate.

*SL Required for Graduation (all students)?* No

*Service Required for Graduation (all students)?* Yes

*Any Co-curricular Service?* Yes

*Any SL Residence Halls or Theme Houses?* No

*SL Degrees Offered:* The university has several departments that require specific numbers of hours to graduate based upon service-learning requirements. Among them are health education, nursing, social work, education, and psychology.

*Number of Undergraduate SL Courses Offered Per Year:* 30

*Number of Graduate SL Courses Offered Per Year:* 6

*Total Number of SL Courses Offered Per Year:* 36

*Number of Instructors Teaching SL Courses Per Year:* 28

*Number of Full-time SL Staff on Campus (not counting instructors):* 7

*Number of Part-time SL Staff on Campus (not counting instructors):* 1

## North Idaho College

1000 West Garden Ave, Coeur d'Alene, ID 83814

*University/College URL:* http://www.nic.edu

*Type of Institution:* public, community college, teaching

*SL Program/Center Name:* Office of Service Learning

*Contact Person Name and Title:* Laurie Olson-Horswill, Fac Coord; Lucy Hein, Placement Coord

*Contact Phone Number:* (208) 769–3403

*Contact Fax Number:* (208) 769–7805

*Contact Email Address:* ljolsonh@nic.edu

*SL Program/Center URL:* http://www.nic.edu/service/service.htm

*SL Online Course Description URL:* http://www.nic.edu/service/service.htm

*Description:* The Office of Service-Learning connects community agencies, faculty, and students. Staff communicate personally with over 50 local agencies in assessing their needs, train faculty on integrating service-learning into their courses, and place students in community agencies according to their interests and their specific course projects. The purpose of the office is to make these service-learning connections as personal, simple, and effective as possible. Moreover, staff continually evaluate and celebrate the efforts of all participants. After initial financial support from the North Idaho College

Foundation in 1996, the office has continued to grow, supported by a small budget which is linked to academics, and by the time of many who believe in giving to this program.

*SL Required for Graduation (all
    students)?* No

*Service Required for Graduation (all students)?* No

*Any Co-curricular Service?* Yes

*Any SL Residence Halls or Theme
    Houses?* No

*Number of Undergraduate SL Courses
    Offered Per Year:* 18–30

*Total Number of SL Courses Offered Per
    Year:* 18–30

*Number of Instructors Teaching SL Courses
    Per Year:* 18

*Number of Full-time SL Staff on Campus
    (not counting instructors):* 2 (the director/
    dean, and a faculty coord, who teaches
    English full-time and helps in the office
    for some release time)

*Number of Part-time SL Staff on Campus
    (not counting instructors):* 1 (a half-time
    placement coord)

## Northampton Community College

3835 Green Pond Rd, Danielsville,
    PA 18038

*University/College URL:* http://www.
    northampton.edu

*Type of Institution:* public, community
    college

*SL Program/Center Name:* Service Learning

*Contact Person Name and Title:* Mardi
    McGuire-Closson, Dean of Students

*Contact Phone Number:* (610) 861–4548

*Contact Fax Number:* (610) 861–5374

*Contact Email Address:*
    MClosson@northampton.edu

*Description:* The Service Learning program began implementation during the Spring 2000 semester. In its early stages, the program will focus on experiences for students in specific courses. The Dean of Students is responsible for coordinating the efforts of the program.

*SL Required for Graduation (all
    students)?* No

*Service Required for Graduation (all students)?* No

*Any Co-curricular Service?* Yes

*Any SL Residence Halls or Theme
    Houses?* No

*Number of Undergraduate SL Courses
    Offered Per Year:* 3 (in Spring 2000)

*Number of Instructors Teaching SL Courses
    Per Year:* 3 (In spring 2000)

*Number of Full-time SL Staff on Campus
    (not counting instructors):* 0

*Number of Part-time SL Staff on Campus
    (not counting instructors):* 1

## Northern State University

1200 S Jay St, Box 794, Aberdeen, SD
    57401–7198

*University/College URL:* http://www.
    northern.edu

*Type of Institution:* public, university, teaching, secular

*SL Program/Center Name:* Aberdeen Service-Learning Center

*Contact Person Name and Title:* Judith
    Rogers Kelsey, Faculty Liaison; Tracy A.
    Russman, Community Liaison

*Contact Phone Number:* (605) 626–2734

*Contact Fax Number:* (605) 626–2984

*Contact Email Address:*
    kelseyj@northern.edu;
    russmat@northern.edu

*SL Program/Center URL:* _ http://www.
    northern.edu/aslc

*Description:* The Aberdeen Service-Learning Center, in collaboration with the Aberdeen Chamber of Commerce and Brown County United Way, facilitates reciprocal service-learning partnerships between area community-based organizations and educational institutions (Aberdeen public and Catholic schools, Presentation College, Northern State University, and the South Dakota School for the Blind and Visually Impaired). The center provides training and technical assistance to educators for integrating service-learning into their curriculum and CBOs for creating effective partnerships that benefit from students as resources. The center also supports student development initiatives such as the Presidents' Student Summits, invitations to area high schools and colleges statewide, and resulting student-organized community-improvement projects such as a local volunteer clearinghouse project. Academic service-learning is integrated into undergraduate and graduate courses in a variety ways: central to or supportive of course objectives; required, optional, or alternative assignments; and extra credit or fourth-credit options.

*SL Required for Graduation (all students)?* No

*Service Required for Graduation (all students)?* No

*Any Co-curricular Service?* No

*Any SL Residence Halls or Theme Houses?* No

*Number of Undergraduate SL Courses Offered Per Year:* 14

*Number of Graduate SL Courses Offered Per Year:* 4

*Total Number of SL Courses Offered Per Year:* 18

*Number of Instructors Teaching SL Courses Per Year:* 12

*Number of Full-time SL Staff on Campus (not counting instructors):* 3

*Number of Part-time SL Staff on Campus (not counting instructors):* 2

## Northern Virginia Community College
6901 Sudley Rd, Manassas, VA 22032
*University/College URL:* http://www.nv.cc.va.us
*Type of Institution:* public, community college, teaching
*Contact Person Name and Title:* Linda J. Simmons, Assoc Prof
*Contact Phone Number:* (703) 257–6688
*Contact Fax Number:* (703) 257–6551
*Contact Email Address:* LSimmons@nv.cc.va.us
*Description:* Service-learning is currently housed in each course, with no center. One faculty member has six hours reassigned time to work with service-learning development. In the "Building Bridges Between Classroom and Community" program, faculty in a variety of academic disciplines include service-learning as an option or mandate in a class.

*SL Required for Graduation (all students)?* No

*Service Required for Graduation (all students)?* No

*Any Co-curricular Service?* Yes

*Any SL Residence Halls or Theme Houses?* No

*Number of Full-time SL Staff on Campus (not counting instructors):* 0

*Number of Part-time SL Staff on Campus (not counting instructors):* 0

## NorthWest Arkansas Community College
One College Dr, Bentonville, AR 72712
*University/College URL:* http://www.nwacc.cc.ar.us
*Type of Institution:* public, community college, teaching
*SL Program/Center Name:* Broadening Horizons in Northwest Arkansas
*Contact Person Name and Title:* Michelle Rieff, Coord, Special Services
*Contact Phone Number:* (501) 619–4232
*Contact Fax Number:* (501) 619–4116
*Contact Email Address:* mrieff@nwacc.cc.ar.us
*Description:* The mission of the service-learning program is to provide an educational experience that combines classroom instruction with community service in order to strengthen the community, individual students, and learning opportunities at NorthWest Arkansas Community College.

*SL Required for Graduation (all students)?* No

*Service Required for Graduation (all students)?* No

*Any SL Residence Halls or Theme Houses?* No

*Number of Undergraduate SL Courses Offered Per Year:* 20

*Total Number of SL Courses Offered Per Year:* 20

*Number of Instructors Teaching SL Courses Per Year:* 6

*Number of Full-time SL Staff on Campus (not counting instructors):* 0

*Number of Part-time SL Staff on Campus (not counting instructors):* 1

**Nova Southeastern University**

Farquhar Center for Undergraduate Studies, 3301 College Ave, Fort Lauderdale, FL 33314

*University/College URL:* http://www. nova.edu

*Type of Institution:* private, university, teaching, research

*SL Program/Center Name:* Community Service Office/SCORE

*Contact Person Name and Title:* Madeline Haug Penna, Coord, Community Service

*Contact Phone Number:* (954) 262–8093

*Contact Fax Number:* (954) 262–3924

*Contact Email Address:* pennam@polaris.nova.edu

*SL Program/Center URL:* http://polaris.nova. edu/SCORE/

*SL Online Course Description URL:* http:// www.polaris.nova.edu/SCORE/courses. html

*Description:* The Office of Community Service and SCORE are resources for students and faculty interested in linking academic experiences with community service. The office maintains a directory of local agencies and projects, creates information and materials for faculty and their students, and offers workshops for campus and community members.

*SL Required for Graduation (all students)?* No

*Service Required for Graduation (all students)?* No

*Any Co-curricular Service?* Yes

*Any SL Residence Halls or Theme Houses?* No

*SL Undergraduate Program Name:* SCORE (Service to the Community, Opportunity, Responsibility and Excellence for students)

*SL Undergraduate Program Description:* SCORE is a four-year service-learning program. Students move from service participants to service "experts" in their freshman to senior years. All students participate in a minimum of nine hours of service per month, complete a service-learning course in their junior year which links service to their professional goals

and design and complete a senior service-learning project. All students share a common general-education program through a set of interdisciplinary core courses which include service-learning.

*Number of Undergraduate SL Courses Offered Per Year:* 12

*Number of Graduate SL Courses Offered Per Year:* 0

*Total Number of SL Courses Offered Per Year:* 12

*Number of Instructors Teaching SL Courses Per Year:* 8

*Number of Full-time SL Staff on Campus (not counting instructors):* 2

*Number of Part-time SL Staff on Campus (not counting instructors):* 0

**Oakton Community College**

1600 East Golf Rd, Des Plaines, IL 60016

*University/College URL:* http://www. oakton.edu

*Type of Institution:* public, community college, teaching, secular

*SL Program/Center Name:* Service-Learning Project

*Contact Person Name and Title:* Gwen Nyden; Alan Rubin

*Contact Phone Number:* (847) 635–1600

*Contact Fax Number:* (847) 63511764

*Contact Email Address:* gnyden@oakton.edu; rubin@oakton.edu

*Description:* The Service-Learning Project began in 1996, with one class and two faculty members. It has grown to include 29 faculty and over 400 students serving in more than 125 Chicago area not-for-profit agencies. The project has been supported in part by the Corporation for National Service as part of their Broadening Horizons through Service-Learning project, which is administered by the American Association of Community Colleges. The goals of the project include increasing students' awareness of their personal and civic responsibilities in building healthier communities.

*SL Required for Graduation (all students)?* No

*Service Required for Graduation (all students)?* No

*Any Co-curricular Service?* Yes

*Any SL Residence Halls or Theme Houses?* No

*Number of Undergraduate SL Courses Offered Per Year:* 40

*Total Number of SL Courses Offered Per Year:* 40

*Number of Instructors Teaching SL Courses Per Year:* 29

*Number of Full-time SL Staff on Campus (not counting instructors):* 0

*Number of Part-time SL Staff on Campus (not counting instructors):* 2

## Oberlin College

70 N Professor St, Oberlin, OH 44074

*University/College URL:* http://www.oberlin.edu

*Type of Institution:* private, college, teaching, secular

*SL Program/Center Name:* Center for Service and Learning

*Contact Person Name and Title:* Daniel Gardner, Dir

*Contact Phone Number:* (440) 775–8055

*Contact Fax Number:* (440) 775–8754

*Contact Email Address:* daniel.gardner@oberlin.edu

*SL Program/Center URL:* http://www.oberlin.edu/~csl

*Description:* The Center for Service and Learning is a comprehensive center for academically based and co-curricular community service. The center supports many initiatives, including the Bonner Scholars Program, the Shouse Non-Profit Leadership Program, the Howard Hughes Science Partnership, the Community Action Fellowship, America Reads, and the Hewlett Common Ground Program.

*SL Required for Graduation (all students)?* No

*Service Required for Graduation (all students)?* No

*Any Co-curricular Service?* Yes

*Any SL Residence Halls or Theme Houses?* No

*Number of Undergraduate SL Courses Offered Per Year:* 19

*Total Number of SL Courses Offered Per Year:* 19

*Number of Instructors Teaching SL Courses Per Year:* 11

*Number of Full-time SL Staff on Campus (not counting instructors):* 4

*Number of Part-time SL Staff on Campus (not counting instructors):* 0

## Ohio State University

301 Ramseyer Hall, 29 W Woodruff Ave, Columbus, OH 43210

*University/College URL:* http://www.coe.ohio-state.edu

*Type of Institution:* public, university, research

*SL Program/Center Name:* Service-Learning Initiatives (School of Educational Policy and Leadership)

*Contact Person Name and Title:* Dr. Susan R. Jones, Assist Prof

*Contact Phone Number:* (614) 688–3095

*Contact Fax Number:* (614) 292–7020

*Description:* Service-learning has been employed on campus for a number of years in both graduate and undergraduate courses. Community service and service-learning occur in a number of settings. Many faculty teach courses with service-learning or community-service components (e.g., one faculty member in the Department of Spanish and Portuguese has been teaching ''Spanish in Ohio'' for many years). In addition, the Service-Learning Scholars Roundtable explores and addresses the future of service-learning on campus (e.g., recommending criteria for identifying courses to be listed as SL courses), and is an integral partner in forwarding service-learning initiatives at the university with the President's Council on Outreach and Engagement. The Student Affairs Leadership Development Institute (including its Minority Service Leaders Program and Reflection Leader Program) also supports service-learning. For example, it is also exploring an indication of service and leadership on the academic transcript. This entry and the next provide details on two primary venues for service-learning and service at Ohio State University: Service-Learning Initiatives in the School of Educational Policy and Leadership; and Community Commitment in Student Affairs, Off-Campus Student Services, Project Community.

Service-Learning Initiatives of the School of Educational Policy and Leadership includes a program which links undergraduate students enrolled in courses with graduate students studying service-learning and community-service agency partners in a curriculum-based opportunity. In addition, Service-Learning Initiatives sponsors a service-learning research team and provides leadership to other faculty interested in learning how to integrate a service component into their courses.

*SL Required for Graduation (all students)?* No

*Service Required for Graduation (all students)?* No

*Any Co-curricular Service?* Yes

*Any SL Residence Halls or Theme Houses?* Yes

*SL Graduate Program Name:* Higher Education and Student Affairs graduate program

*SL Graduate Program Description:* The Higher Education and Student Affairs graduate program offers a service-learning track in the curriculum which provides students with an opportunity for coursework in service-learning, serving as Teaching Assistants/Community Service site leaders for the undergraduate course, and community-based research opportunities. Graduate assistantship opportunities in service-learning are available.

*Number of Undergraduate SL Courses Offered Per Year:* 3 (through the School of Educational Policy and Leadership)

*Number of Graduate SL Courses Offered Per Year:* 3

*Total Number of SL Courses Offered Per Year:* 6

*Number of Instructors Teaching SL Courses Per Year:* 3

*Number of Full-time SL Staff on Campus (not counting instructors):* 0

*Number of Part-time SL Staff on Campus (not counting instructors):* 0

**Ohio State University**
104 E 15th Ave, Columbus, OH 43201
*University/College URL:* http://www.osu.edu

*Type of Institution:* public, university, research

*SL Program/Center Name:* Community Commitment (Student Affairs, Off-Campus Student Services, Project Community)

*Contact Person Name and Title:* Judy Richards, Coord, Project Community

*Contact Phone Number:* (614) 292–0100

*Contact Fax Number:* (614) 292–4786

*Contact Email Address:* projcomm@osu.edu

*SL Program/Center URL:* http://www. osuoffcampus.com

*Description:* Community Commitment is a campus-wide collaboration, short-term introductory service-learning event during Welcome Week for university students. The program is a co-curricular event designed to introduce participants to the surrounding community, engage them in thoughtful community service, and introduce them to the elements of service-learning. The event is similar to an ''into the streets'' service event. Community Commitment engages over 50 local human-service agencies, schools, parks, and neighborhood organizations in a morning of service for more than 1,300 university students, faculty, and staff. Each agency/organization agrees to develop an experience including preparation/orientation, meaningful action, and reflection on-site. Community Commitment, with the assistance of the Ohio Campus Compact, trains more than half of the student site leaders in a four-hour training and introduction to service-learning (and the remainder in a briefer session).

*SL Required for Graduation (all students)?* No

*Service Required for Graduation (all students)?* No

*Any Co-curricular Service?* Yes

*Any SL Residence Halls or Theme Houses?* Yes

*Number of Undergraduate SL Courses Offered Per Year:* 49+ (A survey three years ago identified more than 49 departments self-identifying as teaching one or more service-learning courses.)

*Number of Full-time SL Staff on Campus (not counting instructors):* 0

*Number of Part-time SL Staff on Campus (not counting instructors):* 0

## Ohio University

Center for Community Service, 204 Baker Center, Athens, OH 45701

*University/College URL:* http://www. ohiou.edu

*Type of Institution:* public, university, teaching, research

*SL Program/Center Name:* Learn & Serve Ohio University

*Contact Person Name and Title:* Merle Graybill, Dir, Center for Community Service

*Contact Phone Number:* (740) 593–4028

*Contact Fax Number:* (740) 593–0047

*Contact Email Address:* graybill@ohiou.edu

*SL Program/Center URL:* http://www.ohiou. edu/commserv/servlern/index.htm

*SL Online Course Description URL:* http:// www.ohiou.edu/commserv/servlern/ courses.htm

*Description:* Learn & Serve Ohio University is one of four programs in the Center for Community Service at Ohio University. The other programs are volunteer mobilization, AmeriCorps, and Community Service Federal Work-Study. Faculty interest in service-learning began in 1992 and has increased with each year. In 1997, a Learn & Serve grant enabled an expansion of the service-learning initiative to accomplish five objectives: increase number of courses campus-wide; infusion of curriculum in College of Education; collaboration with community agencies to jointly design effective partnerships; classroom-based research on learning outcomes; and development of student leadership. Annual faculty and community organizations training has yielded 60 service-learning courses in different disciplines. Community organizations, faculty, and students are participating in a year-long dialogue, a Learning Circle, about joint design of service-learning partnerships.

*SL Required for Graduation (all students)?* No

*Service Required for Graduation (all students)?* No

*Any Co-curricular Service?* Yes

*Any SL Residence Halls or Theme Houses?* No

*Number of Undergraduate SL Courses Offered Per Year:* 55

*Number of Graduate SL Courses Offered Per Year:* 5

*Total Number of SL Courses Offered Per Year:* 60

*Number of Instructors Teaching SL Courses Per Year:* 60

*Number of Full-time SL Staff on Campus (not counting instructors):* 1

*Number of Part-time SL Staff on Campus (not counting instructors):* 0

## Olivet College

320 S Main St, Olivet, MI 49076

*University/College URL:* _ http://www. olivetnet.edu

*Type of Institution:* private, college, religious

*SL Program/Center Name:* Service Learning Center, Community Service Programs

*Contact Person Name and Title:* Kathy Fear, Assist Dean, Academic Affairs; Terry Langston, Dir, Student Develop & Youth Outreach Services; Margot Kennard, Dir, Service Learning Center

*Contact Phone Number:* (616) 749–7618 [Fear]; (616) 749–7112 [Langston]; (616) 749–7613 [Kennard]

*Contact Fax Number:* (616) 749–6603 [Fear]; (616) 749–3821 [Langston]

*Contact Email Address:* kfear@olivetnet.edu; tlangston@olivetnet.edu; mkennard@olivetnet.edu

*SL Program/Center URL:* http://www. olivetnet.edu/student.life/ocstl5.html

*Description:* The Service Learning Center promotes faculty integration of community service, service-learning, and volunteerism as a way of building on student learning. In addition, the center promotes faculty development, research, and partnerships.

*SL Required for Graduation (all students)?* Yes

*Service Required for Graduation (all students)?* Yes

*Any Co-curricular Service?* Yes

*Any SL Residence Halls or Theme Houses?* No

*Number of Undergraduate SL Courses Offered Per Year:* 30

*Number of Graduate SL Courses Offered Per Year:* 0

*Total Number of SL Courses Offered Per Year:* 30

*Number of Instructors Teaching SL Courses Per Year:* 12

*Number of Full-time SL Staff on Campus (not counting instructors):* 1

*Number of Part-time SL Staff on Campus (not counting instructors):* 2

## Oswego State University

Route 104, Oswego, NY 13126

*University/College URL:* http://www.oswego.edu

*Type of Institution:* public, college, teaching, research, secular

*SL Program/Center Name:* Office of Experience Based Education

*Contact Person Name and Title:* Dr. Paul Roodin, Dir, Experience Based Education

*Contact Phone Number:* (315) 341–2151

*Contact Fax Number:* (315) 341–5406

*Contact Email Address:* Roodin@oswego.edu

*SL Program/Center URL:* http://www.oswego.edu/Acad_Dept/ebe/

*Description:* Service Learning is an academic program organized through the office of experience-based education. To date, students are all committed to service on behalf of the elderly in the rural upstate New York community. Students may earn from one to three credit hours per semester for their service; the course may be repeated for a maximum of six credit hours. Placements are available in 43 different venues including nursing homes, assisted living, as well as the local YMCA, Meals on Wheels, and in private homes through religious organizations or the county department of social services (adult services). Students have regular reflective assignments, meet for class-based discussions, and have an opportunity to discuss their experiences individually with faculty and with on-site mentors. The common thread to student service is to meet the needs of seniors who are often socially isolated regardless of the residence in which they live.

*SL Required for Graduation (all students)?* No

*Service Required for Graduation (all students)?* No

*Any Co-curricular Service?* Yes

*Any SL Residence Halls or Theme Houses?* Yes

*Number of Undergraduate SL Courses Offered Per Year:* 6–8

*Number of Graduate SL Courses Offered Per Year:* 0

*Total Number of SL Courses Offered Per Year:* 6–8

*Number of Instructors Teaching SL Courses Per Year:* 6

*Number of Full-time SL Staff on Campus (not counting instructors):* 0

*Number of Part-time SL Staff on Campus (not counting instructors):* 2

## Ouachita Baptist University

410 Ouachita St, PO Box 3783, Arkadelphia, AR 71998–0001

*University/College URL:* http://www.obu.edu

*Type of Institution:* private, university, teaching, religious

*SL Program/Center Name:* Ben M. Elrod Center for Family and Community

*Contact Person Name and Title:* Ian Robert Cosh, Dir

*Contact Phone Number:* (870) 245–5320

*Contact Fax Number:* (870) 245–5325

*Contact Email Address:* coshi@alpha.obu.edu

*SL Program/Center URL:* http://www.obu.edu/famcom/

*Description:* The Elrod Center for Family and Community at Ouachita Baptist University is dedicated to serve humankind through the education experience. Ouachita's faculty, staff, and students are equipped, encouraged, and supported in their efforts to be involved in volunteerism, community service, service-learning, research, outreach, and instruction.

*SL Required for Graduation (all students)?* No

*Service Required for Graduation (all students)?* No

*Any Co-curricular Service?* Yes

*Any SL Residence Halls or Theme Houses?* No
*Number of Undergraduate SL Courses Offered Per Year:* 7
*Number of Graduate SL Courses Offered Per Year:* 0
*Total Number of SL Courses Offered Per Year:* 7
*Number of Instructors Teaching SL Courses Per Year:* 7
*Number of Full-time SL Staff on Campus (not counting instructors):* 1

## Pace University
One Pace Plaza, New York, NY 10038
*University/College URL:* http://www.pace.edu
*Type of Institution:* private, university, teaching, secular
*SL Program/Center Name:* VIA PACE (Volunteers in Action at Pace University)
*Contact Person Name and Title:* Debra Greenwood, Service-Learning Coord, Pleasantville; Lilian Barria, Service-Learning Coord, New York City
*Contact Phone Number:* (914) 773–3841; (212) 346–1021
*Contact Fax Number:* (914) 773–3314; (212) 346–1725
*Contact Email Address:* dgreenwood@fsmail.pace.edu; lbarria@fsmail.pace.edu
*SL Program/Center URL:* http://www.pace.edu/dyson/html/body_viapace.html
*Description:* VIA PACE is a program in service-learning and social responsibility, sponsored by the Dyson College of Arts and Sciences at Pace University, designed to engage students in their community throughout the undergraduate experience. VIA PACE serves students in several ways: it provides individual volunteer placements, coordinates events, provides assistance to clubs and organizations in their service events, and promotes service-learning courses. It also serves faculty through ongoing faculty-development opportunities and support in course development.
*SL Required for Graduation (all students)?* No

*Service Required for Graduation (all students)?* No
*Any Co-curricular Service?* Yes
*Any SL Residence Halls or Theme Houses?* No
*Number of Undergraduate SL Courses Offered Per Year:* 35–40
*Number of Graduate SL Courses Offered Per Year:* 10–15
*Total Number of SL Courses Offered Per Year:* 45–60
*Number of Instructors Teaching SL Courses Per Year:* 35
*Number of Full-time SL Staff on Campus (not counting instructors):* 5 (1 dir, 2 service-learning coord, and 2 volunteer coord)
*Number of Part-time SL Staff on Campus (not counting instructors):* 4 (3 student aides and 1 graduate assistant)

## Pacific Lutheran University
Tacoma, WA 98447
*University/College URL:* http://www.plu.edu
*Type of Institution:* private, university, teaching, research, religious
*SL Program/Center Name:* Center for Public Service
*Contact Person Name and Title:* Oney Crandall, Dir
*Contact Phone Number:* (253) 535–7652
*Contact Fax Number:* (253) 535–8752
*Contact Email Address:* crandaie@plu.edu
*Description:* The Center for Public Service is an academic support office established by the university in 1993 to coordinate, encourage, broaden, and strengthen all initiatives for service at PLU. The center supports the university's mission to "empower its students for lives of thoughtful inquiry, service, leadership and care—for other persons, for the community, and for the earth." To accomplish this, the center connects students, staff, and faculty with opportunities to meet community needs at many levels. It encourages thoughtful reflection about service experience, in formats ranging from rigorous academic scholarship ("scholar service") to informal group discussion. It advo-

cates service as a rich source of enlightenment and spiritual growth which blends professional and liberal arts to create lifelong learners with a sense of vocation and civic responsibility. At the same time, the center celebrates the full partnership of community, recognizing the give-and-take of social and human endeavors.

The Center for Public Service supports service-learning at the university; houses the student Volunteer Center; runs several co-curricular mentoring, tutoring, and senior citizen programs; and promotes a variety of service activities across campus during the year. To support service-learning, the center offers faculty incentive awards from time to time, promotes workshop and conference opportunities, maintains an up-to-date library of resource materials on service-learning; arranges service opportunities for students, offers orientation and reflection information as requested by faculty, keeps sample contract agreements, helps with transportation arrangements, surveys faculty and students annually about their service experience, and works with faculty to develop cross-disciplinary strategies for service-learning.

*SL Required for Graduation (all students)?* No

*Service Required for Graduation (all students)?* No

*Any Co-curricular Service?* Yes

*Any SL Residence Halls or Theme Houses?* No

*Number of Undergraduate SL Courses Offered Per Year:* 49 (15 focused in the liberal arts; 34 in the professional schools where students in practica simultaneously offer public service that might otherwise be unavailable, such as in low-income clinics or education classes tutoring in low-income schools)

*Total Number of SL Courses Offered Per Year:* 49

*Number of Instructors Teaching SL Courses Per Year:* 47 (15 in the liberal arts; 32 in the professional schools)

*Number of Full-time SL Staff on Campus (not counting instructors):* 0

*Number of Part-time SL Staff on Campus (not counting instructors):* 1

**Pacific University**
2043 College Way, Forest Grove, OR 97116
*University/College URL:* http://www.pacificu.edu

*Type of Institution:* private, university, teaching, secular (though founded by the United Church of Christ with some remaining connection)

*SL Program/Center Name:* Pacific Humanitarian Center

*Contact Person Name and Title:* Ellen Hastay, Service Learning Coord

*Contact Phone Number:* (503) 359–2914

*Contact Fax Number:* (503) 359–3164

*Contact Email Address:* hastaye@pacificu.edu

*SL Program/Center URL:* http://nellie.pacificu.edu/humctr/index.html

*Description:* The Pacific Humanitarian Center connects students, faculty, and staff with community partners to enhance student learning of academic and civic principles and to promote the common good. The center assists faculty in the development and coordination of service-learning courses and also coordinates a variety of ongoing, student-led service programs and alternative spring breaks. Residence halls, campus clubs, and individual students receive assistance in planning service programs.

*SL Required for Graduation (all students)?* No

*Service Required for Graduation (all students)?* No

*Any Co-curricular Service?* Yes

*Any SL Residence Halls or Theme Houses?* No

*SL Degrees Offered:* N (But service-learning is required for Peace and Conflict Studies Minor and Feminist Studies Minor.)

*Number of Undergraduate SL Courses Offered Per Year:* 10

*Number of Graduate SL Courses Offered Per Year:* 5

*Total Number of SL Courses Offered Per Year:* 15

*Number of Instructors Teaching SL Courses Per Year:* 15

*Number of Full-time SL Staff on Campus (not counting instructors):* 3 (1 full-time

Service Learning Coord, 1 VISTA Student Outreach Coord, and 1 AmeriCorps Team Leader)
*Number of Part-time SL Staff on Campus (not counting instructors):* 2 (1 part-time Faculty Dir of the Humanitarian Center, 1part-time Program Assist)

## Pennsylvania State University

College Ave, University Park, PA 16802
*University/College URL:* http://www.psu.edu
*Type of Institution:* public, university, research
*SL Program/Center Name:* SAIL (Service Action Initiative Leadership), Schreyer Honors College
*Contact Person Name and Title:* Josephine Carubia, PhD, Coord, Student Programs and Service Learning, Schreyer Honors College
*Contact Phone Number:* (814) 863–2635
*Contact Fax Number:* (814) 863–8688
*Contact Email Address:* jmc30@psu.edu
*SL Program/Center URL:* http://nellie.pacificu.edu/humctr/index.html
*Description:* SAIL is an umbrella organization for a variety of service initiatives within the Schreyer Honors College. SAIL's mission is to provide resources and guidance for Honors Scholars to initiate, serve in, and run volunteer efforts. Some of SAIL's current projects are the Student-to-Student Mentor Program, SPEAK (Speaking Practical English for Adults and Kids), Free Music Lessons Project, Upward Bound, SAIL Habitat for Humanity, Food Donation Project, and International Journeys Storyhour.
*SL Required for Graduation (all students)?* No
*Service Required for Graduation (all students)?* No
*Any Co-curricular Service?* No
*Any SL Residence Halls or Theme Houses?* Yes
*Number of Undergraduate SL Courses Offered Per Year:* 5
*Total Number of SL Courses Offered Per Year:* 5
*Number of Instructors Teaching SL Courses Per Year:* 5

*Number of Full-time SL Staff on Campus (not counting instructors):* 0
*Number of Part-time SL Staff on Campus (not counting instructors):* 1

## Pennsylvania State University

201 Carnegie Bldg, University Park, PA 16802
*University/College URL:* http://www.psu.edu
*Type of Institution:* public, university, research, secular
*SL Program/Center Name:* SOURCE (Service, Outreach, Unity, Research, Communications, Education), College of Communications
*Contact Person Name and Title:* Cinda Kostyak, Dir, and Dir, Curricular and Research Management
*Contact Phone Number:* (814) 863–6307
*Contact Fax Number:* (814) 863–8044
*Contact Email Address:* csk2@psu.edu
*SL Program/Center URL:* http://www.psu.edu/dept/comm/source/index.html
*Description:* SOURCE serves as an academic and administrative umbrella for public scholarship and service-learning in the College of Communications. An annual spring institute for students, faculty, staff, and community provides development and reflection among participants. SOURCE provides liaison services between the college and community organizations working with faculty, staff, and students.
*SL Required for Graduation (all students)?* No
*Service Required for Graduation (all students)?* No
*Any Co-curricular Service?* Yes
*Any SL Residence Halls or Theme Houses?* No
*Number of Undergraduate SL Courses Offered Per Year:* 32
*Number of Graduate SL Courses Offered Per Year:* 0
*Total Number of SL Courses Offered Per Year:* 32 (in 1998–99)
*Number of Instructors Teaching SL Courses Per Year:* 28 (in the College of Communications who have taught SL courses in the past 18 months)

*Number of Full-time SL Staff on Campus
(not counting instructors):* 0

*Number of Part-time SL Staff on Campus
(not counting instructors):* 1 (Director has
other duties in addition to SOURCE)

**The Pennsylvania State University
Fayette Campus**
Route 119, PO Box 519, Uniontown,
PA 15401
*University/College URL:* http://www.fe.
psu.edu
*Type of Institution:* public, university,
teaching
*SL Program/Center Name:* Service Learning
Program
*Contact Person Name and Title:* Lynn
Petko, Service Learning Coord
*Contact Phone Number:* (724) 430–4129/
4123/4140
*Contact Fax Number:* (724) 430–4184
*Contact Email Address:* ldp1@psu.edu
*SL Program/Center URL:* http://www.fe.
psu.edu/lec
*Description:* Begun in Fall 1999, the Service
Learning Program is presently housed in the
Learning Enrichment Center. The center coordinator also serves as the service-learning coordinator and is responsible for all aspects of
service-learning assistance, including setting
up service-learning projects; talking with community agencies and organizations; speaking to
classes and students who use or want to use
service-learning in their course work; monitoring ongoing projects; and conducting any necessary follow-ups. Some First-Year Seminar
instructors use service-learning to accomplish
some of the objectives set by the Penn State
University General Education Committee for
First-Year Seminar courses. In Fall 1999, the
Penn Sate Fayette campus enlisted over 150
students in service-learning: students in the
two- and the four-year nursing program, others
in upper-level business courses, and still others
in introductory, general-education courses and
in First-Year Seminar courses, required for
Human Development/Family Studies, Administration of Justice, 4-Year Letters, Arts and
Sciences, Nursing, and Business baccalaureate
degrees. A number of agencies and organiza-

tions have planned projects with Penn State
Fayette: City Missions and other homeless shel-
ters, the Crime Victim's Center, Communities
in Schools, Senior Citizens' Centers, Child-
ren and Youth Services, Community Action,
the Legal Aid Society, the Office of Human
Resources, and the American Heart Associa-
tion. Many more projects and students will be a
part of service-learning in Spring Semester 2000.
*SL Required for Graduation (all
students)?* No
*Service Required for Graduation (all stu-
dents)?* No
*Any Co-curricular Service?* No
*Any SL Residence Halls or Theme
Houses?* No
*Number of Undergraduate SL Courses
Offered Per Year:* 24 (Fall 1999: 10;
Spring 2000: 14)
*Total Number of SL Courses Offered Per
Year:* 24
*Number of Instructors Teaching SL Courses
Per Year:* 24
*Number of Full-time SL Staff on Campus
(not counting instructors):* 0
*Number of Part-time SL Staff on Campus
(not counting instructors):* 0

**Pepperdine University**
24255 Pacific Coast Hwy, Malibu, CA
90263–4143
*University/College URL:* http://www.
pepperdine.edu
*Type of Institution:* private, university, teach-
ing, religious
*SL Program/Center Name:* Service Learning
Center, Seaver College
*Contact Person Name and Title:* Brad
Dudley, Service Learning Coord
*Contact Phone Number:* (310) 456–4143
*Contact Fax Number:* (310) 456–4827
*Contact Email Address:*
bdudley@pepperdine.edu
*SL Program/Center URL:* http://www.
pepperdine.edu/studentaffairs/
volunteercenter/learning.html
*SL Online Course Description URL:* http://
www.pepperdine.edu/studentaffairs/
volunteercenter/classes.html
*Description:* The Pepperdine Service Learning

Center provides support to students, faculty, and community agencies by maintaining a database of Los Angeles-area service opportunities, a growing library of service-learning books, monographs, and journals, and knowledgeable support staff. The Service Learning Office's mission includes three primary objectives: enhance academic discovery and instruction through service-learning activities; promote the Christian ethic of service through expressions of civic and social responsibility; and strengthen collaborative campus/community partnerships which address significant community needs.

*SL Required for Graduation (all students)?* No

*Service Required for Graduation (all students)?* No

*Any Co-curricular Service?* Yes

*Any SL Residence Halls or Theme Houses?* No

*SL Undergraduate Program Name:* N (A proposal is in progress)

*Number of Undergraduate SL Courses Offered Per Year:* 46

*Number of Graduate SL Courses Offered Per Year:* 5

*Total Number of SL Courses Offered Per Year:* 51

*Number of Instructors Teaching SL Courses Per Year:* 25

*Number of Full-time SL Staff on Campus (not counting instructors):* 1

*Number of Part-time SL Staff on Campus (not counting instructors):* 4 (Service Learning Advocates, i.e., students who have developed some expertise and experience in service-learning through both coursework and training in the center)

## Pine Manor College

400 Heath St, Chestnut Hill, MA 02467

*University/College URL:* http://www.pmc.edu

*Type of Institution:* private, college, teaching, secular

*SL Program/Center Name:* Community Service Learning Office

*Contact Person Name and Title:* Community Service Learning Coord

*Contact Phone Number:* (617) 731–7073

*Contact Fax Number:* (617) 731–7199

*Description:* The Community Service Learning Office is a newly established office on campus which serves as a resource for students, faculty, staff, and administrators. The office helps coordinate community service as well as service-learning in response to the college's commitment to inclusive leadership and social responsibility.

*SL Required for Graduation (all students)?* No

*Service Required for Graduation (all students)?* No

*Any Co-curricular Service?* Yes

*Any SL Residence Halls or Theme Houses?* No

*Number of Undergraduate SL Courses Offered Per Year:* 3

*Number of Graduate SL Courses Offered Per Year:* 0

*Total Number of SL Courses Offered Per Year:* 3

*Number of Instructors Teaching SL Courses Per Year:* 3

*Number of Full-time SL Staff on Campus (not counting instructors):* 1

*Number of Part-time SL Staff on Campus (not counting instructors):* 0

## Portland Community College

PO Box 19000, Portland, OR 97217

*University/College URL:* http://www.pcc.edu

*Type of Institution:* public, community college, teaching, secular

*Contact Person Name and Title:* Porter Raper, English Faculty and SL Coord

*Contact Phone Number:* (503) 978–5283

*Contact Fax Number:* (503) 978–5050

*Contact Email Address:* praper@pcc.edu

*Description:* Portland Community College's service-learning initiative is a faculty-based movement without a central office or support staff. There is a faculty coordinator who has been released half-time to promote service-learning, and support faculty who are implementing community-based education. The program has grown quickly over the last two years throughout the multi-campus district.

*SL Required for Graduation (all students)?* No

*Service Required for Graduation (all students)?* No

*Any Co-curricular Service?* Yes

*Any SL Residence Halls or Theme Houses?* No

*Number of Undergraduate SL Courses Offered Per Year:* 60–65

*Number of Graduate SL Courses Offered Per Year:* 0

*Total Number of SL Courses Offered Per Year:* 60–65

*Number of Instructors Teaching SL Courses Per Year:* 55–60

*Number of Full-time SL Staff on Campus (not counting instructors):* 0

*Number of Part-time SL Staff on Campus (not counting instructors):* 0

## Portland State University

1021 SW Broadway Ave, PO Box 751-CAE, Portland, OR 97207–0751

*University/College URL:* http://www.pdx.edu

*Type of Institution:* public, university, teaching

*SL Program/Center Name:* Center for Academic Excellence

*Contact Person Name and Title:* Dilafruz Williams, PhD, Dir, Community-University Partnerships

*Contact Phone Number:* (503) 725–5642

*Contact Fax Number:* (503) 725–5262

*Contact Email Address:* williamsdi@pdx.edu

*SL Program/Center URL:* http://www.oaa.pdx.edu/cae/

*Description:* Portland State University has a curricular-based service-learning program that spans all of the academic disciplines. Portland State has been cultivating institutional commitment to service-learning for a number of years. At this stage, service-learning is embedded into the undergraduate curriculum by requiring all graduating seniors to complete a six-credit service-learning course (Capstone) to address a community identified problem (1,300 students yearly). These courses are with multidisciplinary groups of students working in teams of no more than 20. In addition to this institutional commitment to service in the form of a Capstone

course, students also encounter service-learning as part of their Freshman Inquiry and throughout their academic program in Community-based Learning courses. The key to the university's success in institutionalizing service-learning on campus has been a deliberate effort to connect community service to discipline-based curriculum. Thus students gain relevant community experiences that enhance their classroom learning.

As with undergraduate education, at the graduate level there are many examples of community-based learning courses. Community-based learning is a dimension of educating students in an academic discipline while also preparing them to be contributing citizens. By becoming involved in community activities students benefit others while benefitting themselves, learning about teamwork, civic responsibility, and the application of intellectual skills to community issues. Community-based learning options in regular classes engage students in performing service as a way to gather, test, and apply content and skill from existing courses. Students perform a designated amount of service, and their learning from that experience is evaluated as part of the course. Initial funding for community-based learning came from a Corporation for National Service Learn and Serve grant. Currently the university benefits from Learn and Serve funds, yet a considerable amount of support comes from the university budget.

*SL Required for Graduation (all students)?* Yes

*Service Required for Graduation (all students)?* Yes

*Any Co-curricular Service?* Yes

*Any SL Residence Halls or Theme Houses?* No

*Number of Undergraduate SL Courses Offered Per Year:* 200

*Number of Graduate SL Courses Offered Per Year:* 100

*Total Number of SL Courses Offered Per Year:* 300

*Number of Instructors Teaching SL Courses Per Year:* 100+

*Number of Full-time SL Staff on Campus
(not counting instructors):* 5
*Number of Part-time SL Staff on Campus
(not counting instructors):* 6

## Prestonsburg Community College
One Bert T. Combs Dr, Pike Building,
Room 202A, Prestonsburg, KY 41653
*University/College URL:* http://www.
prestonsburgcc.com
*Type of Institution:* public, community college, teaching
*SL Program/Center Name:* Service Learning
Program
*Contact Person Name and Title:* Paul D.
Thompson, Dir
*Contact Phone Number:* (606) 886–
3863, ext 313
*Contact Fax Number:* (606) 886–8683
*Contact Email Address:* pccsl@pop.uky.edu
*SL Program/Center URL:* _ http://www.
prestonsburgcc.com
*Description:* The Service Learning Program is
staffed by the director and two full-time work-study students. An orientation for students,
faculty, and agencies is held the third week of
each semester, and a celebration is held near the
end of the semester. A handbook is distributed
containing application and agreement forms,
and a time sheet for recording hours worked.
The Service Learning Office also keeps a list of
agencies and provides individual help with
student placement. The office has helped the
Counseling Center set up a database for use by
students. The resulting Service Learning Agency
Listing has job descriptions from places where
students have served. Several courses involve
a service-learning component (either mandatory or extra credit). These include "Basic
Public Speaking," "Interpersonal Communication," "Introduction to Social Services,"
"Introduction to Sociology," "General Psychology," "Introduction to American Education," and "Human Development and Learning." Although service-learning has been most
heavily employed in the Social Science Division, other divisions have offered courses with
a service-learning component, e.g. General
Chemistry, Dental Hygiene, and Biology. In
addition, students can perform service-learning

separate from any particular course by taking
"Experiential Education," in which a student
works 40 hours to earn one Pass/Fail credit. A
reflective journal is required.
*SL Required for Graduation (all
students)?* No
*Service Required for Graduation (all students)?* No
*Any Co-curricular Service?* No
*Any SL Residence Halls or Theme
Houses?* No
*Number of Undergraduate SL Courses
Offered Per Year:* 24
*Number of Graduate SL Courses Offered
Per Year:* 0
*Total Number of SL Courses Offered Per
Year:* 24
*Number of Instructors Teaching SL Courses
Per Year:* 16
*Number of Full-time SL Staff on Campus
(not counting instructors):* 3
*Number of Part-time SL Staff on Campus
(not counting instructors):* 0

## Princeton University
Princeton, NJ 08544
*University/College URL:* http://www.
princeton.edu
*Type of Institution:* private, university, teaching, research, secular
*SL Program/Center Name:* Community-Based Learning Initiative
*Contact Person Name and Title:* Hank
Dobin, Associate Dean of the College
*Contact Phone Number:* (609) 258–3040
*Contact Fax Number:* (609) 258–6371
*Contact Email Address:*
hdobin@princeton.edu
*SL Program/Center URL:* http://www.
princeton.edu/~cbli
*SL Online Course Description URL:* http://
www.princeton.edu/~cbli
*Description:* The Community Based Learning
Initiative is the collaborative effort of students,
faculty, administration, and community experts
working to provide students with opportunities
for community involvement and hands-on research in the classroom. Community-based

learning enriches coursework by encouraging students to apply the knowledge and analytic tools gained in the classroom to the pressing issues that affect local communities. Working with faculty members and community leaders, students develop research projects, collect and analyze data, and share their results and conclusions with the organizations and agencies that need the information, as well as with their professors. Not only does the community benefit, but students' understanding of the subject is also greatly enhanced.

*SL Required for Graduation (all students)?* No

*Service Required for Graduation (all students)?* No

*Any Co-curricular Service?* Yes

*Any SL Residence Halls or Theme Houses?* No

*Number of Undergraduate SL Courses Offered Per Year:* 10

*Number of Graduate SL Courses Offered Per Year:* 0

*Total Number of SL Courses Offered Per Year:* 10

*Number of Instructors Teaching SL Courses Per Year:* 10

*Number of Full-time SL Staff on Campus (not counting instructors):* 0

*Number of Part-time SL Staff on Campus (not counting instructors):* 0 (This past year an alumni organization hired a person to spend most of her time working with CBLI, but she was not hired by the university, nor was she reporting to a university official—she was employed by the alumni organization)

**Providence College**
Providence, RI 02918–0001
*University/College URL:* http://www. providence.edu
*Type of Institution:* private, college, teaching, religious
*SL Program/Center Name:* Feinstein Institute for Public Service
*Contact Person Name and Title:* Dr. Richard Battistoni, Dir

*Contact Phone Number:* (401) 865–2786
*Contact Fax Number:* (401) 865–1206
*Contact Email Address:* rickbatt@providence.edu
*SL Program/Center URL:* http://www. providence.edu/psp/
*SL Online Course Description URL:* http:// www.providence.edu/psp/req.htm
*SL Online Syllabi URL:* http://www. providence.edu/psp/syllabi/index.html
*Description:* The fundamental mission of the Feinstein Institute for Public Service is strengthening communities by integrating public and community service into the liberal arts curriculum. Believing that service bears witness to religious and ethical values central to the college's mission and is at the heart of a liberal arts education in a democratic society, the institute provides an environment for research and reflection on the meaning of public and community service and an educational experience that prepares future leaders for positive change. The Feinstein Institute administers a unique four-year curriculum in Public and Community Service Studies which involves a systemic and rigorous study of the major conceptual themes of comn.unity, service, public ethics, social justice, leadership, and social change.

*SL Required for Graduation (all students)?* No

*Service Required for Graduation (all students)?* No

*Any Co-curricular Service?* Yes

*Any SL Residence Halls or Theme Houses?* No

*SL Degrees Offered:* Bachelor of Arts in Public and Community Service Studies (students can also minor)

*Number of Undergraduate SL Courses Offered Per Year:* 20

*Number of Graduate SL Courses Offered Per Year:* 0

*Total Number of SL Courses Offered Per Year:* 20

*Number of Instructors Teaching SL Courses Per Year:* 15

*Number of Full-time SL Staff on Campus (not counting instructors):* 2

*Number of Part-time SL Staff on Campus (not counting instructors):* 15

## Pueblo Community College
900 W Orman Ave, Pueblo, CO 81004
*University/College URL:* http://www.pcc.cccoes.edu
*Type of Institution:* public, community college, teaching, secular
*SL Program/Center Name:* Service Learning Program
*Contact Person Name and Title:* Gwen Speaks, Service Learning Coord
*Contact Phone Number:* (719) 549–3247
*Contact Fax Number:* (719) 549–3309
*Contact Email Address:* Gwen.Speaks@pcc.cccoes.edu
*SL Program/Center URL:* http://www.pcc.cccoes.edu/ser_net/intro.htm
*Description:* Pueblo Community College students are involved in service-learning on many levels. Most of the programs have service-learning as an option in one or more classes. In some programs it is required. Students have done service in museums, with the local school districts, in nursing homes, with mental-health centers, and many other agencies. Activities are coordinated through the individual instructors and the Service Learning Coordinator.
*SL Required for Graduation (all students)?* No
*Service Required for Graduation (all students)?* No
*Any Co-curricular Service?* Yes
*Any SL Residence Halls or Theme Houses?* No
*Number of Undergraduate SL Courses Offered Per Year:* 20–50
*Number of Graduate SL Courses Offered Per Year:* 0
*Total Number of SL Courses Offered Per Year:* 20–50
*Number of Instructors Teaching SL Courses Per Year:* 15–25
*Number of Full-time SL Staff on Campus (not counting instructors):* 0
*Number of Part-time SL Staff on Campus (not counting instructors):* 1

## Purdue University
1285 Electrical Engineering Bldg, EPICS, West Lafayette, IN 47907
*University/College URL:* http://www.purdue.edu
*Type of Institution:* public, university, teaching, research
*SL Program/Center Name:* EPICS
*Contact Person Name and Title:* Pamela Brown, Prog Coord
*Contact Phone Number:* (765) 494–0639
*Contact Fax Number:* (765) 494–0052
*Contact Email Address:* epics@ecn.purdue.edu
*SL Program/Center URL:* http://epics.ecn.purdue.edu
*SL Online Course Description URL:* http://shay.ecn.purdue.edu/~epics/docs/docs.html
*Description:* EPICS is an innovative new program at Purdue University's School of Electrical and Computer Engineering that places teams of undergraduate engineering students into a partnership with local community-service agencies. This partnership provides many benefits to the students and the community alike.
*SL Required for Graduation (all students)?* No
*Service Required for Graduation (all students)?* No
*Any Co-curricular Service?* Yes
*Any SL Residence Halls or Theme Houses?* No
*Number of Undergraduate SL Courses Offered Per Year:* 19
*Number of Instructors Teaching SL Courses Per Year:* 15
*Number of Full-time SL Staff on Campus (not counting instructors):* 1
*Number of Part-time SL Staff on Campus (not counting instructors):* 3

## Radford University
Route 11 and Norwood St, PO Box 7010, Radford, VA 24142
*University/College URL:* http://www.runet.edu
*Type of Institution:* public, university
*SL Program/Center Name:* Center for Experiential Learning

*Contact Person Name and Title:* Dr. Kevin
  Everett
*Contact Phone Number:* (540) 831–6386
*Contact Fax Number:* (540) 831–6119
*Contact Email Address:* scrump@runet.edu
*SL Program/Center URL:* http://www.runet.
  edu/~srvlearn
*Description:* The mission of the service-learning program is to broaden educational opportunities by involving students in learning experi-
ences in the community. Students' educational
experiences are enriched while meeting community needs. Service-learning objectives are
integrated into individual courses by faculty
members. Radford University funds the program, which is a division of the Center for
Experiential Learning.
*SL Required for Graduation (all*
  *students)?* No
*Service Required for Graduation (all stu-*
  *dents)?* No
*Any Co-curricular Service?* Yes
*Any SL Residence Halls or Theme Houses?*
  Yes (Beginning in 2000, Service-Learning
  month targets one residence hall of
  freshmen. Received a VACOOL grant for
  this project)
*Number of Undergraduate SL Courses*
  *Offered Per Year:* 25–35
*Number of Graduate SL Courses Offered*
  *Per Year:* 5
*Total Number of SL Courses Offered Per*
  *Year:* 30–40
*Number of Instructors Teaching SL Courses*
  *Per Year:* 25–35
*Number of Full-time SL Staff on Campus*
  *(not counting instructors):* 3
*Number of Part-time SL Staff on Campus*
  *(not counting instructors):* 2

**Raritan Valley Community College**
Route 28 and Lamington Rd, North Branch,
  NJ, PO Box 3300, Somerville, NJ 08807
*University/College URL:* http://www.
  raritanval.edu
*Type of Institution:* public, community col-
  lege, teaching
*SL Program/Center Name:* Service Learn-
  ing Office

*Contact Person Name and Title:* Lori Moog,
  Service Learning Coord
*Contact Phone Number:* (908) 526–1200,
  ext 8284
*Contact Fax Number:* (908) 704–3442
*Contact Email Address:*
  lmoog@rvcc.raritanval.edu
*SL Program/Center URL:* _ http://www.rvcc.
  raritanval.edu/servicelearning
*Description:* Service Learning at Raritan Valley Community College links community service to academic courses. Students work in
community agencies as part of their course
assignments, learning real-world applications
and practicing skills that directly relate to their
course goals. RVCC works with over 200 social service agencies, government offices, nonprofit businesses, educational institutions, museums, and various associations. The program
places more than 800 students annually in
service-learning projects.
*SL Required for Graduation (all*
  *students)?* No
*Service Required for Graduation (all stu-*
  *dents)?* No
*Any Co-curricular Service?* Yes
*Any SL Residence Halls or Theme*
  *Houses?* No
*Number of Undergraduate SL Courses*
  *Offered Per Year:* 87
*Number of Graduate SL Courses Offered*
  *Per Year:* 0
*Total Number of SL Courses Offered Per*
  *Year:* 87
*Number of Instructors Teaching SL Courses*
  *Per Year:* 70
*Number of Full-time SL Staff on Campus*
  *(not counting instructors):* 0
*Number of Part-time SL Staff on Campus*
  *(not counting instructors):* 1 (3/4 time)

**Regis University**
Center for Service Learning, E-28, 3333
  Regis Blvd, Denver, CO 80221
*University/College URL:* http://www.
  regis.edu
*Type of Institution:* private, university, teach-
  ing, religious
*SL Program/Center Name:* Center for Serv-
  ice Learning

*Contact Person Name and Title:* Mary Ellen
Carroll, Coord, Regis College; Rhonda
Sims, Coord, School for Health Care
Professions
*Contact Phone Number:* (303) 458–3550;
(303) 458–4188
*Contact Fax Number:* (303) 964–5478; (303)
964–5533
*Contact Email Address:* mcarroll@regis.edu;
rsims@regis.edu
*SL Program/Center URL:* http://www.regis.
edu/service
*Description:* The Center for Service Learning
works with students, faculty, and staff to cultivate an understanding of how one is called to
promote justice and to discern the influence of
one's actions from the perspective of the poor.
In the quest to understand and discern what
justice looks like, one must have the opportunity to hear the voices of those not often heard
in one's culture and educational system: voices
that provide a view of reality from the vantage
point of the dispossessed. Through service one
develops the capacity to listen and to learn from
those at the margins and to grow in solidarity
with them and begin to see society as an integrated whole. As a member and sustaining link
of "this whole," one can no longer forget,
dismiss, or distance oneself from "the other."
One glimpses the interdependent nature of justice. One is transformed and must rise to the
challenge of becoming a positive change agent
in society. The goal, therefore, is not simply to
experience and gain a deeper understanding of
the "voices" of the other, but rather, to learn
about and gain the tools through which the
inequitable systems and structures of society
can be changed.
*SL Required for Graduation (all students)?*
No (It is not a graduation requirement in
the college, but it is a graduation
requirement in the School for Health Care
Professions.)
*Service Required for Graduation (all stu-
dents)?* No (same as above)
*Any Co-curricular Service?* Yes
*Any SL Residence Halls or Theme
Houses?* Yes

*Number of Undergraduate SL Courses
Offered Per Year:* 10–15
*Number of Graduate SL Courses Offered
Per Year:* 8–10
*Total Number of SL Courses Offered Per
Year:* 18–25
*Number of Instructors Teaching SL Courses
Per Year:* 9–20
*Number of Full-time SL Staff on Campus
(not counting instructors):* 2
*Number of Part-time SL Staff on Campus
(not counting instructors):* 1

## Rice University

6100 Main St, PO Box 1892, Houston, TX
77251–1892
*University/College URL:* http://riceinfo.
rice.edu
*Type of Institution:* private, university, teach-
ing, research, secular
*SL Program/Center Name:* Community In-
volvement Center
*Contact Person Name and Title:* Heather
Syrett, Assoc Dir for Community
Involvement
*Contact Phone Number:* (713) 527–4970
*Contact Fax Number:* (713) 737–6165
*Contact Email Address:* heathers@rice.edu
OR service@rice.edu
*SL Program/Center URL:* http://www.ruf.
rice.edu/~cicpage
*Description:* The Community Involvement Center was established in 1995 as the center of
community-service programming for Rice University students, faculty, and staff. The center
seeks to establish a culture of service and an
ethic of social responsibility within the university community by developing one-time and
ongoing service projects, advising student service organizations, and serving as a resource for
students, faculty, and staff interested in community service and service-learning. It coordinates a number of opportunities for community
involvement throughout the year including the
America Reads Tutoring Program, ESL Tutoring, Outreach Days, the Good Works Volunteer and Career Fair, International Service Projects, Alternative Spring Breaks, and many
others. The center also advises and supports 13
student-run service organizations, including the

Rice Student Volunteer Program, the largest student service organization at Rice University.

*SL Required for Graduation (all students)?* No

*Service Required for Graduation (all students)?* No

*Any Co-curricular Service?* Yes

*Any SL Residence Halls or Theme Houses?* No (But there is a service committee in each of the eight residential colleges.)

*Number of Undergraduate SL Courses Offered Per Year:* 10

*Total Number of SL Courses Offered Per Year:* 10

*Number of Instructors Teaching SL Courses Per Year:* 10

*Number of Full-time SL Staff on Campus (not counting instructors):* 2

*Number of Part-time SL Staff on Campus (not counting instructors):* 0

## Royal Roads University

2005 Sooke Rd, Victoria, British Columbia, Canada V9B 5Y2

*University/College URL:* http://www. royalroads.ca

*Type of Institution:* public, university, teaching, secular

*SL Program/Center Name:* Leadership and Training Division

*Contact Person Name and Title:* Dr. P. Gerry Nixon, Dir

*Contact Phone Number:* (250) 391–2569

*Contact Fax Number:* (250) 391–2608

*Contact Email Address:* gerry.nixon@royalroads.ca

*SL Program/Center URL:* http://www. royalroads.ca/oll/malt/

*Description:* The Master of Arts in Leadership and Training at Royal Roads University is a two-year applied program for mid-career leaders working in learning/training environments. The program is structured on the basis of two short residency periods followed by distance courseware and a major consultancy project.

*SL Required for Graduation (all students)?* No

*Service Required for Graduation (all students)?* Yes

*Any Co-curricular Service?* No

*Any SL Residence Halls or Theme Houses?* No

*SL Graduate Program Name:* Master of Arts: Leadership and Training

*Number of Graduate SL Courses Offered Per Year:* 1

*Total Number of SL Courses Offered Per Year:* 1

*Number of Instructors Teaching SL Courses Per Year:* 3 (in 1 team)

*Number of Full-time SL Staff on Campus (not counting instructors):* 0

*Number of Part-time SL Staff on Campus (not counting instructors):* 0

## Rutgers University

New Brunswick, NJ 08901

*University/College URL:* http://www. rutgers.edu

*Type of Institution:* public, university, research, secular

*SL Program/Center Name:* Citizenship and Service Education

*Contact Person Name and Title:* D. Michael Shafer, Dir

*Contact Phone Number:* (732) 932–8660

*Contact Fax Number:* (732) 932–1207

*Contact Email Address:* mshafer@rci.rutgers.edu

*SL Program/Center URL:* http://case. rutgers.edu

*Description:* The Citizenship and Service Education (CASE) program is built on a philosophy of active learning. Central to the program is the belief that citizenship, a service ethic, and an application for American diversity cannot be learned from books alone but must be learned by doing. Therefore, CASE courses typically combine an academically rigorous three-credit classroom course with a one-credit community service-learning placement directly related to the subject matter of the course. CASE courses are taught across the curriculum, but they all require students to do the following: contribute typically 40 hours of community service; confront the complex, ambiguous, human realities that lie behind the abstract concepts and materials they are studying in the classroom; think about, discuss, and practice good citizenship; and forge a link between service and learning, i.e., between the classroom and the real world. CASE is comprised of CASE (New Brunswick), Camden Associates Civic Education (ACE), and CASE (Newark).

*SL Required for Graduation (all students)?* No

*Service Required for Graduation (all students)?* No

*Any Co-curricular Service?* Yes

*Any SL Residence Halls or Theme Houses?* Yes

*Number of Undergraduate SL Courses Offered Per Year:* 78 (50 in New Brunswick, 16 in Newark, and 12 in Camden)

*Total Number of SL Courses Offered Per Year:* 78

*Number of Instructors Teaching SL Courses Per Year:* 59

*Number of Full-time SL Staff on Campus (not counting instructors):* 2 (1 in New Brunswick, 1 in Newark)

*Number of Part-time SL Staff on Campus (not counting instructors):* 25 (21 in New Brunswick, 1 in Newark, 3 in Camden)

## Saint Francis College

PO Box 600, Loretto, PA 15940

*University/College URL:* http://www. sfcpa.edu

*Type of Institution:* private, college, teaching, religious

*Contact Person Name and Title:* Joyce T. Remillard, Dir, Service Learning

*Contact Phone Number:* (814) 472–3343

*Contact Fax Number:* (814) 472–3937

*Contact Email Address:* jremillard@sfcpa.edu

*Description:* All sophomore students are required to take the Faith and Franciscanism course. Within the course is a Service Learning Component in which students are required to perform ten hours of service. Student projects are varied between programs for young people, mentally and physically handicapped, elderly, environment, food kitchens, and construction so that students can choose projects to meet their skills, major, or interest. The reflection process consists of informal discussion in class; a written reflection paper at the end of the course

connecting their service to a theme or theory that has been developed during the course, or connecting the service to their major; and a formal presentation by each student to their peers.

*SL Required for Graduation (all students)?* Yes

*Service Required for Graduation (all students)?* No

*Any Co-curricular Service?* Yes

*Any SL Residence Halls or Theme Houses?* No

*SL Degrees Offered:* A certificate, signed by the university president, is given to all students who perform more than the required 10 hours of service in their Faith and Franciscanism course.

*Number of Undergraduate SL Courses Offered Per Year:* 28

*Total Number of SL Courses Offered Per Year:* 28

*Number of Instructors Teaching SL Courses Per Year:* 12

*Number of Full-time SL Staff on Campus (not counting instructors):* 1

*Number of Part-time SL Staff on Campus (not counting instructors):* 3

## Saint Francis Xavier University

PO Box 5000, Antigonish, Nova Scotia, Canada B2G 2W5

*University/College URL:* http://www.stfx.ca

*Type of Institution:* public, university, teaching, research, secular

*SL Program/Center Name:* Service Learning Program

*Contact Person Name and Title:* Marla Gaudet, Course-based SL Officer; Brenda Riley, Immersion SL Officer

*Contact Phone Number:* (902) 867–2563; 867–5049

*Contact Fax Number:* (902) 867–5395

*Contact Email Address:* mgaudet@stfx.ca; briley@stfx.ca

*SL Program/Center URL:* http://www.stfx. ca/tresearch

*SL Online Course Description URL:* http:// www.stfx.ca/tresearch

*Description:* In Course-Based Service Learning, students complete a variety of service options in the local community as part of their course work. The nature and duration of the service is determined by the professor through the course content and the needs of the community. The service-learning experience is supported by program staff and the students' professor, who prepares them for the experience, helps them reflect on it, and integrates it with their academic knowledge and assignments. Courses with service-learning components vary each year.

In Immersion Service Learning, students become involved in intense service experiences in communities which include inner-city settings and international locations. Immersion projects, led by faculty leaders, engage student groups in educational sessions and service placements that help students understand community issues and community dynamics in a development context. These experiences typically occur during the second-term recess. Students may also choose to integrate an immersion experience with their chosen field of study through research for course credit, or specifically through course IDS 305: Immersion Service Learning. The Service Learning Program is currently funded through a combination of private foundation support, university alumni support, and university administration funding.

*SL Required for Graduation (all students)?* No

*Service Required for Graduation (all students)?* No

*Any Co-curricular Service?* Yes

*Any SL Residence Halls or Theme Houses?* No

*Number of Undergraduate SL Courses Offered Per Year:* 31 (30 courses with an SL option and one SL course)

*Number of Graduate SL Courses Offered Per Year:* 3–4 (The Bachelor of Education post-graduate degree program has 3–4 courses with an SL option.)

*Total Number of SL Courses Offered Per Year:* 35

*Number of Instructors Teaching SL Courses Per Year:* 30

*Number of Full-time SL Staff on Campus (not counting instructors):* 2

*Number of Part-time SL Staff on Campus (not counting instructors):* 2

**Saint Joseph's College**
278 Whites Bridge Rd, Standish, ME 04084
*University/College URL:* http://www. sjcme.edu
*Type of Institution:* private, college, teaching, religious
*SL Program/Center Name:* Community Enhancement Initiative
*Contact Person Name and Title:* Erin D. Swezey, Community Service Dir
*Contact Phone Number:* (207) 893–7794
*Contact Fax Number:* (207) 893–6605
*Contact Email Address:* eswezey@ sjcme.edu
*Description:* Community Enhancement Initiative is a problem-based approach to connecting community service in rural communities with academic study at a small, Catholic, liberal arts college in southern Maine. In less than three years, 15 faculty, 25 community partners, and over 300 students have participated. Each semester, learning and service outcomes are evaluated by students, faculty, and community partners. Faculty from the following academic disciplines are involved: philosophy, English, sociology, psychology, nursing, business, and environmental sciences.

*SL Required for Graduation (all students)?* No

*Service Required for Graduation (all students)?* No

*Any Co-curricular Service?* Yes

*Any SL Residence Halls or Theme Houses?* No

*Number of Undergraduate SL Courses Offered Per Year:* 12

*Total Number of SL Courses Offered Per Year:* 12

*Number of Instructors Teaching SL Courses Per Year:* 12–15

*Number of Full-time SL Staff on Campus (not counting instructors):* 0

*Number of Part-time SL Staff on Campus (not counting instructors):* 1

**Saint Joseph's University**

5600 City Ave, Wolfington Center, Philadelphia, PA 19131

*University/College URL:* http://www.sju.edu

*Type of Institution:* private, university, teaching, religious

*SL Program/Center Name:* Service-Learning Program, Wolfington Center for Ministry, Faith & Service

*Contact Person Name and Title:* Constance McSherry SL Contact Person Name and Title

*Contact Phone Number:* (610) 660–1338

*Contact Fax Number:* (610) 660–1042

*Contact Email Address:* mcsherry@sju.edu

*SL Program/Center URL:* http://www.sju.edu/cas/faith-justice/servlear.html

*Description:* The Service-Learning Pilot Initiative, implemented in 1992, proposed a three-tiered developmental plan to integrate service to the external community within traditional academic courses. The first level begins with a two-semester philosophy course that integrates a year-long service contract with a community agency. The service experience at this level is one of encounter, encouraging empathy and a sense of relatedness to persons of different life circumstances. The second level offers courses in which students engage in critical social analysis that is deepened by the service experience. The third level focuses on the integration of values into lifestyle and emphasizes the ethic of civic responsibility. Students at this level form a relationship with a community group and participate in group discussion and decision-making. They can also serve as mentors for first-level service-learning students. Service-learning has become institutionalized at the university, impacting students' intellectual and moral development, enriching faculty teaching and research, and providing a more reliable and informed service to our community partners.

*SL Required for Graduation (all students)?* No

*Service Required for Graduation (all students)?* No

*Any Co-curricular Service?* Yes

*Any SL Residence Halls or Theme Houses?* Yes

*Number of Undergraduate SL Courses Offered Per Year:* 12

*Total Number of SL Courses Offered Per Year:* 12

*Number of Instructors Teaching SL Courses Per Year:* 10

*Number of Full-time SL Staff on Campus (not counting instructors):* 2

*Number of Part-time SL Staff on Campus (not counting instructors):* 6

**Saint Louis College of Pharmacy**

4588 Parkview Pl, Saint Louis, MO 63021

*University/College URL:* http://stlcop.edu

*Type of Institution:* private, college, teaching

*Contact Person Name and Title:* Thomas D. Zlatic, PhD; Michael S. Maddux, PharmD

*Contact Phone Number:* (314) 367–8700

*Contact Fax Number:* (314) 367–2784

*Contact Email Address:* tzlatic@stlcop.edu

*SL Online Course Description URL:* http://rx.stlcop.edu/~tzlatic/index.html

*SL Online Syllabi URL:* http://rx.stlcop.edu/~tzlatic/sl/sl.html

*Description:* Saint Louis College of Pharmacy offers one service-learning course entitled: "Topics in Pharmaceutical Care: Community Service." In addition, elements of service-learning have been incorporated into the residency program. On campus a number of organizations offer opportunities for volunteering.

*SL Required for Graduation (all students)?* No

*Service Required for Graduation (all students)?* No

*Any Co-curricular Service?* Yes

*Any SL Residence Halls or Theme Houses?* No

*Number of Undergraduate SL Courses Offered Per Year:* 1 (1 course/two semesters)

*Number of Graduate SL Courses Offered Per Year:* 0

*Total Number of SL Courses Offered Per Year:* 1 (1 course/two semesters)

*Number of Instructors Teaching SL Courses Per Year:* 2

*Number of Full-time SL Staff on Campus (not counting instructors):* 0

*Number of Part-time SL Staff on Campus (not counting instructors):* 0

## Saint Louis Community College at Meramec

11333 Big Bend Blvd, CN214, Kirkwood, MO 63122

*University/College URL:* http://www. stlcc.cc.mo.us

*Type of Institution:* private, community college

*SL Program/Center Name:* Service Learning Office

*Contact Person Name and Title:* Donna Halsband, Service Learning Coord

*Contact Phone Number:* (314) 984–7893

*Contact Fax Number:* (314) 984–7010

*Contact Email Address:* dhalsband@mcmail.stlcc.cc.mo.us

*SL Program/Center URL:* http://www.stlcc. cc.mo.us/mc/dept/slp/

*Description:* The Service-Learning program involves faculty from a wide variety of disciplines who offer service-learning projects as a part of their curriculum. English composition classes offer a fourth-hour practicum credit in service-learning, and a one-hour personal development "Learning Through Service" class is offered by the coordinator. Funding for 3/4-time coordinator is a part-time faculty position, seeking other funding.

*SL Required for Graduation (all students)?* No

*Service Required for Graduation (all students)?* No

*Any Co-curricular Service?* No

*Any SL Residence Halls or Theme Houses?* No

*Number of Undergraduate SL Courses Offered Per Year:* 25

*Number of Graduate SL Courses Offered Per Year:* 0

*Total Number of SL Courses Offered Per Year:* 25

*Number of Instructors Teaching SL Courses Per Year:* 20

*Number of Full-time SL Staff on Campus (not counting instructors):* 0

*Number of Part-time SL Staff on Campus (not counting instructors):* 1

## Saint Mary-of-the-Woods College

Saint Mary-of-the-Woods, IN 47876

*University/College URL:* http://www. smwc.edu

*Type of Institution:* private, college, religious

*SL Program/Center Name:* Service Learning Center

*Contact Person Name and Title:* Rosemary Nudd, SP, Service Learning Coord

*Contact Phone Number:* (812) 535–5210

*Contact Fax Number:* (812) 535–5169

*Contact Email Address:* rnudd@smwc.edu

*Description:* The Service Learning Center is working towards full integration of service-learning into the curriculum, with help from a grant from the Lilly Foundation (now in the third year). Service-learning courses are encouraged in all majors, with a minimum of 12 contact hours per semester required. Instructors apply to teach SL courses, confer with the coordinator about course learning goals and appropriate service sites. Together, the coordinator and instructors explain SL to the students (instructors include learning goals, evaluation, and possible service sites in syllabi). Service-learning is required (not optional) in courses which include service-learning. The program has guidelines for faculty, service-learning agreements, applications, placement and procedure sheets, time sheet, and evaluations from service sites for students. The center is working on an assessment instrument and a handbook.

*SL Required for Graduation (all students)?* No

*Service Required for Graduation (all students)?* No

*Any Co-curricular Service?* No

*Any SL Residence Halls or Theme Houses?* No

*Number of Undergraduate SL Courses Offered Per Year:* 10

*Total Number of SL Courses Offered Per Year:* 10

*Number of Instructors Teaching SL Courses Per Year:* 8

*Number of Full-time SL Staff on Campus (not counting instructors):* 0

*Number of Part-time SL Staff on Campus (not counting instructors):* 1

## Saint Mary's University

One Camino Santa Maria, Box 82, San Antonio, TX 78228

*University/College URL:* http://cww. stmarytx.edu

*Type of Institution:* private, university, religious

*SL Program/Center Name:* Service Learning Center

*Contact Person Name and Title:* Judy M. Geelhoed, Dir of Service Learning

*Contact Phone Number:* (210) 431–2108

*Contact Fax Number:* (210) 436–3300

*Contact Email Address:* judyg@stmarytx.edu

*SL Program/Center URL:* http://cww. stmarytx.edu/studev/slc/

*Description:* The Service Learning Center was established in 1994 to help the university further its Marianist Catholic mission of extending the self in service to society. Annually, over 2,000 members of the St. Mary's Community participate in service-learning activities through the center. The center provides curricular and co-curricular service opportunities that enable students to respond to today's complex social realities by reaching out to the community, especially the poor and the marginalized. Through various modes of reflection, students are helped to personally integrate the principles of justice and peace inspired by Gospel values and Catholic social teaching in the Marianist Tradition. The center administers a comprehensive program which includes the community-service work-study program, service- learning course integration, one-time service projects, long-term service placements, regional and international service-immersion trips, and the Marianist Leadership Program.

*SL Required for Graduation (all students)?* No

*Service Required for Graduation (all students)?* No

*Any Co-curricular Service?* Yes

*Any SL Residence Halls or Theme Houses?* No

*Number of Undergraduate SL Courses Offered Per Year:* 15

*Number of Graduate SL Courses Offered Per Year:* 0

*Total Number of SL Courses Offered Per Year:* 15

*Number of Instructors Teaching SL Courses Per Year:* 10

*Number of Full-time SL Staff on Campus (not counting instructors):* 2

*Number of Part-time SL Staff on Campus (not counting instructors):* 2 (1 staff member, plus one graduate assistant)

## Saint Norbert College

100 Grant St, De Pere, WI 54115

*University/College URL:* http://www.snc.edu

*Type of Institution:* private, college, teaching, religious

*SL Program/Center Name:* Department of Leadership, Service and Involvement

*Contact Person Name and Title:* Nancy Mathias, Assoc Dir of Leadership and Service

*Contact Phone Number:* (920) 403–4040

*Contact Fax Number:* (920) 403–4092

*Contact Email Address:* mathnb@mail.snc.edu

*SL Program/Center URL:* http://www. snc.edu/lsi

*Description:* The Department of Leadership, Service and Involvement (LSI) is dedicated to the personal development of students through leadership, community service, and college community involvement opportunities. LSI supports a model of developing students' involvement in social responsibility, and service-learning is an aspect of this model. LSI is supported and funded by Student Life.

*SL Required for Graduation (all students)?* No

*Service Required for Graduation (all students)?* No

*Any Co-curricular Service?* Yes

*Any SL Residence Halls or Theme Houses?* Yes

*Number of Undergraduate SL Courses Offered Per Year:* 8–12

*Number of Graduate SL Courses Offered Per Year:* 0

*Total Number of SL Courses Offered Per Year:* 8–12

*Number of Instructors Teaching SL Courses Per Year:* 5–7

*Number of Full-time SL Staff on Campus (not counting instructors):* 1 (part of the responsibilities of one position)

*Number of Part-time SL Staff on Campus (not counting instructors):* 1

## Salt Lake Community College

4600 South Redwood Rd, PO Box 30808, Salt Lake City, UT 84130–0808

*University/College URL:* http://www.slcc.edu

*Type of Institution:* public, community college, teaching

*SL Program/Center Name:* Emma Lou Thayne Community Service Center

*Contact Person Name and Title:* Susan A. Marchant, Dir

*Contact Phone Number:* (801) 957–4555

*Contact Fax Number:* (801) 957–4958

*Contact Email Address:* marchasu@slcc.edu

*SL Program/Center URL:* http://www.slcc.edu/student/serv_center

*Description:* Established in 1994, the Thayne Community Service Center's purpose is to involve students, staff, and faculty in service opportunities and promote service-learning at Salt Lake Community College. One function of the center is to assist with SLCC's Service-Learning Scholars Program. The center is a department within Student Services. It receives operating funds from the college, student fees, and private donations.

*SL Required for Graduation (all students)?* No

*Service Required for Graduation (all students)?* No

*Any Co-curricular Service?* No

*Any SL Residence Halls or Theme Houses?* No

*SL Undergraduate Program Name:* Service-Learning Scholars Program

*SL Undergraduate Program Description:* The Service-Learning Scholars Program began in 1997, and is open to all students. To be Service-Learning Scholars, students must complete 100 hours of community service while attending the college (these hours are documented through an ongoing, reflective journal reviewed by the Service-Learning Scholars committee); complete 10 hours of service-learning or service-related course work (one credit hour of the 10 is received through an independent study course); meet with the program's academic advisor at least twice per semester; complete an Integrative Service Project of 50 hours during the last year of enrollment (these hours count towards the 100 documented service hours identified above); and maintain a cumulative 3.0 GPA. Students who complete all requirements receive a Certificate of Achievement from Salt Lake Community College, are designated as Service-Learning Scholars on the printed commencement program, and are honored at the Thayne Center Humanitarian Banquet. In addition, Service-Learning Scholar achievement is printed on students' official transcripts. Some requirements transfer directly to the University of Utah Service-Learning Scholars' program.

*SL Degrees Offered:* The Service-Learning Scholar certificate is awarded to all students who complete program requirements.

*Number of Undergraduate SL Courses Offered Per Year:* 35

*Total Number of SL Courses Offered Per Year:* 35

*Number of Instructors Teaching SL Courses Per Year:* 25

*Number of Full-time SL Staff on Campus (not counting instructors):* 2

*Number of Part-time SL Staff on Campus (not counting instructors):* 3

## San Diego State University

5500 Campanile Dr, Mail Code 4495, San Diego, CA 92182–4495

*University/College URL:* http://www.sdsu.edu

*Type of Institution:* public, university, research

*SL Program/Center Name:* Center for Community-Based Service Learning

*Contact Phone Number:* (619) 594–0807
*Contact Fax Number:* (619) 594–0545
*Contact Email Address:* ccbl@mail.sdsu.edu
*SL Program/Center URL:* http://www.sa.
sdsu.edu/ccbsl
*SL Online Course Description URL:* http://
130.191.211.77/ccbl_web/database_web/
courses/course.htm
*Description:* The mission of the Center for
Community-Based Service Learning is to en-
hance learning and civic responsibility through
community involvement.
*SL Required for Graduation (all
students)?* No
*Service Required for Graduation (all stu-
dents)?* No
*Any Co-curricular Service?* Yes
*Any SL Residence Halls or Theme
Houses?* No
*Total Number of SL Courses Offered Per
Year:* 100+
*Number of Full-time SL Staff on Campus
(not counting instructors):* 1
*Number of Part-time SL Staff on Campus
(not counting instructors):* 3

## San Francisco State University

1600 Holloway Ave, San Francisco,
CA 94132
*University/College URL:* http://www.sfsu.edu
*Type of Institution:* public, university, teach-
ing, secular
*SL Program/Center Name:* Office of Com-
munity Service Learning
*Contact Person Name and Title:* Gerald S.
Eisman, Dir
*Contact Phone Number:* (415) 338–6846
*Contact Fax Number:* (415) 338–3284
*Contact Email Address:* ocsl@sfsu.edu
*SL Program/Center URL:* http://thecity.sfsu.
edu/~ocsl
*SL Online Course Description URL:* http://
thecity.sfsu.edu/~ocsl/courses.html
*Description:* The Office of Community Serv-
ice Learning (OCSL) is responsible for coordi-
nating campus efforts to incorporate commu-
nity service-learning into the curriculum at San
Francisco State University. The central goal of

the office's five-year plan is to provide every
San Francisco State student with the opportu-
nity to take a community service-learning course
before graduation.
*SL Required for Graduation (all
students)?* No
*Service Required for Graduation (all stu-
dents)?* No
*Any Co-curricular Service?* Yes
*Any SL Residence Halls or Theme
Houses?* No
*Number of Undergraduate SL Courses
Offered Per Year:* 70
*Number of Graduate SL Courses Offered
Per Year:* 5
*Total Number of SL Courses Offered Per
Year:* 75
*Number of Instructors Teaching SL Courses
Per Year:* 64
*Number of Full-time SL Staff on Campus
(not counting instructors):* 1
*Number of Part-time SL Staff on Campus
(not counting instructors):* 4

## Seattle Central Community College

1701 Broadway, Seattle, WA 98122
*University/College URL:* http://
seattlecentral.org
*Type of Institution:* public, community col-
lege, teaching
*SL Program/Center Name:* Service-Learning
Program, Center for Independent Study
*Contact Person Name and Title:* Michelle
Gherardi, Prog Coord
*Contact Phone Number:* (206) 587–6997
*Contact Fax Number:* (206) 287–5529
*Contact Email Address:*
mghera@sccd.ctc.edu
*SL Program/Center URL:* http://www.sccd.
ctc.edu/~ccslp/
*Description:* The Center for Independent Study's
Service-Learning Program provides technical
support to faculty and students engaged in
service-learning. The program is devoted to the
enhancement and development of the college's
mission, which focuses on lifelong learning,
self-reflection, and community involvement.
Service-Learning is a "Community Service for

Credit'' program offered to students enrolled in college transfer or professional-technical courses. As a component to an individual course, service-learning enables students to earn academic credit through community involvement. Once a student has begun a course with this component, the required hours and activity focus are determined by the faculty. Advantages of service-learning include the opportunity to enhance understanding of course content, build experience for a resume, expand opportunities when transferring, explore career options and earn college credit. One to two transferable elective credits may be earned by completing community-service hours in conjunction with individual coursework such as writing, reading, speaking, and reflection. Service-learning is a coordinated effort between the student, faculty, nonprofit agency, and college. Registration is coordinated by the Service-Learning Program and the faculty of the individual course during the second week of the quarter. Final grades are allocated by the instructor. The program supports five to ten courses per quarter while offering two supplemental credits per student enrolled in discrete courses which incorporate a service-learning component. The service-learning component, more often than not, is offered as an option. On average, about 100 students per quarter make use of this option. The program is funded with 50 percent hard money, which supports a permanent part-time program coordinator.

*SL Required for Graduation (all students)?* No

*Service Required for Graduation (all students)?* No

*Any Co-curricular Service?* No

*Any SL Residence Halls or Theme Houses?* No

*Number of Undergraduate SL Courses Offered Per Year:* 30–40

*Total Number of SL Courses Offered Per Year:* 30–40

*Number of Instructors Teaching SL Courses Per Year:* 20

*Number of Part-time SL Staff on Campus (not counting instructors):* 1

**Seattle University**
900 Broadway, Seattle, WA 98122
*University/College URL:* http://www.seattleu.edu
*Type of Institution:* private, university, teaching, religious
*SL Program/Center Name:* Leadership and Service Office
*Contact Person Name and Title:* Kathryn Hubbard, Dir
*Contact Phone Number:* (206) 296–0257
*Contact Fax Number:* (206) 296–6054
*Contact Email Address:* hubbard@seattleu.edu; serv-learn@seattleu.edu
*Description:* Seattle University's Leadership and Service Office provides opportunities for students to engage in experiences that prepare them to be leaders well able to serve their communities. Students interested in service in the community can access a wide range of agencies, from those working with vulnerable populations to those specializing in environmental concerns. The office also supports the service-learning program, linking academic coursework to the learning laboratory of the surrounding community. In addition, the office provides a variety of leadership programming for students, including workshops to develop leadership skills and opportunities to interact with prominent local and international leaders.

*SL Required for Graduation (all students)?* No

*Service Required for Graduation (all students)?* No

*Any Co-curricular Service?* No

*Any SL Residence Halls or Theme Houses?* No

*Number of Undergraduate SL Courses Offered Per Year:* 30

*Number of Graduate SL Courses Offered Per Year:* 5

*Total Number of SL Courses Offered Per Year:* 35

*Number of Instructors Teaching SL Courses Per Year:* 20

*Number of Full-time SL Staff on Campus (not counting instructors):* 1

*Number of Part-time SL Staff on Campus (not counting instructors):* 2 (half-time graduate student assistants)

## Seattle University

900 Broadway, School of Education, Seattle, WA 98122

*University/College URL:* http://www. seattleu.edu

*Type of Institution:* private, university, teaching, religious

*SL Program/Center Name:* Seattle Community Service-Learning Partnership, School of Education

*Contact Person Name and Title:* Jeffrey Anderson, Assoc Prof, Education

*Contact Phone Number:* (206) 296–5754

*Contact Fax Number:* (206) 296–2053

*Contact Email Address:* janderso@seattleu.edu

*Description:* The Seattle University Community Service-Learning Partnership involves preparing preservice teachers to use service-learning as a pedagogy with their future K-12 students. A second, equally important goal of the partnership is to assist K-12 teachers and students in the design and implementation of high-quality service-learning activities. To achieve these goals all prospective teachers in Seattle University's Master in Teaching (MiT) Program take a required two-credit course titled "Service Leadership." In this course they receive preparation in the use of service-learning as a teaching method and engage in 25 hours of service-learning working with a K-12 school to assist in developing an carrying out a new service-learning activity. The course concludes with a conference at which Seattle University MiT students, K-12 teachers and students, and community agency personnel share their service-learning projects, and reflect on the service-learning process.

*SL Required for Graduation (all students)?* Yes (The Service Leadership course is required to earn the Master in Teaching degree.)

*Service Required for Graduation (all students)?* No

*Any Co-curricular Service?* Yes

*Any SL Residence Halls or Theme Houses?* No

*Number of Graduate SL Courses Offered Per Year:* 4

*Total Number of SL Courses Offered Per Year:* 4

*Number of Instructors Teaching SL Courses Per Year:* 4

## Sinclair Community College (partnered with Wright State University)

140 East Monument Ave, Dayton, OH 45402

*University/College URL:* http://www. sinclair.edu

*Type of Institution:* public, community college, teaching, secular

*SL Program/Center Name:* Center for Healthy Communities, Division of Allied Health Technologies

*Contact Person Name and Title:* Annette Canfield, RN, MS, Assist Dir

*Contact Phone Number:* (937) 775–1114

*Contact Fax Number:* (937) 775–1110

*Contact Email Address:* Annette.Canfield@Wright.edu

*SL Program/Center URL:* http://www.med. wright.edu/som/comminv/chc/serv.html

*Description:* The Center for Healthy Communities is a community academic partnership committed to improving primary-care service delivery and health professions education. Center staff work with faculty and students from allied health, medicine, nursing, psychology, social work, law, and theology to better integrate student learning objectives with community learning objectives using the Service Learning Protocol for Health Professions Schools, which was developed by the center. Staff place over 600 health professions students annually in community-based clinical training sites, providing health care and health education services to over 12,000 people. They work closely with the service-learning offices of the colleges and universities in the Dayton area, and provide Faculty Curricular Development seminars to health professions schools across the state of Ohio. Campus-wide service learning in coordinated through the Community Service Office.

*SL Required for Graduation (all students)?* No

*Service Required for Graduation (all students)?* No

*Any Co-curricular Service?* Yes

*Any SL Residence Halls or Theme Houses?* No

*Number of Graduate SL Courses Offered Per Year:* 7

*Number of Instructors Teaching SL Courses Per Year:* 120

*Number of Full-time SL Staff on Campus (not counting instructors):* 0

*Number of Part-time SL Staff on Campus (not counting instructors):* 2

## Skagit Valley College

2405 E College Way, Mount Vernon , WA 98273

*University/College URL:* http://www.svc. ctc.edu

*Type of Institution:* public, college, teaching

*SL Program/Center Name:* Learning Into Action

*Contact Person Name and Title:* Shawna Chriss

*Contact Phone Number:* (360) 416–7807

*Contact Fax Number:* (360) 416–7868

*Contact Email Address:* chriss@skagit.ctc.edu

*SL Program/Center URL:* http://www.svc. ctc.edu/pub_html/dept/StuServ/ccs/LIA/ PPT/index.htm

*Description:* Service-learning is part of a larger experiential education program, "Learning Into Action," that incorporates internships, cooperative education, and independent study. Learning Into Action is a capstone experience for the two-year Associate in Arts University and College Transfer degree. It is designed to help students apply knowledge and theory gained in the college classroom and relate it to career exploration, continuing education, or the "real world of work." The student, faculty advisor, Learning Into Action Coordinator, and site supervisor work together in supporting student learning objectives related to a specific placement or project. The Learning Into Action program operates under the direction of Career Services. It is located in Counseling and Career Services (Student Services and Student Success).

*SL Required for Graduation (all students)?* No. (However, "Learning Into Action" is required for the Associates in Arts University and College Transfer Degree, and a majority of students choose to perform service as they fulfill this graduation requirement.)

*Service Required for Graduation (all students)?* No

*Any Co-curricular Service?* Yes

*Any SL Residence Halls or Theme Houses?* No

*Total Number of SL Courses Offered Per Year:* 6–10

*Number of Instructors Teaching SL Courses Per Year:* 43

*Number of Full-time SL Staff on Campus (not counting instructors):* 2

*Number of Part-time SL Staff on Campus (not counting instructors):* 2

## Slippery Rock University

214 Spotts World Cultures Bldg, Slippery Rock, PA 16057

*University/College URL:* http://www.sru.edu

*Type of Institution:* public, university, teaching

*SL Program/Center Name:* The Community Service-Learning Institute

*Contact Person Name and Title:* Alice E. Kaiser-Drobney, Dir

*Contact Phone Number:* (724) 738-CARE

*Contact Fax Number:* (724) 738–2314

*Contact Email Address:* alice.kaiser-drobney@sru.edu

*SL Program/Center URL:* http://www.sru. edu/depts/artsci/gov/csli/service.htm

*SL Online Course Description URL:* http:// www.sru.edu/depts/artsci/gov/csli/service. htm

*Description:* Begun in 1993, the Community Service-Learning Institute coordinates curricular and co-curricular service-learning programs at the university, as well as a 55-member AmeriCorps program. The institute's mission is to help students develop and connect intellect, interpersonal skills, and passion for purposeful action. Projects focus on five service areas: education and literacy, environment, health and wellness, human services, and youth advocacy and leadership. All co-curricular programs are managed by AmeriCorps members and are open to all students, faculty, and staff. The institute is funded by the university and various grants, including an Education-Awards-Only AmeriCorps program from the Corporation for National Service.

All elementary education majors are required to show competency in service-learning. This includes professional development in service-learning methodology and completion of two service-learning projects, which are required for certification.

*SL Required for Graduation (all students)?*
No (However, service-learning is required for elementary education majors.)
*Service Required for Graduation (all students)?* No
*Any Co-curricular Service?* Yes
*Any SL Residence Halls or Theme Houses?* Yes
*SL Degrees Offered:* Academic minor in Community Service and Service-Learning, Certificate in Nonprofit Leadership, Certificate from American Humanics
*Number of Undergraduate SL Courses Offered Per Year:* 22
*Number of Graduate SL Courses Offered Per Year:* 5
*Total Number of SL Courses Offered Per Year:* 27
*Number of Instructors Teaching SL Courses Per Year:* 20
*Number of Full-time SL Staff on Campus (not counting instructors):* 5 (VISTA volunteers)
*Number of Part-time SL Staff on Campus (not counting instructors):* 63 (55 AmeriCorps members, plus 8 graduate assistants)

### Sonoma State University

California Institute on Human Services, 1801 E Cotati Ave, Rohnert Park, CA 94928
*University/College URL:* http://www.sonoma.edu
*Type of Institution:* public, college, teaching, research

*SL Program/Center Name:* Service Learning Center
*Contact Person Name and Title:* Julie McClure, Prog Dir
*Contact Phone Number:* (707) 664–4232
*Contact Fax Number:* (707) 664–2417
*Contact Email Address:* julie.mcclure@sonoma.edu
*SL Program/Center URL:* http://www.sonoma.edu/cihs/slc/
*SL Online Course Description URL:* http://www.sonoma.edu/cihs/slc/programs.html
*Description:* California Institute on Human Services is a university-based entity that works with leaders to implement state and federal policies in the field of education and human services, through research, training, and technical assistance.
*SL Required for Graduation (all students)?* No
*Service Required for Graduation (all students)?* No
*Any Co-curricular Service?* No
*Any SL Residence Halls or Theme Houses?* No

### Southern Methodist University

3140 Dyer, PO Box 0355, Dallas, TX 75275–0355
*University/College URL:* http://www.smu.edu
*Type of Institution:* private, university, teaching, research
*SL Program/Center Name:* Office of Community Involvement
*Contact Person Name and Title:* Rebecca Bergstresser, Dir
*Contact Phone Number:* (214) 768–4403
*Contact Fax Number:* (214) 768–4600
*Contact Email Address:* rbergstr@mail.smu.edu
*SL Program/Center URL:* http://www.smu.edu/~vols
*SL Online Course Description URL:* http://www.smu.edu/~vols/courses.html
*Description:* The Office of Community Involvement provides information and resources to the campus and the community in order to facilitate mutually beneficial learning experiences. The office links students, organizations,

faculty, and staff to nonprofit community agencies seeking volunteers or resources. It administers a service-learning support program for faculty integrating service into existing courses. The student organization Mobilization of Volunteer Efforts (MOVE), which creates a variety of service opportunities for all members of the SMU community, is based in the office. The coed service fraternity Alpha Phi Omega is also based in the office.

*SL Required for Graduation (all students)?* No

*Service Required for Graduation (all students)?* No

*Any Co-curricular Service?* Yes

*Any SL Residence Halls or Theme Houses?* Yes

*Number of Undergraduate SL Courses Offered Per Year:* 20–25

*Number of Instructors Teaching SL Courses Per Year:* 15–20

*Number of Full-time SL Staff on Campus (not counting instructors):* 1

*Number of Part-time SL Staff on Campus (not counting instructors):* 5

## Southern Utah University

351 W Center St, Cedar City, UT 84720

*University/College URL:* http://www.suu.edu

*Type of Institution:* public, university, teaching, secular

*SL Program/Center Name:* SUU Service Center

*Contact Person Name and Title:* Alex Herzog, Dir, Student Activities

*Contact Phone Number:* (435) 865–8535

*Contact Fax Number:* (435) 865–8199

*Contact Email Address:* herzog@suu.edu

*Description:* The Service Center opened in Fall 1999, with funding assistance from the Student Activities Office. It acts as a resource center for those interested in curricular service-learning, including faculty, staff, and students. The center is also a clearinghouse for existing volunteer opportunities, it works in conjunction with the Volunteer Center for Iron County, and it helps to connect volunteers with specific service opportunities.

*SL Required for Graduation (all students)?* No

*Service Required for Graduation (all students)?* No

*Any Co-curricular Service?* Yes

*Any SL Residence Halls or Theme Houses?* No

*Number of Undergraduate SL Courses Offered Per Year:* 10

*Number of Graduate SL Courses Offered Per Year:* 0

*Total Number of SL Courses Offered Per Year:* 10

*Number of Instructors Teaching SL Courses Per Year:* 10

*Number of Full-time SL Staff on Campus (not counting instructors):* 1

*Number of Part-time SL Staff on Campus (not counting instructors):* 1

## Southwest Missouri State University

901 S National, Plaster Student Union 208, Springfield, MO 65804–0094

*University/College URL:* http://www.smsu.edu

*Type of Institution:* public, university

*SL Program/Center Name:* Citizenship and Service Learning (CASL)

*Contact Person Name and Title:* Dr. Debra McDowell, Dir

*Contact Phone Number:* (417) 836–4840

*Contact Fax Number:* (417) 836–6429

*Contact Email Address:* dsm259f@mail.smsu.edu

*SL Program/Center URL:* http://www.smsu.edu/casl/

*SL Online Course Description URL:* http://www.smsu.edu/casl/

*Description:* The Citizenship and Service Learning Program (CASL) promotes service-learning as an effective pedagogical method that helps develop educated undergraduate and graduate students and promotes responsible student participation that benefits the community at-large. Working in collaboration with faculty and students of the university, community-based organizations, and other state and national organizations, CASL advocates service-learning as a pedagogical strategy; researches, develops, and disseminates best practices for service-learning; recommends and guides university policy on service-learning;

disseminates service-learning information, training, and resources; supports and strengthens the development of new and/or existing service-learning initiatives; and encourages student and faculty initiative and leadership through the vehicle of service-learning.

CASL is for undergraduates and graduate students. At the undergraduate level, students may take courses in accounting; anthropology; biomedical science (nutrition); chemistry; child and family development; clothing, textiles, and merchandising; communication and mass media; computer science; crime and society; English; finance and general business; French; geography, geology and planning; German; history; journalism; management; marketing and quantitative analysis; mathematics; music; political science; psychology; reading and special education; religious studies; social work; Spanish; technology; and theatre and dance. At the graduate level, students may take courses in communication and mass media; library science; and reading and special education.

*SL Required for Graduation (all students)?* No

*Service Required for Graduation (all students)?* No

*Any Co-curricular Service?* No

*Any SL Residence Halls or Theme Houses?* Yes (a service-learning/citizenship residence hall on campus)

*Number of Undergraduate SL Courses Offered Per Year:* 100+

*Number of Graduate SL Courses Offered Per Year:* 0 (This is a new program, beginning in Spring 2000.)

*Total Number of SL Courses Offered Per Year:* 100+

*Number of Instructors Teaching SL Courses Per Year:* 50

*Number of Full-time SL Staff on Campus (not counting instructors):* 2

*Number of Part-time SL Staff on Campus (not counting instructors):* 2

## Southwestern College
900 Otay Lakes Rd, Chula Vista, CA 91910
*University/College URL:* http://www.swc.cc.ca.us

*Type of Institution:* public, community college, teaching

*SL Program/Center Name:* Service-Learning Center

*Contact Person Name and Title:* Kathy Parrish, Project Dir; Siliva Cornejo-Darcy, Americorps Project Coord

*Contact Phone Number:* (619) 421–6700, ext 5566; ext 5812 (Parrish)

*Contact Fax Number:* (619) 482–6412

*Contact Email Address:* kparrish@swc.cc.ca.us; scornejo@swc.cc.ca.us

*Description:* The Service-Learning Center currently supports two different programs. In Spring 1999, a broad-based Service Learning program was offered in 25 different disciplines, including English, Spanish, environmental studies, history, and psychology. A separate service-learning course is also offered. The center has partnerships with over 50 local agencies. All service-learning students who perform at least 15 hours of service over the course of the semester receive a certificate signed by the college president and mention of this accomplishment on their transcripts. The second area involves the AmeriCorps/America Reads program, which has 40 members per year who act as literacy tutors for pre- and early-grade school children 15 hours per week, and, in addition, take a service-learning course.

*SL Required for Graduation (all students)?* No

*Service Required for Graduation (all students)?* No

*Any Co-curricular Service?* No

*Any SL Residence Halls or Theme Houses?* No

*Number of Undergraduate SL Courses Offered Per Year:* 4

*Number of Graduate SL Courses Offered Per Year:* 0

*Total Number of SL Courses Offered Per Year:* 4

*Number of Instructors Teaching SL Courses Per Year:* 2

*Number of Full-time SL Staff on Campus (not counting instructors):* 1

*Number of Part-time SL Staff on Campus (not counting instructors):* 5

## Stanford University

Haas Center for Public Service, 562
    Salvatierra Walk, Stanford, CA
    94305–8620
*University/College URL:* http://www.
    stanford.edu
*Type of Institution:* private, university,
    research
*SL Program/Center Name:* Haas Center for
    Public Service
*Contact Person Name and Title:* Heather
    Ramírez
*Contact Phone Number:* (650) 723–5719
*Contact Fax Number:* (650) 725–7339
*Contact Email Address:*
    hramirez@leland.stanford.edu
*SL Program/Center URL:* http://haas.
    stanford.edu
*SL Online Course Description URL:* http://
    haas.stanford.edu
*Description:* Established in 1985, the Haas
Center for Public Service represents Stanford's
most visible institutional commitment to the
education for civic responsibility. By engaging
students in the widest variety of service ac-
tivities—through direct service, policy research,
or community problem solving—the center en-
riches their education and inspires them to
commit their lives to improving society.
*SL Required for Graduation (all
    students)?* No
*Service Required for Graduation (all stu-
    dents)?* No
*Any Co-curricular Service?* Yes
*Any SL Residence Halls or Theme
    Houses?* Yes
*Number of Undergraduate SL Courses
    Offered Per Year:* 35
*Total Number of SL Courses Offered Per
    Year:* 35
*Number of Instructors Teaching SL Courses
    Per Year:* 28
*Number of Full-time SL Staff on Campus
    (not counting instructors):* 23
*Number of Part-time SL Staff on Campus
    (not counting instructors):* 0

## State University of New York, College at Oneonta

Oneonta, NY 13820
*University/College URL:* http://www.
    oneonta.edu
*Type of Institution:* public, college, teaching
*SL Program/Center Name:* Center for Social
    Responsibility and Community
*Contact Person Name and Title:* Karen
    Meola, Service-Learning Dir
*Contact Phone Number:* (607) 436–2676
*Contact Fax Number:* (607) 436–2760
*Contact Email Address:*
    meolakl@oneonta.edu
*SL Program/Center URL:* http://www.
    oneonta.edu/~ctrweb/
*Description:* The Center for Social Responsibility and Community (CSRC) is community-
oriented and fosters the union of academic
study and voluntary community service by
providing programs through which students
can participate in a full range of service, volunteer, and philanthropic experiences in local,
state, national, and international communities.
The purpose of the center is to develop a strong
sense of social responsibility and community in
students by giving youth a purpose, and a
voice, and recognizing youth as a valuable
resource. It accomplishes its mission by strengthening the relationship between academic study
and volunteer community service in higher
education through service-learning, thereby ex-
posing all students to the opportunity to grow
as socially responsible community members.
Volunteer and service-learning opportunities
for students are coordinated through the center.
These opportunities may be tailored to meet the
needs of an individual student or designed to
place an entire class in service-learning placements. As the coordinating office for service on
the campus the center tracks all service-related
hours accrued (logged) by students and enters
the data into the college database generating a
record of service for each student.
*SL Required for Graduation (all
    students)?* No
*Service Required for Graduation (all stu-
    dents)?* No
*Any Co-curricular Service?* Yes

*Any SL Residence Halls or Theme Houses?*
No (But there are service theme suites in
residence halls.)

*SL Degrees Offered:* N (However, students
completing 500 hours of service-learning
are honored by the college president at
graduation. Students completing 500 or
750 hours of service are given special
recognition by the college president at
graduation. A Record of Service, documenting the hours and locations of
service, is generated by the CSRC along
with the student's transcript.)

*Number of Undergraduate SL Courses
Offered Per Year:* 35

*Total Number of SL Courses Offered Per
Year:* 35

*Number of Instructors Teaching SL Courses
Per Year:* 35

*Number of Full-time SL Staff on Campus
(not counting instructors):* 1

*Number of Part-time SL Staff on Campus
(not counting instructors):* 0

## Sterling College

Craftsbury Common, VT 05672

*University/College URL:* http://www.
sterlingcollege.edu

*Type of Institution:* private, college, teaching

*SL Program/Center Name:* Work College
Program

*Contact Person Name and Title:* Erik
Hansen, Dean of Work

*Contact Phone Number:* (802) 586–7711

*Contact Fax Number:* (802) 586–2596

*Contact Email Address:*
ehansen@sterlingcollege.edu

*Description:* Sterling College is a member of
the national Work Colleges Consortium. All
resident students participate in a comprehensive work program (at least 60 hours a semester) that includes both on- and off-campus work
and service (10–20 percent of the work done is
in a community-service capacity). Crew positions range from working on the college's farm,
forest, and gardens to serving as mentors in
area schools and doing watershed survey projects to improve water quality in the state.
Students work an average of 4–5 hours a week
and in return receive a reduction of their

tuition. The Work College component comprises an important segment of the college's
service-learning option. While students don't
get academic credit as such for the Work Crew
Program, each job must include learning objectives, evaluation, and a record of work performance that is part of the student's college
record. The work component is a requirement
for graduation in the same way that accruing
academic credit is required. There is also a
major internship requirement, usually a semester each in the second and fourth years, a good
portion of which often involves substantial
service-learning. At least 10 courses in the
Sterling curriculum include service as a regular
component in the academic course of study. In
addition, one class, "Service Learning Project," is required for graduation. The Work
College program is funded in part through
federal work-study funds matched equally by
Sterling College grant assistance.

*SL Required for Graduation (all
students)?* Yes

*Service Required for Graduation (all stu-
dents)?* Yes

*Any Co-curricular Service?* Yes

*Any SL Residence Halls or Theme
Houses?* No

*Number of Undergraduate SL Courses
Offered Per Year:* 10

*Number of Graduate SL Courses Offered
Per Year:* 0

*Total Number of SL Courses Offered Per
Year:* 10

*Number of Instructors Teaching SL Courses
Per Year:* 4

*Number of Full-time SL Staff on Campus
(not counting instructors):* 8

*Number of Part-time SL Staff on Campus
(not counting instructors):* 8

## Stetson University

421 N Woodland Blvd, Unit 8353, DeLand,
FL 32720

*University/College URL:* http://www.
stetson.edu

*Type of Institution:* private, university,
teaching

*SL Program/Center Name:* Community
Service Office

*Contact Person Name and Title:* Courtney W. McIntyre, Coord, Community Service Office

*Contact Phone Number:* (904) 822–7524

*Contact Fax Number:* (904) 822–7227

*Contact Email Address:* cmcintyr@stetson.edu

*Description:* Stetson University is currently in the process of establishing a Community Service Office that coordinates service-learning in the schools of Arts and Sciences, Business Administration, and Music. The office will be a resource and offer workshops to interested faculty.

*SL Required for Graduation (all students)?* No

*Service Required for Graduation (all students)?* No

*Any Co-curricular Service?* Yes

*Any SL Residence Halls or Theme Houses?* No (But an apartment complex focusing on Community Service has been designated, and will house 11 individuals. Target date is Fall 2000.)

## Stonehill College

320 Washington St, Box D149, Easton, MA 20357–6120

*University/College URL:* http://www. stonehill.edu

*Type of Institution:* private, college, teaching, religious

*SL Program/Center Name:* Center for Social Concern

*Contact Person Name and Title:* Paula M. Bozoian, Dir

*Contact Phone Number:* (508) 230–7220

*Contact Fax Number:* (508) 238–9633

*Contact Email Address:* socialconcern@stonehill.edu

*SL Program/Center URL:* http://community. stonehill.edu/cfsc/csc/index.htm

*Description:* At Stonehill College, service-learning has been integrated into courses in sociology, health care administration, and religious studies. The integration of service-learning into coursework is not part of a college-wide initiative or mandate; however, the appropriateness of service-learning to the academic mission of the college is being considered by several col-

lege policy and planning committees. For the past two years, the Center for Social Concern has assisted faculty members in sociology and health care administration with the development of service-learning placements. In addition, through a 1999– 2000 Learn and Serve America sub-grant from Massachusetts Campus Compact, the center has had the opportunity to work with the college's Department of Education to explore the relationship between field-based experience and service-learning.

*SL Required for Graduation (all students)?* No

*Service Required for Graduation (all students)?* No

*Any Co-curricular Service?* Yes

*Any SL Residence Halls or Theme Houses?* No

*Number of Full-time SL Staff on Campus (not counting instructors):* 0

*Number of Part-time SL Staff on Campus (not counting instructors):* 0

## Swarthmore College

500 College Ave, Swarthmore, PA 19355

*University/College URL:* http://www. swarthmore.edu

*Type of Institution:* private, college, secular

*SL Program/Center Name:* Community Service Learning Programs

*Contact Person Name and Title:* Patricia James, Dir

*Contact Phone Number:* (610) 328–7320

*Contact Fax Number:* (610) 328–8617

*Contact Email Address:* pjames1@swarthmore.edu

*SL Program/Center URL:* http://www. swarthmore.edu

*Description:* The Office of Community Service Learning Programs coordinates community-based service and learning initiatives of students, faculty and staff, and is a liaison between the college and the communities in which service is conducted. Initiatives include CIVIC (College Involved in Volunteering In Communities), the Lang Scholars Program, the Swarthmore Foundation, and Summer of Service. The office supports faculty to develop and implement courses and seminars that employ community-based learning, and supports a number of community-based initiatives in areas such as education reform and economic development.

*SL Required for Graduation (all students)?* No

*Service Required for Graduation (all students)?* No

*Any Co-curricular Service?* Yes

*Any SL Residence Halls or Theme Houses?* No

*Number of Undergraduate SL Courses Offered Per Year:* 30

*Total Number of SL Courses Offered Per Year:* 30

*Number of Instructors Teaching SL Courses Per Year:* 10

*Number of Full-time SL Staff on Campus (not counting instructors):* 1

*Number of Part-time SL Staff on Campus (not counting instructors):* 1

## Temple University

Philadelphia, PA 19122

*University/College URL:* http://www.temple.edu

*Type of Institution:* public, university, research, secular

*Contact Person Name and Title:* Lori Shorr, Dir, School and Community Partnerships

*Contact Phone Number:* (215) 204–3773

*Contact Fax Number:* (215) 204–5735

*Contact Email Address:* ShorrL@mail.temple.edu

*SL Program/Center URL:* http://community.temple.edu/outreach/

*SL Online Course Description URL:* http://community.temple.edu/outreach/academic.html

*Description:* The Service Learning Roundtable, a voluntary association of faculty members, attempts to foster service-learning on campus, disseminate information about service-learning, and to put service-learning on the administrative agenda of the school. This year, two academically-based community-service coordinators focus exclusively on encouraging and facilitating service-learning on campus. A full-time administrator and professor also deals with service-learning issues in the context of the position of director of School and Community Partnerships. Some service-learning activities this year include organizing and hosting workshops for students on the service-learning experience (both introducing the concept for new students and reflecting on past service-learning for experienced students), organizing and hosting at least one brown-bag lunch for faculty on structuring service-learning courses, and setting up a database of all offered service-learning courses and putting it online. Additionally, the College of Liberal Arts has appointed a full-time director of Experiential and Service Learning.

*SL Required for Graduation (all students)?* No

*Service Required for Graduation (all students)?* No

*Any Co-curricular Service?* Yes

*Any SL Residence Halls or Theme Houses?* No

*SL Degrees Offered:* N (However, community service can be put on a transcript of extracurricular achievement on Temple record.)

*Number of Undergraduate SL Courses Offered Per Year:* 58+ (not all are offered every year)

*Total Number of SL Courses Offered Per Year:* 58+ (not all are offered every year)

*Number of Part-time SL Staff on Campus (not counting instructors):* 2 (The second is a full-time staff member also responsible for other duties.)

*Number of Part-time SL Staff on Campus (not counting instructors):* 2

## Texas A&M University

125 Koldus, College Station, TX 77843–1236

*University/College URL:* http://www.tamu.edu

*Type of Institution:* public, university, research

*SL Program/Center Name:* Volunteer Services Center

*Contact Person Name and Title:* Lori Deana Salter, Coord

*Contact Phone Number:* (409) 862–3912

*Contact Fax Number:* (409) 847–8854

*Contact Email Address:* lori-s@tamu.edu

*SL Program/Center URL:* http://givem.
    tamu.edu
*SL Online Course Description URL:* http://
    stuact.tamu.edu/289/s-l/
*SL Online Syllabi URL:* http://stuact.tamu.
    edu/289/s-l/syllabus.html
*Description:* The Service-Learning course is a
one-credit class open to all students enrolled at
Texas A&M. Students choose an academic
course in their current schedule, do service in
that subject area, and then reflect on that serv-
ice in the class. The class is funded by the
Department of Student Activities.
*SL Required for Graduation (all*
    *students)?* No
*Service Required for Graduation (all stu-*
    *dents)?* No
*Any Co-curricular Service?* No
*Any SL Residence Halls or Theme*
    *Houses?* No
*Number of Undergraduate SL Courses*
    *Offered Per Year:* 6–8
*Number of Graduate SL Courses Offered*
    *Per Year:* 0
*Total Number of SL Courses Offered Per*
    *Year:* 6–8
*Number of Instructors Teaching SL Courses*
    *Per Year:* 3
*Number of Full-time SL Staff on Campus*
    *(not counting instructors):* 0
*Number of Part-time SL Staff on Campus*
    *(not counting instructors):* 0

**Thiel College**
75 College Ave, Greenville, PA 16125
*University/College URL:* http://www.
    thiel.edu
*Type of Institution:* private, college, teach-
    ing, research
*Contact Person Name and Title:* Joanne
    Schell, Dir, Career Center
*Contact Phone Number:* (724) 589–2014
*Contact Fax Number:* (724) 589–2850
*Contact Email Address:* jschell@thiel.edu
*SL Program/Center URL:* http://www.thiel.
    edu/career/community_svc.htm
*Description:* Service Learning is a joint pro-
gram coordinated through the Community Serv-
ice Department and Academic Services. Most
service learning is in an eight-credit, two-se-

mester Global Heritage class. Through this
course, students are encouraged to "think globally, act locally." Through community-service
involvement, students learn to develop appreciation for cultural diversity and address world,
national, and local problems. This eight-hour
course is a requirement for graduation, usually
taken for two semesters in the sophomore year.
Several other courses also have a built in community-service component.
*SL Required for Graduation (all*
    *students)?* No
*Service Required for Graduation (all stu-*
    *dents)?* No (But the Education Dept.
    requires all of their students to per-
    form community service as a graduation
    requirement.)
*Any Co-curricular Service?* Yes
*Any SL Residence Halls or Theme*
    *Houses?* No

**Thomas Nelson Community College**
99 Thomas Nelson Dr, PO Box 9407,
    Hampton, VA 23670
*University/College URL:* http://www.tncc.
    cc.va.us
*Type of Institution:* public, community col-
    lege, teaching, secular
*SL Program/Center Name:* Service Learning
    in Community Encounters (SLICE)
*Contact Person Name and Title:* Anne
    Andrews, Assis Prof, Human Services,
    Acting SL Program Coord
*Contact Phone Number:* (757) 825–2782
*Contact Fax Number:* (757) 825–3840
*Contact Email Address:*
    andrewsa@tncc.cc.va.us
*SL Program/Center URL:* http://www.tncc.
    cc.va.us/slice
*SL Online Course Description URL:* http://
    www.tncc.cc.va.us/slice
*Description:* In the Fall of 1998, Thomas Nel-
son Community College began to develop and
use experiential education/service-learning
within the college academic offerings. A major
focus was to build and implement service-
learning into courses in all areas of the campus.
In the span of one semester, seven courses were
identified and many other faculty are interested. As of Spring 1999, no specific center has

been established, and a faculty member is serving as coordinator and resource person for the campus.

*SL Required for Graduation (all students)?* No

*Service Required for Graduation (all students)?* No

*Any Co-curricular Service?* No

*Any SL Residence Halls or Theme Houses?* No

*Number of Undergraduate SL Courses Offered Per Year:* 7

*Number of Graduate SL Courses Offered Per Year:* 0

*Total Number of SL Courses Offered Per Year:* 7

*Number of Instructors Teaching SL Courses Per Year:* 5

*Number of Full-time SL Staff on Campus (not counting instructors):* 0

*Number of Part-time SL Staff on Campus (not counting instructors):* 0

## Trinity College

300 Summit St, Hartford, CT 06106

*University/College URL:* http://www. trincoll.edu

*Type of Institution:* private, college

*SL Program/Center Name:* Urban Learning Initiatives

*Contact Person Name and Title:* Elinor Jacobson, Coord

*Contact Phone Number:* (860) 297–4275

*Contact Fax Number:* (860) 297–6206

*Contact Email Address:* elinor.jacobson@mail.cc.trincoll.edu

*SL Program/Center URL:* http://www. trincoll.edu/~cli/

*SL Online Course Description URL:* http:// www.trincoll.edu/prog/cli/models/

*SL Online Syllabi URL:* http://www.trincoll. edu/prog/cli/models/

*Description:* Community Learning Initiatives provides support to the faculty in the development and implementation of community learning components for their courses.

*SL Required for Graduation (all students)?* No

*Service Required for Graduation (all students)?* No

*Any Co-curricular Service?* Yes

*Any SL Residence Halls or Theme Houses?* Yes

*Number of Undergraduate SL Courses Offered Per Year:* 30

*Total Number of SL Courses Offered Per Year:* 30

*Number of Instructors Teaching SL Courses Per Year:* 30

*Number of Full-time SL Staff on Campus (not counting instructors):* 0

*Number of Part-time SL Staff on Campus (not counting instructors):* 3

## Tufts University

Medford, MA 02155

*University/College URL:* http://www. tufts.edu

*Type of Institution:* private, university, teaching, research

*SL Program/Center Name:* University College of Citizenship and Public Service

*Contact Person Name and Title:* Badi Foster, Exec Dir and Prof, Citizenship and Public Affairs

*Contact Phone Number:* (617) 627–3453

*Contact Fax Number:* (617) 627–3401

*Contact Email Address:* bfoste01@tufts.edu

*SL Program/Center URL:* http://www.ase. tufts.edu/lfc

*Description:* Service Learning at Tufts is university-wide with administrative focus at the Lincoln Filene Center for Citizenship and Public Affairs. The service-learning initiative is coordinated with several other programs at the center including school/community collaboration, management and community development, and citizenship participation.

*SL Required for Graduation (all students)?* No

*Service Required for Graduation (all students)?* No

*Any Co-curricular Service?* No

*Any SL Residence Halls or Theme Houses?* Yes

*Number of Undergraduate SL Courses Offered Per Year:* 8–12

*Number of Graduate SL Courses Offered
    Per Year:* 4–8
*Total Number of SL Courses Offered Per
    Year:* 12–16
*Number of Instructors Teaching SL Courses
    Per Year:* 8–12
*Number of Part-time SL Staff on Campus
    (not counting instructors):* 2–3

**Tulane University**
6823 St Charles Ave, New Orleans,
    LA 70118
*University/College URL:* http://www.
    tulane.edu
*Type of Institution:* private, university,
    research
*SL Program/Center Name:* Office of Service
    Learning
*Contact Person Name and Title:* Vincent
    Ilustre, Assist Dir
*Contact Phone Number:* (504) 862–3358
*Contact Fax Number:* (504) 862–8061
*Contact Email Address:*
    vilustr@mailhost.tcs.tulane.edu
*SL Program/Center URL:* http://www.tulane.
    edu/~ServLrng/main.htm
*Description:* Service-learning is part of Tulane's
commitment to forge unique and lasting part-
nerships with the New Orleans community.
The mission of Tulane's Office of Service
Learning is to engage faculty members and
students in an endeavor that combines commu-
nity service with academic learning. Service
Learning aims to benefit students' education,
enhance faculty research and teaching, and
build community goodwill. To achieve this
mission, the office strives to help create a
"classroom without walls" that is beneficial to
faculty, students, the community, and the
university.
*SL Required for Graduation (all
    students)?* No
*Service Required for Graduation (all stu-
    dents)?* No
*Any Co-curricular Service?* No
*Any SL Residence Halls or Theme
    Houses?* Yes
*Number of Undergraduate SL Courses
    Offered Per Year:* 24–36

*Total Number of SL Courses Offered Per
    Year:* 24–36
*Number of Instructors Teaching SL Courses
    Per Year:* 20–30
*Number of Full-time SL Staff on Campus
    (not counting instructors):* 4
*Number of Part-time SL Staff on Campus
    (not counting instructors):* 2

**Tusculum College**
60 Shiloh Rd, PO Box 5041, Greeneville,
    TN 37743
*University/College URL:* http://www.
    tusculum.edu
*Type of Institution:* private, college, teaching
*SL Program/Center Name:* Tusculum Col-
    lege Service-Learning Center
*Contact Person Name and Title:* Dr. John
    Reiff, Dir
*Contact Phone Number:* (423) 636–7327
*Contact Fax Number:* (423) 636–7327
*Contact Email Address:* jreiff@tusculum.edu
*SL Program/Center URL:* http://www.
    tusculum.edu/servlearn
*SL Online Course Description URL:* http://
    www.tusculum.edu/servlearn/servcur.htm
*Description:* The Service-Learning Center
teaches several general-education service-learn-
ing courses and provides support to faculty
who integrate service-learning into courses in
their disciplines. It administers a Learn And
Serve America–Higher Education grant as part
of the East Tennessee Consortium for Service-
Learning. It organizes the annual all-campus
day of service. It works with students to develop a culture of service on the campus, and it
collaborates with community organizations and
with other colleges to promote service.
    Students are introduced to the college's com-
mitment to service through the annual Nettie
Fowler McCormick Service Day, which organizes classes as service teams on a day early each
September. In their general-education requirements, students take a sophomore-level class,
Citizenship and Social Change: Theory and
Practice, which has a class service-learning
project of 10–15 hours built into it. To complete their requirements, students then take one

of three junior-level classes—Service-Learning Practicum (with 50 hours of service in a community organization and regular class meetings and writing assignments), Civic Arts Project (where they work with community members to design and implement a project that addresses a community need), or Service-Learning Immersion (where they travel away from campus for two to three weeks to immerse themselves in service projects and reflection). Students may elect more than one of these courses, and they may also take an Advanced Service-Learning Practicum. An Advanced Service-Learning Project is currently under consideration by the faculty. In addition to these courses in the general education program, numerous faculty have embedded service-learning in their disciplinary courses. For example, a physical education professor teaches PE methods by making the college's facilities available to the local home-schooling association; a professional writing professor is having her class design a Web page for a local nonprofit; and an education professor is teaching creative thinking and problem-solving by having her class work with elementary schoolchildren to design and carry out service-learning projects.

*SL Required for Graduation (all students)?* Yes

*Service Required for Graduation (all students)?* No

*Any Co-curricular Service?* Yes

*Any SL Residence Halls or Theme Houses?* No

*Number of Undergraduate SL Courses Offered Per Year:* 9 courses, 15 sections

*Number of Graduate SL Courses Offered Per Year:* 0

*Total Number of SL Courses Offered Per Year:* 9 courses, 15 sections (in 1998–1999)

*Number of Instructors Teaching SL Courses Per Year:* 10 (in 1998–1999)

*Number of Full-time SL Staff on Campus (not counting instructors):* 2 (includes the SL Center dir, who is split between faculty/administrator.)

*Number of Part-time SL Staff on Campus (not counting instructors):* 2

## United States International University

10455 Pomerado Rd, M-2, San Diego, CA 92131–1799

*University/College URL:* http://www.usiu.edu

*Type of Institution:* private, university, teaching, secular

*SL Program/Center Name:* Department of Orientation and Service-Learning

*Contact Person Name and Title:* Michele Spicer, Dir, Orientation and Service-Learning

*Contact Phone Number:* (858) 635–4847

*Contact Fax Number:* (858) 635–4853

*Contact Email Address:* mspicer@usiu.edu

*SL Program/Center URL:* http://www.usiu.edu/Student/studcomm.htm

*Description:* The department's purpose is to assist and facilitate the coordination of service-learning opportunities with faculty and students. The department informs academic departments of service opportunities and shares syllabi pertaining to the appropriate academic area. Limited funding is available.

*SL Required for Graduation (all students)?* No

*Service Required for Graduation (all students)?* Yes

*Any Co-curricular Service?* Yes

*Any SL Residence Halls or Theme Houses?* No

*Number of Full-time SL Staff on Campus (not counting instructors):* 1 (SL is only part of this person's duties.)

*Number of Part-time SL Staff on Campus (not counting instructors):* 0

## Unity College

Quaker Hill Rd, HC 78, Box 1, Unity, ME 04988

*University/College URL:* http://www.unity.edu

*Type of Institution:* private, college, teaching, secular

*SL Program/Center Name:* Office of Community Service

*Contact Person Name and Title:* Libbey Seigars, Dir, Career Resource Center

*Contact Phone Number:* (207) 948–3131
*Contact Fax Number:* (207) 948–6277
*Contact Email Address:*
   lseigars@unity.unity.edu
*SL Program/Center URL:* http://www.unity.
   edu/ServiceLearning/
*Description:* The Office of Community Service supports both co-curricular and curricular service at Unity College. The office encourages students, faculty, and staff to become full participants in the college and broader communities by participating in service. It works with the community to identify community needs, builds partnerships, matches students to community needs, provides support for faculty to link courses to community issues, and coordinates the college's annual Service Opportunity Fair and Day of Service. The office is primarily funded through the college budget; additional support is provided by grants. It is staffed by a full-time director of Career Resource Center, a director of New Student Orientation and Service Learning, an AmeriCorps VISTA volunteer, and four or more work-study students.

The Unity College educational experience begins with the one-credit wilderness-based New Student Orientation course. The course includes a one-week wilderness trip during which students accomplish a group service project, a weekend orientation program, and a campus engagement component that involves students in the campus and local community. Students select a community-service project to complete during their first semester. The exploration of, and participation in, stewardship continues with Unity College's interdisciplinary core curriculum which includes five sequential courses: "Perspectives on Nature," "Perspectives on Conservation," "Human Ecology I & II" and "Environmental Stewardship." Other service-learning courses within a student's area of emphasis address local and regional environmental and social issues.

*SL Required for Graduation (all students)?* Yes
*Service Required for Graduation (all students)?* Yes
*Any Co-curricular Service?* Yes

*Any SL Residence Halls or Theme Houses?* No
*Number of Undergraduate SL Courses Offered Per Year:* 36+
*Number of Graduate SL Courses Offered Per Year:* 0
*Total Number of SL Courses Offered Per Year:* 36+
*Number of Instructors Teaching SL Courses Per Year:* 26
*Number of Full-time SL Staff on Campus (not counting instructors):* 2.5 (Career Resource Center Director with half time responsibility for service learning)
*Number of Part-time SL Staff on Campus (not counting instructors):* 0

**University of Arizona**
Tuscon, AZ 85721
*University/College URL:* http://www.
   arizona.edu
*Type of Institution:* public, university, research
*SL Program/Center Name:* Center for Service-Learning
*Contact Person Name and Title:* Laura Teso, Service-Learning Coord; Dr. Sue Warnock, Dir of Composition
*Contact Phone Number:* (520) 626–7562 (CSL); (520) 621–1836 (Composition)
*Contact Fax Number:* (520) 621–8158 (CSL); (520) 621–7397 (Composition)
*Contact Email Address:*
   lpteso@u.arizona.edu;
   warnocks@u.arizona.edu
*SL Program/Center URL:* http://w3.arizona.
   edu/~career; http://w3.arizona.edu/~
   guide/sl
*Description:* The Connections program in Career Services addresses the needs of service-learning students from all departments and programs across the campus. Connections assists students with all phases of the process, from brainstorming various possible types of service-learning experiences that will meet the student's needs, to developing a resume and/or personal statement, to providing access to service-learning opportunities through the online CatTraks system. The primary concern of Career

Services is to provide all students with opportunities to gain meaningful experiences based on their needs. Those needs vary from student to student. Some attempt to broaden their perspective and understanding of coursework, while others wish to gain experience for a particular career path.

Teachers in the Composition Program at the university are developing service-learning assignments and support structures for use in the composition courses that are the only universal undergraduate requirement. The goal is to integrate service-learning into the curriculum to provide opportunities for the sort of critical reflection and inquiry into related issues needed to ensure that community work is not mere volunteerism. A Web home page facilitates placements and fosters collaborations among teachers and students. Staff are working with local community organizations to develop other online resources as well.

*SL Required for Graduation (all students)?* No

*Service Required for Graduation (all students)?* No

*Any Co-curricular Service?* Yes

*Any SL Residence Halls or Theme Houses?* No

*Number of Undergraduate SL Courses Offered Per Year:* 25

*Number of Graduate SL Courses Offered Per Year:* 15

*Total Number of SL Courses Offered Per Year:* 40

*Number of Instructors Teaching SL Courses Per Year:* 50

*Number of Full-time SL Staff on Campus (not counting instructors):* 4

*Number of Part-time SL Staff on Campus (not counting instructors):* 4

## University of Balamand
Fares Hall, PO Box 100, Tripoli, Lebanon
*University/College URL:* http://www.balamand.edu.lb
*Type of Institution:* private, university, teaching, secular
*SL Program/Center Name:* The SEED Program (Service Experience: Education through Doing)
*Contact Person Name and Title:* Samer Annous, Assist Dir
*Contact Phone Number:* 00 961 6 400 740, ext 231
*Contact Fax Number:* 00 961 6 400 742
*Contact Email Address:* seed@balamand.edu.lb
*SL Program/Center URL:* http://www.balamand.edu.lb/seed/htm
*Description:* The purpose of the SEED (Service Experience: Education through Doing) program is to nurture a sense of civic responsibility in every student. SEED courses typically combine an academically rigorous three-credit classroom course with a one-credit service-learning placement directly related to the course content. Generally, the student is required to do 40 hours of community service in addition to regular class instruction. An in-class component in the form of presentations, journals, papers, and open forums among others, is provided for reflecting on the service-learning experience.

*SL Required for Graduation (all students)?* No

*Service Required for Graduation (all students)?* No

*Any Co-curricular Service?* Yes

*Any SL Residence Halls or Theme Houses?* No

*Number of Undergraduate SL Courses Offered Per Year:* 15

*Number of Graduate SL Courses Offered Per Year:* 5

*Total Number of SL Courses Offered Per Year:* 20

*Number of Instructors Teaching SL Courses Per Year:* 20

*Number of Full-time SL Staff on Campus (not counting instructors):* 4

*Number of Part-time SL Staff on Campus (not counting instructors):* 3

## University of California-Berkeley
Berkeley, CA 94720
*University/College URL:* http://www.berkeley.edu

*Type of Institution:* public, university, research

*SL Program/Center Name:* Service-Learning Research & Development Center

*Contact Person Name and Title:* Dr. Andrew Furco, Dir

*Contact Phone Number:* (510) 642–3199

*Contact Fax Number:* (510) 642–6105

*Contact Email Address:* afurco@uclink4.berkeley.edu

*SL Program/Center URL:* http://www-gse.berkeley.edu/research/slc

*SL Online Course Description URL:* http://www-gse.berkeley.edu/research/slc/courses.htm

*Description:* The mission of the Service-Learning Research and Development Center is to advance the service-learning field through research, development, and evaluation of programs that integrate community service into the academic curriculum. The center engages in a number of national, state, and local research and evaluation studies to assess the impact of service-learning on students, faculty, and schools at the K-12 and higher education levels. In addition, the center supports faculty who use service-learning in their courses. This support includes instructional mini-grants, curricular materials, reflection and assessment tools, referrals to community agencies, and networking opportunities.

*SL Required for Graduation (all students)?* No

*Service Required for Graduation (all students)?* No

*Any Co-curricular Service?* Yes

*Any SL Residence Halls or Theme Houses?* Yes

*Number of Undergraduate SL Courses Offered Per Year:* 164

*Number of Graduate SL Courses Offered Per Year:* 26

*Total Number of SL Courses Offered Per Year:* 190

*Number of Full-time SL Staff on Campus (not counting instructors):* 3

*Number of Part-time SL Staff on Campus (not counting instructors):* 5

**University of California at Los Angeles (UCLA)**

405 Hilgard Ave, Los Angeles, CA 90095–1361

*University/College URL:* http://www.ucla.edu

*Type of Institution:* public, university, research

*SL Program/Center Name:* Center for Experiential Education and Service Learning (CEESL)

*Contact Person Name and Title:* Parvin Kassaie, Dir

*Contact Phone Number:* (310) 825–2295

*Contact Fax Number:* (310) 267–2482

*Contact Email Address:* parvink@ucla.edu

*SL Program/Center URL:* http://www.oid.ucla.edu/ceesl

*Description:* The Center for Experiential Education and Service Learning (formerly known as Field Studies Development) is a unit of the Office of Instructional Development. It is responsible for coordinating and supporting service-learning programs on campus. The center serves over 1,500 undergraduate students a year in a variety of service-learning and experiential education options, and offers counseling services to approximately 3,500 more. In addition, it provides technical assistance to faculty and departments on all service-learning matters. The center develops and supports a variety of service-learning courses across many disciplines and majors, and has numerous community partners throughout the greater Los Angeles area.

*SL Required for Graduation (all students)?* No

*Service Required for Graduation (all students)?* No

*Any Co-curricular Service?* Yes

*Any SL Residence Halls or Theme Houses?* No

*Number of Undergraduate SL Courses Offered Per Year:* 53

*Total Number of SL Courses Offered Per Year:* 53

*Number of Instructors Teaching SL Courses Per Year:* 193 (including faculty sponsors of Independent Studies)

*Number of Full-time SL Staff on Campus
  (not counting instructors):* 6
*Number of Part-time SL Staff on Campus
  (not counting instructors):* 45–50

## University of Central Florida

College of Education, Department of Educa-
  tional Foundations, Office of Service
  Learning, Orlando, FL 32816–1250
*University/College URL:* http://www.ucf.edu
*Type of Institution:* public, university, teach-
  ing, secular
*SL Program/Center Name:* Office of Service
  Learning, College of Education
*Contact Person Name and Title:* Dr. Jennie
  Loudermilk, Coord and Instruct
*Contact Phone Number:* (407) 823–2042
*Contact Fax Number:* (407) 823–5144
*Contact Email Address:*
  service@pegasus.cc.ucf.edu
*SL Program/Center URL:* http://pegasus.cc.
  ucf.edu/~service
*SL Online Course Description URL:* http://
  pegasus.cc.ucf.edu/~service/pagge3.htm
*Description:* The Service Learning office and
course provide the opportunity for students to
learn through 75 hours of service in two ap-
proved community organizations and/or schools.
The course is best classified as a field study,
and it provides students with the opportunity to
develop a sense of commitment and apply
theories in practice while earning three hours of
university credit.
*SL Required for Graduation (all
  students)?* No
*Service Required for Graduation (all stu-
  dents)?* No
*Any Co-curricular Service?* No
*Any SL Residence Halls or Theme
  Houses?* No
*Number of Undergraduate SL Courses
  Offered Per Year:* 9
*Number of Graduate SL Courses Offered
  Per Year:* 0
*Total Number of SL Courses Offered
  Per Year:* 9
*Number of Instructors Teaching SL Courses
  Per Year:* 1
*Number of Full-time SL Staff on Campus
  (not counting instructors):* 0

*Number of Part-time SL Staff on Campus
  (not counting instructors):* 1

## University of Cincinnati

Mail Location #0205, Language Arts Depart-
  ment, University College, Cincinnati,
  OH 45221
*University/College URL:* http://www.uc.edu
*Type of Institution:* public, university
*SL Program/Center Name:* University Col-
  lege Service-Learning Pilot
*Contact Person Name and Title:* Barbara
  Wallace
*Contact Phone Number:* (513) 556–2021
*Contact Fax Number:* (513) 556–3007
*Contact Email Address:*
  wallacbl@ucmail.uc.edu
*SL Online Course Description URL:* http://
  oz.uc.edu/~wallacbl/Welcome.html
*SL Online Syllabi URL:* http://oz.uc.edu/~
  wallacbl/Welcome.html
*Description:* The University College Service-
Learning Pilot Program includes ''Service-
Learning in English Composition'' courses (101,
102, and 103), which grew out of an American
Association of Higher Education Summer Academy in June 1998. Faculty and administrators
from the University of Cincinnati attended the
summer academy in order to discover ways to
implement service-learning across the university. The resulting courses combine community
service with academic instruction. To increase
students' awareness and knowledge of community social issues, nine social themes are carefully examined: environment, disability, and
pregnant/parenting teens (in 101); poverty, hun-
ger/homelessness, and aging (in 102); and bias
and literacy (in 103). Students participate in
thoughtfully organized service that meets actual community needs and that is integrated
into the academic curriculum; have structured
opportunities for reflection; strengthen their
newly acquired academic skills and knowledge
in real-life situations in the community; and
increase their sense of social/civic responsibility.
*SL Required for Graduation (all
  students)?* No
*Service Required for Graduation (all stu-
  dents)?* No
*Any Co-curricular Service?* No

*Any SL Residence Halls or Theme
    Houses?* No
*Number of Undergraduate SL Courses
    Offered Per Year:* 6
*Number of Graduate SL Courses Offered
    Per Year:* 0
*Total Number of SL Courses Offered
    Per Year:* 6
*Number of Instructors Teaching SL Courses
    Per Year:* 6
*Number of Full-time SL Staff on Campus
    (not counting instructors):* 0
*Number of Part-time SL Staff on Campus
    (not counting instructors):* 0

## University of Colorado at Boulder

1201 17th St, IBS 5, Ste 11, Campus Box
    471, Boulder, CO 80309–0471
*University/College URL:* http://www.
    colorado.edu
*Type of Institution:* public, university, teach-
    ing, research, secular
*SL Program/Center Name:* Service Learning
    Program
*Contact Person Name and Title:* Sally
    Susnowitz, Dir
*Contact Phone Number:* (303) 492–7718
*Contact Email Address:*
    servicel@colorado.edu
*SL Program/Center URL:* http://www.
    colorado.edu/servicelearning
*SL Online Course Description URL:* http://
    www.colorado.edu/servicelearning/
    studcourses.html
*Description:* The Service Learning Program
Office serves as the campus-community liaison
vis-a-vis service-learning. The office works
with faculty, students, community organizations, and other campus programs that offer
students experiential learning and service opportunities. It helps match courses with partner
community organizations, arranges individual
student placements, advises faculty about curriculum design, and provides needed training.
The office also works with related campus
programs, e.g., the Student Leadership Institute, International and National Voluntary Service Training (INVST), Career Services' Internship Program, and the Volunteer Clearing House.
Additionally, office staff actively recruit ad-

ditional participants and write proposals to
fund service-learning opportunities, such as an
Internet writing center for high school students.
*SL Required for Graduation (all
    students)?* No
*Service Required for Graduation (all stu-
    dents)?* No
*Any Co-curricular Service?* Yes
*Any SL Residence Halls or Theme
    Houses?* Yes
*Number of Undergraduate SL Courses
    Offered Per Year:* 50–60
*Total Number of SL Courses Offered Per
    Year:* 50–60
*Number of Instructors Teaching SL Courses
    Per Year:* 35–40
*Number of Part-time SL Staff on Campus
    (not counting instructors):* 4

## University of Colorado at Colorado Springs

1420 Austin Bluffs Prkwy, PO Box 7150,
    Colorado Springs, CO 80933–7150
*University/College URL:* http://www.
    uccs.edu
*Type of Institution:* public, university, teach-
    ing, research, secular
*SL Program/Center Name:* Center for Com-
    munity Development & Design
*Contact Person Name and Title:* Bill
    Leon, Dir
*Contact Phone Number:* (719) 262–3568
*Contact Fax Number:* (719) 262–3040
*Contact Email Address:*
    bleon@mail.uccs.edu
*SL Program/Center URL:* http://ccdd.ufp.
    uccs.edu/
*Description:* The Center for Community Development and Design (CCDD) is a University
of Colorado outreach center that empowers
community members to solve problems by
blending service, education, and research activities to enhance the essence of community.
The center is a partnership between the university and local communities. It responds to requests for planning, design, research, and community development from community groups,
government units, and nonprofit organizations
that cannot afford or do not have the services it
provides. The center joins the efforts of its own

professional staff with those of faculty, students, and community representatives in responding to requests for services. Projects are approved by the center's Cooperative Community Board. Its commitments include the building and strengthening of a community's ability to solve problems. While the center is striving to provide educationally oriented public service to communities, it also affords students a chance to apply classroom learning through professionally supervised field experiences. Faculty working with the center are provided with funding and logistical support for numerous types of research opportunities.

*SL Required for Graduation (all students)?* No

*Service Required for Graduation (all students)?* No

*Any Co-curricular Service?* Yes

*Any SL Residence Halls or Theme Houses?* Yes

*Number of Undergraduate SL Courses Offered Per Year:* 10

*Number of Graduate SL Courses Offered Per Year:* 0

*Total Number of SL Courses Offered Per Year:* 10

*Number of Instructors Teaching SL Courses Per Year:* 10

*Number of Full-time SL Staff on Campus (not counting instructors):* 1

*Number of Part-time SL Staff on Campus (not counting instructors):* 4

## University of Colorado at Denver

Campus Box 199, PO Box 173364, Denver, CO 80217

*University/College URL:* http://www. cudenver.edu

*Type of Institution:* public, university, teaching, research

*SL Program/Center Name:* Service Learning Program

*Contact Person Name and Title:* Audra Beyer, Proj Coord

*Contact Phone Number:* (303) 556–4803

*Contact Fax Number:* (303)556–6477

*Contact Email Address:* abeyer@maroon.cudenver.edu

*Description:* The Service Learning Program's

goal is to assist students developing service projects, or connect them to direct service opportunities by coordinating community contacts, faculty advisors, and resources. The program also provides a network for faculty interested in incorporating service into their courses and/or research. The program is funded by grants. Service-learning courses or components are available in political science, psychology, architecture, anthropology, communications, art, theater, music, biology, philosophy, English/ literature, and education, among others. Students majoring in political science are required to complete service hours as a part of the political science program. "Chancellor's Scholars and Leaders" is a two-year leadership program in which students complete a semester or more of service.

*SL Required for Graduation (all students)?* No

*Service Required for Graduation (all students)?* No

*Any Co-curricular Service?* No

*Any SL Residence Halls or Theme Houses?* Yes

*Number of Instructors Teaching SL Courses Per Year:* 30

*Number of Full-time SL Staff on Campus (not counting instructors):* 1

*Number of Part-time SL Staff on Campus (not counting instructors):* 0

## University of Dayton

300 College Park Dr, Dayton, OH 45469

*University/College URL:* http://www. udayton.edu

*Type of Institution:* private, university, teaching, religious

*SL Program/Center Name:* Service-Learning Resource Center (SLRC)

*Contact Person Name and Title:* Monalisa Mullins, Dir

*Contact Phone Number:* (937) 229– 2752/4716

*Contact Fax Number:* (937) 229–4400

*Contact Email Address:* slrc@udayton.edu

*SL Program/Center URL:* http://www. udayton.edu/~service

*SL Online Course Description URL:* http:// www.udayton.edu/~service

*SL Online Syllabi URL:* http://www.udayton.
edu/~service

*Description:* The Service-Learning Resource
Center provides information and assistance to
faculty, staff, and students interested in service-learning. The center has arranged placements for over 800 students since it first opened
its doors in 1997. It has also been instrumental
in developing course-specific service-learning
projects for faculty in the professional schools
and in the College of Arts and Sciences. The
Service-Learning Resource Center became part
of the new Learning Teaching Center at the
university in January 2000.

*SL Required for Graduation (all
    students)?* No

*Service Required for Graduation (all stu-
    dents)?* No

*Any Co-curricular Service?* Yes

*Any SL Residence Halls or Theme
    Houses?* No

*Number of Undergraduate SL Courses
    Offered Per Year:* 70–80

*Number of Graduate SL Courses Offered
    Per Year:* 0

*Total Number of SL Courses Offered Per
    Year:* 75

*Number of Instructors Teaching SL Courses
    Per Year:* 40–50

*Number of Full-time SL Staff on Campus
    (not counting instructors):* 0

*Number of Part-time SL Staff on Campus
    (not counting instructors):* 3 (1 profes-
    sional, plus 2 work-study students)

## University of Denver

2050 E Evans Ave, Driscoll South, Suite 66,
    Denver, CO 80208

*University/College URL:* http://www.du.edu

*Type of Institution:* private, university

*SL Program/Center Name:* Service Learning
    Program

*Contact Person Name and Title:* Dr. C.
    David Lisman

*Contact Phone Number:* (303) 871–4921

*Contact Fax Number:* (303) 871–3110

*Contact Email Address:* dlisman@du.edu

*SL Program/Center URL:* http://www.
    du.edu/slp

*Description:* The Service Learning Program

works with faculty, staff, and students on creating and building long-term, sustainable, and
mutually beneficial partnerships with community-based organizations in Metro Denver. The
goal is for academically based service-learning
projects to help meet actual community needs
and develop a deeper sense of civic responsibility in students.

*SL Required for Graduation (all
    students)?* No

*Service Required for Graduation (all stu-
    dents)?* No

*Any Co-curricular Service?* Yes

*Any SL Residence Halls or Theme
    Houses?* Yes

*SL Degrees Offered:* N (But service-learning
    is a requirement for some minors, e.g.,
    leadership, international issues, environ-
    mental, and wellness.)

*Number of Undergraduate SL Courses
    Offered Per Year:* 25

*Number of Graduate SL Courses Offered
    Per Year:* 15

*Total Number of SL Courses Offered Per
    Year:* 40

*Number of Instructors Teaching SL Courses
    Per Year:* 23

*Number of Full-time SL Staff on Campus
    (not counting instructors):* 3

*Number of Part-time SL Staff on Campus
    (not counting instructors):* 1

## University of Detroit Mercy

4001 W McNichols, PO Box 19900, Detroit,
    MI 48219–0900

*University/College URL:* http://www.
    udmercy.edu

*Type of Institution:* private, university,
    religious

*SL Program/Center Name:* Leadership
    Development Institute

*Contact Person Name and Title:* Barbara
    Cyr-Roman, Community Service Coord;
    Colleen Kaminski, Dir

*Contact Phone Number:* (313) 993–1776

*Contact Fax Number:* (313) 993–1509

*Contact Email Address:*
    cyrrombc@udmercy.edu;
    kaminscm@udmercy.edu

*SL Program/Center URL:* http://libarts.
udmercy.edu/univ/ldi/

*SL Online Course Description URL:* http://
libarts.udmercy.edu/univ/ldi/academics.
html

*Description:* The Leadership Development Institute integrates the university's values and vision for the future and fosters a particular kind of leadership: leadership in service. This concept of leadership is at the core of the university's mission, which is to ''challenge students to an understanding of their social, leadership and service responsibilities.'' The institute assists students, faculty, and community-service agencies with the logistics, presentations, placement, evaluation, and reflection of service-learning. Service-learning at the university integrates course theory with community-based experiences to help students develop an understanding of community needs, gain valuable insight through practical experience, and grow as educated citizens.

*SL Required for Graduation (all
students)?* No

*Service Required for Graduation (all students)?* No

*Any Co-curricular Service?* Yes (Leadership In Service Program)

*Any SL Residence Halls or Theme Houses?*
Yes (Peace and Social Justice floor)

*Number of Undergraduate SL Courses
Offered Per Year:* 26

*Number of Graduate SL Courses Offered
Per Year:* 8

*Total Number of SL Courses Offered Per
Year:* 34

*Number of Instructors Teaching SL Courses
Per Year:* 26

*Number of Full-time SL Staff on Campus
(not counting instructors):* 3

*Number of Part-time SL Staff on Campus
(not counting instructors):* 1 (1 grad assist
per semester)

**University of Florida**
330 J. Wayne Reitz Union, PO Box 118505,
Gainesville, FL 32611

*University/College URL:* http://www.ufl.edu

*Type of Institution:* public, university, research, secular

*SL Program/Center Name:* The TreeHouse
(Campus Volunteer Center)

*Contact Person Name and Title:* Colette
Taylor, Assist Dir of Student Activities

*Contact Phone Number:* (352) 392–1655

*Contact Fax Number:* (352) 392–6450

*Contact Email Address:*
Colette@union.ufl.edu

*SL Program/Center URL:* http://www.union.
ufl.edu/treehouse/tree.html

*Description:* The TreeHouse serves as the campus clearinghouse for volunteerism. It is specifically designed to foster an atmosphere of giving and community on campus. The TreeHouse provides programs that focus on service, collaboration, networking, and awareness. The goal of the TreeHouse is to educate and socially develop members of the university community through involvement or participation in civic-leadership opportunities. The mission of the Service Learning Program is to develop awareness, understanding, and commitment to service-learning by creating a physical and virtual resource center that facilitates interactions between faculty, graduate, and undergraduate students, student services staff, and community partners. As a part of this mission, the TreeHouse works actively to serve educational institutions, governmental and non-governmental organizations, community agencies, and the UF campus community; organizes educational and training tools to aid the development and implementation of service-learning activities across disciplines; works with faculty to support student learning objectives, and develop successful approaches to establish service-learning teaching strategies through existing networks, mentors, and resources; appreciates service-learning as an academically effective and socially beneficial pedagogy (therefore the center supports the exploration of service-learning through student theses and faculty research); and actively participates in campus, system, statewide, and national movements to promote service-learning as a means for social and intellectual development.

*SL Required for Graduation (all
students)?* No

*Service Required for Graduation (all students)?* No

*Any Co-curricular Service?* Yes

*Any SL Residence Halls or Theme Houses?* Yes

*Number of Undergraduate SL Courses Offered Per Year:* 64

*Number of Graduate SL Courses Offered Per Year:* 2

*Total Number of SL Courses Offered Per Year:* 66

*Number of Instructors Teaching SL Courses Per Year:* 31

## University of Florida

Norman Hall, PO Box 117044, Gainesville, FL 32611–7044

*University/College URL:* http://www.coe.ufl.edu

*Type of Institution:* public, university, teaching, research, secular

*SL Program/Center Name:* College of Education

*Description:* While there is no formal service-learning program within the College of Education, some service-learning courses and projects exist. One such course is "Exceptional People" (EEX 3312), an introductory survey course in Special Education, in which each student is required to do a 20-hour service-learning project coordinated by Dr. Stuart Schwartz (ses@coe.ufl.edu) in the Department of Special Education and the Alachua County Volunteer Center. "Bright Futures" is a tutoring project for students enrolled in their first semester in the Unified Elementary/Special Education preservice teacher-preparation program. Students are required to tutor children who are at risk for success in school. All children are identified and tutored through the public housing projects in Gainesville, Florida. Dr. Elizabeth (Buffy) Bondy (bondy@coe.ufl.edu) teaches, organizes, and supervises this project. In "Project BookTalk" (another project for students enrolled in their first semester in the preservice teacher-preparation program), students read to children in home day care settings. Dr. Linda Lamme (lammel@coe.ufl.edu) coordinates this project.

## University of Hartford

200 Bloomfield Ave, Center for Community Service, West Hartford, CT 01002

*University/College URL:* http://www.hartford.edu

*Type of Institution:* private, university, teaching

*SL Program/Center Name:* Center for Community Service

*Contact Person Name and Title:* Irwin Nussbaum, Dir and Assoc Dean of Students

$11(860) 768–5026

*Contact Fax Number:* (860) 768–5025

*Contact Email Address:* ccs@mail.hartford.edu

*SL Program/Center URL:* http://uhavax.hartford.edu/~ccs

*SL Online Course Description URL:* http://uhavax.hartford.edu/~ccs

*Description:* The Center for Community Service promotes civic responsibility and enhances the educational process through academic service-learning experiences and active participation in community-service programs. The center assists students and faculty in integrating service-learning into the academic experience; develops collaborative partnerships with community agencies and service organizations; and establishes and promotes community-service opportunities for individuals, groups, and classes.

*SL Required for Graduation (all students)?* No

*Service Required for Graduation (all students)?* No

*Any Co-curricular Service?* No

*Any SL Residence Halls or Theme Houses?* Yes

*Number of Undergraduate SL Courses Offered Per Year:* 40

*Number of Graduate SL Courses Offered Per Year:* 5

*Total Number of SL Courses Offered Per Year:* 45

*Number of Instructors Teaching SL Courses Per Year:* 25

*Number of Full-time SL Staff on Campus (not counting instructors):* 0

*Number of Part-time SL Staff on Campus (not counting instructors):* 0

## University of Hawai'i at Manoa

2600 Campus Rd, Student Services Center Rm 213, Honolulu, HI 96822

*University/College URL:* http://www.hawaii.edu

*Type of Institution:* public, university, research

*SL Program/Center Name:* Service Learning Program

*Contact Person Name and Title:* Atina T. Pascua, Coord

*Contact Phone Number:* (808) 956–4641

*Contact Fax Number:* (808) 956–3394

*Contact Email Address:* atina@hawaii.edu

*SL Program/Center URL:* http://www2.hawaii.edu/~slp/

*Description:* The Service Learning Program exists to integrate service-learning into the culture of the university and to enhance the philanthropic consciousness of the university community. The purpose of the program is to facilitate activities which promote social responsibility, provide curricular and co-curricular developmental opportunities, and foster mutually beneficial relationships with the university and local community.

*SL Required for Graduation (all students)?* No

*Service Required for Graduation (all students)?* No

*Any Co-curricular Service?* Yes

*Any SL Residence Halls or Theme Houses?* Yes

*Number of Undergraduate SL Courses Offered Per Year:* 35

*Number of Graduate SL Courses Offered Per Year:* 7

*Total Number of SL Courses Offered Per Year:* 42

*Number of Instructors Teaching SL Courses Per Year:* 42

*Number of Full-time SL Staff on Campus (not counting instructors):* 1

*Number of Part-time SL Staff on Campus (not counting instructors):* 5

## University of Illinois at Urbana-Champaign

1401 West Green St, 284 Illini Union, MC-384, Urbana, IL 61801

*University/College URL:* http://www.uiuc.edu

*Type of Institution:* public, university, research, secular

*SL Program/Center Name:* Office of Volunteer Programs (OVP)

*Contact Person Name and Title:* Thomas Shields, Dir

*Contact Phone Number:* (217) 333–7424

*Contact Fax Number:* (217) 244–4294

*Contact Email Address:* ovp@uiuc.edu

*SL Program/Center URL:* http://www.union.uiuc.edu/ovp

*SL Online Course Description URL:* http://www.union.uiuc.edu/servicelrn

*Description:* The Office of Volunteer Programs' mission since 1989 is to enhance and expand meaningful student involvement in community service and, through it, enrich the educational experience of students at the university. The office serves four main functions on campus. First, it provides a clearinghouse where volunteer opportunities can be matched with willing volunteers. The office continually strives to increase students awareness of the needs of the Champaign-Urbana community. Second, it promotes student leadership in community service through advising Volunteer Illinois and other student community-service organizations which are part of the SERVE Illinois coalition. Third, it sponsors special events to raise awareness and educate the campus community about service-related issues. Events include a nonprofit career fair and Hunger and Homelessness Awareness Week. Fourth, the office supports the development of service-learning courses and programs by consulting and providing information which links such courses to community organizations. The Office of Volunteer Programs is jointly funded by alumni donations to the Student Leadership Fund and by the United Way of Champaign County.

*SL Required for Graduation (all students)?* No

*Service Required for Graduation (all students)?* No

*Any Co-curricular Service?* Yes

*Any SL Residence Halls or Theme Houses?* No

*Number of Undergraduate SL Courses Offered Per Year:* 20

*Number of Full-time SL Staff on Campus (not counting instructors):* 1 (academic professional, about 1/5 of total responsibilities)

*Number of Part-time SL Staff on Campus (not counting instructors):* 5 (1 half-time grad assistant, plus 4 undergrad assistants)

## University of Kentucky

206 Mathews Bldg, Office for Experiential Education, Lexington, KY 40506–0047

*University/College URL:* http://www.uky.edu

*Type of Institution:* public, university, research

*SL Program/Center Name:* Office for Experiential Education

*Contact Person Name and Title:* Louise Stone, Dir

*Contact Phone Number:* (606) 257–3632

*Contact Fax Number:* (606) 257–2378

*Contact Email Address:* elston00@pop.uky.edu

*SL Program/Center URL:* http://www.uky.edu/UExt/experiential_education.html

*Description:* The Service-Learning Program at the University of Kentucky has been in operation since 1973 in the Office for Experiential Education. The programs are all academic, for credit, and involve faculty from the appropriate department. Over 100 faculty participate in various service-learning programs.

*SL Required for Graduation (all students)?* No

*Service Required for Graduation (all students)?* No

*Any Co-curricular Service?* No

*Any SL Residence Halls or Theme Houses?* No (But plans have begun for this.)

*Number of Undergraduate SL Courses Offered Per Year:* 15

*Number of Graduate SL Courses Offered Per Year:* 5

*Total Number of SL Courses Offered Per Year:* 20

*Number of Instructors Teaching SL Courses Per Year:* 100

*Number of Full-time SL Staff on Campus (not counting instructors):* 2

*Number of Part-time SL Staff on Campus (not counting instructors):* 1 (Staff also coordinate a campus-wide internship and shadowing program.)

## University of Louisiana at Lafayette

104 University Cir, PO Box 40198, Lafayette, LA 70504–0198

*University/College URL:* http://www.louisiana.edu

*Type of Institution:* public, university, teaching, secular

*SL Program/Center Name:* Service-Learning Center

*Contact Person Name and Title:* Dr. Charles E. Palmer, Dean of Community Service

*Contact Phone Number:* (337) 482–6044

*Contact Fax Number:* (337) 482–5374

*Contact Email Address:* cep4690@louisiana.edu

*Description:* The Service-Learning Center is connected to the university's AmeriCorps Community Service Program. The center works with any student at the university to establish a service-learning experience with interested faculty members. The Dean of Community Service heads a Service-Learning Council of over 40 faculty.

*SL Required for Graduation (all students)?* No

*Service Required for Graduation (all students)?* No

*Any Co-curricular Service?* No

*Any SL Residence Halls or Theme Houses?* No

*Number of Undergraduate SL Courses Offered Per Year:* 40

*Total Number of SL Courses Offered Per Year:* 40

*Number of Instructors Teaching SL Courses Per Year:* 30

*Number of Full-time SL Staff on Campus (not counting instructors):* 0

*Number of Part-time SL Staff on Campus (not counting instructors):* 1

## University of Louisville

Student Activities Center, W318/Service Learning Office, Louisville, KY 40292

*University/College URL:* http://www. louisville.edu

*Type of Institution:* public, university, teaching, research

*SL Program/Center Name:* Service Learning Program

*Contact Person Name and Title:* Kim K. Lockwood Johnson, Service Learning Coord

*Contact Phone Number:* (502) 852–3436

*Contact Fax Number:* (502) 852–1429

*Contact Email Address:* kkjohn01@gwise.louisville.edu

*SL Program/Center URL:* http://www. louisville.edu/student/life/serv-learn/

*SL Online Course Description URL:* http:// www.louisville.edu/student/life/serv-learn/learn.html

*Description:* The Service Learning Program Office provides resources and support for students, student organizations, and faculty who are involved in service-learning and community service. The office promotes service in the community by forming informal partnerships with community agencies and by providing resource information on local agencies in need of volunteers. It also works directly with faculty, offering training to those interested in incorporating service-learning into their courses, and helping them plan course syllabi and find appropriate sites. The office is in the process of creating criteria for faculty to use in identifying those courses which include a service-learning component. Service-learning courses may be designated as such in the Spring 2000 catalogue, so that students have the option of taking classes with an SL component. The office trains student leaders to incorporate service-learning into their student organizations' community-service projects. It coordinates campus-wide service projects and sponsors or plans the Alternative Spring Break Program in conjunction with Student Life. The office also administers the America Reads Challenge Federal Work Study program, and is responsible for the recruitment, supervision, and training of 50 tutors per semester, who tutor in urban areas of Louisville (e.g., public schools and community centers). The university has an "urban" mission focus, which the Service Learning Program Office coordinates, i.e., it recruits, supervises, helps train, and provides reflection opportunities throughout the semester. In Fall 1999, the office started Service Learning Faculty and Student Advisory Committees to help focus and coordinate efforts to educate the campus about service-learning.

*SL Required for Graduation (all students)?* No

*Service Required for Graduation (all students)?* No

*Any Co-curricular Service?* Yes (Many student and Greek organizations require and encourage community service; the Honors College, along with several on-campus honors societies, are committed to community service projects.)

*Any SL Residence Halls or Theme Houses?* No

*SL Graduate Program Name:* The Samuel L. Greenbaum Public Service Program

*SL Graduate Program Description:* The Samuel L. Greenbaum Public Service Program is part of the Louis Brandeis School of Law (http://www.louisville.edu/brandeislaw), at the University of Louisville. All students are required to perform a minimum of 30 hours of law-related public service prior to graduation. The program also sponsors the IOLTA Public Service Fellowship and the Edwin H. Perry Mediation Fellowship. Programs offered to the community include Consumer Law in KY Seminars and Advice-and-Counsel Clinics, Legal Clinics, Lunch and Learn Programs, and the Prisoner Mediation Project. Most graduate programs (particularly programs through the Kent School of Social Work, the School of Education, Allied Health, Urban Studies and the Medical, Dental, and Nursing Schools) have an internship or practicum requirement in which students apply what they are learning in a community setting. Many of these placements include an equal balance between service and learning, completing projects that meet a community need, and ongoing reflection that is an integral part of service-learning.

*Number of Undergraduate SL Courses Offered Per Year:* 59

*Number of Graduate SL Courses Offered Per Year:* 54

*Total Number of SL Courses Offered Per Year:* 113 (based on 1997 data; a new survey is underway)

*Number of Instructors Teaching SL Courses Per Year:* 64

*Number of Full-time SL Staff on Campus (not counting instructors):* 1

*Number of Part-time SL Staff on Campus (not counting instructors):* 3 (2 federal work study students who work 10–15 hours a week; 1 America Reads payroll clerk—funded by grant—who works 15 hours a week on the America Reads Program)

## University of Maine at Farmington
106 Main St, Farmington, ME 04938
*University/College URL:* http://www.umf.maine.edu
*Type of Institution:* public, college, teaching, secular
*Contact Person Name and Title:* Lucia Swallow, Assoc Dir, Service-Learning
*Contact Phone Number:* (207) 778–7037
*Contact Fax Number:* (207) 778–7196
*Contact Email Address:* swallow@maine.edu
*Description:* Service-learning has been growing at the University of Maine at Farmington for about five years. Interest is particularly strong in the College of Health, Education and Rehabilitation. There is now an associate director of service-learning, whose primary purpose is to work with faculty to implement and institutionalize service-learning at the university. The position and budget are funded through educational and general funds. The associate director reports to the vice president of Student and Community Affairs. Students also find service opportunities on campus through Stu-

dent Life, the Health and Fitness Center, clubs, and organizations.

*SL Required for Graduation (all students)?* No

*Service Required for Graduation (all students)?* No

*Any Co-curricular Service?* Yes

*Any SL Residence Halls or Theme Houses?* No

*Number of Undergraduate SL Courses Offered Per Year:* 40–60 (20–30 per semester)

*Number of Graduate SL Courses Offered Per Year:* 0

*Total Number of SL Courses Offered Per Year:* 40–60 (20–30 per semester)

*Number of Instructors Teaching SL Courses Per Year:* 20–30 (in Liberal Arts, Health, Education, and Rehabilitation)

*Number of Full-time SL Staff on Campus (not counting instructors):* 0

*Number of Part-time SL Staff on Campus (not counting instructors):* 1 (half-time, 9-month, professional staff person with no support staff, only work-study students for 10–15 hrs. per week)

## University of Maine at Presque Isle
181 Main St, Presque Isle, ME 04769
*University/College URL:* http://www.umpi.maine.edu
*Type of Institution:* public, university, teaching
*Contact Person Name and Title:* Srijana Bajracharya, Assoc Prof
*Contact Phone Number:* (207) 768–9436
*Contact Email Address:* Srijana@maine.edu
*Description:* Service-learning has been employed at the University of Maine at Presque Isle for about ten years. There is no central service-learning office: some faculty members pursue it on their own. Service-learning courses exist in health education, criminal justice, and biology. There is an effort underway to develop more service-learning courses on campus. At present, Maine Campus Compact funds some service-learning activities aimed at local school teachers and their inservice training. An AmeriCorps VISTA volunteer is formally organizing the advisory group to initiate addi-

tional service-learning projects on campus, and coordinates the America Reads and America Counts programs.

*SL Required for Graduation (all students)?* No

*Service Required for Graduation (all students)?* No

*Any Co-curricular Service?* Yes

*Number of Undergraduate SL Courses Offered Per Year:* 2

*Total Number of SL Courses Offered Per Year:* 2

*Number of Instructors Teaching SL Courses Per Year:* 3–4

*Number of Full-time SL Staff on Campus (not counting instructors):* 0

*Number of Part-time SL Staff on Campus (not counting instructors):* 0

**University of Maryland**
1195 Stamp Student Union, College Park, MD 20742

*University/College URL:* http://www.umd.edu

*Type of Institution:* public, university, research, secular

*SL Program/Center Name:* Community Service Programs

*Contact Person Name and Title:* Marie Troppe, Coord of Service-Learning

*Contact Phone Number:* (301) 314–5387

*Contact Fax Number:* (301) 314–9874

*Contact Email Address:* mtroppe@accmail.umd.edu

*SL Program/Center URL:* http://www.umd.edu/CSP/s-l

*Description:* The service-learning program at the University of Maryland involves approximately 1,500 students annually. Fifty faculty, from disciplines such as Afro-american studies, botany, education, engineering, English, health education and family studies, psychology, sociology, and Spanish practice service-learning in their courses. The campus offers 40 service-learning courses per year, most during the regular semester and some during the Winter term. In addition, service-learning is a pillar of both University Honors and College Park Scholars. New honors students take Honors 100: ''The Responsibilities of a Liberally Edu-

cated Person,'' which includes a service component. Nine of the 10 College Park Scholars programs engage students in service-learning. While the campus focuses on service-learning opportunities for undergraduates, several graduate courses incorporate service-learning too.

*SL Required for Graduation (all students)?* No

*Service Required for Graduation (all students)?* No

*Any Co-curricular Service?* Yes

*Any SL Residence Halls or Theme Houses?* Yes (College Park Scholars is a living/learning community in which nine of the 10 academic programs incorporate service-learning. A second thematic living and learning program, CIVICUS, allows a small, diverse, and committed group of first-year and upperclass students to examine and create their own unique civil society within one residence hall. CIVICUS is based upon the concepts of leadership, citizenship, scholarship, community service, and the development of a diverse community)

*Number of Undergraduate SL Courses Offered Per Year:* 40

*Number of Graduate SL Courses Offered Per Year:* 4

*Total Number of SL Courses Offered Per Year:* 44

*Number of Instructors Teaching SL Courses Per Year:* 50

*Number of Full-time SL Staff on Campus (not counting instructors):* 1

*Number of Part-time SL Staff on Campus (not counting instructors):* 4 (A portion of each staff member's time goes to support faculty in service-learning.)

**University of Maryland, Baltimore County**
1000 Hilltop Circle, Baltimore, MD 21250

*University/College URL:* http://www.umbc.edu

*Type of Institution:* public, university, research, secular

*SL Program/Center Name:* The Shriver Center

*Contact Person Name and Title:* John S. Martello, Exec Dir

*Contact Phone Number:* (410) 455–2493
*Contact Fax Number:* (410) 455–1074
*Contact Email Address:* martello@umbc.edu
*SL Program/Center URL:* http://www.
    shrivercenter.org
*SL Online Course Description URL:* http://
    www.shrivercenter.org
*Description:* The Shriver Center was created in
1993 in honor of Eunice Kennedy and Sargent
Shriver to harness the resources of the university to attack and solve the most urgent economic, social, and cultural problems that threaten
the vitality of the American city. To that end,
the center seeks to initiate and promote educational programs, institutional structures, and
faculty research that will deepen the mutually
beneficial engagement of the university and the
city. Central to this mission is the creation of
programs which educate a new generation of
citizens committed to working in and caring for
their communities: programs which develop
students' capacity to recognize their values,
insights, and skills and integrate choice, action,
and a concern for the common good at the
fundamental level of the person. These programs are organized under the categories of
service delivery, community service and learning, and professional practice.

The Shriver Center's Community Service
and Learning Program is structured to cultivate
social conscience and civic literacy among
UMBC students. The program places students
in human service and community-action agencies that focus on a variety of social issues
such as mental retardation, juvenile justice,
education, homelessness, aging, and the environment. These community-service and learning placements are highly structured and carefully supervised. Strict criteria are established
to ensure that the service experience meets
academic objectives. Students participate in
structured reflection activities through linked
coursework. In this way, study is enhanced and
service illuminated.

The Shriver Peaceworker Program enables
returned Peace Corps volunteers (RPCVs) to
adapt their experience in the developing world
to the challenges of urban America. Each year,
on a competitive basis, the Peaceworker Program invites a group of RPCVs to participate in
a rigorous, two-year program integrating community service, graduate study, and ethical
reflection. The goal is to prepare citizen leaders
who can creatively respond to the economic,
social, and cultural problems confronting the
United States today.

*SL Required for Graduation (all
    students)?* No
*Service Required for Graduation (all stu-
    dents)?* No
*Any Co-curricular Service?* Yes
*Any SL Residence Halls or Theme
    Houses?* No
*Number of Undergraduate SL Courses
    Offered Per Year:* 10
*Number of Graduate SL Courses Offered
    Per Year:* 1
*Total Number of SL Courses Offered Per
    Year:* 11
*Number of Instructors Teaching SL Courses
    Per Year:* 15
*Number of Full-time SL Staff on Campus
    (not counting instructors):* 2
*Number of Part-time SL Staff on Campus
    (not counting instructors):* 0

**University of Massachusetts-Amherst**
Office of Community Service Learning
    at Commonwealth College, Room 504
    Goodell, UMass, Amherst, MA 01003
*University/College URL:* http://www.
    umass.edu
*Type of Institution:* public, university
*SL Program/Center Name:* Office of Com-
    munity Service Learning at Common-
    wealth College
*Contact Person Name and Title:* Dr. John
    Reife, Dir, Office of Community Service
    Learning
*Contact Phone Number:* (413) 545–2015
*Contact Fax Number:* (413) 545–4469
*Contact Email Address:*
    keene@anthro.umass.edu or
    schimmel@educ.umass.edu
*SL Program/Center URL:* http://www.
    umass.edu/csl
*SL Online Course Description URL:* http://
    www.umass.edu/csl/web/courses.shtml
*Description:* Community service-learning is a

cornerstone of the Commonwealth Honors College. While the Office of Community Service Learning is based in Commonwealth College, it serves as a nexus for community service-learning for the entire campus. Community service-learning opportunities are integrated in a number of honors seminars, offered through stand-alone leadership courses, and available as one-credit additions to academic courses. In addition, "Alternative Spring Break" is a four-credit course offered spring semester though the sponsorship of the Honors College. The office sponsors a number of innovative academic community service-learning programs, including the Citizen Scholars Program, Curricular Altnerative Spring Break, and the new IMPACT freshman community service-learning community. The office advises students on the range of community service-learning opportunities and specific classes, as well as assisting in placement of students with community organizations and agencies. The office also manages the faculty and departmental fellowship programs in community service-learning, as well as the faculty seminar in community service-learning. The office is staffed by a full-time director, two graduate assistants, and a few work-study students, and is run by the director in consultation with a faculty/student advisory board.

*SL Required for Graduation (all students)?* No

*Service Required for Graduation (all students)?* No

*Any Co-curricular Service?* Yes

*Any SL Residence Halls or Theme Houses?* Yes

*SL Undergraduate Program Name:* Citizen Scholar's Program

*SL Undergraduate Program Description:* The Citizen Scholar's Program is a two-year program that combines rigorous academic coursework with service in the community. The program is designed to help students develop the capacity to become leaders and effective agents for social change. Students complete five community service-learning courses over two years, including a gateway course and a capstone course. Students must complete a minimum of 120 hours of community service per year in conjunction with these courses. Service experiences must include direct service, immersion, administrative or public-policy service, and service-based research. Students attend bi-monthly dinner seminars with community and campus leaders. Admission of up to 20 students per year is competitive. Students receive a $1000 scholarship for each year in the program and special recognition upon graduation as Citizen Scholars. The program is open to students from all majors.

*Number of Undergraduate SL Courses Offered Per Year:* 40–50

*Number of Graduate SL Courses Offered Per Year:* 5–10

*Total Number of SL Courses Offered Per Year:* 45–60

*Number of Instructors Teaching SL Courses Per Year:* 60

*Number of Full-time SL Staff on Campus (not counting instructors):* 1

*Number of Part-time SL Staff on Campus (not counting instructors):* 5 (3 plus 2 VISTA volunteers)

## University of Miami

1306 Stanford Dr, UC Room 240, PO Box 249116, Coral Gables, FL 33124–6923

*University/College URL:* http://www.miami.edu

*Type of Institution:* private, university, research

*SL Program/Center Name:* William R. Butler Volunteer Services Center

*Contact Person Name and Title:* Dir of Volunteer Services

*Contact Phone Number:* (305) 284-GIVE

*Contact Fax Number:* (305) 284–4310

*Contact Email Address:* volunteerservices@miami.edu

*SL Program/Center URL:* http://gehon.ir.miami.edu/volunteer-services/faculty.html

*Description:* The mission of the Butler Volunteer Services Center is to actively promote the inclusion of community service in every facet of the university experience by helping students to realize their potential to impact their environment through the power of social action, responsible citizenship, and volunteerism; challenging the university community to seek knowledge and experience outside the classroom; serving as a liaison between the community and the university; encouraging students to apply knowledge from their individual academic concentrations to create a just and peaceful society; and providing placement and support services to individuals involved in community service.

*SL Required for Graduation (all students)?* No

*Service Required for Graduation (all students)?* No

*Any Co-curricular Service?* Yes

*Any SL Residence Halls or Theme Houses?* No

*Number of Full-time SL Staff on Campus (not counting instructors):* 2 (full-time staff in the Volunteer Services Center, who are responsible for running the programs and coordinating the resources as part of their duties in center)

*Number of Part-time SL Staff on Campus (not counting instructors):* 0

## University of Michigan

Ann Arbor, MI 48109

*University/College URL:* http://www. umich.edu

*Type of Institution:* public, university, research, secular

*SL Program/Center Name:* Edward Ginsberg Center for Community Service and Learning

*Contact Person Name and Title:* Jeffrey Howard, Assist Dir for Academic Service Learning

*Contact Phone Number:* (734) 647–7402

*Contact Fax Number:* (734) 647–7464

*Contact Email Address:* jphoward@umich.edu

*SL Program/Center URL:* http://www.umich.edu/~mserve

*Description:* The Center for Community Service and Learning opened its doors in 1997, building upon a tradition of service-learning programs in operation since the early 1970s.

The center has three goals: engage students in learning and leadership through community service and academic study; enable faculty members to integrate service into teaching and to conduct research responsive to community needs; and develop collaborative partnerships with communities. Student programs are of three types: academic courses, co-curricular, and national service opportunities. Programs include Project Community (a sociology service-learning course); Project Serve (a co-curricular program that offers volunteer opportunities); Alternative Break programs (Spring and weekends); program leadership opportunities; America Reads (a work-study literacy service-learning program); and the Michigan Community Service Corps (a paid service program over the summer months in various communities across the state of Michigan). In addition, the center runs an AmeriCorps program, a national service program in which graduate students from a number of different professional schools work in interdisciplinary teams with agencies in the Michigan Neighborhood Partnership in Detroit.

*SL Required for Graduation (all students)?* No

*Service Required for Graduation (all students)?* No

*Any Co-curricular Service?* Yes

*Any SL Residence Halls or Theme Houses?* Yes

*Number of Undergraduate SL Courses Offered Per Year:* 60

*Number of Graduate SL Courses Offered Per Year:* 20

*Total Number of SL Courses Offered Per Year:* 80

*Number of Instructors Teaching SL Courses Per Year:* 70

*Number of Full-time SL Staff on Campus (not counting instructors):* 10

*Number of Part-time SL Staff on Campus (not counting instructors):* 1

## University of Michigan-Flint

303 E Kearsley St, Flint, MI 48502

*University/College URL:* http://www.flint.umich.edu

*Type of Institution:* public, university, teaching

*SL Program/Center Name:* Office of Service Learning and School Partnerships

*Contact Person Name and Title:* Laura Bucklen, Manager of Service Learning

*Contact Phone Number:* (810) 766–6898

*Contact Fax Number:* (810) 237–6501

*Contact Email Address:* bucklen@flint.umich.edu

*SL Program/Center URL:* http://www.umf-outreach.edu

*Description:* The Office of Service Learning and School Partnerships is committed to providing meaningful community-service opportunities for the university through a variety of programs, supporting faculty who choose to use academic service-learning as a teaching method, and developing effective partnerships with local school districts. All projects and partnerships are intended to be mutually beneficial and are designed to provide unique learning experiences for students.

*SL Required for Graduation (all students)?* No

*Service Required for Graduation (all students)?* No

*Any Co-curricular Service?* Yes

*Any SL Residence Halls or Theme Houses?* No

*Number of Undergraduate SL Courses Offered Per Year:* 10–15

*Number of Graduate SL Courses Offered Per Year:* 2–3

*Total Number of SL Courses Offered Per Year:* 12–18

*Number of Instructors Teaching SL Courses Per Year:* 7–10

*Number of Full-time SL Staff on Campus (not counting instructors):* 3

*Number of Part-time SL Staff on Campus (not counting instructors):* 3

**University of Minnesota-Crookston**
2900 University Ave, 120 Bede Student Center, Crookston, MN 56716

*University/College URL:* http://www.crk.umn.edu

*Type of Institution:* public, university, teaching, secular

*SL Program/Center Name:* UMC Service Learning Center

*Contact Person Name and Title:* Pamela Holsinger-Fuchs, Dir of Student Activities/Service Learning

*Contact Phone Number:* (218) 281–8505

*Contact Fax Number:* (218) 281–8504

*Contact Email Address:* pholsing@mail.crk.umn.edu

*SL Program/Center URL:* http://www.crk.umn.edu/people/services/serve-learn/index.htm

*Description:* The mission of the Service Learning Center is to provide all students with the opportunity to have meaningful service-learning experiences prior to graduation. The center's primary focus is incorporating service-learning into the academic curriculum. The center also works with various community-service agencies to support service performed by campus clubs and organizations and to provide opportunities for individual volunteering. The center is funded by the university with support from AmeriCorp and VISTA volunteers.

*SL Required for Graduation (all students)?* No

*Service Required for Graduation (all students)?* No

*Any Co-curricular Service?* Yes

*Any SL Residence Halls or Theme Houses?* No

*Number of Undergraduate SL Courses Offered Per Year:* 35

*Total Number of SL Courses Offered Per Year:* 35

*Number of Instructors Teaching SL Courses Per Year:* 30

*Number of Full-time SL Staff on Campus (not counting instructors):* 1

*Number of Part-time SL Staff on Campus (not counting instructors):* 6

**University of Minnesota-Twin Cities**
Minneapolis, MN 55455

*University/College URL:* http://www.umn.edu

*Type of Institution:* public, university, research

*SL Program/Center Name:* Community Involvement Programs, Career and Community Learning Center

*Contact Person Name and Title:* Laurel Hirt, Interim Coord

*Contact Phone Number:* (612) 626–2044

*Contact Fax Number:* (612) 624–2538

*Contact Email Address:* lhirt@adv.cla.umn.edu

*SL Program/Center URL:* http://www.oslo.umn.edu

*SL Online Course Description URL:* http://www.oslo.umn.edu/Community_Involvement_Programs/relatedcourses.htm

*Description:* Community Involvement Programs (CIP) offers individuals opportunities to learn more about themselves, the communities in which they live, and how to actively participate in community problem-solving. These experiences are meant to not only enrich and enhance learning, but also to fulfill real and often-times urgent community needs. CIP provides a range of services including technical assistance and support to faculty developing or redesigning curricula to integrate a community-based learning component; advertising courses which integrate a community-based component into the academic curriculum to students; individual advising, ongoing support, and reflection sessions for students through the Community Empowerment through Learning and Leadership (CELL) program; opportunities for students with substantial community experience to take on leadership roles within the office through the CELL program Leadership Network; cultivating and strengthening partnerships with local community organizations throughout the Twin Cities area that provide meaningful opportunities for student involvement in their local communities; advocating for, and educating about, best practices when combining community work with learning; and providing information to students, faculty, staff, and community partners on training opportunities, conferences, funding sources, awards, and related programs in the state, region, and nationally that may be of interest to people working on campus-community collaboration efforts.

*SL Required for Graduation (all students)?* No

*Service Required for Graduation (all students)?* No

*Any Co-curricular Service?* Yes

*Any SL Residence Halls or Theme Houses?* No

*SL Degrees Offered:* N (But a minor or certificate are being explored.)

*Number of Undergraduate SL Courses Offered Per Year:* 50

*Number of Graduate SL Courses Offered Per Year:* 10

*Total Number of SL Courses Offered Per Year:* 60

*Number of Instructors Teaching SL Courses Per Year:* 50+

*Number of Full-time SL Staff on Campus (not counting instructors):* 2

*Number of Part-time SL Staff on Campus (not counting instructors):* 11 (1 graduate student, plus 10 undergraduate assistants)

**University of Montana-Missoula**

Volunteer Action Services, Missoula, MT 59812

*University/College URL:* http://www.umt.edu

*Type of Institution:* public, university, teaching, research, secular

*SL Program/Center Name:* Volunteer Action Services

*Contact Person Name and Title:* Andrea Vernon, Dir

*Contact Phone Number:* (406) 243–5159

*Contact Fax Number:* (406) 243–6446

*Contact Email Address:* vernon@selway.umt.edu

*SL Program/Center URL:* http://www.dhc.umt.edu/vas/home.htm

*Description:* Volunteer Action Services is the volunteer clearinghouse and service-learning center for the University of Montana. It refers student volunteers to the community, organizes and implements service projects on campus and in the community, and works with faculty to integrate service-learning in curriculum. Volunteer Action Services receives funding through a variety of sources, including state funds, AmeriCorps funds, foundation funds, and private donations.

*SL Required for Graduation (all students)?* No

*Any Co-curricular Service?* Yes

*Any SL Residence Halls or Theme Houses?* No

*Number of Undergraduate SL Courses Offered Per Year:* 25

*Number of Graduate SL Courses Offered Per Year:* 10

*Total Number of SL Courses Offered Per Year:* 35

*Number of Instructors Teaching SL Courses Per Year:* 12

*Number of Full-time SL Staff on Campus (not counting instructors):* 3

*Number of Part-time SL Staff on Campus (not counting instructors):* 8

## University of Natal

King George V Ave, 4001, University of Natal, Durban, KwaZulu-Natal, South Africa 4041

*University/College URL:* http://www.nu.ac.za

*Type of Institution:* public, university, teaching, research, secular

*SL Program/Center Name:* Office of Community Outreach and Service Learning

*Contact Person Name and Title:* Ms. Frances O'Brien

*Contact Phone Number:* (27) 31 260 2366

*Contact Fax Number:* (27) 31 260 1511

*Contact Email Address:* dicksonj@mtb.und.ac.za

*SL Program/Center URL:* http://www.und.ac.za/und/cadds/cosl.htm

*Description:* Founded in 1999, the Office of Community Outreach and Service Learning (COSL) is a new initiative. Its objectives include integrating service-learning into undergraduate and postgraduate programs within the university; promoting community outreach activities by staff and students; brokering partnerships between community organizations, the public and private sectors, and the university; and establishing joint outreach and service-learning initiatives with international institutions. COSL offers a number of stand-alone service-learning courses and participates in the integration of service-learning into numerous discipline-specific courses such as psychology, community development, music, and drama. It offers these disciplines support in the areas of student orientation, planning and logistics, staff training, and placements. COSL also offers a placement program for international students as part of the university's Winter School (June to August). COSL is funded partly by the university and partly from external sources.

*SL Required for Graduation (all students)?* No

*Service Required for Graduation (all students)?* No

*Any Co-curricular Service?* Yes

*Any SL Residence Halls or Theme Houses?* No

*Number of Undergraduate SL Courses Offered Per Year:* 2 (general service-learning courses; there are also numerous discipline-specific courses)

*Number of Graduate SL Courses Offered Per Year:* 2 (general service-learning courses; there are also numerous discipline-specific courses)

*Total Number of SL Courses Offered Per Year:* 4 (general service-learning courses; there are also numerous discipline-specific courses)

*Number of Instructors Teaching SL Courses Per Year:* 2

*Number of Full-time SL Staff on Campus (not counting instructors):* 1

*Number of Part-time SL Staff on Campus (not counting instructors):* 2

## University of Nebraska-Lincoln

200 Nebraska Union, PO Box 880453, Lincoln, NE 68588–0453

*University/College URL:* http://www.unl.edu

*Type of Institution:* public, university, research

*SL Program/Center Name:* Student Involvement

*Contact Person Name and Title:* Diane L. Podolske, PhD

*Contact Phone Number:* (402) 472–2454

*Contact Fax Number:* (402) 472–8140

*Contact Email Address:* dpodolske1@unl.edu

*SL Program/Center URL:* http://www.unl.edu/sinvolve

*Description:* The Service-Learning Program at the University of Nebraska-Lincoln generates the opportunity for students to promote social change by becoming trustees of their community through service-learning. The program is housed in Student Involvement, which is a division of Student Affairs. It includes faculty support for service-learning courses, training sessions on service-learning pedagogy for community agencies/schools, and support for student-initiated and student-driven service-learning projects. Program staff also coordinate the Pepsi Scholarship for Outstanding Leadership and Service program, which includes a noncredit course on service-learning event programming and community activism. The Service-Learning Program is funded through student fees and through grants from the Nebraska Consortium for Service-Learning in Higher Education.

*SL Required for Graduation (all students)?* No

*Service Required for Graduation (all students)?* No

*Any Co-curricular Service?* Yes

*Any SL Residence Halls or Theme Houses?* No

*Number of Undergraduate SL Courses Offered Per Year:* 25

*Number of Graduate SL Courses Offered Per Year:* 7

*Total Number of SL Courses Offered Per Year:* 32

*Number of Instructors Teaching SL Courses Per Year:* 32–35

*Number of Full-time SL Staff on Campus (not counting instructors):* 1

*Number of Part-time SL Staff on Campus (not counting instructors):* 2

**University of North Carolina-Chapel Hill**
CB# 5210 Carolina Student Union, Chapel Hill, NC 27599–5210

*University/College URL:* http://www.unc.edu

*Type of Institution:* public, university, research, secular

*SL Program/Center Name:* APPLES Service-Learning Program

*Contact Person Name and Title:* Mary Fanning Morrison, Dir

*Contact Phone Number:* (919) 962–0902

*Contact Fax Number:* (919) 843–9685

*Contact Email Address:* apples@unc.edu

*SL Program/Center URL:* http://www.unc.edu/student/orgs/apples

*SL Online Course Description URL:* http://www.unc.edu/student/orgs/apples/academicyear/ay.html

*Description:* APPLES is a service-learning program that incorporates community service into existing university courses. The program also connects service with academic-year and summer internships, spring break experiences, and student-initiated service-learning projects. APPLES is a student-initiated, student-coordinated and student-funded organization.

*SL Required for Graduation (all students)?* No

*Service Required for Graduation (all students)?* No

*Any Co-curricular Service?* Yes

*Any SL Residence Halls or Theme Houses?* No (but in future plans)

*Number of Undergraduate SL Courses Offered Per Year:* 22

*Total Number of SL Courses Offered Per Year:* 22

*Number of Instructors Teaching SL Courses Per Year:* 20

*Number of Full-time SL Staff on Campus (not counting instructors):* 1

*Number of Part-time SL Staff on Campus (not counting instructors):* 0

**University of North Carolina at Charlotte**
9201 University City Blvd, Charlotte, NC 28223–0001

*University/College URL:* http://www.uncc.edu

*Type of Institution:* public, university, teaching, research

*SL Program/Center Name:* Citizenship and Service Practicum

*Contact Person Name and Title:* C. D. Fernald. PhD, Assoc Prof, Psychology

*Contact Phone Number:* (704) 547–4741

*Contact Fax Number:* (704) 547–3096

*Contact Email Address:* cdfernal@email.uncc.edu

*SL Program/Center URL:* http://www.uncc.edu/cdfernal

*SL Online Course Description URL:* http://www.uncc.edu/cdfernal/ARSCmain.html

*SL Online Syllabi URL:* http://www.uncc. edu/cdfernal/3480Sylb.html
*Description:* ''Citizenship and Service Practicum'' (ARSC 3480) is a course which explores issues of citizenship and community needs for the 21st century. On campus, students meet for lectures and seminars to discuss issues such as human needs, social justice, and community service. Beyond the classroom, students complete 40 hours of volunteer work at an agency of their choice in the community.
*SL Required for Graduation (all students)?* No
*Service Required for Graduation (all students)?* No
*Any Co-curricular Service?* Yes
*Any SL Residence Halls or Theme Houses?* No
*Number of Undergraduate SL Courses Offered Per Year:* 1 (with 6 sections)
*Total Number of SL Courses Offered Per Year:* 1
*Number of Instructors Teaching SL Courses Per Year:* 3
*Number of Full-time SL Staff on Campus (not counting instructors):* 0
*Number of Part-time SL Staff on Campus (not counting instructors):* 0

## University of North Florida
4567 St Johns Blurr Rd, South, Jacksonville, FL 32224–2645
*University/College URL:* http://www.unf.edu
*Type of Institution:* public, university
*SL Program/Center Name:* UNF Honors Service Learning Program
*Contact Person Name and Title:* Amy Lohman, Service Learning Coord
*Contact Phone Number:* (904) 620–3933
*Contact Fax Number:* (904) 620–3896
*Contact Email Address:* alohman@unf.edu
*SL Program/Center URL:* http://www.unf. edu/dept/honors/
*SL Online Course Description URL:* http:// www.unf.edu/dept/honors/9908courses. html
*SL Online Syllabi URL:* http://www.unf.edu/ dept/honors/refugee/
*Description:* The Honors Service Learning Program coordinates and facilitates the service-

learning colloquia within the Honors Program. These one-credit-hour colloquia cover a diverse array of service issues, e.g., domestic violence, at-risk youth, environment, refugees, etc. The colloquia provide a structured environment for students to study, reflect, and learn from their service. The honors program requires all incoming first-year honors students to enroll in a colloquium and requires upper-level honors students to enroll in two colloquia. During the 1998–1999 school year, the colloquia provided more than 250 honors students with the opportunity to participate in over 12,000 hours of service.
*SL Required for Graduation (all students)?* No (It is a requirement for completing the Honors Program, however.)
*Service Required for Graduation (all students)?* No
*Any Co-curricular Service?* Yes (Through the UNF Volunteer Center)
*Any SL Residence Halls or Theme Houses?* No
*Number of Undergraduate SL Courses Offered Per Year:* 26 (in 1998–99)
*Number of Graduate SL Courses Offered Per Year:* 0
*Total Number of SL Courses Offered Per Year:* 26 (13 in Fall 1998, 13 in Spring 1999; includes some sections of the same course and some courses, which were offered both semesters)
*Number of Instructors Teaching SL Courses Per Year:* 8
*Number of Full-time SL Staff on Campus (not counting instructors):* 1
*Number of Part-time SL Staff on Campus (not counting instructors):* 0

## University of Northern Iowa
Department of Philosophy and Religion, Cedar Falls, IA 50614–0501
*University/College URL:* http://www.uni.edu
*Type of Institution:* public, university, teaching, secular
*SL Program/Center Name:* Service, Ethical Reflection, Vocational Exploration (SERVE)
*Contact Person Name and Title:* William W.

Clohesy, PhD, Assoc Prof of Philosophy, SERVE Co-Dir

*Contact Phone Number:* (319) 273–6123
*Contact Fax Number:* (319) 273–7095
*Contact Email Address:*
    William.Clohesy@uni.edu
*Description:* In 1995, the Department of Philosophy and Religion received a grant from the W. K. Kellogg Foundation to undertake the SERVE Project. The grant was supplemented in 1998. The SERVE Project's extended purpose has five components: (1) the Ethics Practicum, a service-learning ethics course in which students combine work in a local service agency with a seminar on relevant ethics and social issues; (2) a Faculty Seminar on philanthropy, nonprofit organizations, and volunteerism from the perspective of philosophical ethics and political theory in which an interdisciplinary group of roughly 15 faculty meet. The seminar has brought in nationally known experts in philosophy and other fields to give a public lecture, hold a seminar meeting, and spend informal time with the faculty. Seminar members also present their own research and pedagogical work for one another; (3) mini-grants for faculty to work on salient issues concerning the third sector as it touches upon their fields, or to develop courses or modules on such topics; (4) the development of a workbook and a set of readings for the Ethics Practicum that will make an innovative course available for other philosophers; and (5) intensive research into issues concerning the third sector, philanthropy, and volunteerism to be presented as scholarly papers, journal articles, and eventually as a monograph.

*SL Required for Graduation (all students)?* No
*Service Required for Graduation (all students)?* No
*Any Co-curricular Service?* No
*Any SL Residence Halls or Theme Houses?* No
*Number of Undergraduate SL Courses Offered Per Year:* 3 (Includes the Ethics Practicum, which has been offered every semester thus far, and will be offered annually beginning Fall 2000; and ''Econo-

mics, Ethics, and Society,'' a service-learning course in economics that has developed from SERVE, which is offered each Spring.)
*Number of Graduate SL Courses Offered Per Year:* 0
*Total Number of SL Courses Offered Per Year:* 3
*Number of Instructors Teaching SL Courses Per Year:* 2
*Number of Full-time SL Staff on Campus (not counting instructors):* 0

**University of Notre Dame**
Center for Social Concerns, PO Box 766, Notre Dame, IN 46556
*University/College URL:* http://www.nd.edu
*Type of Institution:* private, university, teaching, research, religious
*SL Program/Center Name:* Center for Social Concerns
*Contact Person Name and Title:* Kathleen Maas Weigert, Assoc Dir, Academic Affairs and Research
*Contact Phone Number:* (219) 631–5319
*Contact Fax Number:* (219) 631–4171
*Contact Email Address:*
    Kathleen.M.Weigert.2@nd.edu
*SL Program/Center URL:* http://www.nd.edu/~ndcntrsc/
*SL Online Course Description URL:* http://www.nd.edu/~ndcntrsc/
*Description:* The Center for Social Concerns is the chief unit through which service-learning is offered and coordinated at Notre Dame. Workshops for faculty are regularly offered to advance an understanding of the pedagogy, thereby increasing the number of courses available for students. Faculty and staff at the center coordinate a number of service-learning courses which are primarily housed in the Department of Theology but are also cross-listed with other departments. The center also provides financial support for Community-based Learning Coordinators (CBLCs) in eight local agencies. The CBLCs are trained by staff at the center and serve as a bridge between campus and community. In their work the CBLCs help faculty make appropriate links to the curriculum; place and monitor students; and provide reports to

the center on course-based and extra-curricular student involvement.

*SL Required for Graduation (all students)?* No

*Service Required for Graduation (all students)?* No

*Any Co-curricular Service?* Yes

*Any SL Residence Halls or Theme Houses?* No

*Number of Undergraduate SL Courses Offered Per Year:* 40

*Number of Graduate SL Courses Offered Per Year:* 2–5

*Total Number of SL Courses Offered Per Year:* 45

*Number of Instructors Teaching SL Courses Per Year:* 30

*Number of Full-time SL Staff on Campus (not counting instructors):* 0

*Number of Part-time SL Staff on Campus (not counting instructors):* 4 + 8 (Within the center, there are 3 faculty positions and 4 staff positions all of which have, as part of their jobs, work on service-learning. In addition, there are 8 ''Community-based Learning Coordinators'' located in eight different agencies in South Bend, paid part-time by the center or from endowment and gifts.)

## University of Oregon

Community Internship Program, 1585 East 13th Ave, Eugene, OR 97403

*University/College URL:* http://www.uoregon.edu

*Type of Institution:* public, university, research

*SL Program/Center Name:* Community Internship Program

*Contact Person Name and Title:* SL Dir

*Contact Phone Number:* (541) 346–4351

*Contact Fax Number:* (541) 346–0620

*Contact Email Address:* intern@darkwing.uoregon.edu

*SL Program/Center URL:* http://darkwing.uoregon.edu/~intern

*Description:* The Community Internship Program is a student-run organization recognized

and funded by students. Students receive credit for volunteering through any one of six divisions including Human Services, Public Schools, Mentorship, Outdoor School, Leadership, and Building Blocks. Students also attend one of six weekly seminars which correspond to their volunteer experience.

*SL Required for Graduation (all students)?* No

*Service Required for Graduation (all students)?* No

*Any Co-curricular Service?* Yes

*Any SL Residence Halls or Theme Houses?* No

*Number of Undergraduate SL Courses Offered Per Year:* 48

*Number of Graduate SL Courses Offered Per Year:* 20

*Total Number of SL Courses Offered Per Year:* 68

*Number of Instructors Teaching SL Courses Per Year:* 20

*Number of Full-time SL Staff on Campus (not counting instructors):* 0

*Number of Part-time SL Staff on Campus (not counting instructors):* 20

## University of Pennsylvania

133 South 36th St, Suite 519, Philadelphia, PA 19104–3246

*University/College URL:* http://www.upenn.edu

*Type of Institution:* private, university, teaching, research, secular

*SL Program/Center Name:* Center for Community Partnerships

*Contact Person Name and Title:* Ira Harkavy, Assoc VP and Dir

*Contact Phone Number:* (215) 898–5351

*Contact Fax Number:* (215) 573–2799

*Contact Email Address:* harkavy@pobox.upenn.edu

*SL Program/Center URL:* http://www.upenn.edu/ccp

*SL Online Course Description URL:* http://www.upenn.edu/ccp/educate.shtml

*Description:* Founded in 1992, the Center for Community Partnerships is Penn's primary vehicle for bringing to bear the broad range of human knowledge needed to solve the complex, comprehensive, and interconnected problems of the American city so that West Philadelphia (Penn's local geographic community), Philadelphia, the university itself, and society benefit. The center, a university-wide initiative, is an outgrowth of the Penn Program for Public Service, which was created in 1989 to replace and expand the Office of Community-Oriented Policy Studies in the school of Arts and Sciences. Through the center, the university currently engages in three types of activities: academically-based community service, direct traditional service, and community development. Academically-based community service is at the core of the center's work. It is service rooted in and intrinsically linked to teaching and/or research, and it encompasses problem-oriented research and teaching, as well as service-learning that emphasizes student and faculty reflection on the service experience. Over 70 courses (from a wide range of disciplines and Penn schools) link Penn students to work in the community.

*SL Required for Graduation (all students)?* No

*Service Required for Graduation (all students)?* No

*Any Co-curricular Service?* Yes

*Any SL Residence Halls or Theme Houses?* Yes

*Number of Undergraduate SL Courses Offered Per Year:* 26

*Number of Graduate SL Courses Offered Per Year:* 12

*Total Number of SL Courses Offered Per Year:* 38

*Number of Instructors Teaching SL Courses Per Year:* 29

*Number of Full-time SL Staff on Campus (not counting instructors):* 11

*Number of Part-time SL Staff on Campus (not counting instructors):* 15

**University of Pennsylvania**
3914 Locust Walk, Civic House, Philadelphia, PA 19104–6152
*University/College URL:* GOTOBUTTON BM_- http://www.upenn.edu

*Type of Institution:* private, university, research, secular

*SL Program/Center Name:* Civic House

*Contact Person Name and Title:* David Grossman, Dir

*Contact Phone Number:* (215) 898–4831

*Contact Fax Number:* (215) 573–3665

*Contact Email Address:* grossman@pobox.upenn.edu

*SL Program/Center URL:* http://www.upenn.edu/civichouse

*SL Online Course Description URL:* http://www.upenn.edu/ccp/educate.shtml

*Description:* Civic House promotes mutually beneficial collaborations between Penn and the West Philadelphia community and beyond. As an impetus for social change, Civic House coordinates and supports Penn's varied service efforts. By linking action with evaluation and reflection, Civic House prepares students for their roles as citizens and leaders. Civic House provides opportunities for students, faculty, and staff to participate in meaningful, effective community service and thus to enlarge their understanding of social issues; offers a setting that encourages student initiative while responding effectively to community needs as identified by community organizations; cooperates with the wide and growing range of service-learning courses; and brings to campus activists and public intellectuals from the community and other universities who give talks, lead discussions, and take part in courses. In all these ways, Civic House supports the academic mission of the university by enriching the intellectual, moral, and academic growth of undergraduate and graduate students, faculty, and staff, while supporting community initiatives.

*SL Required for Graduation (all students)?* No

*Service Required for Graduation (all students)?* No

*Any Co-curricular Service?* Yes

*Any SL Residence Halls or Theme Houses?* Yes

*Number of Full-time SL Staff on Campus (not counting instructors):* 4

*Number of Part-time SL Staff on Campus (not counting instructors):* 12–15

## University of Pittsburgh

Student Volunteer Outreach, 920 William
Pitt Union, Pittsburgh, PA 15260
*University/College URL:* http://www.pitt.edu
*Type of Institution:* public, university
*SL Program/Center Name:* Pennsylvania
Service-Learning Alliance
*Contact Person Name and Title:* Dr.
Terrence Milani, Exec Dir; Dr. Cynthia
Belliveau, Dir; and Cynthia F. Wetmiller,
Western PA Dir
*Contact Phone Number:* (412) 648–1673
*Contact Fax Number:* (412) 648–1492
*Contact Email Address:* cfish@pitt.edu AND
tmilani@pitt.edu
*SL Program/Center URL:* http://www.pitt.
edu/~psla/
*Description:* The Pennsylvania Service-Learn-
ing Alliance is the main technical assistance
and training provider for the Pennsylvania
Department of Education's Learn and Serve
program. With offices at the University of
Pittsburgh Student Volunteer Outreach and the
University of Pennsylvania Center for Com-
munity Partnerships, the alliance conducts workshops on service-learning, and trains teachers in the practice of infusing service-learning
with unique educational subjects and arenas
(e.g., School-to-Work, Character Education,
Youth Leadership, Transition Coordination,
Pregnant and Parenting Teens, Special Education, Alternative Education, and Safe and
Drug Free Schools). The alliance collaborates
throughout the state of Pennsylvania with
AmeriCorps, AmeriCorps VISTA, America's
Promise, PennSERVE (the state commission
on service), Campus Compact, ACUI, and a
large number of nonprofit organizations throughout the state. The Pennsylvania Service-Learning Alliance coordinates the efforts of 20 state
Service-Learning Peer Consultants who individually provide assistance to teachers and
organizations in need of more individualized
service-learning expertise and training. It currently provides training to over 75 school districts each year, and through its newsletter,
*Learning and Serving in Pennsylvania,* students, teachers, and community volunteers help
keep the state connected and in touch with the

classroom and community impact of service-
learning in Pennsylvania from both a K-12 and
Higher Ed perspective.
*SL Required for Graduation (all
students)?* No
*Service Required for Graduation (all stu-
dents)?* No
*Any Co-curricular Service?* Yes
*Any SL Residence Halls or Theme
Houses?* No
*SL Degrees Offered:* Y (Graduate students in
the field of education can do a self-
designed major in service-learning.)
*Number of Undergraduate SL Courses
Offered Per Year:* 0
*Number of Graduate SL Courses Offered
Per Year:* 0
*Total Number of SL Courses Offered
Per Year:* 0
*Number of Instructors Teaching SL Courses
Per Year:* 0
*Number of Full-time SL Staff on Campus
(not counting instructors):* 0
*Number of Part-time SL Staff on Campus
(not counting instructors):* 0

## University of Pittsburgh

200 Lothrop St, E820 Montefiore University
Hospital, Pittsburgh, PA 15213–2582
*University/College URL:* http://www.pitt.edu
*Type of Institution:* public, university, teach-
ing, research
*SL Program/Center Name:* Program for
Health Care to Underserved Popula-
tions, Health Professional Schools Service
Learning Consortium
*Contact Person Name and Title:* Joyce Holl,
Program Admin
*Contact Phone Number:* (412) 692–4840
*Contact Fax Number:* (412) 692–4325
*Contact Email Address:*
holl@genmed.upmc.edu
*Description:* The Program for Health Care to
Underserved Populations is a Learn and Serve
Higher Education Program at the University of
Pittsburgh that brings vital free basic health
care to some of the city's most needy residents.
Service-learning students from the schools of
Medicine, Nursing, and Pharmacy serve at seven
community clinics through the program. Each

clinic is located within, and partnered with, an existing social-service agency. Almost 4,000 patients visits are performed yearly. Over 400 health professional students (including over half of all medical students), 70 internal medicine residents, and 20 faculty and community physicians volunteer in the program.

There also have been several intensive, interdisciplinary instructional experiences called Areas of Concentration (AOC) curricula for students in the health professions. Through this program, students focus on developing their skills in one of six areas of expertise related to underserved communities and/or special-needs populations: homelessness, geriatric, substance abuse and mental health, domestic violence, women's health, and reproductive health care. The goal of the AOC curricula is to enable interested students to develop within an interdisciplinary framework and throughout a continuum of care the skills, knowledge, and attitudes they require to successfully provide health services for individuals who live in distressed communities or have special needs.

*SL Required for Graduation (all students)?* No

*Service Required for Graduation (all students)?* No

*Any Co-curricular Service?* Yes

*Any SL Residence Halls or Theme Houses?* No

*SL Degrees Offered:* Certificate or letter (still pending)

*Number of Instructors Teaching SL Courses Per Year:* 20 (in this program)

*Number of Full-time SL Staff on Campus (not counting instructors):* 4 (in this program)

## University of Redlands
1200 East Colton Ave, PO Box 3080, Redlands, CA 92373–0999

*University/College URL:* http://www. redlands.edu; http://newton.uor.edu

*Type of Institution:* private, university, teaching, secular

*SL Program/Center Name:* Community Service Learning Office

*Contact Person Name and Title:* Tony Mueller, Dir

*Contact Phone Number:* (909) 335–5103

*Contact Fax Number:* (909) 335–5162

*Contact Email Address:* tmueller@uor.edu

*SL Program/Center URL:* http://newton.uor. edu/StudentLife/CommunityService/csl. html

*SL Online Course Description URL:* http:// newton.uor.edu/StudentLife/ CommunityService/slc.html

*Description:* The Office of Community Service Learning supports and promotes the educational benefits of all elements dealing with service-learning, service internships, volunteer opportunities, and nonprofit work-study placements. In the Community Service Activity Course (CSAC), all students must participate in a service activity through service-learning courses or contracted service internships prior to graduation.

*SL Required for Graduation (all students)?* Yes (300 students each year participate in faculty-taught service-learning courses or individual service contracts representing 25 to 30 thousand hours of service worldwide.)

*Service Required for Graduation (all students)?* Yes

*Any Co-curricular Service?* Yes

*Any SL Residence Halls or Theme Houses?* Yes (Three service-learning/community-service honor houses)

*Number of Undergraduate SL Courses Offered Per Year:* 9+

*Total Number of SL Courses Offered Per Year:* 9+

*Number of Instructors Teaching SL Courses Per Year:* 9

*Number of Full-time SL Staff on Campus (not counting instructors):* 1

*Number of Part-time SL Staff on Campus (not counting instructors):* 1

## University of Richmond
Service Learning, G29B Richmond Hall, University of Richmond, Richmond, VA 23173

*University/College URL:* http://www. richmond.edu

*Type of Institution:* private, university, teaching, research, secular

*SL Program/Center Name:* Service-Learning Program

*Contact Person Name and Title:* Elizabeth L. MacNabb, PhD, Assist Dir, Service Learning

*Contact Phone Number:* (804) 289–8686

*Contact Fax Number:* (804) 289–6465

*Contact Email Address:* emacnabb@richmond.edu

*SL Program/Center URL:* http://www.cdc. richmond.edu/service/servlearn.html

*Description:* The Service-Learning Program is aimed primarily at faculty and is still in the early recruiting stages. The institutional location of the program has moved several times: from the LINCS office, which is based in the Jepson Leadership School, to the Career Development Center, to the newly created Teaching, Learning and Technology Center (in Summer 2000). The program is currently attempting to educate most of the campus as to the pedagogical value of service-learning as a method. There are about 10 professors who use service-learning at this time. The program gives incentive mini-grants to faculty who write proposals for incorporating service-learning into their courses. It also organizes forums and guest speakers to give faculty a place to share their work. The Service-Learning Program collaborates with the LINCS office when possible. Since Fall 1998, there has been a salary line for a service-learning coordinator.

*SL Required for Graduation (all students)?* No (But the Jepson School of Leadership Studies requires service-learning of all majors.)

*Service Required for Graduation (all students)?* No

*Any Co-curricular Service?* Yes

*Any SL Residence Halls or Theme Houses?* No

*Number of Undergraduate SL Courses Offered Per Year:* 8–10

*Number of Graduate SL Courses Offered Per Year:* 0

*Total Number of SL Courses Offered Per Year:* 8–10

*Number of Instructors Teaching SL Courses Per Year:* 8–10

*Number of Full-time SL Staff on Campus (not counting instructors):* 1

*Number of Part-time SL Staff on Campus (not counting instructors):* 4 (1 AmeriCorps Assist, 3 student assists)

## University of Saint Thomas

2115 Summit Ave, Saint Paul, MN 55105

*University/College URL:* http://www. stthomas.edu

*Type of Institution:* private, university, teaching, religious

*Contact Person Name and Title:* Dr. Ellen J. Kennedy, Prof and Coord, Service-Learning

*Contact Phone Number:* (651) 962–5082

*Contact Fax Number:* (651) 962–5093

*Contact Email Address:* ejkennedy@stthomas.edu

*Description:* Service-Learning is part of the mission of the University of Saint Thomas as an urban Catholic university. Course-based service-learning initiatives are developed collaboratively with existing community partners and illustrate the university's approach to participate in both service and efforts to alleviate causes of suffering and inequality.

*SL Required for Graduation (all students)?* No

*Service Required for Graduation (all students)?* No

*Any Co-curricular Service?* Yes

*Any SL Residence Halls or Theme Houses?* No

*Number of Undergraduate SL Courses Offered Per Year:* 30–60

*Total Number of SL Courses Offered Per Year:* 30–60

*Number of Instructors Teaching SL Courses Per Year:* 40

*Number of Full-time SL Staff on Campus (not counting instructors):* 0

*Number of Part-time SL Staff on Campus (not counting instructors):* 0

## University of San Diego

5998 Alcala Park, San Diego, CA 92110–2492

*University/College URL:* http://www. acusd.edu

*Type of Institution:* private, university, teaching, religious
*SL Program/Center Name:* Office for Community Service-Learning
*Contact Person Name and Title:* Dr. Judy Rauner, Dir
*Contact Phone Number:* (619) 260–4798
*Contact Fax Number:* (619) 260–2610
*Contact Email Address:* rauner@acusd.edu
*SL Program/Center URL:* http://sa.acusd.edu/comservice
*Description:* USD's Office for Community Service-Learning was founded in 1986. Course-based service-learning began in 1994 and grew out of the administrators' and faculty's desire to use community service as one way to place values into action and enhance academic learning. Community service-learning is divided into three components or pathways to action: Experiential Education, Associated Students Community Service, and the Social Issues Committee. Collaboratively with the Office for Community Service-Learning, students, faculty, administration, and community partners address real community needs by combining service and learning.
*SL Required for Graduation (all students)?* No
*Service Required for Graduation (all students)?* No
*Any Co-curricular Service?* Yes
*Any SL Residence Halls or Theme Houses?* No
*Number of Undergraduate SL Courses Offered Per Year:* 49
*Number of Graduate SL Courses Offered Per Year:* 8
*Total Number of SL Courses Offered Per Year:* 50+
*Number of Instructors Teaching SL Courses Per Year:* 40+
*Number of Full-time SL Staff on Campus (not counting instructors):* 2
*Number of Part-time SL Staff on Campus (not counting instructors):* 2

**University of San Francisco**
2130 Fulton St, San Francisco, CA 94117
*University/College URL:* http://www.usfca.edu

*Type of Institution:* private, university, teaching, religious
*SL Program/Center Name:* Community Service and Service Learning Programs, Dept of Multicultural Opportunities for Developing Excellence in Leadership (MODEL)
*Contact Person Name and Title:* Jack McLean, Coord
*Contact Phone Number:* (415) 422–2156
*Contact Fax Number:* (415) 422–5641
*Contact Email Address:* mclean@usfca.edu
*SL Program/Center URL:* http://www.usfca.edu/MODEL/
*SL Online Course Description URL:* http://www.usfca.edu/MODEL/sltf/html/courses.html
*Description:* The Community Service and Service Learning Program maintains a database of community partners for making community-service placements. As part of an ongoing effort to further integrate service-learning across the curriculum, a Service Learning Task Force helps formulate policy and recommendations. More than 70 courses currently have service-learning components and more courses are being added.
*SL Required for Graduation (all students)?* No
*Service Required for Graduation (all students)?* No
*Any Co-curricular Service?* Yes
*Any SL Residence Halls or Theme Houses?* No
*Number of Undergraduate SL Courses Offered Per Year:* 40
*Number of Graduate SL Courses Offered Per Year:* 30
*Total Number of SL Courses Offered Per Year:* 70
*Number of Full-time SL Staff on Campus (not counting instructors):* 0
*Number of Part-time SL Staff on Campus (not counting instructors):* 1

**University of Scranton (and Marywood University)**
Scranton, PA 18510
*University/College URL:* http://www.uofs.edu

*Type of Institution:* private, university

*SL Program/Center Name:* Collegiate Volunteers of the University of Scranton and Marywood University

*Contact Person Name and Title:* Catherine Mascelli, Service Learning Coord

*Contact Phone Number:* (570) 941–7429

*Contact Fax Number:* (570) 941–7963

*Contact Email Address:* Collegiate-Vols@uofs.edu

*SL Program/Center URL:* http://academic. scranton.edu/department/ministry/volunt. html

*Description:* Collegiate Volunteers is a collaborative program between the University of Scranton and Marywood University. It maintains information on over 125 community organizations and agencies where students can choose to do their service learning. In addition to assisting students in the selection of a service site, Collegiate Volunteers assists faculty in designing service-learning components for their courses. Collegiate Volunteers helps with reflection activities and training events. The program is partially funded through a private endowment.

*SL Required for Graduation (all students)?* No

*Service Required for Graduation (all students)?* No

*Any Co-curricular Service?* Yes

*Any SL Residence Halls or Theme Houses?* Yes

*Number of Undergraduate SL Courses Offered Per Year:* 30

*Total Number of SL Courses Offered Per Year:* 30

*Number of Instructors Teaching SL Courses Per Year:* 15

*Number of Full-time SL Staff on Campus (not counting instructors):* 1

*Number of Part-time SL Staff on Campus (not counting instructors):* 3

## University of Scranton

800 Linden St, Scranton, PA 18510–9949

*University/College URL:* http://www.uofs. edu

*Type of Institution:* private, university, teaching, research, religious

*SL Program/Center Name:* Service Learning Program, Panuska College of Professional Studies

*Contact Person Name and Title:* Patricia A. Bailey, Prof of Nursing

*Contact Phone Number:* (570) 941–4346

*Contact Fax Number:* (570) 941–7903

*Contact Email Address:* Baileyp1@uofs.edu

*SL Program/Center URL:* http://academic. uofs.edu/department/cps/service_learning. html

*SL Online Course Description URL:* http:// academic.uofs.edu/department/cps/ service_learning.html

*Description:* The purpose of the Panuska College of Professional Studies is to contribute to a variety of professional fields by developing values in students while preparing informed, inquiring, and skilled professionals, and to assist in the growth and development of the community served by the university. The vision of the service-learning program at the college is to support a link between community service and academic study so that each enriches the other. The purpose of the program is to provide service to the local community based on its needs and goals while providing students with meaningful learning experiences that are enhanced through academic assignments and reflection. Through an integrated service-learning program, students in the college complete 80 hours of service (20 hours per year) as a requirement for graduation.

*SL Required for Graduation (all students)?* Yes(in the College of Professional Studies)

*Service Required for Graduation (all students)?* Yes (in the college of Professional Studies)

*Any Co-curricular Service?* Yes

*Any SL Residence Halls or Theme Houses?* No

*Total Number of SL Courses Offered Per Year:* 22 courses in 7 departments in the College of Professional Studies at present; SL components are being integrated into an additional 11 courses by 2000–2001)

*Number of Instructors Teaching SL Courses*

*Per Year:* 22 (full-time faculty, plus 7 SL liaisons in departments)
*Number of Full-time SL Staff on Campus (not counting instructors):* 3
*Number of Part-time SL Staff on Campus (not counting instructors):* 1

## University of South Florida
4202 East Fowler Ave, SOC 107
$ Tampa, FL 33629
*University/College URL:* http://usfweb.usf.edu
*Type of Institution:* public, university, teaching, research, secular
*SL Program/Center Name:* Community Experiential Learning (CEL) Program, College of Arts and Sciences
*Contact Person Name and Title:* Robin R. Jones, Dir
*Contact Phone Number:* (813) 974 8452
*Contact Fax Number:* (813) 972 2819
*Contact Email Address:* jones@chuma1.cas.usf.edu
*SL Program/Center URL:* http://www.cas.usf.edu/ADMIN_DEPTS/ACADEMIC_AFFAIRS/community/CommunityExper.htm
*SL Online Course Description URL:* http://www.cas.usf.edu/ADMIN_DEPTS/ACADEMIC_AFFAIRS/community/CommunityExper.htm
*SL Online Syllabi URL:* http://www.cas.usf.edu/ADMIN_DEPTS/ACADEMIC_AFFAIRS/community/CommunityExper.htm
*Description:* The Community Experiential Learning (CEL) Program is part of the College of Arts and Sciences Community Initiative (CI). CI is exploring ways to integrate its teaching, research, and service missions. Thus far the program is an "add-on" within the College of Arts and Sciences. The goal is to conduct a survey of existing courses with a community-based component, catalogue and promote them, and also encourage new additions through "seed" grants.
*SL Required for Graduation (all students)?* No
*Service Required for Graduation (all students)?* No

*Any Co-curricular Service?* Yes
*Any SL Residence Halls or Theme Houses?* No
*Number of Undergraduate SL Courses Offered Per Year:* 4 (within CEL; those located within departments have yet to be surveyed)

## University of Southern California
JEP House, 801 West 34th St, Los Angeles, CA 90089–0471
*University/College URL:* http://cwis.usc.edu
*Type of Institution:* private, university, research
*SL Program/Center Name:* Joint Educational Project (JEP)
*Contact Person Name and Title:* Tammara Anderson, Dir
*Contact Phone Number:* (213) 740–1837
*Contact Fax Number:* (213) 740–1825
*Contact Email Address:* tanderso@usc.edu
*SL Program/Center URL:* http://www.usc.edu/dept/LAS/JEP/
*SL Online Course Description URL:* http://www.usc.edu/dept/LAS/JEP/jeptext/Courses_Fac.htm
*Description:* The Joint Educational Project (JEP) is a service-learning program based in USC's College of Letters, Arts and Sciences. The program is designed to broker between academic courses and schools and service agencies in the university's community. Each year JEP places approximately 1,500 students from college courses in the neighborhood as mentors, mini-course instructors, translators, and assistants to teachers and other helping professionals.
*SL Required for Graduation (all students)?* No
*Service Required for Graduation (all students)?* No
*Any Co-curricular Service?* Yes
*Any SL Residence Halls or Theme Houses?* Yes
*Number of Undergraduate SL Courses Offered Per Year:* 45
*Total Number of SL Courses Offered Per Year:* 45
*Number of Instructors Teaching SL Courses Per Year:* 55

*Number of Full-time SL Staff on Campus
(not counting instructors):* 5
*Number of Part-time SL Staff on Campus
(not counting instructors):* 25

**University of Southern Maine**
96 Falmouth St, PO Box 9300, Portland, ME
04104–9300
*University/College URL:* http://www.usm.
maine.edu
*Type of Institution:* public, university, teach-
ing, research, secular
*SL Program/Center Name:* c/o Center For
Teaching
*Contact Person Name and Title:* John
Bay, Dir
*Contact Phone Number:* (207) 780–4470
*Contact Fax Number:* (207) 780–4055
*Contact Email Address:*
JohnBay@usm.maine.edu
*Description:* The University of Southern Maine
is divided into three geographically separate
campuses, which work very independently from
one another. Over the last few years, individual
faculty at each campus have initiated very
successful collaborations with community, but
there has been no central program to give
support, set standards, or act as a clearinghouse. For the last two years the university has
participated in a Corporation for National Service program through Maine Campus Compact,
which has provided the university with VISTA
volunteers who have, as part of their mission,
encouraged and supported the development of
service-learning. There is now sufficient interest among all stakeholders to create an organizing structure, and the university has applied for
a grant which, if awarded, will allow it (over a
three-year period) to coordinate service-learning across the university, encourage and support faculty, and keep the development of each
campus/community under the direction of local
committees.
*SL Required for Graduation (all
students)?* No
*Service Required for Graduation (all stu-
dents)?* No
*Any Co-curricular Service?* No
*Any SL Residence Halls or Theme
Houses?* No

*Number of Undergraduate SL Courses
Offered Per Year:* 4–8
*Number of Instructors Teaching SL Courses
Per Year:* 4–8
*Number of Full-time SL Staff on Campus
(not counting instructors):* 0
*Number of Part-time SL Staff on Campus
(not counting instructors):* 1

**University of Southern Maine/Lewiston-
Auburn College**
51 Westminster St, Lewiston, ME 04110
*University/College URL:* http://usm.
maine.edu/lac
*Type of Institution:* public, university,
teaching
*Contact Person Name and Title:* Marvin
Druker, Assoc Dean
*Contact Phone Number:* (207) 753–6582
*Contact Fax Number:* (207) 753–6555
*Contact Email Address:*
druker@usm.maine.edu
*Description:* At Lewiston-Auburn College students consult or provide other assistance through
service-learning projects which many classes
now require. In this respect, the college not
only provides benefits for students, but also
fulfills one of its mission's goals, i.e., to act
as a resource for the community. Among the
organizations that students completed service-
learning projects with are United Way, Advo-
cates for Children, FaithWorks, Tri-County
Mental Health, and the Lewiston Police
Department.
*SL Required for Graduation (all
students)?* No
*Service Required for Graduation (all stu-
dents)?* No
*Any Co-curricular Service?* No
*Any SL Residence Halls or Theme
Houses?* No
*Number of Undergraduate SL Courses
Offered Per Year:* 15
*Number of Graduate SL Courses Offered
Per Year:* 0
*Total Number of SL Courses Offered Per
Year:* 15
*Number of Instructors Teaching SL Courses
Per Year:* 4

*Number of Full-time SL Staff on Campus*
    *(not counting instructors):* 0
*Number of Part-time SL Staff on Campus*
    *(not counting instructors):* 1

**University of Surrey Roehampton**
Southlands College, 80 Roehampton Ln,
    London, UK SW15 5SL
*University/College URL:* http://www.
    roehampton.ac.uk
*Type of Institution:* public, university, teach-
    ing, research
*SL Program/Center Name:* Service Learn-
    ing (undegraduate); M.A. in International
    Service (graduate)
*Contact Person Name and Title:* Ms. Jenny
    Iles; Mr David Woodman, Principal
    Lecturer
*Contact Phone Number:* (44) 181 392 3621;
    020 8392 3091
*Contact Fax Number:* (44) 181 392 3518;
    020 8392 3518
*Contact Email Address:*
    J.Iles@roehampton.ac.uk;
    D.Woodman@Roehampton.ac.uk
*SL Program/Center URL:* http://www.
    roehampton.ac.uk/acprog/b/xservice-
    learning.html; http://www.roehampton.ac.
    uk/acprog/m/mdinternationalservice.html
*SL Online Course Description URL:* http://
    www.roehampton.ac.uk/acprog/x-
    listedcourses/b/serc.html#SELH10.001;
    http://www.roehampton.ac.uk/acprog/M/
    mdint.html#SELM60.001
*Description:* There is no center at present, but
there are plans for one which will combine the
undergraduate and postgraduate programs.
*SL Required for Graduation (all*
    *students)?* No
*Service Required for Graduation (all stu-*
    *dents)?* No
*Any Co-curricular Service?* Yes
*Any SL Residence Halls or Theme*
    *Houses?* No
*SL Undergraduate Program Name:* Service
    Learning
*SL Undergraduate Program Description:* The
Service Learning program (or "course" in
U.S. terminology) at Roehampton has been

available to students since 1992. Service Learning is an experiential-based course that enables
students to undertake community service and
gain academic credits for their efforts. The
course links practical experience in an agency
with academic learning and personal growth, as
well as providing students with the opportunity
to expand their awareness of social concerns.
Service-learning students work in various social, community educational, or charitable agencies for a maximum of 120 hours spread over
the course. The course has been carefully designed to serve two functions: to enable students to reflect on their learning for community
service; and to encourage critical thinking about
the ideologies which have underpinned the
shifts in responsibility for people's welfare.
The course uses a variety of teaching methods
that include lectures and support seminars. The
seminars give students the opportunity to exchange their experiences with fellow students
and review their progress. Assessment is based
on both course and placement attendance and
the production of a "Service Placement File."
This file is an ongoing record of the students'
placement experience which includes the keeping of a journal and coursework essays.

Contractually, all American students in the
program (both undergraduate and MA) must
enroll via the International Partnership for Service Learning (please contact IPS-L, not
Roehampton). This course provides practical
experience in a service placement to allow
links between academic study, service in the
community, and personal development. Students work in various social, community, or
charitable agencies at home and abroad. The
actual tasks are agreed by the student, agency,
and tutor. Students are encouraged, where appropriate, to select placements which relate to
their academic studies, e.g., a psychology major
might work in an agency caring for emotionally
disturbed children.
*SL Graduate Program Name:* MA Interna-
    tional Service/Graduate Diploma
*SL Graduate Program Description:* This program prepares 12 students for employment in

national and international not-for-profit organizations and offers the opportunity of combining academic study with practical service in Mexican or Jamaican community and service agencies. The program is also concerned with professional and personal growth. The first semester takes place in either Guadalajara, Mexico, at the Automous University or in Kingston, Jamaica, at the University of Technology. The second semester takes place at Roehampton Institute London, where students continue their placement experiences with UK-based agencies and extend their studies. The dissertation, which has all the features normally contained in a master's dissertation, also contains an outline funding proposal for its in-country agency. This proposal may be used by the in-country agency to attract funds. The program is primarily self-funded. Students completing 180 credits earn the M.A. in International Service. Those completing 120 credits earn the Graduate Diploma.

*SL Degrees Offered:* M.A. in International Service

*Number of Undergraduate SL Courses Offered Per Year:* 2 (one each semester)

*Number of Graduate SL Courses Offered Per Year:* 1

*Total Number of SL Courses Offered Per Year:* 3

*Number of Instructors Teaching SL Courses Per Year:* 6 (1 undergrad; 5 grad)

*Number of Full-time SL Staff on Campus (not counting instructors):* 0

*Number of Part-time SL Staff on Campus (not counting instructors):* 2 (0 undergrad; 2 grad)

## University of Texas at Austin

100 C West Dean Keeton St, SSB 4.102, Austin, TX 78712

*University/College URL:* http://www. utexas.edu

*Type of Institution:* public, university

*SL Program/Center Name:* University Volunteer Center; Students for Service-Learning (Student Organization)

*Contact Person Name and Title:* Glen Baumgart / UVC Coord

*Contact Phone Number:* (512) 471–6161

*Contact Fax Number:* (512) 471–2360

*Contact Email Address:* gbaumgart@mail.utexas.edu

*SL Program/Center URL:* http://www.utexas. edu/depts/dos/uvc/

*Description:* The University Volunteer Center works closely with other university departments and organizations, such as Students for Service-Learning, Student Government, Urban Issues Program, the Texas Center for Service-Learning, the Volunteer Council, and others, enhancing and expanding the use of service-learning. The Volunteer Center is part of the Office of the Dean of Students.

*SL Required for Graduation (all students)?* No

*Service Required for Graduation (all students)?* No

*Any Co-curricular Service?* Yes

*Any SL Residence Halls or Theme Houses?* No

## University of Texas-San Antonio

6900 North Loop 1604 West, San Antonio, TX 78249

*University/College URL:* http://www. utsa.edu

*Type of Institution:* public, university, teaching, secular

*SL Program/Center Name:* Do It! Service-Learning Program

*Contact Person Name and Title:* Mike Kern, Prog Coord for Service Learning

*Contact Phone Number:* (210) 458–4160

*Contact Fax Number:* (210) 458–4734

*Contact Email Address:* mkern@utsa.edu

*SL Program/Center URL:* http://www.utsa. edu/actlc/9Service_Learning_Resources/ service_learning.htm

*Description:* The Do It! Service Learning Program was started in 1995 with the support of an SBC foundation grant as a joint venture with UTSA and the Alamo Community College District. The program is housed in the Office of Student Leadership and Activities. Undergraduates enrolled in service-learning courses choose among the 40 partner community agencies and typically serve in individual placements for 24 hours. Out-of-class reflection sessions, volunteer placements, tracking, and recognition are organized by the service-learning coordinator.

*SL Required for Graduation (all students)?* No

*Service Required for Graduation (all students)?* No

*Any Co-curricular Service?* Yes

*Any SL Residence Halls or Theme Houses?* No

*SL Degrees Offered:* Y (Minor/certification through American Humanics)

*Number of Undergraduate SL Courses Offered Per Year:* 20

*Number of Graduate SL Courses Offered Per Year:* 0

*Total Number of SL Courses Offered Per Year:* 20

*Number of Instructors Teaching SL Courses Per Year:* 16

*Number of Full-time SL Staff on Campus (not counting instructors):* 1

*Number of Part-time SL Staff on Campus (not counting instructors):* 0

## University of Utah

200 Central Campus Dr, #101, Salt Lake City, UT 84112–9100

*University/College URL:* http://www.utah.edu

*Type of Institution:* public, university, teaching, research, secular

*SL Program/Center Name:* Lowell Bennion Community Service Center

*Contact Person Name and Title:* Irene Fisher, Dir

*Contact Phone Number:* (801) 581–4811

*Contact Fax Number:* (801) 585–9241

*Contact Email Address:* ifisher@ssb1.saff.utah.edu

*SL Program/Center URL:* http://www.bennioncenter.org

*SL Online Course Description URL:* http://www.bennioncenter.org/SL/courses.htm

*Description:* The service-learning program at the University of Utah includes over 130 classes which offer service opportunities as part of the curriculum. The Bennion Center supports faculty members by providing them with trained teaching assistants the first time they teach a service-learning class. In addition to service-learning classes for all students, a Service-Learning Scholars designation at graduation has been established for students who want a more concentrated focus on service. Students who choose to graduate as Service-Learning Scholars must complete 400 hours of service, 10 semester hours of service-learning classes, and a final integrative service project which applies their learning and skills in addressing a community need. There are also co-curricular service opportunities in the Bennion Center. The Bennion Center was created in 1987, with a donation from a University of Utah alumnus who became aware of the Haas Center at Stanford University. He gave his contribution to create a center honoring Lowell Bennion, who was an inspiration to many with his service to the community. The funds to support the activities of the Bennion Center are currently divided fairly equally between the university administration, community fund raising, and interest on the endowment.

*SL Required for Graduation (all students)?* No

*Service Required for Graduation (all students)?* No

*Any Co-curricular Service?* Yes

*Any SL Residence Halls or Theme Houses?* No

*SL Undergraduate Program Name:* Service-Learning Scholars Program (see above)

*SL Degrees Offered:* Service-Learning Scholars designation at graduation

*Number of Undergraduate SL Courses Offered Per Year:* 69 (but 42 per semester)

*Number of Graduate SL Courses Offered Per Year:* 0

*Total Number of SL Courses Offered Per Year:* 69

*Number of Instructors Teaching SL Courses Per Year:* 90 (but 50 faculty per semester)

*Number of Full-time SL Staff on Campus (not counting instructors):* 2

*Number of Part-time SL Staff on Campus
(not counting instructors):* 1

## University of Vermont

Service-Learning Internship Program (SLIP),
Career Services—L/L E, Burlington,
VT 05405

*University/College URL:* http://www.
uvm.edu

*Type of Institution:* public, university, teaching, research

*SL Program/Center Name:* Service-Learning
Internship Program (SLIP)

*Contact Person Name and Title:* Courtney
W. Lamontagne, Coord

*Contact Phone Number:* (802) 656–3450

*Contact Fax Number:* (802) 656–0126

*Contact Email Address:*
clamonta@zoo.uvm.edu

*SL Program/Center URL:* http://career.uvm.
edu/interns.htm#slip

*SL Online Course Description URL:* http://
career.uvm.edu/interns.htm#slip

*Description:* The Service-Learning Internship
Program is managed by the Career Services
office and offers academic credit through the
College of Education and Social Services. A
student may earn between one and 12 credits
per semester, and the number of credits chosen
will determine the number of hours the student
will work in his or her agency. The student can
choose between two academic options: The
Seminar option requires that students attend a
weekly seminar class in addition to the time
spent at the community agency; the Field Studies option allows students to reflect on their
own with a self-guided syllabus and reader.

*SL Required for Graduation (all
students)?* No

*Service Required for Graduation (all stu-
dents)?* No

*Any Co-curricular Service?* Yes

*Any SL Residence Halls or Theme
Houses?* Yes

*Number of Graduate SL Courses Offered
Per Year:* 0

*Number of Instructors Teaching SL Courses
Per Year:* 1

*Number of Full-time SL Staff on Campus
(not counting instructors):* 1

*Number of Part-time SL Staff on Campus
(not counting instructors):* 0

## University of Washington

34 Communications, Box 353760, Seattle,
WA 98195

*University/College URL:* http://www.
washington.edu

*Type of Institution:* public, university, teaching, research

*SL Program/Center Name:* Edward E. Carlson Leadership and Public Service Center

*Contact Person Name and Title:* Marilyn
Zucker, Assoc Dir

*Contact Phone Number:* (206) 543–2618

*Contact Fax Number:* (206) 685–8299

*Contact Email Address:*
leader@u.washington.edu

*SL Program/Center URL:* http://www.
washington.edu/students/carlson/

*SL Online Course Description URL:* http://
www.washington.edu/students/carlson/
servlern/students/#courses; http://www.
washington.edu/students/carlson/servlern/
faculty/

*Description:* The mission of the Carlson Center
is to develop and support opportunities for
undergraduates to become involved in effective public service, helping them to gain deepened understandings of complex social, philosophical, economic, and political issues and
instilling in them a life-long commitment to
community service and civic involvement. The
heart of the Carlson Center is its service-learning program, where students can connect their
academic study with community service. Students work two to four hours per week in
positions which allow for a unique perspective
on questions and issues being raised in their
academic classes.

*SL Required for Graduation (all
students)?* No

*Service Required for Graduation (all stu-
dents)?* No

*Any Co-curricular Service?* No

*Any SL Residence Halls or Theme
Houses?* No

*Number of Undergraduate SL Courses
Offered Per Year:* 65

*Total Number of SL Courses Offered Per Year:* 65

*Number of Instructors Teaching SL Courses Per Year:* 30

*Number of Full-time SL Staff on Campus (not counting instructors):* 3

*Number of Part-time SL Staff on Campus (not counting instructors):* 8

**University of West Florida**

11000 University Pkwy, Pensacola, FL 32514

*University/College URL:* http://www.uwf.edu

*Type of Institution:* public, university, teaching, secular

*SL Program/Center Name:* Center for Learning through Organized Volunteer Efforts (CLOVE)

*Contact Person Name and Title:* Toni Whitfield, Dir

*Contact Phone Number:* (850) 474–3114

*Contact Fax Number:* (850) 474–3114

*Contact Email Address:* clove@uwf.edu; twhitfie@uwf.edu

*Description:* The CLOVE Office is both a placement office for volunteers and service-learning students at the University of West Florida. This office acts as a clearinghouse for students who are interested in volunteering, who are taking part in service-learning projects in their classes, or who desire to register for the one to three credit service-learning field study. CLOVE tracks student placement and students receive recognition on their transcripts. CLOVE also works on campus to interest and train faculty to develop service-learning courses by providing one-on-one assistance, workshops, and faculty incentives. In addition, CLOVE offers training workshops for local nonprofit agencies that it serves.

*SL Required for Graduation (all students)?* No

*Service Required for Graduation (all students)?* No

*Any Co-curricular Service?* Yes

*Any SL Residence Halls or Theme Houses?* No

*Number of Undergraduate SL Courses Offered Per Year:* 40 +

*Number of Graduate SL Courses Offered Per Year:* 10

*Total Number of SL Courses Offered Per Year:* 50

*Number of Full-time SL Staff on Campus (not counting instructors):* 1

*Number of Part-time SL Staff on Campus (not counting instructors):* 1

**University of Wisconsin-Eau Claire**

Park and Garfield Aves, PO Box 4004, Eau Claire, WI 54702–4004

*University/College URL:* http://www. uwec.edu

*Type of Institution:* public, university, teaching, secular

*SL Program/Center Name:* Center for Service-Learning

*Contact Person Name and Title:* Robert E. Burns, Dir

*Contact Phone Number:* (715) 836–4649

*Contact Fax Number:* (715) 836–4633

*Contact Email Address:* srvlearn@uwec.edu; burnsre@uwec.edu

*SL Program/Center URL:* http://www.uwec. edu/Admin/SL/

*Description:* All undergraduate students at the University of Wisconsin-Eau Claire complete 30 hours of service-learning activity as a graduation requirement. Students can satisfy this requirement in one of three ways: through requirements established by their academic major (e.g., education, nursing, social work); through 90 individual courses that have service-learning elements; or through independent projects facilitated through the Center for Service-Learning. The center provides clearinghouse services and technical assistance to students, faculty, and community partners to facilitate completion of the student's service-learning requirement.

*SL Required for Graduation (all students)?* Yes

*Service Required for Graduation (all students)?* No

*Any Co-curricular Service?* Yes

*Any SL Residence Halls or Theme Houses?* No

*Number of Undergraduate SL Courses Offered Per Year:* 90

*Total Number of SL Courses Offered Per Year:* 90

*Number of Instructors Teaching SL Courses Per Year:* 90

*Number of Full-time SL Staff on Campus (not counting instructors):* 2

*Number of Part-time SL Staff on Campus (not counting instructors):* 4

## University of Wisconsin-Green Bay

2420 Nicolet Dr, Student Life, Green Bay, WI 54311–7001

*University/College URL:* http://www.uwgb.edu

*Type of Institution:* public, university, teaching, research, secular

*SL Program/Center Name:* Office of Student Life

*Contact Person Name and Title:* Brenda Amenson-Hill, Dir of Student Life

*Contact Phone Number:* (920) 465–2200, ext 40

*Contact Email Address:* hillb@uwgb.edu

*SL Program/Center URL:* http://gbms01.uwgb.edu/~service/

*SL Online Course Description URL:* http://gbms01.uwgb.edu/~service/courses.htm

*Description:* The Office of Student Life develops community service and service-learning programs to cultivate student interest in learning by volunteering, and in making a personal difference in the community and on campus. The office is part of a campus committee working on projects for a Service Learning Grant. Student Life also advises and support Students Serving Society, a registered campus student organization.

*SL Required for Graduation (all students)?* No

*Service Required for Graduation (all students)?* No

*Any Co-curricular Service?* Yes

*Any SL Residence Halls or Theme Houses?* Yes

*Number of Full-time SL Staff on Campus (not counting instructors):* 0

*Number of Part-time SL Staff on Campus (not counting instructors):* 1 (50% position)

## University of Wisconsin-Madison

716 Langdon St, Room 154, Madison, WI 53706–1400

*University/College URL:* http://www.wisc.edu

*Type of Institution:* public, university, research, secular

*SL Program/Center Name:* Morgridge Center for Public Service

*Contact Person Name and Title:* Susan Dibbell, Manager

*Contact Phone Number:* (608) 263–4009

*Contact Fax Number:* (608) 262–0542

*Contact Email Address:* smvandeh@facstaff.wisc.edu

*SL Program/Center URL:* http://www.wisc.edu/union/wud/morgridge/

*Description:* The Morgridge Center for Public Service promotes, organizes, and supports a variety of public service and service-learning opportunities for members of the university. Wisconsin Idea Undergraduate Fellowships create opportunities for students to reach out, share their expertise, serve the community, and learn outside the classroom. The fellowships support special projects in which students, faculty, and community organizations collaborate in activities designed to benefit all of the participants.

*SL Required for Graduation (all students)?* No

*Service Required for Graduation (all students)?* No

*Any Co-curricular Service?* Yes

*Any SL Residence Halls or Theme Houses?* Yes

*Total Number of SL Courses Offered Per Year:* 70 (mix of undergraduate and graduate)

*Number of Instructors Teaching SL Courses Per Year:* 70

*Number of Full-time SL Staff on Campus (not counting instructors):* 3

*Number of Part-time SL Staff on Campus (not counting instructors):* 1

## University of Wisconsin-Milwaukee

PO Box 413, Milwaukee, WI 53201

*University/College URL:* http://www.uwm.edu

*Type of Institution:* public, university, research, secular

*SL Program/Center Name:* Institute for Service Learning

*Contact Person Name and Title:* Dean A. Pribbenow, Dir

*Contact Phone Number:* (414) 229–3702

*Contact Fax Number:* (414) 229–3884

*Contact Email Address:* pribbeno@uwm.edu

*SL Program/Center URL:* http://www.uwm. edu/Dept/ISL

*SL Online Course Description URL:* http:// www.uwm.edu/Dept/ISL/uwmslcourses. html

*Description:* The Institute for Service Learning, currently a part of the Center for Urban Initiatives and Research, is a university-wide program aimed at supporting faculty, students, and community members involved in service-learning. As such, the institute builds upon the university's rich tradition of community engagement. In addition to resources and workshops for faculty, it provides preparation and reflection workshops for students. The institute is currently staffed by one full-time director, a program assistant, and student staff who assist with student placements and tracking service activities.

*SL Required for Graduation (all students)?* No

*Service Required for Graduation (all students)?* No

*Any Co-curricular Service?* Yes

*Any SL Residence Halls or Theme Houses?* No

## University of Wisconsin-River Falls
410 S 3rd St, River Falls, WI 54022

*University/College URL:* http://www. uwrf.edu

*Type of Institution:* public, university, teaching, secular

*SL Program/Center Name:* Service Learning Help Desk

*Contact Person Name and Title:* Sally Berkholder, Career Counselor

*Contact Phone Number:* (715) 425–3572

*Contact Fax Number:* (715) 425–3573

*Contact Email Address:* sally.l.berkholder@uwrf.edu

*SL Program/Center URL:* http://www. uwrf.edu/ccs

*Description:* The Service Learning Help Desk provides faculty members with information on potential service-learning sites in and around the campus community. It is funded through a three-year grant awarded to the university.

*SL Required for Graduation (all students)?* No

*Service Required for Graduation (all students)?* No

*Any Co-curricular Service?* No

*Any SL Residence Halls or Theme Houses?* No

*Number of Instructors Teaching SL Courses Per Year:* 4

*Number of Full-time SL Staff on Campus (not counting instructors):* 0

*Number of Part-time SL Staff on Campus (not counting instructors):* 2

## University of Wisconsin-Whitewater
800 W Main St, Whitewater, WI 53190

*University/College URL:* http://www. uww.edu

*Type of Institution:* public, university, teaching

*SL Program/Center Name:* Students Organized for Service

*Contact Person Name and Title:* Ron Buchholz, Assoc Dir, James R. Connor University Center

*Contact Phone Number:* (414) 472–1950

*Contact Fax Number:* (414) 472–3900

*Contact Email Address:* buchholr@mail.uww.edu

*SL Program/Center URL:* http://uc.uww.edu/ stgroups/sos

*Description:* Students Organized for Service (SOS) is the university's community-service program. SOS offers several specific community-service programs, and in some cases service-learning programs, designed to provide students with the opportunity to learn through service. SOS programs include Alternative Breaks, Adopt-A-School (classroom tutoring), Into the City (SL one-day service trips to various sites in Milwaukee), Make a Difference Day and Into the Streets (service plunge activities), and the VI Volunteer Project (working with developmentally disabled adults). In addition, SOS offers assistance in matching volunteers with community agencies in need of volunteers. SOS has teamed with United Way of Jefferson and Northern Walworth Counties to offer an electronic listing of community-service opportunities in this region of the state. SOS is a student-coordinated, staff-directed program of the university.

*SL Required for Graduation (all students)?* No

*Service Required for Graduation (all students)?* No

*Any Co-curricular Service?* Yes

*Any SL Residence Halls or Theme Houses?* Yes

*Number of Undergraduate SL Courses Offered Per Year:* 7

*Number of Graduate SL Courses Offered Per Year:* 2

*Total Number of SL Courses Offered Per Year:* 9

*Number of Instructors Teaching SL Courses Per Year:* 9

*Number of Full-time SL Staff on Campus (not counting instructors):* 1 (1/4-time)

*Number of Part-time SL Staff on Campus (not counting instructors):* 1 (1/4-time)

**Vanderbilt University**
Nashville, TN 37240
*University/College URL:* http://www.vanderbilt.edu
*Type of Institution:* private, university, teaching, research, secular
*SL Program/Center Name:* Center for Teaching
*Contact Person Name and Title:* Peter Felten, Assist Dir
*Contact Phone Number:* (615) 322–7290
*Contact Fax Number:* (615) 343–8111
*Contact Email Address:* peter.felten@Vanderbilt.edu
*SL Program/Center URL:* http://www.vanderbilt.edu/cft/
*SL Online Course Description URL:* http://www.vanderbilt.edu/cft/sl/s-l_examples.htm
*Description:* Established in 1986, the Center for Teaching has two major missions: to stimulate dialogue about teaching excellence and to help members of the Vanderbilt teaching community gather, analyze, and apply information about their teaching. Over the past two decades, college-level teaching has blossomed into an exciting field of research and practice. This research, drawing on scholarship in learning and cognition, has generated many fresh, highly effective techniques to complement more traditional approaches. The center helps keep Vanderbilt on the forefront of instructional innovation. Vanderbilt expects its faculty and teaching assistants to the meet the highest standards of teaching excellence on every evaluative criterion: student learning, student ratings, peer review, and self-evaluation. The center offers several confidential services to help instructors assess their effectiveness.

Ingram Scholars (http://www.vanderbilt.edu/ingram): The Ingram Scholarship Program challenges students to create and implement substantial service projects in the community. The program sponsors students who are committed to finding their personal roles in the solution of societal problems and who have the maturity and initiative to promote positive social change. Ingram Scholars are expected to devote approximately 20 hours each month during the academic year and at least one of the undergraduate summers to relevant community outreach and service projects.

Mayfield Living/Learning Lodges (http://www.vanderbilt.edu/ResEd/4may_pro.html): Each year, the Office of Housing and Residential Education sets aside several Mayfield Lodges for the purpose of creating the LivingLearning Lodge program. The Lodges are assigned to groups of ten students who live together in order to pursue a self-directed, year-long program of educational activities, including, but not limited to, community-service projects.

*SL Required for Graduation (all students)?* No

*Service Required for Graduation (all students)?* No

*Any Co-curricular Service?* No

*Any SL Residence Halls or Theme Houses?* Yes

*Number of Undergraduate SL Courses Offered Per Year:* 3–5

*Number of Graduate SL Courses Offered Per Year:* 2–3

*Total Number of SL Courses Offered Per Year:* 6–7

*Number of Instructors Teaching SL Courses Per Year:* 8–10

*Number of Full-time SL Staff on Campus (not counting instructors):* 0

*Number of Part-time SL Staff on Campus (not counting instructors):* 1

## Villanova University

800 Lancaster Ave, Villanova, PA 19085

*University/College URL:* http://www. villanova.edu/servlet/Web2000

*Type of Institution:* private, university, teaching, religious

*Contact Person Name and Title:* Mark J. Doorley, PhD, Ethics Program, and Coord, Service/Service-Learning

*Contact Phone Number:* (610) 519–4736

*Contact Fax Number:* (610) 519–6098

*Contact Email Address:* mark.doorley@villanova.edu

*SL Online Syllabi URL:* http://www28. homepage.villanova.edu/mark.doorley/ eth_2050_sec_010_spring_2000.htm

*Description:* There are three service-learning initiatives at Villanova University. In the College of Arts and Sciences, work is underway on a proposal which will institutionalize support for faculty in the development and implementation of service-learning courses. The Ethics Program also has a service component in its Ethics Concentration requirements. The reflective piece is done explicitly through a senior integrative project, with a strong suggestion to journal about the experience. This concentration is just beginning and is being refined over time. Finally, a service-learning Honors community is being developed (slated to begin in the Fall 2000).

*SL Required for Graduation (all students)?* No

*Service Required for Graduation (all students)?* No

*Any Co-curricular Service?* Yes

*Any SL Residence Halls or Theme Houses?* Yes (as of Fall 2000)

*Number of Undergraduate SL Courses Offered Per Year:* 6

*Number of Graduate SL Courses Offered Per Year:* 0

*Total Number of SL Courses Offered Per Year:* 6

*Number of Instructors Teaching SL Courses Per Year:* 4

*Number of Full-time SL Staff on Campus (not counting instructors):* 0

*Number of Part-time SL Staff on Campus (not counting instructors):* 3

## Virginia Commonwealth University

827 W Franklin St, PO Box 842041, Richmond, VA 23284–2041

*University/College URL:* http://www.vcu.edu

*Type of Institution:* public, university, teaching, research

*SL Program/Center Name:* Office of Community Programs

*Contact Person Name and Title:* Dr. Cathy Howard, Dir

*Contact Phone Number:* (804) 828–1831

*Contact Fax Number:* (804) 828–8172

*Contact Email Address:* choward@vcu.edu

*SL Program/Center URL:* http://www.vcu. edu/ocp/ocpdocs/slap.html

*Description:* Service-learning at Virginia Commonwealth University is a course-based, credit-bearing educational experience in which students participate in an organized service activity that meets community-identified needs. Students reflect on the service activity in such a way as to increase understanding and application of course content and to enhance a sense of civic responsibility.

*SL Required for Graduation (all students)?* No

*Service Required for Graduation (all students)?* No

*Any Co-curricular Service?* Yes (Within the College of Humanities and Sciences there is an urban experience requirement which a service-learning course will satisfy.)

*Any SL Residence Halls or Theme Houses?* No

*Number of Undergraduate SL Courses Offered Per Year:* 30+
*Number of Graduate SL Courses Offered Per Year:* 3
*Total Number of SL Courses Offered Per Year:* 33+
*Number of Instructors Teaching SL Courses Per Year:* 15+
*Number of Full-time SL Staff on Campus (not counting instructors):* 3

## Virginia Polytechnic Institute and State University

210 Burruss Hall, 0131, Blacksburg, VA 24061
*University/College URL:* _ http://www.vt.edu
*Type of Institution:* public, university, research, secular
*SL Program/Center Name:* The Service-Learning Center
*Contact Person Name and Title:* Michele James-Deramo, Dir
*Contact Phone Number:* (540) 231–6947
*Contact Fax Number:* (540) 231–6367
*Contact Email Address:* deramo@vt.edu
*SL Program/Center URL:* http://www.majbill.vt.edu/SL/index.html
*SL Online Course Description URL:* http://www.majbill.vt.edu/SL/courses.html
*Description:* The mission of the Virginia Tech Service-Learning Center is to promote the integration of community service with academic study in every college of the university in order to enhance student learning and deepen civic responsibility. Service-learning programs include Community Partnerships with the Christiansburg Institute and the Village of Newport; Distance and Service-Learning in the Sciences; Empowerment of Women and Girls gender-equity program; Service-Learning Extension Project creating service-learning opportunities at cooperative extension sites; STEP (Service Training for Environmental Progress); the Virginia Tech Community Literacy Corps; and VTOPS (Virginia Tech Outreach Program to Schools).
*SL Required for Graduation (all students)?* No
*Service Required for Graduation (all students)?* No

*Any Co-curricular Service?* Yes
*Any SL Residence Halls or Theme Houses?* No
*Number of Undergraduate SL Courses Offered Per Year:* 65–70
*Number of Graduate SL Courses Offered Per Year:* 1–2
*Total Number of SL Courses Offered Per Year:* 75
*Number of Instructors Teaching SL Courses Per Year:* 70
*Number of Full-time SL Staff on Campus (not counting instructors):* 3
*Number of Part-time SL Staff on Campus (not counting instructors):* 3–4 (1 part-time, plus 2–3 graduate assistants)

## Wagner College

One Campus Rd, Staten Island, NY 10301
*University/College URL:* http://www.wagner.edu
*Type of Institution:* private, college, teaching, secular
*SL Program/Center Name:* Experiential Learning Center
*Contact Person Name and Title:* Julia Barchitta, Dean of Experiential Learning
*Contact Phone Number:* (718) 390–3443
*Contact Fax Number:* (718) 390–3217
*Contact Email Address:* jbarchit@wagner.edu
*SL Program/Center URL:* http://www.wagner.edu/prosstud/ugradstud/explearn.html
*Description:* Beginning with the entering class of Fall 1998, Wagner College initiated a new curriculum and new graduation requirements. As part of these requirements, students complete three "Learning Communities" before graduation: one in the freshman year, one during the intermediate years, and one in the senior year in the student's major. These Learning Communities are linked to experiential learning to enhance the liberal arts education by developing critical-thinking skills, a commitment to values, and skills for effective citizenship. The field experiences are directly linked to academic coursework while identifying and meeting the needs of the community. In the freshman year the field experience is based on the theme of the liberal arts courses in the

learning community. In the senior year, the field experience is an internship in the student's major. The communities of Staten Island and Manhattan are part of this partnership with the college. Some 430 freshmen were placed in over 75 nonprofit community agencies including public schools, after-school centers, health care agencies, social service agencies, environmental agencies, political and community organizations, the national park service, museums, and cultural organizations. Each student performed at least three hours of volunteer service per week throughout the semester.

*SL Required for Graduation (all students)?* Yes

*Service Required for Graduation (all students)?* Yes

*Any Co-curricular Service?* No

*Any SL Residence Halls or Theme Houses?* Yes

*Number of Undergraduate SL Courses Offered Per Year:* 32 (plus internships)

*Total Number of SL Courses Offered Per Year:* 32

*Number of Instructors Teaching SL Courses Per Year:* 32

*Number of Full-time SL Staff on Campus (not counting instructors):* 2

*Number of Part-time SL Staff on Campus (not counting instructors):* 0

## Wake Forest University

Benson University Center, Rm 321, Box 7351 Volunteer Services, Winston-Salem, NC 27109

*University/College URL:* http://www.wfu.edu

*Type of Institution:* private, university, teaching, research

*SL Program/Center Name:* Volunteer Services

*Contact Person Name and Title:* Paige Wilbanks

*Contact Phone Number:* (336) 758–4549

*Contact Fax Number:* (336) 758–4744

*Contact Email Address:* wilbanp@wfu.edu

*SL Program/Center URL:* http://www.wfu. edu/Student-Services/Student-Life/volserv/ index.html

*Description:* ACE (Academic and Community Engagement) Fellowship Program is a collaborative effort between the Teaching and Learning Center and Volunteer Services. It is a new initiative linking the university's commitment to academic excellence and service to humanity. At its core, this program seeks to provide opportunities and incentives for faculty fellows to explore and implement service-learning into the existing courses or first-year seminars. In addition to training and educating faculty, the ACE Fellowship Program seeks to increase excitement and enthusiasm about community engagement, teaching, and service throughout campus.

*SL Required for Graduation (all students)?* No

*Service Required for Graduation (all students)?* No

*Any Co-curricular Service?* Yes

*Any SL Residence Halls or Theme Houses?* No

*Number of Undergraduate SL Courses Offered Per Year:* 10–12

*Total Number of SL Courses Offered Per Year:* 10–12

*Number of Instructors Teaching SL Courses Per Year:* 9–10

*Number of Full-time SL Staff on Campus (not counting instructors):* 1

*Number of Part-time SL Staff on Campus (not counting instructors):* 0

## Washington State University

1 SE Stadium Way, Pullman, WA 99164

*University/College URL:* http://www.wsu.edu

*Type of Institution:* public, university, research

*SL Program/Center Name:* Community Service Learning Center

*Contact Person Name and Title:* Melanie Brown, Program Dir

*Contact Phone Number:* (509) 335–7708

*Contact Fax Number:* (509) 335–3400

*Contact Email Address:* melanieb@wsunix.wsu.edu

*SL Program/Center URL:* http://cub.wsu. edu/cslc

*SL Online Syllabi URL:* http://cub.wsu.edu/ cslc/sample_syllabi.htm

*Description:* The Community Service Learning Center serves as the office on campus devoted to promoting and facilitating community service and service-learning. Established in 1993, the center has grown steadily, serving students, faculty, and the local community. Loyal to its mission of service-learning, the center endeavors to intentionally balance the goals of providing meaningful service to the local community and purposeful learning opportunities for student participants. It bridges the gap between campus and community and the boundaries between university units, incorporating an interdisciplinary approach to student learning and campus engagement.

*SL Required for Graduation (all students)?* No

*Service Required for Graduation (all students)?* No

*Any Co-curricular Service?* Yes

*Any SL Residence Halls or Theme Houses?* Yes

*Number of Undergraduate SL Courses Offered Per Year:* 35 (in 1998–99)

*Number of Graduate SL Courses Offered Per Year:* 0

*Total Number of SL Courses Offered Per Year:* 35

*Number of Instructors Teaching SL Courses Per Year:* 25

*Number of Full-time SL Staff on Campus (not counting instructors):* 1 program dir

*Number of Part-time SL Staff on Campus (not counting instructors):* 12 (1 office assist, 4 grad assists, 7 undergrad assists)

## Washtenaw Community College

4800 East Huron River Dr, PO Box D-1, Ann Arbor, MI 48106–1610

*University/College URL:* http://www.washtenaw.cc.mi.us

*Type of Institution:* public, community college

*SL Program/Center Name:* Workplace Learning Center

*Contact Person Name and Title:* Fofie Pappas, Service Learning Advisor

*Contact Phone Number:* (734) 677–5120; 973–3421

*Contact Fax Number:* (734) 677–5444

*Contact Email Address:* fpappas@wccnet.org

*SL Program/Center URL:* http://www.washtenaw.cc.mi.us/info/#workplace

*Description:* The Workplace Learning Center's service-learning advisor provides placement assistance to various faculty who use academic service-learning as part of their curriculum. Course assignments direct students to volunteer at nonprofit agencies for a specified number of hours. Students have specific objectives they must complete as part of their service. For example, a student in political science might determine how government affects an agency; or students in the Human Services program might make career decisions about their areas of concentration. The Workplace Learning Center keeps a file of the various agencies in the community, and the service-learning advisor assists students in finding the best placement for their particular interests and availability.

*SL Required for Graduation (all students)?* No

*Service Required for Graduation (all students)?* No

*Any Co-curricular Service?* No

*Any SL Residence Halls or Theme Houses?* No

*Number of Undergraduate SL Courses Offered Per Year:* 10

*Number of Graduate SL Courses Offered Per Year:* 0

*Total Number of SL Courses Offered Per Year:* 10

*Number of Instructors Teaching SL Courses Per Year:* 5

*Number of Full-time SL Staff on Campus (not counting instructors):* 0

*Number of Part-time SL Staff on Campus (not counting instructors):* 1

## Waynesburg College

51 W College St, Waynebsurg, PA 15370

*University/College URL:* http://www.waynesburg.edu

*Type of Institution:* private, college, religious

*SL Program/Center Name:* Center for Service Leadership

*Contact Person Name and Title:* Patricia J. Delaney, Dir, Bonner Scholars Program, and Coord for Service Learning

*Contact Phone Number:* (724) 852–3318
*Contact Fax Number:* (724) 852–6416
*Contact Email Address:*
  pdelaney@waynesburg.edu
*SL Program/Center URL:* http://waynesburg.
  edu/~commserv/service.htm
*Description:* The Center for Service Leadership

In 1988, Waynesburg College implemented the inaugural service-learning course as a component of its general-education curriculum. The course consisted of a minimum 30-hour service requirement with personal reflections and analysis structured through journals and a final paper. In later years, the course was modified to permit students to enroll in service-learning for anywhere from one to three credit hours. The shift was made from a single administrator supervising the service-learning placement to a decentralized approach with a group of faculty mentors providing guidance and experience and facilitating learning sessions based upon the service experiences of students. These faculty mentors, from various academic disciplines, work as a group to plan and structure learning experiences which occur under their leadership throughout the semester the student is enrolled. Students serve with over 40 agencies and programs that are designed to meet the needs of Greene County and the surrounding area. Outside of Waynesburg and Greene County, groups travel to Nashville to work in soup kitchens, to Italy to tutor English, to India to work in hospitals, and to El Salvador and Mexico to build churches. Students also travel into the city to participate in various urban intensive service experiences such as, ''The Open Door,'' ''East Liberty Saturday Celebration,'' and the ''Pittsburgh Project.'' Service placement ''matches'' are made by staff at the Center for Service Leadership, which is located in the new Stover Campus Center. Students are placed in service sites according to their major field of study and areas of personal interest. Supportive services, orientation, training, and reflection classes are also provided by the center's staff in order to assist students to gain the maximum benefit from their service experiences.

Waynesburg College also participates in the Corella and Bertram F. Bonner Foundation Service Scholarship Program. The program offers selected students financial assistance to supplement the college's aid package, in return for a commitment to service while enrolled at Waynesburg. Bonner Scholars serve an average of 10 hours per week during the school year in community-service programs in order to earn their scholarship benefits. Waynesburg College has an 80-student program that generates 800 hours of community-service per week. Each year, 20 new Bonner Scholars are chosen; they return to the campus, in August, one week earlier than the general student body to participate in an intensive orientation to the program and specialized training.

*SL Required for Graduation (all
  students)?* Yes
*Service Required for Graduation (all students)?* Yes
*Any Co-curricular Service?* Yes
*Any SL Residence Halls or Theme
  Houses?* No
*Number of Undergraduate SL Courses
  Offered Per Year:* 26
*Total Number of SL Courses Offered Per
  Year:* 26
*Number of Instructors Teaching SL Courses
  Per Year:* 13
*Number of Full-time SL Staff on Campus
  (not counting instructors):* 13
*Number of Part-time SL Staff on Campus
  (not counting instructors):* 2

**West Chester University of Pennsylvania**
High and Rosedale Sts, West Chester,
  PA 19383
*University/College URL:* http://www.
  wcupa.edu
*Type of Institution:* public, university,
  teaching
*SL Program/Center Name:* Office of Service-Learning & Volunteer Programs
*Contact Person Name and Title:* Maggie
  Tripp, Dir
*Contact Phone Number:* (610) 436–3379
*Contact Fax Number:* (610) 436–2480
*Contact Email Address:* mtripp@wcupa.edu
*SL Program/Center URL:* http://www.wcupa.
  edu/_SERVICES/stu.slv/
*Description:* The Office of Service-Learning

and Volunteer Programs was created in 1997 and is jointly funded by the Divisions of Academic Affairs and Student Affairs. The office provides assistance to faculty using service-learning and those interested in developing it into an existing course. The office works with approximately 75 area agencies and assists students looking for class placements and extracurricular activities. Each year several major service projects are planned and the entire campus is invited to participate.

*SL Required for Graduation (all students)?* No

*Service Required for Graduation (all students)?* No

*Any Co-curricular Service?* Yes

*Any SL Residence Halls or Theme Houses?* No

*Number of Undergraduate SL Courses Offered Per Year:* 25

*Number of Graduate SL Courses Offered Per Year:* 2

*Total Number of SL Courses Offered Per Year:* 27

*Number of Instructors Teaching SL Courses Per Year:* 30

*Number of Full-time SL Staff on Campus (not counting instructors):* 1

*Number of Part-time SL Staff on Campus (not counting instructors):* 0

## West Virginia University

102 A Stewart Hall, PO 6201, Morgantown, WV 26506

*University/College URL:* http://www.wvu.edu

*Type of Institution:* public, university, teaching, research, secular

*SL Program/Center Name:* Office of Service-Learning

*Contact Person Name and Title:* Dr. Susan Hunter, Dir

*Contact Phone Number:* (304) 293–8761, ext 4484

*Contact Fax Number:* (304) 293–2906

*Contact Email Address:* Shunter2@wvu.edu

*SL Program/Center URL:* http://www.wvu.edu/~oslp/

*SL Online Course Description URL:* http://www.wvu.edu/~oslp/

*Description:* The office of Service-Learning at West Virginia University manages several programs. It coordinates America Reads and America Counts on the campus and also supports Kaleidoscope, a similar reading/mentoring program with local schools. It also provides workshops for faculty, students, community members, and nonprofits; assists with placements; and offers staff support for service-learning courses across campus. In addition, the office, under contract to the West Virginia Board of Education, produces a state-wide service-learning newsletter, which goes to all nonprofit organizations and public schools in the state. West Virginia Campus Compact is housed in the office and produces a state-wide newsletter to college campuses. It also hosts an annual Higher Education Service Learning Symposium. Alternative Break projects are organized under the auspices of Campus Compact, but are funded by the Office of Service-Learning. Finally, the university has the Rural Health Initiative and Health Sciences Technology Academy, which send health sciences students into the communities on three-month rotations with service required. Some of these programs are undergraduate and some are graduate.

*SL Required for Graduation (all students)?* No

*Service Required for Graduation (all students)?* No (However, there are service requirements for some majors.)

*Any Co-curricular Service?* Yes

*Any SL Residence Halls or Theme Houses?* Yes (One dorm has a service-learning theme and all ''Orientation One'' students are expected to work on a service project.)

*Number of Undergraduate SL Courses Offered Per Year:* 20

*Number of Graduate SL Courses Offered Per Year:* 20 (In addition, all health science programs require service learning and several colleges require portfolios which include service.)

*Total Number of SL Courses Offered Per Year:* 50

*Number of Instructors Teaching SL Courses Per Year:* 20

*Number of Full-time SL Staff on Campus
  (not counting instructors):* 3
*Number of Part-time SL Staff on Campus
  (not counting instructors):* 9 (2 part-time,
  2 work-study, and five student interns)

## Western Michigan University
Kalamazoo, MI 49008
*University/College URL:* http://www.
  wmich.edu
*Type of Institution:* public, university, teach-
  ing, secular
*SL Program/Center Name:* Student Volunteer Services
*Contact Person Name and Title:* Katrina
  Chester, Coord
*Contact Phone Number:* (616) 387–3230
*Contact Fax Number:* (616) 387–3903
*Contact Email Address:*
  katrina.chester@wmich.edu
*Description:* Student Volunteer Services oper-
ates as a service-learning resource for the entire
campus. Its main objective is to provide serv-
ice-learning placements for students taking
courses in the Lee Honors College. Others in
the campus community are welcome to use the
services of the office. The office is funded by
the Lee Honors College.
*SL Required for Graduation (all
  students)?* No
*Service Required for Graduation (all stu-
  dents)?* No
*Any Co-curricular Service?* Yes
*Any SL Residence Halls or Theme
  Houses?* No
*Number of Undergraduate SL Courses
  Offered Per Year:* 14
*Number of Graduate SL Courses Offered
  Per Year:* 5
*Total Number of SL Courses Offered Per
  Year:* 19
*Number of Instructors Teaching SL Courses
  Per Year:* 13

## Western Montana College of the University of Montana
710 South Atlantic St, Dillon, MT 59725
*University/College URL:* http://www.
  wmc.edu

*Type of Institution:* public, college, teaching,
  secular
*SL Program/Center Name:* Center for Service-Learning
*Contact Person Name and Title:* Ron-
  nie Monroe
*Contact Phone Number:* (406) 683–7016
*Contact Email Address:*
  R_Monroe@wmc.edu
*SL Program/Center URL:* http://www.wmc.
  edu/academics/special.html#anchor45545
*Description:* The Center for Service-Learn-
ing operates service-learning courses through
the faculty, on-campus and community pro-
grams, and AmeriCorps programs in the schools
(mentoring and America Reads), and with vari-
ous other youth and senior programs.
*SL Required for Graduation (all
  students)?* No
*Service Required for Graduation (all stu-
  dents)?* Yes
*Any Co-curricular Service?* Yes
*Any SL Residence Halls or Theme
  Houses?* No
*Number of Undergraduate SL Courses
  Offered Per Year:* 12
*Number of Graduate SL Courses Offered
  Per Year:* 0
*Total Number of SL Courses Offered Per
  Year:* 12
*Number of Instructors Teaching SL Courses
  Per Year:* 12
*Number of Full-time SL Staff on Campus
  (not counting instructors):* 0
*Number of Part-time SL Staff on Campus
  (not counting instructors):* 4

## Western State College
Service Learning, Union 102, Gunnison,
  CO 81231
*University/College URL:* http://www.
  western.edu
*Type of Institution:* public, college, teaching
*SL Program/Center Name:* Service-Learn-
  ing Center
*Contact Person Name and Title:* Layne
  Nelson, Dir
*Contact Phone Number:* (970) 943–2130
*Contact Fax Number:* (970) 943–2702

*Contact Email Address:*
lnelson@western.edu

*SL Program/Center URL:* http://www.western.edu/srvlrn/Welcome.htm

*Description:* The Service Learning Center develops projects around community needs which are done concurrently with coursework, tied to the objectives of the course. Students learn by doing, through volunteer work in community agencies, schools, nonprofit organizations, and government agencies.

*SL Required for Graduation (all students)?* No

*Service Required for Graduation (all students)?* No

*Any Co-curricular Service?* No

*Any SL Residence Halls or Theme Houses?* No

*Number of Undergraduate SL Courses Offered Per Year:* 20

*Total Number of SL Courses Offered Per Year:* 20

*Number of Instructors Teaching SL Courses Per Year:* 12

*Number of Full-time SL Staff on Campus (not counting instructors):* 0

*Number of Part-time SL Staff on Campus (not counting instructors):* 1

## Westminster College

501 Westminster Ave, Fulton, MO 65251

*University/College URL:* http://www.wcmo.edu

*Type of Institution:* private, college, teaching, religious

*SL Program/Center Name:* Office of Student Life

*Contact Person Name and Title:* Robert N. Hansen, Dir of Counseling & Health Services

*Contact Phone Number:* (573) 592–5361

*Contact Fax Number:* (573) 592–5180

*Contact Email Address:*
hansenr@jaynet.wcmo.edu

*Description:* Westminster College has a decentralized service-learning program with segments coordinated through the Westminster Seminar program, Chapel Leadership Program, and the Counseling and Health Center.

*SL Required for Graduation (all students)?* No

*Service Required for Graduation (all students)?* No

*Any Co-curricular Service?* Yes

*Any SL Residence Halls or Theme Houses?* No

## Westminster College

1840 S 1300 East, Salt Lake City, UT 84105

*University/College URL:* http://www.wcslc.edu

*Type of Institution:* private, college, secular

*SL Program/Center Name:* Volunteer Center

*Contact Person Name and Title:* Carrie Anderson, Volunteer Center Coord

*Contact Phone Number:* (801) 832–2840

*Contact Fax Number:* (801) 484–2462

*Contact Email Address:* volcntr@wcslc.edu

*Description:* The Service-Learning program at Westminster College is coordinated through the Volunteer Center. Faculty interested in teaching service-learning courses may contact the Volunteer Center coordinator for assistance with planning and implementing service-learning in their courses. Service-learning models are also used for monthly service projects coordinated by the Volunteer Center. The center is staffed by AmeriCorps and AmeriCorps*VISTA. It is funded through the Associated Students of Westminster College.

*SL Required for Graduation (all students)?* No

*Service Required for Graduation (all students)?* No

*Any Co-curricular Service?* Yes

*Any SL Residence Halls or Theme Houses?* No

*Number of Undergraduate SL Courses Offered Per Year:* 5–10

*Number of Graduate SL Courses Offered Per Year:* 2–3

*Total Number of SL Courses Offered Per Year:* 7–13

*Number of Instructors Teaching SL Courses Per Year:* 3–5

*Number of Full-time SL Staff on Campus (not counting instructors):* 1

*Number of Part-time SL Staff on Campus
(not counting instructors):* 0

**Westmont College–
San Francisco Urban Program**
3016 Jackson Str, San Francisco, CA 94115
*University/College URL:* http://www.
westmont.edu
*Type of Institution:* private, college, teaching, religious
*SL Program/Center Name:* San Francisco
Urban Program
*Contact Person Name and Title:* Steven
Schultz, Dir
*Contact Phone Number:* (415) 931–2460
*Contact Fax Number:* (415) 931–0212
*Contact Email Address:*
sschultz@westmont.edu
*Description:* This one-semester study program in San Francisco for liberal arts undergraduates provides students with the opportunity to study contemporary urban issues through seminars and field experiences, as well as to be involved in a 24-hour per week service-learning placement related to the student's academic major. Participants receive four units of credit for the urban studies course, and eight units of credit for the service placement, which includes opportunities in organizations working in the following areas: arts, education, medical care, criminal justice, AIDS, international relations, community media, human services, and youth. An additional four units of credit is available to those who take part in an independent-study project, usually tied to the student's academic major. A group of 20 to 24 students per semester live together in a facility that includes faculty offices and classrooms, located in one of the residential neighborhoods of the city.
*SL Required for Graduation (all
students)?* No
*Service Required for Graduation (all students)?* No
*Any Co-curricular Service?* Yes
*Any SL Residence Halls or Theme
Houses?* No
*Number of Full-time SL Staff on Campus
(not counting instructors):* 0
*Number of Part-time SL Staff on Campus
(not counting instructors):* 0

**Wheaton College**
Norton, MA 02766
*University/College URL:* http://www.
wheatonma.edu
*Type of Institution:* private, college
*SL Program/Center Name:* Filene Center for
Work & Learning (the community service
department is a part of the experiential
learning center)
*Contact Person Name and Title:* Grace
Baron, Faculty Fellow for Service
Learning
*Contact Phone Number:* (508) 286–3799
*Contact Fax Number:* (508) 285–8261
*Contact Email Address:*
gbaron@wheatonma.edu
*SL Program/Center URL:* http://www.
wheatoncollege.edu/Filene/Service.html
*SL Online Course Description URL:* http://
www.wheatoncollege.edu/Filene/Service.
html
*Description:* For the past three years, faculty from many disciplines have accepted the college's invitation to transform existing courses into service-learning opportunities. Faculty in the math/science, social science, and humanities now offer over 20 classes in which service is a central component. A Faculty Fellow in Service Learning assists faculty in course design and ongoing course/project evaluation.
*SL Required for Graduation (all
students)?* No
*Service Required for Graduation (all students)?* No
*Any Co-curricular Service?* Yes (All incoming students participate in a day of
service as part of orientation.)
*Any SL Residence Halls or Theme Houses?*
No (However, many residence hall floors
and theme houses have strong voluntary
participation in service.)
*Number of Undergraduate SL Courses
Offered Per Year:* 6
*Number of Graduate SL Courses Offered
Per Year:* 0
*Total Number of SL Courses Offered
Per Year:* 6
*Number of Instructors Teaching SL Courses
Per Year:* 6

*Number of Full-time SL Staff on Campus (not counting instructors):* 1 (One full-time faculty member has a 2/3 time special assignment as Faculty Fellow for Service Learning.)
*Number of Part-time SL Staff on Campus (not counting instructors):* 0

## Wheeling Jesuit University
316 Washington Ave, Wheeling, WV 26003
*University/College URL:* http://www.wju.edu
*Type of Institution:* private, university, teaching, religious
*Contact Person Name and Title:* Carolyn Dalzell, Assoc Dean of Students
*Contact Phone Number:* (304) 243–2257
*Contact Fax Number:* (304) 243–2243
*Contact Email Address:* cgd@wju.edu
*Description:* Service-learning is planned and implemented by individual faculty members, with support from the Offices of Student Life and Academic Affairs. Faculty and students engage in values-based scholarship by integrating academically rigorous course material with meaningful community-service activities. Justice education and the development of ''men and women for others'' is the focus of Wheeling Jesuit's service-learning initiatives. Opportunities for volunteering are offered through the Office of Student Life. Project-based service is coordinated by professional staff as part of the First Year Seminar and the Laut Honors Program, as well as the focus of clubs like the Appalachian Experience club and Excellence in Christian Leadership (EXCEL) program. The Mother Jones house, a community-service residence, was recently established through a cooperative venture of the university and the Laughlin Memorial Chapel, an outreach agency of the First Presbyterian Church in Wheeling. The Mother Jones house is located in an economically challenged neighborhood in Wheeling, and students live and work in outreach to their neighbors through established, ecumenical community agencies. Funding for the house was generously provided by the Frueauff Foundation and further supported by the Bonner Foundation. A progressive wellness clinic is operated by the nursing department in a subsi-dized elder residence, receiving financial support from local private and public donors.
*SL Required for Graduation (all students)?* No
*Service Required for Graduation (all students)?* Yes
*Any Co-curricular Service?* No
*Any SL Residence Halls or Theme Houses?* No (However, there are two service-related residential options. Any student may request to live in the dedicated Community Service hall in Ignatius Hall; juniors and seniors may apply to live in the Mother Jones house.)
*Number of Undergraduate SL Courses Offered Per Year:* 10
*Number of Graduate SL Courses Offered Per Year:* 5
*Total Number of SL Courses Offered Per Year:* 15
*Number of Instructors Teaching SL Courses Per Year:* 6
*Number of Full-time SL Staff on Campus (not counting instructors):* 0
*Number of Part-time SL Staff on Campus (not counting instructors):* 0

## Willamette University
900 State St, Salem, OR 9730–3931
*University/College URL:* http://www.willamette.edu
*Type of Institution:* private, university, teaching, secular
*SL Program/Center Name:* Service Learning Resource Center, Community Outreach Program
*Contact Person Name and Title:* Jessica Glenn, Coord of Community Service Learning
*Contact Phone Number:* (503) 370–6807
*Contact Fax Number:* (503) 370–6407
*Contact Email Address:* jglenn@willamette.edu
*SL Program/Center URL:* http://www.willamette.edu/org/cop/service_learning.html
*SL Online Course Description URL:* http://www.willamette.edu/org/cop/integration.html
*Description:* The goal of the Community Outreach Program is to encourage and facilitate

community involvement in order to help the Willamette Community to become more aware of the issues facing society and to improve the quality of life in the Salem area. The office helps students locate volunteer opportunities, provides support to student-run service organizations, and assists faculty in integrating service-learning into their courses. In addition, the Community Outreach Program organizes special projects such as alternative breaks and an orientation program focused on community service.

The new Latin American Studies major is the first at Willamette that requires students to participate in service-learning. Students can fulfill this requirement at Willamette or while studying abroad. Three of the faculty in this department have integrated service-learning into their courses. The PaCE (Public, Private, and Community Enterprise) Program is in its second year at the university's Atkinson Graduate School of Management. First-year graduate students are assigned to groups in which they research, design, and carry out a business enterprise. As part of this project they partner with a not-for-profit organization and donate 500 hours of community service to the agency. The service experience is then tied back into their core courses on management and organizations.

*SL Required for Graduation (all students)?*
No (But undergraduate majors in Latin American Studies are required to do service-learning.)

*Service Required for Graduation (all students)?* No (But first-year graduate students in the PaCE Program in the Atkinson Graduate School of Management are required to do service.)

*Any Co-curricular Service?* Yes

*Any SL Residence Halls or Theme Houses?* No

*Number of Undergraduate SL Courses Offered Per Year:* 5

*Number of Graduate SL Courses Offered Per Year:* 2

*Total Number of SL Courses Offered Per Year:* 7

*Number of Instructors Teaching SL Courses Per Year:* 6

*Number of Full-time SL Staff on Campus (not counting instructors):* 1 (Coord of the Community Outreach Program; both co-curricular and service-learning)

*Number of Part-time SL Staff on Campus (not counting instructors):* 0

## Wilmington College
251 Ludovic St, Pyle Center Box 1294, Wilmington, OH 45177

*University/College URL:* http://genesis. wilmington.edu

*Type of Institution:* private, college, teaching, religious

*SL Program/Center Name:* Center for Service Learning

*Contact Person Name and Title:* Tara L. Lydy, Coord of Service Learning

*Contact Phone Number:* (937) 382–6661, ext 261

*Contact Fax Number:* (937) 383–8560

*Contact Email Address:* tara_lydy@wilmington.edu

*SL Program/Center URL:* http://www. wilmington.edu/Servlearn.htm

*Description:* The Center for Service Learning offers a variety of service projects. There are ongoing monthly sites where students commit to a set number of hours: animal shelter, homeless shelter, Athenian Tutoring program, Helping Hands, AVOC, Camp Joy, Tot Tales, The Reel Deal, Big Brothers/sisters, Clinton County Youth Council, Adopt-A-Highway, Adopt-A-Grandparent, and Pen-Pals. The center also offers a variety of special projects such as National Make A Difference Day, National Random Acts of Kindness Week, Absolutely Incredible Kid Day, The annual "Quake" and others.

*SL Required for Graduation (all students)?* No

*Service Required for Graduation (all students)?* No

*Any Co-curricular Service?* Yes

*Any SL Residence Halls or Theme Houses?* No

*Total Number of SL Courses Offered Per Year:* 0

*Number of Instructors Teaching SL Courses Per Year:* 0

*Number of Full-time SL Staff on Campus
(not counting instructors):* 1
*Number of Part-time SL Staff on Campus
(not counting instructors):* 0

## Wittenberg University
737 North Fountain Ave, P.O. Box 720,
Springfield, OH 45504
*University/College URL:* http://www.
wittenberg.edu
*Type of Institution:* private, university, teach-
ing, research
*SL Program/Center Name:* The Community
Workshop
*Contact Person Name and Title:*
Cindy Larson
*Contact Phone Number:* (937) 327–7523
*Contact Email Address:*
clarson@wittenberg.edu
*SL Program/Center URL:* http://www.
wittenberg.edu/witt/commservice
*Description:* The Community Workshop is the
locus and clearinghouse for service activity at
Wittenberg. It is staffed by a full-time director,
staff assistant, and 16 part-time student coordinators who mentor 30 to 40 students through all
phases of their service experience each semester. Service has been an institutional requirement at Wittenberg since 1989. The Community Workshop works with approximately 40
community sites. At present, there is one course
in sociology, ''Welfare and Human Services''
that incorporates service-learning. The depart-
ment is funded totally through university monies.
*SL Required for Graduation (all
students)?* Yes
*Service Required for Graduation (all stu-
dents)?* Yes
*Any Co-curricular Service?* Yes
*Any SL Residence Halls or Theme
Houses?* No
*Number of Undergraduate SL Courses
Offered Per Year:* 1
*Number of Graduate SL Courses Offered
Per Year:* 0
*Total Number of SL Courses Offered
Per Year:* 1
*Number of Instructors Teaching SL Courses
Per Year:* 0

*Number of Full-time SL Staff on Campus
(not counting instructors):* 2
*Number of Part-time SL Staff on Campus
(not counting instructors):* 16 part-time
student coordinators (10 hours weekly)

## Wright State University (partnered with Sinclair Community College)
140 East Monument Ave, Dayton,
OH 45402
*University/College URL:* http://www.
wright.edu
*Type of Institution:* public, university, teach-
ing, secular
*SL Program/Center Name:* Center for
Healthy Communities, Division of Health
Professions Education
*Contact Person Name and Title:* Annette
Canfield, Assist Dir
*Contact Phone Number:* (937) 775–1114
*Contact Fax Number:* (937) 775–1110
*Contact Email Address:*
Annette.Canfield@Wright.edu
*SL Program/Center URL:* http://www.med.
wright.edu/som/comminv/chc/serv.html
*Description:* The Center for Healthy Communities is a community academic partnership
committed to improving primary-care service
delivery and health professions education. Center
staff work with faculty and students from allied
health, medicine, nursing, psychology, social
work, law, and theology to better integrate
student learning objectives with community
learning objectives using the Service Learning
Protocol for Health Professions Schools, which
was developed by the center. Staff place over
600 health professions students annually in
community-based clinical training sites, providing health care and health education services to over 12,000 people. They work closely
with the service-learning offices of the colleges
and universities in the Dayton area and provide
Faculty Curricular Development seminars to
health professions schools across the state of
Ohio. At Wright State University, future service-learning initiatives, if any, for other than
health professions schools will be coordinated
through the Service-Learning Resource Program in the Center for Teaching and Learning.

*SL Required for Graduation (all students)?* No
*Service Required for Graduation (all students)?* No
*Any Co-curricular Service?* No
*Any SL Residence Halls or Theme Houses?* No
*Number of Graduate SL Courses Offered Per Year:* 7

*Number of Instructors Teaching SL Courses Per Year:* 120
*Number of Full-time SL Staff on Campus (not counting instructors):* 0
*Number of Part-time SL Staff on Campus (not counting instructors):* 2

# 4
# Service-Learning and Service Organizations, Associations, and Networks

## Service-Learning Organizations, Associations, and Networks

Most of the associations, organizations, networks, foundations, programs, and centers listed below are central to service-learning in higher education in the U.S. and abroad. For the majority, service-learning is either the main focus or it shares the spotlight equally with service. In a few cases, the mandate involves higher education or experiential education. These are included here because their contributions to service-learning are significant. Again, the majority primarily serve institutions and constituencies in higher education; some also serve K-12 audiences. Given the focus of this sourcebook on higher education, those which only serve primary and secondary education institutions and agendas are not included.

### American Association for Higher Education (AAHE)
One Dupont Circle, NW, Suite 360
Washington, DC 20036
(202) 293–6440
fax: (202) 293–0073
e-mail: info@aahe.org
http://www.aahe.org

AAHE's mission involves improving higher education. It has over 9,000 individual members, and it hosts a national conference and several smaller conferences each year. AAHE's Service Learning Project includes an 18-volume monograph series entitled *Series on Service-Learning in the Disciplines.* Each monograph focuses on the integration of service-learning in one discipline or field, including accounting, biology, communication studies, composition, engineering, environmental studies, history, management, medical education, nursing, peace studies, philosophy, political science, psychology, sociology, Spanish, teacher education, and women's studies (see Chapter 2 for more information on this series).

### American Association of Colleges for Teacher Education
Service-Learning and Teacher Education
  Project
Joost Yff, Senior Project Director
1307 New York Ave., NW, Suite 300
Washington, DC 20005–4701
(202) 293–2450, ext 585
fax: (202) 457–8095
e-mail: jyff@aacte.org
http://www.aacte.org

"AACTE is a national, voluntary association of colleges and universities with undergraduate or graduate programs to prepare professional educators." One of its initiatives is the Service-Learning and Teacher Education Project, which helps "develop institutional capacity and interinstitutional infrastructure to incorporate service-learning in teacher education programs. Six subgrantee institutions. . . address various aspects, culminating in a major publication that will be used as the basis for technical assistance to schools, colleges and departments of education seeking to develop such programs." The project is funded by the Corporation for National Service (CNS).

### American Association of Community Colleges (AACC)
Service Learning Clearinghouse
One Dupont Circle, NW, Suite 410

Washington, DC 20036–1176
(202) 728–0200, ext. 254
fax: (202) 833–2467
e-mail: grobinson@aacc.nche.edu
http://www.aacc.nche.edu/initiatives/service/
  service.htm

The American Association of Community Colleges supports and promotes two-year associate degree-granting institutions. Begun in 1920, AACC pursues specific policy initiatives, engages in advocacy and research, provides education services, and coordination of its membership network. One of its initiatives is the Service Learning Clearinghouse, which seeks to advance the development of service-learning at community colleges. The clearinghouse offers various types of support to its member institutions through service-learning projects, national data collection efforts, publications, and technical assistance.

**Association for Experiential
Education (AEE)**
2305 Canyon Boulevard, Suite #100
Boulder, CO 80302
(303) 440–8844
fax: (303) 440–9581
e-mail: bill@aee.org
http://www.aee.org

The Association for Experiential Education seeks to "contribute to making a more just and compassionate world by transforming education." Accordingly, its mission is "to develop and promote experiential education in all settings. The Association is committed to support professional development, theoretical advancement, and evaluation in the field of experiential education worldwide." Begun in the early 1970s, AEE now has a membership of some 2,000 individuals and organizations in over 20 countries. It sponsors an annual international conference and provides awards, publications, a listserv, and other resources to its member.

**The Bonner Scholars Program**
The Corella & Bertram F. Bonner
  Foundation
10 Mercer Street
Princeton, NJ 08540
(609) 924–6663

fax: (609) 683–4626
e-mail: info@bonner.org
http://www.Bonner.org

The Bonner Scholars Program provides a significant number of community-service scholarships to college students. (See Chapter 6 for a detailed entry on this program.)

**Break Away: the Alternative Break
Connection**
2121 W. Pensacola Street, #543
Tallahassee, FL 32304
(850) 644–0986
fax: (850) 644–1435
e-mail:breakaway@alternativebreaks.com
http://www.alternativebreaks.com

Break Away promotes "service on the local, regional, national and international levels through break-oriented programs which immerse students in often vastly different cultures, heighten social awareness and advocate life-long social action." Its services include an annual national conference, training and special events, networking, and access to its Sideband Catalog (which lists community organizations that host alternative break programs). Alternative Break Citizenship schools (ABCs)—new in 2000—are "week-long experiential training sessions which provide student and staff leaders from different campuses with the knowledge and skills necessary to build a quality alternative break program. . . [and] the ABCs training components are themselves presented within the context of a week-long alternative break experience." Break Away publications include *Connections* (their newsletter); the *Break Away Site Leader Survival Manual*, *Break Away: Organizing an Alternative Break;* and *Curriculum-Based Alternative Breaks*, *Break Away: Hosting and Alternative Break.* Founded in June 1991, and located at Vanderbilt University for many years, Break Away recently moved its offices to Tallahassee, FL.

**Campus Compact: The Project for Public
and Community Service**
PO Box 1975
Brown University
Providence, RI 02912
(401) 863–1119

fax: (401) 863–3779
e-mail: campus@compact.org
http://www.compact.org

Campus Compact is a "coalition of college and university presidents committed to helping students develop the values and skills of citizenship through participation in public and community service." Its primary purpose is "to support campus-based public and community service" in higher education. In January 2000, some 15 years after its founding in 1985, Campus Compact includes a national office, 21 state compacts, six "developing" state compacts, a National Center for Community Colleges (based at Mesa Community College in Mesa, Arizona), and a Western Region Campus Compact Consortium Office (at Western Washington University in Bellingham, Washington), and "a membership of 620 public and private two- and four-year colleges and universities, located in 41 states and the District of Columbia." While all "Campus Compact presidents support service learning," it is important to note that a number of these member institutions do not necessarily have service-learning programs our courses at present.

## Campus Compact National Center for Community Colleges (CC NCCC)

Lyvier Conss, Executive Director
Mesa Community College
Downtown Center
145 North Centennial Way, Suite 108H
Mesa, AZ 85201
(602) 461–6258
fax: (602) 461–6218
e-mail: conss@mc.maricopa.edu
web: http://www.mc.maricopa.edu/academic/
  compact

CC NCCC is Campus Compact's national technical assistance center for community colleges. Begun in late 1990 with a sub-grant to Maricopa County Community College District, it is housed at Mesa Community College. CCNCC "serves as a national advocate for community colleges in service learning to sustain service learning as a national movement. . . [and] serves member organizations and others in the promotion and implementation of community service as a means to improve teaching and learning to the ultimate benefit of students and the communities in which they live." As part of its work, CC NCCC hosts an annual conference.

## Campus Outreach Opportunity League (COOL)

37 Temple Place, Suite 401
Boston, MA 02111
(617) 695–2665
fax: (617) 695–0022
e-mail: inquiry@COOL2SERVE.org
http://www.cool2serve.org

COOL, as it is known, is one of the early organizations that has helped shape service and, ultimately, service-learning in the U.S. It was founded in 1984. and it continues to "educate and empower students to strengthen our nation through community service." It has contributed to mobilizing college students and building a network of youth committed to service. It hosts an Annual COOL National Conference on Student Community Service (its 17th is in 2001) and regional meetings, has its own listserv and Web site (including a searchable database called "COOL Tools"), publishes a quarterly newsletter (*What's COOL!*), offers various service awards, and has developed "Into the Streets," its own "model national program designed to introduce students to volunteering through hands-on experience in an area of their choice." Its membership includes individual college students, colleges, and universities.

## The Carnegie Foundation for the Advancement of Teaching

The Carnegie Foundation for the Advancement of Teaching
555 Middlefield Road
Menlo Park, California 94025
(650) 566–5100
fax: (650) 326–0278
clyburn@carnegiefoundation.org
http://www.carnegiefoundation.org/

While not a service-learning organization, per se, the Carnegie Foundation for the Advancement of Teaching has contributed significantly to service-learning. Founded in 1905 by Andrew Carnegie, the Carnegie Foundation for the

Advancement of Teaching works "to do all things necessary to encourage, uphold and dignify the profession of teaching." Its Project on Higher Education and the Development of Moral and Civic Responsibility, directed by Senior Scholars Anne Colby and Tom Ehrlich, "focuses on educational programs that foster moral and civic development in undergraduate students. It seeks to examine and strengthen the means by which American higher education prepares thoughtful, socially responsible, and civically engaged graduates."

## Community-Campus Partnerships for Health

Amy Zechman, Program Coordinator
3333 California Street, Suite 410
San Francisco, CA 94118
(415) 502–7933
fax: (415) 476–4113
fax-on-demand: 1–888-267–9183
e-mail: ccph@itsa.ucsf.edu
http://futurehealth.ucsf.edu/ccph.html

"Community-Campus Partnerships for Health is a nonprofit organization that fosters partnerships between communities and educational institutions that build on each other's strengths and develop their roles as change agents for improving health professions education, civic responsibility and the overall health of communities." It developed "The Principles of Good Community-Campus Partnerships" (see "Partnerships" in Chapter 1). CCPH is involved in numerous programs, including "Health Professions Schools in Service to the Nation Program (HPSISN)" and "Community-Campus Partnerships: A National Study of Academic Health Centers and their Surrounding Communities." CCPH hosts an annual national conference and a Summer Faculty Service-Learning Institute.

## Corporation for National Service (CNS)

1201 New York Avenue, NW
Washington, DC 20525
(202) 606–5000
fax: (202) 565–2781
e-mail: webmaster@cns.gov
http://www.nationalservice.org

In September 1993, the Corporation for National Service and AmeriCorps came into being when President Clinton signed the National and Community Service Trust Act of 1993. At this time, the existing VISTA (Volunteers in Service to America) program begun in 1964, became part of AmeriCorps and was renamed AmeriCorps*VISTA. In the years preceding this legislation, Congress passed the National and Community Service Act of 1990, which authorized two kinds of grants: grants to schools to support service-learning (originally called "Serve America;" now called "Learn and Serve America"); and demonstration grants for national service programs. In 1989–90, the Office of National Service was created in the White House and the Points of Light Foundation was founded to encourage volunteering. In 1985, Youth Service America and the National Association of Service and Conservation Corps were created. Today, CNS has a national office in Washington, DC, and offices in 45 states. It oversees a number of major programs, including AmeriCorps, America Reads, Learn and Serve America, and Senior Corps. The Corporation for National Service has played a significant role in funding service and service-learning efforts across the country and in K-12 and higher education since its inception.

## International Partnership for Service-Learning

815 Second Avenue, Suite 3155
New York, NY 10017
(212) 986–0989
fax: (212) 986–5039
e-mail: pslny@aol.com
http://www.ipsl.org/

The International Partnership for Service-Learning, originally founded as the Partnership for Service-Learning in 1982, runs off-campus programs that link community service and academic study in a number of countries: The Czech Republic, Ecuador, England, France, India, Israel, Jamaica, Mexico, the Philippines, Scotland, and South Dakota in the U.S. The IPS-L also administers a one-year (British) Master's Degree Program in International Service, in cooperation with affiliated universities in Great Britain, Mexico, and Jamaica (see

Chapter 3). In addition, IPS-L promotes service and service-learning by publishing information and hosting annual international conferences. Their eighteenth International Conference took place in Ecuador in February 2000 (see Chapter 5). The organization is supported, in part, by funding from various foundations, including the Ford Foundation, the Johnson Foundation, and the Luce Foundation.

## The Invisible College
c/o Patricia E. O'Connor
Assoc. Prof. English, 312 New North
Georgetown University
Washington, DC 20057
(202) 687–7622
fax: (202) 687–5445
e-mail: invisiblec@gusun.georgetown.edu
http://www.selu.edu/orgs/ic/

The Invisible College grew out of several meetings in the early 1990s at the Highlander Research and Education Center in Tennessee and the Wingspread Conference Center in Wisconsin. The Invisible College, as it came to be known, started out as an organization of and for faculty in higher education who were committed to integrating learning and service within their work and communities. John Wallace notes that the name of the organization "is borrowed from Kenneth Boulding, who, at the time. . . was helping to start the International Peace Studies Association, [and] wrote of the need for 'the development and encouragement of an invisible college,' of people whose work is meaningful to each other and who need to be in communication" (http://www.selu.edu/Academics/ArtsSciences/IC/). The name also originated out of the founders' feeling invisible or marginal in their respective colleges and universities because of their nontraditional pedagogies and philosophies. At first, a small number of members were selected each year to join the organization. This approach later evolved into a more inclusive, growth-oriented, open membership policy. In addition, community partners were welcomed into the organization as "co-educators" and members. Today, the Invisible College includes "university faculty and staff, community partners, and students." It favors the "learning circle format"

(see "learning circles" in Chapter 1) as a means of communication and empowerment. Since May 1995, the Invisible College has held an annual "National Gathering on service-learning as a way to help enrich experiences in community service by hard questioning and deep reflection on all our roles in education."

## The Learn & Serve America National Service-Learning Clearinghouse
University of Minnesota
Department of Work, Community, and Family Education
1954 Burford Avenue, Room R-460
Saint Paul, MN 55108
(800) 808–7378
fax: (651) 625–6277
e-mail: serve@tc.umn.edu
http://www.nicsl.coled.umn.edu

The Learn & Serve America National Service-Learning Clearinghouse is a "comprehensive information system that focuses on all dimensions of service-learning, covering kindergarten through higher education school-based as well as community based initiatives." It is located at the University of Minnesota and is part of a "consortium of thirteen other institutions and organizations." The Clearinghouse is also an adjunct ERIC clearinghouse. Their Web site includes a number of searchable databases (on award grantees, events, programs, literature in their library, and their K-12 listserv), other resources, publications, and a links section. The clearinghouse is funded by The Corporation for National Service.

## The National Council of Teachers of English
1111 West Kenyon Road
Urbana, IL 61801–1096
(800) 369–6283
fax: (217) 328–9645
e-mail: public_info@ncte.org
http://www.ncte.org

The National Council of Teachers of English is "dedicated to improving the teaching and learning of English and the language arts at all levels of education." Founded in 1911, it has about 80,000 individual and institutional members worldwide. Its Web site hosts a "Service-

Learning in Composition'' Web site (http://www.ncte.org/service). See Chapter 2 for more information on this Web site.

### National Society for Experiential Education (NSEE)
1703 North Beauregard St., Suite 400
Alexandria, VA 22311–1714
(703) 933–0017
fax: (603) 250–5852
e-mail: info@nsee.org
http://www.nsee.org

Founded in 1971, the National Society for Experiential Education ''serves as a national resource center for the development and improvement of experiential education programs nationwide. NSEE supports the use of learning through experience for intellectual development, cross-cultural and global awareness, civic and social responsibility, ethical development, career exploration, [and] personal growth.'' While NSEE's mission involves the broader arena of experiential education, its Service-Learning SIG (special interest group) has grown significantly in recent years and service-learning is an important part of NSEE's agenda and conferences. NSEE has a resource center, publishes the *NSEE Quarterly* and a number of service-learning volumes, provides consulting and training, and holds an annual meeting (the one in 2000 is its 29ᵗʰ annual event).

### National Youth Leadership Council (NYLC)
1910 West County Road B
Saint Paul, MN 55113
(651) 631–3672
fax: (651) 631–2955
e-mail: nylcinfo@nylc.org
http://www.nylc.org

Founded in 1983, the National Youth Leadership Council's mission is ''to engage young people in their communities and schools through innovation in learning, service, leadership, and public policy.'' As an advocate of service-learning and youth service, NYLC develops innovative model programs in schools across America, creates curricula and training programs for educators and youth, advocates educational reform and progressive youth policy, conducts ongoing research in youth issues, and maintains networks in support of these measures. NYLC sponsors the annual National Service-Learning Conference.

### New England Resource Center for Higher Education (NERCHE)
University of Massachusetts Boston
Graduate College of Education
Boston, MA 02125–3393
(617) 287–7740
fax: (617) 287–7747
e-mail: narc@umb.edu
http://www.nerche.org

Founded in 1988, the New England Resource Center for Higher Education (NARC) is ''dedicated to improving colleges and universities as workplaces, communities, and organizations.'' NARC's programs focus on faculty roles and rewards, and obstacles to effective service and outreach. It also convenes ''think tanks'' that ''serve not only as a venue for exchanging information and resources, but also as a forum for translating theory into practice as members draw policy implications from their discussions.'' NARC publishes *Working Papers* on educational and workplace concerns and *The Academic Workplace*, a biannual newsletter. It also sponsors the Ernest A. Lynton Award for Faculty Professional Service and Academic Outreach.

### UK Centres for Experiential Learning
Anthony Evans, Director
136 Crackley Bank
Chesterton
Newcastle, STAFFS
ST5 7AA
44 (0) 1782 566179
fax: 44 (0) 1782 566008
e-mail: Ukcentres@BTINTERNET.COM
http://www.btinternet.com/~ukcentres

UK Centres administers three programs: International Community Service (for students not needing academic credit); Westminster College, Oxford Service-Learning (for those requiring integrated credited studies); and Internships. Upon arrival, students in the Westminster

College, Oxford Service-Learning Program spend one orientation week on campus and then are placed in a service agency (there is a wide range from which to choose). Students pursue a course of study that is "part of the total service-learning and cultural experience," participate in three courses ("British Institutions In Society," "Contemporary Britain In Historical Perspective," and "English Literature"), and develop a "Profile of an Agency" (a reflection exercise). Following orientation, students return to campus for three "study days" of one-to-one tutorials with faculty, in order to help them to integrate personal experience in the placement and culture into studies. Students receive 12 to 16 credits; a transcript is provided.

## Virginia Campus Outreach Opportunity League (VA COOL)

RC Box 26
28 Westhampton Way
University of Richmond, VA 23173
(804) 289–8963
fax: (804) 287–6584
e-mail: enorflee@richmond.edu
http://www.richmond.edu/~vacool/

The Virginia Campus Outreach Opportunity League's mission is "to positively affect communities, students and institutions by promoting and enhancing campus-based community service and service-learning initiatives at institutions of higher education across the state of Virginia." Begun in 1989 by students of the University of Richmond, VA COOL offers a variety of programs, including the Virginia Campus-Community Corps (NCCC), Student Mini-Grants and "SEAD" Grants, Faculty Fellows, a Faculty Development Mentorship Program, regional meetings, an Annual Statewide Conference on Service in Higher Education, an Annual Symposium on Integrating Service with the Curriculum, an Annual Think Tank, and the Ambassador Program (in which students serve on the Board of Directors and as representatives of the organization at speaking engagements, publicity campaigns, and training opportunities throughout the state).

## Western Region Campus Compact Consortium

Kevin Kecskes, Program Director
Western Washington University, MS-5291
Bellingham, WA 98225
(360) 650–7554
fax: (360) 650–6895
e-mail: kkecskes@cc.wwu.edu
http://www.ac.wwu.edu/~wrccc/

The Western Region Campus Compact Consortium is "a four state coalition of ninety-two college and university Presidents and Chancellors that seeks to increase campuswide participation in community and public service and to integrate service-learning as a valued component of higher education." The consortium includes the California, Hawaii, Oregon, and Washington state Campus Compacts, and is funded, in part, by the Corporation for National Service (Learn and Serve: Higher Education.). The consortium provides annual mini-grants (renewable for up to three years) to 43 higher education institutions in its region. Since 1998, it has sponsored the annual Continuums of Service Conference.

## Service Organizations, Associations, and Networks

This section includes contact information for—and brief descriptions of—centers, agencies, organizations, and networks that use, promote, or oversee service, volunteer, and internship placements for students (and sometimes for others, too). It is important to note, that there are literally tens of thousands of nonprofit organizations, NGOs, and INGOs (non-governmental organizations and international non-governmental organizations, respectively), foundations, and networks, all of which might reasonably be included here because they use and need volunteers or interns for their own work; promote service, volunteering, or internships as part of their work; or assist in the placement of volunteers or interns in communities or organizations in the U.S. or around the world. Information about this large constellation of organizations can be found in many other places: it is not the purpose of this source book to explore or replicate this immense domain. As a result, many organizations (e.g., the Peace Corps and Peace Brigades International) are not included here. The listings below include two basic kinds of entries: (1) a representative sample of some of the most important organizations that need volunteers or interns in their humanitarian efforts, and (2) the best organizations or database services that promote and/or place volunteers and interns. Both kinds of entries typify sources that service-learning offices on college and university campuses might reasonably use (beyond local community agencies) in their efforts to place service-learning students. Some lesser-known organizations are included to provide some sense of the diversity that exists in this arena. The healthy number of organizations with international service opportunities, as listed below, is representative of the large universe of international offerings, and it reflects the author's desire to encourage service-learning programs in the U.S. to consider the benefits of international and intercultural service experiences for all involved.

*For those with little time who are interested in volunteering or service opportunities in the U.S. or abroad, see the entry (under "Organizations with National and International Service Opportunities") for: **Action Without Borders/Idealist**. It is by far the most comprehensive site on the Web, with listings of 20,000 community and nonprofit organizations in 140 countries.*

## Organizations with Local or Statewide Service Opportunities

### Boulder County LINC

Boulder Community Network
3645 Marine Street
Campus Box 455
Boulder, CO 80309–0455
(303) 492–8176
e-mail: Troy Kilen at
  kilen@bcn.boulder.co.us
http://bcn.boulder.co.us/human-social/linc.
  html

LINC (Local INformation Connection) is Boulder County's online database for human service programs in public agencies and nonprofit organizations. It is hosted by the Boulder Community Network (http://bcn.boulder.co.us) and is listed under Human Services Center. Each agency in the database is responsible for keeping their information current. In February 2000, there were 207 listings covering everything from AARP to the Boulder Country Safehouse to the YWCA. Online users can search by program or keyword. The entire list of programs is also available for browsing.

### Campus Compact: The Project for Public and Community Service

PO Box 1975
Brown University
Providence, RI 02912
(401) 863–1119
fax: (401) 863–3779
e-mail: campus@compact.org
http://www.compact.org

Given that Campus Compact's primary purpose is "to support campus-based public and community service" in higher education, it might not seem a logical first place to look for statewide details on service. However, it has 21 state compacts (and six more "developing" state compacts), all of which are useful contacts for specific, statewide information service alliances, organizations, and networks in their respective states. Compact's national Web site includes contact information (including Web addresses when available) for each of its state offices.

### Global Exchange

2017 Mission Street #303
San Francisco, CA 94110
(415) 255–7296
fax: (415) 255–7498
e-mail: info@globalexchange.org
http://www.globalexchange.org

Volunteering at Global Exchange is representative of the many opportunities students and youth have to serve locally while helping globally. Global Exchange, founded in 1988, is a nonprofit "education, research and action center aimed at forging closer ties between U.S. Citizens and citizens of developing countries who are working for greater social justice."

Although the interns themselves don't gain volunteer experience overseas, they do work on national and international programs while residing in the San Francisco area. Interns can also earn academic credit. Global Exchange programs include "study tours to developing countries, retail stores that promote alternative trade, educational resources development, media outreach, and human and labor rights campaigns."

**Human Service Alliance**
3983 Old Greensboro Road
Winston-Salem, NC 27101
(336) 761–8745; (877) joy 2 giv
fax: (336) 722–7882
e-mail: inquiry@hsa.org
http://www.hsa.org

Human Service Alliance is an all-volunteer organization that offers free "round-the-clock hands-on care for the terminally ill, care for developmentally disabled children, and support/therapy for persons with chronic pain or illness." The HSA Volunteer Program involves full-time, live-in care (volunteers receive meals and lodging on the HSA campus at no charge) and is devoted primarily to HSA's "Care for the Terminally Ill Project."

**Youth Service California (YSCal)**
754 Sir Francis Drake, Suite 8
San Anselmo, CA 94960
(415) 257–3500
fax: (415) 257–5838
e-mail: info@yscal.org
http://www.yscal.org

"Founded in 1990, Youth Service California (YSCal) is a nonprofit, statewide organization that promotes youth service and provides information and assistance to local programs across the State."

**Organizations with National Service Opportunities**

**Alpha Phi Omega National Service Fraternity**
14901 E. 42nd Street
Independence, MO 64055
(816) 373–8667

fax: (816) 373–5975
e-mail: executive.director@apo.org
http://www.apo.org

Alpha Phi Omega of the United States of America is a national service fraternity for college students that seeks to "develop effective leadership skills," "promote fellowship among all people," "provide service to humanity," and "further our acknowledged freedoms"—and to do so, "in the fellowship of principles derived from the Scout Oath and Law of the Boy Scouts of America." It has approximately 350 active chapters.

**Do Something**
423 West 55th Street, 8th Floor
New York, NY 10019
(212) 523–1175
fax: (212) 582–1307
e-mail: mail@dosomething.org
http://www.dosomething.org

Do Something seeks to inspire "young people to believe that change is possible, and trains, funds and mobilizes them to be leaders who measurably strengthen their communities." Do Something sponsors an ongoing national media campaign, an interactive, educational Web site, a BRICK Award for Community Leadership, a Kindness and Justice Challenge (a school-based character education and service learning program that encourages students to perform acts of kindness and to stand up for what is right), a Do Something League (a national leadership program), and a Community Connections Campaign.

**Independent Sector**
1200 Eighteenth Street, Suite 200
Washington, DC 20036
(202) 467–6100
fax: (202) 467–6101
e-mail: info@IndependentSector.org
http://www.indepsec.org

Independent Sector is a "national leadership forum," working to strengthen the nonprofit sector and "encourage philanthropy, volunteering, not-for-profit initiatives and citizen action that help us better serve people and communities." Begun in 1980, it seeks to "promote increased giving and volunteering, active citizenship and community service."

## The Points of Light Foundation

1400 I Street, NW, Suite 800
Washington, DC 20005
(202) 729–8000
fax: (202) 729–8100
e-mail: volnet@pointsoflight.org
http://www.pointsoflight.org

Founded in 1990, the Points of Light Foundation's mission is to "engage more people more effectively in volunteer community service to help solve serious social problems." It has a network of over 500 volunteer centers throughout the U.S.

## The Washington Center for Internships and Academic Seminars

2000 M Street, NW, Suite 750
Washington, DC 20036–3307
(800) 486–8921
fax: (202) 336–7609
e-mail: info@twc.edu
http://www.twc.edu

The Washington Center supports experiential education by providing "internship programs and academic seminars to college students from across the country and around the world." The internship placements are in "major professional fields in the private, public and nonprofit sector" in the Washington, DC area.

## YMCA of the USA

101 North Wacker Drive
Chicago, IL 60606
(312) 977–0031
fax: (312) 977–9063
http://www.ymca.net

The YMCA of the USA's mission is "to build strong kids, strong families and strong communities" by engaging in service in local communities. It is part of the World Alliance of YMCAs, "a nonbinding organization of independent YMCA movements from more than 100 countries," with headquarters in Geneva, Switzerland.

## Organizations with National and International Service Opportunities

### Action Without Borders/Idealist

350 Fifth Avenue, Suite 6614
New York, NY 10118
(212) 843–3973
fax: (212) 564–3377
e-mail: info@idealist.org
http://www.idealist.org

Formerly known as the Contact Center Network, Action Without Borders set out in 1995 to "build a network of neighborhood Contact Centers that would provide a one-stop shop for volunteer opportunities and nonprofit services in communities around the world." What it ended up with was a project called Idealist, a virtual "community of nonprofit and volunteering resources," which also provides a Web presence to those without Web sites. Idealist includes information on 20,000 organizations in 140 countries, which can be searched or browsed by name, location, or mission. Moreover, it has a significant list of organizations that promote global volunteering (i.e., beyond the huge list of organizations where volunteers are placed). It also has job and internship listings in its Nonprofit Career Center; "a directory of companies and consultants that provide products and services to nonprofit organizations; links to the most useful resources. . . on the Web for managing and funding a nonprofit organization; a collection of the most informative and frequently updated Nonprofit News Sites on the Web; and a global directory of Public Internet Access Points in hundreds of schools, libraries, community centers and Internet cafes."

(See Chapter 2: "Online Resources.")

### AFS Intercultural Programs, Inc.

AFS International
71 West 23rd Street, 17th Floor
New York, NY 10010
(212) 807–8686
fax: (212) 807–1001
e-mail: info@afs.org
http://www.afs.org

AFS Intercultural Programs, Inc. was formed in 1947 "to facilitate student and teacher exchanges.'' The organization follows the model begun by its predecessor, the American Field Service ambulance corps, during World Wars I and II. In one AFS program, students (aged 15 to 18) ''live with a family in a community abroad and attend school for a year or semester.'' In another program, young adults (18 and over) ''work in community service organizations or businesses in countries abroad while learning new skills, the language and culture.'' In a third AFS program, teachers ''live with a host family in another country and teach in the local school system.'' As part of the network, host families all over the world provide homes for AFS students.

## American Friends Service Committee (AFSC)

1501 Cherry Street
Philadelphia, PA 19102
(215) 241–7000
fax: (215) 241–7275
e-mail: afscinfo@afsc.org
http://www.afsc.org

''The American Friends Service Committee (AFSC) is a Quaker organization that includes people of various faiths who are committed to social justice, peace, and humanitarian service. Its work is based on the Religious Society of Friends (Quaker) belief in the worth of every person, and faith in the power of love to overcome violence and injustice. . . .Founded in 1917 to provide conscientious objectors with an opportunity to aid civilian victims during World War I, today the AFSC has programs that focus on issues related to economic justice, peace-building and demilitarization, social justice, and youth, in the United States, and in Africa, Asia, Latin America, and the Middle East.'' AFSC's Web site lists over 130 programs, from the Africa Program to the Youth Action Program, located all over the U.S. and around the world. In addition, it has a Web site for volunteer opportunities ( that includes Summer Volunteer Projects in Mexico, Internships in Mexico City, service opportunities with AFSC's Rising Stars Theatre Troupe in Baltimore, MD, for 20 high school students, Summer Youth Leadership Training Programs. In addition, the Quaker Information Center ''offers 16 different lists/categories of volunteer and service opportunities, including workcamps, internships, other potentially transformational experiences, and some perennial jobs—Quaker and non-Quaker; short, medium, and long-term; domestic and international.''

## The American Red Cross

Attn: Public Inquiry Office
11th Floor
1621 N. Kent Street
Arlington, VA 22209
(703) 248–4222; (800)-HELP-NOW
e-mail: info@usa.redcross.org
http://www.crossnet.org

Founded in 1881, the American Red Cross helps victims of disasters and emergencies. It is essentially an all-volunteer, humanitarian organization, with some 1.3 million volunteers. Interested volunteers are invited to sign-up online or contact their local Red Cross (which can be found on their Web site). The American Red Cross is the U.S. member of the International Red Cross and Red Crescent Movement.

## Amizade, Ltd.

7612 N. Rogers, 3rd Floor
Chicago, IL 60626
(773) 973–3719
fax: (773) 973–3731
e-mail: Volunteer@amizade.org
http://www.amizade.org

Amizade is a nonprofit organization that promotes and encourages volunteerism, community service, collaboration, and cultural awareness. It ''collaborates with existing community-based organizations to develop projects which are both beneficial to the community and enjoyable to the volunteers.'' Amizade offers Volunteer Programs in Korrawinga Aboriginal Community, Queensland, Australia; Cochabamba, Bolivia (in the Andes Mountains); Santarém, Brazil (on the Amazon River); the Greater Yellowstone Region, Montana; and the Navajo Nation, Arizona. It also puts together customized ''Alternative Break'' service-learning programs in these areas for groups of six or more.

**Amnesty International**
(International Secretariat)
1 Easton Street
London
WC1X 8DJ
UK
(44) (171) 413 5500
fax: (44) (171) 956 1157
e-mail: amnestyis@amnesty.org
http://www.amnesty.org
(US Offices in NY and Washington, DC)
322 8th Ave.
New York, NY 10001
(212) 807–8400
fax: (212) 463–9193/627–1451
e-mail: admin-us@aiusa.org
http://www.amnesty-usa.org
600 Pennsylvania Ave, SE, 5th Floor
Washington DC 20003
(202) 544–0200
fax: (202) 546–7142
e-mail: admin-us@aiusa.org
http://www.amnesty-usa.org

Amnesty International is "a worldwide campaigning movement that works to promote all the human rights enshrined in the Universal Declaration of Human Rights and other international standards. In particular, Amnesty International campaigns to free all prisoners of conscience; ensure fair and prompt trials for political prisoners; abolish the death penalty, torture and other cruel treatment of prisoners; end political killings and 'disappearances'; and oppose human rights abuses by opposition groups." Begun in 1961, the organization "was founded on the principle that people have fundamental rights that transcend national, cultural, religious, and ideological boundaries." Volunteers maintain much of the organization's campaigns in 162 countries. There is also Amnesty International Volunteers (aiadmin@amnestvolunteer.org; http://www. amnesty-volunteer.org), which is actually an "Online Archive of Resources for Amnesty Volunteers."

**Catholic Network of Volunteer Service**
4121 Harewood Road, NE
Washington, DC 20017–1593
(202) 529–1100; 800–543–5046

fax: (202) 526–1094
email: cnvs@ari.net; tta@cnvs.org
http://www.paulist.org/cnvs/

Originally begun in 1963 as the International Liaison of Lay Volunteers in Mission, Catholic Network of Volunteer Service is a "nonprofit organization representing over 180 domestic and international volunteer programs." CNVS publishes a directory of volunteer programs (*RESPONSE*), and provides "technical assistance resources for volunteer programs, formation workshops, the administration of AmeriCorps Education Awards and the offering of training to AmeriCorps programs, networking of volunteer organizations, and recruitment of volunteers through a toll-free number, volunteer fairs, their web site, and the annual CNVS National Conference."

**Council on International Educational Exchange (CIEE)**
205 East 42nd Street
New York, NY 10017–5706
(212) 822–2600; (800) 40-STUDY
fax: 212–822-2779
e-mail: info@councilexchanges.org
http://www.ciee.org

Begun in 1947, the Council on International Educational Exchange helps young people study, work, and travel abroad. CIEE is now divided into three operations: Council-International Study Programs, Council Exchanges, and Council Travel. Those interested in service-learning may find some opportunities in Council-International Study Programs. Council Travel also includes International Volunteer Projects, which offer "short-term, team oriented projects overseas." Participants "join a group of 10–20 other volunteers from different countries, [and] spend 2–4 weeks working. . . [and] living. . . together while helping a community." There are more than 600 projects in over 30 countries in Africa, Europe, Latin America, Asia, and North America.

**EarthWatch Institute**
3 Clocktower Place, Suite 100
Box 75
Maynard, MA 01754
(978) 461–0081

fax: (978) 461–2332
info@earthwatch.org
http://www.earthwatch.org

Earthwatch Institute is an international non-profit organization, founded in Boston in 1971. Its mission is ''to promote sustainable conservation of our natural resources and cultural heritage by creating partnerships between scientists, educators and the general public.'' Accordingly, Earthwatch ''puts people in the field where they can assist scientists in their field work.'' The purpose of the Earthwatch Volunteer Program is to coordinate the placement of volunteers with scientific research teams all over the world.

**Global Citizens Network**
130 N. Howell Street
Saint Paul, MN 55104
(800) 644–9292; (651) 644–0960
e-mail: gcn@mtn.org
http://www.globalcitizens.org

Global Citizens Network ''sends small teams of volunteers to rural communities around the world to immerse themselves in the daily life of the local culture for several weeks. The teams work on community projects initiated by the local people, such as planting trees, digging irrigation trenches, setting up a schoolroom or teaching commercial skills.'' Projects are located in Belize, Bolivia, Guatemala, Kenya, New Mexico, St. Vincent, and Yucatan.

**Habitat for Humanity International**
121 Habitat Street
Americus, GA 31709
(912) 924–6935, ext. 2551 or 2552
e-mail: public_info@habitat.org
http://www.habitat.org

Founded in 1976, Habitat for Humanity International is a nonprofit, ecumenical Christian housing ministry that ''seeks to eliminate poverty housing from the world and to make decent shelter a matter of conscience and action.'' It addresses the issues of poverty housing by building and rehabilitating houses with—and for—families in need. Habitat's visibility grew substantially in 1984, when Jimmy and Rosalynn Carter joined a Habitat work trip. Habitat has a Campus Chapters Program (with over 500 campus chapters), a Youth Program (for youth ages 5 and up), and a Collegiate Challenge Break Trip Program. In 1994, Habitat for Humanity International became a partner in the AmeriCorps National Service Program. This partnership allows AmeriCorps members to work for Habitat for an 11-month term and receive the benefits available to all those serving in AmeriCorps. Contact information for Habitat*AmeriCorps: Habitat*AmeriCorps, 121 Habitat Street, Americus, GA 31709, (800) 422–4828, ext. 2293, e-mail: HAC@habitat.org.

**Higher Education Consortium for Urban Affairs (HECUA)**
Mail #36 at Hamline University
1536 Hewitt Avenue
St. Paul, MN 55104–1284
(651) 646–8831; (800) 554–1089
fax: (651) 659–9421
e-mail: info@hecua.org
http://www.hecua.org

Founded in 1971, HECUA is a consortium of 15 Midwest colleges and universities that offers ''out-of-classroom educational experiences in urban affairs and social justice issues. With programs in the U.S. and abroad, HECUA examines the systems that create inequality and the ways that social change is made.'' ''All programs include internships or structured field projects as a way to connect theoretical studies with current realities. Scholarships are available.''

**Impact Online, Inc.**
325 'B' Forest Avenue
Palo Alto, CA 94301
(650) 327–1389
fax: (650) 327–1395
e-mail: respond@impactonline.org
http://www.impactonline.org

Impact Online, founded in 1994, is a nonprofit organization that assists volunteerism through the Internet. Visitors to their Web site will find ''VolunteerMatch, a matching service for volunteers and nonprofits; Virtual Volunteering, a research project on volunteer activities which can be completed over the Internet; and information and resources on volunteerism. (See ''Online Resources'' in Chapter 2.)

**International Volunteer Expeditions
(IVEX)**
2001 Vallejo Way
Sacramento, CA 95818
(916) 444–6856
e-mail: ivex@email.com
http://www.espwa.org/ivex.html

International Volunteer Expeditions (IVEX)
is a nonprofit corporation which provides service experiences that support "organizations
and agencies working towards sustainable development." Volunteer placements range from
short- to medium-term, and are located in Africa;
Antigua, West Indies; Bangladesh; Cambodia;
Commonwealth of Dominica, West Indies; Hun-
gary; Indonesia; Italy; Japan; Latvia; Mexico;
Phillippines; South Korea; Thailand; Turkey
(earthquake relief); and the United States.

**International Volunteer Programs
Association (IVPA)**
LaFetra Operating Foundation
1221 Preservation Park Way #100
Oakland, CA 94612
(510) 763–9206
fax: (510) 763–9290
e-mail: Info@lafetra.org
http://www.lafetra.org/ivpa.htm

This new association is an "alliance of nonprofit, non-governmental organizations based
in the Americas, that are involved in international
volunteer and internship exchanges." IVPA
works to promote "excellence and responsibility in the field . . . and . . . public awareness of
and greater access to international volunteer
programs." It sponsors a national conference
and "expo" on international volunteer opportunities, working groups, roundtable meetings,
professional-development workshops, a listserv,
and its Web site, which includes a planned
searchable database on international volunteer
and internship opportunities

**JustAct: Youth Action for Global Justice**
333 Valencia Street, Suite 101
San Francisco, CA 94103
(415) 431–4204
fax: (415) 431–5953
e-mail: info@justact.org
http://www.justact.org

JustAct is the new name for the Overseas
Development Network (ODN), which was
founded by students in 1983. JustAct promotes
youth leadership and action for global justice
through its four major programs (education,
alternative opportunities, bike aid, and partnerships). The Education Program involves "a
network of chapters and student activists across
the country who are bringing development education and action to their respective campuses."
As part of this program, JustAct convenes
regional and international conferences. It also
produces numerous publications and sponsors
national speaking tours. The Alternative Opportunities Program is a volunteer and internship
clearinghouse for placements in Appalachia,
Bangladesh, Belize, Bolivia, Chile, Guatemala,
India, Jerusalem, Mexico, the Philippines, and
Zimbabwe. The "clearinghouse service refers
individuals to private voluntary organizations
in the U.S. which send volunteers overseas, or
helps individuals build their own volunteer
positions by referring them directly to community-based organizations seeking volunteers."
JustAct also has a Summer Internship Program
in San Francisco.

**Oxfam America**
26 West Street
Boston, MA 02111
(800) 77-OXFAM
fax: (617) 728–2594
e-mail: info@oxfamamerica.org
http://www.oxfamamerica.org

Oxfam America is a privately funded organization that works to create "lasting solutions to
hunger, poverty and social injustice through
long-term partnerships with poor communities
around the world." Started in 1970, Oxfam
America disburses "program funding and technical support to hundreds of partner organizations in Africa, Asia, the Caribbean and the
Americas, including the United States."

**Peacework: Programs in International
Volunteer Service and Exchange**
305 Washington Street, SW
Blacksburg, VA 24060–4745
(540) 953–1376
fax: (540) 552–0119

e-mail: sdarr@compuserve.com
http://www.peacework.org

Peacework offers ''short-term volunteer opportunities in international development for
people around the world and to bridge cultural
and political divisions through one-on-one interactions.'' Peacework's first project was in
Nicaragua in 1989: it ''brought together representatives of two former adversaries—volunteers from the former Soviet Union and the
United States. Together they worked to build
houses for refugees from active Contra war
zones in the highlands.'' Projects are from one
to four weeks long and take place in Mexico,
Belize, Costa Rica, Cuba, the Dominican Republic, El Salvador, Honduras, Nicaragua, Russia,
the Ukraine, the U.S., and Vietnam. Volunteers' ages range from 16 to 76 years old; the
average volunteer is college-aged or a graduate
student.

### School for International Training

Kipling Road
P.O. Box 676
Brattleboro, VT 05302–0676
(802) 257–7751
fax: (802) 258–3248
e-mail: info@sit.edu
http://www.sit.edu

Initially known as the U.S. Experiment in
International Living, The School for International Training (SIT) ''began sending students
abroad for international learning experiences in
1932.'' SIT ''offers master's degrees, study
abroad, extension courses, educational system
reform initiatives, management development
and peace and conflict resolution training.''
One SIT master's degree is in ''International
and Intercultural Service.'' Their study abroad
and international exchange programs offer the
possibility of internships and community service.

### Youth Service America (YSA)

1101 15th Street, NW, Suite 200
Washington, DC 20005
(202) 296–2992
fax: (202) 296–4030
e-mail: feedback@ysa.org
http://www.ysa.org

Youth Service America is a resource center
and alliance of over 200 organizations working
to increase ''the quantity and quality of opportunities for young Americans to serve locally,
nationally, or globally.'' One of YSA's programs is SERVEnet (http://www.servenet.org), a
Web site that brings ''volunteers and community organizations together online'' (see Chapter 2: ''Online Resources'').

## Organizations with International Service Opportunities

### Accord Cultural Exchange

750 La Playa
San Francisco, CA 94121
(415) 386–6203
fax: (415) 386–0240
e-mail: leftbank@hotmail.com
http://www.cognitext.com/accord

ACCORD sends American college students
to work and study in Europe: as au pairs, as
''guest teachers'' in Spain, or as Interns with a
company in London (work areas include marketing, engineering, communications, computer
technology, finance, environmental studies, and
others).

### Alliances Abroad

409 Deep Eddy Ave.
Austin, TX 78703
(888) 622–7623; (512) 457–8062
e-mail: nrossi@alliancesabroad.com
http://www.alliancesabroad.com

Alliances Abroad offers volunteer and internship programs, au pair opportunities, language tutor programs, and homestay programs.
Their volunteer programs are in Australia, Costa
Rica, Ecuador, Ghana, Mexico, and Senegal.
Volunteers are matched with projects and live
with local families. Volunteers may take language courses as part of the program. Volunteers in Ghana may take summer classes at the
University of Ghana. Allicances Abroad also
offers paid and unpaid international internships
in a number of countries. Like Amerispan,
Alliances Abroad encourages students wanting
academic credit for their volunteering or internships to check with their academic advisors in
advance.

**The American Refugee Committee**
ARC International Headquarters USA
2344 Nicollet Avenue, South, Suite 350
Minneapolis, Minnesota 55404
(612) 872–7060
fax: (612) 872–4309
e-mail: pr@archq.org
http://www.archq.org

Founded in 1978, the American Refugee Committee (ARC) works on behalf of "refugees, displaced persons, and those at risk, and seeks to enable them to rebuild productive lives of dignity and purpose, striving always to respect the values of those served. ARC is an international nonprofit, non-sectarian organization." The primary beneficiaries are "women and children in Bosnia and Croatia, Thailand and Cambodia, Honduras, Guinea, Kenya, Liberia, Rwanda, and Sudan." Unpaid internships in the Minneapolis office and short-term overseas positions "may be available depending on qualifications." There also may be employment opportunities overseas (most positions require a one-year commitment).

**Amerispan Unlimited**
PO Box 40007
Philadelphia, PA 19106–0007
(800) 879–6640; (215) 751–1100
fax: (215) 751–1986
e-mail: info@amerispan.com
http://www.amerispan.com
AmeriSpan Guatemala
6a Avenida Norte, #40
Antigua, Guatemala
(502) 832–0164/4846
fax: (502) 832–1896
e-mail: amerispan@guate.net
http://www.amerispan.com/guatemala

AmeriSpan offers Spanish immersion, volunteer/intern, and educational travel programs throughout Mexico, the Caribbean, Central America, South America and Spain. Volunteer/intern placements last from two weeks to six months depending on the placement. There is also a mandatory four week language/culture component before the work placement. Students wanting academic credit for their intern-

ships or volunteering are advised to check with their academic advisors in advance.

**Amigos de las Américas**
International Office
5618 Star Lane
Houston, TX 77057
(800) 231–7796; (713) 782–5290
fax: (713) 782–9267
e-mail: info@amigoslink.org
http://www.amigoslink.org

Amigos de las Américas prepares U.S. high school and college students in leadership and language training programs prior to placing them as volunteers in "ongoing community health projects throughout Latin America" for a summer. The projects are in Brazil, Bolivia, Costa Rica, the Dominican Republic, Ecuador, Honduras, Mexico, and Paraguay.

**Centro de Estudios Interamericanos (CEDEI)**
**(Centers for Interamerican Studies)**
PO Box 668
Peoria, AZ 85380–0668
(888) 522–6486
fax: (888) 522–6486
e-mail: info@cedei.org
http://www.cedei.org
Centro de Estudios Interamericanos
Gran Colombia 11–02 & General Torres
Casilla 597
Cuenca, Ecuador
(593–7) 839–003
fax: (593–7) 833–593
interpro@cedei.org
http://www.cedei.org

CEDEI is a nonprofit "institution of higher learning, dedicated to the study of American languages and cultures" and founded in 1992. In addition to English and Spanish programs, it also offers service-learning and internship programs. In both programs, students work as volunteers for community-based organizations in and around the city of Cuenca, Ecuador. In the Service Learning Program, students combine service and learning "in ways that are appropriate to both the local region and students." The service is integrated into CEDEI courses "through discussions, written essays and shared reflection. Typically, a three-credit Service Learning experience will comprise 30 hours of service in a community-based organization and 24 hours of class meetings.''

## Cross Cultural Solutions

47 Potter Avenue
New Rochelle, NY 10801
(800) 380–4777; (914) 632–0022
fax: (914) 632–8494
e-mail: info@crossculturalsolutions.org
http://www.crossculturalsolutions.org

Cross-Cultural Solutions is a nonprofit organization ''that employs humanitarian volunteer action to empower local communities, foster cultural sensitivity and understanding, and further social progress in India, Ghana, and Peru and through the women's cultural tour of India.'' Volunteers work in small groups of two three people for three weeks.

## Global Service Corps

300 Broadway #28
San Francisco, CA 94133–3312
(415) 788–3666, ext. 128
fax: (415) 788–7324
e-mail: gsc@igc.org
http://www.globalservicecorps.org

Global Service Corps provides ''cross-cultural learning and community service adventures for adults in Costa Rica, Kenya and Thailand. Short-term (two to four weeks), long-term (two to six months), and student internship programs are available.'' Their programs target three primary project areas: Environment, Health, and Education.

## Global Volunteers

375 E. Little Canada Road
St. Paul, MN 55117–1627
(800) 487–1074; (651) 407–6100
fax: (651) 482–0915
email@globalvolunteers.org
http://www.globalvolnteers.org

The goal of Global Volunteers is to help ''establish a foundation for peace through mutual international understanding.'' It does so by coordinating ''teams of volunteers who participate on short-term human and economic development projects worldwide in Africa, Asia, the Caribbean, Europe, Latin America, and the Pacific.'' Global Volunteers was founded in 1984.

## Middle East Children's Alliance (MECA)

905 Parker Street
Berkeley, California 94710
(510) 548–0542
fax: (510) 548–0543
e-mail: meca@peacenet.org
http://www.mecaforpeace.org

The Middle East Children's Alliance works ''for peace and justice in the Middle East; focusing on Palestine, Israel, Lebanon and Iraq.'' MECA's approach emphasizes ''the need to educate North Americans about the Middle East and U.S. foreign policy, and to support projects that aid and empower communities.'' It believes ''in insuring the human rights of all people in the region, especially focusing on the rights of children.'' MECA's programs include a Playgrounds for Peace project, and Volunteers for Peace in Palestine: a ''volunteer opportunity clearinghouse and placement service program for people interested in living and working in the West Bank.'' Volunteers for Peace in Palestine places North Americans who want to ''work for peace and human rights groups in Jerusalem and the West Bank.''

## The Odyssey: World Trek for Service and Education

650 Townsend Street, Suite 375
San Francisco, CA 94103
(415) 659–3178
fax: (415) 659–3201
e-mail: worldtrek@hotmail.com
http://www.worldtrek.org

The Odyssey is quite different from all of the other entries in this section of the book: its ''World Trek'' team members engage in service as part of their two-year trek around the world. The trek and the service are shared with students in hundreds of classrooms, thereby educating students about local organizations, NGOs and INGOs, and the issues they confront. (See ''Online Resources'' in Chapter 2 for a more detailed entry.)

**People to People International**
501 E. Armour Blvd.
Kansas City, MO 64109
(816) 531–4701
fax: (816) 531–7502
e-mail: ptpi@ptpi.org
http://www.ptpi.org

People to People International (PTPI) is a "cultural and educational exchange organization founded [in 1956] by former U.S. President Dwight D. Eisenhower to provide opportunities for private citizens to promote international understanding through direct people-to-people contacts." PTPI has two goals: "enhancing tolerance and understanding among all peoples and supporting youth development and the needs of youth." Their Collegiate and Professional Studies Program offers internships (which give "upper level undergraduate and graduate students an opportunity to participate in two-months, full-time, unpaid work assignments") and traveling seminars. Academic credit is offered for both.

**Service Civil International (SCI)**
International Secretariat
St-Jacobsmarkt 82
B-2000 Antwerpen, Belgium
(32–3) 2265727
fax: (32–3) 2320344
e-mail: sciint@xs4all.be
http://www.ines.org/sci

Service Civil International (SCI), founded in 1920, is a voluntary service organization with 33 branches and groups worldwide. SCI's goals are "to promote peace, international understanding and solidarity, social justice, sustainable development, and respect for the environment." It works toward these goals by sponsoring international workcamps in Europe, Asia, and Africa. The workcamps involve "short term projects" (usually two to three weeks) and are open to anyone over 18 years of age.

**Studyabroad.com**
1450 Edgmont Ave., Suite 140
Chester, PA 19013
(610) 499–9200
fax: (610) 499–9205

e-mail: webmaster@studyabroad.com
http://www.studyabroad.com

Studyabroad.com is a comprehensive "online study abroad information resource." It includes listings for a very large number of study-abroad programs in over 100 countries (see "Online Resources" in Chapter 2).

**VFP International Workcamps**
1034 Tiffany Rd.
Belmont, VT 05730–0202
(802) 259–2759
fax: (802) 259–2922
e-mail: vfp@vfp.org
http://www.vfp.org

VFP programs "foster international education, voluntary service and friendship" by coordinating international workcamps. VFP was founded as a nonprofit organization in Vermont in 1982. The average age of VFP workcampers is 21–25, but anyone 18 or older is welcome to join a workcamp, which usually lasts 2–3 weeks.

**Vision Resource Centre**
International Leadership Program
director@visionresource.org
http://www.visionresource.org

The Vision Resource Centre is a new nonprofit organization that hosted its first annual "International Leadership Program: Leadership and the Community" June 19–July 21, 2000, in Prague, Czech Republic. The five-week, summer study-abroad program is designed for undergraduate students from around the world who wish to study leadership and participate in community service and cultural activities. Academic credit is earned at the University of Economics, Prague. Available courses include "Philosophies of Leadership," "Comparative Government of East and Central Europe," "Central European Managerial Systems," "Environmental Economics and Policy ," and "Elementary Czech." All courses are taught in English and are worth three semester credits each. The community-service activities in the program, "performed in conjunction with local nonprofits," do not appear to be integrated into the coursework. The Vision Resource Centre does not include a phone or fax number, or a postal address in its communications and can only be found via Web and e-mail.

**WorldTeach**
c/o Center for International Development
Harvard University
79 JFK Street
Cambridge MA 02138
(617) 495–5527; (800) 483–2240
fax: (617) 495–1599

e-mail: info@worldteach.org
http://www.worldteach.org

Established by a group of Harvard students in 1986, WorldTeach ''provides opportunities for individuals to make a meaningful contribution to international education by living and working as volunteer teachers in developing countries.'' WorldTeach is a nonprofit organization located at the Center for International Development at Harvard University.

# 5
# Conferences, Colloquia, Institutes, and Academies

The events below represent the main offerings in service-learning. All of them are annual meetings, unless otherwise noted. The few that are not annual are included here to illustrate the diversity of constituencies and thematic interests in service-learning and related areas. Themes of recent conferences, and, whenever possible, themes, dates, and locations of conferences in 2001 are provided in the conference abstracts.

At one time, the main conferences were markedly different from one another, primarily because there were fewer to choose from and they catered to different (or at best, overlapping) constituencies. In recent years, however, the number of service-learning conferences has grown significantly, and today it seems less easy to differentiate among them. A fair number are marketed as *the* national service-learning or community-service conference of the year. Each conference remains unique in its theme, of course, but many appear to seek similar outcomes, promise similar offerings, and are open to all comers: faculty, staff, students, community partners, funders, and interested agencies.

## Conferences and Colloquia

### AAHE Assessment Conference
American Association for Higher Education (AAHE)
One Dupont Circle, NW, Suite 360
Washington, DC 20036
(202) 293–6440
fax: (202) 293–0073
e-mail: info@aahe.org
http://www.aahe.org

Just as AAHE's focus is higher education in general, this conference on assessment is not limited to assessing service-learning, but service-learning is one of the foci. The conference explores assessment and its role in helping higher education institutions meet the demands they face. It is about assessment theory and methods, and assessing learning and pedagogies, including learning communities, collaborative learning, service-learning, and "technology-supported and distributed learning." Themes of past conferences include "Assessment as Evidence of Learning: Serving Student and Society" (June 1999); and "Rising Expectations For Assessment" (June 2000). The 2001 conference was held on June 22–25, 2001 at Adam's Mark Denver Hotel, CO.

### AAHE Conference on Faculty Roles and Rewards
American Association for Higher Education (AAHE)
One Dupont Circle, NW, Suite 360
Washington, DC 20036
(202) 293–6440
fax: (202) 293–0073
e-mail: info@aahe.org
http://www.aahe.org

This conference attracts those in higher education interested in the ways faculty are rewarded, one way or another, in their work. While not restricted to service-learning, service-learning is one set of pedagogies that comes into play here. For example, service-learning faculty are interested in how innovation, scholarship, teaching, and research in service-learning can be counted—or counted more—in faculty reviews, promotions, tenure decisions, etc.

The theme of the February 2000 conference was "Scholarship Reconsidered: Update and New Directions." The ninth annual conference was held on February 1–4, 2001 at Tampa Waterside Marriott, FL.

## AAHE National Conference on Higher Education

American Association for Higher Education (AAHE)
One Dupont Circle, NW, Suite 360
Washington, DC 20036–1110
(202) 293–6440, ext 793
fax: (202) 293–0073
e-mail: info@aahe.org
http://www.aahe.org

Like its Assessment Conference and its Conference on Faculty Roles and Rewards, AAHE's annual National Conference on Higher Education focuses on issues pertinent to higher education in general, rather than on service-learning in particular. Each year this national conference focuses on a new set of contemporary issues and concerns in higher education. The conference in March 2000 celebrated the association's 30th anniversary. Its theme was "To Form a More Perfect Union: Diversity & Learning." The conference "reexamine[d] the nature of the social contract that makes an unum of the American pluribus. It. . . focus[ed] in particular on higher education's role in creating not only the national union but the union between diversity and learning." The conference theme in 2001 is "Private Gain, Public Good: The Challenge of Balance." "With tensions building between higher education's pursuit of Private Gain and its responsibility for the larger Public Good, the 2001 National Conference on Higher Education will explore what balance can be struck between these seemingly irreconcilable demands."

The conference was held on March 24–28, 2001 at Marriott Wardman Park, Washington, DC.

## Association for Experiential Education International Conference

Association for Experiential Education
(AEE) International Office
Cheryl Schwartz, Director of Conference
Services
2305 Canyon Boulevard, Suite #100
Boulder, CO 80302
(303) 440–8844, ext 12
fax: (303) 440–9581
e-mail: cheryl@aee.org
http://www.aee.org

AEE's international conference is about the broader field of experiential education, not service-learning, per se. As a subset of experiential education pedagogies, service-learning is certainly included. Unfortunately, except for information about themes, dates, and locations, there is no information available about the general purpose and structure of the conferences. The theme of the conference in November 2000 was "A Celebration of Learning: Explore the Vision—Experience the Journey." The 29th international conference will be held November 1–4, 2001, in Charleston, WV.

## Annual Conference of Campus Compact National Center for Community Colleges

Campus Compact National Center for Community Colleges (CCNCCC)
Mesa Community College
Downtown Center
145 N. Centennial Way, Suite 108
Mesa, AZ 85201
(480) 461–6280
fax: (480) 461–6218
e-mail:
  gloria.schoonover@mcmail.maricopa.edu
http://www.mc.maricopa.edu/academic/
  compact/

CCNCCC's conferences are intended primarily for its constituency of community colleges. The theme of the ninth annual conference in May 2000 was "Celebrating a Decade of Success In a Civil Society." It was intended to "honor. . . both the hard work and commitment of those who have been pioneers in the field of service learning while embracing the enthusiasm and excitement of those new to the field." The conference "incorporat[ed] the best practices and lessons learned throughout the past decade. . . [and]. . . provide[d] many formal and informal opportunities for participants to model successful programs, network with sea-soned and new colleagues, and of course learn strategies for implementing and enhancing new and existing programs.''

## A Boyer Center Conference: Strengthening Service-Learning at Faith Based Colleges

Boyer Center, Messiah College
John W. Eby
Messiah College
Grantham, PA 17027
(717) 766–2511
fax: (717) 796–5221
e-mail: JEby@messiah.edu
http://www.boyercenter.org

''There is a particularly strong 'fit' between Service-Learning and liberal arts colleges and universities which have a strong faith/value base, an emphasis on service, and student cen-tered, holistic educational philosophies. This conference [was designed to identify and ex-plore] critical issues in service-learning at these kinds of colleges.'' Held in June 2000, this conference was the first of its kind and does not appear to be intended as an annual event.

## Break Away National Conference

Co-sponsor (for the March 2000 confer-ence): Campus Outreach Opportunity League (COOL)

Break Away
37 Temple Place, Suite 401
Boston, MA 02111
(617) 695–2665
fax: (617) 695–0022
e-mail: breakaway@alternativebreaks.com
http://www.alternativebreaks.com

Break Away's annual national conference ''is an. . . opportunity to bring students, staff, administrators and community organizations together to improve the quality of alternative break programs. The conference provides. . . information through workshops, speakers, and special events such as the Service Exhibition. Participants can get information to start a pro-gram or share their expertise with schools across the country. Break Away's sixth national con-ference, in March 2000, was jointly sponsored by Campus Outreach Opportunity League (COOL). The theme was ''Sit In, Speak Up, Take a Stand: Uniting Activism With Advo-cacy.'' See COOL's conference listing, below, for more information on this event.

## The California Service & Volunteerism Leadership Conference

Sponsors and Supporters (of the February 2000 conference): Youth Service California, The Volunteer Centers of California, Califor-nia Campus Compact, The California Com-mission on Improving Life Through Service, Corporation for National Service—CA State Office, CA Conservation Corps, CA Associa-tion of Local Conservation Corps (CALCC), CA Community Colleges-Chancellor's Office, CA Department of Education—CalServe, CA State University—Office of the Chancellor, Service Learning 2000 Center at Stanford Uni-versity, Volunteer Bureau, Office of the Mayor, City of Los Angeles, The James Irvine Founda-tion, and The William and Flora Hewlett Foundation.

Youth Service California (YSCal)
S&V Conference Planning Committee
754 Sir Francis Drake, Suite 8
San Anselmo, CA 94960
(415)257–3500
fax: (415) 257–5838
info@yscal.org
http://www.yscal.org
also: The CSUS Business Services Group
(916) 278–4960; (800) 858–7743

While not a service-learning conference, this statewide conference on service is an important part of the service/service-learning network. Its purpose is ''to strengthen alliances that will advance service and volunteerism throughout California in the twenty-first century.'' The February 2000 conference theme was ''Con-necting the Pieces.'' The Draft Report of Con-ference Proceedings on their Web site indicates that participants at the conference discussed everything from ''common themes'' to ''diver-sity issues'' to ''infrastructure'' to ''organizing politically'' to ''Web sites.''

**Campus Compact Presidents' Leadership Colloquium, Higher Education for Democracy**

Co-sponsor (of the June 2000 colloquium): The University of Pennsylvania

Campus Compact
PO Box 1975
Brown University
Providence, RI 02912
(401) 863–1119
fax: (401) 863–3779
e-mail: campus@compact.org
http://www.compact.org

The colloquium in June 2000 was "a follow-up to last year's successful meeting at the Aspen Institute, where 51 presidents drafted and endorsed the Presidents' Declaration on the Civic Responsibility of Higher Education, now endorsed by more than 300 presidents." The theme in 2000 was "Strategies for Civic Engagement."

**CCPH National Conference**

Community-Campus Partnerships for Health (CCPH)

Amy Zechman, Program Coordinator
3333 California Street, Suite 410
San Francisco, CA 94118
(415) 502–7933
fax: (415) 476–4113
fax-on-demand: 1–888-267–9183
e-mail: ccph@itsa.ucsf.edu
http://futurehealth.ucsf.edu/ccph.html

The goal of this conference is to "broaden and deepen participants' understanding of the policies, processes and structures that affect community- campus partnerships, civic responsibility, and the overall health of communities. . . .[and] enhance participants' ability to advance these policies, processes and structures." More than 500 conference participants were expected to attend the fourth annual conference in April–May 2000, including "representatives of community agencies, government, foundations, health care delivery organizations, and leaders from educational institutions (i.e. academic administrators, faculty, staff, and students)." The theme of the 2000 conference was "From Community-Campus Partnerships to Capitol Hill: A Policy Agenda for Health in the 21st Century." The 2001 conference was held on May 5–8, in San Antonio, TX.

**Continuums of Service Conference**

Sponsors: California, Hawaii, Oregon and Washington State Campus Compacts

Co-Sponsor (of the 2000 conference): University of Washington
Kevin Kecskes
Program Director
Western Region Campus Compact Consortium
Western Washington University, MS-5291
Bellingham, WA 98225
(360) 650–7554
fax: (360) 650–6895
e-mail: kkecskes@cc.wwu.edu
http://www.ac.wwu.edu/~wrccc/events.htm

The Continuums of Service conference is an "inclusive gathering for higher education service-learning practitioners and their community, school, and campus-based partners." The theme of the third annual conference in April 2000 was "Relationships, Rigor, and Responsibility: Service-Learning in the New Century." The state compacts (California, Hawaii, Oregon and Washington) that comprise the Western Region Campus Compact Consortium are the primary sponsors of this annual conference. Portland State University and California State University-Fullerton co-sponsored the first and second annual conferences, respectively. Other "collaborative organizations" involved in the conferences include, in part the American Association of Community Colleges, the W.K. Kellogg Foundation, the Corporation for National Service (Learn and Serve America Higher Education), and the California State University Chancellors Office.

**COOL National Conference on Student Community Service**

Co-sponsor (of the 2000 conference): Break Away

Campus Outreach Opportunity League (COOL)
37 Temple Place, Suite 401
Boston, MA 02111
(617) 695–2665

fax: (617) 695–0022
e-mail: conference@COOL2SERVE.org
e-mail: inquiry@COOL2SERVE.org
http://www.cool2serve.org

COOL has hosted an annual conference on "student community service" since it was founded in 1984. Its March 1999 conference (theme: "If Not Us, Then Who?") featured Dolores Huerta, Harris Wofford, Adam Werbach, Jared Raynor, and Jeremy Woodrum. COOL's 16th conference (theme: "Sit In, Speak Up, Take a Stand: Uniting Activism With Advocacy") in March 2000, was jointly held with Break Away. The conference "encompass[ed] the dynamics of activism partnered with advocacy" and "unite[d] those who sit in and take a stand with those who speak up." The conference featured William Upski Wimsatt, the author of "No More Prisons" and "Bomb the Suburbs"; Eric Saperston, the founder of Journey Productions; the East Timor Action Network; an Oxfam Hunger Banquet; a student keynote address; workshops; an opportunities fair; and a variety of pre-conferences.

### International Conference (International Partnership for Service-Learning)

Co-sponsors (of the 2000 conference): Campus Compact, International Volunteer Programs Association, and Fundacion Ninez Internacional—Ecuador

International Partnership for Service-
  Learning
815 Second Avenue, Suite 3155
New York, NY 10017
(212) 986–0989
fax: (212) 986–5039
e-mail: pslny@aol.com
http://www.ipsl.org/

This biennial conference is the main international gathering on service-learning. It is devoted to service-learning and international education. The international conference attracts "educators and service agency supervisors from around the world," including IPS-L's own member programs. The theme of the February 2000 conference held in Guayaquil and Quito, Ecuador was "Service-Learning: Education with a Difference, Making a Difference." Confer-

ence organizers invited a diverse group of participants: college and university administrators; study-abroad directors; international studies faculty; service-learning coordinators and faculty; field study, cooperative education, off-campus and experiential study advisors; Latin American studies specialists; service providers; college and university students; and IPS-L alumni. Participants attended the conference in order to "examine the purposes of higher education and to work together to re-form education to better address human and social needs in local communities, in nations, and in the world." The 19th international conference is scheduled for April 2002, in Prague, Czech Republic.

### The National Community Service Conference (Points of Light Foundation)

Co-sponsors: Corporation for National Service, United Parcel Service

The Points of Light Foundation
1400 I Street, NW, Suite 800
Washington, DC 20005
(202) 729–8000
fax: (202) 729–8100
e-mail: volnet@pontsoflight.org
http://www.pointsoflight.org

The Points of Light Foundation hosts this annual conference in partnership with the Corporation for National Service. It is a "training event for volunteer management, community volunteering and national service leaders in nonprofit organizations, businesses, government agencies and Volunteer Centers." The conferences in 1999 and 2000 were held in June.

### National Gathering (The Invisible College)

Co-sponsors: Campus Compact, Georgetown University Center for Urban Research and Teaching, Georgetown Program for Justice and Peace, and the Georgetown Volunteer and Public Service Center

The Invisible College
Jennifer Guerin, Coordinator
312 New North
Georgetown University
Washington, DC 20057
(202) 687–7622
fax: (202) 687–5445
e-mail: invisiblec@gusun.georgetown.edu

http://www.selu.edu/orgs/ic/

The first "National Gatherings" were intended for faculty in higher education only. Today they are an opportunity for "all service-learning educators to connect (and re-connect!) with others through reflection, action, and hard questioning." A day of interactive workshops precedes the main event "two days of sustained conversation in learning circles-small, participant-generated discussion groups that allow members to teach and learn from each other. These circles-where discussion unfolds from initial questions framed by facilitators, based on participants' concerns-are at the core of the National Gathering, and of the Invisible College itself." The conference is open to anyone. The theme of the conference in June 2000, was "Bridging the Gap: Service Learning to Social Justice." The seventh National Gathering took place June 21–24, 2001, at Indiana University Purdue University Indianapolis (IUPUI).

## National Service-Learning Conference (National Youth Leadership Council)

Co-Sponsors (of the 2000 conference): Campus Compact; City Year Rhode Island; Feinstein Institute for Public Service, Providence College; Howard R. Swearer Center for Public Service, Brown University; Massachusetts Service Alliance; Public Education Fund, Rhode Island; Rhode Island Department of Education; and Rhode Island Service Alliance.

National Youth Leadership Council (NYLC)
2010 West County Road B
Roseville, MN 55113
(651) 631–3672
fax: (651) 631–2955
e-mail: conference@nylc.org
http://www.nylc.org/conference2000
Also: Amy Umstadter
Rhode Island Service Alliance
PO Box 72822
Providence, RI 02907
(401)331–2298
e-mail: amy_umstadter@yahoo.com

"The National Service-Learning Conference highlights and promotes service-learning as a way of teaching and learning that builds aca-demic and citizenship skills while renewing communities. It is the only major national education conference that provides service-learning professional development to a diverse audience of K-H educators, administrators, pre-service teacher education staff and faculty, researchers, youth leaders, parents, national service practitioners, community-based organization staffs, and corporate and foundation officers."

The conference theme in March 2000 was "Leadership for the Common Good." The theme of the 12$^{th}$ annual conference is "Partnerships for a Civil Society." It took place on April 4–8, 2001 in Denver, CO.

## National Society for Experiential Education National Conference

National Society for Experiential Education
1703 North Beauregard Street, Suite 400
Alexandria, VA 22311–1714
(703) 933–0017
fax: (603) 250–5852
e-mail: conference@nsee.org
http://www.nsee.org

NSEE's annual conference reflects the organization's broader interests in experiential education, but in recent years service-learning has grown to be a significant component of NSEE's agenda and conferences. The October 2000 conference was its 29$^{th}$ annual event. The theme was "Experiential Education: Connecting Classrooms, Workplaces and Communities." The opening keynote speaker was anthropologist and author Dr. Mary Catherine Bateson (George Mason University).

## RACE: Relevance of Assessment and Culture in Evaluation (College of Education and Division of Psychology in Education, Arizona State University)

Co-sponsors (of the 2000 conference): United Nations Educational, Scientific, Cultural Organization–Principal Regional Office for Asia and the Pacific (UNESCO-PROAP), and Asian-Pacific Centre of Educational Innovation for Development (ACEID)

College of Education & Division of Psychology in Education, Arizona State University

Vivian Ota Wang & Stafford Hood, Conference Co-Directors
(480) 727–6933; 965–6556
PO Box 870611
Tempe, AZ 85287–0611
e-mail: race2000@asu.edu
http://race2001.asu.edu

"RACE is a national meeting devoted to
issues of culture in the context of educational
assessment, psychological assessment, pedagogy, and counseling as it applies to both
research and practice." Main themes include
Assessment and Pedagogy in the Context of
Culture; Program Evaluation and Policy; and
Multicultural Competence, Assessment, and
Training.

The first annual RACE conference was held
in January 2000.

## Institutes and Academies

Institutes and academies are primarily venues
for faculty development (although some include students, and two of the offerings, below,
are intended for students only). Most of them
are offered in the summer. (For additional
training opportunities, see Chapter 6: Awards
and Funding.) There are also a fair number of
workshops offered each year, again for the
purpose of faculty development. Workshops
are not included here because they tend to be
one-time events rather than annual offerings.

### AAHE Annual Summer Academy
American Association for Higher Education (AAHE)
Co-sponsor (of the academy in 2000): The
American Council on Education (ACE)
Contact: Teresa Antonucci, Program Manager AAHE
One Dupont Circle, Suite 360
Washington, DC 20036
(202) 293–6440, ext 34
fax: (202) 293–0073
e-mail: tantonucci@aahe.org
http://www.aahe.org

AAHE's Annual Summer Academy focuses
on "learning about student-centeredness." Participation is organized in terms of 30–35 campus
teams (of 6–8 members). Each campus team

develops a "project that contributes to 'Organizing for Learning.'" These campus teams then
return to their institutions to implement action
plans intended to "influence their institution's
next steps in undergraduate academic reform."
The theme of the fifth annual academy, held in
July 2000, was "Organizing for Learning."

### Assessment Institute
Indiana University-Purdue University
  Indianapolis
Contact: Trudy W. Banta
Vice Chancellor, Planning and Institutional
  Improvement
Indiana University-Purdue University
  Indianapolis
355 N Lansing St, AO 140
Indianapolis, IN 46202–2896
(317) 274–4111
fax: (317) 274–4651
e-mail: banta@iupui.edu
http://www.jaguars.iupui.edu/plan/confernc.
  html

Like the assessment conferences mentioned
above, the Assessment Institute is not specifically about assessment in service-learning. It
attracts those interested in assessment method-
ologies, instruments, and innovations. For example, the 1999 institute included sessions on
the following: Using the Grading Process for
Departmental and General Education Assessment; Prior Learning Assessment; Developing and Implementing Assessment Surveys;
Activity-Based Costing; Web Applications in
Assessment; Assessment of General Education; Design and Delivery of Distance Delivered Competence-Based Degree Programs; Institutional Effectiveness; Assessment in Student
Affairs; Communicating Assessment Results;
Faculty Involvement in Assessment; and Port-
folio Assessment. The annual institute includes
Pre-Institute Workshops and a "Best Practice
Fair." The institutes are held in November, at
the University Place Conference Center and
Hotel in Indianapolis, Indiana. Past themes of
the institute include "Technology: Best New
Hope for Assessment?" (1996); "Collabora-
tion: Key to Assessment" (1998); and "Have
We Made a Difference? And What About the
Future?" (1999).

## CCPH Summer Faculty Service-Learning Institute

Community-Campus Partnerships for
  Health (CCPH)
Contact: Amy Zechman, Program
  Coordinator
3333 California Street, Suite 410
San Francisco, CA 94118
(415) 502–7933
fax: (415) 476–4113
fax-on-demand: 1–888-267–9183
e-mail: ccph@itsa.ucsf.edu
http://futurehealth.ucsf.edu/ccph.html

"During intensive, interactive workshops and small group sessions, participants learn about the pedagogy of service-learning—theoretical foundations and current practices, similarities and differences with other forms of community-based learning; effective curricular models of service-learning in a variety of health professions disciplines, including interdisciplinary models; strategies for promoting reflection, building community-campus partnerships and assessing service-learning outcomes; strategies for institutionalizing service-learning into the health professions curriculum; [and] service-learning as a vehicle for knowledge transformation and social change. . . . A unique and effective aspect of the Institute's approach is inclusion of the mentoring model—participants will work in small groups and as individuals with mentors to further shape their own action plans for developing service-learning curricula." The theme of the June 2000 institute was "Advancing Education Innovations for Improved Student Learning and Community Health" (Beginner Level). The 6th annual institute, "Fostering Leadership for Service-Learning Sustainability" (Advanced Level) was held on January 27–30, 2001 in Middleton, SC.

## Institute in Social Movements and Strategic Nonviolence

Peace and Justice Studies, Tufts University
Co-Sponsor (of the tenth annual institute
  in 2000): The New Century Leadership Project
Dale Bryan, Assistant Director, Peace and
  Justice Studies
109 Eaton Hall

Tufts University
Medford, MA 02155
(617) 627–2261
fax: (617) 627–3032
e-mail: dbryan@tufts.edu
http://ase.tufts.edu/pjs

"The institute explores both the limits and potential of strategic nonviolence in peace movement, in particular, and the prevailing social science theories about social movements, generally. To more fully accomplish its objectives, the institute provides internships at organizations advocating social change and public agencies implementing policy on key peace and security issues." The theme of the 10th institute, held from May to August 2000, was "An Experiential Inquiry into Peace Action."

## Institute on College Student Values

Anne Kaiser, Institute Director
Center for the Study of Values in College
  Student Development
Florida State University
313 Westcott Building
Tallahassee, FL 32306–1340
(850) 644–3691
fax: (850) 644–6297
e-mail: akaiser@admin.fsu.edu
http://www.fsu.edu/~staffair/institute/

"The Institute. . . examine[s] the variety of initiatives being taken by college and university leaders to encourage the development of higher ethical standards of personal and social responsibility on the part of students and other members of the campus community." The theme of the February 2000 institute was "What College Presidents Are Doing to Promote Moral Character and Civic Responsibility." The theme of the 11th annual institute is "Colleges that Care: A National Workshop on Campus Strategies for Fostering Moral and Civic Responsibility in College Students." The 2001 institute was held on February 8–10, 2001 at Florida State University, Tallahassee, FL.

## Institute on Voluntary Service and Philanthropy

Academic Sponsor: Indiana University Center on Philanthropy, Indiana University-Purdue University, Indianapolis

Organizational Sponsor: The Fund for American Studies

Martel Plummer, Administrator of the Institute
Indiana University Center on Philanthropy
550 W. North Street, Suite 301
Indianapolis, IN 46202–3272
(317) 274–4200
fax: (317) 684–8900
e-mail: mkplumme@iupui.edu.
http://www.philanthropy.iupui.edu/Institute2000.htm
The Fund for American Studies
IU Summer Institute on Philanthropy and Voluntary Service
1526 18th Street, NW
Washington, D.C. 20036
(800) 741–6964

fax: (202) 986–0390

This is a six-week residential program for 30 college undergraduates (juniors and seniors). ''It is designed for the growing number of students engaged in tutoring, mentoring, and other kinds of service programs on and off their campuses. It will enable participants to deepen their understanding of the history and ethics of philanthropy and volunteering; explore the role of philanthropy and voluntary service in American society; participate in an internship with a leading nonprofit organization; meet nationally prominent leaders in philanthropy and voluntary service; and identify opportunities for fulfilling careers in the nonprofit sector.'' Students earn six credit hours from Indiana University for successfully completing the Institute. Begun in 1999, the institutes are held in June and July.

# 6

# Awards, Scholarships, Fellowships, Internships, and Grants

The number of public and community service-related awards, scholarships, fellowships, internships, and grants is quite large and beyond the scope of this resource book. What is of interest here are: (1) national awards, scholarships, etc, for service-learning in higher education, and (2) those national community service awards, scholarships, etc., that are directly relevant and applicable to faculty, students, or community partners engaged in service-learning programs, projects, or courses.

In the section below on awards, those directly related to service-learning are listed first; relevant service awards are second. It is worth noting that some colleges and universities have their own service-learning awards, scholarships, etc. With the exception of the Indiana University Ehrlich Award for Teaching Service-Learning, awards unique to individual colleges and universities are not included in this section. For more information about the sponsoring organizations, see Service-Learning and Service Organizations, Associations, and Networks in Chapter 4.

## Awards: Service-Learning

### Ernest A. Lynton Award for Faculty Professional Service and Academic Outreach

Sponsor: The New England Resource Center for Higher Education (NERCHE), Graduate College of Education, University of Massachusetts Boston, Boston, MA 02125–3393; (617) 287–7740; fax: (617) 287–7747; e-mail: nerche@umb.edu; http://www.nerche.org.

This annual award honors the memory of Ernest Lynton, the academic vice president for the University of Massachusetts's three-campus system in 1973, and a founding member of the New England Resource Center for Higher Education (NERCHE) at the University of Massachusetts Boston. "Dr. Lynton's work championed a vision of service that embraced collective responsibility and a vision of colleges and universities as catalysts not only in the discovery of new knowledge but also in its application throughout society." (Burack, Cathy. E-mail message to the Service-Learning Discussion Group ["Lynton Award Winners Announced!"]. 05 January, 1999.)

### Howard R. Swearer Student Humanitarian Award

Sponsor: Campus Compact: The Project for Public and Community Service, PO Box 1975, Brown University, Providence, RI 02912; (401) 863–1119; fax: (401) 863–3779; e-mail: campus@compact.org; http://www.compact.org.

The Howard R. Swearer Student Humanitarian Award "honors five students annually for their outstanding community and public service, and supports their continued efforts to address societal needs." Nominees must be undergraduates at Campus Compact member institutions, and must be nominated by their college or university president or chancellor. Winners receive $1,500 each, which "supports service programs designed or chosen by the recipients." (*Campus Compact*, http://www.compact.org. May 2000.)

### Indiana University Ehrlich Award for Teaching Service-Learning

Sponsor: Office of Community Partnerships in Service-Learning, Franklin Hall 004, Indiana University, Bloomington, IN 47405; (812) 856–6011; fax: (812) 855–8404.

This award is intended for outstanding faculty who "have implemented service-learning in a manner consistent with good practice, improved the course, reflected upon it, taken on leadership in their department, campus, and/or discipline and had an impact on students and the community both in and out of the classroom . . . [and] have supported the integration of community or public service into the curriculum and made efforts to institutionalize service-learning." The recipient of the award becomes the university's nominee for the national Thomas Ehrlich Award for Service Learning (see below) the following year. (Campbell, Joann Louise. E-mail message to the Service-Learning Discussion Group ["Faculty Award"]. 15 December 1999.)

### Thomas Ehrlich Faculty Award for Service-Learning

Sponsor: Campus Compact: The Project for Public and Community Service, PO Box 1975, Brown University, Providence, RI 02912; (401) 863–1119; fax: (401) 863–3779; e-mail: campus@compact.org; http://www.compact.org.

The Thomas Ehrlich Faculty Award "recognizes one faculty member whose teaching, scholarship, and leadership—on campus and in the community—exemplify exceptional service-learning practices. The individual and collective work of the nominees is a testament to the impact of service-learning on teaching and learning, community renewal, and the academy."

Each year, Campus Compact invites the president or chancellor of each of its member colleges and universities to nominate one faculty member for the award. The first award was given in 1995. (Campus Compact, http://www. compact.org. May 2000.)

## Awards: Service

### Daily Points of Light Award

Sponsor: Points of Light Foundation (1400 I Street, NW Suite 800, Washington, D.C. 20005; (202) 729–8000; fax: (202) 729–8100;

e-mail: awards@PointsofLight.org; http://www. pointsoflight.org).

The Daily Points of Light Awards are given to exceptional volunteers "who have made a commitment to connect Americans through service to help meet critical needs in their communities, especially focused on the goals for children and youth set by the Presidents' Summit for America's Future." The awards are given each out weekday (including holidays); 2000 awards were given out in the year 2000. (Points of Light Foundation, http://www. pointsoflight.org, May 2000.)

### Do Something Brick Award

Sponsor: Do Something (423 West 55 St, 8th Floor, New York, NY 10019; (212) 523–1175; fax: (212) 582–1307; e-mail: brick@ dosomething.org; http://www.dosomething.org/.

Do Something's BRICK Award "recognize[s] and support[s ten] outstanding leaders under the age of 30 who measurably strengthening their communities. . . .Award winners each receive a $10,000 grant to support their community work, and a national grand prize winner receives a $100,000 grant." Applicants are evaluated on "leadership and entrepreneurial skills, long-term vision for their community and the measurable results of how their efforts have created lasting, positive change." Applications are due in May. The Brick Award program started in 1996. (Do Something, http:// www.dosomething.org/. May 2000.)

### J.W. Saxe Memorial Prize

Sponsor: J.W. Saxe Memorial Fund, 1524 31t Street NW, Washington, DC 20007

The J.W. Saxe Memorial Prize provides $1,000 to one or more students (undergraduate or graduate) working toward a career in public service. The award is intended to allow recipients to gain practical experience in public service by taking a nonpaying or low-paying job or internship during the summer or other term. Preference is given to those applicants who have already found such a position but who require additional funds. The deadline for applications is in March. (Campus Compact, http:// www.compact.org. May 2000.)

## Models That Work (MTW) Award

Sponsor: Models That Work (MTW) Campaign, C/O PSA, Inc., 6066 Leesburg Pike, Suite 200, Falls Church, Virginia 22041.

The Models That Work Award "honor[s] and recognize[s] outstanding programs, or health systems, that demonstrate innovation, quality and outcomes in primary health care. This award is designed to acknowledge and promote the innovative models of service delivery that create health, social and economic benefits for vulnerable and underserved populations." Winners receive "national recognition, an expense paid trip to Washington, D.C. for the awards ceremony, technical assistance opportunities and honoraria for promoting their innovations at national conferences and workshops." The fourth MTW competition was held in November, 2000. (Ikeda, Elaine. E-mail message to the Service-Learning Discussion Group ["Models that Work Competition 2000"]. 11 January, 2000.)

## President's Service Award

Sponsor: Points of Light Foundation (http://www.pointsoflight.org).

Since 1982, this award is the "nation's highest honor for volunteer service." It recognizes "outstanding individuals, families, groups, organizations, businesses and labor unions engaged in voluntary community service addressing unmet human service, educational, environmental and public safety needs." These awards are normally presented to recipients by the President at a White House ceremony during National Volunteer Week every April. (*Points of Light Foundation*, http://www.pointsoflight.org, May 2000).

## President's Student Service Awards

Sponsor: Corporation for National Service (http://www.cns.gov/challenge/; http://www.student-service-awards.org/); administered by the Points of Light Foundation's Youth Outreach department (http://www.pointsoflight.org) in partnership with the American Institute for Public Service and Youth Service America, President's Student Service Awards, P.O. Box 189, Wilmington, DE 19899–0189; (302) 622–9107; fax: (302) 622–9106; E-mail: pssainfo@dca.net.

The President's Student Service Awards and the President's Student Service Scholarships comprise the President's Student Service Challenge, begun in December 1998. The awards honor young people (ages 5 to 25), "who complete at least 100 hours of service to their community within a 12-month period. Students receive a gold pin, certificate, and letter from the President. There is also a silver level award for youth ages 5 to 14 who complete 50 hours within a 12-month period." (*Points of Light Foundation*, http://www.pointsoflight.org, May 2000).

## Romney Volunteer Center Excellence Award

Sponsor: Points of Light Foundation (http://www.pointsoflight.org).

Since 1996, the Romney Volunteer Center Excellence Award has been given to member volunteer centers "that have demonstrated deliberate and significant progress in implementing the VC2000/Connect America mission: the Volunteer Center of the future mobilizes people and resources to deliver creative solutions to community problems." Honorees receive $1,000 at the Points of Light Foundation's annual National Community Service Conference. (*Points of Light Foundation*, http://www.pointsoflight.org, May 2000).

## Samuel Huntington Public Service Award

Sponsor: The Samuel Huntington Fund, 25 Research Drive, Westborough, MA 01582; (508) 389–2125).

The Samuel Huntington Public Service Award is a $10,000 stipend that is given nationally to one or two graduating college seniors "who wish to pursue public service for up to one year." The stipends may be used for "any activity that furthers the public good" (e.g., individual projects or those involving "established charitable, religious, education, governmental, or other public service organizations"). The application deadline is February 15 of each year (*Mount Holyoke College Career Development Center*, http://www.mtholyoke.edu/offices/careers/fellows/service.htm, May 2000.)

## Scholarships

### The Bonner Scholars Program

Sponsor: The Corella & Bertram F. Bonner Foundation, 10 Mercer St, Princeton, NJ 08540; (609) 924–6663; fax: (609) 683–4626; e-mail: info@bonner.org; http://www.Bonner.org.

The Bonner Scholars Program is one of two main programmatic areas of the Corella & Bertram F. Bonner Foundation. The mission of the program is to "transform the lives of students at 24 colleges and universities and the life of their campuses, their local communities, and the nation through the service and leadership of college students." Accordingly, the Bonner Foundation offers "four-year community service scholarships to approximately 1500 students (who are referred to as Bonner Scholars) annually." All Bonner Scholars have a significant financial need and are committed to service; they "receive up to $4,000 per year to supplement the financial aid package provided by the school. The Bonner Scholars Program began at Berea College in Kentucky in 1990–91. It has continued to grow and now includes 25 colleges and universities in 12 states in the Southeast and Midwest.

### President's Student Service Scholarships

Sponsor: Corporation for National Service (http://www.cns.gov/challenge/); administered by Connect America partner Citizens' Scholarship Foundation of America, (President's Student Service Scholarships, 1505 Riverview Road, P.O. Box 68, St. Peter, MN 56082; (888) 275–5018; fax: (507) 931–9168; e-mail: RDCSFA@aol.com.

The President's Student Service Scholarships and the President's Student Service Awards comprise the President's Student Service Challenge. The scholarships and awards "recognize and encourage young people who are making positive contributions to their communities." "Each high school in the country may select two juniors or seniors to each receive a $1,000 scholarship for outstanding service to the community. The Corporation for National Service provides $500 for each scholarship matched with $500 from the community. In addition to the scholarship, students receive a scholarship certificate, a letter from the President, and the President's Student Service Award gold pin." Applications for the latest cycle of scholarships are available in January, 2001. (*Points of Light Foundation*, http://www.pointsoflight.org, May 2000.)

## Fellowships

### Coro Fellows Program in Public Affairs

Sponsor: Coro (Coro Northern California Center, 220 Sansome Street, 4th Floor, San Francisco, CA 94104; (415) 986–0521; fax: (415) 986–5522; e-mail: tjones@coro.org; http://www.coro.org).

Coro is a "private, non-profit, and non-partisan educational institution." The Fellows Program in Public Affairs chooses 60 fellows per year for its "nine-month, full-time, postgraduate experiential leadership training program which introduces. . . young public servants to all aspects of the public affairs arena. Field assignments, site visits, interviews and special individual and group projects and consultancies prepare Coro Fellows to translate their ideals into action for improving their own communities. . . The Fellows Program. . . is conducted in San Francisco, Los Angeles, St. Louis, New York and Pittsburgh." Application deadlines are in February each year. (*Coro*, http://www.coro.org, May 2000.)

### Echoing Green Public Service Fellowship

Sponsor: Echoing Green Foundation 198 Madison Ave, 8th Floor, New York, NY 10016; (212) 689–1165; fax: (212) 689–9010; e-mail: general@echoinggreen.org; http://www.echoinggreen.org.

The Echoing Green Foundation provides up to nine "full-time fellowships to emerging social entrepreneurs" every year. The foundation "applies a venture capital approach to philanthropy by providing seed money and technical support to individuals creating innovative public service organizations or projects that seek to catalyze positive social change. Echoing Green invests in entrepreneurs' organizations and projects at an early stage, before most funders are willing to do so, and then provides them with support to help them grow beyond start-up. The Echoing Green community currently includes over 300 Fellows working domestically and internationally on a wide range of social issues.'' The next application cycle begins in June, 2001. (*Echoing Green Foundation*, http://www.echoinggreen.org, May 2000.)

### The Mickey Leland Hunger Fellows Program

Sponsor: The Congressional Hunger Center 229½ Pennsylvania Avenue, SE, Washington, D.C. 20003; (202) 547–7022; fax: (202) 547–7575; e-mail: mlhfp@aol.com; http://www.hungercenter.org; in partnership with Ameri-Corps* VISTA.

The Mickey Leland Hunger Fellows Program is a leadership development program and a year-long service-learning opportunity. ''Begun in partnership with VISTA in 1994, the. . . Program is a project of the Congressional Hunger Center, founded by Congressman Tony P. Hall after the demise of Congress' Select Committee on Hunger. Fellows are chosen each year to honor the work of former U.S. Representative Mickey Leland, who perished in an air crash while visiting hunger-stricken areas in Africa in 1989.''

''Leland Fellows spend six months gaining hands-on experience with grassroots hunger-relief organizations around the country. The following six months are spent in Washington, D.C. at national nonprofit organizations working on hunger and poverty policy. While in D.C., Fellows take part in weekly professional development days, trainings, and a retreat experience.'' They ''receive a living allowance that averages $8000 for the year (designed to experience living at the poverty level), health insurance, and an education award of $4,725 for use toward further education or repayment of student loans. Housing is provided in the host community during the six month field placement, and assistance in locating housing in Washington, D.C. is offered for the policy placement segment of the program. Program travel expenses are provided as well.''

A majority of the participants are recent college graduates or current college students, but the program is open to anyone. Application deadlines are in January; the program begins in mid-August each year. (*Congressional Hunger Center, Mickey Leland Hunger Fellows Program*, http://www.hungercenter.org/mlhf.html, May 2000.)

### National Service Fellows Program

Sponsor: Corporation for National Service, 1201 New York Avenue, NW, Washington, DC 20525; (202) 606–5000; fax: (202) 565–2781; e-mail: fellowships@cns.gov; http://www.nationalservice.org/jobs/fellowships/index.html.

The purpose of the National Service Fellows Program is to ''improve the quality of service through the talents of a diverse, self-managed team that will learn with the Corporation for National Service and will contribute to the future of national service.'' The first 12 National Service Fellowships were awarded in September of 1997. ''The Fellows. . . contract. . . with. . . CNS to produce a product or outcome of value to the Corporation or broadly to the field of service. . . [and] are attached to an office of the Corporation or an affiliated state organization.'' (*Corporation for National Service*, http://www.nationalservice.org/jobs/fellowships/index.html, May 2000.)

## Internships

### Coro Summer Internship in Public Affairs

Sponsor: Coro Coro Kansas City, mailing address: P.O. Box 32976, Kansas City, MO 64171; street address: 701 Westport Road, Kansas City, MO, 64111; (816) 931–0751; fax: (816) 756–0924; e-mail: corokc@aol.com; http://www.coro.org.

The Summer Internship in Public Affairs at Coro Kansas City helps ''develop future community leaders through exposure to community issues, skill development, civic leaders and organizations. . . Each intern is assigned a brief, individual internship in business, government, labor, media, and not-for-profit organizations.'' The program ''is a full-time, ten-week summer program for college juniors or seniors primarily from Kansas City and other Midwest cities. The program is designed to give participants first-hand experience in dealing with the issues

and problems facing Kansas City leaders.''
(*Coro*, http://www.coro.org, May 2000.)

**Corporation for National Service Internships**

Sponsor: Corporation for National Service, Intern Coordinator, Corporation for National Service, 1201 New York Avenue, NW, Washington, DC 20525; (202) 606–5000; fax: (202) 565–2784; e-mail: internships@cns.gov; http://www.nationalservice.org/jobs/internships/index.html.

The CNS Internship Program offers ''students with differing education levels and backgrounds an opportunity to complete substantive projects from a wide range of fields within a federally funded corporation. Summer interns broaden their learning experience by participating in a weekly speakers series featuring specialists in the community service field; in addition, interns may familiarize themselves with the Corporation's initiatives by partaking in a variety of service projects.'' Internships are available in AmeriCorps Recruitment Chief Financial Office Learn & Serve America, AmeriCorps*NCCC Chief Operating Office Planning & Program Integration, AmeriCorps*State/National Congressional Relations Public Affairs, AmeriCorps*VISTA Evaluation & Effective Practices Public Liaison, and Chief Executive Office General Counsel Senior Corps. CNS does not give ''stipends, relocation or housing assistance.'' (*Corporation for National Service*, http://www.nationalservice.org/jobs/internships/index.html, May 2000.)

# Grants

## Corporation For Public Service Grants

Sponsor: Corporation for National Service, 1201 New York Avenue, NW, Washington, DC 20525; (202) 606–5000; fax: (202) 565–2781; http://www.nationalservice.org.

The Corporation for National Service is essentially a grant-giving agency, and IT is the primary source of funding for service-learning grants. Each year it gives many kinds of grants related to a wide spectrum of initiatives in service and service-learning. Grants specifically for service-learning in higher education

are administered through the Learn and Serve America–Higher Education program. The grants come in many forms and have regular annual cycles. The best way to learn about currently available service-learning grants in higher education is to visit the corporation's Web page.

## Everett Public Service Internship Program Grants

Sponsor: Everett Public Service Internship Program, c/o Co-op America, 1612 K Street NW, Suite 600, Washington, DC 20006; (202) 872–5335; fax: 202–331-8166; e-mail: info@everettinternships.org; http://www.everettinternships.org.

Begun in 1989, the Everett Public Service Internship Program ''encourages students' future involvement in public service by acquainting them with the challenges and rewards of public interest work. . . [and] provides the public interest community, which too often functions on limited resources, with the dedication, energy, and idealism that interns bring to their work.''

The program ''also offers grants to those organizations interested in hosting Everett Interns.'' The grants cover the weekly stipends paid to interns. Only undergraduate and graduate students who are enrolled in 2001 may apply for Everett Internships in summer 2001. Each summer, close to 200 Everett Interns work in about 55 organizations dedicated to improving the world. Internships are ten weeks long and each intern receives $210 per week to help with expenses.

## New Voices Grants

Sponsor: Program funding comes from the Ford Foundation; program is administered by the Academy for Educational Development, AED/New Voices, 1825 Connecticut Ave, N.W, Washington, D.C. 20009, (202) 884–8051; e-mail: newvoice@aed.org; http://www.aed.org; http://198.69.134.142/home.html.

New Voices is a relatively new national program that helps ''non-profit organizations bring innovative new talent to their staffs'' and helps train new leaders. Begun in 1999, New Voices ''awards salary-support grants to community-based and nonprofit organizations demonstrating a commitment to cultivating and strengthening the leadership potential of 'new voices.' Through the mentoring and professional development of the Fellows, organizations. . . deepen and extend their participation and that of the New Voices Fellows in the community devoted to human rights and international cooperation.'' (Schadewald, Paul John. E-mail message to the Service-Learning Discussion Group [''NPO Fellowship Program (fwd)'']. 27 December 1999.)

# Appendix: E-mail Questionnaire Used for Directory Entries (Chapter 3)

University/College Name
Street Address
P.O. Box or Mailing Address
City
State
Zip
University/College URL (Website address)
Type of Institution: (select those that apply; delete others)
(a) public (b) private
(c) university (d) college (e) community college (f) teaching (g) research
(h) secular (i) religious
Service-Learning (SL) Program/Center Name
SL Contact Person Name and Title
SL Contact Phone Number
SL Contact Fax Number
SL Contact Email Address
SL Program/Center URL (Website address)
SL Online Course Description URL, if any
SL Online Syllabi URL, if any
SL Program/Center: Brief Description (one paragraph)
(this should include, at minimum, the following information: what it is, what it does, how it works, who it's aimed at, who funds it, other)
Service-Learning Required for Graduation (all students)?

Yes (Y) No (N)
Service Required for Graduation (all students)?
Yes (Y) No (N)
Any Co-curricular Service?
Yes (Y) No (N)
Any service-learning residence halls or theme houses?
Yes (Y) No (N)
SL Undergraduate Program Name, if any
SL Undergraduate Program Description
SL Graduate Program Name, if any
SL Graduate Program Description
SL Degrees Offered, if any (includes majors, minors, certificates, etc. in Service-Learning or something closely related)
Number of Undergraduate SL Courses Offered Per Year
Number of Graduate SL Courses Offered Per Year
Total Number of Service-Learning Courses Offered Per Year
Number of Instructors Teaching Service-Learning Courses Per Year
Number of Full-time SL Staff on Campus (not counting instructors)
Number of Part-time SL Staff on Campus (not counting instructors)

# Bibliography

Albert, Gail. "Intensive Service-Learning Experiences." In *Service-Learning in Higher Education: Concepts and Practices*, edited by Barbara Jacoby and Associates. San Francisco: Jossey-Bass, 1996.

Althaus, Jennifer. "Service-Learning and Leadership Development: Posing Questions Not Answers." *Michigan Journal of Community Service Learning* 4, (1997): 122–129.

*America Reads*, http://www.nationalservice.org/areads/index.html; http://www.ed.gov/inits/americareads/, April 2000.

*America Counts*, http://www.ed.gov/americacounts/, April 2000.

American Association for Higher Education (AAHE). *Service-Learning in the Disciplines*. Monograph Series. Washington, DC: AAHE, 1997–2000.

American Association for Higher Education Assessment Forum, "Principles of Good Practice for Assessing Student Learning." Washington, DC: AAHE, 1992.

*American Association of Community Colleges Service Learning Clearinghouse: Resources/Publications*, http://199.75.76.16/initiatives/SERVICE/b_resour.htm, May 2000. (Online).

*An Annotated Bibliography of Service-Learning: A Partial List of Resources Held by the Center for Teaching Library*, (Center for Teaching Library, Vanderbilt University, October 1998), http://www.vanderbilt.edu/cft/sl/bibliography.pdf, May 2000.

Astin, Alexander W., Lori J. Vogelgesang, Elaine K. Ikeda, and Jennifer A. Yee. *How Service Learning Affects Students: Executive Summary*. Los Angeles: Service Learning Clearinghouse Project, Higher Education Research Institute, University of California. January 2000. http://www.gseis.ucla.edu/slc/rhowas.html, April 2000.

Barrows, Howard S. "Problem-Based Learning in Medicine and Beyond: A Brief Overview." In *Bringing Problem-Based Higher Education: Theory and Practice: New Directions for Teaching and Learning*, edited by L. Walkerton and W. H. Gijselaers. San Francisco: Jossey-Bass, 1996.

Battistoni, Richard M., and William E. Hudson, eds. *Experiencing Citizenship: Concepts and Models for Service-Learning in Political Science*. Washington, DC: American Association for Higher Education, 1997.

Belbas. Brad, and Robert D. Shumer. *Frequently Cited Sources in Service Learning*. St. Paul: National Service-Learning Cooperative Clearinghouse (NSLC), 1993. (Online: NSLC, http://www.nicsl.coled.umn.edu/res/bibs/bibs.htm).

*Bennion Center, University of Utah,* http://www.bennioncenter.org, February 2000.

Berg, Deanna. E-mail message to the Service-Learning Discussion Group ("Collecting Service Hours"). 24 February, 1999.

Berson, Judith S. E-mail message to the Service-Learning Discussion Group ("Study Results Announced"). 25 August, 1997.

*Best Practices in Cyber-Serve: Integrating Technology With Service-Learning Instruction.*

Blackburn, VA: Virginia Tech Service-Learning Center, Virginia Polytechnic Institute and State University, 1999.

Billingsley, Ronald G. "Leadership Training and Service Learning." In *Building Community: Service Learning in the Academic Disciplines*, ed. Richard J. Kraft and Marc Swadener. Denver: Colorado Campus Compact, 1994.

Bonar, Linda, Renee Buchanan, Irene Fisher, and Ann Wechsler. "Annotated Bibliography." In *Service-Learning in the Curriculum: A Faculty Guide to Course Development,* Linda Bonar, Renee Buchanan, Irene Fisher, and Ann Wechsler. The Lowell Bennion Community Service Center, University of Utah, 1996.

Bonar, Linda, Renee Buchanan, Irene Fisher, and Ann Wechsler. *Service-Learning in the Curriculum: A Faculty Guide to Course Development*. The Lowell Bennion Community Service Center, University of Utah, 1996.

Boyer, Ernest L. "Creating the New American College." *Chronicle of Higher Education* (Mar 9, 1994): 48.

Boyer, Ernest L. *Scholarship Reconsidered: Priorities of the Professoriate*. Princeton: Carnegie Foundation for the Advancement of Teaching, 1990.

Boyte, Harry, and Elizabeth Hollander. "Wingspread Declaration on Renewing the Civic Mission of the American Research University." 1998–99. *Campus Compact*, http://www.compact.org, January 2000.

*Break Away*, http://www.alternativebreaks.com, January 2000.

Bringle, R.G., R. Games, C. Ludlum, R. Osgoode, and R. Osborne. "Faculty Fellows Program: Enhancing Integrated Professional Development Through Community Service." *American Behavioral Scientist* 43, no. 5 (2000): 882–894.

Bringle, R.G., and J.A. Hatcher. "A Service-Learning Curriculum for Faculty." *Michigan Journal of Community Service Learning* 2 (1995): 112–122.

Bringle, R.G., JA Hatcher, and R. Games. "Engaging and Supporting Faculty in Service Learning." *Journal of Public Service and Outreach* 2 (1997): 43–51.

Buckley, Honora. E-mail message to the Service-Learning Discussion Group ("Curriculum-Based Immersion Programs"). 29 April, 1999.

Baric, Cathy. E-mail message to the Service-Learning Discussion Group ("Lynton Award Winners Announced!"). 5 January, 1999.

Campbell, Joann Louise. E-mail message to the Service-Learning Discussion Group ("Faculty Award"). 15 December 1999.

Campus Compact, *Best Practices in Campus-Based Mentoring: Linking College Students and At-Risk Youth*. Providence: Campus Compact, 1993.

Campus Compact, *Community Service Learning: Essential Reading Bibliography*. Caron, Barbara. E-mail message to the Service-Learning Discussion Group ("'Best of' resources for Service Learning/Heidi Bitter's request"). 21 December, 1999. (Online: *Service-Learning: The Home of Service-Learning on the World Wide Web: The Service-Learning Discussion Group*, http://csf.colorado.edu/mail/service-learning/, December 1999.)

*Campus Compact*, http://www.compact.org, January, May 2000.

Campus Compact, *Introductory Service-Learning Toolkit*. Providence: Campus Compact, 1999. *Campus Compact*, http://www.compact.org/toolkit_new.html, May 2000.

Campus Compact, *Knowing You've Made a Difference: Strengthening Campus-Based Mentoring Programs through Evaluation and Research*. Providence: Campus Compact, 1990.

Campus Compact, *Resource Manual for Campus-Based Youth Mentoring Programs*. Providence: Campus Compact, 1993.

Campus Outreach Opportunity League. *Into the Streets: Organizing Manual*. St. Paul: COOL Press, 1993.

*Center for Problem-Based Learning Research and Communications*, http://www.samford. edu/pbl, February 2000.

*The Center for Public Service and Leadership*, http://cpsl.iupui.edu, April 2000.

*Center For Social Concerns*, http://www.nd. edu/~ndcntrsc, April 2000.

Colorado State University, Office for Service-Learning and Volunteer Programs, Service Integration Project. *SIP Manual.* http://www.colostate.edu/Depts/SLVP/ sipman.htm.

*Community-Campus Partnerships for Health, "Principles of Good Community-Campus Partnerships,"* http://futurehealth.ucsf.edu/ ccph.html, January 2000.

*Community Service in Higher Education: A Decade of Development.* Providence: Providence College, 1996.

*Congressional Hunger Center, Mickey Leland Hunger Fellows Program*, http://www. hungercenter.org/mlhf.html, May 2000.

Constitutional Rights Foundation. *Civic Participation Service Learning: A Brief Bibliography.* Los Angeles: Constitutional Rights Foundation, 1994.

Cook, Charles C. *African-American, Hispanic, and Latino Youth in Service Topic Bibliography.* National Service-Learning Cooperative Clearinghouse (NSLC), 1999. (Online: NSLC, http://www.nicsl.coled.umn. edu/res/bibs/bibs.htm).

Cook, Charles C., and Robert Shumer. *Literacy and Service-Learning: A "Links" Piece, Connecting Theory and Practice.* National Service-Learning Cooperative Clearinghouse (NSLC), 1998. (Online: NSLC, http://www.nicsl.coled.umn.edu/ res/bibs/bibs.htm).

Cooper, Mark. *The Big Dummy's Guide to Service-Learning: 27 Simple Answers to Good Questions on: Faculty, Programmatic, Student, Administrative, & Non-Profit Issues.* Miami: Volunteer Action Center, Florida International University, http://www.fiu.edu/~time4chg/Library/ bigdummy.html, May 2000.

*Coro*, http://www.coro.org, May 2000.

*Corporation for National Service*, http://www. nationalservice.org, January 2000.

*Corporation for National Service*, http://www. nationalservice.org/jobs/fellowships/ index.html, May 2000.

*Corporation for National Service*, http://www. nationalservice.org/jobs/internships/ index.html, May 2000.

Corporation for National Service. *The Internet Guide To National Service Networking.* Washington, DC: Corporation for National Service, 1996.

*Corporation for National Service: Learn & Serve America!*, http://www.nationalservice. org/learn/index.html, April 2000.

*Corporation for National Service, Learn & Serve:Research,*http://www.nationalservice. org/learn/research/index.html, April 2000.

*Corporation for National Service, Martin Luther King Day*, http://www.mlkday.org, April 2000.

Council of Chief State School Officers. *Service Learning Annotated Bibliography.* Washington DC: Council of Chief State School Officers, 1993.

Crews, Robin J. "Learning about Peace through Service: Introduction to Peace and Conflict Studies at the University of Colorado at Boulder." In *Teaching for Justice: Concepts and Models for Service-Learning in Peace Studies*, edited by Kathleen Maas Weigert and Robin J. Crews. Washington, DC: American Association for Higher Education 1999.

Crews, Robin J. "Peace Studies, Pedagogy, and Social Change." In *Teaching for Justice: Concepts and Models for Service-Learning in Peace Studies*, edited by Kathleen Maas Weigert and Robin J. Crews. Washington, DC: American Association for Higher Education 1999.

Crews, Robin J., and Kathleen Maas Weigert. "Peace Studies and Service-Learning: Pedagogy and Possibilities." Roundtable, Eighth Annual Meeting of the Peace Studies Association. Richmond, IN: Earlham College, April 1996.

Crews, Robin J., Kathleen Maas Weigert, Nadinne Cruz, Dale Bryan, and Robert Seidel. "Service-Learning and Peace Studies: Connections Between Academic Neighbors." Roundtable, NSEE National Conference. New Orleans: November 1995.

Cruz, Nadinne. "Proposed Diversity Principles of Good Practice in Combining Service and Learning." In *Service-Learning in Higher Education: Concepts and Practices*, edited by Barbara Jacoby and Associates. San Francisco: Jossey-Bass, 1996.

Cumbo, Kathryn Blash, and Jennifer A. Vadeboncouer. "What are Students Learning? Assessing Cognitive Outcomes in K-12 Service-Learning." *Michigan Journal of Community Service Learning* 6, (1999): 84–96.

Deans, Thomas. *Writing Partnerships: Service-Learning in Composition.* New York: NCTE Press 2000.

Dewey, John. *How We Think.* Boston: Heath, 1933.

Dewey, John. *Experience and Education.* New York: Collier Books, 1938.

*Do Something*, http://www.dosomething.org/. May 2000.

Doorley, Mark. E-mail message to the Service-Learning Discussion Group ("A Request"). 15 September, 1999.

Driscoll, Amy, Barbara Holland, Sherril Gelmon, and Seanna Kerrigan. "An Assessment Model for Service-Learning: Comprehensive Case Studies of Impact on Faculty, Students, Community, and Institution." *Michigan Journal of Community Service Learning* 3 (1996): 66–71.

*Echoing Green Foundation*, http://www. echoinggreen.org, May 2000.

Ehrlich, Thomas. "Foreword." In *Service-Learning in Higher Education: Concepts and Practices*, edited by Barbara Jacoby and Associates. San Francisco: Jossey-Bass, 1996.

Ehrlich, Thomas, and Elizabeth Hollander. "Presidents' Fourth of July Declaration on the Civic Responsibility of Higher Education Declaration." 1999. *Campus Compact*, http://www.compact.org, January 2000.

Enos, Sandra L., and Marie L. Troppe. "Service-Learning in the Curriculum." In *Service-Learning in Higher Education: Concepts and Practices*, edited by Barbara Jacoby and Associates. San Francisco: Jossey-Bass, 1996.

ERIC Clearinghouse on Higher Education. *Community Service Learning. ERIC Critical Issues Bibliography.* 1997. (Online: ERIC Clearinghouse on Higher Education, http:// www.gwu.edu/~eriche/Library/ CRIB59a2.html).

*Essential Characteristics for Course Inclusion in the Service Integration Project.* Fort Collins: Colorado State University, 1994.

Eyler, Janet, and Dwight E. Giles, Jr. *Where's the Learning in Service-Learning?* San Francisco: Jossey-Bass, 1999.

Eyler, Janet, Dwight E. Giles, Jr., and Angela Schmiede. *A Practitioner's Guide to Reflection in Service-Learning: Student Voices & Reflections.* Nashville: Vanderbilt University, 1996.

Eyler, Janet, Dwight E. Giles, Jr., and Angela Schmiede. "Reflection Bibliography." In *A Practitioner's Guide to Reflection in Service-Learning: Student Voices & Reflections*, Janet Eyler, Dwight E. Giles, Jr., and Angela Schmiede. Nashville: Vanderbilt University, 1996.

Eyler, Janet, Dwight E.Giles, Jr. and Charlene J. Gray. *At A Glance: What We Know about The Effects of Service-Learning on Students, Faculty, Institutions and Communities 1993–1999.* National Service-Learning Cooperative Clearinghouse (NSLC) 1999. (Online: NSLC, http://www. nicsl.coled.umn.edu/res/bibs/bibs.htm).

Eyler, Janet, Dwight E. Giles, Jr., and John Braxton. "The Impact of Service-Learning on College Students." *Michigan Jour-*

*nal of Community Service Learning* 4, (1997): 5–15.

Fisher, Irene S. "Integrating Service-Learning Experiences into Postcollege Choices." In *Service-Learning in Higher Education: Concepts and Practices*, edited by Barbara Jacoby and Associates. San Francisco: Jossey-Bass 1996.

Flueckiger, Anne. E-mail message to the Service-Learning Discussion Group ("Waivers, etc. for Overseas Travel"). 4 April 2000.

Foos, C., and J.A. Hatcher. *Service Learning Curriculum Guide for Campus-Based Workshops*. Indianapolis: Indiana Campus Compact 1999.

*Gainesville College Co-Curricular Transcript*, http://troy.gc.peachnet.edu/www/ssmith/cct/what.html, April 2000.

Galiardi, Shari. E-mail message to the Service-Learning Discussion Group ("Here's what they said. . . "). 13 March 2000.

Galura, Joseph, Jeffrey Howard, Dave Waterhouse, and Randy Ross. *Praxis III: Voices in Dialogue*. Ann Arbor: University of Michigan, OCSL Press 1995.

Galura, Joseph, Rachel Meiland, Randy Ross, Mary Jo Callan, and Rick Smith, eds. "Bibliography" in *Praxis II: Service-Learning Resources for University Students, Staff and Faculty*. Ann Arbor: University of Michigan, OCSL Press 1993.

Galura, Joseph, Rachel Meiland, Randy Ross, Mary Jo Callan, and Rick Smith, eds. *Praxis II: Service-Learning Resources for University Students, Staff and Faculty*. Ann Arbor: University of Michigan, OCSL Press 1993.

Giles, Jr., Dwight E., and Janet Eyler. "The Theoretical Roots of Service-Learning in John Dewey: Toward a Theory of Service-Learning." *Michigan Journal of Community Service Learning* 1, no. 1 (1994): 77–85.

*Gonzaga University Office of Service-Learning*, http://www.gonzaga.edu/service/gvs/service_learning/courses/index.html, May 2000.

Gray, Maryann J., Elizabeth H. Ondaatje, and Laura Zakaras. *Combining Service and Learning in Higher Education: Summary Report*. Santa Monica: Rand 1999.

Grusky, Sara. E-mail message to the Service-Learning Discussion Group ("international sl"). 15 May 1998.

Hatcher, J.A., ed. *Service Learning Tips Sheets: A Faculty Resource Guide*. Indianapolis: Indiana Campus Compact 1998.

Hengel, Madeleine S., and Robert Shumer. *School-To-Work and Service-Learning: A "Links" Piece, Connecting Theory and Practice*. National Service-Learning Cooperative Clearinghouse (NSLC), 1997. (Online: NSLC, http://www.nicsl.coled.umn.edu/res/bibs/bibs.htm).

Hengel, Madeleine S., and Robert Shumer. *A Summit Summary: An Annotated Bibliography on Civic Service-Learning, National Service, Education, and Character Education*. National Service-Learning Cooperative Clearinghouse (NSLC), 1997. (Online: NSLC, http://www.nicsl.coled.umn.edu/res/bibs/bibs.htm).

Hesser, Garry. "Faculty Assessment of Student Learning: Outcomes Attributed to Service-Learning and Evidence of Changes in Faculty Attitudes About Experiential Education." *Michigan Journal of Community Service Learning* 2, (1995): 33–42.

Hockenbrought, Charles D. *Service-Learning Bibliography*. E-mail message to Robin Crews ("Bibliography"). 14 April 1995. (Online: *Service-Learning: The Home of Service-Learning on the World Wide Web: Service-Learning Bibliographies*, http://csf.colorado.edu/sl/biblios.html, February 1999.)

Howard, Jeffrey. "Bibliography." In *Praxis I: A Faculty Casebook on Community Service Learning*, edited by Jeffrey Howard. Ann Arbor: University of Michigan, OCSL Press, 1993.

Howard, Jeffrey. "Community Service Learning in the Curriculum." In *Praxis I: A Faculty Casebook on Community Service Learning,* edited by Jeffrey Howard. Ann Arbor: University of Michigan, OCSL Press, 1993.

Howard, Jeffrey, ed. *Praxis I: A Faculty Casebook on Community Service Learning.* Ann Arbor: University of Michigan, OCSL Press, 1993.

Ikeda, Elaine. E-mail message to the Service-Learning Discussion Group ("Evaluation & Assessment Resources"). 13 February 2000.

Ikeda, Elaine K. E-mail message to the Service-Learning Discussion Group ("Mandatory Community Service"). 20 February 2000.

Ikeda, Elaine. E-mail message to the Service-Learning Discussion Group ("Models that Work Competition 2000"). 11 January 2000.

*Impacts and Effects of Service-Learning.* National Service-Learning Cooperative Clearinghouse (NSLC), No date. (Online: NSLC, http://www.nicsl.coled.umn.edu/res/bibs/bibs.htm).

*International Partnership for Service-Learning,* http://www.ipsl.org, April 2000.

Jackson, Katherine, ed. *Redesigning Curricula: Models of Service Learning Syllabi.* Providence: Campus Compact, 1994.

Jacoby, Barbara "Service-Learning in Today's Higher Education." In *Service-Learning in Higher Education: Concepts and Practices*, edited by Barbara Jacoby and Associates. San Francisco: Jossey-Bass, 1996.

Jacoby, Barbara, and Associates, eds. *Service-Learning in Higher Education: Concepts and Practices.* San Francisco: Jossey-Bass, 1996.

James-Deramo, Michele. E-mail message to Deanna Berg; included in Deanna Berg's message to the Service-Learning Discussion Group ("Collecting Service Hours"). 24 February 1999.

James-Deramo, Michele. "Hunger for Justice: Service-Learning in Feminist/Liberation Theology." In *Teaching for Justice: Concepts and Models for Service-Learning in Peace Studies*, edited by Kathleen Maas Weigert and Robin J. Crews. Washington, DC: American Association for Higher Education, 1999.

Kendall, Jane C., and Associates, eds. *Combining Service and Learning: A Resource Book for Community and Public Service.* Volumes I-II. Raleigh: National Society for Internships and Experiential Education, 1990.

Kezar, Adrianna. E-mail message to the Service-Learning Discussion Group ("Outcomes Assessment"). 20 July 1999.

Kolb, David A. *Experiential Learning: Experience as the Source of Learning and Development.* Englewood Cliffs: Prentice-Hall, 1984.

Klosterman, Gail. *Guides to Developing Service-Learning Programs.* National Service-Learning Cooperative Clearinghouse (NSLC), 1996. (Online: NSLC, http://www.nicsl.coled.umn.edu/res/bibs/bibs.htm).

Kraft, Richard J., and Marc Swadener, eds. *Building Community: Service Learning in the Academic Disciplines.* Denver: Colorado Campus Compact, 1994.

Kraft, Richard J. "A Comprehensive Resource List/Bibliography." In *Building Community: Service Learning in the Academic Disciplines*, ed. Richard J. Kraft and Marc Swadener. Denver: Colorado Campus Compact, 1994.

Kraft, Richard J., and James Krug. "Review of Research and Evaluation on Service Learning in Public and Higher Education." In *Building Community: Service Learning in the Academic Disciplines*, ed. Richard J. Kraft and Marc Swadener. Denver: Colorado Campus Compact, 1994.

Kupiec, Tamar Y., ed. *Rethinking Tradition: Integrating Service and Academic Study on College Campuses*. Providence: Campus Compact, 1993.

Lowell Bennion Community Service Center. *Building An Engaged Campus: A Four-Year Plan to Strengthen Community Partnerships and Service-Learning and Encourage Community-Based Scholarship at the University of Utah*. Salt Lake City: University of Utah, 1998.

Luce, Janet, ed. *Service-Learning: An Annotated Bibliography. Linking Public Service with the Curriculum*. Volume III of *Combining Service and Learning: A Resource Book for Community and Public Service*. Raleigh: National Society for Internships and Experiential Educa-Education, 1988.

*Mandatory Community Service: Citizenship Education or Involuntary Servitude?* Issue Paper. Denver: Education Commission of the States, 1999.

Masters, Ellen L. E-mail message to the Service-Learning Discussion Group ("Cocurricular Transcripts"). 15 November 1999.

McElhaney, Kellie, and Adrianna Kezar. *Community Service Learning in Higher Education: Outcomes Reassessed and Assessment Realigned*. ASHE-ERIC Higher Education Report Series. San Francisco: Jossey-Bass Publishers, 2001.

Miller, Jerry. "The Impact of Service-Learning Experiences on Students' Sense of Power." *Michigan Journal of Community Service Learning* 4 (1997): 16–21.

Miller, Jerry. "Linking Traditional and Service-Learning Courses: Outcome Evaluations Utilizing Two Pedagogically Distinct Models." *Michigan Journal of Community Service Learning* 1 (1994): 29–36.

Mitzel, Meg. E-mail message to the Service-Learning Discussion Group ("Faculty Incentives"). 12 May 1999.

Moore, Amanda. *Annotated Bibliography: Service Learning and Related Issues*. Columbia, SC: University of South Carolina, 1996.

*Mount Holyoke College Career Development Center*, http://www.mtholyoke.edu/offices/careers/fellows/service.htm, May 2000.

*National Society for Experiential Education*, http://www.nsee.org/sigs.htm, January 2000.

Nonprofit Risk Management Center, *State Liability Laws for Charitable Organizations and Volunteers*. Washington, DC: Nonprofit Risk Management Center, 1996.

*Office of Community Outreach and Service Learning, University of Natal*, http://www.und.ac.za/und/cadds/cosl.htm, February 2000.

Office for Service-Learning and Volunteer Programs, Service Integration Project. *Service-Learning Faculty Manual*. Fort Collins: Colorado State University, 1996.

O'Meara, KerryAnn, Robin J. Crews, and Carol Maybach. "Reflections on the Causes of Injustice and Their Relationship to Service-Learning Programs." Roundtable. NSEE National Conference. Snowbird, UT: October 1996.

Peters, Vincent. E-mail message to the Service-Learning Discussion Group ("Journals publishing articles on Service-Learning"). 9 November 1999.

*Points of Light Foundation*, http://www.pointsoflight.org, May 2000.

Porter Honnet, Ellen, and Susan J. Poulsen. *Principles of Good Practice for Combining Service and Learning. Wingspread Special Report*. Racine, WI: Johnson Foundation, 1989.

*Portland State University, Center for Academic Excellence*, http://www.oaa.pdx.edu/cae/, May 2000.

Portland State University, Center for Academic Excellence. *Assessing the Impact of Service Learning: A Workbook of Strategies and Methods*. Portland, OR: Portland State University, Center for Academic Excellence, 1998.

Renner, Tanya, and Michele Bush. *Evaluation and Assessment in Service-Learning*. Mesa,

AZ: Campus Compact National Center for Community Colleges, 1997.

Roswell, Barbara. E-mail message to the Service-Learning Discussion Group (''Reflections—Call for Papers''). 14 February 2000.

Roufs, Andrea. E-mail message to the Service-Learning Discussion Group (''FAQ: Risk Management, Liability, Insurance and Service''). 13 December 1999.

Rypkema, Pam. *Avoiding a Crash Course: Auto Liability, Insurance and Safety for Nonprofits*. Washington, DC: Nonprofit Risk Management Center, 1995.

Rypkema, Pamela J., Herschel Dungey, and Eileen Cronin. *Grievance Procedures for AmeriCorps*USA*. Washington, DC: Nonprofit Risk Management Center, 1997.

Rypkema, Pamela J., and Melanie L. Herman. *Crisis Prevention: Effective AmeriCorps Program Management*. Washington, DC: Nonprofit Risk Management Center, 1997.

Schadewald, Paul John. E-mail message to the Service-Learning Discussion Group [''NPO Fellowship Program (fwd)'']. 27 December 1999.

Scheinberg, Cynthia. ''Learning Circles.'' *Invisible College*, http://www.selu.edu/orgs/ic, January 2000.

Scheuermann, Cesie Delve. ''Ongoing Cocurricular Service-Learning.'' In *Service-Learning in Higher Education: Concepts and Practices*, edited by Barbara Jacoby and Associates. San Francisco: Jossey-Bass, 1996.

*School for International Training in Brattleboro*, http://www.sit.edu, February 2000.

Schultz, Steven. ''Book Review: Where's the Learning in Service-Learning?'' *Michigan Journal of Community Service Learning* 6, (1999): 142–143.

Seidman, Anna. *Negotiating the Legal Maze to Volunteer Service*. Washington, DC: Nonprofit Risk Management Center, 1998.

Seidman, Anna, and Charles Tremper. *Legal Issues for Service-Learning Programs*.

Washington, DC: Nonprofit Risk Management Center, 1994.

Seifer, Sarena. E-mail message to the Service-Learning Discussion Group (''National Learn and Serve Evaluation''). 21 June 1996.

*Service-Learning and Evaluation: A Brief Review of Issues and the Literature. A ''Link'' Piece: Connecting Theory With Practice*. National Service-Learning Cooperative Clearinghouse (NSLC), No date. (Online: NSLC, http://www.nicsl.coled.umn.edu/res/bibs/bibs.htm).

Service-Learning Faculty Council. ''Policy on Service-Learning Placements.'' In *The University of Colorado at Boulder Service-Learning Handbook*. Boulder: Student Employment & Service-Learning Center, University of Colorado–Boulder, 1995.

*Service-Learning: The Home of Service-Learning on the World Wide Web: Benefits of Service-Learning*, http://csf.colorado.edu/sl/benefits.html, April 2000.

*Service-Learning: The Home of Service-Learning on the World Wide Web: Service-Learning Handbooks and Manuals*, http://csf.colorado.edu/sl/handbooks.html, April 2000.

*Service-Learning: The Home of Service-Learning on the World Wide Web: Service-Learning Syllabi By Discipline*, http://csf.colorado.edu/sl/syllabi/index.html, May 2000.

*Shelf List of Research Resources*. National Service-Learning Cooperative Clearinghouse (NSLC), 1996. (Online: NSLC, http://www.nicsl.coled.umn.edu/res/bibs/bibs.htm).

Sigmon, Robert. ''Service-Learning: Three Principles.'' *Synergist* 8, no.1 (1979): 10.

Silcox, H. C. *A How-To Guide to Reflection: Adding Cognitive Learning to Community Service Programs*. Philadelphia: Brighton Press, 1993.

Smith, Marilyn W. *Bibliography and Annotated Bibliography of Research: the Effects of Service Learning Participation on Stu-*

*dents Who Serve*. St Paul: Minnesota Commission on National and Community Service, 1992.

Stanton, Timothy K., Dwight E. Giles, Jr., and Nadinne I. Cruz. ''Helps, Hindrances, and Accomplishments.'' In *Service-Learning: A Movement's Pioneers Reflect on Its Origins, Practice, and Future*, ed. Stanton, Timothy K., Dwight E. Giles, Jr., and Nadinne I. Cruz. San Francisco: Jossey-Bass, 1999.

Stanton, Timothy K., Dwight E. Giles, Jr., and Nadinne I. Cruz. *Service-Learning: A Movement's Pioneers Reflect on Its Origins, Practice, and Future*. San Francisco: Jossey-Bass, 1999.

Student Employment and Service-Learning Center. *The University of Colorado at Boulder Service-Learning Handbook*. Boulder: University of Colorado—Boulder, 1995, 1996.

Stukas, A. A., M. Snyder, and E. G. Clary. ''The Effects of 'Mandatory Volunteerism' on Intentions to Volunteer.'' *Psychological Science* 10, no.1 (1999): 59–64.

Stukas, Art. E-mail message to the Service-Learning Discussion Group (''Mandatory Community Service''). 20 February 2000.

Syrett, Heather C. E-mail message to the Service-Learning Discussion Group (''Position Announcement''). 1 April 1998.

Thorpe, Sima. E-mail message to the Service-Learning Discussion Group (''Co-curricular transcript development''). 27 July 1999.

Treacy, Ann. E-mail message to the Service-Learning Discussion Group (''Articles on Service-Learning [NSEE Quarterly]''). 24 January 2000.

Treacy, Ann. *Service Learning as a Tool for Violence Prevention: an Annotated Topic Bibliography*. National Service-Learning Cooperative Clearinghouse (NSLC), 1999. (Online: NSLC, http://www.nicsl.coled. umn.edu/res/bibs/bibs.htm).

Tremper, Charles, and Anna Seidman. *Special Legal Issues for AmeriCorps\*USA*. Washington, DC: Nonprofit Risk Management Center, 1994.

Tremper, Charles, Anna Seidman, and Suzanne Tufts. *Managing Volunteers Within the Law*. Washington, DC: Nonprofit Risk Management Center, 1994.

Tremper, Charles, and Pamela Rypkema. *Insurance Basics for Community-Serving Programs*. Washington, DC: Nonprofit Risk Management Center, 1994.

Troppe, Marie, ed. *Connecting Cognition and Action: Evaluation of Student Performance in Service Learning Courses*. Providence: Campus Compact, 1995.

Tufts, Suzanne, and Charles Tremper. *Legal Barriers to Volunteer Service*. Washington, DC: Nonprofit Risk Management Center, 1994.

*UCLA Service-Learning Clearinghouse Project*, http://www.gseis.ucla.edu/slc/, April 2000.

*UK Centres for Experiential Learning*, http:// www.btinternet.com/~ukcentres, February 2000.

*University of Wisconsin-Green Bay Service Learning Site Bibliography*, http://gbms01. uwgb.edu/~service/biblio.htm, May 2000. (Online).

*VA COOL*, http://www.student.richmond.edu/ ~jmarsh/, April 2000.

Vernon, Andrea, and Kelly Ward. ''Campus and Community Partnerships: Assessing Impacts and Strengthening Connections.'' *Michigan Journal of Community Service Learning* 6 (1999): 30–37.

*Villanova University*, http://www.villanova.edu/ servlet/Web2000, February 2000.

Vue-Benson, Robin, and Robert Shumer. *Individuals with Disabilities Performing Service Topic Bibliography*. 1994. Updated by Madeleine S. Hengel and Craig Hollander in 1997. National Service-Learning Cooperative Clearinghouse (NSLC), 1994, 1997. (Online: NSLC, http://www.nicsl.coled. umn.edu/res/bibs/bibs.htm).

Vue-Benson, Robin, and Robert Shumer. *Intergenerational Service Topic Bibliography*. 1995. Revised by Madeleine S. Hengel and Craig Hollander in 1997.

National Service-Learning Cooperative Clearinghouse (NSLC), 1995, 1997. (Online: NSLC, http://www.nicsl.coled.umn.edu/res/bibs/bibs.htm).

Vue-Benson, Robin, and Robert Shumer. *Topic Bibliography of Sources Related to Service-Learning by ESL/Bilingual Students.* National Service-Learning Cooperative Clearinghouse (NSLC), 1994. (Online: NSLC, http://www.nicsl.coled.umn.edu/res/bibs/bibs.htm).

Vue-Benson, Robin, and Robert Shumer. *Topic Bibliography on English Language Arts and Service.* National Service-Learning Cooperative Clearinghouse (NSLC), 1995. (Online: NSLC, http://www.nicsl.coled.umn.edu/res/bibs/bibs.htm).

Vue-Benson, Robin, and Robert Shumer. *Topic Bibliography on Resiliency and "At Risk" Youth.* National Service-Learning Cooperative Clearinghouse (NSLC), 1994. (Online: NSLC, http://www.nicsl.coled.umn.edu/res/bibs/bibs.htm).

Vue-Benson, Robin, and Robert Shumer. *Topic Bibliography on Service with Math and Science Education.* National Service-Learning Cooperative Clearinghouse (NSLC), 1994. (Online: NSLC, http://www.nicsl.coled.umn.edu/res/bibs/bibs.htm).

Vue-Benson, Robin, and Robert Shumer. *Topic Bibliography on Sources Related to Mentoring and Service.* National Service-Learning Cooperative Clearinghouse (NSLC), 1994. (Online: NSLC, http://www.nicsl.coled.umn.edu/res/bibs/bibs.htm).

Vue-Benson, Robin, and Robert Shumer. *Topic Bibliography on Sources Related to Service and the Environment.* National Service-Learning Cooperative Clearinghouse (NSLC), 1994. (Online: NSLC, http://www.nicsl.coled.umn.edu/res/bibs/bibs.htm).

Weigert, Kathleen Maas, and Robin J. Crews. eds. *Teaching for Justice: Concepts and Models for Service-Learning in Peace Studies.* Washington, DC: American Association for Higher Education, 1999.

Welch, M. "The ABCs of Reflection: A Template for Students and Instructors to Implement Written Reflection in Service-Learning." *NSEE Quarterly*, 25, no. 2 (1999): 23–25.

Whitaker, Urban. *Assessing Learning: Standards, Principles, and Procedures.* Chicago: Council for Adult and Experiential Learning (CAEL), 1989.

Whitfield, Toni S. "Connecting Service- and Classroom-Based Learning: The Use of Problem-Based Learning." *Michigan Journal of Community Service Learning* 6 (1999): 106–111.

Willingham, Warren W. *Principles of Good Practice in Assessing Experiential Learning.* Chicago: Council for Adult and Experiential Learning (CAEL), 1977.

# Index

AAHE. *See* American Association for Higher Education

Academic credit, 1–2, 6, 26

*Academic Exchange Quarterly* (AEQ), 49, 50

Academic legitimacy, 3, 16, 25, 66

Accord Cultural Exchange, 259

*Acting Locally,* 45

*Action in Teacher Education,* 49

Action Without Borders/Idealist, 43, 60, 252, 254

Adler-Kassner, Linda, 45

*Adolescence,* 50

*African-American, Hispanic, and Latin Youth in Service Topic Bibliography,* 53

AFS Intercultural Programs, Inc., 254–55

Albert, Gail, 27

Alliances Abroad, 259

Alpha Phi Omega National Service Fraternity, 253

Alternative break programs, vii, 3–4, 12, 22, 25

*Alternative Higher Education,* 49

Althaus, Jennifer, 27

American Association of Colleges for Teacher Education, 245

American Association of Community Colleges (AACC), 52, 58, 245–46

*American Association of Community Colleges Service Learning Clearinghouse: Resources/ Publications,* 52

American Association for Higher Education (AAHE), ix, 6; Annual Summer Academy, 271; Assessment Conference, 5, 265; Conference on Faculty Roles and Rewards, 266–67; National Conference on Higher Education, 266; *Series on Service-Learning in the Disciplines,* ix, 18, 36, 45–46, 53, 245

*American Behavioral Scientist,* 50

*American Educator,* 49

American Friends Service Committee (AFSC), 255

*American Journal of Education,* 49

*American Journal Research Journal,* 49

*American Psychologist,* 50

American Red Cross, 255

American Refugee Committee, 260

America Reads and America Counts Programs, 4–5, 248

AmeriCorps, 5, 248

Amerispan Unlimited, 260

Amigos de las Américas, 260

Amizade, Ltd., 255

Amnesty International, 256

Anderson, Jeffrey B., 46

*Annotated Bibliography: Service Learning and Related Issues,* 53

*An Annotated Bibliography of Service-Learning: A Partial List of Resources Held by the Center for Teaching Library,* 52

*Assessing the Impact of Service Learning: A Workbook of Strategies and Methods,* 7

Assessment and evaluation, 5–7, 13

Assessment Institute, 5, 271–72

Association for Experiential Education (AEE), 246; International Conference, 266

Astin, Alexander W., 6, 9

*At a Glance: What We Know about the Effects of Service-Learning on Students, Faculty, Institutions and Communities,* 53

Awards, scholarships, fellowships, internships and grants: The Bonner Scholars Program, 278; Coro Fellows Program In Public Affairs, 278; Coro Summer Internship in Public Affairs, 279–80; Corporation For Public Service Grants, 280; Corporation for National Service Internships, 280; Daily Points of Light Award, 276; Do Something Brick Award, 276; Echoing Green Public Service Fellowship, 278–79; Ernest A. Lynton Award for Faculty Professional Service and Academic Outreach, 275; Everett Public Service Internship Program Grants, 280; Howard R. Swearer Student Humanitarian Award, 275; Indiana University Ehrlich Award for Teaching Service-Learning,

275–76; J.W. Saxe Memorial Prize, 276; The
Mickey Leland Hunger Fellows Program, 279;
Models That Work (MTW) Award, 277;
National Service Fellows Program, 279; New
Voices Grants, 280–81; President's Serv-
ice Aware, 277; President's Student Serv-
ice Award, 277; President's Student Service
Scholarships, 278; Romney Volunteer Center
Excellence Award, 277; Samuel Huntington
Public Service Award, 277; Thomas Ehrlich
Faculty Award for Service-Learning, 276

Balliet, Barbara, 46
Barrows, Howard S., 40
Battistoni, Richard M., 46, 53
Belbas, Brad, 53
Benefits and outcomes, 9–10, 11–12
Berson, Judith S., 9
Best Buy Co., Inc., 33
*Best Practices in Campus-Based Mentoring:
    Linking College Students and At-Risk
    Youth,* 33
*Best Practices in Cyber-Serve: Integrating Tech-
    nology With Service-Learning Instruction,* 55
*Beyond the Tower,* 46
Bibliographies: *African-American, Hispanic, and
    Latin Youth in Service Topic Bibliography,*
    53; *American Association of Community Col-
    leges Service Learning Clearinghouse:
    Resources/Publications,* 52; *Annotated Bibli-
    ography: Service Learning and Related Issues,*
    53; *An Annotated Bibliography of Service-
    Learning: A Partial List of Resources Held by
    the Center for Teaching Library,* 52; *At a
    Glance: What We Know about the Effects of
    Service-Learning on Students, Faculty, Institu-
    tions and Communities,* 53; *Bibliography and
    Annotated Bibliography of Research: The
    Effects of Service Learning Participation on
    Students Who Serve,* 54, 55; *Building Commu-
    nity: Service Learning in the Academic
    Disciplines,* 53; *Civic Participation Service
    Learning: a Brief Bibliography,* 55; *Combin-
    ing Service and Learning: A Resource Book
    for Community and Public Service,* 54;
    *Community Service Learning: Essential Read-
    ing Bibliography,* 53; *Community Service
    Learning. ERIC Critical Issues Bibliography,*
    55; *Experiencing Citizenship: Concepts and
    Models for Service-Learning in Political Sci-
    ence,* 53; *A Faculty Casebook on Commu-
    nity Service Learning,* 53; *Frequently Cited
    Sources in Service Learning,* 53; *Guides to
    Developing Service-Learning Programs,* 54;

*Impacts and Effects of Service-Learning,* 54;
    *Individuals with Disabilities Performing Serv-
    ice Topic Bibliography,* 54; *Intergenerational
    Service Topic Bibliography,* 54; *Literacy and
    Service-Learning: A "Links" Piece, Connect-
    ing Theory and Practice,* 53; *A Practitioner's
    Guide to Reflection in Service-Learning:
    Student Voices & Reflections,* 55; *School-To-
    Work and Service-Learning: A "Links" Piece,
    Connecting Theory and Practice,* 53–54;
    *Service-Learning: An Annotated Bibliography.
    Linking Public Service with the Curriculum,*
    52; *Service Learning Annotated Bibliography,*
    52; *Service Learning Bibliography,* 53; *Serv-
    ice-Learning in the Curriculum: A Faculty
    Guide to Course Development,* 46, 52, 55;
    *Service-Learning and Evaluation: A Brief
    Review of Issues and the Literature. A "Link"
    Piece Connecting Theory with Practice,* 54;
    *Service-Learning Resources for University
    Students, Staff, and Faculty,* 53; *Service
    Learning as a Tool for Violence Prevention:
    An Annotated Topic Bibliography,* 54; *Shelf
    List of Research Resources,* 55; *A Summit
    Summary: An Annotated Bibliography on
    Civic Service-Learning, National Service, Edu-
    cation, and Character Education,* 54; *Topic
    Bibliography on English Language Arts and
    Service,* 54; *Topic Bibliography on Resiliency
    and "At Risk" Youth,* 54; *Topic Bibliography
    on Service with Math and Science Education,*
    54; *Topic Bibliography on Sources Related to
    Mentoring and Service,* 54; *Topic Bibliog-
    raphy on Sources Related to Service and
    the Environment,* 54; *Topic Bibliography of
    Sources Related to Service-Learning by ESL/
    Bilingual Students,* 54; *University of Wiscon-
    sin-Green Bay Service Learning Site Bibliog-
    raphy,* 53
*Bibliography and Annotated Bibliography of
    Research: The Effects of Service Learning
    Participation on Students Who Serve,* 54, 55
Billingsley, Ronald G., 27–28
Bonar, Linda, 46, 52, 55
The Bonner Scholars Program, 246, 278
Books: *Acting Locally,* 45; *Best Practices in
    Campus-Based Mentoring: Linking College
    Students and At-Risk Youth,* 33; *Best Practices
    in Cyber-Serve: Integrating Technology With
    Service-Learning Instruction,* 55; *Beyond the
    Tower,* 46; *Building Community: Service
    Learning in the Academic Disciplines,* 48, 53;
    *Caring and Community,* 46; *Combining Serv-
    ice and Learning: A Resource Book for*

*Community and Public Service,* 18, 29, 30, 47, 52, 54; *Community Service in Higher Education: A Decade of Development,* 46; *Connecting Cognition and Action: Evaluation of Student Performance in Service Learning Courses,* 6; *Construyendo Puentes (Building Bridges),* 46; *Creating Community-Responsive Physicians,* 45; *Cultivating the Sociological Imagination,* 46; *Experiencing Citizenship: Concepts and Models for Service-Learning in Political Science,* 46, 53; *A Faculty Casebook on Community Service Learning,* 48–49, 53; *The Internet Guide to National Service Networking,* 56; *Introductory Service-Learning Toolkit,* 18; *Knowing You've Made a Difference: Strengthening Campus-Based Mentoring Programs through Evaluation and Research,* 33; *Learning by Doing,* 45; *Learning by Serving,* 45; *Learning with the Community,* 46; *Life, Learning & the Community,* 45; *A Practitioner's Guide to Reflection in Service-Learning: Student Voices & Reflections,* 41, 46–47, 55; *Praxis* series, 48–49, 53; *Redesigning Curricula: Models of Service Learning Syllabi,* 47, 48; *Resource Manual for Campus-Based Youth Mentoring Programs,* 33; *Rethinking Tradition: Integrating Service and Academic Study on College Campuses,* 47, 48; *Service-Learning: A Movement's Pioneers Reflect on Its Origins, Practice, and Future,* 48; *Service-Learning: An Annotated Bibliography. Linking Public Service with the Curriculum,* 47–48, 52; *Service-Learning in the Curriculum: A Faculty Guide to Course Development,* 46, 52, 55; *Service-Learning in the Disciplines,* ix, 18, 36, 45, 45–46, 53, 245; *Service-Learning in Higher Education: Concepts and Practices,* 47; *Service-Learning Resources for University Students, Staff, and Faculty,* 48–49, 53; *Teaching for Justice,* 46; *Voices in Dialogue,* 48–49; *Voices of Strong Democracy,* 45; *With Service in Mind,* 46; *Writing the Community,* 45
Boulder County LINC, 252
Boulding, Kenneth, 249
A Boyer Center Conference: Strengthening Service-Learning at Faith Based Colleges, 267
Boyer, Ernest L., 3, 11, 23, 51
Boyte, Harry, 12
Braxton, John, 6, 10
Break Away: the Alternative Break Connection, 3–4, 246; National Conference, 267
Bringle, Robert G., 46
Brubaker, Dave, 45

Buchanan, Renee, 46, 52, 55
*Building Community: Service Learning in the Academic Disciplines,* 48, 53
*Business Communication Quarterly,* 50

The California Service & Volunteerism Leadership Conference, 267
California State University Service Learning Internet Community (SLIC), 55–56
Callan, Mary Jo., 48–49, 53
Campus Compact: The Project for Public and Community Service, 18, 23–24, 33, 47, 48, 58, 246–47, 252, 268
Campus Compact National Center for Community Colleges (CCNCCC), 247; Annual Conference, 266–67
Campus Compact Presidents' Leadership Colloquium, Higher Education for Democracy, 268
Campus Outreach Opportunity League (COOL), 12–13, 20, 58, 247, 268–69
*Caring and Community,* 46
The Carnegie Foundation for the Advancement of Teaching, 247–48
Caron, Barbara, 53
Catholic Network of Volunteer Service, 256
CCNCCC. *See* Campus Compact National Center for Community Colleges
CCPH. *See* Community-Campus Partnerships for Health
Centro de Estudios Interamericanos (CEDEI), 260–61
*Change,* 50
CIEE. *See* Council on International Educational Exchange
Citizenship, civic and social responsibility, and civil education, 11–12
*Civic Participation Service Learning: a Brief Bibliography,* 55
CNS. *See* Corporation for National Service
Co-curricular service, vii, 12, 27, 64, 65–66
*College Composition and Communication,* 50
Colleges and universities with service-learning programs: Adrian College, 66; Albuquerque TVI Community College, 66–67; Allan Hancock College, 67; Alma College, 67–68; Alvernia College, 68; American Research University, 11–12; American University, 68–69, 69; Appalachian State University, 69–70; Arizona State University, 70, 270–71; Ashland University, 70–71; Auburn University, 71; Augsburg College, 22, 71–72; Augustana College, 72; Azusa Pacific University, 72–73; Baldwin-Wallace College, 22, 73; Ball State University, 28,

73–74; Barry University, 74; Barstow College, 74–75; Bates College, 75; Belmont University, 75–76; Bentley College, 26, 65, 76; Bethel College, 76–77; Binghamton University, 77; Birmingham-Southern College, 77; Bloomsburg University of Pennsylvania, 78; Boston College, 78–79; Brevard Community College, 17, 79; Bridgewater College, 79–80; Brigham Young University, 80; Brooklyn College of the City University of New York, 80–81; Brown University, 81–82; Bucknell University, 82–83; California Polytechnic State University, 83; California State Polytechnic University, Pomona (Cal Poly Pomona), 83; California State University, 84; California State University at Monterey Bay, 86–87; California State University, Chico, 17, 21–22, 84; California State University, Fresno, 84–85; California State University, Fullerton, 85; California State University, Long Beach, 85–86; California State University, Los Angeles, 86; California State University, Northridge, 87–88; California State University, Sacramento, 88; California State University, San Marcos, 88–89; Calvin College, 89; Case Western Reserve University, 89–90; Centenary College of Louisiana, 90–91; Chaminade University of Honolulu, 91; Chandler-Gilbert Community College, 91–92; Chapman University, 92; Chatham College, 65, 92–93; Chattanooga State Technical Community College, 65, 93; City College of San Francisco, 93–94; City University of New York, 80–81; Clarion University, 94–95; Clark College, 95; Clemson University, 95–96; Colby College, 96; College of the Atlantic, 97–98; College of Eastern Utah, 96–97; College of Saint Benedict/Saint Johns University, 17, 97; College of William and Mary, 98–99; Collin County Community College, 99; Colorado College, 99; Colorado Mountain College, 99–100; Colorado State University, 18, 39, 100; Community College of Aurora, 100–101; Community College of Denver, 101; Community College of Rhode Island, 101–2; Connecticut College, 102–3; Cornell University, 20, 103; Cowley College, 103–4; Creighton University, 22, 104; Del Mar College, 104–5; Denison University, 105; DePaul University, 105–6; Duke University, 106–7; Earlham College, 107; Eastern College, 107–8; Eastern Michigan University, 20, 108; Eckerd College, 108–9; Elizabethtown College, 109; Elon College, 109–10; Emory

University, 110; Florida Atlantic University, 110–11; Florida Gulf Coast University, 111; Florida International University, 11, 111–12; Florida State University, 11, 112–13; Fort Lewis College, 113; Gadsden State Community College, 113–14; Gainesville College, 17, 114; Gannon University, 114–15; GateWay Community College, 115; George Fox University, 115–16; George Mason University, 28, 116–17; Georgetown University, 118; George Washington University, 64, 117–18; Georgia State University, 118–19; Gettysburg College, 22, 119; Gonzaga University, 17, 29, 119–20; Goshen College, 22; Goucher College, 22, 66, 120; Grand Rapids Community College, 121; Grand Valley State University, 121–22; Grossmont College, 122; Hamline University, 122–23; Hocking College, 123; Holyoke Community College, 123–24; Honolulu Community College, 124; Humboldt State University, 28, 65, 124–25; Indiana University, Bloomington, 125; Indiana University of Pennsylvania, 28, 125–26; Indiana University-Purdue University Indianapolis, 18, 20, 28, 126; International Partnership for Service-Learning, 65, 126–27; Iowa Wesleyan College, 127; Jacksonville University, 127–28; James Madison University, 28, 128; John Carroll University, 128–29; Johnson & Wales University, 129–30; Johnson County Community College, 130; Juniata College, 130–31; Kansas State University, 131; Kean University, 22, 131–32; Kennebec Valley Technical College, 132; Lafayette College, 133; LaGrange College, 28, 133–34; La Salle University, 132–33; Lehigh University, 134; Lethbridge Community College, 64, 134–35; Longwood College, 135; Louisiana State University, 135–36; Loyola College in Maryland, 22, 28, 136; Loyola University Chicago, 137; Lycoming College, 137; Macalester College, 137–38; Marian College, 138; Marquette University, 138–39; Marywood University, 139, 220–21; Massachusetts College of Liberal Arts, 139–40; Massachusetts College of Pharmacy and Health Sciences, School of Pharmacy-Worcester, 140; McHenry County College, 140–41; Mesa Community College, 141; Messiah College, 141–42; Metropolitan State College of Denver, 142; Miami-Dade Community College, 143; Miami University, 142–43; Michigan State University, 143–44; Millikin University, 144–45; Mills College, 145; MiraCosta College, 65, 145–46; Moravian College, 146; Mount St. Mary's College (MD), 22, 147–48; Mount St. Mary's College (CA), 20, 146–47; Mount Wachusett Community College, 65, 148; Nebraska Methodist College of Nursing and Allied Health, 148–49; Neumann College, 149; New College of University of South Florida, 149–50; Niagara University, 150; Northampton Community College, 152; North Carolina Central University, 64, 150–51; Northern State University, 22, 152–53; Northern Virginia Community College, 153; North Idaho College, 151–52; NorthWest Arkansas Community College, 153; Nova Southeastern University, 154; Oakton Community College, 154–55; Oberlin College, 155; Ohio State University, 65, 155–57; Ohio University, 157; Olivet College, 157–58; Oswego State University, 158; Ouachita Baptist University, 158–59; Oxford University, 26, 250–51; Pace University, 17, 159; Pacific Lutheran University, 159–60; Pacific University, 65, 160–61; Pennsylvania State University, 161–62; Pennsylvania State University, Fayette Campus, 162; Pepperdine University, 162–63; Pine Manor College, 163; Portland Community College, 163–64; Portland State University, 7, 164–65; Prestonsburg Community College, 165; Princeton University, 165–66; Providence College, 64, 65, 166–67; Pueblo Community College, 167; Purdue University, 167; Radford University, 167–68; Raritan Valley Community College, 168; Regis University, 168–69; Rice University, 22, 26, 169–70; Royal Roads University, 28, 64, 65, 170; Rutgers University, 170–71; Saint Francis College, 21, 171; Saint Francis Xavier University, 22–23, 64, 171–72; Saint John's University, 17, 97; Saint Joseph's College, 172; Saint Joseph's University, 173; Saint Louis College of Pharmacy, 173–74; Saint Louis Community College at Meramec, 174; Saint Mary-of-the-Woods College, 174; Saint Mary's University, 22, 23, 175; Saint Norbert College, 175–76; Salt Lake Community College, 65, 176; San Diego State University, 176–77; San Francisco State University, 177; Seattle Central Community College, 177–78; Seattle University, 28, 178–79; Sinclair Community College, 179–80, 243–44; Skagit Valley College, 180; Slippery Rock University, 64, 180–81; Sonoma State University, 181; Southern Methodist University, 181–82; Southern Utah University, 182; Southwestern College, 183–84; South-

west Missouri State University, 11, 182–83; Stanford University, 33, 184; State University of New York, College at Oneonta, 65, 184–85; Sterling College, 185; Stetson University, 185–86; Stonehill College, 186; SUNY College, 17; Swarthmore College, 186–87; Temple University, 187; Texas A&M University, 187–88; Thiel College, 188; Thomas Nelson Community College, 188–89; Trinity College, 189; Tufts University, 11, 189–90; Tulane University, 190; Tusculum College, 22, 23, 190–91; United States International University, 191; Unity College, 191–92; University of Arizona, 192–93; University of Balamand, 64, 193; University of California at Los Angeles (UCLA), 59–60, 194–95; University of California-Berkeley, 7, 193–94; University of Central Florida, 195; University of Cincinnati, 195–96; University of Colorado at Boulder, 18, 28, 37, 57–58, 59, 196; University of Colorado at Colorado Springs, 196–97; University of Colorado at Denver, 197; University of Dayton, 197–98; University of Denver, 65, 198; University of Detroit Mercy, 28, 43, 198–99; University of Florida, 199–200; University of Hartford, 200–201; University of Hawai'i at Manoa, 201; University of Illinois at Urbana-Champaign, 201–2; University of Kentucky, 202; University of Louisiana at Lafayette, 202–3; University of Louisville, 65, 203–4; University of Maine at Farmington, 204; University of Maine at Presque Isle, 204–5; University of Maryland, 205; University of Maryland, Baltimore County, 205–6; University of Massachusetts-Amherst, 206–7; University of Miami, 207–8; University of Michigan, 48–49, 208; University of Michigan-Flint, 208–9; University of Minnesota, 33, 249; University of Minnesota-Crookston, 209; University of Minnesota-Twin Cities, 65, 209–10; University of Montana-Missoula, 210–11; University of Natal, 26, 64, 211; University of Nebraska-Lincoln, 211–12; University of North Carolina at Charlotte, 212–13; University of North Carolina-Chapel Hill, 212; University of Northern Iowa, 213–14; University of North Florida, 213; University of Notre Dame, vii, 22, 23, 214–15; University of Oregon, 215; University of Pennsylvania, 11, 215–16; University of Pittsburgh, 64, 65, 217–18; University of Redlands, 218; University of Richmond, 28, 218–19; University of Saint Thomas, 219; University of San Diego, 219–20; University

of San Francisco, 220; University of Scranton, 139, 220–22; University of Southern California, 222–23; University of Southern Maine, 223; University of Southern Maine/Lewiston-Auburn College, 223–24; University of South Florida, 149–50, 222; University of Surrey Roehampton, 64, 65, 224–25; University of Texas at Austin, 225; University of Texas-San Antonio, 64, 65, 225–26; University of Utah, 14, 15, 20, 41, 46, 65, 226–27; University of Vermont, 227; University of Washington, 28, 227–28; University of West Florida, 228; University of Wisconsin-Eau Claire, 228–29; University of Wisconsin-Green Bay, 53, 229; University of Wisconsin-Madison, 229; University of Wisconsin-Milwaukee, 229–30; University of Wisconsin-River Falls, 230; University of Wisconsin-Whitewater, 230–31; Vanderbilt University, 231–32; Villanova University, 22, 232; Virginia Commonwealth University, 232–33; Virginia Polytechnic Institute and State University, 17, 55, 233; Wagner College, 233–34; Wake Forest University, 20, 234; Washington State University, 234–35; Washtenaw Community College, 235; Waynesburg College, 28, 235–36; West Chester University of Pennsylvania, 236–37; Western Michigan University, 238; Western Montana College of the University of Montana, 238; Western State College, 238–39; Westminster College (MO), 239; Westminster College of Oxford University, 26, 250–51; Westminster College (UT), 239–40; Westmont College-San Francisco Urban Program, 240; West Virginia University, 237–38; Wheaton College, 20, 240–41; Wheeling Jesuit University, 241; Willamette University, 241–42; Wilmington College, 242–43; Wittenberg University, 243; Wright State University, 179–80, 243–44
*College Teaching,* 49
*Combining Service and Learning: A Resource Book for Community and Public Service,* 18, 29, 30, 47, 52, 54
Communications for a Sustainable Future (CSF), 57–58, 59
Community-Campus Partnerships for Health (CCPH), 35, 248; National Conference, 268; Summer Faculty Service-Learning Institute, 272
*Community College Journal,* 49, 50
*Community Education Journal. Perfect Match: Community Education and Service Learning,* 50

Community Service, 12–13, 27
*Community Service in Higher Education: A Decade of Development,* 46
*Community Service Learning: Essential Reading Bibliography,* 53
*Community Service Learning. ERIC Critical Issues Bibliography,* 55
Conferences, colloquia, institutes and academies: AAHE Annual Summer Academy, 271; AAHE Assessment Conference, 5, 265; AAHE Conference on Faculty Roles and Rewards, 266–67; AAHE National Conference on Higher Education, 266; Annual Conference of Campus Compact National Center for Community Colleges, 266–67; Assessment Institute, 5, 271–72; Association for Experiential Education International Conference, 266; A Boyer Center Conference: Strengthening Service-Learning at Faith Based Colleges, 267; Break Away National Conference, 267; The California Service & Volunteerism Leadership Conference, 267; Campus Compact Presidents' Leadership Colloquium, Higher Education for Democracy, 268; CCPH National Conference, 268; CCPH Summer Faculty Service-Learning Institute, 272; Continuums of Service Conference, 268; COOL National Conference on Student Community Service, 268–69; Institute on College Student Values, 272; Institute in Social Movements and Strategic Nonviolence, 272; Institute on Voluntary Service and Philanthropy, 273; International Conference (International Partnership for Service-Learning), 269; National Community Service Conference (Points of Light Foundation), 269; National Gathering (The Invisible College), 269–70; National Service-Learning Conference (National Youth Leadership Council), 270; National Society for Experiential Education National Conference, 270; RACE: Relevance of Assessment and Culture in Evaluation (College of Education and Division of Psychology in Education, Arizona State University), 270–71
*Connecting Cognition and Action: Evaluation of Student Performance in Service Learning Courses,* 6
Connolly, Charlene, 46
Constitutional Rights Foundation, 55
*Construyendo Puentes (Building Bridges),* 46
Continuums of Service Conference, 268
Cook, Charles C., 53

COOL. *See* Campus Outreach Opportunity League
Coro Fellows Program In Public Affairs, 278
Coro Summer Internship in Public Affairs, 279–80
Corporation For Public Service Grants, 280
Corporation for National Service (CNS), 4, 5, 30, 33, 55, 59, 248, 280; Learn and Serve America—Higher Education, 20, 28, 58
Corporation for National Service Internships, 280
Council on International Educational Exchange (CIEE), 256
Course development, 15–16
*Creating Community-Responsive Physicians,* 45
Crews, Robin J., 41, 46, 57–58
Crooks, Robert, 45
Cross Cultural Solutions, 261
Cruz, Nadinne I., viii, 3, 33, 39–40, 41, 48
*Cultivating the Sociological Imagination,* 46
Cumbo, Kathryn Blash, 7
*Curriculum Inquiry,* 49

Daily Points of Light Award, 276
Degrees in service-learning, 16, 64–65
*Democracy and Education,* 49
Dewey, John, 41, 45
Documentation of service, 16–17
Donovan, Bill, 45
Do Something, 253; Brick Award, 276; Kindness & Justice Challenge, 33
Driscoll, Amy, 6
Droge, David, 45
Duffy, Donna K., 46

EarthWatch Institute, 256–57
Echoing Green Public Service Fellowship, 278–79
*Education,* 49
Educational Directories Unlimited, Inc., 61
*Educational Record,* 49
Educational Resources Information Center (ERIC), 7; Clearinghouse on Higher Education, 55
*Education Digest,* 49
*Education Leadership,* 49
*Education and Urban Society,* 49, 50
*Education Week on the Web, Educational Evaluation and Policy Analysis,* 49
EESE. *See* Evaluation System for Experiential Education
Ehrlich, Thomas, viii–ix, 12, 47
Enos, Sandra L., 27, 46
Erickson, Joseph A., 46

ERIC. *See* Educational Resources Information Center
Ernest A. Lynton Award for Faculty Professional Service and Academic Outreach, 275
Evaluation System for Experiential Education (ESEE), 7
Everett Public Service Internship Program Grants, 280
*Experiencing Citizenship: Concepts and Models for Service-Learning in Political Science,* 46, 53
*Experiential Education,* 49
Experiential learning, viii
Eyler, Janet, vii, 6, 10, 41, 45, 46–47, 53, 55

Faculty: development, 18, 19; fellows, 19–20; incentives for, 21
*A Faculty Casebook on Community Service Learning,* 48–49, 53
Fellowships, 19–20, 278–79
First Book, 33
Fisher, Irene S., 33, 46, 48, 52, 55
Foster Grandparent Program, 34
Fourth credit options, 21–22, 25
*Frequently Cited Sources in Service Learning,* 53

Galura, Joseph, 48–49, 53
Gelmon, Sherril, 6
*Generator,* 49
*The Generator: Journal of Service-Learning and Service Leadership,* 49, 50–51
Giles, Dwight E, Jr., vii, viii, 3, 6, 10, 33, 41, 45, 46–47, 48, 53, 55
Global Citizen Network, 257
Global Exchange, 252–53
Global Service Corps, 261
Global Volunteers, 261
Godfrey, Paul C., 45
Grasso, Edward T., 45
Gray, Charlene J., 53
Gray, Maryann J., 6, 10
Greater Kalamazoo Evaluation Project, 7
*Guides to Developing Service-Learning Programs,* 54
Guide to: College and University Service-Learning Programs Including Links to Online Course Lists and Syllabi, 58, 65

Habitat for Humanity International, 33, 257
Harkavy, Ira, 45, 48
*Harvard Educational Review,* 49
Harvey, Irene E., 46
HECUA. *See* Higher Education Consortium for Urban Affairs

Heffernan, Kerry, 46
Hellebrandt, Josef, 46
Hengel, Madeleine S., 53–54, 54
Hermanns, Kris, 45
Hesser, Garry, 6, 46
Higher Education Consortium for Urban Affairs (HECUA), 257
Hockenbrought, Charles D., 53
Holland, Barbara, 6
Hollander, Craig, 54
Hollander, Elizabeth, 11–12
Howard, Jeffrey, 2, 38, 48–49, 53
Howard R. Swearer Student Humanitarian Award, 275
Hudson, William E., 46, 53
Human Service Alliance, 253

Idealist, 43, 60, 252, 254
Ikeda, Elaine K., 6
Immersion programs, vii, 12, 22–23, 25
Impact Online, Inc., 60, 257
*Impacts and Effects of Service-Learning,* 54
Independent Sector, 253–54
Indiana University Ehrlich Award for Teaching Service-Learning, 275–76
*Individuals with Disabilities Performing Service Topic Bibliography,* 54
*Innovative Higher Education,* 49
Institute on College Student Values, 272
Institute in Social Movements and Strategic Nonviolence, 272
Institute on Voluntary Service and Philanthropy, 273
*Instructor,* 49
*Intergenerational Service Topic Bibliography,* 54
International Partnership for Service-Learning, 248–49; International Conference, 269
International service-learning, 26, 30, 248–49, 252, 254–63, 269
International Studies Association (ISA), 59
International Volunteer Expeditions (IVEX), 258
International Volunteer Programs Association (IVPA), 258
*The Internet Guide to National Service Networking,* 55
Internships, 1, 12, 25, 27, 37, 279–80
*Introductory Service-Learning Toolkit,* 18
The Invisible College, 29–30, 58, 249; National Gathering, 269–70
IVEX. *See* International Volunteer Expeditions
IVPA. *See* International Volunteer Programs Association

Jackson, Katherine, 47, 48

Jacoby, Barbara, viii, 41, 47
James-Deramo, Michele, 29
*Journal of Adolescence,* 50
*Journal of Adolescent Research,* 50
*Journal of Business Education,* 50
*Journal of Business Ethics,* 50
*Journal of Career Development,* 50
*Journal of College Student Development,* 49
*Journal of Cooperative Education,* 49
*Journal on Excellence in College Teaching,* 49, 51
*Journal of Health Education,* 50
*Journal of Higher Education,* 50
*Journalism Educator,* 50
*Journal of Moral Education,* 50
*Journal of Nursing Education,* 50
*The Journal of Public Service & Outreach,* 49, 51
*Journal of Research and Development in Education,* 50
Journals: *Academic Exchange Quarterly* (AEQ), 49, 50; *Action in Teacher Education,* 49; *Adolescence,* 50; *Alternative Higher Education,* 49; *American Behavioral Scientist,* 50; *American Educator,* 49; *American Journal of Education,* 49; *American Journal Research Journal,* 49; *American Psychologist,* 50; *Business Communication Quarterly,* 50; *Change,* 50; *College Composition and Communication,* 50; *College Teaching,* 49; *Community College Journal,* 49, 50; *Community Education Journal. Perfect Match: Community Education and Service Learning,* 50; *Curriculum Inquiry,* 49; *Democracy and Education,* 49; *Education,* 49; *Educational Record,* 49; *Education Digest,* 49; *Education Leadership,* 49; *Education and Urban Society,* 49, 50; *Education Week on the Web, Educational Evaluation and Policy Analysis,* 49; *Experiential Education,* 49; *Generator,* 49; *The Generator: Journal of Service-Learning and Service Leadership,* 49, 50–51; *Harvard Educational Review,* 49; *Innovative Higher Education,* 49; *Instructor,* 49; *Journal of Adolescence,* 50; *Journal of Adolescent Research,* 50; *Journal of Business Education,* 50; *Journal of Business Ethics,* 50; *Journal of Career Development,* 50; *Journal of College Student Development,* 49; *Journal of Cooperative Education,* 49; *Journal on Excellence in College Teaching,* 49, 51; *Journal of Health Education,* 50; *Journal of Higher Education,* 50; *Journalism Educator,* 50; *Journal of Moral Education,* 50; *Journal of Nursing Education,* 50; *The Journal of Public Service & Outreach,* 49, 51; *Journal of*

*Research and Development in Education,* 50; *Liberal Education,* 50; *Metropolitan Universities,* 50; *Michigan Journal of Community Service Learning,* 45, 49, 51; *NSEE Quarterly,* 49, 51–52, 250; *Phi Delta Kappan,* 50; *PS: Political Science and Politics,* 50; *Reflections on Community-Based Writing Instruction,* 49, 52; *Service: a Journal for Academically Based Public Service,* 50; *Social Policy,* 50; *Synergist,* 50; *Teaching Sociology,* 50; *Theory and Research in Social Education,* 50; *Thrust,* 50

JSL List (Journal of Service Learning), 56

JustAct: Youth Action for Global Justice, 258

J.W. Saxe Memorial Prize, 276

Kendall, Jane C., 18, 29, 30, 47, 54

Kerrigan, Seanna, 6

Kezar, Adrianna, 7

King, Martin Luther, Jr., 32–33

Klosterman, Gail, 54

*Knowing You've Made a Difference: Strengthening Campus-Based Mentoring Programs through Evaluation and Research,* 33

Koerner, JoEllen, 46

Kolb, David A., 1–2

Kraft, Richard J., 6, 48, 50, 53

Krug, James, 6

Kupiec, Tamar Y., 47, 48

Lappe, Frances Moore, 47

Leadership, 27–28

Learning agreements and service contracts, 29

*Learning by Doing,* 45

*Learning by Serving,* 45

Learning circles, 29–30

*Learning with the Community,* 46

Learn and Serve America—Higher Education (LSAHE), 10, 58; National Service-Learning Clearinghouse (NSLC), 28, 33, 41, 50, 53–55, 56, 59, 249

Lewis, Judy, 45

Liability, 30

*Liberal Education,* 50

*Life, Learning & the Community,* 45

Lisman, C. David, 46

Listservs: American Association of Community Colleges, 58; Campus Compact, 58; JSL List (Journal of Service Learning), 56; Learn and Serve America—Higher Education (LSAHE), 58; NSLCK-12 Listserv, 46, 57; Service-Learning Discussion Group (Service-Learning List), 5, 13, 24, 41, 56, 57–58, 59; Service-Learning and Writing, 56–57; Vir-

ginia Campus Outreach Opportunity League (COOL), 58

*Literacy and Service-Learning: A "Links" Piece, Connecting Theory and Practice,* 53

LSAHE. *See* Learn and Serve America—Higher Education

Luce, Janet, 47–48, 52

Martin Luther King Day of Service, 32–33

McElhaney, Kellie, 7

MECA (Middle East Children's Alliance), 261

Meiland, Rachel, 48–49, 53

Mentoring and tutoring, 5, 33

*Metropolitan Universities,* 50

*Michigan Journal of Community Service Learning,* 45, 49, 51

The Mickey Leland Hunger Fellows Program, 279

Middle East Children's Alliance (MECA), 261

Miller, Jerry, 10

Models That Work (MTW) Award, 277

Moore, Amanda, 53

Morton, Keith, 48

Murphy, Bren Ortega, 45

NAFSA: Association of International Educators, 30

National Civilian Community Corps (NCCC), 5

National and Community Service Act of 1990, 248

National Community Service Conference (Points of Light Foundation), 269

National and Community Service Trust Act of 1993, 248

National Council of Teachers of English, 249–50

National Gathering (The Invisible College), 269–70

National Science Foundation, 4

National Senior Service Corps, 34, 248

National Service Fellows Program, 279

National Service-Learning Conference (National Youth Leadership Council), 270

National Society for Experiential Education (NSEE), 36, 49, 51–52, 250; National Conference, 270

National Youth Leadership Council (NYLC), 250, 270

NCCC. *See* National Civilian Community Corps

New England Resource Center for Higher Education (NERCHE), 250

New Voices Grants, 280–81

Nonprofit Risk Management Center, 30

Norbeck, Jane S., 46

*NSEE Quarterly,* 49, 51–52, 250

NSEE. *See* National Society for Experiential
Education
NSLCK-12 Listserv, 46, 57
NYLC. *See* National Youth Leadership Council

The Odyssey: World Trek for Service and
Education, 60–61, 261
Ondaatje, Elizabeth H., 6, 10
One credit options. *See* Fourth credit options
One-time service events, 12
Online resources. *See* Listservs; Web sites
Orientation, 4, 12
Ostroff, Joel, 45
Ostrow, James, 46
Oxfam America, 258

Palmer, Parker, 48
Partnerships, 34–35, 248
Payment vs. academic credit, 1, 2
PBL. *See* Problem-based learning
Peace studies, 35–36
Peace Studies Association, 36
Peacework: Programs in International Volunteer
Service and Exchange, 258–59
People to People International, 262
Peters, Vincent, 49–50
*Phi Delta Kappan,* 50
Placement issues, 37
Points of Light Foundation, 33, 254, 269
Porter Honnet, Ellen, 38
Poulsen, Susan J., 38
*A Practitioner's Guide to Reflection in Service-
Learning: Student Voices & Reflections,* 41,
46–47, 55
*Praxis* series, 48–49, 53
President's Student Service Award, 277
President's Student Service Scholarships, 278
Principles of good community-campus partner-
ships, 35, 248
Principles of good practice, 2, 6, 27, 38–40
Problem-based learning (PBL), 40
Promise Fellows Program, 5
*PS: Political Science and Politics,* 50

Questionnaire, 63, 283

RACE: Relevance of Assessment and Culture in
Evaluation (College of Education and Division
of Psychology in Education, Arizona State
University), 5, 270–71
Rama, D. V., 45
Ramsey, William, vii
Rand, 10

*Redesigning Curricula: Models of Service Learn-
ing Syllabi,* 47, 48
Reflection, 4, 13, 27, 41, 46–47
*Reflections on Community-Based Writing Instruc-
tion,* 49, 52
Reorientation, 4
Residence halls and theme housing, 42–43, 64
*Resource Manual for Campus-Based Youth
Mentoring Programs,* 33
Resources on service-learning. *See* Bibliograph-
ies; Books; Journals; Listservs; Web sites
*Rethinking Tradition: Integrating Service and
Academic Study on College Campuses,* 47, 48
Retired and Senior Volunteer Program
(RSVP), 34
Romney Volunteer Center Excellence Award, 277
Roper, Don, 57–58, 59
Ross, Randy, 48–49, 53

Samuel Huntington Public Service Award, 277
Scheinberg, Cynthia, 29
Scheuermann, Cesie Delve, 12
Schmiede, Angela, 41, 46, 55
School for International Training, 26, 65, 259
*School-To-Work and Service-Learning: A "Links"
Piece, Connecting Theory and Practice,* 53–54
Schultz, Steven, 10
SCI (Service Civil International), 262
Seifer, Sarena D., 10, 45
Senior Companion Program, 34
*Service: a Journal for Academically Based Public
Service,* 50
Service Civil International (SCI), 262
Service contracts. *See* Learning agreements and
service contracts
Service-learning: academic credit for, 1–2, 6, 26;
academic legitimacy of, 3, 16, 25, 66;
alternative break programs, vii, 3–4, 12, 22,
25; assessment and evaluation of, 5–7, 13;
benefits and outcomes of, 9–10, 11–12;
changes in programs, 63; and co-curricular
service, vii, 12, 27, 64, 65–66; community
relations in, 12, 37; and community service,
12–13, 27; contemporary issues and topics in,
13; course criteria and designations, 14–15;
course development, 15–16; curriculum integration of, vii, 14, 25; definitions of, vii-ix,
14–15; degrees in, 16, 64–65; documentation
of, 16–17; as experiential learning, viii, 1;
fourth credit options in, 21–22, 25; immersion
programs, vii, 12, 22–23, 25; institutionalization of, 14, 23–25, 32; as interdisciplinary, 3,
25; international opportunities in, 26, 248–49,
252, 254–63, 269; and internships, 12, 25, 27,

37; and leadership, 27–28; as learning, vii-viii; learning agreements and service contracts, 29; liability issues in, 30; mentoring and tutoring, 5, 33; one-time service events, 12; orientation for, 4, 12; partnerships in, 34–35, 248; and peace studies, 35–36; as pedagogy, vii, viii, 1, 3, 9, 27–28, 32, 36, 38; placement issues in, 37; principles of good community-campus partnerships, 35, 248; principles of good practice in, 2, 6, 27, 38–40; and reflection, 4, 13, 27, 41, 46–47; reorientation in, 4; as required for graduation, 32, 64; and social change, vii, 3, 32; training for, 4, 12; types of service, 43; and volunteering, 3, 12–13, 27, 31–33. *See also* Awards, scholarships, fellowships, internships and grants; Bibliographies; Books; Colleges and universities with service-learning programs; Conferences, colloquia, institutes and academies; Journals; Listservs; Service-learning organizations, associations and networks; Service organizations, associations and networks; Web sites

*Service-Learning: A Movement's Pioneers Reflect on Its Origins, Practice, and Future,* 48

*Service-Learning: An Annotated Bibliography. Linking Public Service with the Curriculum,* 47–48, 52

*Service-Learning and Evaluation: A Brief Review of Issues and the Literature. A "Link" Piece Connecting Theory with Practice,* 54

Service-Learning and Writing, 56–57

*Service Learning Annotated Bibliography,* 52

*Service Learning as a Tool for Violence Prevention: An Annotated Topic Bibliography,* 54

*Service Learning Bibliography,* 53

Service-Learning Discussion Group (Service-Learning List), 5, 13, 24, 41, 56, 57–58, 59

*Service-Learning in the Curriculum: A Faculty Guide to Course Development,* 46, 52, 55

*Service-Learning in the Disciplines,* ix, 18, 36, 45–46, 53, 245

*Service-Learning in Higher Education: Concepts and Practices,* 47

Service-learning organizations, associations and networks, 245–251; American Association of Colleges for Teacher Education, 245; American Association of Community Colleges (AACC), 245–46; American Association for Higher Education (AAHE), ix, 5, 6, 18, 36, 45–46, 53, 245, 265, 266–67, 271; Association for Experiential Education (AEE), 246; The Bonner Scholars Program, 246; Break Away: the Alternative Break Connection, 3–4, 246; Campus Compact: The Project for Public and

Community Service, 18, 23–24, 33, 47, 48, 58, 246–47; Campus Compact National Center for Community Colleges (CCNCCC), 247, 266–67; Campus Outreach Opportunity League (COOL), 12–13, 20, 58, 247, 268–69; The Carnegie Foundation for the Advancement of Teaching, 247–48; Community-Campus Partnerships for Health (CCPH), 35, 248, 268; Corporation for National Service (CNS), 4, 5, 20, 28, 30, 33, 34, 55, 58, 59, 248, 280; International Partnership for Service-Learning, 26, 248–49; The Invisible College, 29–30, 58, 249, 269–70; The Learn and Serve America National Service-Learning Clearinghouse, 28, 33, 41, 249; National Council of Teachers of English, 249–50; National Society for Experiential Education (NSEE), 36, 49, 51–52, 250, 270; National Youth Leadership Council (NYLC), 250, 270; New England Resource Center for Higher Education (NERCHE), 250; UK Centres for Experiential Learning, 26, 250–51; Virginia Campus Outreach Opportunity (VA COOL), 20, 58, 251; Western Region Campus Compact Consortium, 251. *See also* Service organizations, associations and networks

Service-Learning Research and Development Center at UC-Berkeley, 7

*Service-Learning Resources for University Students, Staff, and Faculty,* 48–49, 53

Service-Learning: The Home of Service-Learning on the World Wide Web, 29, 53, 58–59

Service organizations, associations and networks, 251–63; Accord Cultural Exchange, 259; Action Without Borders/Idealist, 43, 60, 252, 254; AFS Intercultural Programs, Inc., 254–55; Alliances Abroad, 259; Alpha Phi Omega National Service Fraternity, 253; American Friends Service Committee (AFSC), 255; American Red Cross, 255; American Refugee Committee, 260; AmeriCorps, 5; Amerispan Unlimited, 260; Amigos de las Américas, 260; Amizade, Ltd., 255; Amnesty International, 256; Boulder County LINC, 252; Campus Compact: The Project for Public and Community Service, 18, 23–24, 33, 47, 48, 58, 246–47, 252, 268; Catholic Network of Volunteer Service, 256; Centro de Estudios Interamericanos (CEDEI), 260–61; Council on International Educational Exchange (CIEE), 256; Cross Cultural Solutions, 261; Do Something, 33, 253, 276; EarthWatch Institute, 256–57; First Book, 33; Global Citizen Network, 257; Global Exchange, 252–53;

Global Service Corps, 261; Global Volunteers, 261; Habitat for Humanity International, 33, 257; Higher Education Consortium for Urban Affairs (HECUA), 257; Human Service Alliance, 253; Impact Online, Inc., 257; Independent Sector, 253–54; International Volunteer Expeditions (IVEX), 258; International Volunteer Programs Association (IVPA), 258; JustAct: Youth Action for Global Justice, 258; Martin Luther King, Jr. center for Nonviolent Social Change, Inc., 33; Middle East Children's Alliance (MECA), 261; Oxfam America, 258; Peacework: Programs in International Volunteer Service and Exchange, 258–59; People to People International, 262; Points of Light Foundation, 33, 254, 269; School for International Training, 26, 65, 259; Service Civil International (SCI), 262; Studyabroad.com, 61, 262; United Way of America, 33; VFP International Workcamps, 262–63; Vision Resource Centre, 262; The Washington Center for Internships and Academic Seminars, 254; WorldTeach, 263; YMCA of the USA, 254; Youth Service America (YSA), 33, 61, 259; Youth Service California (YSCal), 253. *See also* Service-learning organizations, associations and networks
SERVnet, 61, 259
*Shelf List of Research Resources,* 55
Shumer, Robert D., 53, 54
Sigmon, Robert L., vii, 38, 48
Silcox, Harry, 41
Smith, Marilyn W., 54, 55
Smith, Rick, 48–49, 53
Social change, vii, 3
*Social Policy,* 50
Stanton, Timothy K., viii, 3, 33, 41, 48
Student-supervisor contracts, 29
Studyabroad.com, 61, 262
*A Summit Summary: An Annotated Bibliography on Civic Service-Learning, National Service, Education, and Character Education,* 54
Swadener, Marc, 48
*Synergist,* 50

*Teaching for Justice,* 46
*Teaching for Peace,* 45
*Teaching Sociology,* 50
Theme housing, 42–43, 64
*The Theoretical Roots of Service-Leaning in John Dewey: Toward a Theory of Service-Learning,* 45
*Theory and Research in Social Education,* 50

Thomas Ehrlich Faculty Award for Service-Learning, 276
*Thrust,* 50
*Topic Bibliography on English Language Arts and Service,* 54
*Topic Bibliography on Resiliency and "At Risk" Youth,* 54
*Topic Bibliography on Service with Math and Science Education,* 54
*Topic Bibliography on Sources Related to Mentoring and Service,* 54
*Topic Bibliography on Sources Related to Service and the Environment,* 54
*Topic Bibliography of Sources Related to Service-Learning by ESL/Bilingual Students,* 54
Training, 4, 12
Treacy, Ann, 54
Troppe, Marie L., 6, 27
Troxell, Wade, 45
Tsang, Edmund, 45
Tutoring and mentoring, 5, 33

UCLA Service-Learning Clearinghouse Project, 59–60
UK Centres for Experiential Learning, 26, 250–51
United Way of America, 33
*University of Wisconsin-Green Bay Service Learning Site Bibliography,* 53
U.S. Department of Education, 4

VA COOL. *See* Virginia Campus Outreach Opportunity League
Vadeboncouer, Jennifer A., 7
Varona, Lucia T., 46
Vernon, Andrea, 7, 35
VFP International Workcamps, 262–63
Virginia Campus Outreach Opportunity League (VA COOL), 20, 58, 251
Vision Resource Centre, 262
VISTA. *See* Volunteers in Service to America
Vogelgesang, Lori J., 6, 9
*Voices in Dialogue,* 48–49
*Voices of Strong Democracy,* 45
Volunteerism, 3, 12–13, 27, 31–33, 60–61
Volunteers in Service to America (VISTA), 5, 248
Vue-Benson, Robin, 54

Ward, Harold, 45
Ward, Kelly, 7, 35
The Washington Center for Internships and Academic Seminars, 254
Waterhouse, Dave, 48–49
Watters, Ann, 45

Web sites, 55–56, 58–61; *Academic Exchange Quarterly,* 50; *American Association of Community Colleges Service Learning Clearinghouse: Resources/Publications,* 52; American Association for Higher Education (AAHE), 46; American Friends Service Committee (AFSC), 255; *An Annotated Bibliography of Service-Learning: A Partial List of Resources Held by the Center for Teaching Library,* 52; Break Away, 4; California State University Service Learning Internet Community (SLIC), 55–56; Campus Compact, 252; *Community College Journal,* 50; Corporation for National Service (CNS), 5, 28; ERIC Clearinghouse on Assessment and Evaluation, 7; ERIC Clearinghouse on Higher Education, 55; Evaluation System for Experiential Education (ESEE), 7; *The Generator: Journal of Service-Learning and Service Leadership,* 50; Greater Kalamazoo Evaluation Project, 7; growth of, 14, 18, 58; Guide to: College and University Service-Learning Programs Including Links to Online Course Lists and Syllabi, 58, 65; Idealist, 43, 60, 252, 254; Impact Online, Inc., 60, 257; International Studies Association (ISA), 59; *Journal on Excellence in College Teaching,* 51; *The Journal of Public Service & Outreach,* 51; Learn and Serve America National Service-Learning Clearinghouse (NSLC), 50, 53–55, 56, 59; *Michigan Journal of Community Service Learning,* 51; NAFSA: Association of International Educators, 30; National Society for Experiential Education, 52; Nonprofit Risk Management Center, 30; The NSLCK-12 Listserv, 56; The Odyssey: World Trek for Service and Education, 60–61, 261; SERVEnet, 61, 259; Service-Learning: The Home of Service-Learning on the World Wide Web, 29, 53, 58–59; with service-learning agreements and contracts, 29; Service-Learning Research and Development Center at UC-Berkeley, 7; Studyabroad.com, 61, 262; UCLA Service-Learning Clearinghouse Project, 59–60; *University of Wisconsin-Green Bay Service Learning Site Bibliography,* 53

Wechsler, Ann, 46, 52, 55
Weigert, Kathleen Mass, 46
Weinberg, Carol, 66
Western Region Campus Compact Consortium, 251
Whitaker, Urban, 6
Whitfield, Toni S., 40
*With Service in Mind,* 46
WorldTeach, 263
*Writing the Community,* 45

Yee, Jennifer A., 6, 9
YMCA of the USA, 254
Youth Service America (YSA), 33, 61, 259
Youth Service California (YSCal), 253

Zakaras, Laura, 6, 10
Zlotkowski, Edward, 46

## About the Author

ROBIN J. CREWS is visiting associate professor and acting director of the Peace Studies Program and special assistant to the academic dean at Goucher College. He is also an international faculty member of the M.A. Program in Peace and Development Studies at the Universitat Jaume I, Castellon, Spain, and the European Peace University, Stadtschlaining, Austria. Dr. Crews is founder and list owner of the Service-Learning Discussion Group and the Peace Studies Discussion Group on the Internet; founder and Web site owner of "Service-Learning: The Home of Service-Learning on the World Wide Web" (http://csf.colorado.edu/sl) and "Peace and Conflict: The Home of Peace Studies on the World Wide Web" (http://csf.colorado.edu/peace); and a founding editor of *Communications for a Sustainable Future* (CSF), located at the University of Colorado at Boulder.